RAND

LECTURES ON INTERNATIONAL TRADE

second edition

LECTURES ON INTERNATIONAL TRADE

second edition

Jagdish N. Bhagwati
Arvind Panagariya
T. N. Srinivasan

The MIT Press
Cambridge, Massachusetts
London, England

Published 1983. Second edition 1998.

This book was set in Times New Roman on the Monotype "Prism Plus" PostScript Image-setter by Asco Trade Typesetting Ltd., Hong Kong.

Printed and bound in the United States of America.

Library of Congress Cataloging-in-Publication Data

Bhagwati, Jagdish N., 1934–
  Lectures on international trade. — 2nd ed. / Jagdish N. Bhagwati,
Arvind Panagariya, T. N. Srinivasan.
    p.   cm.
  Includes bibliographical references and index.
  ISBN 0-262-02443-8 (hc : alk. paper)
  1. International trade—Econometric models. 2. Commercial policy—
Econometric models. I. Panagariya, Arvind. II. Srinivasan, T. N.,
1933–   . III. Title.
HF1379.B5   1998
382—dc21
                                                        98-10303
                                                          CIP

Contents

Preface to the Second Edition

In this revised edition, we have added nine new chapters and introduced new sections to several existing chapters. The revised book contains a systematic treatment of all the important developments that have taken place in international trade theory since the publication of the original edition. Like its predecessor, this edition is intended for graduate-level courses, but it could be readily used for undergraduate courses by selecting chapters to suit the needs of the course.

The original edition of the book had benefited greatly from careful readings of the manuscript and comments by Richard Brecher and Robert Feenstra. We had also received useful comments on parts of the book by Gene Grossman and Murray Kemp, and Kar-Yiu Wong had assisted in the preparation of recommended readings and corrections to the manuscript.

In preparing this revised edition, we have further benefited from careful comments by Subhayu Bandyopadhyay, Donald Davis, Vivek Dehejia, and Pravin Krishna. We are especially grateful to Poonam Gupta and Deepak Mishra for comments and assistance at all stages in preparing this edition. Rupa Dutta-Gupta, Praveen Kumar, Vandana Sipahimalani, Beata Smarzynska, and Varsha Venkatesh were generous with their assistance in proofreading the manuscript.

Over the years we have naturally benefited from discussions and conversations with and the scholarly writings of many economists. In particular, we wish to acknowledge our intellectual debt to James Anderson, Kym Anderson, Kyle Bagwell, V. N. Balasubramanyam, Robert Baldwin, Richard Baldwin, Magnus Blomström, Pranab Bardhan, Christopher Bliss, Eric Bond, James Brander, William Branson, Richard Brecher, Drusilla Brown, Alessandra Casella, John Chipman, Max Corden, Satya Das, Alan Deardorff, Avinash Dixit, Slobadan Djajic, Jaime de Melo, Elias Dinopoulos, Jonathan Eaton, Richard Eglin, Wilfred Ethier, Robert Feenstra, Raquel Fernandez, Henry Flam, Rod Falvey, David Feldman, Joseph Francois, Jeffrey Frankel, Ross Garnaut, David Greenaway, Earl Grinols, Gene Grossman, Koichi Hamada, Gordon Hanson, James Harrigan, Tatsuo Hatta, Elhanan Helpman, Henrik Horn, Douglas Irwin, Murray Kemp, Ken Kletzer, Paul Krugman, Kala Krishna, Anne Krueger, Sajal Lahiri, Edward Leamer, James Levinsohn, Philip Levy, Assar Lindbeck, Staffan Linder, Robert Lipsey, Peter Lloyd, Patrick Low, Rodney Ludema, James Markusen, Giovanni Maggi, Wolfgan Mayer, Rachel McCulloch, John McMillan, James Melvin, Chris Milner, Michael Mussa, Peter Neary, Victor Norman, Torsten Person, Thomas Prusa, David Richardson, Martin Richardson, James Rauch, Raymond Riezman, Dani Rodrik, Peter Rosendorff, Andre Sapir, Hirofumi Shibata, Matthew Slaughter, Alasdair Smith, Richard Snape, Bo Södersten, Barbara Spencer, Robert Staiger, Robert Stern, Sethput Suthiwart-Narueput,

Lars Svensson, Costas Syropoulos, Wendy Tackacs, Scott Taylor, P. K. M. Tharakan, Marie Thursby, Edward Tower, Daniel Trefler, Anthony Venables, David Weinstein, John Whalley, Sheng-Jin Wei, John Wilson, Alan Winters, Martin Wolf, Kar-Yiu Wong, Paul Wonnacott, Ron Wonnacott, and Ian Wooton.

Jagdish Bhagwati
Arvind Panagariya
T. N. Srinivasan

1   Introduction

1.1 Pure Theory of Trade

The theory of international trade divides traditionally into two disciplines distinguished by their theoretical frameworks of analysis: the pure theory and the monetary theory. In this volume we will primarily be concerned with the pure theory of trade, which in essence is an extension of value-theoretic analysis in the Walras-Hicks tradition.

1.2 Distinguishing Features of International Trade Theory

Why do we study international economics as a separate branch of economic theory? Can we truly differentiate it from other disciplines relating to the analysis of "closed" economies? Such methodological questions have been fashionable from time to time among international economists. The classical economists thought that the distinction we are looking for consisted in the "fact" that factors of production were mobile within a country but not across countries so that international economic analysis was distinguished by the novel assumption of factor immobility. This was largely fiction, even at the time of the classical writings: Colonies were being opened up and populated, and through the latter half of the nineteenth-century capital and labor were to play a major role in the development of the New World. Nor was it always the case that factors were perfectly mobile within countries. Indeed, from a strictly theoretical point of view, the analysis that we pursue often allows for international factor mobility, whereas the positive and welfare aspects of domestic factor immobility have equally been brought within the purview of analysis by recent trade theorists.

If there are striking differences between "closed-economy" and "open-economy" analyses, they are to be found elsewhere. There are two political, decision-making aspects of the international economy that, although they are relevant to intranational analysis, have not received equal emphasis outside of trade-theoretic analysis. First, it is inescapable that trade theory should focus, at least in part, on the welfare effects of alternative economic policies (free trade, customs unions, etc.) on individual nations within the international economy. Indeed, it has never been enough for the trade economists to look at world welfare. The individual nations as political units make policy decision in their "national" (as distinct from "world") interest, so many trade problems have eventually had to be looked at from a national viewpoint as well. On the other hand, identical tools of economic analysis, when deployed to examine intranational problems, have generally been addressed to the question of national welfare as distinct from the welfare of individual units (e.g., producers or consumers) within the nation. While the problem of income distribution has been raised as well, it has been largely from the viewpoint of the conceptual difficulties raised by income-distribution changes in ranking alternative policies. In fact, until recently, a lacuna of modern, closed-economy theory has been that welfare problems of individuals and groups within a nation state have not generally received the attention that they deserve as social questions of importance. Second, there are differences at the "monetary" level in "adjustment mechanisms" between countries and within a country. The central points of difference are that (1) the "exchange rate" adjustment is not meaningful within a country with a single currency, whereas in general it is admissible between countries (but can be ruled out by the presence of currency blocks or the operation of the gold standard), and (2) the general improbability of using "adjustment" measures such as tariffs and quota restrictions between regions within a country, whereas tariffs and restrictions have sometimes been used within countries (although international trade is sometimes conducted, as in free-trade areas, under rules that preclude the use of such tariffs and restrictions).

The qualifications to each of these attempted distinctions between trade and other theories underline the central conclusion that they are based on contrasts between intranational (i.e., among regions or sectors within a country) and international economic relations—contrasts pertaining to factor mobility, focus on units within the overall economy, and permissible adjustment mechanisms—that can by no means be drawn firmly.

1.3   Positive and Normative Aspects

Throughout the volume we will draw a sharp distinction between the positive and the normative (or welfare) aspects of trade theory. For example, when discussing the theory of comparative advantage, we will distinguish between the theories that attempt to explain the pattern of trade and the theories that relate to the gains from trade. These distinctions are not always drawn as sharply as they should be. Reputed economists have fallen into the trap of taking the Heckscher-Ohlin theorem—which states that a country will export that commodity that uses its abundant factor intensively—to imply that a labor-abundant country ought (on welfare grounds) to export labor-intensive commodities.

1.4 Organization of the Volume

Part I is addressed to an extended analysis of the general-equilibrium analysis of international trade, involving alternative theories of the pattern of trade (the central focus being on the Ricardian and Heckscher-Ohlin theorems) and the depiction of free-trade equilibrium under different assumptions relating to technology, income distribution, perfection in the factor and commodity markets, and variability of the factor endowments. New theories of trade involving imperfect competition and product creation are also discussed there.

Part II discusses the comparative statics of trade-theoretic analysis, focusing on tariffs and transfers. Two important areas of recent attention —tariffs versus quotas and effective protection—are also considered there.

Part III is concerned with the welfare propositions of trade theory and deals broadly with the questions relating to optimal trade and nontrade policies under alternative assumptions relating to foreign trade opportunities and imperfections in the domestic markets (e.g., involving externalities in production or consumption). The analysis is also extended to the question of optimal policy intervention when noneconomic objectives such as defense production, reduction of import dependence, or maintenance of labor force in a sector (e.g., agriculture in advanced countries or industry in underdeveloped countries) constitute additional constraints subject to which optimal policy would have to be devised in a trading economy. Questions of optimal policy intervention in the presence of capital mobility and labor migration are also considered.

Part IV takes up a number of analytical issues that have recently been raised in the literature on trade, growth, and development. This part also systematizes a great deal of recent work on lobbying for tariffs or import-license premia and on illegal trade.

Our primary emphasis is on intuitive arguments and on simple geometric expositions and illustrations. Policy aspects and the relevance of theoretical arguments are often discussed in detail. At the same time the underlying formal structure of the argumentation is developed mathematically in a number of chapters. Some of the more mathematical proofs of propositions developed less formally in the text are explored in the three appendixes.

1.5 Standardized Notation

There is no standard notation in the literature on international trade theory; unfortunately, the student will have to become familiar with the particular notation used in virtually every journal paper that must be read in the original. However, we have standardized our notation in this volume. For the bulk of the text, where the traditional trade-theoretic model with two traded goods and two primary factors is used, we will use the following notation:

I, II	Countries (sometimes referred to as home and foreign countries, respectively; country II's variables are distinguished by an asterisk)
$1, 2$	Traded goods (commodities, sectors or industries, interchangeably)
K, L	Primary factor endowments of capital and labor, respectively
w, r	Wage and rental rate on capital, respectively, in terms of the numéraire
ω	Wage/rental ratio
p	Relative price of good 2 in terms of the numéraire good 1 (also the domestic relative price in country I)
p^*	Relative price of good 2 in country II (also the world relative price of good 2)
p_P	Relative price faced by producers in country I
p_C	Relative price of good 2 faced by consumers in country I
Q_1, Q_2	Outputs of goods 1 and 2, respectively
F, G	Production functions of goods 1 and 2, respectively
f, g	Average-product-of-labor production functions
k_1, k_2	capital-labor ratios in the production of goods 1 and 2, respectively
k	K/L endowment ratio
C_1, C_2	Consumption levels of goods 1 and 2, respectively
E, M	Exports and imports, respectively (sometimes E_1 and M_2 are used to identify explicitly the goods being exported and imported)
D_i	Domestic income
D_e	Domestic expenditure
B	Balance of payments
U_C	Social indifference curve (where no ambiguity is possible, U is used without a subscript)
U_T	Trade-indifference curves

t_1, t_2 Tariffs and trade subsidies on goods 1 and 2, respectively

t_l Tax on labor

t_k Tax on capital

t_{C_1}, t_{C_2} Tax on consumption of goods 1, and 2, respectively

t_{P_1}, t_{P_2} Tax on production of goods 1 and 2, respectively

Additional notation will be introduced as necessary—for example, for models of economies of scale and oligopoly and those based on duality and intermediate inputs. In analyses of models with many goods and many factors, modified notation permitting more general treatment will be used, with clear warning.

I   THEORIES OF INTERNATIONAL TRADE

2 Model and Analytic Relationships in Ricardian Theory

In this chapter we consider the basic analytical relationships that obtain in the Ricardian model. These provide the propositions that underlie the Ricardian theorem relating to the pattern of trade, which is that *a country will export that commodity in which it has comparative labor productivity advantage*.

Here we will be considering the Ricardian model in its barest essentials, using a two-commodity, two-country framework.[1] Not until chapter 4 will the extensions to a multicommodity, multicountry system be considered, and the formal proof of the Ricardian theorem is deferred until chapter 3.

2.1 Ricardian Model

The Ricardian model has the following features:

Production. One factor of production whose endowment is fixed. There are two commodities characterized by constant and hence identical marginal and average factor/output ratios in production.

Demand. No specific assumption regarding the demand functions. Trade is balanced, implying that the economywide spending equals income.

Trade. There are two countries that can trade the two goods free of transport costs. The factor is immobile internationally.

Market structure. There is perfect competition in all markets.

2.2 Supply Relations

In this highly simplified general-equilibrium model, the supply relations are readily derived.

Production-Possibility Curve

In figure 2.1, assume that all of the available factor (e.g., labor) is used to produce commodity 1. Then OA represents the maximum amount of commodity 1 that can be produced given the labor supply and the technological relationship between labor and output of commodity 1. Similarly we could derive OB as the maximum amount of commodity 2 that can be produced if all the available labor is deployed to produce it. With constant labor/output ratios in both commodities 1 and 2, it follows that the

---

1. Papers by Samuelson (1964), Metcalfe and Steedman (1973), and Steedman and Metcalfe (1973) on time-phased Ricardian models raise capital-theoretic issues in an essential way.

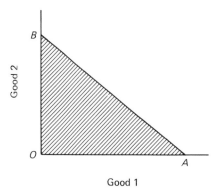

Figure 2.1

economy will produce any linear combination of these two output levels while employing the available labor fully. Hence the line AB represents the locus of feasible full-employment production points, given the labor supply and the technology.

The shaded area OAB represents the set of production possibilities. Any point in OAB but not on AB involves some unemployment. Hence the locus AB, described variously as the *production-possibility curve*, the *production-possibility frontier*, or the *transformation locus*, is the Pareto-efficient locus of production possibilities. This means that from a point on AB, one cannot increase the production of one commodity without having to reduce that of the other. On the other hand, from any point inside OAB and off the line AB, since there is unemployed labor available, one can always move northeast and get more of one good and no less of the other. The locus AB is therefore technologically efficient.

The production-possibility curve exhibits a constant rate of transformation between commodities 1 and 2. No matter which point one starts from on AB, a unit reduction (increase) in the production of one commodity will always permit a unique increase (reduction) in the production of the other. This follows quite simply in the Ricardian model because a given reduction in the output of a commodity always leads to the same scale-free release of labor, and this released labor always leads to the same scale-free increase in the output of the other commodity.

Competitive System

So far we have been discussing the purely technological aspects of the Ricardian production model. We now turn to a different question: How will the production levels be determined for a perfectly competitive economy? This question is no longer purely technological but relates to the working of a particular institutional system: the perfectly competitive economy. It can be shown that the economy will operate on the production-possibility curve and that, at equilibrium points of production involving incomplete specialization in production, the commodity-price ratio will be tangential to the production-possibility curve.

The economy must operate on the production-possibility curve (AB in figure 2.1) because there will be unemployed labor if it is off this locus, and the presence of unemployed labor is incompatible with the assumption of perfect competition in the Ricardian model. Further the commodity-price ratio p ($= p_2/p_1$) will be tangential to the production-possibility curve at all points of incomplete specialization in production. This follows simply from the assumption of perfect competition, which means that the price of a commodity being produced in positive amounts will equal its average (labor) cost. Thus, for incomplete specialization in production,

$$p = \frac{L_2/Q_2}{L_1/Q_1},$$

where L_1/Q_1 and L_2/Q_2 are the labor/output ratios in 1 and 2. (The wage rates, being identical in both goods, cancel out on the right-hand side.) Hence, By rearranging terms, we get

$$p = \frac{Q_1/L_1}{Q_2/L_2}.$$

But this labor-productivity ratio is also the (constant) rate at which commodity 2 is transformed into commodity 1. Hence the production-possibility curve and the commodity-price ratio will overlap. In figure 2.2, for example, the tangent of angle OBA gives both the price ratio p and the constant rate of transformation between commodities 2 and 1 as

$$\frac{Q_1/L_1}{Q_2/L_2}.$$

We can now exhaust all possibilities relating the commodity-price ratio to production. Take the price ratio Ap_1 as representative of all price ratios steeper than AB. For such price ratios, production will be completely specialized at A, involving zero production of commodity 2 and deployment of all labor to produce commodity 1. The reason for this specialization in production on commodity 1 is that any shift out of 1 into 2 will be along AB, whereas the price ratio in the market is Ap_1. This means that the revenue lost by reducing the output of 1 will be greater than the revenue earned by increasing the output of 2. Thus the shifting of production, at the margin, into 2 will not be profitable. Similarly we can

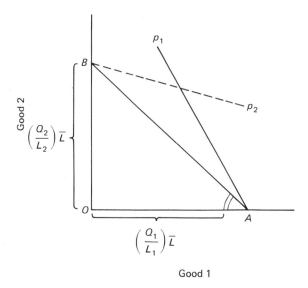

Figure 2.2

show that for price ratios that are flatter than AB, as is Bp_2, there will be complete specialization in producing 2 at B. We thus have three sets of possibilities: complete specialization in commodity 1 for all price ratios steeper than AB; complete specialization in commodity 2 for all price ratios flatter than AB; and incomplete specialization, plus complete specialization in either commodity, for price ratio AB.

A few other implications of analytical interest need to be elaborated at this stage. First, relative commodity prices depend in this model only on comparative labor productivities if we impose the condition that supply and demand for commodities 1 and 2 are positive and equal in equilibrium, thus ruling out the possibility of international trade. In this case the "self-sufficiency" equilibrium will be at some point of incomplete specialization on AB, thus implying a price ratio equaling the slope of AB (appropriately measured). For complete specialization at A or B (in which case there is only one commodity being both consumed and produced), the comparative labor productivity determines a lower or an upper bound on relative prices, depending on the point of specialization. Remember that in this model, demand conditions will determine only the production point, from among the different possibilities on AB; they will not affect the commodity-price ratio if there is positive demand for both commodities. Here we have the general-equilibrium analogue of the Marshallian long-run case where demand determines output but the price is determined by the horizontal supply curve. If there is specialization, the

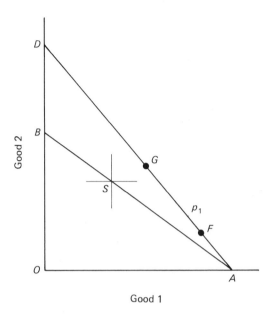

Figure 2.3

demand conditions determine the upper or the lower bound for the price ratio while the supply conditions (i.e., comparative labor productivities) determine the lower or the upper bound, depending on the point of specialization. Similarly the level of factor supply will not affect the commodity prices. An increase in labor supply will shift AB outward but will not affect its slope; the rate of transformation between commodities, and the commodity-price ratio, will still be the same and reflect the unchanged labor productivities.

Yet another implication is that the Ricardian labor theory of value will break down if we allow for international trade. Thus, if our example were a small country trading at given international prices Ap_1, production would be specialized in commodity 1 at A, and the economy would exchange 1 for 2 at this price ratio and reach equilibrium in consumption at some point such as G on line Ap_1 in figure 2.3. Thus this economy could have price ratios other than AB if international trade were allowed, and hence the labor theory of value would break down. This presumably explains why Ricardo attached so much significance to his analysis of international trade.

Ricardo appears to have put this simple model to still another elemental use to provide antimercantilist proof that trade could improve a country's welfare. In figure 2.3 production and consumption at point S under self-sufficiency is dominated by consumption at point G (which is reached through production at A and then trade along line Ap_1D), in the sense that G lies to the northeast of S. Ricardo essentially provided a simple demonstration of the superiority of trade without raising the difficult questions of modern welfare analysis (e.g., the question of what would happen if G were to the southeast, as at F). Indeed, for Ricardo's times and for his essential purposes, this simple model and the related demonstration of the superiority of trade were totally adequate.

2.3   Self-sufficiency Equilibrium

In depicting equilibrium of supply and demand, either under self-sufficiency or under trade, we have to introduce demand relations in a systematic fashion. In putting down the self-sufficiency equilibrium at S and the trade equilibrium at G and F in figure 2.3, we were essentially using only one property of the Ricardian model: that the economy should not spend more than it earns. Thus, under trade, at price ratio Ap_1D, production will be at A, and the social-budget line will therefore be defined by AD. By choosing a consumption point such as G, we are therefore using the assumption that the consumption expenditure will equal the income earned; thus the valuation of consumption at the market prices will be OA and so also will be the valuation of production. If we were to allow expenditure to exceed earned income, as with a transfer from abroad, we would depict this by shifting the budget line outward from AD by the amount of the transfer and then choosing a consumption point on this expanded social-budget line.

How should we choose the actual consumption point, given the social-budget line? There are a number of ways. At this stage we will depict two alternative ways, both of which will be used later. One procedure is to assume a single-person economy, or a set of consumers with identical tastes and incomes, or a set of individuals with identical, homothetic (constant-returns-to-scale) tastes, or to assume that by lump-sum transfers a Samuelson-type social-indifference map is generated.[2] In each of these cases, we could assume that consumption is chosen by the tangency of the social-budget line with a social-indifference curve, as in figure 2.4a, where G_s is the self-sufficiency consumption point and G_F the trade consumption point.

Alternatively, we could take income distribution into account directly. For example, figure 2.4b shows a two-person-economy equilibrium. The

2. The concept of social-indiffernece curves is discussed in chapter 18.

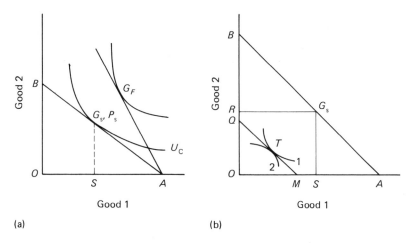

Figure 2.4

total social income, measured in units of good 1, is OA. This income is divided between individuals 1 and 2 so that individual 1 gets OM and individual 2 gets MA units. The dimensions of the box ORG_sS define the total consumption as also the consumption of each commodity for society in the aggregate. Measuring from G_s as the origin, we can draw in the indifference curves of individual 2; similarly from O as the origin we sketch in the indifference curves of individual 1. The point of common tangency with the commodity-price ratio QM (which is parallel to AB) then indicates the respective allocation of the consumption bundle G_s among the two at the point of tangency T. Thus each possible distribution of total income determines a particular point of consumption on line BA.

2.4 Trade Equilibrium and Offer Curves

With the single-person-economy depiction of demand, which is generally used in this book, we can now portray trade equilibrium. The trade equilibrium we propose to portray is one where the economy is engaging in "free trade"—that is, there is no impediment to trade. We also assume that there are no domestic taxes and subsidies or quantitative restrictions. In later chapters we will analyze equilibrium under alternative assumptions relating to commercial and domestic policy.

If we wish to portray free-trade equilibrium under the assumptions of the Ricardian model, as set out at the beginning of this chapter, we can do it simply as in figure 2.5. Suppose that the goods-price ratio in free-trade

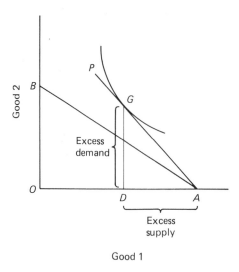

Figure 2.5

equilibrium is the slope of AP.[3] Then production in this Ricardian economy is at A, the social-budget line becomes AP, consumption is at G, and hence there is an excess demand for GD units of good 2 and an excess supply of AD units of good 1. The assumption that the slope of AP is the equilibrium price ratio implies that in the second country in this Ricardian two-country world, the same price ratio results in an excess supply of GD units of good 2 and an excess demand for AD units of good 1. Then, in this Ricardian world without transport costs, the equilibrium price ratio (terms of trade) that corresponds to matching "trade offers," and hence to the clearance of world markets in both commodities, would be AP and figure 2.5 would be portraying "trade equilibrium" in the world economy.

The traditional technique for determining the trade-equilibrium price ratio, however, is by the intersection of the Marshallian offer curves of the two countries. The offer curve of a country is merely the locus of the excess supplies and demands for commodities that are generated at different commodity-price ratios or terms of trade. Figure 2.6 illustrates the offer curve for a Ricardian economy, showing different offers of good 1 for good 2 (or different excess supplies of good 1 and associated excess demands for good 2) in the first quadrant and the reverse offers in the third quadrant. It is derived quite simply as follows: Refer back to figure 2.4a. Quote the price ratio AB to the economy. We know, from our

---

3. To avoid repetition, we denote by AP, AB, etc., both the lines and their slopes, leaving the reader to infer from the context the sense in which it is meant.

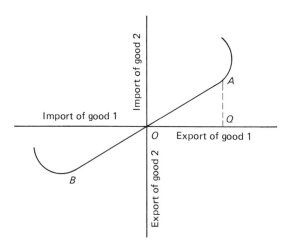

Figure 2.6

earlier analysis, that the economy can produce anywhere along *AB* when this price ratio is quoted; we have here a case of multiple production equilibria. On the other hand, consumption is uniquely chosen at G_s under our demand assumptions. If we now confine ourselves to possible production equilibria along the stretch AG_s, we have corresponding excess demands for good 2 and associated excess supplies of good 1. The excess supplies and demands are zero when production coincides with G_s. When production coincides with *A*, there is an excess supply of *AS* of good 1 and an excess demand of G_sS for good 2. These "offers" can then be plotted in figure 2.6 in the first quadrant, with *O* representing the self-sufficiency equilibrium and the entire line *OA* representing the possible trade offers of good 1 for good 2 at the price ratio given by the tangent of angle *QOA* (which is the same as the price ratio *AB* in figure 2.4a).

Similarly, if we next consider the stretch BG_s in figure 2.4a, which also shows possible points of production when the price ratio quoted is *AB*, we have production of good 2 exceeding its consumption. Hence we are in the situation of a reversed pattern of trade. The country will be "offering" good 2 for good 1. By an argument analogous to the good-1-for-good-2 case, the stretch of the offer curve (now drawn as *OB* in the third quadrant, which shows reversed pattern of trade) will be equal to the length BG_s in figure 2.4a.

For prices steeper than *AB* in figure 2.4a, implying a higher relative price for good 1 there will be complete specialization in producing that good. Hence the pattern of trade can only be the export of good 1 for the import of good 2, so the offer curve for these prices will lie in the

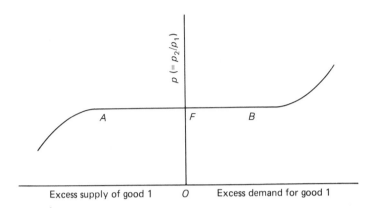

Figure 2.7

first quadrant. Similarly, for price ratios flatter than AB in figure 2.4a (implying a higher relative price for good 2), there is complete specialization in the production of good 2. Hence trade offers can only be the export of good 2 for the import of good 1, and the offers will lie in the third quadrant in figure 2.6.

Before we discuss the shapes of the offer curves for price ratios implying complete specialization in production of either commodity, let us discuss briefly the relationship of the offer curve to the ordinary Marshallian demand curve. The Marshallian demand curve for (say) tea shows the quantities of tea demanded for different prices. This, however, can be converted into an offer curve showing money being offered for tea. Similarly the offer curve can be mapped into a diagram such as figure 2.7, with the relative price of commodities on the vertical axis and the quantity of good 1 demanded and supplied on the horizontal axis.[4]

Now return to the offer curve. By rotating the price line to the left, indicating increasing relative price of good 1, we can investigate the shape of the offer curve in the first quadrant in figure 2.8. Essentially this involves analyzing the effect of the changing goods-price ratio on equilibrium production and consumption of the two goods. Remembering that throughout the analysis the production of good 1 will remain fixed and that the production of good 2 is zero and that therefore any change in the consumption of each commodity involves an identical change in the trade offer (i.e., excess supply or demand) of that commodity, we can reach the following conclusions:

4. This diagram of excess demand may be a bit confusing if interpreted as a Marshallian demand curve, since as the price of 2 relative to 1 goes up the amount demanded of 1 may fall. However, this "abnormal" shape is perfectly legitimate, as is explained later in the text.

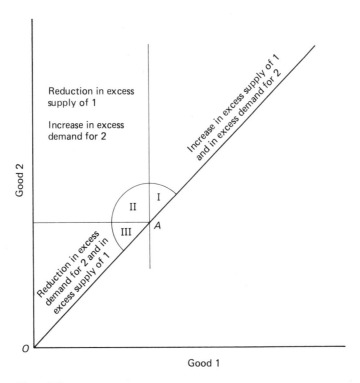

Figure 2.8

• As the price line is slightly rotated left from *OA*, the offer curve can move into one of three regions: zone I, where there is an increase in the excess supply of good 1 and in the excess demand for good 2; zone II, where there is a reduction in the excess supply of good 1 but an increase in the excess demand for good 2; and zone III, where there is a reduction in both the excess demand for good 2 and the excess supply of good 1.

• The three zones are shown in figure 2.9 as well, on the assumption that the price ratio shifts from *QAB* to *QRMS*. If the new equilibrium consumption is on *SN*, we are in zone I; if on *NM*, then in zone II; and if on *MR*, then in zone III.

• Noting that increased price of good 1 entails increased real income (in view of the specialization in the production of 1), we conclude that even if inferior goods are excluded, the offer curve can enter zones I and II in the immediate neighborhood of *A*. Since real income increases and the relative price of good 1 has increased, the demand for good 2 can only increase, whereas that for good 1 may rise or fall, if inferior goods are excluded. It also follows that zone I will necessarily be entered if good 1

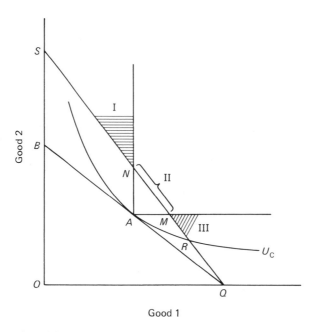

Figure 2.9

is an inferior good and that zone III can only be entered if good 2 is an inferior good and that it is entered if and only if 2 is a Giffen good.

2.5 Trade-Indifference Curves

Trade-indifference curves are used extensively in the geometric analysis of gains from trade, in considerations of optimal tariff under monopoly power in trade and in related discussions. These curves are essentially a useful device for analyzing welfare questions in the same diagrams as the offer curves we have been discussing. In fact the offer curve can be derived by rotating the price line and taking the locus of tangencies with the trade-indifference curves.

Although Meade (1952) extended the derivation of trade-indifference curves to a model allowing for changing production (along a production-possibility curve), they are derived simply, and their economic essence is understood most readily through the use of a pure exchange model where the economy has a fixed endowment of one good. Thus in figure 2.10 we take the case of an economy with a given endowment of $O\overline{X}$ of good 1. The social-indifference curves are also drawn (partially, between the two vertical lines) with the standard properties (e.g., relating to convexity). The diagram indicates satiation for good 1, at point $\overline{X}$, for utility curve

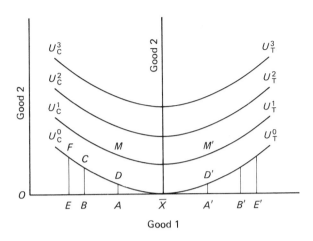

Figure 2.10

U_C^0; however, this is, not essential to the argument. Let us consider more closely the utility curve U_C^0. Looking left from $\overline{X}$, note that if this society were to give up $\overline{X}A$ of good 1 and get AD of good 2 in trade, then it would be on the same level of welfare at U_C^0. Similarly the economy would equally be indifferent between export of $\overline{X}B$ of good 1 for import of BC of good 2 and export of $\overline{X}E$ for import of EF. It follows that the entire consumption-indifference curve U_C^0 is in fact a trade-indifference curve if only we take $\overline{X}$ as the origin and measure the quantity of good 1 traded leftward from it. An identical argument applies to the other consumption-indifference curves. Trade of $\overline{X}A$ of commodity 1 will leave the country on the higher indifference curve U_C^1 if AM of commodity 2 is obtained in exchange, and so on.

In effect the entire set of consumption-indifference curves, drawn with O as the origin, becomes a corresponding set of trade-indifference curves, with $\overline{X}$ as the origin. We can then "turn the page over" and draw the mirror images of these trade-indifference curves with $\overline{X}$ as the origin but now measuring the quantities of 1 exported to the right. This yields the complete set of trade-indifference curves drawn in the customary first quadrant. Any point on a trade-indifference curve then represents the quantities of commodities 1 and 2 that would have to be exchanged to bring the economy, with its initial endowment of $O\overline{X}$ of commodity 1, to the welfare level represented by that indifference curve.

It also follows that the offer curve can be derived by merely rotating a commodity-price ratio and joining up the points of its tangency with the different trade-indifference curves. We have drawn three of the trade-indifference curves in the right part of figure 2.11. The left part of the figure, spanned by the space between the two vertical lines, gives the

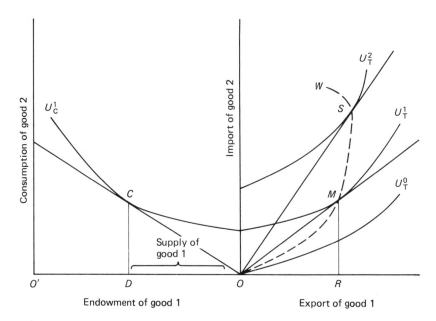

Figure 2.11

endowment of commodity 1 as $O'O$, indicates a price ratio OC, and shows consumption at point C on consumption-indifference curve U_C^1. Therefore the actual trade offer, at this price ratio, implies the supply of OD of good 1 for the import of CD of good 2. An identical result can be obtained in the trade-indifference diagram. Price ratio OM, which is identical with price ratio OC, is tangential at point M to the trade-indifference curve U_T^1, which corresponds to the consumption-indifference curve U_C^1 in terms of welfare level; this also implies an export of good 1 by amount OR (which equals OD) and an import of good 2 by amount MR (which equals CD). Thus the tangency of the price ratio with this trade-indifference curve represents the trade offer of good 1 for good 2 that will emerge at that price ratio. This argument applies to all price ratios and the corresponding tangencies, since we picked our price ratio arbitrarily. Hence it follows that the offer curve $OMSW$ can be derived by rotating the price line and joining up the resulting tangencies with the trade-indifference curves.

We can now derive the trade-indifference curves in the fashion of Meade (1952), confining ourselves essentially to the procedure involved and drawing attention to some of the central properties that will be utilized in the later chapters. Figure 2.12 shows how the trade-indifference curves can be derived, in the case of variable production, by sliding the production-possibility block $O'RSF$ along each social-indifference curve

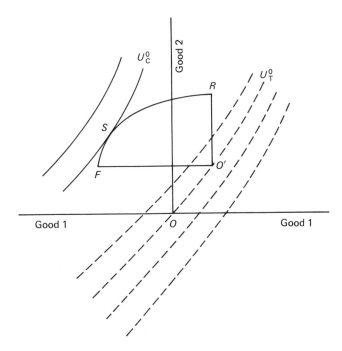

Figure 2.12

and maintaining $O'R$ vertical and $O'F$ horizontal. The trade-indifference curve U_T^0 going through the origin O is seen to be derived by sliding the production block along the social-indifference curve U_C^0. Similarly higher (lower) trade-indifference curves are derived by sliding the production block along the higher (lower) social-indifference curves. The trade-indifference curves are traced out by the movement of the origin of the production block (O') as the block slides along the social-indifference curve, and the level of social utility implied by the trade-indifference curve naturally corresponds to that implied by the social-indifference curve along which the production block slides in order to generate the trade-indifference curve in question.

Figure 2.13 illustrates the central property of the trade-indifference curves: that the tangent to any trade-indifference curve, as at O' to U_T^0, is parallel to the tangent to the social-indifference curve and the production-possibility curve at the "corresponding" point, as at S. In a competitive system this tangent corresponds to the price ratio between the two goods, which is both the world and the domestic price ratio when no impediments to trade are present. (The cases where tariffs or quotas make it necessary to distinguish between domestic and world prices will be discussed later in chapters 12 and 13.)

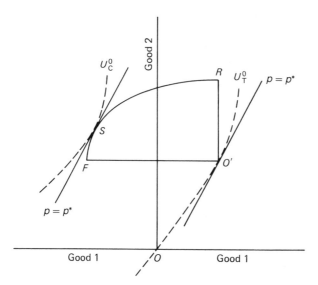

Figure 2.13

Next we will show that the foreign-offer curve of this economy can be generated by rotating the price line with O as pivot and taking the locus of all the points of tangencies between the various price lines and the trade-indifference curves, as before. In this case the shape of the trade-indifference curves is not parallel to that of the corresponding social-indifference curves. These curves would be parallel in the exchange model or if the production of both goods were fixed, but when production is variable, the movement in O' corresponding to the movement in S as the production block slides will reflect not only moves along the social-indifference curve but also moves along the production block. It follows that once the production block has shifted to a point of complete specialization in either good, any further tracing out of the trade-indifference curve will reflect only changes in consumption, and hence, beyond such points of complete specialization, the social- and trade-indifference curves will become parallel.

Meade also notes that the exclusion of inferior goods imposes restrictions on the shapes of the trade-indifference curves. In figure 2.12 the exclusion of inferior goods implies that any vertical movement from an arbitrary point such as O' will cut successively steeper trade-indifference curves and any horizontal movement to the left from any such point will cut successively flatter trade-indifference curves.[5] This property is of some importance, for the presence or absence of inferior goods will later be

5. For a proof, see Meade (1952, pp. 15–16).

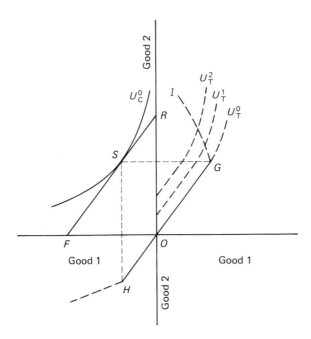

Figure 2.14

seen to be central to the phenomenon of multiple equilibrium and hence
to both positive and welfare questions in trade theory.

Since this chapter is addressed primarily to the Ricardian model, note
the shapes of the trade-indifference curves in this case. Figure 2.14 shows
that where the Ricardian production block is $ORSF$, the Meade technique will lead to trade-indifference curves with straight segments. Thus
U_T^0 will clearly have the linear stretch OG equal to FS, and for the third
quadrant (reversed offers of good 2 for good 1) U_T^0 will have the linear
stretch OH equal to RS. The linear stretch GH on U_0^T will equal the
linear stretch RF on the Ricardian production block. Points G and H
represent the points of complete specialization, beyond which (as discussed above) the trade-indifference curve U_0^T will follow the shape of the
social-indifference curve U_C^0.

Finally the Ricardian offer curve will be derived by rotating the price
line and joining up the locus of its tangencies with such trade-indifference
curves. It will therefore follow OG and then turn left in the familiar
manner, tracing a locus such as OGI.

2.6   Formal Notes on the Ricardian Model

We can now treat the Ricardian analysis algebraically. Let the labor
input per unit of good i be denoted by l_i $(i = 1, 2)$. Let p denote the

relative price of good 2 in terms of the numéraire good 1, and let w be the wage rate in terms of good 1. Clearly, if good i can be produced at a constant (average and marginal) input of l_i per unit of output, under competition, producers of good 1 will produce nothing when $wl > 1$ (i.e., when wage cost of production exceeds unit price), will produce any amount between 0 and ∞ when $wl_1 = 1$, and will want to produce an infinite amount when $wl_1 < 1$. Similarly producers of commodity 2 will produce nothing when $p < wl_2$, will produce any amount between 0 and ∞ when $p = wl_2$, and will want to produce an infinite amount when $p > wl_2$. Hence, if positive amounts of both commodities are produced under competition, $wl_1 = 1$ or $w = 1/l_1$ and $p = wl_2 = l_2/l_1$; that is, the wage rate in terms of the numéraire is the marginal (and average) productivity of labor in the production of numéraire good 1. The relative price of good 2 in terms of good 1 is the ratio of productivity of labor in producing good 1 to that in producing good 2.

If there is specialization in good 1 (i.e., if a positive amount of good 1 is produced and zero amount of good 2), we have $wl_1 = 1$ and $p < wl_2$ (or $p < l_2/l_1$). Similarly, if $p > l_2/l_1$, there is specialization in good 2. Given an endowment of labor of L units, the maximal amount of good i that can be produced is L/l_i. Thus we can summarize the production levels of good $i(Q_i)$ in a Ricardian world under competition as follows:

$$p < \frac{l_2}{l_1}, \quad Q_1 = \frac{L}{l_1}, \quad Q_2 = 0, \quad w = \frac{1}{l_1},$$

$$p = \frac{l_2}{l_1}, \quad Q_2 = \frac{L - Q_1 l_1}{l_2}, \quad 0 \le Q_1 \le \frac{L}{l_1}, \quad w = \frac{L}{l_1},$$

$$p > \frac{l_2}{l_1}, \quad Q_1 = 0, \quad Q_2 = \frac{L}{l_2}, \quad w = \frac{p}{l_2}.$$

Given a social-utility function $U(C_1, C_2)$, where C_i is the consumption of good i, we can derive the offer curve relating net exports of good 1 $(Q_1 - C_1)$ to net imports of good 2 $(C_2 - Q_2)$ by maximizing $U(C_1, C_2)$ subject to

$$C_1 + pC_2 = Q_1 + pQ_2, \qquad 0 < p < \infty$$

where (Q_1, Q_2) for each given p is as above.

We can derive the trade-indifference curve, given that the economy is specialized (say) in good 1, as follows. Let

$$E_1 = (Q_1 - C_1) = \left(\frac{L}{l_1}\right) - C_1$$

be the exports of good 1. Let the imports of good 2 be

$$M_2 = (C_2 - Q_2) = C_2.$$

Then, to achieve welfare $\overline{U}$, we must have

$$U\left(\frac{L}{l_1} - E_1, M_2\right) = \overline{U},$$

and the corresponding terms of trade will be E_1/M_2. Writing

$$U\left(\frac{L}{l_1} - E_1, M_2\right) \equiv W[E_1, M_2],$$

we obtain trade-indifference curves by setting $W = \overline{W}$. It is then easily verified that since U is monotonically increasing in C_1 and C_2 and is concave, W is also monotonically increasing in M_2, decreasing in E_1, and concave. Maximizing U subject to

$$C_1 + pC_2 = Q_1 + pQ_2$$

with $Q_1 = L/l_1$ and $Q_2 = 0$ (i.e., $p < l_2/l_1$) is equivalent to maximizing W subject to $E_1 = pM_2$. In other words, the offer curve for $p < l_2/l_1$ can be derived by obtaining the tangency point of the highest trade-indifference curve with the terms of trade line. For $p \geq l_2/l_1$, the modifications are obvious.

Recommended Readings

Bhagwati, J. The pure theory of international trade: A survey. *Economic Journal* 74 (1964): 1–84.

Brecher, R. A., and I. C. Parker. Time structure of production and the theory of international trade. *Journal of International Economics* 7 (1977): 385–402.

Caves, R. E. *Trade and Economic Structure.* Cambridge: Harvard University Press, 1960, ch. 2.

Chipman, J. S. A survey of the theory of international trade: Part 1, The classical theory. *Econometrica* 33 (1965): 477–519.

Graham, F. D. The theory of international values reexamined. *Quarterly Journal of Economics* 38 (1923): 54–86. Reprinted in *Readings in the Theory of International Trade*, ed. by H. Ellis and L. Metzler. Philadelphia: Blakiston, 1949.

Graham, F. D. The theory of international values. *Quarterly Journal of Economics* 46 (1932): 581–616.

Leontief, W. The use of indifference curves in the analysis of foreign trade. *Quarterly Journal of Economics* 47 (1933): 493–503. Reprinted in *International Trade*, ed. by J. Bhagwati. Baltimore: Penguin, 1969.

McKenzie, L. W. On equilbrium in Graham's model of world trade and other competitive systems. *Econometrica* 22 (1954): 147–61.

Meade, J. E. *A Geometry of International Trade.* London: Allen and Unwin, 1952, chs 1, 2, 4.

Metcalfe, J. S., and I. Steedman. Heterogeneous capital and the Heckscher-Ohlin-Samuelson theory of trade. In *Essays in Modern Economics: The Proceedings of the Association of University Teachers of Economics*, ed. by M. Parkin. London: Longmans, Green, 1973.

Metzler, L. A. Graham's theory of international values. *American Economic Review* 40 (1950): 301–22.

Mill, J. S. *Principles of Political Economy*, ed. by W. J. Ashley. London: Longmans, Green, 1917, book 3, chs 17, 18.

Samuelson, P. A. Theoretical notes on trade problems. *Review of Economics and Statistics* 46 (1964): 145–54.

Samuelson, P. A. Trade pattern reversals in time-phased Ricardian systems and intertemporal efficiency. *Journal of International Economics* 5 (1975): 309–64.

Steedman, I., and J. S. Metcalfe. On foreign trade. *Economia Internationale* 26 (1973): 516–27.

We are now in a position to derive formally the Ricardian theorem relating to the pattern of trade: *A country exports that commodity in which it has comparative labor-productivity advantage.* We will also derive simultaneously the associated proposition, attributed to John Stuart Mill: *The equilibrium terms of trade will lie in the range spanned by the self-sufficiency price ratios in the two trading countries.*

Figure 3.1 shows excess demand for commodity 2 in two countries, I and II, at different goods/price ratios. The price ratio *OE* is the self-sufficiency price ratio in country II, and also the price ratio at which excess supply and demand for each good can materialize. Point *Q* corresponds to complete specialization in production of good 1, and point *R* to complete specialization in production of good 2. Similarly *OF* is the self-sufficiency price ratio in country I.

We noted in the preceding that the excess-demand curves may show increasing, decreasing, or constant excess demand for good 2 as *p* increases in the immediate neighborhood of *R*. Assume now that as the price of good 2 is raised to infinity, nowhere does the excess-demand curve touch the vertical axis above *OE*. (We will discuss later in this chapter the precise demand assumptions that ensure this result.) Note, however, that no matter what we assume about demand, the curve cannot cut across into the other quadrant as *p* rises; this would imply excess supply of good 1, which is impossible given the specialization in production of commodity 2 at all *p* above *OE*. Similarly, as the relative price of good 2 falls, the excess-demand curve will bend in or out in the immediate neighborhood of *Q*; again we assume that nowhere does the curve bend back so far as to touch the vertical axis below *OE*.

It follows that for each country in this Ricardian world, the only possible equilibrium requires that the excess demand for each commodity be zero for the world as a whole and be in the range *EF*, which is spanned by the self-sufficiency price ratios of the two countries. For any price ratio above *OF*, there will be world excess demand for good 1; for price ratios below *OE* there will be world excess demand for good 2. By continuity, there will therefore be an equilibrium price ratio, in the range *EF*, at which the world markets will be cleared for each good—hence Mill's proposition that the equilibrium terms of trade lie between (though they may overlap with one of) the self-sufficiency price ratios of the two trading countries.

It also follows that country I will export good 1 and import good 2, and that country II will export good 2 and import good 1. Thus the country with the cheaper (relative) price of good 1 in self-sufficiency will export good 1 and import good 2. However, as soon as we combine this proposition with the earlier proposition that the self-sufficiency price

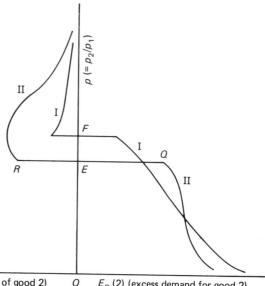

Figure 3.1

ratios will reflect the labor-productivity ratios, we arrive at the Ricardian theorem. Thus country I will export good 1 and import good 2 when $p > p^*$ in self-sufficiency. But

$$p = \frac{L_2/Q_2}{L_1/Q_1}$$

in self-sufficiency; therefore country I will export good 1 and import good 2 when

$$\left(\frac{L_2/Q_2}{L_1/Q_1}\right) > \left(\frac{L_2/Q_2}{L_1/Q_2}\right)^*.$$

Rewriting this, we get the standard theorem: If

$$\frac{(Q_1/L_1)}{(Q_1/L_1)^*} > \frac{(Q_2/L_2)}{(Q_2/L_2)^*},$$

then country I will export good 1 and import good 2; that is, *each country will export that good in which it enjoys comparative labor-productivity advantage.*

The analysis does not rule out multiple trade equilibria. Figure 3.2 shows how there may be a price range, such as *SU*, over which world supply and demand are equal in each market. Any price ratio in that range represents a possible trade equilibrium.

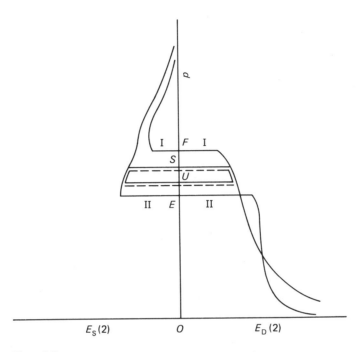

Figure 3.2

All these propositions can be illustrated in terms of the Marshallian offer-curve technique. Figure 3.3 illustrates Mill's and Ricardo's propositions by showing how the equilibrium terms of trade (OF) lie between the self-sufficiency price ratios of the two countries $(OW$ and $OZ)$. In particular, the fact that the third quadrant does not contain an intersection of the two offer curves implies that the pattern of trade cannot be reversed from what the Ricardian theorem predicts, for the same reasons that this was ruled out when we were considering the diagrammatic technique for excess demand of good 2.

In general, the excess demand curves can meet the vertical axis more than once, giving rise to multiple zero-trade equilibria. This possibility can arise when indifference curves meet one or both axes. For example, suppose that they meet the horizontal axis and that at the point of complete specialization in good 1, the indifference curve that meets the horizontal axis is steeper than the production-possibilities frontier. The pretrade equilibrium at the point of complete specialization in good 1 is then compatible with all prices lying between the marginal rate of substitution at that point and the marginal rate of transformation. It is then possible for both Ricardo's and Mill's theorems, as stated above, to break down. Without demonstrating this result, we offer two solutions to the problem. The first solution involves restricting demands in such a way as

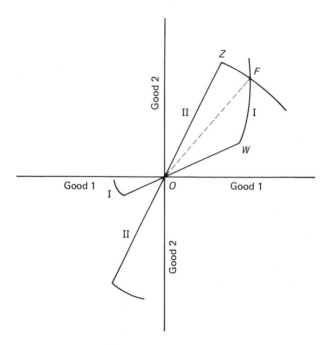

Figure 3.3

to rule out multiple equilibria; the second one weakens the statement of the Ricardian theorem to rule out the case in which zero-trade multiple equilibria arise.

3.1 Alternative Demand Assumptions

The following demand restrictions would eliminate multiple no-trade equilibria in the Ricardian model.

• If we assume the existence of a set of community-indifference curves, it is enough to assume positive demand for both goods at the self-sufficiency prices ratio in each country. Then, given the specialization in production at every other price ratio and the nonintersection of the indifference curve, we cannot have termination of demand for the commodity being produced under specialization at any given price ratio. Hence we cannot have zero excess demand at prices other than the unique commodity-price ratio that equals the productivity-determined transformation rate between commodities.

• A stronger sufficient condition would be to assume interminable demand for each commodity at all price ratios in each country—that is, community-indifference curves do not touch either axis.

3.2   Weaker Formulation of Ricardian Theorem

It follows from the last remark that we can restate the Ricardian theorem, without having to invoke the two preceding demand restrictions, by merely adding the qualification that the Ricardian theorem applies "when trade arises." Because the excess-demand curves cannot cross over into either quadrant more than once in the Ricardian model, it is impossible to have, say, a positive-trade equilibrium that contradicts the Ricardian theorem. Thus, *if the opening to trade leads to positive quantities of trade, each country exports that commodity in which it has comparative labor-productivity advantage.*[1]

Recommended Readings

Bhagwati, J. Proofs of the theorems on comparative advantage. *Economic Journal* 77 (1967): 75–83.

Bhagwati, J., and H. G. Johnson. Notes on some controversies in the theory of international trade. *Economic Journal* 70 (1960): 74–93.

Mill, J. S. *Principles of Political Economy*, ed. by W. J. Ashley. London: Longmans, Green. 1917. Book 3, chs. 17, 18.

Ricardo, D. *On the Principles of Political Economy and Taxation* (The Works and Correspondence of David Ricardo, vol. 1), ed. by P. Sraffa. Cambridge: Cambridge University Press, 1951, ch. 7.

1. The Mill theorem is also then satisfied.

This chapter extends the Ricardian analysis to cases where there are more than two countries, cases where there are more than two goods, cases where transport costs are allowed, and cases where tariffs are permitted. In principle, we can also generalize the Ricardian theory to two or more factors by considering Hicks-neutral technical differences across countries in the production functions for each industry. We defer this, however, until chapter 7.

4.1   Multiple Countries

As soon as we introduce more than two countries while sticking to the other Ricardian assumptions, we have to weaken our formulation of the Ricardian theorem to read as follows: *If all countries are ranked according to their labor-productivity ratios, $(Q_1/L_1)/(Q_2/L_2)$, the country with the highest ratio will export good 1, the country with the lowest ratio will import good 1. Countries in the intermediate range may export or import good 1, although all countries exporting good 1 will have higher labor-productivity ratios than all countries importing good 1.*

This proposition is demonstrated in figure 4.1. We show there the excess-demand curves for three countries, I, II, and III, with the proviso that there is a unique self-sufficiency equilibrium price ratio p for each country: OD, OF, and OE for countries I, III, and II, respectively.

It is immediately clear from figure 4.1 that any price ratio p higher than OD will lead to world excess supply of good 2 and any price ratio lower than OE will lead to world excess demand for good 2. Hence the feasible price-ratio range is DE, which implies that country I must export good 1 and country II must export good 2. However, if the trade equilibrium involves a price ratio higher than OF, country III will export good 2, and at price ratio lower than OF, country III will export good 1. Thus the trade pattern is indeterminate for country III but predictable for countries I and II. More generally, if countries are ranked according to their self-sufficiency price ratios p, then the country with the lowest price ratio must export good 2 and the country with the highest price ratio must import good 2. But countries in the intermediate range may export or import good 2, although all countries exporting good 2 must have lower self-sufficiency price ratios than all countries importing good 2. Since the self-sufficiency price ratios reflect the labor-productivity ratios, the Ricardian proposition stated at the outset of the present analysis follows.

Even though we rule out multiple pretrade price equilibria, this is not sufficient to rule out the possibility of the intermediate countries having

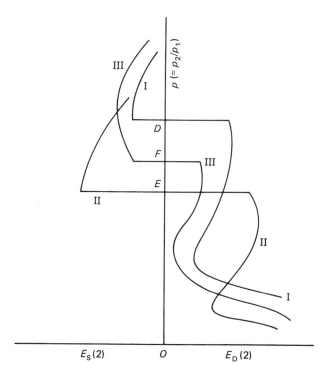

Figure 4.1

both patterns of trade feasible. This is best seen by comparing the aggregate excess-demand curve for countries I and II against the excess-demand curve for the intermediate country, III. Figure 4.2 shows the case where there is a unique pattern of trade for country III. The self-sufficiency price ratios in countries I and II are OD and OE. At OD, there is excess supply of good 2. The aggregate excess-demand curve for countries I and II together therefore passes through the vertical axis at T, going from M to N. When the excess-demand curve for country III is included, we have a unique pattern of trade established in the range TF, with country III importing good 2. The quantities of good 2 exchanged are $QS = RS$, and the terms of trade are OS. As before, there may be multiple post-trade equilibria, but the pattern of trade will be uniquely determined by whether OF exceeds or is exceeded by OT.

In figure 4.3 we illustrate the case where the aggregate excess-demand curve for countries I and II together cuts across the vertical axis more than once, as indeed can happen. In this case the pattern of trade for country III may involve export of good 2 (as at the equilibrium price ratio OG) or import of good 2 (as at the equilibrium price ratio OF).

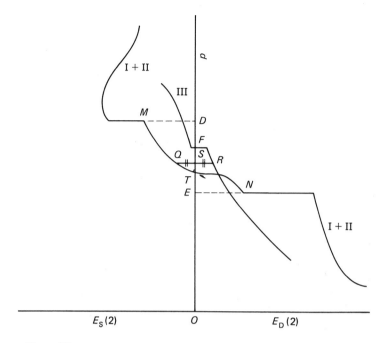

Figure 4.2

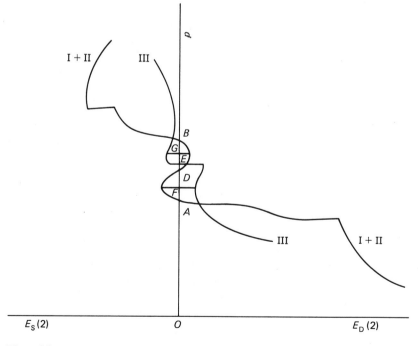

Figure 4.3

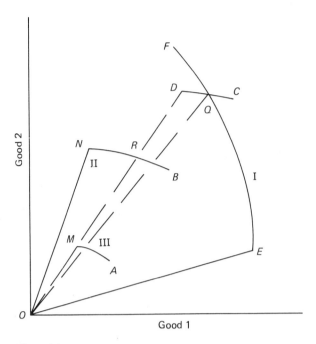

Figure 4.4

Becker (1952) proposed that the pattern of trade of the intermediate country will be determined by the "cost and utility" considerations of the extreme countries, but only by the cost conditions of the intermediate country. This proposition clearly holds for the case where the intermediate country's pattern of trade is uniquely derived, as in figure 4.2. The sum of the excess-demand curves of the extreme countries, I and II, then defines the pattern of trade when considered with respect to only the price ratio at which the intermediate country III has its self-sufficiency (which reflects only cost conditions). But when the intermediate country can have reversed patterns of trade, as in figure 4.3, it is clear that the shape of the excess-demand curve of the intermediate country, and not just its self-sufficiency price ratio, will determine in general the pattern of trade of the intermediate country.

All the results derived here can be presented with the aid of the Marshallian offer curves. The diagrammatic technique that can be deployed for this purpose is illustrated in figure 4.4. Here the offer curves of countries II and III—ONB and OMA, respectively—are aggregated to arrive at a joint offer curve for these countries: $ONRDQC$.[1] Following Becker,

1. The length RD equals OM. The aggregation relates to quantities offered at different terms of trade.

we are carrying out the aggregation on the assumption that only the offers of good 2 for good 1 are being added. Hence we are not deriving a "net" schedule of offers from countries II and III together, at different terms of trade, against which we can compare country II's offer curve ($OEQF$) to arrive at the equilibrium terms of trade for the entire international economy. If we were doing the latter (as we will in figures 4.6 and 4.7), at terms of trade lying in the range of ON to OM we would have to subtract the offers of good 1 for good 2 (from country III, not shown in the third quadrant) from the offers of good 2 for good 1 (from country II) to arrive at the "net," aggregate offer curve of countries II and III. Bearing this caveat in mind, we can use this illustration to show the international terms of trade at OQ, with countries II and III exporting good 2 for good 1 and country I exporting good 1 for good 2.

We can infer from the diagram the amounts of good 2 exported by countries II and III individually. In figure 4.4, with three countries, we can infer also the amounts traded by each country with every other country. However, once we go beyond three countries, we cannot in general infer the actual traded amounts for each bilateral group of countries. This is seen from figure 4.5, which generalizes figure 4.4. Here we show export of good 2 for import of good 1 by five countries whose self-sufficiency price ratios are OA, BC, DE, FG, and HK and export of good 1 for import of good 2 for four countries with self-sufficiency price ratios of OP, RS, TM, and NS. The international terms of trade are at OQ, and the total amounts transacted are correspondingly inferred as the coordinates of point Q. We can also infer the amounts transacted by each country with the outside world *in toto*, but we cannot infer what each country transacts with each other country.

We now turn to the derivation of the net, aggregate offer curve of countries II and III together so that we can compare it directly against the offer curve of country I to obtain the free-trade equilibrium. Two cases are distinguished depending on whether country II's self-sufficiency price ratio gets into the first or the third quadrant when the net, aggregate offer curve is drawn. In figure 4.6, by successively rotating the terms-of-trade line from the left of OA clockwise through OC and beyond, we can take the offers of country II (as revealed by its offer curve $HGOAQB$) and of country III (as revealed by its offer curve $FJEOCD$) and add them up to derive the net, aggregate offer curve of countries II and III together: $WNJGKMOCQRS$.[2] Similarly we derive the aggregate offer curve as $RQGOMNSTW$ in figure 4.7, starting from $FEOCD$ as the offer curve of country III and $HGOMASB$ as the offer curve of country II. The

2. The lengths OC and QR are equal; so are OG and JN.

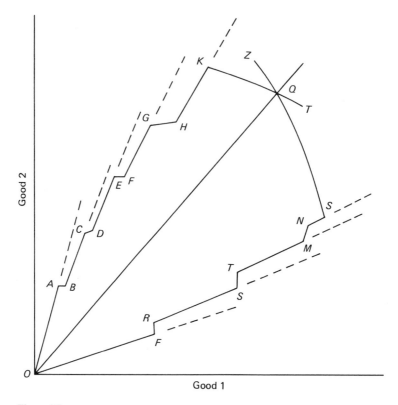

Figure 4.5

difference between the two figures is that whereas country II's self-sufficiency price ratio is in the same relative position with respect to that of country III in both, the aggregate offer curve for the price range between the two self-sufficiency price ratios is in the third quadrant in figure 4.6 and in the first quadrant in figure 4.7. In either case it is clear that an increase in the number of countries tends to increase the elasticity of the aggregate offer curve derived, either by increasing the straight segments as in figure 4.6 or by increasing the overall length over which these linear stretches operate. The result is that as Graham was the first to point out and as Becker has subsequently emphasized, the effect of an increase in the demand of country I on the terms of trade is likely to be diminished.

4.2 Multiple Goods

Let us now revert to two countries but consider multiple goods. When we do this, we can again rescue a weaker formulation of the Ricardian theorem:

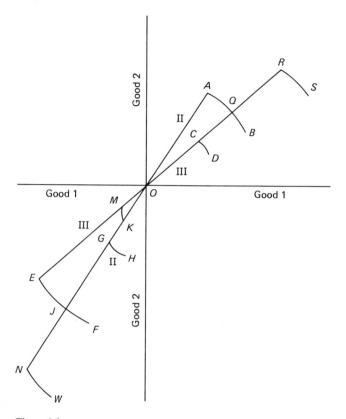

Figure 4.6

• *If every good is ranked according to its comparative labor-productivity advantage as between the two countries,* for example,

$$\frac{(Q_1/L_1)}{(Q_1/L_1)^*} > \frac{(Q_2/L_2)}{(Q_2/L_2)^*} > \frac{(Q_3/L_3)}{(Q_3/L_3)^*},$$

then each country must export the good in which it has the greatest comparative advantage (e.g., country I will export good 1 and country II will export good 3), these being the goods at the end of the "chain."[3]

• Nothing can be asserted in general about the other goods in the middle of the chain; demand conditions have to be specified to determine which of these will be exported and imported. However, the chain cannot be "crisscrossed"; each exported good must have a comparative labor-productivity advantage over each imported good.[4]

---

3. The proposition, as stated, requires the explicit demand assumption that the demand for either good does not terminate.

4. This proposition, as stated, is valid even when the demand for (and hence the production of) a good will terminate in equilibrium.

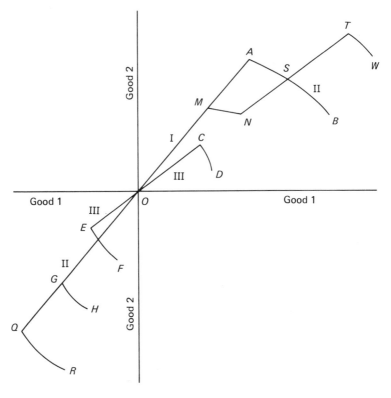

Figure 4.7

4.3 Transportation Costs

Samuelson (1954) suggested a simple way in which transportation costs could be introduced into two-good models without having to add a third good called "transportation." This is done by adopting the "iceberg" view of transportation: Of each unit of a good leaving an origin, only a fraction reaches the destination (as if a part of an iceberg melts away in transit). The fraction lost in transportation is the transportation cost. We can utilize this device to introduce transportation costs into the Ricardian model.

Assume that our two countries exchange their exportables for their importables at an international market midway between them, and that only a fraction g_i of each unit of good i leaving an origin (e.g., either country or the international market) reaches its destination (the international market or either country). Consider exporting good 1 and importing good 2, given an international price ratio p^W for good 2 in terms of good 1. With the transportation costs, only g_1 of each unit of good 1 exported reaches the international market, where it is exchanged for g_1/p^W units of good 2. When transported back home as imports, only g_2g_1/p^W units of good 2 reach home. Thus, using the international market involves obtaining g_2g_1/p^W units of good 2 for each unit of good 1. Given self-sufficiency exchange ratios of $1/p$ and $1/p^*$, respectively, in the two countries, exporting good 1 will be worthwhile only if $g_2g_1/p^W \geq 1/p$ (i.e., $p^W \leq g_2g_1p$) for country I and $p^W \leq g_2g_1p^*$ for country II. By analogous argument, it follows that exports of good 2 will take place only if $g_1g_2p^W \geq p$ in the case of country I and only if $g_1g_2p^W \geq p^*$ in the case of country II. Hence, if $g_1g_2p < p^W < p/g_1g_2$, country I will not want to enter international markets, whereas if $g_1g_2p^* < p^W < p^*/g_1g_2$, country II will not want to enter international markets—as contrasted with a situation of zero transportation costs ($g_1 = g_2 = 1$).

For a country to want to trade, the presence of transportation costs implies that it is no longer sufficient for the international price ratio merely to differ from the self-sufficiency price ratio. The difference has to be large enough to outweigh the effect of the transportation costs. For this to translate into actual trade, a further necessary condition is that the two countries export different goods. This requires, in addition to $p^* < p$, that $p^*/g_1g_2 \leq p^W < g_1g_2p$ before country I will export good 1 and country II will export good 2. However, sufficiently high transportation costs (i.e., sufficiently low g_1g_2) can result in $g_1g_2p < p^*/g_1g_2$ though $p > p^*$. In other words, sufficiently high transportation costs can eliminate trade altogether. Thus, even though both goods are tradable, they will not be traded.

It follows that in the two-country Ricardian model with more than two goods, it should be possible to have a subset of nontraded goods determined endogenously once transportation costs are admitted. This will be demonstrated later in this chapter.

Finally, for the two-good case, we should be able to show trade taking place in the usual way by using offer curves whose intersection yields the equilibrium world price ratio p^W. Such an offer curve for each country can be derived, as illustrated in figure 4.8,[5] by noting that p^W corresponds to an FOB price of $g_1g_2p^W$ for exports of good 2 and a CIF price of p^W/g_1g_2 for imports of good 2. These offer curves of the two countries will intersect if and only if the condition established above for non-elimination of trade is satisfied.

---

5. The dashed line is the offer curve for positive transportation costs; solid line is the offer curve for zero transportation costs.

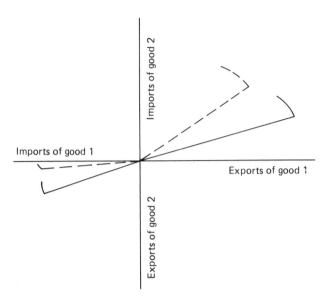

Figure 4.8

4.4 Tariffs

Tariffs too can eliminate trade. In Samuelson's phraseology they are "artificial" impediments to trade, just as transportation costs are "natural" impediments. We consider the implications of the imposition of an import tariff by one country in a Ricardian model[6] in figure 4.9. AB is the production-possibility curve, and the country is specialized in the production of good 1 under free trade. Assume that the tariff on the import of good 2 does not raise the relative price of good 2 so much as to induce the country to produce good 2. Then, in figure 4.9, at the initial free-trade relative price of good 2, the economy consumes at C^F. With the terms of trade unchanged but the tariff in place, production continues to be specialized in good 1 and consumption shifts to C^T on the same terms-of-trade line, where the slope of the social-indifference curve equals the tariff-inclusive price of good 2. Thus only DC^T units of good 2 are imported under the tariff, compared with GC^F under free trade. It is also seen from figure 4.9 that while national income at factor cost is OB in units of good 1, national expenditure (the value of the consumption

6. The tariff analysis below for the Ricardian case is only a special case of the more general tariff analysis in chapter 12.

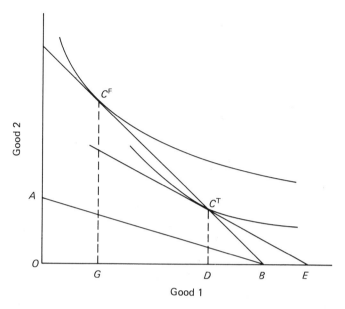

Figure 4.9

bundle at domestic prices) is OE; the difference BE is the tariff revenue that is assumed to be returned to consumers in a lump-sum transfer. That BE is the tariff revenue is also seen from the fact that the value of imports of DC^T of good 2 is valued at DB units of good 1 at world prices, whereas at domestic prices the value is DE. In sum, at world prices represented by the slope of BC^T and a tariff-inclusive price represented by the sloped of EC^T, the economy offers to export BD units of good 1 in return for DC^T units of good 2.

Now, for production to be specialized in good 1, and with the *ad valorem* tariff set at rate t, the domestic tariff-inclusive price $p = p^*(1 + t)$ of good 2 has to be lower than its autarky price p^A; that is, $p^*(1 + t) < p^A$. Thus, by keeping the tariff fixed at t and varying p^* in the interval $0 < p^* < p^A/(1 + t)$, we can plot the resulting tariff-ridden offer curve of the economy in the quadrant where it exports good 1. This is shown in figure 4.10. It is clear that one can similarly derive a tariff-ridden offer curve in the quadrant where the economy exports good 2 instead. Hence, if the government announces a tariff at an *ad valorem* rate of t on imports regardless of whether good 1 or good 2 will be imported and if the world price p^* happens to be in the interval $p^A/(1 + t) \leq p^* \leq p^A(1 + t)$, the two countries will not trade.

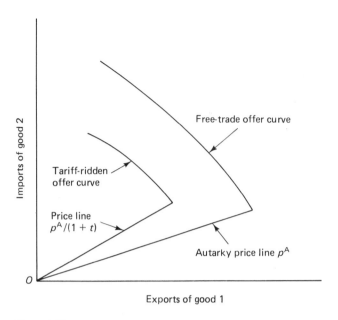

Figure 4.10

4.5   Nontraded Goods

So far we have shown how tariffs and transport costs can be incorporated into the Ricardian model. We have also shown how these costs can eliminate trade altogether. However, it follows immediately that if we introduce more than two goods into the Ricardian model and allow such impediments to trade, it should be simple to established that one or more goods (in the three-or-more-goods model) could become unprofitable to trade in equilibrium. That is, it should be possible to show that the nontraded goods are endogenously determined in the Ricardian model.

To see this, consider the Ricardian model but allow three goods in a two-country framework. Let a_i and a_i^* denote the labor needed to produce a unit of good i in countries I and II, respectively. If w and w^* are the wage rates (in terms of a common numéraire) in the two countries, it is clear that in the absence of tariffs or transport costs, country I would like to produce good i at home rather than import it if $wa_i \leq w^* a_i^*$ (i.e., if $w/w^* \leq a_i^*/a_i$). Now denote w/w^* by ω and a_i^*/a_i by A_i, and assume (without loss of generality) that goods are ranked according to the comparative advantage of country I (i.e., $A_1 > A_2 > A_3$). We can then claim that for a determinate international trade equilibrium, we must have $A_3 \leq \omega \leq A_1$. If, for instance, $\omega > A_1$ $(< A_3)$, country I (II) will want to import all three commodities, which is clearly infeasible. The demand conditions determine where the equilibrium value of ω (e.g., $\tilde{\omega}$) will lie in the interval (A_3, A_1). If $\tilde{\omega}$ is such that $A_3 < \tilde{\omega} < A_2$, then country II specializes in good 3 and country I produces goods 1 and 2.

Suppose now that because of transportation costs, only a fraction g of a unit of any good exported from one country to the other reaches its destination. It is then clear that country I will produce rather than import good i if $wa_i \leq w^*a_i^*/g$ (i.e., $\omega \leq A_i/g$). Similarly country II will produce rather than import good i if $w^*a_i^* \leq wa/g$ (i.e., $gA_i \leq \omega$). Now consider an ω such that $gA_2 < \omega < A_2/g$. At such an ω, both countries will not import but produce (and consume what they produce) good 2. Thus good 2 becomes a nontraded good. Again demand conditions will determine the equilibrium ω. Therefore, while all goods are tradable in this model, whether a good is actually traded or not is determined endogenously in general equilibrium. This contrasts with other models in which some goods are exogenously classified as nontradable and hence not traded.

If $\omega < A_3/g$, country I will produce all three goods and import none. Similarly, if $\omega > gA_1$, country II will produce all three goods and import none. With sufficiently high transportation costs (i.e., with sufficiently low g), we will have $gA_1 < A_3/g$. There then cannot be an equilibrium with positive trade; that is, both countries will stay in their autarky equilibrium. Thus sufficiently high transportation costs can eliminate trade altogether, as indeed we showed earlier for the two-good Ricardian model.

4.6   The Continuum-of-Goods Model

All the multiple-goods models that we have considered so far leave demand outside the analysis and, as a result, are unable to determine the relative wages between the two countries and hence the pattern of trade in products other than those lying at the end points of the chain of comparative advantage. A particularly neat model that introduces demand explicitly and lends itself to straightforward comparative statics analysis is due to Dornbusch, Fischer, and Samuelson (DFS 1977).

Though the DFS model assumes a continuum of goods, it is instructive to introduce it with the help of the model considered in section 4.2. Suppose that there are two countries and n goods. As in the previous section, let a_i and a_i^* be labor per-unit of good i ($i = 1, 2, \ldots, n$) required in countries I and II, respectively. Index goods such that

$$\frac{a_1^*}{a_1} > \frac{a_2^*}{a_2} > \cdots > \frac{a_n^*}{a_n}.$$

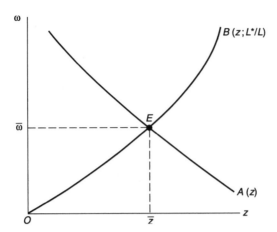

Figure 4.11

As we saw in section 4.2, in this model country I has a comparative advantage in good 1 and country II in n, while the comparative advantage in the remaining goods cannot be determined unless we explicitly introduce demand conditions.

Suppose now that there are infinitely many goods indexed by variable z over interval $[0, 1]$ on the real line. Letting $a(z)$ and $a^*(z)$ be labor per unit of good z $(0 \leq z \leq 1)$ in countries I and II, respectively, and arranging goods such that country I's comparative advantage declines with a rise in z, we have

$$A(z) = \frac{a^*(z)}{a(z)}, \qquad A'(z) < 0. \tag{4.1}$$

The assumption $A'(z) < 0$ indicates that country I's comparative advantage declines as z increases. The relationship is shown in figure 4.11 by the curve labeled $A(z)$.

Letting w and w^* be the wage in terms of common numéraire in countries I and II, respectively, the former will produce z provided $a(z) \cdot w \leq a^*(z) \cdot w^*$, or $\omega \leq a^*(z)/a(z)$ where, for purposes of this chapter, $\omega \equiv w/w^*$. For a given ω, country I has a comparative advantage in commodities z such that $0 \leq z \leq \tilde{z}(\omega)$ where $\tilde{z}$ is given by

$$\omega = a(z) \quad \text{or} \quad \tilde{z} = A^{-1}(\omega). \tag{4.2}$$

Country II specializes in products z given by $\tilde{z}(\omega) \leq z \leq 1$.

To determine $\tilde{z}$, we must determine ω. This in turn requires the introduction of demand conditions. DFS do this by assuming preferences to be Cobb-Douglas and identical across individuals and across countries.

They define the constant expenditure share as

$$b(z) = \frac{P(z) \cdot c(z)}{Y} > 0, \quad b(z) = b^*(z), \tag{4.3}$$

where $P(z)$ and $c(z)$ represent prices and consumption of z, respectively, and Y is income. The expenditure shares satisfy the usual constraint

$$\int_0^1 b(z)dz = 1. \tag{4.4}$$

The fraction of income spent on country I's goods is given by

$$\phi(\tilde{z}) = \int_0^{\tilde{z}} b(z)dz > 0,$$

$$\phi'(\tilde{z}) = b(\tilde{z}) > 0. \tag{4.5}$$

The fraction of income spent on country II's goods is

$$1 - \phi(\tilde{z}) = \int_{\tilde{z}}^1 b(z)dz > 0. \tag{4.5'}$$

In equilibrium, country I's income must equal the total expenditure on its goods. That is,

$$wL = \phi(\tilde{z})(wL + w^*L^*). \tag{4.6}$$

Dividing by w^* on both sides and rearranging, we can rewrite equation (4.6) as

$$\omega = \frac{\phi(\tilde{z})}{1 - \phi(\tilde{z})} \frac{L^*}{L} \equiv B\left(\tilde{z}, \frac{L^*}{L}\right). \tag{4.6'}$$

This relationship is shown by curve $B(z, L^*/L)$ in figure 4.11. It is easily verified from (4.6') that $B(\cdot)$ passes through the origin, slopes upward, and approaches infinity as z approaches unity.

There are at least two ways to interpret the $B(\cdot)$ schedule. Seen one way, it is a representation of demand conditions. Accordingly it says that an increase in the range of goods produced in country I increases the demand for labor in that country and hence requires an increase in its relative wage to clear the labor market at the fixed labor supply.

The second interpretation of (4.6') is in terms of the trade balance condition. For this, rewrite it as

$$[1 - \phi(\tilde{z})]wL = \phi(\tilde{z})w^*L^*. \tag{4.6''}$$

The left-hand side of this equation represents expenditures by country I on country II's goods, while the right-hand side represents II's expenditure on I's goods. To ensure a balance in trade, these two must be equal. Looking at the condition this way, a rise in the range of goods produced by country I reduces its imports and increases its exports. The resulting trade surplus must be eliminated through an increase in I's wage, which will increase its demand for imports and reduce the supply of its exports.

In equilibrium, we have

$$\tilde{\omega} = A(\tilde{z}) = B\left(\tilde{z}; \frac{L^*}{L}\right). \tag{4.7}$$

Thus the key variables of the system are determined.

So far we have not said anything about relative prices. For z and z' both produced in country I, the relative price between them is given by

$$\frac{P(z)}{P(z')} = \frac{w \cdot a(z)}{w \cdot a(z')} = \frac{a(z)}{a(z')}, \qquad z, z' \leq \tilde{z}. \tag{4.8}$$

For z produced in country I and z'' produced in II, the relative price is given by

$$\frac{P(z)}{P(z'')} = \frac{w \cdot a(z)}{w^* a^*(z'')} = \omega \frac{a(z)}{a^*(z'')}, \qquad z < \tilde{z} < z''. \tag{4.9}$$

The equilibrium in this model, as usual, depends on technology, tastes, and factor supplies. Therefore shifts in these parameters will lead to a shift in the range of goods produced in the two countries and the relative wage which, given Cobb-Douglas preferences and no distortions, also determines the relative well-being of individuals in a country. We illustrate the working of the model with the help of one comparative statics exercise: a rise in the relative size of country II's labor force.

An increase in L^*/L has no effect on schedule $A(\cdot)$ but shifts schedule $B(\cdot)$ up in proportion to the shift in the relative size. The reason is that *on the demand side represented by $B(\cdot)$ schedule*, at the initial $\tilde{z}$, the increase in country II's labor force increases the demand for its imports and reduces the supply of its exports. The resulting trade deficit is corrected by a decline in its wage, which lowers its demand for imports and raises its supply of exports. Because income is the product w^*L^*, a 10 percent rise in L^* is exactly offset by a 10 percent fall in w^* explaining why the upward shift in $B(\cdot)$ is in proportion to the rise in L^*.

Because the fall in II's wage triggers a shift in the goods produced in the latter's favor, the net change in its relative wage is proportionately less than the rise in the labor force. This is verified easily with the help of figure 4.12. Essentially, at the initial relative wage and $\tilde{z}$, the increase in

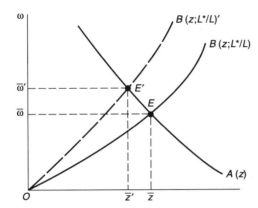

Figure 4.12

L^* leads to an excess supply of labor and trade deficit in II and excess demand for labor and trade surplus in I. The decline in II's wage corrects these imbalances but also lowers its unit labor costs, thus giving it comparative advantage in some of the goods previously produced by I. Because the relative wages also determine the relative welfare of workers, this change is accompanied by a rise in the welfare of workers in country I relative to that of workers in country II.

As DFS show, the model can also be employed to study the effects of a change in technology which shifts the $A(z)$ schedule, a change in demand which shifts the $B(\cdot)$ schedule, and a transfer by one country to another which shifts neither curve. The model can also be extended to allow for nontraded goods, transport costs that give rise to endogenous equilibrium for nontraded goods in the spirit of section 4.5 above, and tariffs.

Recommended Readings

Becker, G. A note on multi-country trade. *American Economic Review* 42 (1952): 558–68.

Dornbusch, R., S. Fischer, and P. A. Samuelson, Comparative advantage, trade, and payments in a Ricardian model with a continuum of goods. *American Economic Review* 47 (1977): 823–39.

Samuelson, P. A. The transfer problem and transport costs: Analysis of effects of trade impediments. *Economic Journal* 64 (1954): 264–89. Reprinted in *Readings in International Economics*, ed. by R. E. Caves and H. G. Johnson. Homewood, IL: Irwin, 1968.

Samuelson, P. A. Theoretical notes on trade problems. *Review of Economics and Statistics* 46 (1964): 145–54.

5   Model and Analytic Relationships under the Heckscher-Ohlin Theory

In this chapter we consider the basic analytical relationships that obtain in the Heckscher-Ohlin model. These provide the propositions that underlie the Heckscher-Ohlin theorem relating to the pattern of trade: *A country will export that commodity which intensively uses its abundant factor.* We will be considering the Heckscher-Ohlin model in its barest essentials, using a two-good, two-country, two-factor framework. The extensions to a multicountry, multigood, multifactor framework will be considered in chapter 7, and the formal proof of the Heckscher-Ohlin theorem is deferred until chapter 6. The analysis of the Heckscher-Ohlin model is exclusively based on geometric and intuitive reasoning, as in many of the journal papers on the subject. It is supplemented by a strictly theoretical statement of the basic mathematics of the 2×2 model in appendix A.

5.1   Heckscher-Ohlin Model

The Heckscher-Ohlin model has the following features:

Production.   Two factors of production, given supplies of these primary factors; constant-returns-to-scale production functions in each of two goods; identical technological know-how (i.e., identical production functions) in each industry internationally; nonreversibility of factor-intensity ranking for the two commodities (as explained in section 5.2).

Demand.   Balanced trade obtains, requiring that the economy spend no more than its earned income. The restrictions on the shape of the demand functions vary with the definition of factor-abundance used (as we will see in chapter 6 when we state the formal proof of the Heckscher-Ohlin theorem).

Trade.   No transportation costs; two countries; two traded goods; factors immobile internationally.

Institutional assumptions.   Pure competition.

The precise Heckscher-Ohlin model, as stated here, is essentially the handiwork of Paul Samuelson, who used it to derive several interesting theorems. It is derived from the original work of the distinguished Swedish economists Eli Heckscher and Bertil Ohlin, who emphasized the role of relative factor abundance in determining the pattern of trade (in contrast to the Ricardian theory which instead focused on international differences in know-how as the determinants of the trade pattern). Consequently this model is referred to here as the HOS (Heckscher-Ohlin-Samuelson) model.

5.2 Supply Relations

In this general-equilibrium model, the supply relations are more complex than in the highly simplified, one-factor Ricardian model. As in the Ricardian analysis, we first focus on the purely technological properties of this model and next derive the analytic relationships that obtain in the model when perfect competition is introduced.

Production-Possibility Curve

With a given technology and specified factor endowments, we can work with the well-known Edgeworth-Bowley diagrammatic technique of the "box diagram."

Box Diagram

In figure 5.1 the dimensions of the box diagram represent the given quantities of the two factors, capital and labor. The factor quantities employed in good 1 are measured with O_1 as the origin; those employed in good 2 are measured with O_2 as the origin. The isoquants for good 1 are sketched moving outward from O_1; those for good 2 are drawn moving southwest from O_2.

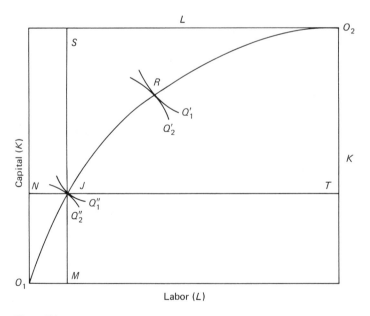

Figure 5.1

The locus of tangencies between the isoquants for goods 1 and 2 then represents a set of Pareto-efficient allocations of the given factors between the two goods. In other words, if we read off the good-1 and good-2 quantities along this locus and then plot them in the 1–2 space, we simply get the production-possibility curve. Thus, on this locus, a point such as J represents a Pareto-efficient allocation of resources, with amounts NJ of labor and JM of capital going to production of good 1 and JT of labor and JS of capital going to production of good 2. The amounts of goods 1 and 2 produced can then be read off the isoquants. Further this is a Pareto-optimal production point because any other allocation of factors produces, subject to the same output level of good 1, a lower amount of good 2. This is seen most simply by "going off" point J and moving along isoquant Q_1'', whose intersection with different good-2 isoquants would then give the quantities of good 2 that could be produced by alternative factor allocations. The rule then is this: If you are off the efficient locus (often called the Edgeworth locus or curve), get back on it if you want to have more of one good produced with no less of the other. Alternatively, if you are on the Edgeworth locus, you cannot get (by reshuffling factors) more of one good without giving up some of the other. The Pareto efficiency of the Edgeworth locus, O_1JRO_2, is also seen readily by noting that the tangency between the isoquants for goods 1 and 2 satisfies the well-known first-order conditions for maximizing good-1 output subject to a given good-2 output.

Savosnick Technique

Although the production-possibility curve can be derived by reading off the isoquant numbers from the Edgeworth locus, a useful diagrammatic technique has been devised by Savosnick (1958) in which the production-possibility curve is drawn right into the box diagram. This technique is demonstrated in figure 5.2. If we use the box diagram there to measure the output of good 2 to the left from O and the output of good 1 to the north from O, we can deduce that the production-possibility curve corresponding to the factor supplies defining the size of the box will be O_1JPO_2. This is done by using the intersections of the good-1 isoquants with the diagonal (O_1O_2) to project good-1 output (and those of the good-2 isoquants to project good-2 output) on the vertical (horizontal) scale, respectively. In view of constant returns to scale, an arbitrarily chosen good-1 isoquant, Q_1', will intersect the diagonal at a distance from O_1 that is λ times the distance at which the $(1/\lambda) \cdot Q_1'$ isoquant cuts the diagonal. Hence the vertical scale from O will uniformly measure changes in the output of good 1 if we project the intersections of the good-1 isoquants with the diagonal onto this vertical axis, and similarly for the

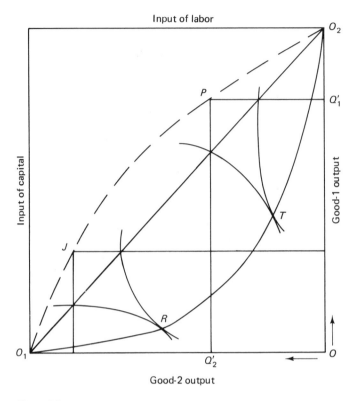

Figure 5.2

good-2 output, which will correspondingly be measured uniformly on the horizontal axis. This technique is illustrated in figure 5.2 for points T and R on the Edgeworth locus, which yield points P and J, respectively, on the production-possibility curve. The output levels corresponding to T and P are OQ_1' on the vertical axis and OQ_2' on the horizontal axis.[1]

Convexity of the Production-Possibility Curve

In figure 5.2 we have drawn the production-possibility curve as (mathematically) convex. This reflects a general property of the production-possibility curve in the model we are using: The production functions for each of the two goods show constant returns to scale and diminishing returns along isoquants. In fact it can be shown that for such a technology the production-possibility curve will be convex; the limiting case is a Ricardian, straight-line, "nonstrictly convex" production-possibility curve with a constant rate of transformation.

1. For further discussions, see Melvin (1971) and Krauss, Johnson, and Skouras (1973).

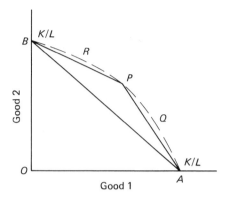

Figure 5.3

To derive this proposition heuristically, we may argue, after Samuelson, as follows: In figure 5.3 let all the available capital and labor be devoted to producing good 2, leading to point B. Similarly we can generate point A on the production-possibility curve by deploying all the available resources to produce good 1. It then follows that we can, by sticking to the K/L technique in each activity, produce any combination of good-1 and good-2 outputs on the line linking A and B.

Now, in the limiting case where the factor endowments and the technology happen to be such that the Edgeworth locus coincides with the diagonal, as in case I and Edgeworth locus O_1FRO_2 illustrated in figure 5.4, the production-possibility curve will necessarily be characterized by a unique factor proportion (equivalent to the overall factor-endowment ratio K/L), and hence the straight line AB will itself be the production-possibility curve.

In general, however, the Edgeworth locus will be characterized either by good 1 having a capital/labor ratio greater than commodity 2, except at points of complete specialization (as with case III in figure 5.4), or by commodity 2 being capital-intensive instead (as with case II in figure 5.4). In either case, the production-possibility curve will be convex, lying outside of AB, as with APB in figure 5.3.

The argument proceeds then by indicating that except in the limiting Ricardian case, the ratios of marginal productivities of the two factors in goods 1 and 2 will be unequal if we move down BA. Hence it should be possible to find a better way of transforming 2 into 1, starting from B, than by moving down BA. This would involve, of course, different factor proportions from K/L. In essence, therefore, we are merely arguing that the possibility of factor substitution makes it possible to find a point to the northeast of AB (e.g., P, as in figure 5.3) on the production-possibility

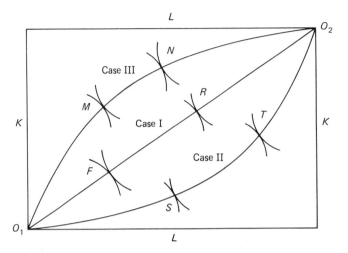

Figure 5.4

curve. Since points A and B are on the production-possibility curve as well, the curve must be convex somewhere; moving outward from B, it must return to A.[2]

The heuristic argument, however, can be carried all the way. Any points on the line segments AP and PB are also feasible production points. This can be seen as follows. Any point on AP is a convex combination of the outputs at A and at P. Thus, by using two techniques for producing good 1 corresponding to the capital/labor ratios at A and P, respectively, but choosing the outputs to be produced by each technique suitably and by using the technique at P for producing good 2 but scaling down its output level as compared to P, any point on AP between A and P can be reached. A similar argument establishes the feasibility of any outputs along PB. Once again, as we move up AP or PB the ratios of the two factors in producing goods 1 and 2 will be different except in a limiting use. Thus there must be points on the production curve to the northeast of AP and PB—say, Q and R, respectively. It is clear that this argument can be used once again with the points Q and R on the curve, thus leading up to the convexity of the curve.

5.3 Competitive System

We can now introduce the assumption of a perfectly competitive economy and analyze the price relationships that will obtain in our model.

---

2. A geometrical proof of this can be found in Worswick (1957).

Since the Heckscher-Ohlin theorem involves two definitions of factor intensity and factor abundance, we begin with them.

Factor Abundance

There are two alternative ways of defining factor abundance. For two countries I and II and two factors K and L, we can define country I as K-abundant if either

$$\left(\frac{K}{L}\right) > \left(\frac{K}{L}\right)^* \quad \text{(''physical'' definition)}$$

or

$$\omega > \omega^* \quad \text{(''price'' definition)},$$

where K and L are the endowments of factors and ω is the wage-rental ratio.

Where the factor endowments are fixed in each country, the "physical" definition is unambiguous. However, if we had variable, national factor supplies that changed with factor rewards (as with work and leisure, or owing to international factor mobility in response to differential rewards across countries), we would have to specify the equilibrium situation at which we make our comparison. Factor-abundance rankings might well reverse, depending on the equilibrium chosen. This problem arises directly with the latter definition, since it defines the K abundance of country I in terms of the (relative) cheapness of K in country I as against its price in country II. Indeed international trade could well lead to equalization of factor prices, although in self-sufficiency there is no such equality. Hence we have to choose an equilibrium situation at which to compare factor prices. In the Heckscher-Ohlin theory the definition will relate to the self-sufficiency situation.

Factor Intensity

Identical problems arise with the definition of factor intensity of activities. If we had Leontief-type, fixed coefficients in each of the two activities, the ranking of activities by their factor intensity (that is, by their K/L ratios) would naturally be unambiguous. But as soon as we introduce the possibility of factor substitution, as with the smoothly convex isoquants in figure 5.5, we cannot rank factor intensities unless we manage to narrow down the choice in some way. This is done simply by considering a competitive economy in which entrepreneurs choose their technique (i.e., their K/L ratios) so as to minimize costs. Then, we can take our comparisons at a common factor-price ratio. Thus, at the common factor-price ratio

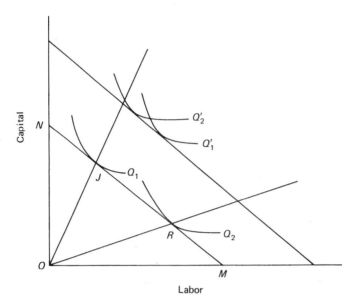

Figure 5.5

MN in figure 5.5, we can say that good 1 will be *K*-intensive because the techniques chosen will be at *J* and *R* for goods 1 and 2, respectively.[3]

Now, if we assume constant returns to scale, it does not matter which pair of 1 and 2 isoquants we take, for the technique chosen will be determined exclusively by the factor-price ratio and will be scale-free. However, if the technique chosen were not scale-free, then it is clearly possible that, depending on the scale of output, good 1 may be *K*-intensive or *L*-intensive even though we specified one factor-price ratio. This possibility is demonstrated by (Q_1, Q_2) and (Q'_1, Q'_2) at factor-price ratio *MN* in figure 5.5.

Even if we assume technique to be scale-free, as will be the case with the Heckscher-Ohlin assumption of production functions with constant returns to scale, we must recognize the possibility that good 1 may be *K*-intensive at one factor-price ratio and *L*-intensive at another. In other words, we may have factor-intensity reversals. Figure 5.6 shows a pair of 1 and 2 isoquants characterizing a technology that permits such a reversal. At factor-price ratio *MN*, both 1 and 2 have an equal factor ratio at *R*. For lower (relative) prices of *L*, to the right of *OR*, good 1 is *K*-intensive and

3. This use of the factor-intensity notion, though standard in the literature on international trade, is the opposite of Ricardo's in his theory of rent. There, using land intensively meant using more of the nonland factors on land, whereas when we say land is used intensively we mean a higher land/nonland ratio.

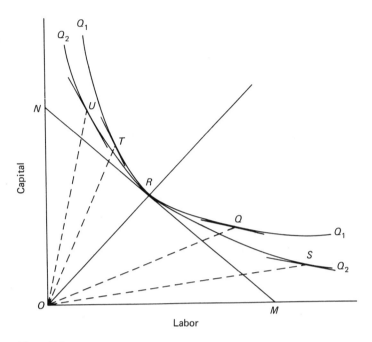

Figure 5.6

good 2 is *L*-intensive (as illustrated at Q and S); for higher (relative) prices of *L*, to the left of *OR*, good 1 is *L*-intensive and good 2 is *K*-intensive (as illustrated at T and U).

We can specify production functions that will lead to such reversals. Consider the following constant-elasticity-of-substitution (CES) production function:

$$Q_1 = [(1 - \alpha_1)K_1^{-\beta} + \alpha_1 L_1^{-\beta}]^{-1/\beta}, \qquad 0 < \alpha_1 < 1, \beta \geq -1,$$

where Q_1 is the output produced by inputs of K_1 and L_1 and where $(1 - \alpha_1)$, α_1, and β are given parameters. We can show that the elasticity of substitution in this case is $\sigma = 1/(\beta + 1)$ and that if we have two activities 1 and 2, each characterized by such a CES production function, then if their elasticities of substitution are unequal ($\sigma_1 \neq \sigma_2$) there must be factor-intensity reversals.[4]

A Brief Statement of the Relationships

We are now in a position to consider four key relationships in the Heckscher-Ohlin model: between goods prices and factor returns, between

---

4. When both goods have Cobb-Douglas production functions and therefore $\sigma_1 = \sigma_2 = 1$, factor-intensity reversals are impossible.

factor endowments and outputs, between goods prices and outputs, and between technological change and outputs. At constant goods prices a change in factor endowments has no effect on factor returns. Therefore this relationship does not figure in our discussion below. A technological change, on the other hand, does lead to a change in factor prices (as analyzed in chapter 10).

We first offer a brief statement of each of these relationships.

Stolper-Samuelson Theorem

The relationship between goods prices and factor returns was derived originally by Stolper and Samuelson (1941) and is known as the Stolper-Samuelson theorem. According to this theorem, an increase in the relative price of the labor intensive good leads to a rise in the relative as well as the real return of labor and a decline in the relative and real return to capital.

Rybczynski Theorem

The relationship between factor endowments and outputs is known as the Rybczynski theorem after Rybczynski (1955). According to this theorem, an increase in the endowment of capital leads to an expansion of the capital-intensive sector and a contraction of the labor-intensive sector. Alternatively, a rise in the K/L ratio leads to a rise in the Q_1/Q_2 ratio. Once again, in this chapter we will focus on the relative version of the Rybczynski theorem.

Goods Prices and Outputs

An increase in the relative price of a good leads to an expansion of the output of that good and a reduction in the output of the other good. Thus the relative output of the good whose price rises also increases.

Technical Change and Outputs

The effect of a technical change on outputs naturally depends on the nature of technical change. As shown originally by Johnson (1955), for a Hicks-neutral technical change we can obtain output effects that essentially mirror the Rybczynski theorem. Thus, at constant goods prices, a Hicks-neutral technical change in an industry leads to an expansion of that industry and a contraction of the other industry. Alternatively, a proportionately larger Hicks-neutral technical progress in an industry leads to an increase in the relative output of that industry.

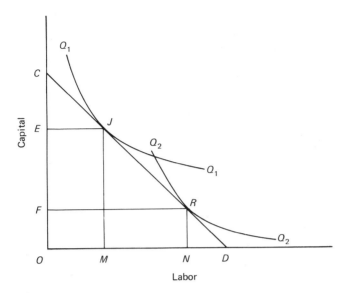

Figure 5.7

Factor Prices and Commodity Prices

We can now investigate the relationship between factor-price and goods-price ratios in our production model. Figure 5.7 shows a pair of iso-quants that are tangential to the same factor-price-ratio line, CD. The tangencies at J and R indicate that in producing Q_1 units of good 1 OM units of labor and OE units of capital are employed, whereas in producing Q_2 units of good 2 ON units of labor and OF units of capital are used. However, at the factor-price ratio CD, OF ($= RN$) units of capital are equivalent to ND units of labor. Thus, in all, $ON + ND = OD$ units of labor are the cost of producing Q_2 units of 2. By an identical argument, $OM + MD = OD$ units of labor are the cost of producing Q_1 units of good 1. Therefore Q_1 units of good 1 will exchange for Q_2 units of good 2 in the marketplace. Thus, given the factor-price ratio, we can readily deduce the associated commodity-price ratio in equilibrium by putting the same factor-price-ratio line tangential to a pair of 1 and 2 isoquants and reading off the isoquant numbers.

This technique, originated by Lerner and revived by Findlay and Grubert (1959), can be used to show that a lowering of the relative price of K will be associated with a lowering of the relative price of the K-intensive good. This is seen from figure 5.8, where a shift in the factor-price ratio from CD to AB leads to Q_1 exchanging for Q_2' ($> Q_2$), implying a lower (relative) price for good 2 (the L-intensive commodity). Note that the old tangencies, with CD at M for good 1 and at N for

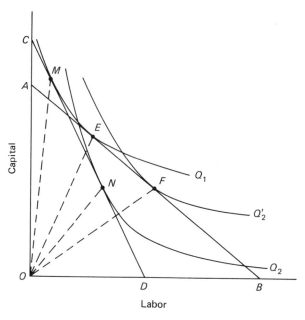

Figure 5.8

good 2, are now replaced by new tangencies, with AB at E for good 1 and at F for good 2.

The relationship between factor-price and goods-price ratios that obtains if factor-intensity reversals are ruled out is then readily illustrated, as in figure 5.9, through the use of a celebrated diagrammatic technique introduced by Samuelson (1948, 1949). The upper quadrant depicts the "strong" factor-intensity assumption, ruling out factor-intensity reversals: $k_1 > k_2$ (i.e., good 1 is K-intensive) at all factor-price ratios, ω. The lower quadrant depicts the relation just derived, where lower ω values imply lower p values because good 1 is the K-intensive good. On the other hand, if factor-intensity reversals are allowed, it no longer follows that p will be a monotonically increasing function of ω. As illustrated in figure 5.10, the p–ω curve will bend back on itself at the critical ω value, OA, where factor intensities reverse themselves. (The relationship between the goods-price ratio and the factor-price ratio is derived mathematically in appendix B.)

Figures 5.8 to 5.10 show the effect of a reduction in the price of good 2 on the *relative* factor returns. We may also ask, as Stolper and Samuelson (1941) did in their original analysis, how the *real* factor returns are affected by the price change. The issue is important because a decline in the relative wage need not imply that the wage declines in real terms. If the decline in the wage is proportionately less than the decline in the price, the wage in

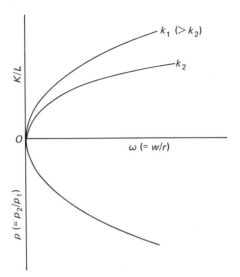

Figure 5.9

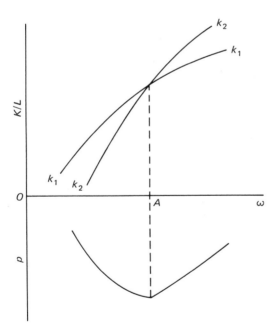

Figure 5.10

terms of good 2 may still rise. Moreover, if workers spend most of their income on good 2, they may still be better off due to the price decline. Stolper and Samuelson showed that this possibility is ruled out. The wage must decline in terms of both goods and the return to capital must rise in terms of both goods as well.

We take up the relationship between goods prices and real factor returns formally in chapter 10. But the basic result can be explained intuitively. Because the relative return to labor declines when p_2 is lowered, the capital-to-labor ratio declines in both sectors. This means that the marginal product of labor must decline in both sectors. But since the wage equals the value of the marginal product in sector i $(i = 1, 2)$, the marginal product represents the wage in terms of good i. Thus wage declines in terms of both goods. Analogously the decline in the capital-to-labor ratio implies a rise in the marginal product of capital and hence a rise in the rental income in terms of both goods.

Factor Endowments

We can conceive of all factor-price ratios for an economy. However, for an economy with a given endowment of factors (K/L), the feasible factor-price-ratio range is only a subset of all the conceivable ratios. In figure 5.11, with the endowment ratio K/L, the feasible factor-price-ratio range is EF. This is obtained by drawing a horizontal line to the right from K/L and dropping vertical lines from its intersection with the k_1 and k_2 schedules. We can demonstrate the impossibility of any price ratios outside this range EF.

For any finite factor-price ratio, there must be full employment of both factors in equilibrium. Furthermore, the overall factor-endowment ratio must be a weighted average of the factor ratios in the two activities, 1 and 2. This is shown in the identity

$$\frac{K}{L} \equiv k_1 \cdot \left(\frac{L_1}{L}\right) + k_2 \cdot \left(\frac{L_2}{L}\right),$$

which follows from the facts that $L_1 + L_2 = L$ and $K_1 + K_2 = K$, and where L_1/L and L_2/L are therefore weights adding up to unity. It then follows that at ω values greater than OF, both k_1 and k_2 will be greater than the overall ratio K/L. However, in view of the identity, this is impossible. Similarly, for ω values lower than OE, both k_1 and k_2 will be lower than K/L. This too is impossible. Hence the only feasible factor-price ratios must lie between OE and OF.

Furthermore at the factor-price ratio OF there can be no allocation of factors to (and hence production of) commodity 1; thus production is specialized in good 2. Similarly at price ratio OE there must be special-

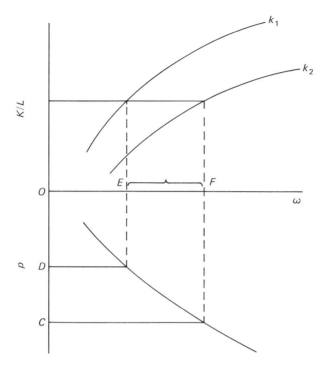

Figure 5.11

ization in producing good 1. Thus in the production-possibility diagram 5.12 the factor-price ratio OF of figure 5.11 will obtain at production point A, and factor-price ratio OE will obtain at production point B. For factor-price ratios between OE and OF, there will be incomplete specialization in production; thus these ratios will correspond to points on the production-possibility curve AB in figure 5.12 other than A and B.

For the goods-price ratios there is no equivalent restriction on feasibility. In figure 5.11 the goods-price ratios corresponding to the factor-price ratios OE–OF are OD–OC. That we can admit higher p values than OC only implies that the economy remains specialized in producing good 2 but gets better terms of trade; similarly at lower p values than OD the economy will remain specialized in producing 1 but will get better terms of trade. This is illustrated in figure 5.12, where the goods-price ratio BQ (which corresponds to OD in figure 5.11) represents a tangency with production-possibility curve AB at B, and where equilibrium production will be at B for all lower p values ranging from BQ to BS (where p tends to zero). Similarly, for p value AP (corresponding to OC in figure 5.11), there is tangency with AB at A, and for goods-price ratios AP–AR (where p tends to infinity), the economy will remain specialized in good 2.

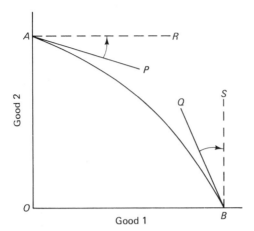

Figure 5.12

If we have the possibility of factor-intensity reversal, two important points need to be noted. If the overall factor-endowment ratio is such that the feasible factor-price-ratio range collapses into a single point, then we are essentially in a Ricardian world. In this case we have a unique factor-price ratio and a unique factor proportion in the economy. In terms of the box diagram, the Edgeworth locus is a straight line coinciding with the diagonal. If, however, the overall factor-endowment ratio is on either side of the crossover point, then the economy will, *de facto*, be in a world where a good is always K-intensive or always L-intensive. Factor-intensity reversals, when possible, cannot actually occur in an economy with a given factor-endowment ratio.

Factor Abundance and Commodity Outputs

We investigate next the question of what effect an increment in the overall endowment ratio (K/L) will have, at any given goods-price ratio, on the composition of output (Q_1/Q_2). We can show in fact that (i) an increase in the endowment of a factor will increase the output of the good using it intensively and reduce the output of the other good,[5] and (more generally) that (ii) an increase in the endowment ratio of a factor (K/L) will increase the ratio of production of the good using that factor intensively (i.e., Q_1/Q_2 when $k_1 > k_2$).[6]

5. This theorem was originally derived by Rybczynski (1955).

6. These propositions have been formulated with reference to incomplete specialization in production. If we assume goods-price ratios where the economy is already specialized in producing the K-intensive good 1, an increment in K supply will only reinforce the production of good 1.

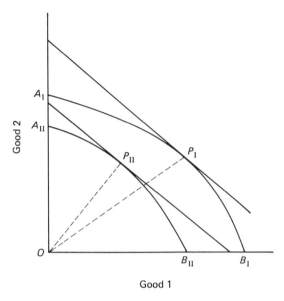

Figure 5.13

By analogy, we can extend these propositions to two different countries, one of which has a higher K/L factor-endowment ratio and is hence defined as K-abundant. In figure 5.13, $A_I B_I$ and $A_{II} B_{II}$ represent the production-possibility curves of countries I and II. Since country I is assumed to be K-abundant and good 1 is assumed to be K-intensive, proposition ii implies that the proportion of good 1 to good 2 produced will be higher in country I than in country II (at a common commodity-price ratio). Indeed, this is seen to be the case.

The proofs of propositions i and ii are fairly straightforward.[7] Assuming the standard technology assumed so far, but also assuming that factor-intensity reversals are ruled out, we can work with the identity

$$\frac{K}{L} \equiv k_1 \cdot \frac{L_1}{L} + k_2 \cdot \frac{L_2}{L}$$

to derive the two propositions. Since the goods-price ratio is fixed, k_1 and k_2 are also fixed, and $k_1 > k_2$ for all factor-price ratios, by assumption. Then, if K increases while L supply is unchanged, the identity can be satisfied only by shifting the weights (L_1/L and L_2/L) in favor of the K-intensive activity, 1. This implies that L_2 must fall. However, with k_2 constant, K_2 must also fall. Since both factors employed in good 2 have

---

7. For mathematical derivations, see appendix B.

fallen, output Q_2 must also fall. The net result is that the output of good 2 has fallen and that of good 1 has increased. Hence the production ratio Q_1/Q_2 will also have increased.[8]

The second and more general proposition then follows simply by virtue of the fact that we can decompose the growth of the two factors K and L into proportional growth (which leads to expansion of good-1 and good-2 output by the same proportion) at the rate of growth of the factor that has grown at the lesser rate plus the incremental growth of the faster-growing factor in excess of this rate. The effect of the excess rate of growth of the faster-growing factor can then be analyzed just as we have analyzed the preceding case. This establishes our second proposition. For example, where K has grown faster than L, there will be a proportionate growth of both 1 and 2 output by the rate of growth of L. In addition the excess growth of K will increase the output of 1 (which is K-intensive) and reduce the output of 2. The net effect therefore will be expansion in the output of 1 and a slower expansion (and possibly a net reduction) in the output of 2. Hence the production ratio Q_1/Q_2 will have increased, demonstrating proposition ii.

Technical Progress and Commodity Outputs

As was noted earlier, if we consider a Hicks-neutral technical progress in one activity, the effect of this on the outputs of the progressive industry and the other industry parallels the effect of factor augmentation, which we have just considered. Thus, again, we can establish two propositions: (i) Hicks-neutral progress in one industry will, at constant goods-price ratio, lead to an expansion of the output of that industry and a reduction in the output of the other.[9] More generally, (ii) greater Hicks-neutral progress in one industry than in another will increase the ratio of production of the former to the latter at constant goods-price ratio.

Hicks-neutral progress implies mere renumbering of isoquants so that the factor proportions chosen in response to any factor-price ratio remain unchanged for all factor-price ratios. Thus in figure 5.14 we have equilibrium initially, with the goods-price ratio exchanging Q_1 for Q_2, the factor-price ratio at ABR, factor proportions in 1 and 2 indicated by points A and B, respectively, and $k_1 > k_2$ at all factor-price ratios. With Hicks-

8. Where the increment of K supply is sufficiently large, the result could be complete specialization in the production of the K-intensive good 1. Also we need to rule out factor-intensity reversals; otherwise, the increasing K supply could, in principle, lead the economy from the left of the crossover point in figure 5.10 to the right, which clearly invalidates the argument in the text and the two propositions being established.

9. This theorem was originally derived by Johnson (1955).

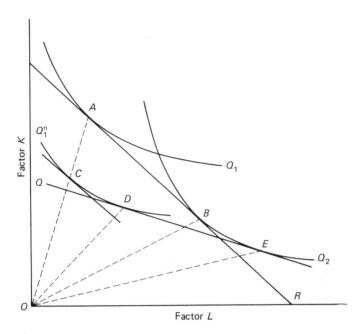

Figure 5.14

neutral technical progress in the production of good 1, the good-1 isoquants are renumbered upward; for example, the new Q_1 isoquant, Q_1^n,
lies below the old Q_1 isoquant for the same level of output. But with the
goods-price ratio fixed at the initial level in the exercise, we can now
derive the new equilibrium factor-price ratio that will follow. This will be
QDE, with factor proportions in 1 and 2 at D and E, respectively. This
factor-price ratio is tangential to the new Q_1^n isoquant and the Q_2 isoquant, and hence implies (as we have seen earlier) the same goods-price
ratio as in the pre-technical-progress equilibrium.

But we must then have a lower ω and thus lower K/L ratios in both
activities. If we again keep in mind the identity

$$\frac{K}{L} \equiv k_1 \cdot \frac{L_1}{L} + k_2 \cdot \frac{L_2}{L}$$

and the fact that the overall K/L ratio has not changed, it follows that
with both k_1 and k_2 falling, there must be an increase in the weight
assigned to the K-intensive commodity, 1. Therefore L_2 must fall. But
with k_2 also fallen, K_2 must also have fallen. Industry 2 thus loses both
factors, has no technical progress, and therefore must have an absolute
decline in its output. Correspondingly industry 1 gains both factors, has
neutral technical progress, and thus has an expansion of its output.

Hence the relative production of 1, the progressive industry, must also have increased; Q_1/Q_2 will have increased.

Proposition ii follows by mere extension of this argument to the case where there is Hicks-neutral progress in both industries but at different rates. In this case, there must be no change in relative outputs as long as we notionally think of technical progress at the same rate in both industries as the rate experienced by the less progressive industry. Beyond this, the incremental progress of the more progressive industry must have the effect considered in the preceding analysis, thus establishing proposition ii.

5.4   Depiction of Free-Trade Equilibrium

As discussed in chapter 3, the production model can be used in conjunction with demand conditions to derive and depict free-trade equilibrium. This can be done in a variety of ways. We proceed to demonstrate alternative techniques developed by a number of writers, using community-indifference curves to represent demand conditions. The mathematical formulation of the model is given in appendix B.

Offer Curves

Plotting the intersection of the offer curves of one country and the rest of the world is the standard technique. The only difference from the Ricardian case is that the production-possibility curve is generally convex in the Heckscher-Ohlin model, so that we no longer get the linear stretch in the offer curve that a constant rate of transformation in domestic production entails.[10]

Figure 5.15 shows such a free-trade equilibrium. The offer curves OI all OII of countries I and II intersect at F, yielding OF as the international terms of trade and OQ as the exports of good 1 by country I to country II for FQ as the imports of good 2 in exchange for them.

Because the offer curves can also be derived by rotating the price line and taking the locus of its tangencies with the trade-indifference curves of a country, it follows that the price line OF must be tangential at F to a trade-indifference curve of both countries I and II. This follows from the fact that F is a point on the offer curves of both countries. Hence OF is tangential to the trade-indifference curve U_T^I of country I and to the trade-indifference curve U_T^{II} of country II.

10. Because production would vary in response to price change, without necessarily entailing specialization, the discussion of the shape of the offer curve would also have to take this into account.

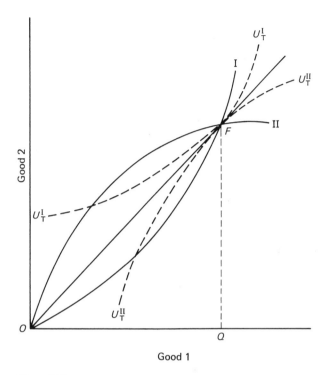

Figure 5.15

Baldwin Technique

The free-trade equilibrium can also be represented through an ingenious technique introduced by Baldwin (1948). Essentially this technique consists in superimposing a country's foreign offer curve on its production-possibility curve.

Consider figure 5.16. AB is the production-possibility curve. Production takes place at the international price ratio PCF (which, under free trade, is also the domestic price ratio), consumption is at C, and the country therefore exports PQ of commodity 1 in exchange for imports of QC of commodity 2. Using P as the origin but facing leftward, we draw in the offer curve from the outside world, PCD; this indicates that at the price ratio PCF the outside world makes a matching offer of CQ of good 2 for PQ of good 1. Thus, in effect, the price ratio PCF represents the equilibrium terms of trade.

Using this idea of superimposing the outside world's offer curve on a country's production-possibility curve, Baldwin derives an availability locus, which corresponds under trade to the production-possibility locus under autarky. This locus, EGF in figure 5.17, is derived under the

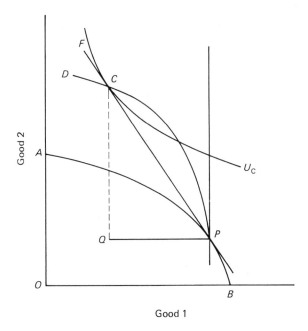

Figure 5.16

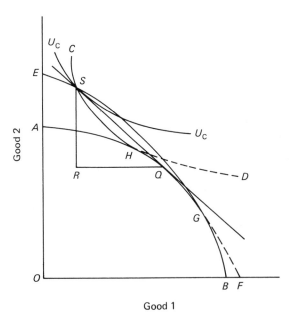

Figure 5.17

assumption that the economy will engage in free trade. The best locus of availabilities to the economy will, in general, lie outside this locus derived under the restrictive assumption that free trade is the policy under which the trade opportunity is being exploited by this economy.

The locus *EGF* in figure 5.17 is derived as follows: Take any terms of trade and discover the offer of trade which this economy, characterized by the production-possibility curve *AB*, would obtain from the outside world (given the curve for the outside world's offer to this country). Assume then that, at the terms of trade *QS*, the outside country offers *SR* of good 2 for *QR* of good 1. This triangle can then be superimposed on *AB* by choosing *Q* so that *QS* is tangential to *AB* at *Q*. This defines the position of *S*. By quoting different terms of trade and following the same procedure in each case, we can then trace out a locus *ESGF*. For example, at *G* the terms of trade would be given by the tangent to *AB* at *G*, and at these terms of trade the outside world is self-sufficient and the offer is therefore zero. To the left of *G* the outside world offers good 2 for good 1; to the right of *G* it offers good 1 for good 2 (as indicated by the dashed segment). Clearly *EF* is the locus of availabilities for our country on the assumption that the domestic goods-price ratio in production must equal the foreign price ratio. This is the free-trade assumption as far as domestic production is concerned. What we have done therefore is nothing more than to discover the different production points at different foreign prices (equal to domestic prices, which in turn determine production under the competitive rules of the game which we have already discussed earlier) and to derive availabilities of goods 1 and 2 by trading therefrom the quantities determined by the foreign offer curve at these terms of trade. Hence *ESGF* is the free-trade locus of availabilities for our country.

International (free-) trade equilibrium can then be depicted by deriving a locus (*CSHD* in figure 5.17) that represents the different demands for goods 1 and 2 generated in the economy at different goods-price ratios. For example, *H* represents the demand vector corresponding to the self-sufficiency price ratio of the country. Similarly, at price ratio *SQ*, the economy would have a consumption vector represented by point *S*. There is a social-indifference curve U_C tangential at *S* to the price ratio *SQ*. To the left of *H*, this locus will represent demand vectors involving exports of good 1 for imports of good 2 by our country; to the right of *H*, for the dashed segment *HD*, the trade pattern will be reversed.

It is clear then that an intersection of the loci *CSHD* and *ESGF* represents the free-trade equilibrium because then the availabilities will equal the demands for both goods. This point is clearly *S* in figure 5.17. Furthermore the intersection between the two loci must involve matching offers of trade for both our country and the outside world; this means that the intersection of the two loci must be between the continuous segments or between the dashed segments.

Lerner Technique

An alternative technique of portraying free-trade equilibrium was suggested by Lerner (1952). Essentially it amounts to aggregating the production-possibility curves of the two countries in a two-country world economy and comparing the aggregate production-possibility curve against a world indifference curve to arrive at world equilibrium outputs and terms of trade. The disadvantage of the technique consists in the difficulty of identifying trade flows without reintroducing the country equilibria.

Meade Technique

The most sophisticated (and cumbersome) technique for portraying free-trade equilibrium is that of Meade (1952). Using several quadrants, it manages to bring into one diagram nearly all aspects of trade equilibrium: offer curves, trade-indifference curves, production-possibility curves, and consumption-indifference curves. The essence of this technique was conveyed in chapter 2; further details should be obtained from Meade's original volume.

Recommended Readings

Baldwin, R. E. Equilibrium in international trade: A diagrammatic analysis. *Quarterly Journal of Economics* 62 (1948): 748–62.

Bhagwati, J. Proofs of the theorems on comparative advantage. *Economic Journal* 77 (1967): 75–83.

Bhagwati, J. Protection, real wages and real incomes. *Economic Journal* 69 (1959): 733–48.

Findlay, R., and H. Grubert. Factor intensity, technological progress, and the terms of trade. *Oxford Economic Papers* 2 (1959): 111–21.

Heckscher, E. The effect of foreign trade on the distribution of income. In *Readings in the Theory of International Trade*, ed. by H. S. Ellis and L. A. Metzler. Philadelphia: Blakiston, 1949.

Johnson, H. G. Economic expansion and international trade. *Manchester School* 23 (1955): 95–112. Reprinted in H. G. Johnson, *International Trade and Economic Growth*. London: Allen and Unwin, 1958.

Jones, R. W. The structure of simple general equilibrium. *Journal of Political Economy* 73 (1965): 557–72.

Jones, R. W. Factor proportions and the Heckscher-Ohlin model. *Review of Economic Studies* 24 (1956–57): 1–10. Reprinted in *International Trade*, ed. by J. Bhagwati. Baltimore: Penguin, 1969.

Krauss, M. B., H. G. Johnson, and T. Skouras. On the shape and location of the production possibility curve. *Economica* 40 (1973): 305–10.

Lancaster, K. The Heckscher-Ohlin trade model: A geometric treatment. *Economica*, N. S., 24 (1957): 19–39. Reprinted in *International Trade*, ed. by J. Bhagwati. Baltimore: Penguin, 1969.

Lerner, A. P. The diagrammatical representation of cost conditions in international trade. *Economica* 12 (1932): 246–56. Reprinted in A. P. Lerner, *Essays in Economic Analysis*. London: Macmillan, 1953.

Lerner, A. P. Factor prices and international trade. *Economica* 19 (1952): 1–15. Reprinted in A. P. Lerner, *Essays in Economic Analysis*. London: Macmillan, 1953.

Meade, J. E. *A Geometry of International Trade*. London: Allen and Unwin, 1952, chs. 1–3.

Melvin, J. R. On the derivation of the production possibility curve. *Economica* 38 (1971): 281–94.

Minhas, B. S. The homohypallagic production function, factor intensity reversals, and the Heckscher-Ohlin theorem. *Journal of Political Economy* 70 (1962): 138–56. Reprinted in *International Trade*, ed. by J. Bhagwati. Baltimore: Penguin, 1969.

Mussa, M. The two-sector model in terms of its dual: A geometric exposition. *Journal of International Economics* 9 (1979): 513–26.

Robinson, R. Factor proportions and comparative advantage: Part I. *Quarterly Journal of Economics* 70 (1956): 169–92. Reprinted in *Readings in International Economics*, ed. by R. E. Caves and H. G. Johnson. Homewood IL: Irwin, 1968.

Robinson, R. Factor proportions and comparative advantage: Part II. *Quarterly Journal of Economics* 70 (1956): 346–63.

Rybczynski, T. N. Factor endowment and relative commodity prices. *Economica*, N. S., 12 (1955): 336–41. Reprinted in *Readings in International Economics*, ed. by R. E. Caves and H. G. Johnson. Homewood, IL: Irwin, 1968.

Samuelson, P. A. International trade and the equalisation of factor prices. *Economic Journal* 58 (1948): 181–97.

Samuelson, P. A. International factor-price equalisation once again. *Economic Journal* 59 (1949): 181–97.

Savosnick, K. M. The box diagram and the production possibility curve. *Ekonomisk Tidsskrift* 60 (1958): 183–97.

Stolper, W., and P. A. Samuelson. Protection and real wages. *Review of Economic Studies* 9 (1941): 58–73. Reprinted in *International Trade*, ed. by J. Bhagwati. Baltimore: Penguin, 1969.

Worswick, G. D. The convexity of the production possibility function. *Economic Journal* 67 (1957): 748–50.

Pattern of Trade and the Heckscher-Ohlin Theory

We are now in a position to derive formally the Heckscher-Ohlin theorem, which is that a country abundant in the endowment of a factor will export the commodity that uses this factor intensively. Because factor abundance can be defined in two alternative ways (the physical and the price definition) and because the assumptions that we must make to deduce the Heckscher-Ohlin theorem vary with these definitions, we will take each definition in turn.

6.1 Heckscher-Ohlin Theorem with Physical Definition of Factor Abundance

Given the Heckscher-Ohlin model (stated at the outset of chapter 5), we can deduce the Heckscher-Ohlin theorem as follows.[1]

Of two countries, I and II, let I be K-abundant so that $(K/L) > (K/L)^*$. Let 1 be the K-intensive good and 2 be the L-intensive good at all factor price ratios so that $k_1 > k_2$ at every ω. Then we know from the Rybczynski theorem that country I will have advantage in the production of good 1: $(Q_1/Q_2) > (Q_1/Q_2)^*$ at all goods-price ratios (when incomplete specialization obtains).

Let P^S in figure 6.1 be the self-sufficiency price ratio for country I. By putting it tangential to the dashed production-possibility curve $A_I B_I$ of country I, we have the self-sufficiency equilibrium production P_I and the consumption C_I at the same point.

If now we were to quote the same price ratio P^S for country II, we would get P_{II} (the equilibrium production at the tangency point with $A_{II} B_{II}$ in country II) at a point to the left of the ray OR, because country II has an advantage, as we have proved, in the production of good 2.

What about the consumption point for country II at price ratio P^S? Let us now make the explicit demand assumption that countries I and II have an identical consumption pattern (C_1/C_2, the ratio of good-1 consumption to good-2 consumption) at common goods-price ratios. This would be the case if we had homothetic indifference curves, and it is clearly a more restrictive assumption than requiring that tastes be merely identical between the two countries. Under this assumption, C_{II} will clearly be on the ray OR, which passes through C_I. It then follows (as is clear from the offer triangle formed by P_{II} and C_{II}) that at the self-sufficiency goods-price ratio of country I, country II will have an excess demand for good 1 and an excess supply of good 2.

1. The proof requires suitable restrictions on demand, which we will spell out where necessary in the statement of the proof.

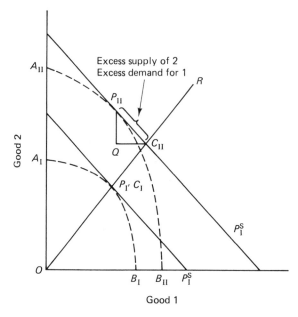

Figure 6.1

If we then rule out multiple pretrade equilibria, so that there is a unique self-sufficiency price ratio in each country, it follows that the self-sufficiency price ratio in country II, P_{II}^S, will have a lower p (relative price of good 2) than P_I^S, and therefore the international free-trade equilibrium will involve the export of good 2 by country II and the export of the K-intensive good 1 by the K-abundant country I. Hence the Heckscher-Ohlin theorem will hold.

That the absence of multiple pretrade equilibria implies that P_{II}^S will have a lower price of good 2 than P_I^S is shown by figure 6.2. We have there the unique self-sufficiency price ratio P_I^S and the excess-demand-for-good-2 curve for country I. At P_I^S the excess demand for good 2 in country II is negative, at level QP_I^S. It follows that the excess-demand-for-good-2 curve for country II should cut the vertical axis below P_I^S, therefore implying the Heckscher-Ohlin pattern of trade (as illustrated at price ratio OE). This is because there must be a crossover into the right quadrant of the excess-demand curve of country II at a price below P_I^S; at some lower p the economy must specialize in producing good 1 and thus have positive excess demand for good 2. But, if so, a crossover to the north of P_I^S is ruled as well out by the assumption that there is only a unique pretrade equilibrium.

A sufficient condition for this uniqueness is that we have social indifference curves with interminability in consumption of either good. This

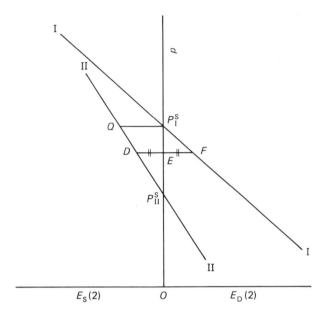

Figure 6.2

means that indifference curves should not meet either axis. To see why this matters, assume that indifference curves do meet the horizontal axis along which we measure good 1. We will then have an indifference curve that meets the production possibilities curve at the point of complete specialization in good 1. Assume for one of the countries that at this point the indifference curve is steeper than the production-possibilities curve. The pretrade equilibrium in this country is then compatible with the entire range of prices lying between the marginal rate of substitution and the marginal rate of transformation at the point of complete specialization in good 1. If the pretrade price in the other country, associated with an incompletely specialized equilibrium, now happens to lie within this range, when the two countries open to trade, the international price will coincide with the second (incompletely specialized) country's pretrade price, but no trade will actually take place. Thus the Heckscher-Ohlin theorem, as stated in the text, which is that each country *exports* the product that uses its abundant factor more intensively, breaks down. Hence a sufficient demand restriction for the validity of the Heckscher-Ohlin theorem as stated above is that we have identical, homothetic indifference curves characterized by interminability of consumption of either good.

Consider briefly the argument that with the negative output elasticity of supply of the capital-intensive commodity when labor is augmented (the Rybczynski theorem, which as we have seen underlies the Heckscher-Ohlin theorem), it should be sufficient to assume that tastes (characterized by social-indifference curves) are identical between countries and that neither good is inferior in consumption. This argument, however, is invalid because it does not allow for the fact that scale differences in the two countries can produce, in the absence of homotheticity, enough incremental output of the labor-intensive commodity in the capital-abundant country that there is an excess supply of the labor-intensive commodity (despite the absence of inferiority in consumption of either good) at the self-sufficiency price ratio of the labor-abundant country, thus invalidating the Heckscher-Ohlin theorem. This can be seen from the fact that it is possible to reverse the relative positions of P_{II} and C_{II} in figure 6.1 while keeping C_{II} to the northeast of C_I and keeping OP_{II} steeper than OP_I.

6.2   Heckscher-Ohlin Theorem with Price Definition of Factor Abundance

The derivation of the Heckscher-Ohlin theorem with the price definition of factor abundance requires less restrictive demand assumptions. Indeed it has been customary to argue (erroneously) that no demand restriction is necessary to prove the theorem in this case. It can be shown readily that the assumption of community-indifference curves with interminability of demand for either good is sufficient to deduce the Heckscher-Ohlin theorem in this instance.

From the relationship established earlier between goods-price and factor-price ratios, it is evident that if country I is defined as K-abundant because $\omega > \omega^*$, it follows equally that $p > p^*$, since $k_1 > k_2$. The fact that multiple self-sufficiency equilibria are ruled out by the demand restriction mentioned in the preceding paragraph implies that country I will export the capital-intensive good 1. Thus it is clear in figure 6.3 that the uniqueness of the pretrade equilibrium in each country ensures that the international terms of trade will lie in the range QR, spanned by the two self-sufficiency price ratios, and that country II will export an amount $JS = SK$ of commodity 2 to country I.

Suppose, however, that we do not have unique pretrade equilibria. This invalidates the Heckscher-Ohlin theorem even when trade does materialize.[2] Thus in figure 6.4 let the excess-demand curve for country II have three self-sufficiency equilibrium price ratios: R_1, R_2, and R_3. (Equilibria R_1 and R_3 are stable, and R_2 is unstable, if we assume that the

2. See Inada (1967) and Bhagwati (1967).

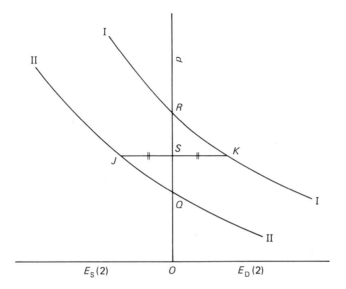

Figure 6.3

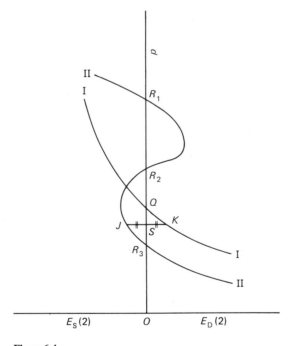

Figure 6.4

"auctioneer" raises price when there is positive excess demand.[3]) In this case, if the self-sufficiency price ratio in country II is R_1 and that in country I is (uniquely) Q, then the trade equilibrium will be at S (and stable) and country I will import the labor-intensive good 2 and export the capital-intensive good 1, although $Q < R_1$ (i.e., $p < p^*$) in self-sufficiency, and therefore country I is labor-abundant by the price definition of factor abundance. Hence the Heckscher-Ohlin theorem is contradicted in this instance and ceases to be logically true. As Inada has pointed out, however, a weaker formulation may then be salvaged: that a pretrade self-sufficiency price ratio (R_3 in figure 6.4) will exist in the multiple-equilibrium situation, which will yield the correct Heckscher-Ohlin pattern of trade.

6.3 Factor-Price Equalization

So far we have focused on the pattern-of-trade issue in the Heckscher-Ohlin model. We now consider the effect of trade on factor prices. For this assume initially that the conditions for the validity of the Heckscher-Ohlin theorem under physical factor abundance definition are satisfied. In addition assume that in the post-trade equilibrium, each country continues to produce both goods.

Consider figure 6.5 which builds on figure 5.11. The endowment ratios of countries I and II are indicated by $\bar{k}$ and $\bar{k}^*$, respectively. For country I, given technology, the endowment ratio sets the upper and lower limits of $\bar{\omega}$ and $\underline{\omega}$, respectively, on the wage-rental ratio. At goods prices $\bar{p}$ or higher, the country is completely specialized in good 2 and the wage-rental ratio is frozen at $\bar{\omega}$. Note that $\bar{\omega}$ is given by the slope of the good-2 isoquant at $k_2 = \bar{k}$. Any price increases beyond $\bar{p}$ leave the economy specialized in good 2 with the wage and rental rate in terms of good 1 rising in exact proportion to the increase in p, leaving their ratio at $\bar{\omega}$. At goods prices $\underline{p}$ or below, country I is completely specialized in good 1 and the wage-rental ratio is frozen at $\underline{\omega}$. Similar description applies to country II, although we do not show the relevant goods prices for her in figure 6.5 to avoid clutter.

In the pretrade equilibrium, the labor-intensive good, good 2, is more expensive in country I which is capital abundant. Thus country I's pretrade or autarky price ratio, p_A, is higher than that of country II, p_A^*. Correspondingly the pretrade wage-rental ratio in country I is higher

---

3. This stability condition is discussed in appendix B.

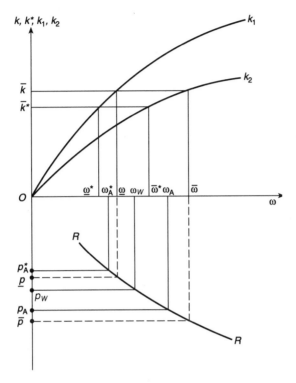

Figure 6.5

than that in country II, $\omega_A > \omega_A^*$. Moreover, since the higher wage-rental ratio leads to a higher capital-labor ratio in each sector in country I, the value of marginal product of labor measured in a common unit is higher and the value of marginal product of capital is lower in that country. Equivalently the real wage is higher and the real rental rate is lower in country I.

Opening to trade leads to a decline in the price of good 2 in country I and a rise in it in country II. It is then immediate from figure 6.5 that the wage-rental ratio declines in country I and rises in country II. Indeed, we know from the Stolper-Samuelson theorem that the real wage falls and the real rental rate rises in country I while the opposite happens in country II. Thus trade leads to a convergence of factor prices across countries in relative as well as in real terms.

The important question is, How far will this convergence go? As Samuelson (1948, 1949) demonstrated a half century ago, as long as the international price ratio is such that both countries continue to produce both goods, factor prices will be equalized completely in relative as well as in real terms. Workers will receive the same wage everywhere and the return to capital will also be the same everywhere. Thus free trade in goods will eliminate all incentives for factors to move internationally.

The equality of relative factor prices under incomplete specialization can be illustrated readily with the help of figure 6.5. Thus, if the international (world) price ratio settles at p_W the wage-rental ratio settles at ω_W in both countries. The equalization of relative factor prices also leads to the equalization of capital-labor ratios in the respective sectors and, hence, of real returns, measured in a common numéraire, of each factor across countries. World efficiency is achieved purely via free trade and no movement of the factors of production.

It is important to note that a relaxation of any one of the assumptions made explicitly or implicitly to establish the factor-price-equalization theorem can lead to its break down. Thus consider the following:

1. If tariffs or transportation costs are present, goods prices will converge but fail to equalize. Correspondingly the factor prices will also converge but fail to equalize.

2. If the relative factor endowments are sufficiently diverse, in the international equilibrium, one of the two countries may become completely specialized.

Then, unless the international price happens to just coincide with the slope of the completely specialized country's production possibilities curve at the point of complete specialization, factor prices will converge but fail to equalize completely. For example, in figure 6.5, holding the world endowments constant, if we make country I more capital abundant and country II more labor abundant, one of the two countries will eventually become completely specialized. Factor prices will equalize up to the point at which the country is just completely specialized. Any further redistributions of endowments will fail to produce such equalization. This last point will become clearer when we consider below the integrated-equilibrium approach to factor price equalization.

3. If factor-intensity reversals exist and endowment ratios of the two countries are sufficiently diverse, factor-price equalization will not happen. In terms of figure 5.10, with sufficiently diverse endowment ratios, wage-rental ratios relevant to country I could lie to the right of point A and those relevant to country II lie to the left of A. It is then immediate that free trade will fail to equalize factor prices. Indeed in this case they may even diverge from each other as a result of free trade.

4. In general, factor prices do not equalize in the presence of scale economies (see chapter 11). Thus the assumption of constant returns is also crucial to achieving factor-price equalization. In terms of figure 6.5,

the relationship between goods prices and factor prices in the presence of scale economies also depends on factor endowments. Thus we have different curves in the lower half of figure 6.5 for each country except in the trivial case of identical factor endowments.

5. Factor prices also fail to equalize if technologies differ between the two countries. Once again, the relationship between goods prices and factor prices in the lower half of figure 6.5 differs between the two countries, and equalization of goods prices does not equalize factor prices.

6. The equality of the number of goods and factors is also important for factor-price equalization. For example, as we will see in the next chapter, if there are more factors than goods as in the specific-factors model, trade will not equalize factor prices.

6.4 Integrated-Equilibrium Approach

Building on Samuelson's (1953) seminal contribution, Dixit and Norman (1980) forcefully advocate using what they call the "integrated-equilibrium" approach to factor-price equalization. Anticipating the problems arising from complete specialization and factor-intensity reversals, they approach the question in the reverse of the traditional approach. Rather then take the factor endowments of the two countries as given and look for conditions (e.g., incomplete specialization, no factor-intensity reversals) under which free trade equalizes factor prices, they ask how a given set of world endowments can be divided so as to give rise to a trading equilibrium in which factor prices are equalized.

Figure 6.6, taken from Dixit and Norman (1980, p. 112), illustrates the integrated-equilibrium technique. Dimensions of the box represent world endowments with labor measured along the horizontal axis and capital along the vertical axis. Assume for a moment that the world economy is fully integrated with resources and goods free to move anywhere. We can then obtain a price ratio and the corresponding factor prices at which world goods and factor markets are cleared. Suppose, at these factor prices, OA_1 and OA_2 represent the equilibrium capital-labor ratios in sectors 1 and 2, respectively.

The question we ask now is what divisions or allocations of the world endowments between countries I and II can reproduce this integrated equilibrium under free trade. Because goods are allowed to be traded freely and we want to reproduce the factor and goods prices obtained in the integrated equilibrium, the essential idea is to look for factor allocations across countries that will leave the total world supply unchanged. To proceed, construct first the parallelogram $OC_1O'C_2$. We know that

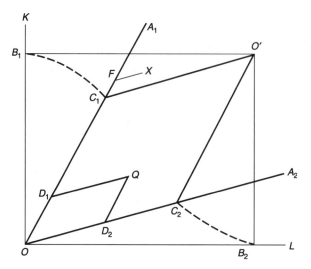

Figure 6.6

resources shown by point C_1 are employed in producing good 1 and those shown by C_2 are used in producing good 2. By construction, the sum of these resources equals the dimensions of the box.

It is easy to see that any division of world resources that lies on or inside the parallelogram $OC_1O'C_2$ is capable of producing the integrated equilibrium. For example, consider point Q. Suppose that the coordinates of Q with O as the origin represent country I's endowments and the remaining endowments belong to country II. Construct the parallelogram OD_1QD_2. Suppose that $OD_1 = (\frac{1}{3})OC_1$ and $OD_2 = (\frac{1}{2})OC_2$. Then country I can produce one-third of the world supply of good 1 and one-half that of good 2, while country II produces the rest. At the prices prevailing in the integrated equilibrium, markets will clear under free trade.

At allocations outside parallelogram $OC_1O'C_2$, the integrated equilibrium cannot be reproduced. For example, take point X as representing country I's endowments. With this endowment, if we were to reproduce the factor prices prevailing in the integrated equilibrium, country I will employ resources indicated by point F in sector 1 and end up supplying more than the total quantity demanded. The only way to reproduce the integrated equilibrium will be for country II to produce a negative quantity of good 1, which is ruled out by assumption.

Observe that all allocations strictly inside parallelogram $OC_1O'C_2$ yield diversified equilibria in both countries. Points on the parallelogram itself, except C_1 and C_2, represent allocations at which one country just specializes completely in one commodity. At C_1 and C_2, both countries just specialize completely. Thus incomplete specialization (ruling out the boundary cases of just complete specialization as in the context of figure 6.5) turns out to be a natural property of the allocations that yield factor-price equalization.

We may ask what happens at allocations outside the parallelogram. We know that the integrated equilibrium cannot be reproduced at these allocations. Further Dixit and Norman also point out that if we make the assumptions of identical homothetic demands and no factor-intensity reversals, the resulting free-trade equilibrium, which naturally results in different goods and factor prices than those characterizing the integrated equilibrium, is accompanied by complete specialization by at least one country in one commodity. They note that the region can be divided into four areas using symmetrically placed curves C_1B_1 and C_2B_2. Inside OB_1C_1, country I is specialized completely in good 1 and country II is diversified. Inside $O'B_1C_1$, country II is specialized completely in good 2 and country I is diversified. Regions OB_2C_2 and $O'B_2C_2$ can be interpreted similarly. On the dividing boundaries, both countries are specialized completely. In general, when factor intensity reversals are allowed or tastes are not identical and homothetic, free-trade equilibria characterized by diversification in both countries can exist.

How do we relate this analysis to factor-intensity reversals? In the manner which the integrated-equilibrium approach proceeds, factor-intensity reversals are automatically ruled out. When the possibility of such reversals exists as in figure 5.10, allocations in parallelogram $OC_1O'C_2$ in figure 6.6 place both countries either to the left of point A in figure 5.10 or to the right of it, and they are compatible with incomplete specialization in both countries.

Finally it is useful to relate the integrated-equilibrium approach to McKenzie's (1955) "diversification cone" approach to factor-price equalization. McKenzie had shown that for incomplete specialization, each country's endowment ratio should lie, on an isoquants diagram such as that in figure 5.5, inside the diversification cone formed by production techniques at the given factor-price ratio. Parallelogram $OC_1O'C_2$ in figure 6.6, which contains all allocations of factor endowments within which factor prices equalize, is clearly formed by the diversification cones of the two countries.

The integrated-equilibrium approach adds two critical elements to the story, however. First, in general, the diversification cone itself depends on the factor prices; for each factor-price ratio, there is a different diversification cone. Which of these many cones should be used to define the relevant endowment ratios? By solving for goods prices and hence factor prices first, the integrated-equilibrium approach is able to identify the particular diversification cone that must be used to determine endowment allocations yielding factor-price equalization. Second, contrary to what the diversification cone approach implies and as we will see in the context of a three-good, two-factor model in chapter 8, for factor-price equalization it is not sufficient to require that the endowment ratio of each country lie within its diversification cone. Market-clearing conditions impose further restriction on these ratios.

Recommended Readings

Bhagwati, J. Proofs of the theorems of comparative advantage. *Economic Journal* 77 (1967): 75–83.

Dixit, A., and V. Norman. *Theory of International Trade*. Cambridge: Cambridge University Press, 1980, ch. 4.

Inada, K. A note on the Heckscher-Ohlin theorem. *Economic Record* 43 (1967): 88–96.

Johnson, H. G. Factor endowments, international trade and factor prices. *Manchester School of Economic and Social Studies* 25 (1957): 270–83. Reprinted in *Readings in International Economics*, ed. by R. E. Caves and H. G. Johnson. Homewood, IL: Irwin, 1968.

Jones, R. W. Factor proportions and the Heckscher-Ohlin theorem. *Review of Economic Studies* 24 (1956–57): 1–10.

Lancaster, K. The Heckscher-Ohlin trade model: A geometric treatment. *Economica* 24 (1957): 270–83.

McKenzie, L. W. Equality of factor prices in world trade. *Econometrica* 23 (1955): 239–57.

Samuelson, P. International trade and the equalisation of factor prices. *Economic Journal* 58 (1948): 163–84.

Samuelson, P. International factor-price equalization once again. *Economic Journal* 59 (1949): 181–97.

Samuelson, P. Prices of factors and goods in general equilibrium. *Review of Economic Studies* 21 (1953): 1–20.

7 Specific-Factors Model

Two key features that drive the basic properties of the 2×2 model are (1) the equality of the number of goods and factors and (2) constant returns to scale. These features are essential for establishing a one-to-one relationship between factor prices and goods prices which, in turn, helps establish the Rybczynski, factor-price equalization, and Heckscher-Ohlin theorems.

Constant returns imply that the average cost of production is independent of the *scale* of output. More to the point, the unit cost function in sector i, $c^i(w, r)$, contains factor prices as the only arguments and is concave and linear homogeneous in them.[1] Given free and costless entry, we obtain the zero-profit condition $c^i(w, r) = p_i$. If we now impose the assumption that the number of sectors in the economy is the same as the number of factors, we have as many zero-profit conditions as there are factor prices.[2] Ruling out multiple solutions (i.e., factor-intensity reversals), we can solve these conditions to obtain a one-to-one relationship between factor prices and goods prices. From this, the factor-price equalization theorem follows immediately.

A one-to-one relationship between factor prices and goods prices implies that factor prices are invariant with respect to changes in factor endowments. Fixity of factor prices, in turn, implies fixity of capital-labor ratios. Then, given full employment conditions, the Rybczynski theorem follows. Combining the Rybczynski theorem with identical homothetic tastes across countries yields the Heckscher-Ohlin pattern of trade.

In this chapter and chapter 11, we show that the introduction of more factors than sectors and economies of scale can alter the general equilibrium relationships within an economy in a fundamental way. Using a simple, three-factor, two-sector model where each sector uses a sector-specific and a common factor, we show that the one-to-one relationship between factor prices and goods prices no longer holds.[3] This model, referred to as the Ricardo-Viner or specific-factors (SF) model in the literature, generates the so-called neoclassical ambiguity whereby an increase

---

1. Properties of the unit-cost function are explained in detail in chapter 9.

2. Note that though the point is being made for the 2×2 model, it applies equally well to the $n \times n$ case where n is larger than 2.

3. The case involving more sectors than factors is not very interesting. In this case, as in the Ricardian model, there are flats in the production surface and a strong tendency for specialization in as many sectors as there are factors. Even if the number of goods produced exceeds the number of factors as, for example, under autarky, the number of independent goods prices must equal the number of factors. Zero-profit conditions associated with these independent prices allow us to solve for factor prices as functions of the latter. The remaining goods prices are then determined by the zero-profit conditions associated with them. Because the factor prices are functions of the independent goods prices, these prices are also functions of the latter.

in the relative price of a good leads to a fall in wages in terms of that good but a rise in terms of the other good. The model yields neither factor-price equalization nor a clear-cut relationship between factor endowments and the pattern of trade.

In the next chapter we will see that economies of scale also undermine the one-to-one relationship between factor prices and goods prices. More important, they can serve as an independent basis of gainful trade between nations. Furthermore, if scale economies are combined with product differentiation, we can generate the widely observed phenomenon of intra-industry trade.[4]

7.1 Specific-Factors Model: Basic Analysis

The SF model was used widely prior to the ascendancy of the Heckscher-Ohlin model and can be traced in the writings of Haberler (1936), Harrod (1939), Ohlin (1933), and Viner (1937). Influential writings of Samuelson during 1940s and 1950s put the Heckscher-Ohlin model at the forefront of trade theory and pushed the SF model into the background. The model was revived during 1970s, however, by Jones (1971) and, indeed, Samuelson (1971a, 1971b) himself. Later Neary (1978a, 1978b) and Mussa (1978), viewing the SF model as a short-run version of the Heckscher-Ohlin model, neatly united it with the latter. The SF model has since become a part of the standard theory of international trade.[5]

As already noted, the SF model has three factors of which two are sector-specific and one is common to both sectors. Because sector-specific factors do not flow between sectors, they are also referred to as fixed or immobile factors. By analogy, the factor common to the two sectors is called the *mobile factor*. Sector-specific factors are frequently labeled as capital and land or, corresponding to the two sectors, sector-1 and sector-2 capital. The mobile factor is usually referred to as labor. In some contexts it may be more appropriate to label the mobile factor as capital and fixed factors as sector-1 and sector-2 labor.

To introduce the model formally, denote the factor specific to sector i by K_i and the mobile factor by L. Because the K_i are now *different*

---

4. Intraindustry trade refers to the phenomenon that countries export and import similar products. For example, the United States exports *as well as imports* automobiles, shoes, textiles, wines, and so on.

5. Although the main results of the model can be found in the papers by Jones (1971) and Samuelson (1971a), papers by Mayer (1974), Mussa (1974), and Amano (1977) contributed further to the revival of the model.

factors, returns to them are also different. We denote these latter by r_i. The number of zero-profit conditions, $c^i(w, r_i) = p_i$, is now smaller than the number of factor prices. We cannot establish a one-to-one relationship between factor prices and goods prices. As we will see shortly, to solve for factor prices, we must take into account other variables including factor endowments.

Because there is only one factor used in both sectors, the allocational problem in the SF model is quite simple. In each sector the value of marginal product of labor gives us the demand for labor. Setting the sum of the two demands equal to the endowment of labor, we obtain the equilibrium allocation of labor and the wage rate. Once we have the wage rate, we can use zero-profit conditions to determine the rental rates on sector-specific factors.

The production function in sector 1 is written $Q_1 = F(K_1, L_1) = L_1 f(k_1)$, where K_1 is now fixed. From this, the value of marginal product of labor (VMPL) may be written $V_1 = p_1(g(k_1) - k_1 g'(k_1))$. It is easy to verify that, holding p_1 and K_1 fixed, this is a negative function of L_1. That is to say, the VMPL or demand-for-labor curve is negatively sloped.

In figure 7.1, introduced by Mussa (1974), we let $O_1 O_2$ represent the total endowment of labor in the economy. We measure L_1 horizontally to the right and V_1 vertically up from O_1. Along the vertical axis we also measure the wage rate. The VMPL or demand-for-labor curve in sector 1 is represented by $V_1 V_1$. The demand-for-labor curve in sector 2 exhibits properties similar to $V_1 V_1$. In figure 7.1 we measure L_2 horizontally to the left and V_2 vertically up from O_2. We then represent the VMPL or

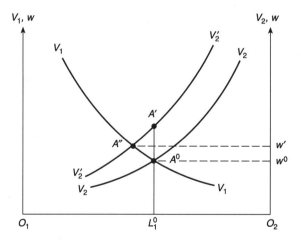

Figure 7.1
V_1, V_2, and w are measured in terms of good 1, the numéraire.

demand-for-labor curve in sector 2 by $V_2 V_2$. As expected, this curve looks like the mirror image of a conventional demand curve when the mirror is placed along the vertical axis.

Each sector equates its VMPL to the wage rate. Moreover, because labor is intersectorally mobile, a single wage must prevail in the two sectors. It follows that the equilibrium will obtain at point A^0 where $V_1 V_1$ and $V_2 V_2$ intersect. The height of point A^0 gives the equilibrium wage rate, while its horizontal distances from O_1 and O_2, respectively, give equilibrium allocations of L_1 and L_2. Given the equilibrium wage rate, zero-profit conditions allow us to determine the rental rates on sector-specific factors. Likewise, substituting the equilibrium values of L_1 and L_2 in the production functions for goods 1 and 2, respectively, we obtain equilibrium outputs. Thus all variables in the economy are determined.

Figure 7.1 has another intuitive interpretation. Relative to origin O_2, horizontal distances along $V_2 V_2$ give the demand for labor in sector 2 at different wage rates. But because $O_1 O_2$ equals the total supply of labor, horizontal distances along $V_2 V_2$ *relative to origin O_1*, give supplies of labor available to sector 1 at different wage rates. Interpreted this way, relative to O_1, $V_2 V_2$ represents the supply of labor available to sector 1. Therefore, point A^0 represents the intersection of demand for and supply of labor in sector 1.

We next consider the comparative statics of the specific-factors model. Before doing so, it may be noted that the concept of relative factor intensities so crucial to comparative statics in the 2×2 model is irrelevant to the specific-factors model. Since K_1 and K_2 are wholly immobile across sectors, they can be viewed as *different* factors, say, capital and land. It is then clear that a comparison of the labor-capital ratio in sector 1 with the labor-land ratio in sector 2 is not particularly meaningful. Only later, when we interpret the model as a short-run version of the 2×2 model, will the concept of relative factor intensities becomes meaningful again.

7.2 Comparative Statics: A Change in Goods Prices

Given the simple nature of the allocational problem, we can derive virtually all comparative statics properties of the SF model using the construction in figure 7.1. Consider first a 10% increase in the price of good 2. This will shift the $V_2 V_2$ curve vertically up to $V_2' V_2'$ by exactly 10 percent. In *absolute* terms, the shift will be larger at higher wages, and vice versa. Point A', directly above A^0, indicates a wage exactly 10 percent higher than the initial equilibrium wage. The new equilibrium obtains at point A'' where the wage is less than 10 percent higher than at the initial equilibrium. Thus the *real* wage declines in terms of good 2 but rises in terms of good 1. This result is referred to as the *neoclassical ambiguity* in the literature. An implication of the result is that if good 2 is the import good, the effect of a tariff on the workers' welfare is ambiguous in general. Welfare is likely to rise or fall as the workers have a strong preference for good 1 or 2.

The reason for a less than proportionate increase in the wage is straightforward. After the price increase, at the initial equilibrium, the VMPL in sector 2 rises 10 percent above that in sector 1. Sector 2 begins to bid labor away from sector 1. The reallocation of labor from sector 1 to 2 raises the VMPL in the former sector and lowers it in the latter. The process comes to a stop when VMPLs in the two sectors are equalized once again. The equality is obtained at a wage that is less than 10 percent higher than the original wage. As expected, the price increase expands sector 2 and contracts sector 1.

We can also establish that a 10 percent price increase in sector 2 is accompanied by a more than 10 percent increase in the rental on the specific factor in that sector and a decline in the return to the other specific sector. Recall that $c^i(w, r_i) = p_i$, where the $c^i(\cdot)$ are linear homogeneous in w and r. With no change in the price of good 1 and a rise in the wage, r_1 must decline in order to satisfy the zero-profit condition for sector 1. Likewise, with a 10 percent increase in p_2 and a less than 10 percent increase in the wage, r_2 must rise by more that 10 percent. These results can also be inferred from figure 7.1 where the capital-labor ratio falls in sector 2 and rises in sector 1 due to a reallocation of labor from the latter to the former sector. This means that the marginal product of capital rises in sector 2 and falls in sector 1. Because the price rises in sector 2, this means that the real rent rises in sector 2 and falls in sector 1 in terms of both goods.[6]

The effects of the price change on factor prices can be summarized as follows:

PROPOSITION 1   In the SF model an increase in the price of a factor raises the real return to the specific factor in that sector, lowers that to the other specific factor, and has an ambiguous effect on the real return to the mobile factor.

---

6. By cost minimization, marginal products of sector-specific factors equal r_1/p_1 and r_2/p_2. A rise in p_2 lowers the former and raises the latter. This means that r_1/p_2 must fall and r_2/p_1 must rise.

7.3   Comparative Statics: A Change in Factor Endowments

We now hold goods prices constant and allow factor endowments to change. Begin with a 10 percent increase in the supply of K_2. In figure 7.2 we reproduce the initial equilibrium A^0 as in figure 7.1. We know from the zero-profit condition in sector 2 that given constant goods prices, the return to the specific factor cannot change unless the wage is changed. Therefore, holding the wage rate fixed, the capital-labor ratio remains unchanged in response to an increase in K_2. The implication is that at each wage rate in figure 7.2, the 10 percent increase in K_2 shifts $V_2 V_2$ horizontally to the left by exactly 10 percent. This is shown by $V_2' V_2'$. A 10 percent horizontal shift translates into larger *absolute* shift at higher levels of L_2, and vice versa.

If the wage rate were to remain unchanged at its initial equilibrium level, L_2 and hence Q_2 would rise by exactly 10 percent. But in order to bid labor away from sector 1, sector 2 must offer a higher wage. The result is a less than 10 percent increase in L_2 and hence Q_2. The Rybcxynski effect observed in the 2×2 model disappears in the present model. Because sector 1 loses labor, its output declines.

As already noted, the increase in K_2 increases the wage. Remembering that we are holding the goods prices constant, it follows from zero-profit conditions that returns to both sector-specific factors must decline in terms of each good. This can also be seen from figure 7.2 where the capital-labor ratios rise in both sectors. (Sector 1 loses labor, while the increase in labor employment in sector 2 is proportionately less than the exogenous increase

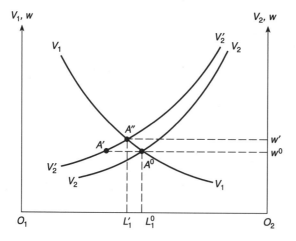

Figure 7.2

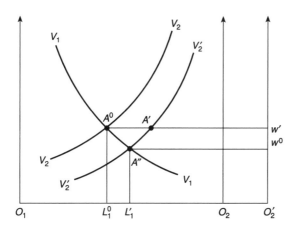

Figure 7.3

in capital.) The rise in capital-labor ratios implies a decline in the marginal products of capital.

The effects of an increase in K_1 are similar to those of an increase in K_2. Therefore, we can state the following general proposition with respect to an increase in endowments of sector-specific factors.

PROPOSITION 2   An increase in the endowment of a factor specific to a sector leads to a less than proportionate increase in the output that sector and a decline in the output of the other sector. The return to the mobile factor rises, while those to sector-specific factors decline.

Next, let us consider an increase in the supply of labor. In figure 7.3 a 10 percent increase in labor endowment shifts the origin O_2 to the right by 10 percent. Correspondingly, the VMPL curve in sector 2, $V_2 V_2$, shifts parallelly to the right by the full amount of the increase in labor endowment. At the original wage rate, there is an excess supply of labor. The wage rate declines, and the additional supply of labor is absorbed partially by sector 1 and partially by sector 2. By zero-profit conditions, rental rates rise in both sectors.

We see from figure 7.3 that both sectors expand in response to the rise in the supply of the mobile factor. Once again, this is different from what is predicted by the Rybczynski theorem. We cannot say in general which of the two sectors will expand more. It is evident from figure 7.3 that labor employment rises proportionately more in the sector with the higher elasticity of demand for labor. In addition, because the elasticity of *output* also depends on labor's share in cost, the sector with higher elasticity of demand weighted by labor's cost share expands relatively more. This result is derived mathematically in chapter 10. We state these results as follows:

PROPOSITION 3   An increase in the endowment of the mobile factor lowers the return to that factor and increases those to sector specific factors. Outputs of both sectors rise. The sector with the higher elasticity of demand for labor weighted by labor's share in income expands relatively more.

The implications of the specific-factors model are quite different from those of the 2×2 model. This raises the important question: Which of the two models should we rely on? Although the choice of the model depends on the nature of the problem at hand—an issue we turn to shortly—it may not always be necessary to consider the two models as competitive. By this latter view, developed in detail in Neary (1978a, 1978b) and Mussa (1978), the specific-factors model can be interpreted as the short-run version of the 2×2 model. To show how this is done in the Neary framework, in section 7.4 we look closely at the short- and long-run effects of a rise in the relative price of good 2. Mussa's formulation, which requires algebra, will be taken up in chapter 10.

7.4   Interpreting the SF Model as the Short-Run Version of the 2×2 Model

In figure 7.4, the lower half represents the 2×2 model and the upper half the SF model. We assume that capital is intersectorally immobile in the short run but perfectly mobile in the long run. Initially, given an exogenous price ratio, the economy is in the long-run equilibrium at point B_1 in the lower panel. Taking the allocation of capital at this point, we can draw the VMP-of-labor curves in sectors 1 and 2 in the upper panel. The intersection of these curves at point A_1 determines the wage rate.

Suppose now that the price of good 2 rises by 10 percent. In the short run, this moves the economy to point A_2 which lies less than 10 percent above A_1. The allocation of capital remains unchanged so that the equilibrium in the lower panel moves to B_2 in the lower panel. At point A_2 the wage has risen by less than 10 percent in terms of good 1. Therefore the return to capital which is immobile in the short run rises by more than 10 percent in sector 2 and falls in sector 1.

In the intermediate run, capital reallocates itself from the lower-return sector to the higher-return sector, namely from sector 1 to sector 2. At the factor prices associated with point B_2, as sector 1 sheds capital, it also sheds labor. Because sector 1 is capital intensive, it sheds less labor per unit of capital than sector 2 demands. The wage rises further. Recalling that the goods price is fixed at its new level during the adjustment pro-

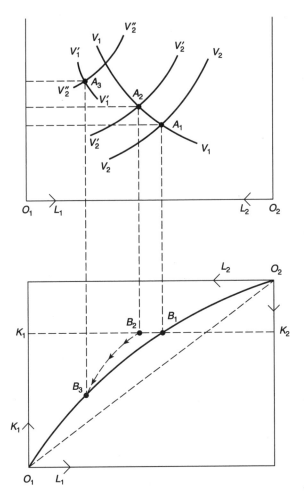

Figure 7.4

cess, the rise in the wage is accompanied by a decline in the return to capital in each sector. During adjustment, the capital-labor ratio in each sector rises, implying an adjustment path marked by arrows in the lower panel of figure 7.4. The new equilibrium obtains at points A_3 and B_3 in upper and lower panels, respectively, where the wage has risen by more than 10 percent and the rental rate on capital, equalized once again across sectors, has fallen in terms of both goods.

How can we be sure that the process of adjustment between points B_2 and B_3 is convergent? More precisely, how do we know that as the economy moves along the path B_2B_3, the difference between the two rental rates declines and eventually disappears? To answer, recall that at B_2, the rental rate is higher in sector 2 than in sector 1. Because sector 2 is labor

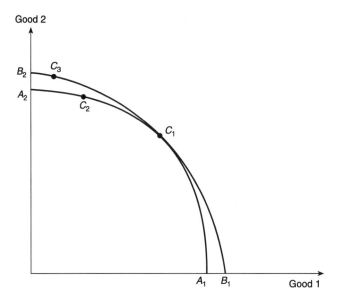

Figure 7.5

intensive, by the zero-profit condition, a given increase in the wage leads to a larger reduction in the rental rate in this sector than in sector 1. The difference between the two rental rates declines and the process is convergent.

Figure 7.5 shows the short- and long-run effects of a price change in the output space. $B_2 B_1$ shows the economy's long-run production-possibility curve corresponding to the efficiency locus $O_1 O_2$ in the lower half of figure 7.4. Initially the economy is at point C_1 in figure 7.5, which corresponds to B_1 in figure 7.4. In the short run, the economy's production possibilities are given by frontier $A_2 A_1$. This frontier is generated by holding capital in each sector fixed at its initial level, namely by tracing the outputs along the horizontal line $K_1 K_2$ in figure 7.4. Except at B_1 which corresponds to C_1 in figure 7.5, each of these combinations is off the efficiency locus and hence inferior to some point on the latter. This is why $A_2 A_1$ lies everywhere strictly inside $B_2 B_1$ except at point C_1. Diminishing returns to labor ensure that $A_2 A_1$ is strictly concave to the origin.[7]

An increase in p_2 moves the economy to point C_2 in the short run and to C_3 in the long run. The slope of $A_2 A_1$ at C_2 equals that of BB at C_3. As expected, the supply response in the short run is smaller than that in the long run. Stated differently, at a long-run equilibrium, the curvature

7. We can draw a short-run production frontier corresponding to each point along the long-run frontier $B_2 B_1$.

of the short-run frontier is higher than that of the long-run frontier. This property derives ultimately from the fact that in the 2×2 model the number of factors is equal to the number of goods, whereas in the SF model it is larger. A more extreme example is that of the Ricardian model where the number of factors is less than the number of goods and the frontier is a straight line.

7.5   Source of Factor Specificity and the Choice of a Model

The SF model explains better why capitalists tend to lobby for protecting their own industry instead of being united as a class along the lines of the Stolper-Samuelson argument. In practice, however, as Magee (1982) has documented, both capital and labor seem to vote with the industry in which they are located, so they may both be acting as if they were sector-specific. If that were indeed true, the most appropriate model would be also the most trivial one—one where both factors are wholly immobile, exactly as in the Haberler (1950) analysis of the gains from trade under factor immobility. We would then have a kink in the production-possibility curve, as at P in figure 7.6, and any decline in a good's relative price would immediately lead to a deterioration in the real return enjoyed by every factor therein (insofar as such factor does not consume solely what it produces). That is, a shift from PS to PR in the goods-price ratio would leave production unchanged at P and all factors

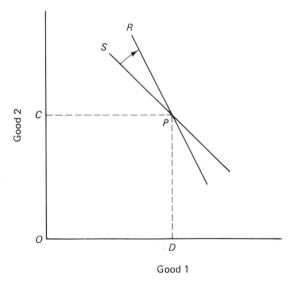

Figure 7.6

in the production of good 2 generally worse off and those in good 1 better off.

Both the trivial all-factors-specific model and the SF model with one factor wholly mobile and the other wholly specific are very special cases with few counterparts in reality, for factors do move in response to changing rewards. The really interesting questions are why factors of production move at different speeds and how we should model the underlying reasons for such differential mobility and examine their differential outcomes for such mobility and for factor remuneration, and the like, in the presence of such changes as intensification of import competition. In short, we have to ask why one or more factors are wholly confined to an industry in the SF type analysis, since the answer to that question will yield different implications for modeling. In other words, we have to examine more closely what exactly is meant by "specificity."

There are in fact two types of sectoral specificity that one could distinguish: *preferential* specificity, in which a factor of production (e.g., homogeneous labor) prefers being employed in one sector to being employed in another such that, for instance, a premium is demanded in the marketplace to be employed in the unpreferred sector, and *aptitudinal* specificity such that a factor of production has a comparative aptitude, in some well-defined sense, in producing one good rather than another. Where a factor of production has an infinite preference for a sector or an infinite incompetence or inaptitude for producing in the other sector, the result will be the pure SF model, and the distinction between the two underlying reasons for immobility of this factor to the other sector will not matter in a comparative static analysis. But it should be evident that the two underlying reasons are conceptually distinct and, short of the extreme example just given, lead to very different models. To see this, consider two very different conceptions: one where the factor of production being considered for specificity is treated as homogeneous (labor is labor, capital is capital, etc.) and one where the factor of production is defined with possibility of heterogeneity (labor consists of different kinds of labor with different degrees of attitudinal or preferential specificity, capital is clay with different kinds of capital goods in different sectors, etc.).

Homogeneous Factors

Preferential specificity of a factor of production may be considered to lead to the wage-differential model of chapter 25 below: Labor may prefer to be employed in the sector producing good 1 rather than good 2 so that, in perfect competition, it accepts wage w_1 in good 1, which is equal to λw_2 where $\lambda < 1$. The analyst can ask what the response of factor prices, factor allocations, and so on, would be to a change in the goods-price ratio in this case as contrasted with the case where there is no such preferential specificity and therefore $\lambda = 1$. Aptitudinal specificity is not easy to contemplate in the case of homogeneous factors of production, and it is more naturally thought of in relation to heterogeneous factors within a class, as discussed below. However, it is clear that Samuelson's concept and definition of factor-intensity differentials come close in some sense to the notion of aptitudinal specificity defined between different homogeneous factors. It is interesting that Samuelson's pioneering of the concept of factor-intensity differentials arose from the fact that until then trade theorists had been forced to invoke the presence of Jones-type specific factors to get the concave implicit transformation functions (to get a "bowed-out" production-possibility curve exhibiting increasing marginal cost of transformation). The assumption of such specific factors yielded the diminishing returns to outward mobility of the nonspecific factors noted in Haberler's classic treatment of the problem (1933, pp. 178–79). The problem with that approach was that it could not distinguish between mobility of a factor between sectors and its "specificity" or aptitudinal efficiency in this instance. It can be said that Samuelson essentially restored mobility to the model but introduced the concept of factor-intensity differences to get at the notion of aptitudinal-efficiency specificity. In that interpretation the wider the factor-intensity difference between two activities or sectors, the more the model is characterized by specificity of the aptitudinal-efficiency type. Again, as Krauss and Johnson (1974) and others have done, we can then proceed to ask a variety of questions: What effect will a widening of factor-intensity differentials have on the outputs of the two sectors at any given goods-price ratio? How will the effect of a change in goods price on the allocation of factor supply to the sector whose price has risen differ if the factor-intensity differential is wider and there is thus more specificity of the aptitudinal type in the system?

Heterogeneous Factors

Here, we consider a factor of production to consist of a variety of heterogeneous subfactors. Typical analytical examples would be vintage capital models which embody the assumption that capital consists of heterogeneous capital goods that are imperfect substitutes for one another but are all "capital" in the sense that, over time, one can be transformed into another. Again, as we just saw in section 7.4, the SF model can be thought of as applicable to a dynamic time-path analysis of an economy where labor moves instantaneously in response to rewards but capital (being clay) moves only gradually as depreciation permits reinvestment of funds (putty) in more appropriate capital form. Insofar as labor contains "human capital," labor can also be construed as consisting of different types of labor with aptitudinal differences among them.

We can explore a model where, say, labor is arrayed in a continuum $\{l_1, \ldots, l_n\}$ such that the preference for being employed in sector 1 rather than sector 2, represented by the wage differential $\lambda < 1$, is correspondingly $\{\lambda_1, \ldots, \lambda_n\}$.

By contrast, we can also consider a model where different kinds of labor or capital can be arrayed in the same manner by their aptitudinal efficiency differences. A simple model that builds such differences into the labor market is the Bhagwati-Srinivasan (1977) model of education, with a job-ladder specification of the labor market and a fairness-in-hiring theory of education in which educated labor can be bumped down from sector 1 into sector 2 when jobs for the educated are less numerous than the educated labor force, but then in sector 2 the educated and the uneducated will have the same productivity. In this model educated labor evidently has comparative aptitudinal efficiency in sector 1 and uneducated labor (which is not employable in sector 1) has it in sector 2. This basic approach to aptitudinal efficiency has been elegantly explored in the trade-theoretic context by Grossman (1983). His model postulates a continuum of capital goods, and he indexes units of capital by i, where $i \in [0, 1]$, such that comparative advantage in supplying efficiency units to sector 1 relative to sector 2 is nonincreasing in i. Thus, denoting $\alpha_1(i)$ and $\alpha_2(i)$ as the potential contributions of unit i to efficient capital in each sector and writing $A_i = \alpha_1(i)/\alpha_2(i)$, he has $A' = dA/di \leq 0$. With factor-intensity differentials between sectors defined in conventional Samuelsonian fashion on efficiency units of capital, Grossman is then able to generate neat results showing that comparative-statics results such as the effect of a change in goods price on factor rental (the Stolper-Samuelson question) depend not only on the factor-intensity differential but also on the aptitudinal-efficiency differences that influence whether the induced transfers of capital to the expanding sector involve an efficiency loss at the margin. It is intuitive that where there is no such loss, the factor-intensity differential will determine the outcome wholly (as in the HOS model with homogeneous capital) and that where this loss is infinite the result will be identical to that in the model where capital is wholly sector-specific at initial allocations. Grossman's analysis applies to these two extremes and all the cases in between.

Recommended Readings

Amano, A. Specific factors, comparative advantage, and international investment. *Economica* 44 (1977): 131–44.

Bhagwati, J. N., and T. N. Srinivasan. Education in a "job ladder" model and the fairness-in-hiring rule. *Journal of Public Economics* 7 (1977): 1–22.

Grossman, G. N. Partially mobile capital: A general approach to two sector trade theory. *Journal of International Economics* 14 (1983): 1–17.

Haberler, G. *The Theory of International Trade*. Hodge, London, 1936.

Haberler, G. Some problems in the pure theory of international trade. *Economic Journal* 60 (1950): 223–40.

Harrod, R. F. *International Economics*. Chicago University of Chicago Press, 1939.

Jones, R. W. A three-factor model in theory, trade and history. In Bhagwati et al., (eds.,) *Trade, Balance of Payments and Growth: Essays in Honor of C.P. Kindleberger*. Amsterdam: North Holland, 1971.

Magee, S. P. The Political Economy of Protectionism: Comment. In J. N. Bhagwati, ed., *Import Competition and Response*. Chicago: University of Chicago Press, 1982.

Mayer, W. Short-run and long-run equilibrium for a small open economy. *Journal of Political Economy* 82 (1974): 955–67.

Mussa, M. Tariffs and the distribution of income: The importance of factor specificity, substitutability, and intensity in the short and long run. *Journal of Political Economy* 82 (1974): 1191–1204.

Mussa, M. Dynamic adjustment in the H-O-S model. *Journal of Political Economy* 86 (1978): 775–91.

Neary, P. Short-run capital specificity and the pure theory of international trade. *Economic Journal* 88 (1978a): 488–510.

Neary, P. Dynamic stability and the theory of factor-market distortions. *American Economic Review* 68 (September 1978b): 671–82.

Ohlin, B. *Interregional and International Trade*. Cambridge: Harvard University Press, 1933.

Samuelson, P. An exact Hume-Ricardo-Marshall model of international trade. *Journal of International Economics* 1 (1971a): 1–18.

Samuelson, P. Ohlin was right. *Swedish Journal of Economics* 73 (1971b): 365–384.

Viner, J. *Studies in the Theory of International Trade*. New York: Harper, 1937.

Generalizations and Empirical Verification of the Heckscher-Ohlin Theory

We have already dealt, in many specific problems, with models involving higher dimensions in terms of the numbers of goods and factors. Samuelson's classic 1953 paper opened up the question forcefully. Subsequently Ethier (1974), Jones and Scheinkman (1977), and Jones (1976) have addressed the limitations of "twoness" fairly systematically in relation to some of the standard propositions of traditional theory (e.g., the Stolper-Samuelson and Rybzynski theorems). What can one say, in light of these and several other papers, about the strengths and limitations of $2 \times 2 \times 2$ models?

Some of the "standard" results of the $2 \times 2 \times 2$ model (or its $1 \times 2 \times 2$ Ricardian predecessor) are misleading if not altogether inapplicable in a model of higher dimensions. However, it is also true that often the "standard" results are not the only ones that are consistent with the standard model but have acquired their "standard" character through the tendency to ignore other possibilities or characterize them as unlikely to be observed. For instance, in the standard Ricardo-Mill version of the $1 \times 2 \times 2$ model the equilibrium terms of trade are portrayed as lying strictly between the limits determined by unit cost ratios in the two countries. Even in this model, equilibrium terms of trade can coincide with the unit cost ratio in one of the countries—a possibility seen more easily in a multicountry extension. But this possibility is treated as extreme, not just in a mathematical sense of terms of trade coinciding with one extreme point of an interval within which it can lie, but as if it is unlikely to be observed. Similarly, in the Heckscher-Ohlin-Samuelson $2 \times 2 \times 2$ model, incomplete specialization in equilibrium is considered the norm and complete specialization, a possibility again extreme in a mathematical sense, is treated as an unlikely event.

However, certain problems cannot be handled very well in a $2 \times 2 \times 2$ framework. One of these is the treatment of nontraded goods. Although, as Jones points out, the distinction between tradables and nontradables corresponds to what he calls "twoness" in a functional sense, and although many analytical results can be derived by using the Komiya-Salter model for a small country facing fixed world relative prices of traded goods in which there are two goods (a single traded composite and a nontraded good) and two factors, it is not easy to handle neatly changes in the relative prices within the basket of traded goods and tariffs applicable only to a subset of traded goods. Indeed any discussion of a tariff structure as contrasted with a tariff on a single good calls for a departure from the standard model. These departures often lead, as in the theory of effective protection (chapter 15), to results that are termed paradoxical only in comparison with the standard model. In a model with nontraded goods, it is easier to see that an increase in the relative price of the exportable good in terms of the importable good (i.e., an improvement in the terms of trade) may lead to a fall in domestic output of the exportable. However, an identical result in the standard model in a region when the domestic offer curve is "backward-bending" is often treated as extreme. Aggregating goods into a basket can make it easy to confuse the effect of a change (e.g., 10 percent) in the price of one good in the basket with the effect of similar and simultaneous changes in the prices of each good in the basket. Another standard result of the two-good trade model, the Lerner symmetry theorem, can be misleading in a model with several traded goods unless carefully interpreted; a tariff on some imported good need not be equivalent to a tax on some exportable in any relevant sense.

Let us consider the standard results of the $2 \times 2 \times 2$ HOS theory in higher dimensions: the Stolper-Smauelson, Rybczynski, factor-price equalization, and Heckscher-Ohlin theorems. The dimensionality can be increased along any of the three characteristics: goods, factors, and countries. We limit ourselves largely to goods and factors, proceeding systematically by first considering more than two goods, then more than two factors, and then many goods and many factors.

8.1   Many Goods, Two Factors

Stolper-Samuelson Theorem

The Stolper-Samuelson theorem generalizes with minor modifications to more than two goods as long as the number of factors is limited to two. This is illustrated with the help of figure 8.1 where we allow for three goods and two factors. The initial goods prices are such that quantities $\bar{Q}_1, \bar{Q}_2,$ and $\bar{Q}_3$ exchange for one another. The prices have been chosen to ensure that all three goods are produced in the initial equilibrium. Suppose now that the price of good 2 rises such that a smaller quantity, $\bar{Q}_2'$, now exchanges for the original quantities of goods 1 and 3. It is clear that good 2 which has risen in price will be necessarily produced. In addition at most one another good will be produced, though we cannot determined with the available information which good that will be. If it is good 1, the new factor-price ratio is given by CD and if it is good 3, the new factor-price ratio is EF. In either case the Stolper-Samuelson theorem is validated in two respects. The price change leads to an increase in the return to one factor and a decrease in the return to the other factor in terms of all goods. Moreover, between the goods that continue to be produced after the price change, the factor used intensively in the good whose price rises gains, and the other factor loses.

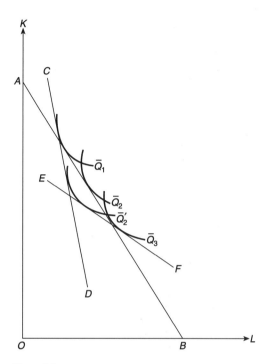

Figure 8.1

Other possibilities can be analyzed similarly. For example, suppose that the isoquant representing $\bar{Q}_3$ lies outside AB initially. Then good 3 will not be produced initially. If the price of good 3 rises now but not enough to justify its production, returns to both factors will fall in terms of good 3 but not change in terms of the other two goods. This result is quite similar to the one encountered in the 2×2 model when the economy is specialized completely in one good.

With three or more goods, one more possibility can arise, however, which does not arise in the two-good case. Thus, in the three-goods case, suppose that initial prices happen to be such that it is profitable to produce only one good, say, good 1. If the price of good 2 rises and that of good 3 falls but both remain unprofitable to produce, returns to both factors fall in terms of good 2 but rise in terms of good 3. Changes in real returns come to depend on the good in which we measure them. This problem can also arise when two of the three goods are produced and prices of one produced and one unproduced good change simultaneously.[1]

---

1. This possibility is noted by Ethier (1984) on which we draw leisurely in this chapter.

Rybczynski Theorem

Leaving aside the possibilities noted in the previous paragraph, the Stolper-Samuelson theorem generalizes to the two-factor, many-goods case. But the Rybczynski theorem runs into a more serious problem. To see this, assume, once again, that the economy produces three goods with their capital intensities ranked as in figure 8.1. Then, holding the goods prices constant, the factor prices and, hence, capital-labor ratios will also be constant. The full employment constraint for capital can be written as

$$K = k_1 L_1 + k_2 L_2 + k_3 L_3. \tag{8.1}$$

Suppose now that the supply of capital rises. Total differentiation of (8.1) yields,

$$dK = k_1 dL_1 + k_2 dL_2 + k_3 dL_3, \tag{8.2}$$

where we make use of the fact that capital-labor ratios do not change as we change factor endowments. With capital-labor ratios held fixed, the output of a sector moves in the same direction as the quantity of labor in that sector. Since we are holding the labor endowment constant, we have $dL_1 + dL_2 + dL_3 = 0$. But this constraint does not preclude equation (8.2) being consistent with L_1 falling or L_3 rising—and hence X_1 falling and X_3 rising—though both cannot happen. To see this, make use of the full employment constraint to rewrite (8.2) as

$$dK = (k_1 - k_2)\, dL_1 - (k_2 - k_3)\, dL_3. \tag{8.2'}$$

Given the assumed relative factor intensities and $dK > 0$, this condition can be satisfied when L_1 falls as long as L_3 also falls. Alternatively, it is also satisfied if L_3 rises as long as L_1 also rises. Thus the increase in the endowment of a factor is consistent with a decline in the output of the sector using that factor most intensively or an increase in the output of the sector using the factor least intensively but not both. This failure of the Rybczynski theorem underlies the breakdown of the so-called chain proposition on the pattern of trade in a many-good, two-factor model in the presence of factor-price equalization (see below).

Factor-Price Equalization Theorem

As long as two countries produce two common commodities and there are no factor-intensity reversals with respect to them, factor-price equalization obtains in the usual manner. Thus the conditions of factor-price equalization in the many-goods, two-factors case do not appear to be more stringent than in the 2×2 model.

Looking at the problem slightly differently, it may appear, however, that with three or more commodities, the factor-price equalization reduces to a mere coincidence. Thus, in the case shown in figure 8.1, factor-price equalization requires that equilibrium goods prices be such that quantities $\bar{Q}_1$, $\bar{Q}_2$, and $\bar{Q}_3$ exchange for one another. If goods prices at the trading equilibrium deviate from this configuration even slightly, in a two-country world, for all goods to be produced somewhere, factor prices will have to differ across countries.

A moment's reflection shows, however, that the case for factor-price equalization is not quite so weak. The key point is that goods prices are not chosen randomly; they are themselves endogenous and depend critically on relative factor endowments. Recall that even in the two-good case, we require that the goods prices be such that it is profitable to produce both goods in both countries. What ensures that this condition is satisfied? It is the requirement that both countries are incompletely specialized which, in turn, follows from the assumption that relative factor endowments of the two countries are not too diverse. This same assumption in the three-goods model ensures that equilibrium goods prices are just right for the production of all goods to be profitable in both locations.

This point is made most clearly and forcefully by Dixit and Norman (1980) using the integrated equilibrium technique. Assume initially that the world economy is fully integrated. Solve for the market-clearing goods and factor prices and, hence, production techniques. In figure 8.2, taken from Dixit and Norman (1980), we measure labor along the horizontal axis and capital along the vertical axis. Ray OA_i ($i = 1, 2, 3$) represents the production technique for goods i in the integrated equilibrium. Point C_i represents the allocation of capital and labor to commodity i necessary to produce the quantity demanded at the integrated equilibrium. The vector sum of the OC_i equals OO', the economy's endowment vector.

To determine the allocations of capital and labor between countries I and II which will reproduce the integrated equilibrium, draw lines C_1H and C_3G and complete the parallel-sided hexagon $OC_1HO'GC_3O$. This hexagon represents the allocations we are looking for. It is easy to check that using the techniques OA_i and employing all factors fully, the two countries can supply the quantities demanded in the integrated equilibrium from any of the allocations in the hexagon. Output bundles produced individually by the two countries are not unique. It is also not necessary for all goods to be produced by both countries, even though such production structure may be consistent with the integrated equilibrium.

At any allocation outside hexagon $OC_1HO'GC_3O$, full employment of all factors in each country using the production techniques of the integrated equilibrium fails to generate output supplies that equal demand

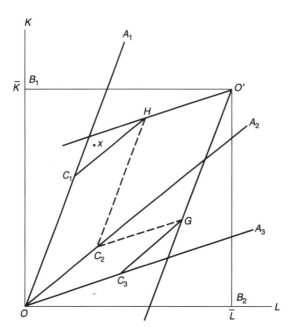

Figure 8.2

without violating nonnegativity constraints on outputs. Thus, even though, at allocation X, each country's endowment lies in its diversification cone, the allocation cannot reproduce the integrated equilibrium and is incompatible with factor-price equalization. In general, it is not sufficient for each country's factor endowment to lie in its diversification cone for factor-price equalization to obtain.

Heckscher-Ohlin Theorem: The "Chain Proposition"

Consider now the Heckscher-Ohlin theorem. The discussion of this theorem in the many-goods, two-factors case takes the form of a "chain proposition." Later we will introduce a "factor content proposition" that holds for the multi-good, multi-factor case and hence can be applied to the present multi-good, two-factor case.

By analogy with the Ricardian model, Jones (1956) proposed that the following chain proposition would also hold in the many-good, two-factor case:

Ordering the commodities with respect to the capital-labor ratios employed in production is to rank them in order of comparative advantage. Demand conditions merely determine the dividing line between exports and imports; it is not possible to break the chain of comparative advantage by exporting, say, the third and fifth commodities and importing the fourth when they are ranked by factor intensity.

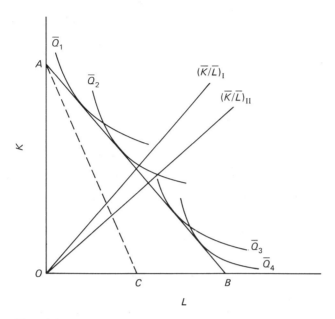

Figure 8.3

Bhagwati (1972), however, showed that this chain proposition would not hold where factor-price equilization has occurred; the chain could then be crisscrossed. The basic argument here is illustrated in figure 8.3. Let there be two countries, I and II, with endowments of two factors, K and L, as shown by the two rays from the origin, such that country I is K-abundant and country II is L-abundant in the physical sense. Assume that there are four goods, 1, 2, 3, and 4, all of them characterized by production functions with the standard restrictions. Strong Samuelson factor-intensity rankings obtain, such that the four goods can be ordered unambiguously according to their K/L ratios. Let the K/L ratios decline successively for goods 1, 2, 3, and 4. Using the Lerner-Findlay-Grubert technique (see chapter 5), we can now take the case where the goods-price ratio that obtains in free-trade equilibrium is one where $\bar{Q}_1$, $\bar{Q}_2$, $\bar{Q}_3$, and $\bar{Q}_4$ exchange for one another on the market. This goods-price ratio also leads, in figure 8.2, to factor-price ratio AB. Since all four goods are viable at these prices in each country on the assumption of internationally identical production functions, multiple production equilibria are possible in each country. Assume then that country I produces goods 1 and 3, whereas country II produces goods 2 and 4. Assuming further that each country consumes some of each good (an assumption consistent with identical, homothetic tastes across countries), we have country I exporting goods 1 and 3 while country II exports goods 2 and 4. However, goods are ordered in a chain of K/L ratios such that $K_1/L_1 > K_2/L_2 > K_3/L_3 > K_4/L_4$, and the chain proposition would imply that since $(\bar{K}/\bar{L})_{\mathrm{I}} > (\bar{K}/\bar{L})_{\mathrm{II}}$, with homothetic tastes, all of country I's exports would be K-intensive in relation to all of that country's imports. But this is not so. The "comparative advantage" chain is thus seen to be criss-crossed by the actual trade pattern in this example.

Deardorff (1979), in an important contribution, provided a formal proof of the non–factor-price-equalization case, where the chain proposition holds, and showed that the proof can accommodate the presence of intermediate goods. He also showed, in an extension to the many-country case, that each of a country's exports will be at least as capital-intensive as each of the exports of all less–capital-abundant countries and at least as labor-intensive as each of the exports of all less–labor-abundant countries (using the physical or the price definition of factor abundance).

8.2 Two Goods, Many Factors

In the last chapter we already examined a model with two goods and three factors. The presence of more factors than goods leads to results that are quite different from those obtained in the 2×2 model. In particular, factor prices are no longer independent of factor endowments. Given this modification, the "standard" theorems of the 2×2 model fail to generalize to the many-factors, two-goods case. Given this conclusion and the fact that we have already covered the most popular 2×3 model in the last chapter, we do not pursue this case further.[2]

8.3 Many Goods, Many Factors

As Jones and Scheinkman (1977) point out, the 2×2 model is special in two ways: It has an equal number of goods and factors, and this number is fixed at two. We have already seen the consequences of raising the number of goods and factors separately. In both cases the number of goods differs from the number of factors. Models with this property are called "odd" in contrast to "even" models which have an equal number of goods and factors. The broad conclusion we can derive from the odd

2. Jones and Easton (1983) analyze the properties of a three-factor model in which all factors are used in all sectors. In this model both relative factor intensities and the elasticities of substitution are crucial to outcomes on how the changes in goods prices and factor endowments impact factor prices and outputs.

models just considered is that though less damage is done to the standard 2×2 theory when we increase the number of goods than when we increase the number of factors, generalizations run into difficulties in either case.

Not surprisingly, generalizations of results derived from the 2×2 Heckscher-Ohlin theory remain difficult when we consider "odd" models of general, $n \times m$, dimensions. Even when we restrict ourselves to even models, the results that can be obtained either require strong restrictions on technological coefficients or are considerably weaker than those obtained in the 2×2 model.

Stolper-Samuelson and Rybczynski Theorems

As Jones (1977) notes, there are two approaches to generalizing the results of 2×2 theory to many-goods, many-factors models. First, we could look for additional restrictions on technology that permit the strong results of the 2×2 model to be replicated in the $n \times m$ model. For example, we could ask under what conditions would each factor be associated with a good such that an increase in the price of that good raises the return to the factor in terms of all goods and lowers the return to all other factors in terms of all goods. Or, under what circumstance, could we associate each good with a factor such that an increase in the supply of that factor raises the output of the good more than proportionately and lowers the outputs of all other goods. Second, we could make the same general assumptions as the standard 2×2 theory and look for weaker results that are as close to the standard results as possible. For example, we could ask whether a price increase necessarily raises the real return to one factor and lowers it to some other factor.

The first approach, pioneered by Chipman (1969) and Uekawa (1971), leads to very limited success. To begin with, for most part, the analysis must be restricted to the even model. Even then, to prove the types of results noted in the previous paragraph, highly complex conditions on technological coefficients that do not lend themselves to a straightforward economic interpretation, must be imposed.

Furthermore one particular aspect of the Stolper-Samuelson and Rybczynski theorems turns out to be impossible to obtain under *any* restrictions on technology. Recall that a change in the relative price unambiguously benefits one factor and hurts the other factor. One possible generalization of this result in the multi-good, multi-factor model is that for *any* change in relative goods prices, the return to each factor either rises or falls in terms of all goods. As Ethier (1984) notes, there are no restrictions on technology in models with dimensions exceeding 2×2 in which this result can be shown to hold true. In the presence of more than two goods, we can always find *some* change in relative goods prices that increases the reward of *some* factor in terms of some goods and reduces it in terms of others.

The second approach to generalizations imposes no more restrictions on technology than the standard 2×2 theory but seeks to prove weaker propositions. At least one interesting and intuitive result obtains for the fully general, $n \times m$ case: Every good is a "friend" to some factor and "enemy" to some other factor in the sense that a rise in the price of the good makes some factor unambiguously better off and some other factor unambiguously worse off.

To show this result, let w_j denote the return to jth factor. Assuming that good 1 is produced initially, the unit-cost-pricing condition for it must hold, $p_1 = c^1 (w_1, \ldots, w_m)$. Allow now the price of good 1 to rise while other prices are held fixed. Using a caret ($^\wedge$) over a variable to denote the proportionate change in that variable, we necessarily have

$$\hat{p}_1 \leq \sum_{j=1}^{m} \theta_{1j} \hat{w}_j, \tag{8.3}$$

where θ_{1j} denotes the distributive share of factor j in sector 1. If good 1 continues to be produced after the price change, (8.3) holds as an equality and, if not, as an inequality. Because positive profits cannot exist under perfect competition, the opposite inequality of the one shown in (8.3) is impossible.

Given the fact that the θ_{1j} are nonnegative and sum to unity, (8.3) necessarily implies that there is at least one factor price, say w_1, that rises proportionately more than p_1. That is to say,

$$\hat{w}_1 \geq \hat{p}_1 > 0 = \hat{p}_2 = \cdots = \hat{p}_n.$$

Thus a rise in the price of a good initially produced must raise the return to some factor in terms of every other good and lower it in terms of no good.

Next, suppose that factor 1 is used in at least one another good, say, good 2, which is produced in the post-price-change equilibrium. For this good we have

$$0 = \hat{p}_2 \geq \sum_{j=1}^{m} \theta_{2j} \hat{w}_j. \tag{8.4}$$

If the good was also produced before the price change, (8.4) holds as an equality. If it was not produced before but is produced after the change, the cost must have fallen to make it profitable to produce now, and hence (8.4) holds as a strict inequality. Because factor 1 is used in good 2 by assumption, $\theta_{21} > 0$. Moreover we have already shown that $\hat{w}_1 > 0$. Then, since the θ_{2j} are nonnegative and sum to unity, (8.4) implies that there is some factor price, say w_2, for which we have

$$\hat{w}_2 < 0 = \hat{p}_2 = \hat{p}_3 = \cdots \hat{p}_n < \hat{p}_1.$$

Thus, in the Scheinkman and Jones (1976) terminology, good 1 is an "enemy" to factor 2.

Similar generalizations cannot be obtained for the Rybczynski theorem in the $n \times m$ case when the number of factors exceeds the number of goods as, for example, in the specific-factors model.[3] The reason lies in the fact that when there are more factors than goods, factor prices are sensitive to endowment changes. But if we restrict ourselves to the case where the number of produced goods is equal to or larger than the number of factors so that factor prices do not change when endowments change at constant goods prices, it can be shown that each factor endowment is a "friend" to the output of some good and an "enemy" to the output of another good. That is to say, if we increase the endowment of a factor, there is a good whose output rises relative to all other factors and falls relative to none, and there is another good whose output falls absolutely. The proof of this result exploits full-employment conditions much in the way we just exploited unit-cost-pricing conditions.

Some additional results obtain if we restrict the number of goods to equal the number of factors. Thus it can be shown that each factor has an enemy in the sense that there is a good such that if that good's price rises, the real return to the factor falls in terms of all goods. But each factor does not necessarily have a friend.

Factor-Price Equalization

We already know from the specific-factors model that with more factors than goods, factor-price equalization is not very likely. When $m > n$, migration of some factors is likely to be needed to equalize factor prices and hence achieve global efficiency in production.

As we have already seen in the case of many goods and two factors, circumstances are more favorable to factor-price equalization when the number of goods exceeds the number of factors. Starting with the even case, we can determine the integrated equilibrium and ask whether there are factor allocations between countries that are capable of reproducing

---

3. One general result that can be obtained in the presence of more factors than goods, however, is that every good has a factor who is its enemy in the sense that an increase in the endowment of the factor reduces the good's output.

the integrated equilibrium. Ruling out linear dependence across columns of input-output matrix where each column contains input-output co-efficients associated with a sector, the answer is in the affirmative.[4] Dixit and Norman also demonstrate that starting with the even model, as we increase the number of goods, there is no presumption that the set of factor allocations permitting factor-price equalization will expand or contract.

Heckscher-Ohlin Theorem: The "Factor-Content" Proposition

Once we get past two factors, ranking goods by factor intensities becomes a complex task and then to related trade flows to endowments on the basis of that ranking even more so. Not surprisingly, when dealing with multi-good, multi-factor settings, the empirically useful literature has proceeded along an alternative route. Rather than focus on specific commodities, they have focused on the net "content" of factors in exports and imports.[5]

The key result is due to Vanek (1968), and it has been extended by Horiba (1974), Leamer (1980), Brecher and Choudhri (1982a), Trefler (1993), and most recently Davis, Weinstein, Bradford, and Shimpo (1997) and Davis and Weinstein (1996).[6] According to this result, known as the Heckscher-Ohlin-Vanek (HOV) theorem, countries are net exporters of the services of their abundant factors and net importers of the services of their scarce factors embodied as factor content in the goods they trade. Because this result has played an important role in empirical work, drawing on Leamer (1980), we discuss it in greater detail before turning to its extensions in the context of empirical work in the next section.

Consider a two-country world with at least as many goods as factors, $n \geq m$. Make the usual assumptions of identical homothetic tastes, identical technologies across countries, perfect competition, and no transportation costs. Assume that goods are traded freely internationally but that factors are not. Factor endowments are sufficiently similar to yield factor-price equalization. Then, according to the HOV theorem,

$$\mathbf{AT} = \mathbf{V} - \alpha(\mathbf{V} + \mathbf{V}^*) \equiv \mathbf{V} - \alpha \mathbf{V}^W, \tag{8.5}$$

where $\mathbf{A}$ is the $m \times n$ matrix of technology coefficients whose typical element, a_{ji}, represents the quantity of jth factor per-unit of ith good, $\mathbf{T}$ is

---

4. Ruling out this linear dependence in the $n \times n$ case is equivalent to ruling out identical factor intensities across industries in the 2×2 case.

5. Deardorff (1982) and Dixit and Norman (1980, pp. 96–100) develop some average relationships between factor endowments and pretrade prices.

6. Among the early contributors, mention must also be made of Melvin (1968) and Travis (1964).

the $n \times 1$ vector of net exports, $\mathbf{V}$ is country I's $m \times 1$ endowment vector, $\mathbf{V}^*$ is country II's $m \times 1$ endowment vector, and α is country I's share in total world expenditure. Vector $\mathbf{V}^W$ ($\equiv \mathbf{V} + \mathbf{V}^*$) is the world endowment vector.

Before we outline the proof of (8.5), it is useful to explain what it says. Suppose that the first factor in vectors $\mathbf{V}$ and $\mathbf{V}^W$ is capital. Then the first equation in (8.5) is represented by

$$K_T \equiv \sum_i a_{ki} T_i = K - \alpha K^W, \tag{8.6a}$$

where K_T represents capital contained in net exports and T_i net exports of good i by country I. According to (8.6), $K_T > 0$ if and only if $K/K^W > \alpha$. That is to say, country I is a net exporter of capital services if and only if its share in world capital is larger than its share in world expenditure or income (under balanced trade). Because the share in world capital relative to the share in world income can be reasonably defined as a measure of a country's capital abundance, (8.6) can be thought of as saying that country I is a net exporter of capital services if it is capital abundant relative to the world. This definition is, of course, different from that used in the 2×2 Heckscher-Ohlin model where abundance in a factor is defined relative to the *other factor*.

To prove (8.5), introduce the output and consumption vectors, $\mathbf{Q}$ and $\mathbf{C}$. By definition, $\mathbf{T} = \mathbf{Q} - \mathbf{C}$ so that we have

$$\mathbf{AT} = \mathbf{AQ} - \mathbf{AC}. \tag{8.5'}$$

Given full employment of resources,

$$\mathbf{AQ} = \mathbf{V}. \tag{8.7}$$

Moreover, given identical homothetic tastes, free trade and no transportation costs,

$$\mathbf{AC} = \alpha \mathbf{AC}^W = \alpha \mathbf{AQ}^W, \tag{8.8}$$

where $\mathbf{C}^W$ and $\mathbf{Q}^W$ are the world consumption and output vectors, respectively. Factor-price equalization, combined with the assumption of identical technology, gives us the last step needed: Matrix $\mathbf{A}$ represents the technology coefficients for the entire world. We have

$$\mathbf{AQ}^W = \mathbf{V}^W. \tag{8.9}$$

Substituting from (8.9) into (8.8), we obtain

$$\mathbf{AC} = \alpha \mathbf{V}^W. \tag{8.8'}$$

Finally substituting from (8.7) and (8.8') into (8.5'), we obtain (8.5).

8.4   Empirical Verification of the Heckscher-Ohlin Theory

We do not offer here a full-scale treatment of empirical literature on the Heckscher-Ohlin theory, which is vast. For that, we refer the reader to detailed surveys of empirical work in international trade by Deardorff (1984) and Leamer and Levinsohn (1995). Instead, we consider the literature that has developed around the factor content theorem.

In a two-factor framework, which is essentially what Leontief (1954) employed in what has become perhaps the most famous empirical finding in economics, the HOV theory can be pushed to yield something akin to the standard Heckscher-Ohlin theory. To show this, let labor be the second factor. Corresponding to (8.6a), we have

$$L_T \equiv \sum_i a_{Li} T_i = L - \alpha L^W. \tag{8.6b}$$

We can now define factor abundance in relative terms as in the standard 2×2 theory. Country I is abundant in capital relative to labor if and only if its share in the world endowment of capital is larger than its share in the world endowment of labor, $K/K^W > L/L^W$ or

$$\frac{K}{L} > \frac{K^W}{L^W}. \tag{8.9}$$

Solving (8.6a) and (8.6b) for K^W and L^W, substituting into (8.9), and simplifying, we can obtain

$$-K \cdot L_T > -L \cdot K_T. \tag{8.10}$$

With only two factors, if trade is balanced, one of K_T and L_T must be positive and the other negative. [They cannot both be zero because that will violate equation 8.10.] Given this fact, inequality (8.10) implies that $L_T < 0$ and $K_T > 0$.

The total value of labor contained in exports can be written $L_E = l_E \cdot E$ where l_E is the labor content of a million dollar's worth of exports and E is the total values of exports in million dollars. Using similar notation, we can define the labor content of imports as $L_M = l_M \cdot M$. Then, $L_T = L_E - L_M = l_E \cdot E - l_M \cdot M < 0$ implies that

$$\frac{l_E}{l_M} < \frac{M}{E} = 1. \tag{8.11a}$$

Similarly, denoting by κ_E and κ_M capital used in a million dollars worth of exports and imports, let $K_E = \kappa_E \cdot E$ and $K_M = \kappa_M \cdot M$ be total capital used in exports and imports, respectively. Then $K_T = K_E - K_M =$

$\kappa_E \cdot E - \kappa_M \cdot M > 0$ implies that

$$\frac{\kappa_E}{\kappa_M} > \frac{M}{E} = 1. \tag{8.11b}$$

Inequalities (11a) and (11b) lead to the conclusion[7]

$$\kappa_E / l_E > \kappa_M / l_M. \tag{8.12}$$

Thus, given balanced trade, in the two-factor, many-goods world the capital-labor ratio in a million dollar's worth of exports is larger than the capital-labor ratio in a million dollar's worth of imports. This is precisely the test Leontief applied.

Combining input-output data with the U.S. trade data for 1947, Leontief found the following values of the ratios shown in (8.11a) and (8.11b): $\kappa_E / \kappa_M = 0.83$ and $l_E / l_M = 1.07$. These ratios violated inequalities (8.11a) and (8.11b), and hence (8.12).

This surprising finding has come to be known as the "Leontief paradox" in the literature. During the last four decades, a large body of literature has developed to explain it. Most investigators focus on alternative factors of production as better suited to explaining the U.S. trade. For example, Vanek (1963) focuses on natural resources arguing that certain categories of trade depend on the availability of such resources rather than on capital-labor ratios. Similarly Keesing (1965, 1966) finds labor skills to be the key determinant of the U.S. trade, while Kenen (1965) stresses a measure of human capital.

But as Deardorff (1984) correctly points out, *if we assume balanced trade*, the presence of additional factors cannot make the paradox in Leontief's numbers go away. Leontief finds $\kappa_E / \kappa_M = 0.83 < 1$ and $l_E / l_M = 1.07 > 1$. If trade is balanced, these inequalities imply that $K_E / K_M < 1$ and $L_E / L_M > 1$ or, equivalently, $K_T < 0$ and $L_T > 0$. Making use of (8.6a) and (8.6b), these last inequalities can be shown to imply that $K / L < K^W / L^W$; that is to say, the United States is relatively capital scarce.

As it happens, Leontief calculated and reported the values of K_T and L_T in his data. It turns out that both of these figures are positive, implying that the United States is a net exporter of both labor and capital. This finding by itself can be reconciled with the theory by assuming either three or more factors or trade surplus or both. We have already seen, however, that assuming a third factor will not do the trick, since the

7. Note that the assumption of balanced trade is not necessary to obtain (8.12) from (8.11a) and (8.11b). But it is needed to obtain opposite signs of K_T and L_T and hence (8.11a) and (8.11b) themselves.

assumption of balanced trade combined with capital labor ratios in million dollars' worth of exports and imports reported above lead to $K_T < 0$ and $L_T > 0$. Therefore the search for an explanation points toward trade surplus.

Leamer (1980) takes this route. Because we required the assumption of balanced trade to derive inequalities (8.11a), (8.11b), and (8.12), these latter inequalities can no longer serve as the "correct" test. Assuming the United States to be capital abundant, inequality (8.10), nevertheless, remains valid. Given $K_T, L_T > 0$, this inequality leads to

$$\frac{K_T}{L_T} > \frac{K}{L}. \tag{8.13a}$$

Moreover, letting K_C and L_C be capital and labor contained in consumption and remembering that K and L are capital and labor contained in production, we have $K = K_C + K_T$ and $L = L_C + L_T$. Making use of these relationships, (8.13a) is equivalent to

$$\frac{K_T}{L_T} > \frac{K_C}{L_C}. \tag{8.13b}$$

Thus, given $K_T, L_T > 0$, the test in (8.12), applied by Leontief, is not the correct test. Instead, we must apply (8.13a) and (8.13b). According to these tests, if the United States is relatively capital abundant, the ratio of capital contained in net exports to labor contained in net exports must exceed the capital-labor ratio in production and in consumption. Combining the calculations provided by Leontief with those done by Travis (1964), Leamer (1980) checks these relationships and finds that they are both valid. The paradox seems to disappear.

Yet, as Brecher and Choudhri (1982b) point out, the positivity of L_T in Leontief's calculations is itself paradoxical. For, given (8.6b), it implies that per-capita expenditure in the United States is lower than in the world as a whole. Citing data, these authors show that this was far from true for the year 1947.

A considerable volume of subsequent research has lent support to Leontief's conclusion by rejecting the HOV model. Thus, working with data different from Leontief's, Maskus (1985), Bowen, Leamer, and Sveikauskas (1987), Brecher and Choudhri (1988), Staiger (1988), and Kohler (1991) have all failed to find support for the HOV theory.

Three recent studies—Trefler (1993), Davis et al. (1997) and Davis and Weinstein (1996)—have reached conclusions more favorable to the Heckscher-Ohlin-Vanek theory, however. Trefler (1993), whose results have been challenged recently in an as yet unpublished paper by Gabaix

(1997), concludes that the assumption of factor-price equalization in terms of measured units of factors rather than efficiency units is at the heart of the problem. Once the traditional factor-price equalization is replaced by the equalization of prices of factors measured in efficiency units, the rest of the HOV model does quite well. Davis et al. (1997) carefully analyze different components of the theory—production, consumption, and trade—and conclude that the failure arises due to the break down of factor-price equalization. Finally Davis and Weinstein (1996) compare the performance of the HOV model against a competing theory based on economies of scale and find that it performs remarkably well. Because these studies make methodological advances, we discuss them, specially the first two, in detail here.

In trying to explain his own results, Leontief had offered international differences in labor productivity as the main culprit. He reasoned that due to its much higher productivity, in efficiency units the United States is likely to be labor abundant compared to its trading partners. Trefler (1993) explores this hypothesis in detail using data for 33 countries, 10 factors of production, and 79 sectors.

Trefler's main innovation is to introduce a productivity parameter for each factor in each country in the HOV model outlined above. Because he deals with many countries, we now introduce a country index $s = 1, \ldots, S$, where S is the total number of countries in the sample. The analysis can be illustrated in terms of one factor, say, labor. Denote the productivity parameter associated with labor in country s by π_L^s. This parameter converts observed units of labor into efficiency units via the relationship $\tilde{L}^s = \pi_L^s \cdot L^s$ ($s = 1, \ldots, S$). Correspondingly we can define technology coefficients in efficiency units such that $\tilde{a}_{Li}^s = \pi_L^s a_{Li}^s$. By the choice of units, we can set the efficiency parameter in country S arbitrarily. Setting $\pi_L^S \equiv 1$, we obtain $\tilde{a}_{Li}^S = a_{Li}^S$. Then, assuming factor-price equalization in terms of efficiency units, we have $\tilde{a}_{Li}^s = a_{Li}^S$ for all s. Assuming further identical homothetic tastes, for each s, we can derive a relationship such as (8.6b) in terms of efficiency units of labor:

$$\tilde{L}_T^s \equiv \sum_i \tilde{a}_{Li}^S T_i^s = \tilde{L}^s - \alpha^s \sum_s \pi_L^s L^s, \qquad s = 1, \ldots, S, \qquad (8.14a)$$

where we have introduced the country superscript s where relevant and used a tilde ($\sim$) to indicate that the variable is measured in efficiency units. We denote the observed wage in s by w^s and that per unit of labor measured in efficiency units by $\tilde{w}^s = w^s / \pi_L^s$. Because we have chosen the efficiency in country S as the numeraire, the wage per unit of labor measured in efficiency units there is the same as the observed wage there, $\tilde{w}^S = w^S$. The equalization of factor prices in efficiency units then implies

$$\frac{w^s}{w^S} = \pi_L^s, \qquad s = 1, \ldots, S-1. \tag{8.14b}$$

Equations (8.14a) and (8.14b) (and similar equations for other factors) form the cornerstone of Trefler's analysis. In (8.14a) values of all variables can be calculated from data except π_L^s. Since $s = 1, \ldots, S$ (8.14a) give us S equations in S unknown π_L^s's. But recalling that we have already set $\pi_L^S \equiv 1$, it appears that there is one more equation than unknowns. It turns out, however, that since $\sum_s \alpha^s = 1$, only $S - 1$ equations in (8.14a) are actually independent. Thus they can be solved to obtain productivity parameters. Once we have these parameters, we can use them to test whether they are consistent with (8.14b). The test is to verify whether the productivity differences revealed by factor contents of trade are consistent with factor-price differences across countries.

Trefler applies this test to aggregate labor and capital for which factor-price data are available.[8] The first point to note is that, in principle, (8.14b) can yield negative values of some π_L^s. But in the case of aggregate labor and capital, for which reliable data are available, these productivity parameters all turn out to be positive. But more important, the correlation between the two sides of (8.14b) turns out to be 0.90 for aggregate labor and 0.68 for capital. Regressions between the two variables on the two sides of (8.14b) also reveal a close and statistically significant relationship between the relative wages and productivity differences, and the same for capital.[9]

A recent paper by Gabaix (1997) raises serious doubts about Trefler's empirical findings by reversing Trefler's procedure. Gabaix uses equation (8.14b) to predict productivities and then tests whether the left-hand side of equation (8.14a) matches the right-hand side. His finding is in the negative.

Davis et al. (1997) offer the most careful and systematic investigation of the HOV theory to-date. Their approach is to essentially unbundle various components of the theory and check which component performs poorly. For this, they use detailed data for ten regions of Japan and 21 countries. They assume throughout that preferences are identical and homothetic and factor prices equalize across regions within Japan. These assumptions are tested against the assumptions of identical homothetic preferences and factor-price equalization across the entire world. The tests are carried out separately for production, consumption, and trade.

8. For other factors, factor-price data being not available, he resorts to weaker and somewhat *ad hoc* tests which, nevertheless, uniformly support the model.

9. Theory predicts that in a loglinear regression the coefficient attached to π_L^s must be 1. The coefficient turns out to be less than one, however.

The authors explicitly allow for the presence of intermediate inputs to take into account indirect factor content in trade. For expositional simplicity, in our presentation of the HOV model, we have suppressed intermediate inputs.[10] We will continue to do so with respect to the analysis of Davis et al.

Denote by r a region in Japan and by J the set containing all r. Let $\mathbf{A}^J$ be Japan's factor-input-coefficients matrix. Because factor prices are equalized across r, we have

$$\mathbf{A}^J \mathbf{Q}^r = \mathbf{V}^r, \qquad r \in J. \tag{8.15a}$$

If we assume factor-price equalization (FPE) for the world as a whole, $\mathbf{A}^J$ applies to all countries, and we additionally have

$$\mathbf{A}^J \mathbf{Q}^s = \mathbf{V}^s, \qquad s \in W \ (\text{FPE—world}), \tag{8.15b}$$

where s indexes countries and W is the set containing all countries in the world.

Next, consider the demand theory. Two demand models are considered. Assume first that the assumption of identical homothetic preferences applies to the regions of Japan alone. Letting α^r be the share of region r in world expenditure and α^J that of Japan as a whole so that $\sum_r \alpha^r = \alpha^J$, we have

$$\mathbf{C}^r = \left(\frac{\alpha^r}{\alpha^J}\right)\mathbf{C}^J, \qquad r \in J. \tag{8.16a}$$

Second, suppose that identical homothetic preferences (IHP) apply to the entire world. We can now represent the consumption vector of entity $h = r \in J, s \in W$ by

$$\mathbf{C}^h = \alpha^h \mathbf{C}^W, \qquad h = r \in J, s \in W \ (\text{IHP—world}). \tag{8.16b}$$

Finally, we can turn to trade relationships. Given (8.16a) which requires IHP for regions within Japan only, the factor content of consumption is

$$\mathbf{A}^J \mathbf{C}^r = \left(\frac{\alpha^r}{\alpha^J}\right)\mathbf{A}^J \mathbf{C}^J, \qquad r \in J.$$

With factor contents in production given by (8.15a) under FPE in regions

---

10. The introduction of intermediate inputs in the analysis is straightforward. All we need to do is premultiply matrix A everywhere by $(\mathbf{I} - \mathbf{B})^{-1}$, where $\mathbf{B}$ is the $n \times n$ input-output coefficients matrix whose ijth element represents the amount of good i used in jth good. The same modification can be applied to the expressions obtained below to obtain precise correspondence with the expressions in Davis et al. Observe that the matrix we denote by $\mathbf{A}$ is denoted by $\mathbf{B}$ by Davis et al., and vice versa.

of Japan only, the factor content of net exports can be written as

$$\mathbf{A}^J(\mathbf{Q}^r - \mathbf{C}^r) = \mathbf{V}^r - \left(\frac{\alpha^r}{\alpha^J}\right)\mathbf{A}^J\mathbf{C}^J, \qquad r \in J. \tag{8.17a}$$

This is the factor content equation equivalent to (8.5) under the assumption that IHP and FPE hold across regions in Japan only.

If we extend IHP to the whole world, (8.16b) holds, and the factor content in consumption is given by

$$\mathbf{A}^J\mathbf{C}^r = \alpha^r\mathbf{A}^J\mathbf{C}^W, \qquad r \in J \text{ (IHP—world)}.$$

Putting $\mathbf{C}^W = \mathbf{Q}^W$ in this equation and combining it once again with (8.15a), the factor content of net exports can be written

$$\mathbf{A}^J(\mathbf{Q}^r - \mathbf{C}^r) = \mathbf{V}^r - \alpha^r\mathbf{A}^J\mathbf{Q}^W, \qquad r \in J \text{ (IHP—world)}. \tag{8.17b}$$

Finally, assume that in addition to IHP, FPE also holds for the world. Then matrix $\mathbf{A}^J$ also applies to the world, and we obtain $\mathbf{A}^J\mathbf{Q}^W = \mathbf{V}^W$. Substituting this into (8.17b), we obtain

$$\mathbf{A}^J(\mathbf{Q}^r - \mathbf{C}^r) = \mathbf{V}^r - \alpha^r\mathbf{V}^W, \qquad r \in J \text{ (IHP, FPE—world)}. \tag{8.17c}$$

Equations (8.15a) and (8.15b) are used to test production theory, (8.16a) and (8.16b) demand theory, and (8.17a)–(8.17c) HOV theory. In each of these seven equations, the left-hand side gives a *measured* value and the right-hand side *predicted* value of the variable in question. Tests involve a comparison between the two sets of numbers and a comparison of how well these relationships do when IHP and/or FPE are assumed for the regions of Japan only and when they are assumed for the entire world.

To explain the nature of tests, take (8.15a). Here we have m equations —one for each factor—corresponding to each region. Under the assumption of FPE across regions in Japan, for each factor for each region, we have a measured and a predicted factor content in production. Tests can involve a simple correlation or a rank correlation between the two sets of numbers. If FPE holds for the entire world, (8.15b) is valid, and we can apply similar tests to all countries in the sample. We can then compare the first set of results against the second set of results to see whether FPE for the entire world works as well as FPE over the regions of Japan only.

Equations (8.16a) and (8.16b) allow us to do similar tests for the IHP assumption. Here (8.16a) gives us n equations—one for each commodity —corresponding to each region in Japan. Under the null hypothesis that IHP holds for Japan, these equations give us a measured and predicted quantity of consumption for each good for each region. Once again, we can do simple and rank correlations. Under IHP for all countries, we can use (8.16b) to do similar tests and then compare these results with the results for (8.16a).

Finally, take (8.17a)–(8.17c). In each of these sets of equations, we have m equations—one for each factor—corresponding to each region. Here, in addition to correlation tests, we can also do sign tests. Factor content of trade can be positive or negative for a factor. We can ask whether the signs of predicted factor contents match the sign of measured factor content. Comparing the results of (8.17a) with those of (8.17b) and (8.17c), we can judge how well the factor content of trade is predicted under FPE and IHP for Japan only, IHP for the world, and IHP and FPE for the world.

The authors' conclusions can be summarized as follows: The production model performs remarkably well for (8.15a) but not for (8.15b), suggesting that FPE for Japan is a good assumption but for the world it is not. The assumption of IHP works equally well for (8.16a) and (8.16b), suggesting that identical homothetic tastes are perhaps not at the heart of the failure of earlier studies to find support for the HOV theory. Tests of the relationships of factor content of trade, equations (8.17a)–(8.17c), reinforce both of these conclusions. Equations (8.17a) and (8.17b) predict the measured factor content of the regions' trade equally well but (8.17c) does it poorly.

In yet another important paper, Davis and Weinstein (1996) contrast the performance of the HOV model against economies-of-scale models. They argue that the key feature that distinguishes the latter models from factor endowments models is what is called the "home-demand" bias in exports. Whereas the models based on constant returns predict that goods for which the demand in a country is stronger than abroad are imported, economies-of-scale models predict the opposite. They take a specific scale economies model with transport costs and embed it into the HOV model. They then test the resulting predictions on output structure using trade and production data of 13 OECD countries at the four-digit level and 22 OECD countries at three-digit level. They find that the structure of OECD manufacturing production is best explained by factor endowments at all levels of classification. There is some indication of home-demand effects in a specification in which the HOV theory determines output structure at three-digit level while home-market effects do so at four-digit level. But these effects are not robust. Allowing endowments to matter for production at the four-digit level eliminates the home-market effect.

In sum, contributions by Davis et al. (1997) and Davis and Weinstein (1996) lend strong support to the production structure assumed by the HOV theory. These studies clearly raise the question why so many earlier studies failed to find support for the theory. One explanation, offered by Davis et al. (1997) is the failure of the universal factor-price equalization which is a central assumption made by all previous studies. An additional problem, at least in the case of some studies, may lie in the input-coefficients matrices used in the studies. To predict trade patterns well, at a minimum the input-output matrix should predict the factor content of production for the country for which the matrix is constructed reasonably well. If this is not true, the matrix can hardly be expected to predict the factor content of partner countries' production or trade well. Unfortunately, the U.S. input-output matrix used by Bowen, Leamer, and Sveikauskas (1987, n. 14) predicted the U.S. factor content in production rather poorly.

Recommended Readings

Bhagwati, J. The Heckscher-Ohlin theorem in the multi-commodity case. *Journal of Policital Economy* 80 (1972): 1052–55.

Bowen, H. P., E. E. Leamer, and L. Sveikauskas. Multicountry, multifactor tests of the factor abundance theory. *American Economic Review* 77 (1987): 791–809.

Brecher, R. A., and E. U. Choudhri. The factor content of international trade without factor-price equalization. *Journal of International Economics* 12 (1982a): 277–84.

Brecher, R. A., and E. U. Choudhri. The Leontief paradox, continued. *Journal of Political Economy* 90 (1982b): 820–23.

Brecher, R. A., and E. U. Choudhri. The factor content of consumption in Canada and the United States: A two-country test of the Heckscher-Ohlin-Vanek model. In *Empirical Methods for International Trade*, ed. by R. C. Feenstra. Cambridge: MIT Press, 1988.

Chipman, J. S. Factor price equalization and the Stolper-Samuelson theorem. *International Economic Review* 10 (1969): 399–406.

Davis, D. R., and D. E. Weinstein. Does economic geography matter for international specialization. Working Paper 5706, National Bureau of Economic Research, Inc. (1996). Cambridge, MA.

Davis, D. R., D. E. Weinstein, S. C. Bradford, and K. Shimpo. Using international and Japanese regional data to determine when the factor abundance theory of trade works. *American Economic Review* 87 (1997): 421–46.

Deardorff, A. V., Weak links in the chain of comparative advantage. *Journal of International Economics* 9 (1979): 513–26.

Deardorff, A. V. The general validity of the Heckscher-Ohlin theorem. *American Economic Review* 72 (1982): 683–94.

Deardorff, A. V. Testing trade theories and predicting trade flows. In *Handbook of International Economics*, vol. 1, ed. by R. W. Jones and P. B. Kenen. Amsterdam: North-Holland, 1984.

Dixit, A., and V. Norman. *Theory of International Trade*. Cambridge: Cambridge University Press, 1980, ch. 4.

Ethier, W. J. Some of the theorems of international trade with many goods and factors. *Journal of International Economics* 4 (1974): 199–206.

Ethier, W. J. Higher dimensional issues in trade theory. In *Handbook of International Economics*, vol. 1, ed. by R. W. Jones and P. B. Kenen. Amsterdam: North-Holland 1984.

Gabaix, X. The factor content of trade: A rejection of the Heckscher-Ohlin-Leontief hypothesis. Mimeo. Harvard University, May 20, 1997.

Horiba, Y. General Equilibrium and the Heckscher-Ohlin theory of trade: The multi-country case. *International Economic Review* 15 (1974): 440–49.

Jones, R. W. Factor proportions and the Heckscher-Ohlin theorem. *Review of Economic Studies* 24 (1956–57): 1–10.

Jones, R. W. "Two-ness" in trade theory: Costs and benefits. Frank Graham Memorial Lecture. Special Papers in International Economics, 12. International Finance Section, Princeton University, 1977.

Jones, R. W., and S. Easton. Factor intensities and factor substitution in general equilibrium. *Journal of International Economics* 15 (1983): 65–99.

Jones, R. W., and J. Scheinkman. The relevance of the two-sector production model in trade theory. *Journal of Political Economy* 85 (1977): 909–35.

Keesing, D. B. Labor skills and international trade: Evaluating many trade flows with a single measuring device. *Review of Economics and Statistics* 47 (1965):

Keesing, D. B. Labor skills and comparative advantage. *American Economic Review* 56 (1966): 249–58.

Kenen, P. B. Nature, capital and trade. *Journal of Political Economy* 73 (1965): 437–60.

Kohler, W. How robust are sign and rank order tests of the Heckscher-Ohlin-Vanek theorem? *Oxford Economic Papers* 43 (1991): 158–71.

Leamer, E. E. The Leontief paradox, reconsidered. *Journal of Political Economy* 86 (1980): 495–503.

Leamer, E., and J. Levinsohn. International trade theory: The evidence. In *Handbook of International Economics*, vol. 3 ed. by G. Grossman, and K. Rogoff. Amsterdam: North-Holland, 1995.

Leontief, W. Domestic production and foreign trade: The american capital position re-examined. *Economia Internationale* 7 (1954): 3–32.

Maskus, K. E. A test of Heckscher-Ohlin-Vanek theorem: The Leontief commonplace. *Journal of International Economics* 19 (1985): 201–12.

Melvin. J. Production and trade with two factors and three goods. *American Economic Review* 58 (1968): 1249–68.

Samuelson, P. A. Prices of factors and goods in general equilibrium. *Review of Economic Studies* 21 (1953–54): 1–20.

Staiger, R. E. A specification test of the Heckscher-Ohlin theory. *Journal of International Economics* 25 (1988): 129–41.

Trefler, D. International factor price differences: Leontief was right! *Journal of Political Economy* 101 (1993): 961–87.

Uekawa, Y. Generalization of the Stolper-Samuelson theorem. *Econometrica* 39 (1971): 197–217.

Vanek, J. The natural resource content of United States foreign trade, 1870–1955. Cambridge: MIT Press, 1963.

Vanek, J. The factor proportions theory: The *N*-factor cases. *Kyklos* 21 (1968): 749–56.

9 Dual Approach: Basic Tools

Up to this point, we have presented the standard theory relying primarily on diagrammatic techniques. We now introduce some mathematical analysis. In this chapter we introduce tools of analysis based on the dual approach to trade theory. These tools simplify considerably solutions to a variety of problems. In the next chapter we derive the results of the Heckscher-Ohlin and specific factors models using the "hat" calculus popularized by Jones (1965, 1971).

An exceptionally clear and detailed treatment of the dual approach can be found in the text by Dixit and Norman (1980).[1] We confine our attention to three main tools: the unit-cost function, the revenue function, and the expenditure function. We conclude the chapter by illustrating briefly the usefulness of the last two of these tools; the first one is employed extensively in chapter 10. We begin with an explanation of the envelope theorem and the envelope function, which are at the heart of all dual analysis.[2]

9.1 Envelope Theorem and Enveloped Function

We illustrate the main points with the help of a simple, two-variable, one-parameter, and one-constraint maximization problem. The propositions we state generalize to a multivariable, multiparameter, and multiconstraint problem in a straightforward manner. Indeed these generalizations can be inferred from our discussion by reinterpreting the variables, parameter, and constraint as vectors.

Let x and y be two variables and b a parameter. Denote the objective function and constraint by $h(x, y, b)$ and $\phi(x, y, b) = 0$, respectively. We solve the problem

$$\max_{x, y, \lambda} L(x, y; b, \lambda) = h(x, y; b) - \lambda \phi(x, y; b), \tag{9.1}$$

where λ is the usual Lagrange multiplier, and we minimize with respect to it. The first-order conditions of optimization are

$$L_x(x, y; b, \lambda) \equiv h_x(x, y; b) - \lambda \phi_x(x, y; b) = 0,$$

$$L_y(x, y; b, \lambda) \equiv h_y(x, y; b) - \lambda \phi_y(x, y; b) = 0, \tag{9.2}$$

$$L_\lambda(x, y; b, \lambda) \equiv -\phi(x, y; b) = 0.$$

---

1. Two key contribution pioneering the application of the dual approach to trade theory are by Woodland (1977, 1980).

2. Our approach is intuitive. We do not attempt to provide complete proofs of the propositions, nor do we try to state sufficiency conditions for maximization.

These three first-order conditions can be solved for optimal values of the three choice variables, x, y, and λ, as functions of parameter b. Substituting the optimal values of x and y into $h(x, y; b)$, we obtain the maximized value of the objective function as a function of b alone. Denote this maximized value by $v(b)$; that is, $v(b)$ is the value of $h(x, y; b)$ when x and y are chosen optimally. Then, according to the envelope theorem, the following remarkable property holds true:

$$v_b(b) = L_b(x, y; b), \tag{9.3}$$

where $L_b(\cdot)$ is evaluated at the optimum. This property is referred to as the *envelope property*, and function $v(b)$ is called the *envelope function*.

The simplifying power of the envelope property can hardly be overstated. It tells us that if we want to assess the impact of a change in a parameter on the value of the objective function at the optimum, we can do so by simply differentiating *partially* the Lagrangean expression with respect to the parameter. The alternative is to differentiate the objective function $h(x, y; b)$ with respect to b, taking into account the fact that at the optimum x and y are also functions of b. Fortunately, the envelope property makes this complicated exercise unnecessary.

Frequently we deal with problems in which certain parameters appear in the objective function only. In this important special case, (9.3) reduces to

$$v_b(b) = L_b(x, y; b) = h_b(x, y; b). \tag{9.3'}$$

That is, the *total* effect of a change in b on $h(\cdot)$ can be obtained by simply differentiating the latter *partially* with respect to b. It turns out that the net effect of a change in b on $h(\cdot)$ through x and y is zero! To prove this result, note that

$$v_b(b)db = h_x(\cdot)\,dx + h_y(\cdot)\,dy + h_b(\cdot)\,db, \tag{9.4}$$

where derivatives are evaluated at the optimum. From the first-order conditions, we have

$$h_x(x, y; b) = \lambda\phi_x(x, y),$$

$$h_y(x, y; b) = \lambda\phi_y(x, y), \tag{9.5}$$

$$\phi(x, y) = 0.$$

Differentiating totally the last of these conditions and making use of the first two, we have

$$\frac{h_x(\cdot)}{\lambda}\,dx + \frac{h_y(\cdot)}{\lambda}\,dy = 0. \tag{9.6}$$

Thus, as was noted above, the net change in $h(\cdot)$ through endogenous change in x and y at the optimum is zero. Substituting from (9.6) into (9.4), we obtain (9.3$'$).

Two additional properties of the envelope function are worth noting. First, suppose that b enters only the objective function. Suppose further that $h(x, y; b)$ is concave in x and y and convex in b for all values of x and y. If we now maximize $h(\cdot)$ subject to a constraint that does not have b as an argument, the resulting envelope function is convex in b. Second, suppose that b appears exclusively in the constraint. In this case, if the objective function is concave in the choice variables and the constraint is convex in the variables and b, the envelope function obtained by maximizing the objective function is concave in b.

Similar results hold for minimization problems. For example, if b does not enter the constraint and the objective function is concave in b, the envelope function obtained from a minimization problem is concave in b.

The envelope theorem and some properties of the envelope function are illustrated in figure 9.1 for the case where parameter b appears in the objective function only. Suppose that $h(x, y; b)$ is concave in x and y and convex in b. We maximize $h(\cdot)$ with respect to x and y subject to a constraint that does not depend on b. Denoting by $\tilde{b}$ a specific value of b and by $(\tilde{x}, \tilde{y})$ the corresponding optimal solution, we have $v(\tilde{b}) = h(\tilde{x}, \tilde{y}; \tilde{b})$. Because b does not enter the constraint, $(\tilde{x}, \tilde{y})$ remains feasible for values of b other than $\tilde{b}$. It follows that $v(b)$ must be at least as large as $h(\tilde{x}, \tilde{y}; b)$ for all values of b. If b is different from $\tilde{b}$, however, the optimal solution will, in general, be different from $(\tilde{x}, \tilde{y})$ and the corresponding value of $v(b)$ strictly larger than $h(\tilde{x}, \tilde{y}; b)$. Therefore in figure 9.1, $v(b)$ is tangent to $h(\tilde{x}, \tilde{y}; b)$ at $\tilde{b}$ in conformity with (9.3$'$); everywhere else, it lies above the latter. Moreover, since $h(\tilde{x}, \tilde{y}; b)$ is assumed to be convex in b, $v(b)$ is also convex in b.

The unit-cost function, revenue function, and expenditure function, considered below, are all envelope functions and their main properties follow directly from the envelope property (9.3) and the properties just described.

9.2   Unit-Cost Function

The unit-cost function gives the minimum per-unit cost of production of a good as a function of factor prices. To derive it, recall that the production function in sector 1 is written $Q_1 = F(L_1, K_1)$. Because the production function is linear homogeneous in its arguments, we can rewrite it as $1 = F(a_{L1}, a_{K1})$, where a_{L1} and a_{K1}, respectively, are labor-output and

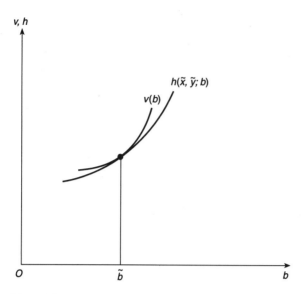

Figure 9.1

capital-output ratios in sector 1. A representative firm's problem is to choose a_{L1} and a_{K1} so as to minimize the unit cost of production, given the technology and factor prices. The Lagrangean for this problem is written

$$\min_{a_{K1},a_{L1},\lambda} L(a_{L1},a_{K1};w,r;\lambda) = wa_{L1} + ra_{K1} + \lambda[1 - F(a_{L1},a_{K1})], \qquad (9.7)$$

where $wa_{L1} + ra_{K1}$, the unit cost of production, is the objective function. We obtain three first-order conditions that allow us to solve for the three choice variables in terms of w and r. Putting the solution values back into the objective function, we obtain the envelope function which contains only w and r as arguments. We denote the envelope function by $c^1(w,r)$ and refer to it as the unit-cost function. The unit-cost function $c^1(w,r)$ is concave in parameters w and r. This follows from the fact that $c^1(w,r)$ is derived by minimizing a function that is concave in parameters that do not appear in the constraint. It can also be shown that $c^1(\cdot)$ is linear homogeneous in its arguments.[3] Finally, by the envelope property, the first partials of $c^1(\cdot)$ with respect to w and r yield optimal values of a_{L1} and a_{K1}, respectively. Stated explicitly,

3. Intuitively, if both w and r increase by a constant proportion, the wage-rental ratio is unchanged. Given linear homogeneity of the production function, this leaves the optimal choices of a_{L_1} and a_{K_1} unchanged. It follows that the unit cost must rise in the same proportion as factor prices.

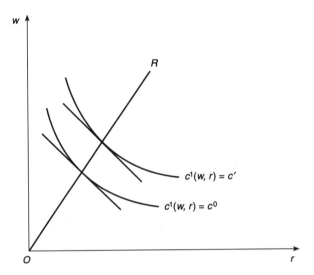

Figure 9.2

$$c_w^1(w,r) = a_{L1} \quad \text{and} \quad c_r^1(w,r) = a_{K1} \tag{9.8}$$

For a given level of unit costs, we can draw a unit cost curve in the (r, w) space. In figure 9.2 we show two such curves. The curve lying farther away from the origin is associated with a higher unit cost. Setting the total differential of $c^1(w, r)$ equal to zero and making use of (9.8), we obtain the slope of the unit-cost curve,

$$\frac{dw}{dr} = -\frac{c_r^1(\cdot)}{c_w^1(\cdot)} = -\frac{a_{K1}}{a_{L_1}} = -\frac{K_1}{L_1}. \tag{9.9}$$

Thus the unit-cost curve is negatively sloped, and the absolute value of its slope at a point gives the equilibrium capital-labor ratio at that point. The curve is also drawn strictly convex to the origin indicating that, due to positive but finite substitutability between factors, the capital-labor ratio rises as we increase the wage and lower the rental rate. If the substitutability between capital and labor is zero (i.e., isoquants are L-shaped), a change in factor prices has no effect on the capital-labor ratio; unit-cost curves are straight lines. If capital and labor are perfect substitutes (i.e., isoquants are straight lines), the capital-labor ratio can vary between zero and infinity at a fixed set of factor prices; the unit-cost curve is L-shaped. Linear homogeneity implies that if we double w and r, unit costs double and the capital-labor ratio remains unchanged. Along a ray through the origin, the slopes of unit-cost curves are constant.

9.3   Revenue Function

The revenue function represents the maximized value of outputs for a given set of commodity prices, technology, and factor endowments. We introduce the revenue function for a n-good, m-factor model and state its properties. In the next chapter we describe briefly specific forms of the revenue function for 2×2 capital-labor and 2×3 specific-factors models.

Let $(Q_1, Q_2, \ldots, Q_n)$ be the output vector, $(V^1, V^2, \ldots, V^m)$ the factor-endowments vector, V_i^j $(i = 1, 2, \ldots, n; j = 1, \ldots, m)$ the quantity of factor j used in sector i, and $Q_i = F_i$ $(V_i^1, V_i^2, \ldots, V^m{}_i)$ the production function of good i. The revenue function is the maximized value of $\Sigma_i p_i Q_i$ subject to the technology and factor-endowments constraint. Formally we solve the problem

$$\max_{V_i^j, \Psi_j} L(V_j^i; p_1, \ldots, p_n; V^1, \ldots, V^m)$$

$$= \Sigma_i p_i F_i(V_i^1, V_i^2, \ldots, V_i^m) - \Sigma_j \Psi_j \Sigma_i (V_i^j - V^j)$$

$$i = 1, 2, \ldots, n, \quad j = 1, 2, \ldots, m. \quad (9.10)$$

The first-order conditions of maximization consist of $m \times n$ equalities setting values of marginal products of different factors equal to their shadow prices (the Ψ_j's) and n full-employment conditions. These can in turn be solved for the V_i^j and Ψ_j as functions of goods prices and factor endowments. Putting the solution values of the V_i^j back into the objective function, $\Sigma p_i F_i(\cdot)$, we obtain the revenue (or GDP) as a function of goods prices and factor endowments. This function, denoted R $(p_1, p_2, \ldots, p_n; V^1, V^2, \ldots, V^m)$, is convex in prices and concave in factor endowments. It is also linear homogeneous in each set of parameters separately.[4] Most important, the first partial of $R(\cdot)$ with respect to the ith price yields the supply of ith output and that with respect to the jth factor gives its shadow price which, in a competitive equilibrium, equals the factor price. We note below the last two of these properties explicitly:

$$R_i(\cdot) \equiv \frac{\partial R(\cdot)}{\partial p_i} = Q_i(p, V), \qquad i = 1, 2, \ldots, n, \quad (9.11)$$

$$R_j(\cdot) \equiv \frac{\partial R(\cdot)}{\partial V^j} = \rho_j(p, V), \qquad j = 1, 2, \ldots, m. \quad (9.12)$$

---

4. Prices appear only in the objective function, and endowments only in the constraints. Therefore the revenue function is convex in prices and concave in factor endowments. The intuitive reasoning behind linear homogeneity is similar to that behind linear homogeneity of the unit-cost function in w and r.

Here ρ_j $(= \Psi_j)$ is the competitive return on factor j, and p and V are shorthand notation for the price and factor-endowments vectors, respectively. A subscript following a function denotes a partial derivative. Unless otherwise noted, i refers to a good or goods price and j to a factor or factor price.

Convexity of the revenue function in prices and concavity in factor endowments, respectively, imply that

$$R_{ii}(\cdot) \equiv \frac{\partial^2 R}{\partial p_i^2} = \frac{\partial Q_i(p, V)}{\partial p_i} \geq 0, \tag{9.13}$$

$$R_{jj}(\cdot) \equiv \frac{\partial^2 R}{\partial V^{j^2}} = \frac{\partial \rho_j(p, V)}{\partial V^j} \leq 0. \tag{9.14}$$

In economic terms, the first inequality says that the supply of a good is a nondecreasing function of its own price. The second inequality says that the return to a factor is a nonincreasing function of its own supply.

An additional useful property—the Samuelson reciprocity relation—concerns the second cross-partials between prices and factors. We know that

$$\frac{\partial^2 R}{\partial p_i \partial V^j} = \frac{\partial^2 R}{\partial V^j \partial p_i}.$$

In view of (9.13) and (9.14), this leads to

$$\frac{\partial \rho_j}{\partial p_i} = \frac{\partial Q_i}{\partial V^j}. \tag{9.15}$$

That is to say, the effect on the price of the jth factor of a unit change in the ith good price is exactly the same as the effect on the ith output of a unit change in the jth factor.

Nothing more can be said about other cross-partials of the revenue function in the general $m \times n$ case. More properties can be established, however, once the production structure is specified in greater detail. This is illustrated in the next chapter for the 2×2 model and n-good version of the specific factors model.

9.4 Expenditure Function

The revenue function neatly summarizes all the information on the supply side. The same task is performed on the demand side by the expenditure function. It is derived by minimizing the expenditure required to achieve a specified level of utility at a given set of prices. Formally we solve the following problem:

$$\min_{C_i, \lambda} L(C_1, \ldots, C_n; p_1, \ldots, p_n; \overline{U}; \lambda) = \Sigma_i p_i C_i + \lambda[U(C_1, \ldots, C_n) - \overline{U}],$$

$$(9.16)$$

where C_i denotes the consumption of good i, $U(\cdot)$ is a standard utility function, and $\overline{U}$ is the minimum level of utility sought. The value of $\Sigma_i p_i C_i$ when the C_i are optimally chosen is the expenditure function and is denoted $H(p_1, p_2, \ldots, p_n; \overline{U})$.[5] Because the problem of minimizing expenditures is very similar to that of minimizing unit costs, properties of the expenditure function mirror those of the unit-cost function. It is concave and linear homogeneous in prices and its first partial with respect to the ith price yields the compensated demand curve for the ith good. That is to say,

$$C_i = H_i(p_1, \ldots, p_n; \overline{U}). \qquad (9.17)$$

Direct second partials of the expenditure function are negative due to concavity implying that compensated demand curves are negatively sloped. Cross-partials in prices are positive or negative as the goods are Hicks substitutes or complements. The first partial with respect to $\overline{U}$ is the inverse of the marginal utility of income. Cross-partials between utility and prices are usually assumed to be positive. This assumption says that the compensated demand rises with the level of utility.

9.5 Equilibrium

Using the dual approach, the equilibrium in a small open economy can be summarized in one equation, namely

$$H(p_1, p_2, \ldots, p_n; U) = R(p_1, p_2, \ldots, p_n; V^1, V^2, \ldots, V^m). \qquad (9.18)$$

According to this equation, income and expenditure must be equal. Given the commodity prices from the world markets, there is only one endogenous variable, U. After we solve (9.18) for U, partial derivatives of the expenditure function with respect to the prices can be used to determine the quantities demanded and consumed. The quantities produced are given by the partial derivatives of the revenue function with respect to the prices. Factor prices are obtained by differentiating the revenue func-

5. A more common notation for the expenditure function is E. But in this book E is used for exports.

tion partially with respect to factor endowments. Thus the entire equilibrium is determined.

Observe that in view of the linear homogeneity of the expenditure and revenue functions in prices, we can rewrite (9.18) as

$$\Sigma_i p_i H_i(\cdot) = \Sigma_i p_i R_i(\cdot). \tag{9.18'}$$

The partial derivatives of the expenditure and revenue functions with respect to a price of a good yield the quantities consumed and produced of that good, respectively. Therefore, defining $H_i(\cdot) - R_i(\cdot) = C_i - Q_i \equiv Z_i$, where Z_i denotes net imports of good i (negative if exports), we see that (9.18') says that the country's net imports are zero. Thus the equilibrium condition (9.18) is equivalent to the trade balance condition.

We can also use the expenditure and revenue functions to represent the equilibrium in a two-country world in a compact form. Label the countries as Home and Foreign countries and distinguish the variables associated with the latter by an asterisk. An equilibrium in the two-country model can be represented by

$$H(p_1, \ldots, p_n; U) = R(p_1, \ldots, p_n; V^1, \ldots, V^m),$$

$$H^*(p_1, \ldots, p_n; U^*) = R^*(p_1, \ldots, p_n; V^{1*}, \ldots, V^{m*}), \tag{9.19}$$

$$H_i(\cdot) + H_i^*(\cdot) = R_i(\cdot) + R_i^*(\cdot), \qquad i = 1, \ldots, n.$$

The first two conditions give budget constraints or trade-balance conditions in the two countries. The remaining n equations represent the market-clearing conditions for n goods. By Walras's law, we can drop one of these market-clearing conditions. By the same token, we can choose one of the goods as the numeraire and set its price equal to unity. Thus we have a total of $n + 1$ equations in $n - 1$ relative prices and two utilities. The model is exactly determined.

There is a further simplification of (9.19) which proves convenient in analyzing situations that do not involve domestic policy interventions (e.g., taxes on production and consumption). Define an "excess expenditure" function $z(\cdot)$ such that

$$Z(p_1, \ldots, p_n; U; V^1, \ldots, V^m) \equiv H(p_1, \ldots, p_n; U)$$

$$- R(p_1, \ldots, p_n; V^1, \ldots, V^m),$$

$$Z_i(\cdot) \equiv H_i(\cdot) - R_i(\cdot), \qquad i = 1, \ldots, n, \tag{9.20}$$

$$Z_j(\cdot) \equiv - R_j(\cdot), \qquad j = 1, \ldots, m,$$

$$Z_U(\cdot) \equiv H_U(\cdot).$$

Recall that a subscript after a function is used to denote a partial derivative and that i refers to a good or goods price and j to a factor or factor price. $Z_i(\cdot)$ is the excess demand for good i and is positive if the good is imported and negative if it is exported. Analogous to (9.20), we can define a $Z^*(\cdot)$ function for the foreign country. Then the system in (9.19) can be rewritten as

$$Z(p_1, \ldots, p_n; U; V^1, \ldots, V^m) = 0,$$

$$Z^*(p_1, \ldots, p_n; U^*; V^{1*}, \ldots, V^{m*}) = 0, \tag{9.19$'$}$$

$$Z_i(\cdot) = -Z_i^*(\cdot), \qquad i = 1, \ldots, n.$$

The small-country model in (9.18) and the two-country model in (9.19) or (9.19$'$) can be subject to a number of comparative statics exercises. For example, we can allow one of the factor supplies to change and study its effects on welfare and, in the case of the two-country model, commodity prices. We can also introduce tariffs or quotas and analyze their effects on welfare, outputs, and so on. After slight modifications the system in (9.19) or (9.19$'$) can also be used to study the effects of factor movements and transfers between the two countries. We can also allow for nontraded goods. We will look at some of these comparative statics exercises and modifications in later chapters. Presently we consider a few useful elasticity relations and stability analysis in a two-country model.

9.6   Trade Elasticities and Stability in a Two-Good Model

Let us revert back to the two-good case, and set $p_1 \equiv 1$. By linear homogeneity, we have $Z_1(\cdot) + p_2 \cdot Z_2(\cdot) = Z(\cdot)$. Since $Z(\cdot) = 0$ from (9.19), this reduces to $-Z_1(\cdot) = p_2 \cdot Z_2(\cdot)$. Letting good 1 be the export good and good 2 the import good, this is equivalent to the familiar trade balance condition, $E_1 = p_2 \cdot M_2$ where we have replaced $-Z_1(\cdot)$ by E_1 and $Z_2(\cdot)$ by M_2. Taking ln on each side and differentiating, we obtain

$$\hat{E}_1 = \hat{p}_2 + \hat{M}_2, \tag{9.21}$$

where a hat ($\hat{}$) over a variable is used to denote the proportionate change in that variable. Dividing throughout by $\hat{p}_2$, (9.21) leads to

$$\varepsilon_s = \varepsilon - 1, \tag{9.22}$$

where ε_s is the elasticity of supply of exports of good 1 and ε is the absolute value of the elasticity of demand for imports of good 2 in the home country. By definition,

$$\varepsilon_s \equiv \frac{\hat{E}_1}{(1/\hat{p}_2)} = -\frac{E_1}{\hat{p}_2}, \quad \varepsilon \equiv -\frac{\hat{M}_2}{\hat{p}_2} \tag{9.23}$$

We have a relationship analogous to (9.22) for the foreign country:

$$\varepsilon_s^* = \varepsilon^* - 1. \tag{9.24}$$

Taking advantage of these elasticities, we can now derive a stability condition for the two-country, two-good model. Assume that prices adjust slowly so that the world market fails to clear instantaneously. Assume further that the price responds positively to the excess demand in the world market

$$\dot{p}_2 = \mu(Z_2(\cdot) + Z_2^*(\cdot)), \tag{9.25}$$

where μ is the speed of adjustment and is exogenously given. For stability, the effect of an exogenous change in p_2 on $\dot{p}_2$ is negative. Differentiating with respect to p_2, we have

$$\frac{d\dot{p}_2}{dp_2} = \mu\left(\frac{dZ_2}{dp_2} + \frac{dZ_2^*}{dp_2}\right). \tag{9.26}$$

Substituting $Z_2 = M_2$ and $Z_2^* = -E_2^*$, multiplying throughout by p_2/M_2, recognizing that $Z_2 = -Z_2^*$ at the equilibrium, and taking into account the definitions of the elasticities in (9.23), we have

$$\frac{p_2}{M_2}\frac{d\dot{p}_2}{dp_2} = -\mu(\varepsilon + \varepsilon_s^*) = -\mu(\varepsilon^* + \varepsilon - 1). \tag{9.27}$$

The last equality makes use of (9.24). According to this equality, the equilibrium is stable if and only if the sum of the import-demand elasticities in the two countries exceeds unity. This condition is often referred to as the Marshall-Lerner condition in the literature.

We conclude this chapter by relating the "total" import-demand elasticity to the compensated import-demand elasticity and the marginal propensity to consume. This relationship is the equivalent of the Slutsky equation in international trade. Recall that $M_2 \equiv Z_2(\cdot)$ and $Z(\cdot) \equiv 0$. Differentiating these identities, we obtain

$$\frac{dM_2}{dp_2} = Z_{22}(\cdot) + Z_{2U}(\cdot)\frac{dU}{dp_2},$$

$$Z_2(\cdot) + Z_U(\cdot)\frac{dU}{dp_2} = 0. \tag{9.28}$$

Solving and making use of the notation introduced above, we can obtain

$$\frac{dM_2}{dp_2} = \frac{\partial M_2}{\partial p_2} - M_2 \frac{H_{2U}}{H_U}. \tag{9.29}$$

Multiplying throughout by p_2/M_2, this may be rewritten as

$$\varepsilon = \varepsilon' - m, \tag{9.30}$$

where ε' is the compensated (i.e., holding utility and factor endowments constant) elasticity of demand for imports and the second term is the marginal propensity to spend on the import good, good 2. The last term is derived as follows:

$$m \equiv p_2 \frac{\partial H_2}{\partial H} = p_2 \frac{\partial H_2}{\partial U} \frac{\partial U}{\partial H} = p_2 \frac{\partial H_2}{\partial U} \frac{1}{\partial H/\partial U} = p_2 \frac{H_{2U}}{H_U}. \tag{9.32}$$

In obtaining the equality before the last one, we make use of the chain relating indirect utility to income, which in turn equals expenditure and that

$$\frac{\partial H}{\partial U} \cdot \frac{\partial U}{\partial H} = 1. \tag{9.33}$$

Analogous to (9.30), for the foreign country, we have

$$\varepsilon^* = \varepsilon^{*\prime} - m^*, \tag{9.34}$$

where $\varepsilon^{*\prime}$ is the foreign compensated elasticity of demand for good 1 and m^* its marginal propensity to spend on its importable, good 1.

Recommended Readings

Dixit, A., and Norman, V. *Theory of International Trade* Cambridge: Cambridge University Press, 1980.

Jones, R. W. The structure of general equilibrium models. *Journal of Political Economy* 73 (1965): 557–72.

Jones, R. W. A three-factor model in theory, trade and history. In *Trade, Balance of Payments and Growth: Essays in Honor of C. P. Kindleberger*, ed. by J. Bhagwati et al. Amsterdam: North Holland, 1971.

Woodland, A. D. A dual approach to equilibrium in the production sector in international trade theory. *Canadian Journal of Economics* 10 (1977): 50–68.

Woodland, A. D. Direct and Indirect trade utility functions. *Review of Economic Studies* 47 (1980): 907–26.

Using the unit-cost function and its properties, the 2×2 capital-labor and 2×3 specific-factors models can be written mathematically in a compact form. We do this below and subject the models to comparative statics with respect to changes in prices and factor endowments. We present the analysis in terms of the socalled "hat calculus" popularized by Jones (1965, 1971).

10.1 The 2 × 2 Model

The 2×2 model can be summarized in the following equations:

$$c^i(r, w) = p_i, \qquad i = 1, 2, \tag{10.1}$$

$$a_{Ki} = c_r^i(\cdot), \tag{10.2}$$

$$a_{Li} = c_w^i(\cdot), \tag{10.3}$$

$$a_{K1} Q_1 + a_{K2} Q_2 = K, \tag{10.4}$$

$$a_{L1} Q_1 + a_{L2} Q_2 = L, \tag{10.5}$$

where $c^i(\cdot)$ is the unit-cost function, a_{Ki} the capital-output ratio, and a_{Li} the labor-output ratio in sector i. K and L are exogenously given endowments of labor and capital, respectively. Equations (10.1) to (10.3) embody all information contained in technology, cost-minimization conditions, and competitive behavior. Thus equations (10.1) represent average-cost pricing conditions resulting from free entry of firms and equations (10.2) and (10.3) result from cost-minimization behavior, given technology and factor prices. As shown in the last chapter, the latter represent the envelope property of the unit-cost function, also known as the Shephard's lemma. Equations (10.4) and (10.5) are the full-employment condition.

Embedded in the system represented by (10.1) through (10.5), there are eight equations in eight endogenous variables, w, r, a_{K1}, a_{L1}, a_{K2}, a_{L2}, Q_1, and Q_2. Thus the small-country model is exactly determined. In the following, we use the model to study the effects of exogenous changes in the goods prices, factor endowments, and technical change on factor prices and outputs.

Goods Prices and Factor Prices

Taking the p_i as exogenously given, (10.1) represents two equations in two endogenous variables, r and w. The equations can be solved to obtain w and r as functions of goods prices. Thus in the present two-factor, two-goods model, factor prices are independent of factor endowments and depend exclusively on goods prices.[1]

Differentiation (10.1) totally, and making use of (10.2) and (10.3), we obtain

$$a_{Ki}\,dr + a_{Li}\,dw = dp_i$$

Multiplying and dividing the first term by r and the second term by w and dividing the entire equation by p_i, we can transform this equation into

$$\Theta_{Ki}\hat{r} + \Theta_{Li}\hat{w} = \hat{p}_i, \qquad i = 1, 2. \tag{10.6}$$

where a hat $(^\wedge)$ over a variable is used to denotes the proportionate change in it (e.g., $\hat{r} \equiv dr/r$) and Θ_{Ki} and Θ_{Li} are income (or cost) shares of capital and labor in sector i (e.g., $\Theta_{Ki} \equiv ra_{Ki}/p_i$). It is easily verified that $\Theta_{Ki} + \Theta_{Li} = 1$. A simple interpretation of (10.6) is that the proportionate change in the unit-cost of production (or the price) equals the weighted sum of proportionate changes in factor prices where the weights are relevant cost shares.

Let us rewrite the system of equations represented by (10.6) in the matrix form:

$$\begin{pmatrix} \Theta_{K1} & \Theta_{L1} \\ \Theta_{K2} & \Theta_{L2} \end{pmatrix} \begin{pmatrix} \hat{r} \\ \hat{w} \end{pmatrix} = \begin{pmatrix} \hat{p}_1 \\ \hat{p}_2 \end{pmatrix}. \tag{10.6'}$$

We denote the determinant of the 2×2 matrix in (10.6′) by Θ. The determinant can be written in three alternative but equivalent forms by making use of the property $\Theta_{Ki} + \Theta_{Li} = 1$. Thus

$$\Theta = \Theta_{K1}\Theta_{L2} - \Theta_{L1}\Theta_{K2} = \frac{wra_{L1}a_{L2}}{p_1p_2}\left(\frac{K_1}{L_1} - \frac{K_2}{L_2}\right)$$

$$= \Theta_{K1} - \Theta_{K2}$$

$$= \Theta_{L2} - \Theta_{L1}. \tag{10.7}$$

According to the last equality in the first line, Θ is positive if and only if sector 1 is capital intensive in physical terms. According to the equality in

1. This result generalizes to the multiple-factors, multiple-goods model in the sense that if the number of factors is the same as the number of goods (i.e., the model is "even"), factor prices depend exclusively on goods prices. If the number of factors exceeds the number of goods (i.e., the model is "odd") as in the specific-factors model, factor prices depend on commodity prices as well as factor endowments. In the remaining case where the number of factors is less than the number of goods as in the Ricardian model, the economy is likely to specialize in as many goods as there are factors, and we are back in the "even" model. If specialization is incomplete, only as many commodity prices as there are factors can be independent. Once again we get into the "even" case where the number of factor prices to be determined equals the number of independent goods prices.

the second line, Θ is positive if and only if capital's income share is larger in sector 1 than in sector 2 or, equivalently, sector 1 is capital-intensive in value terms. Finally, according to the equality in the third line, Θ is positive if and only if labor's income share is larger in sector 2 than in sector 1 or, equivalently, sector 2 is labor-intensive in value terms. The equalities in the three lines are all equivalent in the sense that one of them necessarily implies the other two.

Given our assumption that sector 1 is capital-intensive, Θ is positive. Letting good 1 be numéraire, we can set $\hat{p}_1 = 0$ and solve (10.6′) to obtain

$$\hat{r} = -\frac{\Theta_{L1}}{\Theta}\hat{p}_2, \tag{10.6a}$$

$$\hat{w} = \frac{\Theta_{K1}}{\Theta}\hat{p}_2. \tag{10.6b}$$

Assuming that $\hat{p}_2 > 0$ and remembering that $\Theta = \Theta_{K1} - \Theta_{K2}$, (10.6b) yields $\hat{w} > \hat{p}_2$. Then, taking (10.6a) into account, we can conclude that

$$\hat{w} > \hat{p}_2 > \hat{p}_1(= 0) > \hat{r}. \tag{10.8}$$

This is what Jones (1965) refers to as the "magnification effect." It was identified earlier as the Stolper-Samuelson theorem: A 1 percent increase in the relative price of good 2 raises the price of the factor used more intensively in that good, labor, by more than 1 percent in terms of the numéraire. The return to the other factor declines. The magnification effect is of course the Stolper-Samuelson theorem in another guise.

Mussa (1979) provides a neat diagrammatic interpretation of the magnification effect. In figure 10.1 we represent the unit-cost functions in the (w, r) space. Each contour gives combinations of w and r that yield a fixed unit cost in terms of the numéraire. In view of the Shephard's lemma, the slope of the contour gives the equilibrium labor-capital ratio in the sector at the specified wage and rental rate. As drawn, sector 2 is relatively labor intensive.

Because of its role as the numéraire, in the case of good 1, we show only the contour which sets unit costs equal to 1. For sector 2 we show two contours. The initial contour sets $c^2(w, r) = p_2^0$ while the second one sets $c^2(w, r) = p_2'$ such that p_2' exceeds p_2^0 by 1 percent. If both goods are produced at the initial price p_2^0, the wage and rental must be at A^0. (The steeper slope of $c^2(\cdot)$ than $c^1(\cdot)$ at A^0 reflects the fact that good 2 is labor-intensive.) A 1 percent increase in p_2^0 shifts the $c_2(\cdot)$ contour radially outward by 1 percent. For example, the slope of $c^2(\cdot)$ at A' is the same as at A^0, and A' lies exactly 1 percent away from the latter. This is because,

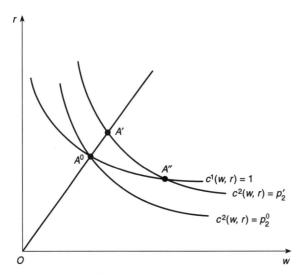

Figure 10.1

with a 1 percent increase in p_2, we can raise the returns to labor and capital both by 1 percent, hold the labor capital ratio at the original level, and still satisfy the zero-profit condition.

If, after the rise in p_2, the wage and rental rate were to actually move to A_2, there will be no magnification effect. But at A' it is unprofitable to produce good 1. Assuming the economy remains incompletely specialized after the price increase, the new wage and rental rate must be at A''. Since w is higher at A'' than at A', it follows that it rises by more than 1 percent relative to point A^0. Also, in view of the negative slope of $c_1(\cdot)$, the rental rate at A'' is lower than at A^0. Thus the inequality in (10.8) is proved.

Factor Endowments and Outputs

Before we derive the effect of a price increase on outputs, it is instructive to derive the effect of a change in factor endowments on outputs, holding goods prices constant. Recall that at constant goods prices, changes in factor endowments have no effect on factor prices. Therefore, as we change factor endowments, the a_{Ki} and a_{Li} do not change. We can solve (10.4) and (10.5) for outputs as functions of factor endowments. Differentiating (10.4) at constant goods prices, we have

$$a_{K1}\, dQ_1 + a_{K2}\, dQ_2 = dK.$$

Multiplying and dividing the first term by Q_1 and the second term by Q_2 and dividing both sides by K, we obtain

$$\lambda_{K1}\hat{Q}_1 + \lambda_{K2}\hat{Q}_2 = \hat{K}, \tag{10.9}$$

where λ_{Ki} $(\equiv K_i/K)$ is the allocative share of capital in sector i and $\lambda_{K1} + \lambda_{K2} = 1$. Analogous to (10.9), differentiating (10.5) at constant goods prices, we obtain,

$$\lambda_{L1}\hat{Q}_1 + \lambda_{L2}\hat{Q}_2 = \hat{L}, \tag{10.10}$$

where $\lambda_{L1} + \lambda_{L2} = 1$. Denoting by λ the determinant of the matrix formed by the coefficients of $\hat{Q}_1$ and $\hat{Q}_2$ in (10.9) and (10.10) in that order, we can show that

$$\lambda = \lambda_{K1}\lambda_{L2} - \lambda_{K2}\lambda_{L1} = \frac{L_1 L_2}{LK}\left(\frac{K_1}{L_1} - \frac{K_2}{L_2}\right)$$

$$= \lambda_{K1} - \lambda_{L1}$$

$$= \lambda_{L2} - \lambda_{K2}. \tag{10.11}$$

These equalities have interpretations analogous to those in (10.7). The most important point is that λ is positive if and only if sector 2 is labor-intensive. Solving (10.9) and (10.10), we can obtain,

$$\hat{Q}_1 = \frac{1}{\lambda}[\lambda_{L2}\hat{K} - \lambda_{K2}\hat{L}], \tag{10.12a}$$

$$\hat{Q}_2 = \frac{1}{\lambda}[-\lambda_{L1}\hat{K} + \lambda_{K1}\hat{L}]. \tag{10.12b}$$

Suppose that we allow L to rise proportionately more than K, namely $\hat{L} > \hat{K}$. Then, in view of relationships in (10.11) and the fact that $\lambda > 0$, we have

$$\hat{Q}_2 > \hat{L} > \hat{K} > \hat{Q}_1. \tag{10.13}$$

Once again we get a magnification effect such that a rise in the labor-capital endowment ratio leads to a proportionately larger increase in the output of the labor-intensive good and a proportionately smaller increase in the output of the capital-intensive good. This of course is the essence of the Rybczynski theorem.

A diagrammatic representation of the relationship between factor endowments and outputs is instructive. In figure 10.2 we plot equations (10.4) and (10.5) for a given set of commodity prices and factor endowments. KK is the full-employment constraint for capital and LL for labor. Assuming full employment of both factors, production will take place at A_1. Suppose now that the endowments of both capital and labor rise by exactly 1 percent. KK and LL will shift out by 1 percent to $K'K'$ and $L'L'$, respectively, and outputs of both goods will rise by 1 percent to A_2.

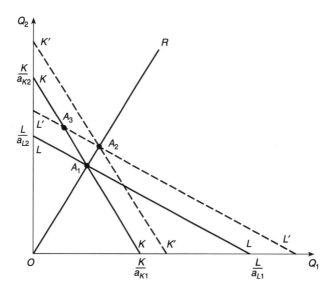

Figure 10.2

Assuming now, however, that the endowment of capital rises by less than 1 percent, the new capital employment constraint will lie inside $K'K'$ and the new production point will lie northwest of A_2 on $L'L'$. That is to say, good 2 will expand more than 1 percent, while good 1 will expand less than 1 percent or actually contract. In the special case when capital is held fixed at its original level, the shift in LL to $L'L'$ yields A_3 as the production point. As expected, the labor-intensive good expands and capital-intensive good contracts.

An additional useful point follows immediately from figure 10.2. The slope of the Rybczynski line—the locus of outputs generated by successive increases in the endowment of a factor—is given by the capital-employment constraint for increases in labor and by the labor-employment constraint for increases in capital. Formally

$$\frac{dQ_2}{dQ_1}\bigg|_{R_L R_L} = -\frac{a_{K1}}{a_{K2}}, \quad \frac{dQ_2}{dQ_1}\bigg|_{R_K R_K} = -\frac{a_{L1}}{a_{L2}}, \tag{10.14}$$

where $R_L R_L$ is used to denote the Rybczynski line corresponding to expansion of labor and analogous interpretation applies to $R_K R_K$. We will see shortly that the slope of the production frontier lies between the slopes of the two Rybczynski lines. This fact has the useful implication that the Rybczynski line associated with the expansion of capital is flatter than the production frontier, while that associated with expansion of labor is steeper than the latter.

To show that the slope of the production frontier lies between the slopes of the two Rybczynski lines, observe that the average-cost pricing conditions allow us to write[2]

$$\frac{p_2}{p_1} = \frac{a_{L2}w + a_{K2}r}{a_{L1}w + a_{K1}r}$$

$$= \frac{a_{L2}/a_{L1}}{1 + (\Theta_{K1}/\Theta_{L1})} + \frac{a_{K2}/a_{K1}}{1 + (\Theta_{L1}/\Theta_{K1})}$$

$$= \Theta_{L1}\left(\frac{a_{L2}}{a_{L1}}\right) + \Theta_{K1}\left(\frac{a_{K2}}{a_{K1}}\right). \tag{10.15}$$

The last equality is a weighted sum of absolute values of the slopes of the two Rybczynski lines and the weights are positive and sum to unity. It follows that the left-hand side must lie between the slopes of the two Rybczynski lines.

Goods Prices and Outputs

We can now consider the remaining relationship in the model: the effect of a change in the relative price on outputs. Purely from the viewpoint of mathematical derivation, this is the most complex relationship. This is because we must now solve all eight equations simultaneously. We begin by differentiating (10.4) and (10.5), holding L and K constant. It is a straightforward matter to differentiate and convert (10.4) and (10.5) into

$$\lambda_{K1}\hat{Q}_1 + \lambda_{K2}\hat{Q}_2 = -[\lambda_{K1}\hat{a}_{K1} + \lambda_{K2}\hat{a}_{K2}], \tag{10.16}$$

$$\lambda_{L1}\hat{Q}_1 + \lambda_{L2}\hat{Q}_2 = -[\lambda_{L1}\hat{a}_{L1} + \lambda_{L2}\hat{a}_{L2}]. \tag{10.17}$$

Next we differentiate (10.3). In terms of proportionate changes, we have

$$\hat{a}_{Li} = \frac{wc_{ww}^i(\cdot)}{c_w^i(\cdot)}\hat{w} + \frac{rc_{wr}^i(\cdot)}{c_w^i(\cdot)}\hat{r}.$$

Since $c^i(\cdot)$ is linear homogeneous, $c_w^i(\cdot)$ is homogeneous of degree zero in its arguments. Therefore we have

$$wc_{ww}^i(\cdot) + rc_{wr}^i(\cdot) = 0.$$

In addition the elasticity of substitution between labor and capital in

---

2. The second equality in (10.15) is obtained by splitting the right-hand side into two, dividing the numerator and denominator of the first term by w/a_{L1} and of the second term by r/a_{K1}, and substituting $wa_{L1}/ra_{K1} = \Theta_{L1}/\Theta_{K1}$. In deriving the last equality, we make use of the condition $\Theta_{L1} + \Theta_{K1} = 1$.

sector i is given by

$$\sigma_i = \frac{C^i(\cdot)C^i_{rw}(\cdot)}{C_w(\cdot)C_r(\cdot)}.$$

Making use of these relationships and recalling that $\Theta_{Ki} = ra_{Ki}/p_i = rc^i_r(\cdot)/c^i(\cdot)$, we can write the proportionate change in the a_{Li} as

$$\hat{a}_{Li} = -\Theta_{Ki}\sigma_i(\hat{w} - \hat{r}). \tag{10.18}$$

Differentiating (10.2), we can derive the analogous equation

$$\hat{a}_{Ki} = \Theta_{Li}\sigma_i(\hat{w} - \hat{r}). \tag{10.19}$$

Subtracting (10.6a) from (10.6b), we obtain $\hat{w} - \hat{r} = (\hat{p}_2/\Theta)$. Using this in conjunction with (10.18) and (10.19), we can rewrite (10.16) and (10.17) as

$$\lambda_{K1}\hat{Q}_1 + \lambda_{K2}\hat{Q}_2 = -\frac{\Delta_K}{\Theta}\,\hat{p}_2, \tag{10.16'}$$

$$\lambda_{L1}\hat{Q}_1 + \lambda_{L2}\hat{Q}_2 = \frac{\Delta_L}{\Theta}\,\hat{p}_2, \tag{10.17'}$$

where $\Delta_L \equiv \lambda_{L1}\Theta_{K1}\sigma_1 + \lambda_{L2}\Theta_{K2}\sigma_2$ and $\Delta_K \equiv \lambda_{K1}\Theta_{L1}\sigma_1 + \lambda_{K2}\Theta_{L2}\sigma_2$. Solving (10.16') and (10.17'), we obtain

$$\hat{Q}_1 = -\frac{\lambda_{K2}\Delta_L + \lambda_{L2}\Delta_K}{\Theta\lambda}\,\hat{p}_2, \tag{10.20a}$$

$$\hat{Q}_2 = \frac{\lambda_{K1}\Delta_L + \lambda_{L1}\Delta_K}{\Theta\lambda}\,\hat{p}_2. \tag{10.20b}$$

As expected, an increase in the relative price of good 2 reduces the output of good 1 and increases that of good 2. A useful outcome of (10.20a) and (10.20b) is

$$\frac{\hat{Q}_2 - \hat{Q}_1}{\hat{p}_2} = \frac{\Delta_L + \Delta_K}{\lambda\Theta} > 0. \tag{10.21}$$

Since prices equal marginal and average costs of production, according to (10.21) an increase in the output of good 2 relative to good 1 is accompanied by an increase in the relative marginal cost of production of good 2. Remembering that there are no distortions in the model, private costs of production coincide with social costs. Therefore we can infer from (10.21) that social opportunity costs of production of a good rise locally as the output of that good rises. That is to say, the production possibilities frontier is locally strictly concave to the origin. Thus we have an alternative proof of the concavity of the production frontier.

Technical Change and Factor Prices

We now hold the goods prices and factor endowments constant but allow technology to change. At first, technical change may appear to be fundamentally no different from a change in factor supplies. But that turns out to be incorrect, since, unlike endowment changes, technical change leads to an adjustment in factor prices.

Let us introduce technical-change parameters μ_{L1} and μ_{K1} and write the production function for good 1 as $Q_1 = F(\mu_{L1}L_1, \mu_{K1}K_1)$ or $1 = F(\mu_{L1}a_{L1}, \mu_{K1}a_{K1}) \equiv F(\tilde{a}_{L1}, \tilde{a}_{K1})$. Minimization of $wa_{L1} + ra_{K1}$ with respect to a_{L1} and a_{K1} subject to the production function is equivalent to minimization of $\tilde{w}_1\tilde{a}_{L1} + \tilde{r}_1\tilde{a}_{K1}$ with respect to $\tilde{a}_{L1}$ and $\tilde{a}_{K1}$, where $\tilde{w}_1 \equiv w/\mu_{L1}$ and $\tilde{r}_1 = (r/\mu_{K1})$ subject to the same constraint. It is then immediate that the solution to the problem can be represented by a cost function $c^1(\tilde{w}_1, \tilde{r}_1) \equiv c^1(w/\mu_{L1}, r/\mu_{K1})$ with partial derivatives $c_{\tilde{w}}^1 = \tilde{a}_{L1}$ and $c_{\tilde{r}}^1 = \tilde{a}_{K1}$. Letting μ_{L2} and μ_{K2} represent the technical-change parameters for good 2 and repeating this exercise for sector 2, we can obtain an analogous unit-cost function for sector 2. Differentiating the unit-cost-pricing conditions for the two sectors with respect to technical-change parameters and manipulating them in the now familiar manner, we obtain

$$\Theta_{Li}(\hat{w} - \hat{\mu}_{Li}) + \Theta_{Ki}(\hat{r} - \hat{\mu}_{Ki}) = 0, \qquad i = 1, 2. \tag{10.22}$$

We can solve these two equations for changes in w and r due to exogenous changes in various technical-change parameters.

To get a fix on some of the results, suppose that technical change in both sectors is of Hicks-neutral variety, namely $\hat{\mu}_{Li} = \hat{\mu}_{Ki} \equiv \hat{\mu}_i$. Because unit-cost functions are linear homogeneous in their arguments, unit-cost pricing conditions reduce to $c^i(w, r) = \mu_i p_i$. Thus Hicks-neutral technical change operates essentially like a change in the price. For example, a 10 percent rise in μ_2 shifts the unit-cost curve for good 2 in figure 10.1 radially out by 10 percent and raises the wage and lowers the rental rate. The difference with the price change, however, is that if both μ_1 and μ_2 rise, it is possible for both wages and rental rate to rise in real terms. For example, a 10 percent increase in μ_1 and μ_2 shifts both unit-cost curves radially out by 10 percent and increases real wages and rental by 10 percent.

Consider next a biased technical change. This is accomplished most simply by setting $\mu_{L1} = \mu_{L2} = 1$ and allowing only μ_{k1} and μ_{K2} to change.

In figure 10.1 a 10 percent rise in μ_{Ki} shifts the units-cost curve for good i vertically up by 10 percent.[3] This means that if both μ_{K1} and μ_{K2} rise by 10 percent, both unit-cost curves will shift vertically up by 10 percent and the rental rate will rise by 10 percent, but wage rate will be unchanged.

In the context of the ongoing debate on trade and wages, it is interesting to note that if we replace capital by skilled labor in this model, a rise in the technical-change parameter associated with skilled labor need not necessarily raise skilled to unskilled wages. The sector in which such progress takes place matters. Thus in figure 10.1 suppose that technical progress takes place in the labor-intensive sector via a rise in μ_{K2}. This will shift the unit-cost curve for good 2 vertically up and *lower* the skilled to unskilled wage. Intuitively the technical change in sector 2, whether associated with skilled or unskilled labor, increases the demand for unskilled labor and pushes the unskilled wage up and skilled wage down.

Hicks-Neutral Technical Change and Outputs

The output effects of a technical change, like factor-price effects, depend on the nature of the change. Here we confine ourselves to Hicks-neutral technical progress. We will see that the output effects of this type of technical progress follow the Rybczynski theorem in the sense that such a change in the labor-intensive sector expands the labor-intensive sector and contracts the capital-intensive sector. A key difference, however, is that the path along which outputs change due to the technical change is not linear.

With factor prices changing, formal derivation of output effects due to a technical change is more complicated than that due to endowment changes. Equations (10.2) and (10.3) are now replaced by corresponding equations with a tilde ($\sim$) over the variables. Equations (10.4) and (10.5) remain unchanged. Thus, in differential form, our system consists of (10.16), (10.17), (10.22), and

$$\hat{a}_{Li} = -\Theta_{Ki}\sigma_i(\hat{w} - \hat{r}) - \hat{\mu}_i, \tag{10.23}$$

$$\hat{a}_{Ki} = \Theta_{Li}\sigma_i(\hat{w} - \hat{r}) - \hat{\mu}_i. \tag{10.24}$$

We solve (10.22) for $\hat{w} - \hat{r}$, substitute it into (10.23) and (10.24), and plug these equations in turn into (10.16) and (10.17). We thus obtain two linear equations in output changes as functions of changes in technical-change parameters:

3. Recalling that $c^1(w/\mu_{L1}, r/\mu_{K1}) = p_1$, a 10 percent rise in μ_{K1} is offset by a 10 percent rise in r at the original value of w, and the unit-cost pricing condition is restored.

$$\lambda_{K1}\hat{Q}_1 + \lambda_{K2}\hat{Q}_2 = \frac{\Delta_K}{\Theta}(\hat{\mu}_1 - \hat{\mu}_2) + (\lambda_{K1}\hat{\mu}_1 + \lambda_{K2}\hat{\mu}_2), \tag{10.25}$$

$$\lambda_{L1}\hat{Q}_1 + \lambda_{L2}\hat{Q}_2 = -\frac{\Delta_L}{\Theta}(\hat{\mu}_1 - \hat{\mu}_2) + (\lambda_{L1}\hat{\mu}_1 + \lambda_{L2}\hat{\mu}_2). \tag{10.26}$$

Solutions for two special cases of (10.25) and (10.26) are worth considering. First, setting $\hat{\mu}_2 = 0$ and solving, we have

$$\hat{Q}_1 = \left(1 + \frac{\lambda_{L2}\Delta_K + \lambda_{K2}\Delta_L}{\Theta\lambda}\right)\hat{\mu}_1, \quad \hat{Q}_2 = -\frac{\lambda_{L1}\Delta_K + \lambda_{K1}\Delta_L}{\lambda\Theta}\hat{\mu}_1. \tag{10.27}$$

That is, a Hicks-neutral technical improvement in sector 1 raises the output of sector 1 but lowers that of sector 2. Intuitively, at the original allocation, the technical change expands sector 1 by a proportionate amount as shown by 1 in the first of the above equations. In addition, due to increased profitability at the original factor prices, sector 1 draws resources out of sector 2. The second term in the right-hand side of the first equation and the right-hand side of the second equation capture the effects of this resource shift.

Next, let us allow both μ_1 and μ_2 to change and calculate the effect on relative outputs. Straightforward manipulations yield

$$\hat{Q}_1 - \hat{Q}_2 = \left(1 + \frac{\Delta_L + \Delta_K}{\lambda\Theta}\right)(\hat{\mu}_1 - \hat{\mu}_2) > 0. \tag{10.28}$$

Thus the ratio of Q_1 to Q_2 rises or falls as the proportionate technical progress in sector 1 is larger or smaller than that in sector 2. Intuitively, even at the original factor allocations, sector 1 expands proportionately more if the proportionate rise in μ_1 is larger than that in μ_2. In addition, due to greater profitability, the sector draws resources from the latter. The two effects are captured by the first and second terms of (10.28), respectively.

Revenue Function for the 2 × 2 Model

Let us now briefly consider the form of the revenue function in the 2 × 2 model. It is more convenient in this case to write the revenue (GDP) in terms of factor income: $wL + rK$. We can solve the average-cost pricing conditions ($c^i(w,r) = p_i$) for the wage and rental rate in terms of the goods prices. We can then substitute these back into the expression for factor income to obtain the revenue function.[4] We have

---

4. In this form the revenue function is obtained by solving the following problem: $\min wL + rK$ subject to $c^i(w,r) \geq p_i$. For a proof of equivalence between the revenue function derived in this way and that derived at the beginning of this section, see Dixit and Norman (1980, pp. 44–47).

$$R = w(p_1, p_2)L + r(p_1, p_2)K, \tag{10.29}$$

where $w(p_1, p_2)$ and $r(p_1, p_2)$ are solutions for the wage and rental rate obtained from the average-cost pricing conditions. Since the $c^i(w, r)$ are strictly concave in w and $r, w(p_1, p_2)$ and $r(p_1, p_2)$ are strictly convex in prices. Therefore the revenue function is also shown to be strictly convex in prices.

A more distinguishing feature of the revenue function, however, is that it is linear in factor endowments. Remembering that the equilibrium value of a factor price is obtained by differentiating partially the revenue function with respect to the factor, we immediately see from (10.29) that as a consequence of the linearity property just noted, factor prices depend exclusively on goods prices. From this the factor price equalization follows easily as long as there are no factor-intensity reversals.

Using the revenue function in conjunction with the Stolper-Samuelson properties of functions $w(p_1, p_2)$ and $r(p_1, p_2)$ derived earlier in this chapter, we can also prove the Rybczynski theorem. Thus recall that the output of good 2 is

$$Q_2 = \frac{\partial w(\cdot)}{\partial p_2} L + \frac{\partial r(\cdot)}{\partial p_2} K. \tag{10.30}$$

Consider the proportionate effect on Q_2 of a rise in L. We have

$$\frac{L}{Q_2}\frac{\partial Q_2}{\partial L} > \frac{L_2}{Q_2}\frac{\partial Q_2}{\partial L} = \frac{L_2}{Q_2}\frac{\partial w}{\partial p_2}$$

$$= \Theta_{L2}\frac{p_2}{w}\frac{\partial w}{\partial p_2}$$

$$= \frac{\Theta_{L2}\Theta_{K1}}{\Theta} > 1. \tag{10.31}$$

Thus a 1 percent increase in L leads to a more than 1 percent increase in Q_2. Observe that the middle equality in (10.31) is obtained by multiplying and dividing by p_2/w and the last one by substituting from (10.6b). The last inequality follows from the definition of Θ in (10.7).

10.2   The 2 × 3 Specific-Factors Model

We now turn briefly to the specific-factors model. It can be summarized in the following set of equations:

$$c^i(w, r_i) = p_i, \qquad i = 1, 2, \tag{10.32}$$

$$a_{Li} = c^i_w(w, r_i), \tag{10.33}$$

$$a_{Ki} = c^i_r(w, r_i), \tag{10.34}$$

$$a_{L1}Q_1 + a_{L2}Q_2 = L, \tag{10.35}$$

$$a_{Ki}Q_i = K_i. \tag{10.36}$$

Here (10.32) is the average-cost pricing condition, (10.33) and (10.34) are the envelope properties of the unit-cost function, and (10.35) and (10.36) are full-employment conditions. There are nine equations in nine endogenous variables: w, r_1, r_2, a_{L1}, a_{K1}, a_{L2}, a_{K2}, Q_1, and Q_2.

Observe that the return to capital in sector 1 is, in general, different from that in sector 2. This is because capital is intersectorally immobile. From (10.32) we gather that the solution for factor prices can no longer be obtained exclusively in terms of goods prices. The entire model must be solved simultaneously. Differentiating (10.32) to (10.36) and converting in terms of rates of changes, we have

$$\Theta_{Li}\hat{w} + \Theta_{Ki}\hat{r}_i = \hat{p}_i, \tag{10.37}$$

$$\hat{a}_{Li} = -\Theta_{Ki}\sigma_i(\hat{w} - \hat{r}_i), \tag{10.38}$$

$$\hat{a}_{Ki} = \Theta_{Li}\sigma_i(\hat{w} - \hat{r}_i), \tag{10.39}$$

$$\lambda_{L1}\hat{Q}_1 + \lambda_{L2}\hat{Q}_2 = \hat{L} - (\lambda_{L1}\hat{a}_{L1} + \lambda_{L2}\hat{a}_{L2}), \tag{10.40}$$

$$\hat{Q}_1 = \hat{K}_i - \hat{a}_{Ki}. \tag{10.41}$$

Goods Prices and Factor Prices

Consider first a change in the price, holding endowments constant. We begin by solving for a change in the return to the mobile factor, labor. The first step is to substitute the value of the proportionate change in output from (10.41) into (10.40). We have

$$\lambda_{L1}(\hat{a}_{L1} - \hat{a}_{K1}) + \lambda_{L2}(\hat{a}_{L2} - \hat{a}_{K2_i}) = 0. \tag{10.42}$$

Subtract (10.39) from (10.38),

$$\hat{a}_{Li} - \hat{a}_{Ki} = -\sigma_i(\hat{w} - \hat{r}_i). \tag{10.43}$$

Rewrite (10.37) as

$$\hat{r}_i = \frac{1}{\Theta_{Ki}}(\hat{p}_i - \Theta_{Li}\hat{w}). \tag{10.37'}$$

Substitute (10.37′) into (10.43),

$$\hat{a}_{Li} - \hat{a}_{Ki} = -\frac{\sigma_i}{\Theta_{Ki}}(\hat{w} - \hat{p}_i). \tag{10.44}$$

At this point it is useful to introduce the elasticity of demand for labor in sector i. This elasticity, to be denoted e_{Li}, is defined as the absolute value of the percentage change in the demand for labor in sector i, L_i, due to a 1 percent change in the wage rate, holding p_i and K_i constant. Setting $\hat{K}_i = \hat{p}_i = 0$ in (10.44), we see that $e_{Li} = \sigma_i/\Theta_{Ki}$. Making use of this elasticity, we can rewrite (10.44) as

$$\hat{a}_{Li} - \hat{a}_{Ki} = -e_{Li}(\hat{w} - \hat{p}_i). \tag{10.44′}$$

Substituting (10.44′) into (10.42), we obtain

$$\lambda_{L1}e_{L1}(\hat{w} - \hat{p}_1) + \lambda_{L2}e_{L2}(\hat{w} - \hat{p}_2) = 0,$$

or finally

$$\hat{w} = \frac{\lambda_{L1}e_{L1}}{\Delta}\hat{p}_1 + \frac{\lambda_{L2}e_{L2}}{\Delta}\hat{p}_2, \tag{10.45}$$

where $\Delta = \lambda_{L1}e_{L1} + \lambda_{L2}e_{L2}$. It can be verified that Δ is the aggregate, general-equilibrium elasticity of demand for labor in the economy (i.e., the proportionate change in $L_1 + L_2$ due to a 1 percent change in w, holding K_1 and K_2 constant).

From (10.45) the proportionate change in w is a weighted sum of proportionate changes in the two prices such that the weights are positive and sum to unity. Therefore the proportionate change in w is trapped between the two price changes. For $\hat{p}_2 > \hat{p}_1$, we have $\hat{p}_2 > \hat{w} > \hat{p}_1$. In economic terms a change in the relative price lowers the real return to labor in terms of the good whose relative price increases but increases it in terms of the other good. The effect of a given price change on labor's welfare depends on its consumption basket. This result is referred to in the literature as the neoclassical ambiguity.

We can solve explicitly for the effect of a change in the relative-price ratio on the r_i by substituting for $\hat{w}$ from (10.45) into (10.37′). But this is unnecessary. The essential qualitative result can be inferred from equation (10.37) after taking into account (10.45). Thus, setting $\hat{p}_1 = 0$ and assuming that $\hat{p}_2 > 0$, we see from (10.37) that for $i = 2$, given $\hat{w} < \hat{p}_2$, we have $\hat{r}_2 > \hat{p}_2$. Analogously, for $i = 1$, given $\hat{w} > \hat{p}_1$, we have $\hat{r}_1 < \hat{p}_1$. In compact form, we can write

$$\hat{r}_2 > \hat{p}_2 > \hat{w} > \hat{p}_1(= 0) > \hat{r}_1. \tag{10.46}$$

The qualitative effects of the price change on output can also be inferred similarly. Continue to assume that the relative price of good 2 rises. Then, according to (10.46), the rental in sector 2 rises and that in sector 1 falls relative to the wage rate. Combining (10.39) and (10.41), we can deduce that the output of good 2 rises and that of good 1 falls. Observe that since there are no distortions, this result also implies that the social opportunity costs rise along the production frontier; that is to say, the latter is locally strictly concave to the origin.

Factor Endowments, Factor Prices, and Outputs

Next let us consider the effects of changes in factor endowments on endogenous variables. As before, the first step is to solve for the effect on w. Setting $\hat{p}_i = 0$ in (10.37), substitute the resulting value of $\hat{r}_i$ into (10.38) and (10.39) to obtain

$$\hat{a}_{Li} = -\sigma_i \hat{w}, \tag{10.47}$$

$$\hat{a}_{Ki} = \Theta_{Li} e_{Li} \hat{w}. \tag{10.48}$$

Putting from (10.41), (10.47), and (10.48) into (10.40), we obtain

$$\hat{w} = -\frac{1}{\Delta}[\hat{L} - (\lambda_{L1}\hat{K}_1 + \lambda_{L2}\hat{K}_2)]. \tag{10.49}$$

Thus an increase in the supply of labor reduces the wage, while that in specific factors does the opposite. In view of the zero-profit condition (10.37) and the fact that $\hat{p}_i = 0$ by assumption, effects on returns on specific factors are opposite those on the common factor, labor.

For a moment, it is useful to define $\hat{S} \equiv \lambda_{L1}\hat{K}_1 + \lambda_{L2}\hat{K}_2$. Then we can think of $\hat{L} - \hat{S}$ as the proportionate change in the supply of labor relative to an "aggregate" of the specific factors. Then (10.49) says that if the supply of labor rises relative to aggregate supply of specific factors, the wage declines, and vice versa.

Finally consider briefly the effect on outputs of changes in endowments. Substituting from (10.48) and (10.49) into (10.41), we can obtain

$$\hat{Q}_i = \hat{K}_i + \frac{\Theta_{Li} e_{Li}}{\Delta}[\hat{L} - (\lambda_{L1}\hat{K}_1 + \lambda_{L2}\hat{K}_2)]. \tag{10.50}$$

From (10.50) we can deduce that an increase in the supply of the mobile factor, labor, increases the outputs of both goods; in other words, the effect is qualitatively different from the Rybczynski theorem in the 2 × 2 model. The sector with the higher elasticity of demand for labor weighted by labor's share in income expands proportionately more in response to an increase in the supply of labor. Setting $i = 1$ in (10.50), it is also easy to verify that the effect on output of an increase in "own" specific factor (K_1) is positive while that of the increase in the "other" specific factor (K_2) is negative. It can also be shown that a 1 percent increase in the supply of the "own" specific factor increases the output by less that 1 percent. Thus the Rybczynski effect does not hold for sector-specific factors either.

Revenue Function for the Specific-Factors Model

In the specific-factors model, we cannot get a clean, explicit expression for the revenue function of the type shown in (10.29) in the case of the 2×2 model. This is because factor prices depend on goods prices as well as factor endowments. The revenue function is not linear in factor endowments.

This fact notwithstanding, the specific-factors model has the nice property of being generalized conveniently to n-good, $n + 1$-factor context. This enables us to sign all cross-partials of the revenue function. Without providing proofs, which are straightforward and can be found in Dixit and Norman (1980), we note these properties below. We denote by $V^j (j = 1, \ldots, n)$ the factor specific to sector j, ρ_j the return to it, L the mobile factor and w the return to it:

$$\frac{\partial^2 R}{\partial p_k \partial p_i} = \frac{\partial Q_i}{\partial p_k} < 0, \qquad i, k = 1, \ldots, n, \ i \neq k, \tag{10.51a}$$

$$\frac{\partial^2 R}{\partial L \partial p_i} = \frac{\partial Q_i}{\partial L} = \frac{\partial w}{\partial p_i} > 0, \tag{10.51b}$$

$$\frac{\partial^2 R}{\partial V^i \partial p_i} = \frac{\partial Q_i}{\partial V^i} = \frac{\partial \rho_i}{\partial p_i} > 0, \tag{10.51c}$$

$$\frac{\partial^2 R}{\partial V^j \partial p_i} = \frac{\partial Q_i}{\partial V^j} = \frac{\partial \rho_j}{\partial p_i} < 0, \qquad i, j = 1, 2, \ldots, n, \ i \neq j, \tag{10.51d}$$

$$\frac{\partial^2 R}{\partial V^j \partial V^i} = \frac{\partial \rho_i}{\partial V^j} < 0. \tag{10.51e}$$

10.3   Dynamic Adjustment with Adjustment Costs

In chapter 7 we considered Neary's analysis of how the SF model can be interpreted as a short-run version of the Heckscher-Ohlin model. Neary (1978) assumes that there are no costs of adjustment and that expectations are static. In the absence of adjustment costs, the speed of adjustment is entirely exogenous. Mussa (1978) introduces these costs which allow him to determine the speed of adjustment endogenously. He also makes explicit distinction between static expectations considered by Neary and rational expectations. Here we briefly introduce his model.

Assume that labor adjusts instantaneously so that wages are equalized continuously across sectors. The movement of capital require real resources. Mussa assumes that the activity that transforms sector 1 capital into sector 2 capital, and vice versa, uses labor and a specific factor. The production function for this activity, called "capital movement," is assumed to be[5]

$$\dot{K} = \left[\left(\frac{1}{b} \right) L_I \right]^{1/2}, \qquad b > 0, \tag{10.52}$$

where the dot over the variable denotes the time derivative of that variable, and $\dot{K} \equiv |\dot{K}_1| = |\dot{K}_2|$ measures the rate of capital movement. Given the specific factor, the capital movement activity is characterized by diminishing returns to labor which lead to rising marginal costs. The rise in marginal costs in turn places a limit on the amount of capital that can be transformed profitably at any instant. The total cost of moving capital is $wL_I = wb\dot{K}^2$. Because each firm can take the wage rate as given, the marginal cost is written $d(wL_I)/d\dot{K} = 2bw\dot{K}$. The marginal benefit of moving capital is the difference in the income streams generated by a unit of capital in the two industries denoted v_1 and v_2, respectively. These streams depend on the expectations of capital owners to be considered shortly. In equilibrium the marginal cost of capital movement is equated to the marginal benefit from it. Thus

$$2bw\dot{K} = |v_1 - v_2| \equiv |v|. \tag{10.53}$$

Given the wage rate v_1 and v_2, this equation determines $\dot{K}$. The wage itself is determined by equating the demand for labor to its supply. The demand for labor in sector i $(i = 1, 2)$ depends on K_i, the relative goods price, and the wage rate. From (10.52) the total demand for labor in capital-moving activity, L_I, equals $b\dot{K}^2$. Therefore the total demand for labor, $L_1 + L_2 + L_I$, depends on $K_1, K_2 \ (= K - K_1), w, P,$ and $\dot{K}$. The full-employment-of-labor constraint then allows us to solve for the wage rate as a function of $K_1, \dot{K}, L, K,$ and P. Since $L, K,$ and P are held fixed, we suppress these are arguments and write

5. Because of the presence of a factor specific to capital transformation activity, the production function exhibits decreasing returns to labor. This specification does imply that the specific factor has no use in the steady state.

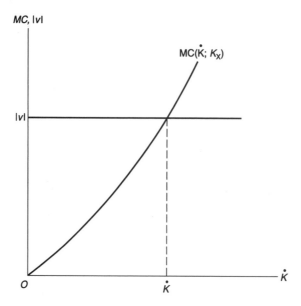

Figure 10.3

$$w = \tilde{w}(\dot{K}, K_1);$$

$$\frac{\partial \tilde{w}(\dot{K}, K_1)}{\partial \dot{K}} > 0, \tag{10.54}$$

$$\frac{\partial \tilde{w}(0, K_1)}{\partial K_1} < 0.$$

The second inequality in the above follows from the fact that at a long-run equilibrium, an expansion of sector 1, the capital-intensive sector, leads to a decline in the wage rate.

The determination of $\dot{K}$ is shown in figure 10.3. Recall that the marginal cost of capital movement is given by the left-hand side of (10.53). In view of $\partial w / \partial \dot{K} > 0$ (see equation 10.54), this expression rises with $\dot{K}$ as shown by the curve labeled $MC(\dot{K}, K_1)$ in figure 10.3. Given the absolute difference between v_1 and v_2, we are then able to determine the rate of capital movement. An increase in $|v|$ leads to an increase in $\dot{K}$.

The $MC(\cdot)$ curve, as shaped in figure 10.3, lends the adjustment process three useful properties. First, with the rising marginal cost, there is an incentive to distribute adjustment over time rather than do it all at once. Second, since the marginal cost at $\dot{K} = 0$ is zero, the economy does converge to the HO model in the long run. Finally, since in the neighborhood of $\dot{K} = 0$, the marginal cost is approximated by a ray through the origin, the rate of capital movement will be approximately proportional to the difference between v_1 and v_2.

We now need to determine income streams v_1 and v_2. Under static expectations, capital owners expect the current wage rate and rental rates to persist indefinitely. Remembering that the current rental rate is related to the wage rate through the unit-cost pricing condition, $p_i = c^i(w, r_i)$, we can write

$$v_i = \frac{r_i(w)}{\rho}, \qquad i = 1, 2, \tag{10.55}$$

where ρ is the exogenously given interest rate used for discounting and the goods price, assumed to be fixed, has been suppressed as an argument. Combining (10.53), (10.54), and (10.55), we can now solve for $w, \dot{K}$, and v_1 and v_2 as functions of K_1. Because we are interested in the behavior of v rather than v_1 and v_2 individually, it is useful to first define

$$v = Q(w) \equiv \frac{1}{\rho}[r_1(w) - r_2(w)], \qquad Q'(w) > 0. \tag{10.56}$$

Note that $Q'(w) > 0$ follows from the fact that sector 1 is capital-intensive. We know that at constant goods prices $dr_i/dw = -L_i/K_i$, yielding $Q'(w) = [(L_2/K_2) - (L_1/K_1)]$. To avoid the confusion in differentiation arising from absolute quantities, let us consider the case where $\dot{K}_1$ and v are positive. We can then replace $\dot{K}$ by $\dot{K}_1$ and $|v|$ by v. Differentiating (10.53) and (10.54) after taking (10.55) and (10.56) into account, we can obtain

$$\left[2wb - \left(Q'(w) - \frac{Q(w)}{w}\right)\frac{\partial \tilde{w}}{\partial \dot{K}_1}\right]\frac{d\dot{K}_1}{dK_1} = \left(Q'(w) - \frac{Q(w)}{w}\right)\frac{\partial \tilde{w}}{\partial K_1}, \tag{10.57}$$

$$\frac{dw}{dK_1} = \frac{\partial \tilde{w}}{\partial \dot{K}_1}\frac{d\dot{K}_1}{dK_1} + \frac{\partial \tilde{w}}{\partial K_1}. \tag{10.58}$$

In deriving (10.57), we have substituted $2b\dot{K}_1 = Q(w)/w$ using (10.53), (10.55), and (10.56). In the neighborhood of a long-run equilibrium, $Q(w)$ is near 0 and $\partial \tilde{w}/\partial K_1 < 0$. We also have $\partial \tilde{w}/\partial \dot{K}_1 > 0$. Therefore from (10.57) we have $d\dot{K}_1/dK_1 < 0$, and the equilibrium is stable as long as b is sufficiently large. Given this result we immediately obtain $dw/dK_1 < 0$ from (10.57). We then also obtain $dv/dK_1 = Q'(w)(dw/dK_1) < 0$, demonstrating that income streams in the two sectors converge as the economy converges to the long-run equilibrium. It is worthwhile to note that if b is large, from (10.52), the instantaneous adjustment is small, and the model behaves like the specific sectors model in the short run.

Static expectations are incorrect in the present context, since along the adjustment path the wage rate and rental rates are changing continuously but agents continue to assume that they will not change. Mussa therefore goes on consider adjustment under rational expectations which, in the absence of uncertainty, coincides with perfect foresight. Income streams v_1 and v_2 are now equal to the discounted sum of all future returns on capital. Formally, equations (55) and (56) are now replaced by

$$v_i = \int_t^\infty r_i[w(s)]e^{-\rho(s-t)}\,ds, \tag{10.55'}$$

$$v(t) = v_1 - v_2. \tag{10.56'}$$

Equations (10.53) and (10.54) continue to hold as before. Without reproducing the entire analysis, we note that this system yields the same path of adjustment as that under static expectations but that the speed of adjustment is lower. Of course the faster convergence under static expectations is not a virtue: As Mussa shows in the appendix to his paper, since the value of output is maximized under rational expectations, the latter process is welfare superior.

Recommended Readings

Dixit, A., and V. Norman. *Theory of International Trade.* Cambridge: Cambridge University Press, 1980.

Jones, R. W., "The Structure of General Equilibrium Models." *Journal of Political Economy* 73 (1965): 557–72.

Jones, R. W. A three-factor model in theory, trade and history. In *Trade, Balance of Payments and Growth: Essays in Honor of C. P. Kindleberger,* ed. by Bhagwati et al. Amsterdam: North Holland, 1971.

Mussa, M. Dynamic adjustment in the H-O-S model. *Journal of Political Economy* 86 (1978): 775–91.

Mussa, M. The two-sector model in terms of its dual: A geometrical exposition. *Journal of International Economics* 9 (1979): 513–26.

Neary, P. Short-run capital specificity and the pure theory of international trade. *Economic Journal* 88 (1978): 488–510.

11 Economies of Scale

Models of economies of scale can be divided into three broad categories: (1) those that maintain the assumption of perfect competition, (2) those that allow for monopolistic competition, and (3) those that allow for oligopoly behavior. In this chapter, we restrict ourselves to model types 1 and 2. Oligopoly is a separate topic in its own right and is taken up in a later chapter in the context of trade policy.

11.1 Models of Perfect Competition

There is a long tradition of trade models based on economies of scale. Summaries of the earlier literature on the subject can be found in the classic surveys of trade theory by Caves (1960) and Chipman (1965). More recent contributions to the literature include Jones (1968), Kemp (1969), Panagariya (1980, 1981, 1986a), Markusen and Melvin (1981), and Ethier (1982a).[1] Panagariya (1981) and Ethier (1982a) analyze the patterns of trade and specialization in one-factor models, while Markusen and Melvin do the same in the capital-labor model. Jones (1968), Kemp (1969), and Panagariya (1980) derive the implications of scale economies for income distribution in the 2×2 model, while Panagariya (1986a) does the same in the specific factors (SF) model.

We begin by spelling out conditions under which scale economies are consistent with perfect competition. There are two alternative assumptions that are sufficient: (1) scale economies are external to the firm and there are many firms in the industry, or (2) scale economies are internal to the firm but markets are contestable. If assumption 1 holds, each firm behaves as though it is subject to constant returns to scale and employs factors of production up to the point where factor payments exactly exhaust output. If assumption 2 holds, in equilibrium, there is only one firm in the industry, but the fear of potential entry forces it to price the product at average cost. In either case we obtain a zero-profit equilibrium.[2]

Scale Economies in the SF Model

The flavor for scale economies can be best given by introducing them into the SF model. For clarity of exposition, we cast the analysis in terms of external economies. We assume that scale economies are present in sector 2 only and that they are external to the firm but internal to the industry.

---

1. Helpman (1984) provides an excellent survey of the modern literature on scale economies.

2. An excellent modern treatment of external economies in a closed economy model can be found in Chipman (1970).

We also make the usual assumption that the industry-level production function is homothetic.

The production function facing firm j in sector 2 is written

$$Q_2^j = b(Q_2)G(K_2^j, L_2^j) \equiv b(Q_2)L_2^j g(k_2^j), \tag{11.1}$$

where $G(\cdot)$ is linear homogeneous, Q_2 is industrywide output, and k_2^j is firm j's capital-labor ratio. Function $b(Q_2)$, whose properties are detailed below, introduces external economies or diseconomies. Because all firms face the same technology and factor prices under perfect competition, they choose the same k_2^j ratio which, in turn, coincides with the industry k_2 ratio. Summing over all firms, the industry production function can be written

$$Q_2 = b(Q_2)G(K_2, L_2) \equiv b(Q_2)L_2 g(k_2). \tag{11.2}$$

As just noted, function $b(Q_2)$ introduces variable returns to scale. Returns to scale are increasing, constant, or decreasing as $b'(Q_2)$ is positive, zero, or negative. We assume that returns to scale are increasing, that $b'(Q_2) > 0$. To make sure that more output requires more inputs, $b(Q_2)$ must be restricted such that its elasticity is strictly less than 1. Thus, denoting $\varepsilon \equiv b'Q_2/b$, we have $0 < \varepsilon < 1$.

Since the firm takes the industry output Q_2 as given, it employs labor and capital up to the point where

$$p_2 b(Q_2)g'(k_2^j) = r_2,$$
$$p_2 b(Q_2)[g(k_2^j) - k_2^j g'(k_2^j)] = w, \tag{11.3}$$

respectively. Due to the externality, the firm does not take into account the effect of the change in $b(Q_2)$ on marginal physical product. That is to say, the firm equates the price of each factor to its "private" (firm-level) value of marginal product which is less than the factor's "social" (industry-level) value of marginal product. This enables the firm to satisfy the zero-profit condition despite the presence of increasing returns to scale.

Given that the firm's capital labor ratio is the same as that of the industry, we can replace the firm-level variables by industry-level variables and carry out the rest of the analysis in terms of the latter. We rewrite (11.3) as

$$p_2 b(Q_2)g'(k_2) = r_2,$$
$$p_2 b(Q_2)[g(k_2) - k_2 g'(k_2)] = w. \tag{11.3'}$$

As in chapter 7 we can present the analysis with the help of the value-of-marginal-product-of-labor (VMPL) curve. Private VMPL is given by the left-hand side of the second equation in (11.3). Denoting this by V_2, we have

$$V_2 \equiv p_2 b(Q_2)[g(k_2) - k_2 g'(k_2)]. \tag{11.4}$$

By contrast, social VMPL is obtained by differentiating (11.2) with respect to L_2 and multiplying it by p_2. Simple manipulations allow us to show that

$$V_2^s = \frac{V_2}{(1 - \varepsilon)}, \tag{11.5}$$

where V_2^s stands for social VMPL. As noted earlier, social VMPL exceeds private VMPL as long as ε is positive.

The competitive equilibrium is determined by the behavior of (11.4). Let us examine the effect of an increase in L_2 on it, holding K_2 fixed. Differentiating (11.4), we have

$$\frac{dV_2}{dL_2} = \frac{p_2 b}{L_2}\left[k_2^2 g'' + \frac{\varepsilon}{1 - \varepsilon} \frac{(g - k_2 g')^2}{g} \right]. \tag{11.6}$$

As we increase L_2, we increase the labor-capital ratio as well as the scale of output. The first term in square brackets in equation (11.6) captures the effect on V_2 due to the rise in labor-capital ratio, holding output constant. As under constant returns to scale, this effect, called the "factor-intensity effect," is negative. The second term captures the effect due to the rise in the level of output, holding labor-capital ratio constant. This effect, called the "scale effect," is positive. The larger is ε, the stronger the scale effect. Depending on whether the factor-intensity effect or scale effect dominates, V_2 may fall or rise as we increase L_2.

Figure 11.1 illustrates the factor-intensity and scale effects with the help of an isoquants diagram. Holding K_2 fixed at 15, suppose that we increase L_2 from A_1 to A_2. This movement can be divided into two parts: A_1 to A_1' and A_1' to A_2. Between A_1 and A_1', the labor-capital ratio rises but output remains constant. Therefore the marginal product of labor declines. Between A_1' and A_2, the labor-capital ratio is constant but output rises. This is accompanied by an increase in the marginal product. Whether the marginal product rises or falls as we move from A_1 and A_2 depends on which of these two effects dominates.

We are now ready to illustrate the implications of economies of scale in the SF model. To make the discussion interesting, assume that scale economies are sufficiently strong to make the $V_2 V_2$ curve in figure 11.2 positively sloped (when viewed with reference to O_2) over some intermediate

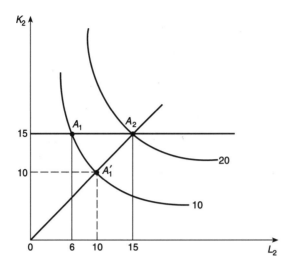

Figure 11.1

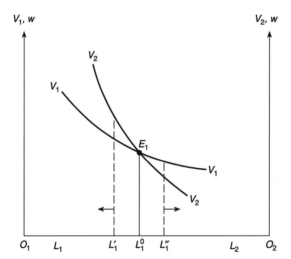

Figure 11.2

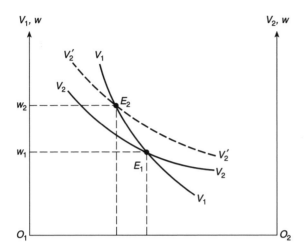

Figure 11.3

range.[3] Indeed, assume that scale economies are so strong that the curve is steeper than the V_1V_1 curve at equilibrium E_1. Now suppose that the price of good 2 rises. This will shift the V_2V_2 curve up (not shown in figure 11.2), yielding a *decline* in Q_2 at the new equilibrium. The output-price relationship is negative.

The negative output-price response raises the possibility of instability.[4] In the present small-country context, this, indeed, happens under a plausible adjustment mechanism.[5] Thus suppose that the allocation of labor in the economy is initially to the left of E_1, say, at L_1'. Also assume that labor moves toward the sector with higher VMPL. It is then immediate that the economy will move away from rather than toward E_1 in figure 11.2.

Figure 11.3 considers briefly the stable case. A rise in p_2 in this case raises the output of good 2. More interestingly, it raises the wage proportionately more than the rise in p_2. This means that the wage rises unambiguously; the neoclassical ambiguity disappears. Furthermore, since the K_2/L_2 ratio falls, the return to K_2 also rises unambiguously. An implication is that if freeing up of trade is associated with a rise in p_2,

3. Given Inada conditions, it can be shown that near $Q_2 = 0$, the VMPL curve is necessarily negatively sloped.

4. As we show a little later, the issue of stability is rather complex. Our discussion relies on a Marhallian adjustment used popularly in the literature.

5. In a closed economy or a large open economy, a negative output-price relationship can be consistent with stability. The condition required for stability under such circumstances generally is that the relevant demand curve be steeper than the supply curve at the equilibrium. See Panagariya (1986b) for details.

both labor and K_2 benefit unambiguously. The return to K_1 falls in terms of both goods because sector 1 is subject to constant returns to scale and wage rises proportionately more than p_2.[6]

Three additional points, to be brought out explicitly in Section 11.3, are worth noting. First, as shown in equation (11.5), social VMPL exceeds V_2 by a factor of $1/(1 - \varepsilon)$. Therefore the output of good 2 is below its socially optimal level. This property manifests itself in a lack of tangency between the price line and the production possibilities frontier. Second, we are likely to obtain multiple equilibria in the presence of scale economies. This can be verified using a construction similar to that in figure 11.2. Finally scale economies make complete specialization a real possibility.

Scale Economies in the 2 × 2 Model

In the 2×2 model the implications of scale economies can be explained most simply by recourse to the unit-cost function. For this, think of the production function in equation (11.1) as involving the production of $G(\cdot)$ by the firm which is then augmented by proportion $b(Q_2)$ via the external economy. We can imagine the firm producing $G(\cdot)$ for which it receives the price $p_2 b(Q_2)$.[7] Then, denoting by $c^2(w, r)$ the unit-cost function associated with $G(\cdot)$, we have

$$c^2(w, r) = p_2 b(Q_2). \tag{11.7}$$

A more conventional interpretation of (11.7) can be given as follows: Because $c^2(w, r)$ is the unit-cost of producing $G(\cdot)$, unit cost of producing Q_2 is $c^2(w, r)/b(Q_2)$. Hence (11.7) says that the unit-cost of production of Q_2 is equated to p_2.

For now let good 1 continue to be produced under constant returns to scale. Denote by $c^1(w, r)$ its unit-cost function. Also assume that good 1 is capital-intensive relative to good 2. In figure 11.4, $c^1(w, r)$ shows various combinations of w and r that allow the production of good 1 at $p_1 = 1$. By Shephard's lemma the slope of this curve equals the optimal labor-capital ratio at the given combination of w and r (see chapter 9).

To determine the equilibrium w and r, we also need to draw, in figure 11.4, $c^2(w, r)$ satisfying equation (11.7). But this requires the knowledge of the equilibrium level of output. For an exogenously given price, p_2^0, suppose that we solve for the equilibrium level of output in the background. We can then substitute this output, say Q_2^0, in (11.7) and draw

---

6. This model can also be used to show that immigration at constant terms of trade can raise rather than lower the wage.

7. This interpretation is due to Helpman (1984).

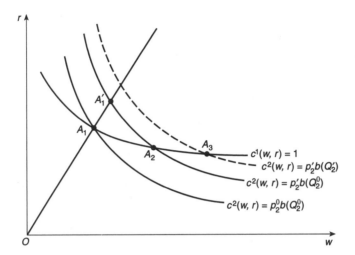

Figure 11.4

the relevant $c^2(w, r)$ contour. In figure 11.4, this contour is marked by $c^2(w, r) = p_2^0 b(Q_2^0)$. Given that both goods are produced, the wage and rental rate must be those associated with point A_1. Note that as drawn, the $c^2(\cdot)$ contour is steeper than the $c^1(\cdot)$ contour at A_1, indicating that good 2 is labor-intensive relative to good 1.

Now suppose that p_2 rises by 10 percent. Holding the output of Q_2 unchanged for a moment, this will shift the $c_2(\cdot)$ contour radially out by 10 percent. The wage and rental will move to A_2. Noting that A_1' represents an exactly 10 percent rise in both w and r, A_2 represents a more than 10 percent increase in w and a decline in r. This is the standard Stolper-Samuelson result.

The story would end here if returns to scale were constant or if output did not adjust. But given increasing returns in good 2 and a change in the output, the $c^2(\cdot)$ must shift further. In the small-country case stability ensures that the output of good 2 rises when its price rises.[8] Therefore $c^2(\cdot)$ contour must shift further out. Essentially, with a rise in the industry-level output, the scale-effect leads to a rise in marginal physical products, permitting further increases in factor returns. The final equilibrium is at A_3 where the Stolper-Samuelson result holds even more strongly than when outputs were held fixed.

This neat result can be modified in many ways. We provide two examples. First, say we assume that the economy is large in the sense that its terms of trade are determined endogenously. Then stability is no longer

8. See Mayer (1974).

sufficient to rule out a negative output-price response (see note 4 at the end of Section 1.1). If returns to scale are sufficiently strong, letting good 2 be the import good, a tariff can actually lower the price of this good. Essentially the expansion of good 2 lowers the unit-cost so much that the domestic price of the good actually declines. Under some assumptions it can be shown that the price decline is associated with an unambiguous rise in the return to labor and decline in the return to capital; the Stolper-Samuelson theorem is reversed.[9] In terms of figure 11.4, the decline in the price shifts the $c^2(\cdot)$ curve toward the origin, but the expansion of output shifts it back out. Under the assumed conditions the latter change dominates, and the Stolper-Samuelson result is turned on its head.

Second, suppose that in addition to scale economies in sector 2, there are external diseconomies of scale in sector 1.[10] Revert back now to the small-country assumption so that a negative output-price response is ruled out by stability. As before, a rise in p_2 shifts the unit-cost function to the dotted line in figure 11.4. But in addition, since the output of good 1 shrinks, $c^2(\cdot)$ also shifts out. It is then entirely possible for both w and r to rise by more than the price increase; namely both factors can be made unambiguously better off.[11]

Similar results can be obtained for increases in factor endowments at constant prices. One important point to note is that as endowments change, factor prices will change, even though goods prices are held constant. In the small-country case with increasing returns, stability will ensure the validity of the Rybczynski theorem. But, in general, it is possible for outputs of both goods to rise in response to an increase in the supply of one of the factors. The diagrammatic technique used in chapter 10 to prove the Rybczynski theorem can be adapted to illustrate these results.

Multiple Equilibria, Stability, and Welfare: The Small-Country Case

To consider the implications of increasing returns for trade and specialization, we rely on a simpler model than those considered above. The reason is that with nonconvexities, there are multiple equilibria and without specific functional forms of production functions, it is difficult to

9. See Jones (1968), Kemp (1969), and Panagariya (1980) for a statement of the assumptions that lead to this reversal.

10. It may be noted that firm-level diseconomies are inconsistent with industry-level diseconomies. If diseconomies are internal to the firm, perfect competition forces each firm to operate at the minimum scale of operation. Any expansion of the industry takes place through entry of new firms operating at the minimum scale, and we obtain constant returns at the level of the industry.

11. For a formal proof, see Panagariya (1980).

trace all potential equilibria. Fortunately the simple model, developed originally by Panagariya (1981) in a slightly different form, is sufficiently rich to bring out most of the important elements introduced by scale economies into the analysis.

Assume that sector 1 is subject to constant returns and uses one specific factor, K_1, and labor, L_1. Sector 2 is subject to increasing returns and uses only labor. Production functions are written

$$Q_1 = K_1^\alpha L_1^{(1-\alpha)},$$
$$Q_2 = Q_2^\varepsilon L_2. \tag{11.8}$$

At the industry level, the production function for sector 2 is homogeneous of degree $1/(1-\varepsilon)$. At the level of the firm, the production functions exhibit constant returns and should be written along the lines of equation (11.1). Letting L be the total supply of labor and assuming full employment, we have

$$L_1 + L_2 = L. \tag{11.9}$$

Equations (11.8) and (11.9) define the economy's production possibilities frontier which is shown in figure 11.5.[12] Differentiating these equations for a fixed L, we can obtain the slope of the frontier:

$$\frac{dQ_2}{dQ_1} = -\frac{(L - L_1)^{\varepsilon/(1-\varepsilon)}}{1 - \varepsilon} \frac{L_1^\alpha}{(1-\alpha)K_1^\alpha}. \tag{11.10}$$

The following properties of the slope can be verified. The slope approaches 0 as either Q_1 or Q_2 approaches 0. Starting from $Q_1 = 0$, as we increase Q_1, the slope increases, reaches a maximum at the point of inflexion, I, and declines thereafter. The production frontier is strictly concave to the origin near the Q_2-axis and strictly convex to the origin near the Q_1-axis with exactly one point of inflexion in the intermediate range. That is, the opportunity cost rises near the Q_2-axis and declines near the Q_1-axis. This property derives from the fact that near the Q_2-axis, the output of good 1 is small, making diminishing returns in that sector more important than increasing returns in sector 2. Near the Q_1-axis, the output of good 2 is small, and the converse holds true.

At a competitive equilibrium, each sector equates the wage to the value of marginal product. In sector 2, by analogy with (11.3'), the appropriate

12. As was noted earlier, this model is a slightly modified version of the model in Panagariya (1981). The only difference is in the specification of the production function for sector 1. Panagariya assumes that this sector uses only one factor, labor, which exhibits decreasing returns to scale. This is equivalent to the assumption of constant returns and a specific factor in the sector.

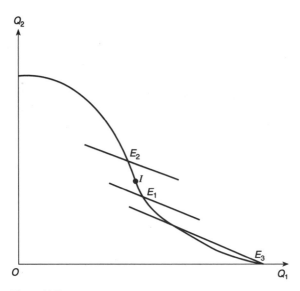

Figure 11.5

value of marginal product is the private one. We have

$$w = \frac{p_1(1-\alpha)K_1^\alpha}{L_1^\alpha} = p_2(L-L_1)^{\varepsilon/(1-\varepsilon)} \tag{11.11}$$

From (11.10) and (11.11) the relationship between the slope of the frontier and the price line is immediate. Setting $p_1 \equiv 1$ by the choice of numéraire, we have

$$\frac{dQ_2}{dQ_1} = -\frac{1}{(1-\varepsilon)p_2}. \tag{11.12}$$

Due to external economies, the social marginal cost of production of good 2 is lower than its price. Hence the price line cuts the production frontier from below.

Let $(dQ_2/dQ_1)_I$ denote the slope of the frontier at the point of inflexion and define $(1/p_2^I) \equiv -(1-\varepsilon)(dQ_2/dQ_1)_I$. Then for $\infty > p_2 > p_2^I$ there are two incompletely specialized and one completely specialized production equilibria. For one such price, these equilibria are shown by three different budget lines in figure 11.5. The income associated with these budget lines rises with the output of the increasing-returns good.[13] For $0 < p_2 < p_2^I$ there is only equilibrium, involving complete specialization in good 1.

---

13. It can be shown that the budget line associated with the completely specialized equilibrium lies necessarily inside the other two budget lines (Panagariya 1981).

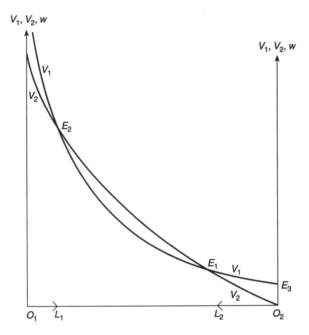

Figure 11.6

Observe that an immediate implication of these properties of equilibria is that the economy will never specialize completely in the increasing-returns good. Because the slope of the frontier near $Q_1 = 0$ is 0, p_2 will have to be ∞ for the economy to produce at $Q_1 = 0$. Intuitively the marginal product of labor in sector 1 is infinite in the neighborhood of $Q_1 = 0$. Therefore it remains profitable to produce a positive quantity of good 1 unless p_2 is ∞ (i.e., $p_1 = 0$).

Presently we restrict ourselves to the small-country context. Assuming the world price to be such that $\infty > p_2 > p_2^I$, we can translate the three production equilibria in figure 11.5 into equilibria in the labor market. This is done in figure 11.6 in which $V_1 V_1$ approaches the vertical axis at O_1 asymptotically and has a normal, negative slope. The $V_2 V_2$ curve, by contrast, has a perverse shape in the sense that as we move from O_2 toward O_1, increasing L_2, VMPL in sector 2 rises. As in figure 11.5, we have three equilibria, E_1, E_2, and E_3.

The natural question that must now be answered is, Which of these three equilibria is likely to obtain in reality? Using the type of stability argument that we employed earlier to sign the comparative statics, it is easy to show that equilibrium E_1 is unstable while E_2 and E_3 are stable. Thus, assuming that labor moves toward the sector that is able to offer a higher current wage, a slight disturbance of labor allocation at E_1 sends the economy to E_3 if the disturbance is to the right of E_1 and to E_2 if it is to the left of the latter. By contrast, slight disturbances of E_2 and E_3 send the economy back to these respective equilibria.

But even if we rule out E_1, the choice between E_2 and E_3 is not obvious. At E_3 the economy is completely specialized in the constant returns sector, while at E_2 it is diversified. The wage and the economywide income are both higher at E_2. The type of stability argument we have used gives history the determining role. If the initial equilibrium happens to be to the left of E_1, the increasing returns sector expands and takes the economy to the superior equilibrium at E_2. If the economy starts to the right of E_1, it ends up with no increasing returns sector and a lower national income and wage.

In a recent interesting paper Krugman (1991a) questions this decisive role played by history in the determination of the economy's equilibrium. He argues that if workers can move costlessly, irrespective of the initial allocation of labor, they will move to the sector that they expect to yield the higher wage, which is the sector to which they expect all other workers to move. Thus, in the absence of adjustment costs, either equilibrium may obtain as a self-fulfilling prophecy.

Krugman goes on to argue that to make the initial allocation of labor matter, it is necessary to introduce adjustment costs. Once this is done, however, the worker's decision to move becomes an *investment* decision, which in turn depends on the current as well as expected future wage rates. With expectations thus playing a role, the possibility of self-fulfilling prophecy is introduced. Krugman goes on to capture this possibility formally in a simplified version of the present model in which labor is the only factor of production. Because the analysis is complex, we choose not to reproduce it here. Instead, we note that Krugman's main conclusion is that while there are paths that validate the ad hoc analysis giving history the decisive role, there are also paths along which this may not be true. In particular, there can be a range around a point such as E_1 over which expectations have the decisive role, while outside that range, history prevails.[14]

Because this type of analysis becomes mathematically complex as we increase the number of factors, the Marshallian stability adjustment has remained the main vehicle for identifying and ruling out unstable equilibria. Indeed in his important work on economic geography, discussed later in this chapter, Krugman (1991b) himself chooses to rely on the

14. That is, within that range, called "overlap" by Krugman, the economy can end up at E_2, even though the initial allocation of labor is to the right of E_1, and at E_3, even though the initial allocation may be to the left of E_1.

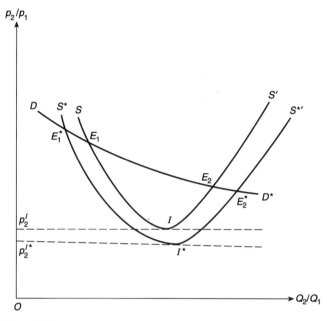

Figure 11.7

Marshallian adjustment to identify stable equilibria. In the following, we will continue to follow this practice.

Let us now consider briefly the effect of the opening of trade on welfare taking the terms of trade as exogenously given. In figure 11.7 we plot the output of good 2 relative to good 1 as a function of p_2. The vertical axis showing $Q_2/Q_1 = 0$ is a production equilibrium for all prices. At prices above p_2^I there are two additional production equilibria. These are shown by curve SS' (ignore $S^*S^{*\prime}$ for now). The range SI is associated with the convex-to-the-origin range and IS' with the concave-to-the-origin range of the production frontier.

To identify the autarky equilibrium, we must introduce demand. Assuming homothetic preferences, let DD^* represent the relative demand in figure 11.7. As drawn, there are two incompletely specialized equilibria. Of these, E_1 is unstable under the Marshallian adjustment process according to which the sector facing a demand price higher than the supply price expands.[15] Therefore let us focus on E_2. If the world price of good 2 is

15. Under this mechanism output rises or falls as the demand price is higher or lower than the supply price. As shown systematically in Panagariya (1986b), the equilibrium is also unstable under the alternative adjustment assumption that labor moves toward the sector able to offer the higher current wage.

above the autarky equilibrium, the increasing returns sector expands. Using a construction similar to figure 11.5, it can be shown that the country necessarily benefits in this case. If the world price is below the autarky price, however, the increasing-returns sector contracts. In this case the effect on welfare is ambiguous. Though there are the usual gains from efficient exchange, contraction of the increasing-returns good, whose output is below Pareto efficient level to begin with, leads to losses. The net effect depends on the relative strength of these two effects. If the world price of good 2 happens to be below p_2^I, the economy necessarily specializes completely in good 1.

Finally consider the possibility that the relative-demand curve is sufficiently steep that it crosses the relative-supply curve in its negatively sloped range. In this case we do not have an autarky equilibrium in the positively sloped range of the supply curve but the one in the negatively sloped range is Marshallian stable. If the exogenously given price of good 2 is below its autarky price, the economy will move toward good 1 and end up at the completely specialized equilibrium. The effect on welfare will be ambiguous.

Two-Country Model: Home-Demand Bias in Exports

Let us now revert back to the case, shown in figure 11.7, in which the stable and incompletely specialized autarky equilibrium lies in the positively sloped range of the relative-supply curve. Introduce another country such that the two countries are identical in all respects except size. Suppose that foreign country has a larger labor force and capital stock by a constant proportion. Without proof, we note that foreign country's relative-supply curve will be as shown by $S^*S^{*\prime}$. It is then clear that at the stable autarky equilibrium, the price of the increasing-returns good will be lower in foreign than home country. When trade opens, foreign country will export the increasing returns good while home country will import it. Thus increasing returns provide an independent basis for trade and specialization.

In the trading equilibrium the foreign country, which is larger, exports the increasing-returns good. Put this way, the pattern of trade seems hardly surprising. Looked at another way, the trade pattern is surprising, however. Note that in the autarky equilibrium, even the *relative* demand for the increasing returns good in the larger country is stronger than in the smaller country. In models with constant returns and increasing costs, a strong demand for a good predisposes that good to be an import good. In the present model it is quite the opposite! Increasing returns introduce a "home-demand" bias in exports rather than imports.

In the case shown in figure 11.7, the home-demand bias in exports is still weak due to the fact that, despite increasing returns, the opportunity costs are increasing at the autarky equilibria. If relative-demand curves are allowed to differ, the bias in demand at a given price in favor of the increasing returns good will still work toward predisposing it to be an import good. A more dramatic home-demand bias in exports appears, however, if we consider stable equilibria in the decreasing-costs range of the supply curve. Thus suppose that the relative-demand curve is sufficiently steep, that it intersects the supply curves in the decreasing-costs range from above. The autarky price of the increasing returns good will still be lower in the larger (foreign) country, and the home-demand bias in exports will obtain. What is more interesting is that if differences in relative demands are introduced such that at a given price the larger country has a larger demand for the increasing returns good, home-demand bias in exports will be reinforced. Indeed it is now possible obtain a home-demand bias even if the two countries are of the same size. This is partially in the spirit of Linder (1961) who hypothesized that countries are likely to export goods that are in greater demand at home.

What can we say about the gains from trade in this two-country model? Recall that foreign country exports the increasing returns good. Therefore that sector expands, and the country necessarily gains. In the home country the increasing-returns good contracts. Following the logic of the small-country case, the welfare effect of trade on that country is ambiguous.[16]

We can also consider briefly the effects of international mobility of K_1 at a free-trade equilibrium. Because the increasing returns good is produced on a larger scale in foreign than in home country and prices are equal across countries, the real wage is higher in foreign country. A comparison of average-cost pricing conditions in sector 1 in the two countries then implies that the return to K_1 is lower in foreign country. Therefore K_1 flows from foreign to home country. Suppose we allow a small amount of K_1 to move from foreign to home country. Holding prices constant, this leads to an expansion of the increasing-returns good in foreign country and of constant-returns good in home country. In each country the exportable expands and importable contracts. This normally leads to a

16. Krugman (1981a) provides a parallel to this result in a two-region, dynamic model based on capital accumulation. Assuming that capital and labor requirements per unit of manufactures decline with the stock of capital and agriculture, which uses only labor, is characterized by constant per-unit labor requirement, he shows that an initial higher capital-labor endowment ratio in a region turns it into a capital-rich industrial region, while the other region becomes a capital-poor industrial region.

further expansion of trade. Thus factor mobility and trade complement rather than substitute for each other.[17]

We conclude this section by noting that in the small-country version of the present model, the optimal policy is to subsidize the production of the increasing returns good. If the initial equilibrium is at E_2 in figure 11.5, a permanent subsidy at rate ε will be optimal. If the country happens to be specialized completely in the constant-returns good at E_3, it may have to give a "big push" to the increasing returns industry, move the equilibrium to E_2, and then subsidize it at rate ε. This analysis is reminiscent of Frank Graham's case for protection, which led to a great deal of controversy during 1920s and was revived during 1980s in papers by Panagariya (1981) and Ethier (1982a).

11.2   Models of Monopolistic Competition

We now turn to models of increasing returns based on monopolistic competition. A distinguishing feature of these models is that they necessarily give rise to intraindustry trade, also called two-way trade or trade in similar products.

Three main approaches to modeling monopolistic competition can be identified. The first one is based on the pioneering work of Dixit and Stiglitz (1977) and has been introduced in international trade by Krugman (1979). Important applications of this approach include Krugman (1980, 1981b, 1982, 1991b), Helpman and Krugman (1985), Markusen (1986), and Krugman and Venables (1995). The second approach draws on the major work of Lancaster (1979, 1980) and is developed principally by Helpman (1981). A book-length treatment of this approach is available in Helpman and Krugman (1985). The third approach is associated with Ethier (1982b).

It may be noted at the outset that all trade models of monopolistic competition assume perfect symmetry across varieties in production as well as consumption. This assumption cannot be relaxed without fundamentally altering the models and their conclusions (see Chipman 1982; Lancaster 1982). Our discussion below begins with a detailed exposition of Krugman's approach. Because this approach is the simplest and has been the most influential, we develop it in greater detail than the other two approaches.

17. See Markusen and Melvin (1981) and Panagariya (1992) for the analysis of factor mobility in the presence of increasing returns.

Krugman's Approach

Krugman's approach is based on two key assumptions. First, each consumer derives utility from product variety; for a given income the greater the variety, the higher the utility. Second, the production of each variety is subject to internal economies of scale. These assumptions, combined with free entry, give rise to monopolistic competition. The presence of scale economies ensures that in equilibrium only a finite number of varieties of the good are produced. In a two-country setting, intraindustry trade is the natural outcome. Gains from trade arise through increased product variety as well as a greater exploitation of scale economies. In the following, we discuss in detail the basic model as outlined in Krugman (1979) and provide a summary treatment of many of its extensions.

Basic Model

Consider a one-sector economy producing a differentiated good with a large number of potential varieties. There is strong symmetry in both production and consumption. Each variety has the same weight in the consumer's utility function and is produced using the same production function. The utility function of a representative consumer is written

$$U = \sum_{i=1}^{N} v(c_i), \qquad v'(c_i) > 0, \quad v''(c_i) < 0, \tag{11.13}$$

where c_i is the individual's consumption of good i and N is the number of potential varieties. The actual number of varieties, denoted n, is endogenous and less than N. Observe that function $v(\cdot)$ is identical across varieties. In Krugman (1980), $v(c_i)$ is replaced by the specific function c_i^θ, giving the utility function CES form. This simplifies the analysis considerably but also limits the role scale economies play in the determination of the gains from trade.

Labor is the only factor of production. The cost function for variety i is given by

$$l_i = \alpha + \beta x_i, \qquad i = 1, \ldots, n, \tag{11.14}$$

where α is the fixed cost, β the marginal cost, x_i the output, and l_i the total amount of labor used. With $\alpha > 0$, the average cost l_i/x_i is a declining function of output. Note the strong assumption that α and β are identical across i; thus all varieties are perfect substitutes in production. This assumption is essential and cannot be relaxed without altering the model and its implications fundamentally.

There are L individuals in the economy, each supplying one unit of labor. The market-clearing condition for each variety then requires

$$x_i = c_i L, \qquad i = 1, \ldots, n. \tag{11.15}$$

The full-employment condition is written

$$\sum_{i=1}^{n} l_i = L. \tag{11.16}$$

There are three sets of variables that we want to determine: the price of each good relative to the wage, p_i/w, the output of each good, x_i, and the number of varieties, n. In view of the symmetry in both production and consumption, all prices and outputs will be the same. Therefore we can simply replace p_i and x_i by p and x, respectively, and carry out the rest of the analysis in terms of a representative variety. Henceforth we drop the subscript i from p, x, and c.

Given the unlimited thirst for variety on the part of consumers and perfect substitution in production, each firm produces a different product. This makes each firm the monopolist of its particular variety. Therefore, the equilibrium quantity and price are found by equating the marginal cost and marginal revenue facing the firm. The marginal cost is $w\beta$. The derivation of marginal revenue is more complicated and requires the determination of the elasticity of demand.

Utility maximization by an individual subject to the budget constraint yields $v'(c) = \lambda p$, where λ is the representative individual's marginal utility of income. Since c is per capita consumption of the representative variety (see equation 11.15), this condition yields the inverse demand function facing the firm producing x.

$$p = \frac{v'(x/L)}{\lambda}. \tag{11.17}$$

In general, λ is a function of all prices and the individual's income. But if n is large, the pricing decision of one firm will not affect this variable. In calculating the elasticity of demand facing the firm, we can treat λ as a constant. It is then immediately obvious that the absolute value of the elasticity of total demand facing the firm is

$$\varepsilon(c) \equiv -\frac{p\,dx}{x\,dp} = -\frac{v'(c)}{c \cdot v''(c)}. \tag{11.18}$$

Not surprisingly, given the symmetry, the elasticity of market demand is the same as the elasticity of individual demand. It is assumed that ε is a declining function of c. A sufficient condition for this is $v''' = 0$. In the special case when preferences are of CES form (Krugman 1980), the elasticity is constant.

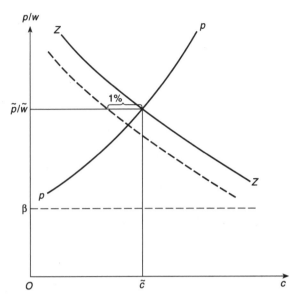

Figure 11.8

The marginal revenue curve facing the firm can now be written $p(\varepsilon - 1)/\varepsilon$. Equating the marginal revenue and marginal cost, we obtain

$$p = \frac{\varepsilon(c)}{\varepsilon(c) - 1} \beta w. \tag{11.19}$$

This equation gives us one relationship between p/w and c. Given the assumption that ε is a declining function of c, according to (11.19), p/w and c are positively related. The relationship is shown by curve PP in figure 11.8. The price is above marginal cost everywhere to ensure that losses do not exceed fixed costs. The price rises with c because the elasticity of demand falls with c, giving the firm more monopoly power. In the special case of CES preferences (Krugman 1980), ε is constant and equation (11.19) is sufficient by itself to determine the price in wage units. In terms of figure 11.8, curve PP is a horizontal straight line.

In the general case where ε varies with c, we need one more equation in p/w and c to determine p/w. This equation is provided by the average-cost pricing condition resulting from free entry of firms. Thus we have

$$\frac{p}{w} = \frac{\alpha}{x} + \beta = \frac{\alpha}{cL} + \beta, \tag{11.20}$$

where we use equation (11.15) to obtain the second equality. According to (11.20), p/w and c vary inversely. The relationship is shown by curve

ZZ in figure 11.8. The curve is a rectangular hyperbola above β, ensuring that the total revenue equals total cost. A rise in c (or, equivalently, x) allows the firm to spread fixed costs more thinly and hence lower the price. The intersection of *ZZ* with *PP* yields equilibrium levels of per-capita consumption and price, $\tilde{c}$ and $(\tilde{p}/\tilde{w})$. The equilibrium output is $\tilde{x} = \tilde{c}L$.

There is only one important variable left to be determined: the number of varieties. In view of the symmetry, after substitution from (11.14), equation (11.16) yields

$$n^* = \frac{L}{\alpha + \beta x^*}. \tag{11.21}$$

Thus all endogenous variables of interest are determined.

Consider now a 1 percent increase in L. In view of (11.19) this change leaves PP unaffected. But according to (11.20) *ZZ* shifts horizontally to the left by exactly 1 percent. Intuitively the zero-profit condition requires that at a given value of p/w, we must also hold the average cost constant. To do so requires that x be held fixed or, equivalently, c be reduced by 1 percent to satisfy $cL = \tilde{x}$ at the 1 percent higher value of L.

The leftward shift in *ZZ* curve implies that the rise in L lowers c as well as p/w. Since the shift is 1 percent and *PP* slopes upward, c falls by less than 1 percent. Recalling that L was increased by 1 percent, the total output x rises, though by less than 1 percent. Given scale economies, the unit cost declines, and in view of the zero-profit condition, p/w declines as well. Finally, from (11.21), since L rises by 1 percent and x by less than 1 percent, n rises. Each individual gains from the decline in costs as well as the rise in variety.

Next, suppose that there are two economies of the type analyzed above. Assume that they are identical in terms of tastes and technology but may differ in size. In this setting the effect of moving from autarky to free trade on each country is the same as that of an increase in labor force. In the post-trade equilibrium, the quantity produced of each good and the associated price is the same across all products and across countries. This means that wages are also equalized across countries, and thus free trade reproduces the integrated world equilibrium. It is as if labor was fully mobile and we are in a single world economy. Recalling that x rises with the size of labor force and the relevant labor force now is $L + L_*$, each product is produced at a larger scale; gains from trade accrue on account of scale economies. The number of varieties is $n = L/(\alpha + \beta x)$ in home country and $n^* = L^*/(\alpha + \beta x)$ in foreign country. With x having gone up, each of n and n^* falls but their sum, $n + n^*$ is larger than pre-trade values of each of n and n^*. And since the consumer has access to all $n + n^*$ varieties in the post-trade equilibrium, his welfare rises on that count as well. Thus the gains from trade arise from increased access to variety as well as expanded scale of production.

Since all varieties have the same price in the post-trade equilibrium, expenditures on each country's goods are proportional to the country's labor force. That is to say, the proportion of each country's (and, hence, the world's) income spent on the home country's goods is $L/(L + L^*)$ and on the foreign country's goods is $L^*/(L + L^*)$. This means that the value of the home country's imports is $M = wL \cdot L^*/(L + L^*) = M^*$. Trade is necessarily balanced. The pattern of trade is of course indeterminate.

We can also consider briefly the relationship between trade and factor mobility more directly. We have already seen that free trade reproduces an integrated world equilibrium that implies that trade and factor mobility are substitutes in this model. This point can also be made by disallowing trade in goods and opening the economies to factor mobility. Given identical technologies, under autarky, the wage is higher and there are more varieties in the country with larger labor force. Therefore, maintaining the assumption of autarky in trade, if we allow international labor mobility, the larger country will receive labor from the smaller country. This will raise the wage in the larger country further and lower it in the smaller country. The process will come to rest only after all labor is concentrated in the larger country. The equilibrium obtained will coincide with that obtained under free trade.

An interesting possibility arises if technologies are allowed to differ across countries. Thus suppose that the smaller country has a superior technology represented by a lower β. This will have the effect of raising the wage under autarky in that country. Yet, if the other country is sufficiently large, the wage there may continue to exceed the wage in the smaller country. If we now allow labor to move internationally, it will go from smaller to larger country. In equilibrium all labor will get concentrated in the country with inferior technology.

We conclude this subsection by introducing the basic model in Krugman (1980) which is a special case of the model just considered. Because of its simplicity this special case has been used extensively by Krugman himself and others. Krugman (1980) replaces $v(c)$ by c^θ $(0 < \theta < 1)$. Given this form of the utility function, the elasticity of demand in (11.18) becomes constant and the PP curve in figure 11.8 becomes horizontal. An increase in labor supply now has no impact on p/w. Moreover a 1 percent increase in L that shifts ZZ in figure 11.8 to the left by 1 percent lowers c by exactly 1 percent and leaves x unchanged. With x unchanged, (11.21) yields a 1 percent increase in n. All extra labor is used up in producing new varieties. Now the only source of the gains from trade is larger variety. Since x is unchanged, the average production cost and hence p/w remains unchanged.

Because the recent literature employs the Krugman (1979, 1980) model extensively, it is useful to summarize it here. The model is quite simple. Given the symmetry, full employment and market-clearing conditions require $L = n(\alpha + \beta x)$ and $x = cL$, respectively. These are two equations in three variables x, c, and n. Fixing any one of the variables determines the remaining variables. Alternatively, we need a third equation. Under the behavioral assumptions made by Krugman, this condition comes from the firm's profit maximization behavior requiring marginal revenue equal to marginal cost pricing $[p(\varepsilon - 1)/\varepsilon = \beta w]$ and free entry leading to average-cost pricing $[p = (\alpha/x)w + \beta w]$. In Krugman (1979), $(\varepsilon - 1)/\varepsilon$ is an implicit function of c so that the solution is defined implicitly. Krugman (1980) is much simpler: With $\varepsilon = \sigma$ which is constant, the firm's profit maximization condition and average-cost pricing condition combine to yield $\beta\sigma/(\sigma - 1) = (\alpha/x) + \beta$, or $x = \alpha(\sigma - 1)/\beta$.

Inter- and Intraindustry Trade and Income Distribution

Krugman (1981) applies the basic Krugman (1980) model to address the income-distribution effects of trade. He shows that contrary to the Stolper-Samuelson result, it is not essential for trade to hurt at least some factor. He begins with a two-sector economy such that each sector produces a differentiated good with many potential varieties. Denoting the sectors by 1 and 2 and the numbers of potential varieties by N_1 and N_2, preferences of an individual are written

$$U = \ln\left(\sum_{i=1}^{N_1} c_{1i}^{\theta}\right)^{(1/\theta)} + \ln\left(\sum_{j=1}^{N_2} c_{2j}^{\theta}\right)^{1/\theta}. \tag{11.22}$$

According to (11.22), preferences are symmetric across goods in the sense that the consumer divides his expenditure equally between them. Individuals are identical in terms of their preferences but differ in their ability to produce the two goods. Total labor force is normalized at 2 of which $2 - z$ is specific to sector 1 and z to sector 2. The only asymmetry between sectors arises from a value of z different from 1. Otherwise, the model is completely symmetric. Symmetry in preferences has already been noted. Production functions are also identical in that fixed and variable costs (α and β) are identical across varieties and sectors. Therefore, if $2 - z = z = 1$, we have complete symmetry and prices, wages, output, and the number of varieties across sectors are equalized.

Given identical values of α and β and identical elasticities of demand, the output of each variety is equalized across sectors. Moreover, in the spirit of Krugman (1980), the output of each variety is invariant with respect to the supply of labor available to produce it. Therefore, assuming that $2 - z < 1$, the number of varieties produced in sector 1, n_1, is less than that in sector 2, n_2. Because expenditures are divided equally across sectors, this leads to a higher price and wage in sector 1 than in sector 2.

Call the country just described home country and introduce a foreign country. Assume that foreign country is identical to home country in all respects except *relative* factor endowments. Specifically, assume that foreign country's relative endowments are a mirror image of those of home country. Formally foreign country's labor force specific to sector 1 is z and that specific to sector 2 is $2 - z$. Given the assumption $2 - z < 1$, home country is scarce in the labor specific to sector 1 relative to foreign country. Under autarky we obtain $w_1 > w_2$ and $p_1 > p_2$ in home country and $w_1^* < w_2^*$ and $p_1^* < p_2^*$ in foreign country. The physical and factor-price definitions of factor endowments coincide with each other.

Opening to free trade gives rise to a world economy in which there are two units of each type of labor. Prices and wages are equalized across sectors and countries. The number of varieties of each product in each country remains unchanged after trade, however. Therefore home country is a net importer of good 1 and net exporter of good 2. There is also intra-industry trade in that each country exports and imports each variety. The extent of the two types of trade depends on the value of z. At one extreme, if the two countries are completely diverse such that $z = 2$ (i.e., $2 - z = 0$), home country produces none of good 1 and foreign country produces none of good 2; all trade is interindustry type. At the other extreme, if the two countries are identical in relative endowments such that $z = 1$, they produce equal varieties of each product, and net exports of each product are zero; all trade is intraindustry type. More generally, intra-industry trade expands proportionately with increased similarity in relative factor endowments.

A final point concerns the income distribution effect of trade. We know that given $2 - z < 1$, under autarky $w_1 > w_2$ in home country. Because the country is a net importer of good 1 and net exporter of good 2, trade lowers w_1 and raises w_2. From this it may seem that trade necessarily hurts the scarce factor and benefits the abundant factor as in the Heckscher-Ohlin model. But this turns out to be untrue. Trade generates gains through increased variety and also through reduction in the price of the net importable. Krugman shows that if $\theta < 0.5$, trade necessarily increases the utility of the scarce factor (and the abundant factor, of course). If $\theta > 0.5$, the effect on the utility of the scarce factor is ambiguous in general. The closer is z to 1, the more likely the scarce factor benefits. For $z = 1$, ex post the model reduces to Krugman (1980) and both factors necessarily benefit. Thus the more similar the countries, the larger the intraindustry trade and the more likely everyone benefits from it.

Three-Region Model

Markusen (1986) develops a three-region model in which he combines Krugman's (1980) model with factor-endowments model and non-homothetic preferences. His objective is to construct a model capable of generating simultaneously a large volume of intraindustry trade between rich countries and interindustry trade between rich and poor countries. The three regions are referred to as West, East, and South where West is identified with North America, East with Western Europe, and South with developing countries. West and East are assumed to be identical in all respects and are together referred to as North.

The basic structure of the model is as follows: There are two goods, a differentiated good denoted x and a homogeneous good denoted y. Preferences are identical across individuals and countries and take the form

$$U = \left[\left(\sum_i x_i^\alpha \right)^{(1/\alpha)} \right]^\beta (y - \gamma)^{(1-\beta)}, \tag{11.23}$$

where γ is a constant and represents the subsistence level of y. This feature introduces nonhomotheticity in preference.

There are two factors of production, labor and capital. A representative product x_i is produced using a composite factor which is itself produced via a linear homogeneous production function of capital and labor. This composite factor replaces the factor "labor" in Krugman (1980). The remainder of technological specification in sector x is the same as in Krugman. Given the utility function (11.23), we obtain an equilibrium in the differentiated goods sector much like that in Krugman.

Good y is produced via a standard linear homogeneous production function. This good is labor-intensive relative to the composite input or, equivalently, relative to x. Population is identified with labor and ownership of capital is distributed (not necessarily evenly) among workers. Nonhomotheticity in tastes implies that the expenditure on y declines proportionately as incomes rise.

In this general setting, in the spirit of Helpman (1981) (see below), Markusen shows that the volume, type (intraindustry vs. interindustry), and direction of trade depend critically on relative endowments of the regions. Thus assume that the relative endowments of East and West are the same, while South is labor-abundant relative to them. Because y is labor-intensive, these relative endowments give South a comparative advantage in y. In addition the higher capital endowment ratio leads to a higher per-capita incomes in North (East and West combined) and hence larger demand for x there than in South. This reinforces the North–South trade generated by factor-endowment differences. Given the demand for variety, there is also intraindustry trade among the three regions. Trade between East and West is primarily of the intraindustry variety. Taking specific values of parameters, Markusen shows that holding total world endowments of factors constant, if we make North more capital-abundant and South more labor-abundant, volumes of East–West and North–South trade both rise, but the former rises more.

Economic Geography

Perhaps the most interesting applications of the Krugman model are in the area of economic geography. The initial application had been provided by Krugman (1980) himself. Rather than begin with that application, however, it is more instructive to begin with a slight variation of the application provided by Helpman and Krugman (1985). Thus take the Krugman (1979) model discussed above in detail and add another homogeneous good to it. Assume that this good is subject to constant returns and, like the differentiated good, uses only labor. Assume that the preferences between differentiated and homogeneous good are Cobb-Douglas, while the subutility function associated with the differentiated good has the form shown by the right-hand side of equation (11.13).

Next, introduce a foreign country which is larger in size but otherwise identical to the country we call the home country. Given equal expenditure shares due to identical Cobb-Douglas preferences, under autarky, the two countries employ equal *shares* of their labor force in the differentiated (and homogeneous) good. This translates into a larger absolute quantity of labor in the differentiated sector in the larger country. Given the conclusions at the start of this section, this will lead to a larger variety and output of each variety in that country. In addition the price of each variety relative to the homogeneous good will be lower.

Suppose now that we open the countries to trade. It is tempting to conclude from these autarky relative prices that in the trading equilibrium, the larger country will become a net exporter of the increasing returns good and net importer of the constant returns good precisely as in the external-economies model considered in section 11.1, and we will obtain the home-demand bias in exports. Yet this is a false conclusion.

To see why, observe that free trade in this model equalizes the prices of all differentiated varieties and wages in terms of the homogeneous good.

Given identical technologies and identical equilibrium outputs of different varieties, they can be produced at identical costs in either country. The production structure is indeterminate: We could have the smaller country produce a large number of varieties and a small quantity of the homogeneous good, the larger country to do the opposite, and vice versa. As long as they can trade freely, the consumption basket of an individual consumer will be independent of the location of production. Home market bias is far from compelling.

Why does the home-market bias we saw in the external-economy model of section 11.1 not arise in this model? The answer is twofold. First and principally, in this model the scale economy is independent of the location: Production costs do not depend on who else is operating in the same location. Second, trade equalizes wages, eliminating any possibility of cost advantage for a location. In the external-economy model, by contrast, costs depend on the location: *Ceteris paribus*, the larger is the size of the *local* industry, the lower the costs. The only way the sector in the smaller country remains internationally competitive in the final equilibrium is through lower wages relative to the larger country.

Krugman (1980) suggests a clever device that helps break this indeterminacy in the production structure in the type of model under consideration and resurrects home-market effects. Thus suppose that it is costly to transport the differentiated good internationally. This feature generates an externality that gives the larger country a comparative advantage in the production of the differentiated good. *Ceteris paribus*, transportation costs make it more profitable to locate production in the location with larger market and serve the location with smaller market through exports. Indeed, as Helpman and Krugman (1985, ch. 10) show for preferences characterized by $v(c_i) = c_i^\theta$ and "iceberg" type of transportation costs (i.e., only a fraction of the quantity exported arrives in the importing country), for sufficiently low transportation costs (or, equivalently, countries of sufficiently dissimilar size), all production of the differentiated good gets concentrated in the larger country. For higher transportation costs (or sufficiently similar countries), diversification is possible, with the smaller country importing the differentiated good on a net basis and exporting the homogeneous good.

Krugman (1980) offers a more dramatic example of home-market effects by combining internal scale economies with transportation costs in a model with two differentiated products sectors. He introduces a two-sector economy in which each sector has its own perfectly substitutable set of differentiated products. Production technology is the same not only across varieties within each sector but also across sectors. Labor can move freely between the two sectors. There are two groups of consumers such that one group is specialized in the consumption of one commodity and the other in the consumption of the remaining commodity. Parameter θ is the same across the two groups of consumers, however. These assumptions imply that prices are identical for both types of goods and varieties. Only the number of varieties differs across commodities. Denoting the two commodities by 1 and 2 and the groups by type 1 and type 2, the larger the type 1 groups relative to type 2 group, the larger the number of varieties produced of good 1 relative to good 2. If the two groups are equal in size, the number of varieties of the two commodities is the same.

Next, introduce another country. Call the two countries home country and foreign country. Assume that the two countries are identical in all respects except that home country has a larger proportion of type 1 consumers than foreign country. Then, under autarky, home country will produce a larger variety of good 1 relative to 2 while foreign country will do the opposite. When trade opens, home country will be a net exporter of good 1 and a net importer of good 2. Thus there is a so-called home-demand bias in exports.

The presence of transportation costs plays a crucial role in obtaining this last conclusion. If these costs were not present, given wage equalization across countries, production structure will be indeterminate across countries as in the simpler variant of Helpman-Krugman (1985) example given above. Krugman goes on to show that if the two countries are sufficiently dissimilar in terms of the division of their populations between type 1 and type 2 consumers, each country specializes completely in the good of home-demand bias.

Krugman (1991b) develops yet another model of economic geography to explain how a country can come to be divided into an industrialized "core" and agricultural "periphery." This analysis is inspired by the observation, for example, that though the United States is generally sparsely populated, a quarter of her population resides on the East-Coast corridor. The model works through an externality generated by the interaction of internal economies of scale in manufactures, demand for them, and transportation costs. Internal scale economies call for concentration of production of a variety in one place, and transportation costs dictate that the concentration be where demand is. But demand itself is where the bulk of population is concentrated, namely where manufactures production is concentrated. There is a circularity in causation.

Formally Krugman postulates a two-region (denoted 1 and 2), two-factor model in which the individual utility function is represented by equation (11.23) with the modification $\gamma = 0$. The x_i are different varieties of manufactures, and y denotes agriculture. Each sector uses only one factor of production that is specific to that sector. Thus agriculture uses only "peasants," while manufactures use only "workers." Peasants and workers have the same preferences. The peasant population is assumed completely immobile between regions.

The production technology in manufactures is the same as in Krugman (1980) while agriculture is characterized by constant returns. To keep the model simple and tractable, it is assumed that agricultural output can be transported costlessly while manufactures are subject to Samuelson's "iceberg" transport costs whereby only a fraction of the output transported arrives at the other end.

Krugman (1991b) shows that in this setting it is possible, though not necessary, that workers will concentrate in one of the regions. To make the argument heuristically, suppose that initially the regions have equal number of workers and hence half of the manufactures. Given identical number of peasants by assumption, this makes the two regions identical with real wages equalized.

The critical question is whether this equilibrium is stable. To answer, suppose that we perturb the equilibrium by a slight movement of workers from, say, region 2 to region 1. The equilibrium is stable if this realloca- tion leads to a decline in the real wage in region 1 relative to that in region 2 inducing the workers to move back to region 2; otherwise, it is unstable. Both outcomes are possible.

A larger labor force in region 1 gives rise to two opposing effects on relative real wages of the regions. The "home market" effect raises the real wage in region 1, but increased competition for the local peasant market lowers it.[18] If, on balance, the former effect dominates, the equilibrium is unstable, and the perturbation leads to more outflow of workers toward region 1 yielding geographical concentration. If the latter effect dominates, the regions do not diverge. Because the model becomes analytically intractable beyond this general conclusion, Krugman offers some simulation results. For the particular parameters he uses, he finds that the lower transport cost leads to divergence (geographical concen- tration) while the higher transport cost leads to convergence (geographical diversification).

Krugman goes on to ask whether a situation in which all workers are concentrated in one region is an equilibrium. He shows that with low enough transportation costs, a high enough share of income spent on manufactures, and strong enough economies of scale, circular causation

18. There is an additional "price index" effect that helps raise the real wage in region 1 relative to region 2. The proportion of locally produced varieties, which are priced lower than "imported" varieties due to transport costs, rises. This lowers the price index in region 1 relative to that in region 2.

sets in and manufacturing concentrates in whichever region gets a head start.

A final interesting application in this area is due to Krugman and Venables (1995). These authors set out to explain how globalization resulting from declining transportation costs can give rise to different effects on incomes and production patterns in the North and South at different *levels* of transportation costs. The essential story, based on numerical simulations and, hence, valid for only certain parameter values of the model, is as follows: There are two regions, North and South. Each region consumes two goods, a homogeneous good called agriculture and a differentiated good called manufactures. There is one primary factor of production, labor. Manufactures are subject to increasing returns and produced using labor and a differentiated intermediate input as in Ethier's model (see below). The latter is itself produced under increasing returns to scale. North and South are equally proficient in all good with no initial comparative advantage in any good. There are no transportation costs for agriculture, but they exist for trade in manufactures and intermediate inputs.

Initially transport costs are so high that each region produces its own supply of all goods. Now suppose that transport costs decline. Two-way trade in manufactures (including intermediate inputs) will emerge. If this equilibrium is perturbed such that one region, North, acquires a larger manufacturing sector, given transport costs, that region becomes a more attractive place to locate intermediate inputs production ("backward linkage" in production). This will in turn lower production costs in manufacturing, expand that sector ("forward linkage"), and make the location of intermediate inputs further attractive. A circular causation sets in, and the world economy is organized into an industrialized North and deindustrialized South. The real wages in North rise due to lower prices of manufactures than in South.

Finally, suppose that transport costs decline further. This lowers the importance of being close to the market and, hence, of backward and forward linkages. Producers can take advantage of the lower real wage in South so that manufactures sector now expand in South and contracts in North. Real wages rise in South and fall in North, and there is convergence of living standards.

While models of geography, by exploiting the three-way link among scale economies, transportation costs, and demand generate rich set of stylized facts, empirical support for them has not been found. As was noted in chapter 8, Davis and Weinstein (1996) take up this task. They embed a variant of the home-market effects model in Krugman (1980) into the traditional Heckscher-Ohlin-Vanek (HOV) model and test for home-market effects for the OECD countries where they are most likely to be present. At all levels of classification, they find factor endowment as the principal explanatory variable determining outputs. They find some indication of home-market effects in the specification in which HOV determines output structure at the three-digit level and economic geography does so at the four-digit level. But these results are not robust. Allowing endowments to matter for production at the four-digit level eliminates the home-market effects.

Helpman Model

In Helpman's model there are two goods, manufactures (x) and food (y), and two factors, capital and labor. Food is homogeneous and labor-intensive, while manufactures are differentiated and capital-intensive. There is a continuum of potential varieties of manufactures represented by points on the circumference of a circle with radius $1/\pi$. Each consumer has an "ideal" variety of manufactures. *Ceteris paribus*, the consumer is equally happy with x units of his ideal variety or $h(v) \cdot x$ units of a variety located on the circle at a distance v from his ideal variety. The function $h(v)$ is such that $h(0) = 1$, $h(v) > 1$ for $v > 0$; $h'(0) = 0$, $h'(v) > 0$ for $v > 0$; and $h''(v) > 0$.

Denote by $x(v)$ the quantity of the manufactured product located at a distance v from a consumer's ideal product that is being consumed by him. Letting y be the quantity of food consumed, the consumer's utility function is written $u(x(v)/h(v), y)$ where $u(\cdot)$ is increasing in both arguments, homothetic, and strictly quasi-concave. Holding the quantities x and y constant, a decline in v increases utility. Consumers, identified by their ideal variety, are distributed uniformly over the circle. This yields a constant density of consumers with a given ideal type. It is further assumed that consumers own the same fraction of all factors of production. This yields the same income for all consumers and, given their uniform distribution over the circle, leads to complete symmetry across varieties on the demand side.

On the production side, both goods use both factors of production. Food (y) is subject to constant returns to scale, while manufactures are subject to increasing returns. Though the cost function for a given variety is quite general, it exhibits perfect symmetry across varieties. This, combined with the symmetry on the demand side, yields identical equilibrium prices and quantities of different varieties of manufactures much as in Krugman's models.

Derivation of the producer equilibrium in manufactures turns out to be vastly more complicated than in Krugman's model. Rather than reproduce it here, we simply note that the elasticity of demand facing a representative producer of manufactures in the model depends on own price, the price of y, and the total number of varieties available. Helpman makes the plausible assumption that the elasticity rises with the number of varieties available.[19] In an autarky equilibrium, both the number of varieties and the output of a variety depend on factor endowments.

Helpman's main concern is to study the positive properties of trading equilibria in a two-country model.[20] For concreteness, it is useful to reproduce a subset of equations describing the equilibrium in the two-country model. For home country, we have

$$p_Y = c_Y(w, r), \tag{11.24a}$$

$$p_X = \frac{C_X(w, r, X)}{X}, \quad C_{XX}(\cdot) \equiv \frac{\partial C_X(\cdot)}{\partial X} \tag{11.24b}$$

$$R(p_X, p_Y, N) = \theta(w, r, X) \equiv \frac{C_X(\cdot)}{X C_{XX}(\cdot)} \tag{11.24c}$$

$$c_{Yw}(w, r) Y + C_{Xw}(w, r, X) n = L, \tag{11.24d}$$

$$c_{Yr}(w, r) Y + C_{Xr}(w, r, X) n = K. \tag{11.24e}$$

Here all variables except N are home-country variables. Y stands for the economywide output of food, X for the output of the representative variety of manufactures, and n for the number of varieties produced. N $(\equiv n + n^*)$ is the number of varieties of manufactures produced in the two countries combined. Other variables have the usual definitions. $c_Y(\cdot)$ is the unit-cost function for Y, $C_X(\cdot)$ the *total*-cost function for X, $\theta(\cdot)$ the ratio of average cost of X to its marginal cost, and $R(\cdot)$ the ratio of average revenue to marginal revenue of X. Given increasing returns in X, $\theta(\cdot) > 1$.

Equations (11.24a) and (11.24b) are average-cost pricing conditions in Y and X, respectively. Taking (11.24b) into account, (11.24c) says that the marginal revenue of X is equal to its marginal cost. The remaining two equations are full-employment conditions. The complete model contains five analogous equations for foreign country, two market-clearing conditions and the relationship $N = n + n^*$. Thus there are 13 equations in all. Setting $p_Y \equiv 1$, they can be solved for 13 variables, X, Y, n, p_X, w, r, six analogous foreign-country variables, and N.

---

19. The assumption is necessarily valid if preferences are of Cobb-Douglas form or if the number of varieties available is very large.

20. Helpman does not present any welfare analysis.

The first result follows immediately from (11.24a)–(11.24c) and three analogous foreign-country equations. If technologies are identical across countries, the mapping from (w, r, X) to (p_X, p_Y, N) in these equations is univalent, and both goods are produced in both countries; w, r, and X are equalized internationally. Thus the factor-price equalization theorem extends to this model.

Next assume that home country is labor-abundant, Y is labor-intensive, and population coincides with the labor force. Then, in a trading equilibrium, home country produces a higher quantity of Y and a lower variety of X *in per-capita terms.* Both countries export and import X but on a net basis, home country exports Y and imports X. Holding the world endowments constant, if we reallocate resources in such a way that home country becomes more labor-abundant and foreign country becomes more capital-abundant without disturbing commodity prices and factor rewards, the share of interindustry trade rises and that of intraindustry trade declines. By contrast, if we make factor endowments more similar, the share of intraindustry trade rises. In the extreme case, if relative endowments becomes identical, interindustry trade is eliminated entirely, and all trade becomes intraindustry type. These results are similar in spirit to those of Krugman (1981b) discussed in section 11.2.

We can state two additional results that relate relative country size to the volume of trade. First, if we reallocate resources such that home country becomes more labor-abundant without a change in the GDP and the goods and factor prices are not disturbed, the volume of trade increases. Second, if the two countries have identical absolute endowments of both factors initially and we reallocate resources such that relative factor endowments are preserved but country sizes become more and more unequal, the volume of trade becomes smaller and smaller.

Ethier's Model

Like Helpman (1981), Ethier (1982b) also works with a model with two final goods and two factors. But his approach is quite different from either Helpman's or Krugman's. The two goods are labeled wheat (W) and manufactures (M). The former is produced under constant returns and the latter under increasing returns. The production of M involves two stages, and increasing returns appear at each stage, albeit of a different variety. First primary resources are used to produce a differentiated intermediate input, called components, under internal economies of scale. Then components are combined to produce M under external economies. The source of externality is the number of components available. The larger the number of components, the greater the degree of specialization and the lower the cost of production of M.

This structure introduces three elements into the model that are absent in models of Krugman and Helpman. First, product differentiation and internal economies appear in intermediate inputs production. Therefore intraindustry trade takes place in inputs rather than final products. Second, in addition to internal economies and product differentiation at the intermediate inputs stage, there are external economies at final-goods-production stage. This introduces some of the features of the models encountered in section 11.1 into the analysis. Finally, since trade permits each country to use the inputs of the other country, the external economy at the final stage of M becomes international in scope. The degree of specialization is determined not by the domestic but world market.

To introduce the model formally, let the two primary factors of production be labor and capital. These factors are first combined to produce W and a hypothetical resource m which serves as the sole input in the production of components. Assuming constant returns in both W and m and assuming that W is relatively labor-intensive, we can obtain a strictly concave transformation curve

$$W = T(m), \qquad T'(m) < 0, T''(m) < 0. \tag{11.25}$$

As just noted, input m is used to produce components denoted x_i. Production functions of the x_i are similar to those used by Krugman with m replacing labor. Thus

$$m_i = b + ax_i. \tag{11.26}$$

The fixed and marginal costs are constant and identical across components. The x_i are combined to produce M via the production function

$$M = n^\alpha \left[\sum_i^n \frac{x_i^\gamma}{n} \right]^{1/\gamma}, \qquad \alpha > 1, 0 < \gamma < 1. \tag{11.27}$$

Ceteris paribus, the larger the variety of inputs available the lower the cost of production of the final product. The underlying idea is that the larger the number of components, the greater the economies of specialization à la Adam Smith. Because n is parametric for a firm producing M, the scale economy is external to it. The production function is linear homogeneous in the firm's choice variables x_i. Note that if the x_i were subject to constant returns, it will pay to produce infinite many varieties to take advantage of economies of specialization in M. The presence of fixed costs limits the number of components produced, however.

In deriving the equilibrium of a component producer, it is helpful to draw an analogy between Krugman (1980) and Ethier (1982b). In Krugman (1980) the demand function facing a representative producer can be derived by minimizing expenditure, $\sum p_i c_i$, subject to a fixed utility where the utility is given by (11.13) after replacing $v(c_i)$ by c_i^θ. As Ethier (1982b) shows, denoting by q_i the price of component x_i, the demand function facing the producer of a representative x_i can be derived by minimizing the cost of producing M, $\sum q_i x_i$, subject to a fixed output where output is given by (11.27). Analytically these problems are identical. Therefore the solutions to them are identical as well. The elasticity of demand facing the producer of x_i equals $1/(1-\gamma)$ which is the same as (11.18) if we replace $v(c)$ by c^θ. The corresponding marginal revenue is $q_i\gamma$. The marginal cost of production is $p_m a$, where, letting W be the numéraire, p_m is the price of m. Under perfect competition, $p_m = -T'(m)$. Equating the marginal revenue and marginal cost, we have

$$\gamma q = -T'(m)a, \tag{11.28}$$

where, taking advantage of the symmetry across varieties, we have dropped the subscript i. Equation (11.28) determines q as a function of m. The zero-profit condition yields

$$x = \frac{b\gamma}{a(1-\gamma)}. \tag{11.29}$$

Thus x is determined independently of m as in Krugman (1980). Changes in m affect the number of varieties only and not x. Summing (11.26) over i, we have $m = bn + anx$. Substituting x from (11.29), we obtain

$$n = \frac{m(1-\gamma)}{b}. \tag{11.30}$$

As expected, a 1 percent increase in m increases n by exactly 1 percent.

We still need to determine m and M. For this we look at the equilibrium in the production of M. Since the scale economy via n is external, we will obtain the zero-profit condition. Given the symmetry across the x_i, (11.27) reduces to $M = n^\alpha x$. Therefore, denoting by p_s the supply price, the average-cost pricing condition ($p_s M = qnx$) leads to

$$p_s = \left[\frac{m(1-\gamma)}{b}\right]^{1-\alpha}\left(-\frac{T'(m)a}{\gamma}\right), \tag{11.31}$$

where we use (11.29) and (11.30). Equation (11.31) determines p_s (which is in fact the average cost of production of M) as a function of m. Note that a rise in m need not raise p_s. Due to the usual factor-intensity effect, the second term in (11.31) rises with a rise in m. But the first term declines due to the scale effect. Thus it is possible for the supply of manufactures implicit in (11.31) to be negatively sloped. This feature, similar to that encountered in models based on homogeneous goods and perfect competition, makes the analysis substantially more complicated than in Krugman and Helpman. In particular, there can be multiple equilibria, and complete specialization becomes a real possibility. Moreover stability is not always guaranteed.

The last step in completing the description of the autarky equilibrium is to find the demand price p_d and equate it to p_s. Assuming Cobb-Douglas preferences and denoting by ψ the expenditure share of M, we have $p_d M = \psi(p_d M + W)$, or, using (11.25) and $M = n^\alpha x$,

$$p_d = \frac{\psi}{1 - \psi} \frac{T(m)}{n^\alpha x}. \tag{11.32}$$

Remembering that n depends on m only and x is determined in terms of parameters of the model (see equation 11.29), we have here p_d as a function of m alone. Equating p_s in (11.31) to p_d, we can solve for m and the remaining variables. Thus the description of the autarky equilibrium is complete. Ethier (1982b) shows that when the supply curve implicit in (11.31) is negatively sloped at the equilibrium, it is necessarily flatter than the demand curve implicit in (11.32). This ensures that the autarky equilibrium is Marshallian stable.

We can now introduce a second country. Assume that home country just described is labor-abundant, while foreign country is capital-abundant. Let foreign country's transformation curve between W^* and m^* be $S(m^*)$. For a given ratio of wheat to m, foreign country's transformation curve will be flatter $(-T' > -S')$. It may seem that under autarky, assuming identical tastes, manufactures will be cheaper in foreign country. But because the supply price depends both on scale and factor-intensity differences, this is not necessarily true. If home country is sufficiently bigger than foreign country, its autarky price of manufactures may be lower even though it is labor abundant.

Despite this ambiguity with respect to relative autarky prices, we can derive some conclusions regarding trading equilibria on the basis of *relative* factor endowments. Thus let us focus on a trading equilibrium involving incomplete specialization in both countries. The first point to note is that free trade gives each country access to the other's components and lowers the production cost of M (and M^*) in a discrete fashion. This is the international aspect of scale economies. If there are no factor-intensity reversals, free trade leads to factor-price equalization. Because the prices of m and m^* are also equalized, $m^*/W^* > m/W$, and indeed $M^*/W^* > M/W$. Tastes being identical across countries, home country exports W and imports M. For trade in final products, the Heckscher-Ohlin pattern holds.

The trading equilibrium is more complex than this, however. The two countries will also trade components. Each country imports all components produced by the other. As in Helpman, holding the world endowments fixed, if we redistribute primary factors such that relative endowments become more similar, intraindustry trade expands. The opposite happens if factor endowments are made dissimilar. In the extreme cases, if factor endowments are sufficiently dissimilar, one country is completely specialized in W and all trade is interindustry type. At the other extreme, if the endowments of the two factors are identical in absolute terms, all trade is intraindustry type.

Recommended Readings

Caves, R. E. *Trade and Economic Structure: Models and Methods.* Cambridge: Harvard University Press, 1960, pp. 169–74.

Chipman, J. S. A survey of the theory of international trade: Part 2, the neoclassical theory. *Econometrica* 33 (1965): 685–760.

Chipman, J. S. External economies of scale and competitive equilibrium. *Quarterly Journal of Economics* 34 (1970): 347–85.

Chipman, J. S. Trade in differentiated products and political economy of trade liberalization: Comment. In *Import Competition and Response*, ed. by J. Bhagwati. Chicago: University of Chicago Press, 1982, pp. 218–21.

Davis, D. R., and D. E. Weinstein. Does economic geography matter for international specialization. Working Paper 5706, National Bureau of Economic Research. Cambridge, MA, 1996.

Dixit, A. K., and J. E. Stiglitz. Monopolistic competition and optimum product diversity. *American Economic Review* 67 (1977): 297–308.

Ethier, W. J. Decreasing costs in international trade and Frank Graham's argument for protection. *Econometrica* 50 (1982a): 243–68.

Ethier, W. J. National and international returns to scale in the modern theory of international trade, *American Economic Review* 72 (1982b): 389–405.

Helpman, E. International trade in the presence of product differentiation, economies of scale and monopolistic competition: A Chamberlin-Heckscher-Ohlin approach. *Journal of International Economics* 11 (1981): 305–40.

Helpman, E. Increasing returns, imperfect markets and trade theory. In *Handbook of International Economics*, vol. 1, ed. by R. W. Jones and P. B. Kenen. Amsterdam: North-Holland, 1984.

Helpman, E., and P. R. Krugman. *Market Structure and Foreign Trade. Increasing Returns, Imperfect Competition, and the International Economy.* Cambridge: MIT Press, 1985.

Jones, R. W. Variable returns to scale in general equilibrium theory. *International Economic Review* 9 (1968): 261–72.

Kemp, M. C. *The Pure Theory of International Trade and Investment* Englewood Cliffs, NJ: Prentice Hall, 1969, ch. 8.

Krugman, P. Increasing returns, monopolistic competition, and international trade. *Journal of International Economics* 9 (1979): 469–79.

Krugman, P. Scale economies, product differentiation, and the pattern of trade. *American Economic Review* 70 (1980), 950–59.

Krugman, P. Trade, accumulation, and uneven development. *Journal of Development Economics* 8 (1981a): 149–61.

Krugman, P. Intraindustry specialization and the gains from trade. *Journal of Political Economy* 89 (1981b): 959–73.

Krugman, P. Trade in differentiated products and political economy of trade liberalization. In *Import Competition and Response*, ed. by J. Bhagwati. Chicago: University of Chicago Press, 1982, pp. 197–208.

Krugman, P. History versus expectations. *Quarterly Journal of Economics* 106 (1991a): 651–67.

Krugman, P. Increasing returns and economic geography. *Journal of Political Economy* 99 (1991b): 483–99.

Krugman, P., and A. J. Venables. Globalization and the inequality of nations. *Quarterly Journal of Economics* 110 (1995): 857–80.

Lancaster, K. *Variety, Equity, and Efficiency*. New York: Columbia University Press, 1979.

Lancaster, K. Intra-industry trade under perfect monopolistic competition. *Journal of International Economics* 10 (1980): 151–75.

Lancaster, K. Trade in differentiated products and political economy of trade liberalization: Comment. In *Import Competition and Response*, ed. by J. Bhagwati. Chicago: University of Chicago Press, 1982, pp. 218–21.

Linder, S. *An Essay on Trade and Transformation*. New York: Wiley, 1961.

Markusen, J. R. Explaining the volume of trade: An eclectic approach. *American Economic Review* 76 (1986): 1002–11.

Markusen, J. R., and J. R. Melvin. Trade, factor prices and gains from trade with increasing returns to scale. *Canadian Journal of Economics* 14 (1981): 450–69.

Mayer, W., Variable returns to scale in general equilibrium theory: A comment. *International Economic Review* 15 (1974): 225–35.

Panagariya, A. Variable returns to scale in general equilibrium theory once again. *Journal of International Economics* 10 (1980): 499–526.

Panagariya, A. Variable returns to scale in production and patterns of specialization. *American Economic Review* 71 (1981): 221–30.

Panagariya, A. Increasing returns and the specific factors model. *Southern Economic Journal* 53 (1986a): 1–17.

Panagariya, A. Increasing returns, dynamic stability, and international trade. *Journal of International Economics* 20 (1986b): 43–63.

Panagariya, A. Factor mobility, trade and welfare: A north–south analysis with economies of scale. *Journal of Development Economics* 39 (1992): 229–45.

II TRADE INTERVENTIONS AND TRANSFERS

12 Tariffs and Trade Equilibrium

In this chapter, and in chapter 16 on the transfer problem and parts of chapter 29 on growth, we will deploy the so-called classical model with two primary factors producing two goods traded between two countries. We will examine in this model the effect of a tariff on the external and the domestic terms of trade. (The latter determine the protective effect of the tariff). Finally we will discuss geometric derivations of tariff-distorted offer curves under alternative assumptions concerning the disposal of tariff revenues, as in Meade's classic 1952 work on the geometry of international trade.

12.1 Free-Trade Version of the Classical Model

This model is set out fully in appendix C, with twelve independent equations and twelve unknowns. Briefly, for convenient reference, the twelve equations are given here as (12.1)–(12.12). The production functions are

$$Q_1 = Q_1\left(\frac{1}{p}\right), \tag{12.1}$$

$$Q_2 = Q_2\left(Q_1\left(\frac{1}{p}\right)\right), \tag{12.2}$$

$$Q_1^* = Q_1^*\left(\frac{1}{p}\right), \tag{12.3}$$

$$Q_2^* = Q_2^*\left(Q_2^*\left(\frac{1}{p}\right)\right), \tag{12.4}$$

where the capital letters refer to production levels and subscripts to goods. With Walras's law holding, we next have

$$D_i = Q_1 + pQ_2, \tag{12.5}$$

$$D_e = C_1 + pC_2, \tag{12.6}$$

$$D_i = D_e, \tag{12.7}$$

$$D_i^* = Q_1^*/p + Q_2^*, \tag{12.8}$$

$$D_e^* = C_1^*/p + C_2^*, \tag{12.9}$$

$$D_i^* = D_e^*, \tag{12.10}$$

where D_i and D_i^* are the national incomes measured at factor cost in countries I (home) and II (foreign) and D_e and D_e^* are the national expenditures at market prices. Then we have two demand equations:

$$C_2 = C_2(D_e, p), \tag{12.11}$$

$$C_1^* = C_1^*\left(D_e^*, \frac{1}{p}\right). \tag{12.12}$$

These twelve equations determine the twelve unknowns Q_1, Q_2, Q_1^*, Q_2^*, C_1, C_2, C_1^*, C_2^*, D_i, D_e, D_i^*, and D_e^* if p is specified exogenously. To determine p, we then can add one more equation from the following three equivalent equations:

$$(C_2 + C_2^*) - (Q_2 + Q_2^*) = 0 \tag{12.13a}$$

or

$$(C_2 - Q_2) = (Q_2^* - C_2^*) \tag{12.13b}$$

or (by Walras's law)

$$(C_2 - Q_2) = \frac{1}{p}(C_1^* - Q_1^*). \tag{12.13c}$$

Writing $M \equiv (C_2 - Q_2)$ for imports of good 2 by the home country I and $M^* \equiv (C_1^* - Q_1^*)$ for imports of good 1 by the foreign country II, we can rewrite the last equation as

$$M = \left(\frac{1}{p}\right)M^*. \tag{12.13c'}$$

Then the free-trade solution will determine the values of the twelve unknowns and the terms of trade p.

12.2   Effect of a Tariff on External and Domestic Terms of Trade

Now introduce a tariff by country I into this model, at *ad valorem* rate t. This tariff generates revenue which, in the algebraic analysis below, we assume to be returned to the nongovernmental sector for spending. (Our geometric illustrations will include the case where the government spends the revenue.) The tariff drives a wedge between the foreign (p^*) and the domestic (p) terms of trade (i.e., goods-price ratio). Besides, national expenditure will now differ from national income by the amount of the tariff revenue.

Trade theorists use a beautiful technique for getting to the criterion for the effect on the terms of trade of this tariff: first, hold the external goods-price ratio p^* constant and compute the excess demand that would materialize for a good. Second, compute the change in terms of trade necessary to eliminate this excess demand. We will use this two-stage derivation in the analysis below.

With initial free trade (i.e., $t = 0$), the tariff will result, at constant p^*, in a full change in the domestic terms of trade, p. The effect of this price change in reducing import demand can be decomposed in the usual way (see appendix C) into a compensated price effect plus the income effect. But the redistributed revenues generate an offsetting income effect on the demand for imports, leaving the aggregate effect as simply a reduced demand for imports from the compensated term, which is definitely signed. This reduction in the excess demand for imports, given stability, will lead in the second-stage argument to an improvement in the terms of trade (except in the limiting case where the country is small in the Samuelson sense and the terms of trade do not change).

Algebraically this result can be obtained by simply differentiating $M^* - pM = 0$ with respect to t, after modifying equations (12.3), (12.4), (12.7)–(12.9), and (12.12). (In equations 12.3, 12.4, and 12.12 we should now write p^* for p, and equations 12.8–12.9 should be modified for this and also to allow for expenditure (D_e) to exceed income (D_i) by the amount of the tariff revenue ($M \cdot dt$).) This yields

$$\frac{dp^*}{dt} = \frac{-\varepsilon'}{\varepsilon + \varepsilon^* - 1}$$

$$< 0 \quad \text{if } \varepsilon + \varepsilon^* > 1. \tag{12.14}$$

The tariff therefore will worsen the external terms of trade if we assume stability (i.e., $\varepsilon + \varepsilon^* > 1$).

The effect on the domestic terms of trade is derived simply by noting that

$$\frac{dp}{dt} = \frac{d(p^*(1 + t))}{dt} = p^* + (1 + t)\frac{dp^*}{dt}. \tag{12.15}$$

Substituting (12.15) into (12.14) and assuming that $t = 0$ because of initial free trade and $p^* = 1$ by choice of units, we get

$$\frac{dp}{dt} = 1 - \frac{\varepsilon'}{\varepsilon + \varepsilon^* - 1} = \frac{m + (\varepsilon^* - 1)}{\varepsilon + \varepsilon^* - 1}. \tag{12.16}$$

Here we see that well-known Metzler (1949) paradox: A tariff may actually lower the relative domestic price of the importable. This paradox will evidently arise, consistent with stability, if the numerator of (12.16) is negative, which requires that the importable in the country enacting the tariff be an inferior good or that $\varepsilon^* - 1 < 0$ (i.e., that the foreign-offer curve be inelastic).

12.3   Geometry of Tariffs

Chapter 6 of Meade 1952 is directly addressed to our present subject. The geometry, especially of how offer curves shift with tariffs, is critical to an understanding of many important papers in the theory of international trade. We present below some of that essential geometry and argumentation in order to make the treatment reasonably self-sufficient, since Meade's classic volume is becoming increasingly difficult to find.

Like Meade, we begin with the case where the government has a separate spending function (which contrasts with the algebra in the preceding section); then we turn to the case where the government returns the tariff revenue in a costless lump-sum fashion to private consumers, with their demand and utility representable by well-behaved social-indifference curves. The novel case where revenues result in revenue-seeking activities by lobbies is analyzed in chapter 34, though it is referred to at the end of the present chapter.

Government Spending of Revenue

Import Duty in Country I

Let us take first the case of an import duty in country I (figure 12.1) where OI is the offer curve of country I. The problem is to derive the tariff-ridden offer curve from OI. To do this, it is sufficient to concentrate on an arbitrary point such as R on OI, with associated terms of trade α. The import duty is levied at rate RK/JK. With this duty in place, we have the producers and consumers in country I facing price ratio α. However, given the duty, the foreigners get to trade only at price ratio β, since when OV of exportables are traded to buy $RV = JO$ of importables in the marketplace, RK of the exportables go to the government as tariff revenue and the foreigners get only JK. It follows that the domestic and external terms of trade, α and β, are defined by the import duty. The pencil $\beta O \alpha$ can therefore be rotated around O to yield alternative R points and corresponding tariff revenues (RK). However, to get the exact shift in the offer curve corresponding to R and α, we need to know the quantities traded and not just the price β. So we need to introduce the government's demand function. This is done by taking R as the origin and drawing in a government indifference curve U_G tangent to KM at S. Thus the government, which can spend its tariff revenues exclusively on

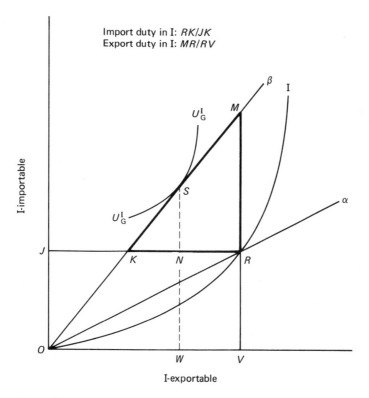

Figure 12.1

I-exportable goods and hence as *RK* or exclusively on I-importable goods and hence as *RM* or in any combination of the two goods along *MK*, chooses *S*. The government winds up consuming *RN* of the exportable and *SN* of the importable. Therefore, given the private "export" of *JR* minus government's demand for *RN* exportables, the net export is *JN* = *OW*. The private import of *OJ* must be added to the government's demand of *NS* to yield *SW* net imports. Therefore the offer curve shifts so that *S* on the tariff-ridden offer curve corresponds to *R* on the free-trade offer curve. This procedure can be repeated for other points on *OI*, such as *R*, until the complete tariff-inclusive offer curve is traced out.

Export Duty in I

The same technique can be used to shift the offer curve *OI* when the duty is on exports rather than on imports. In fact an export duty at the rate *MR/RV* in figure 12.1 is identical to the rate *RK/JK* at which the import duty was considered above. However, the export duty at this identical rate will yield to the government revenue of *MR* in I-importables. At

price ratio β, in the domestic economy, consumers and producers will
again exchange OV for VR at price ratio α but the foreigners have to
pay, for OV of I-exportables, MV of I-importables at price ratio β, with
MR accruing to the government of country I. At price ratio β this will
yield again the government budget line KM, and with government's indifference curve U_G the government will consume at S with reference to
origin R. Therefore the offer curve, with export duty at rate MR/RV,
will shift identically as with an import duty at an identical rate KR/JK.
This proposition, which is due to Lerner (1936) and is known as the
Lerner symmetry theorem, is discussed more directly in section 12.6.

Import Subsidy In Country I

Now consider an import subsidy in country I at rate KR/JK in figure
12.2. Again take an arbitrary point R on county I's offer curve OI with
price ratio α. At this price ratio consumers and producers will exchange
(or have "offers" or excess demand and supply of) RV importables for
OV exportables. However, the foreigners give MV of I-importables
at price ratio β for only JK of I-exportables, and the extra RK of I-

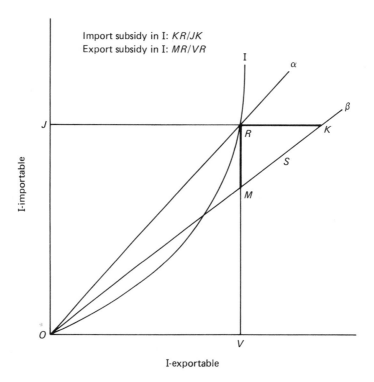

Figure 12.2

exportables have to come from the government subsidy at rate KR/JK. The relationship between α and β, both measured as the domestic and foreign relative price of the importable, is simply

$$\alpha = \frac{JR}{JO},$$

$$\beta = \frac{JK}{JO},$$

$$\alpha = \beta(1 - s).$$

Put even more concisely,

$$JR = JK\left(1 - \frac{KR}{JK}\right).$$

Depending on how the government chooses to combine the supply of the two goods, at identical values along MK the offer curve will shift from R to any point on MK, such as S. The Lerner symmetry theorem on import and export duties, which says that an import duty is equivalent to an export tax at the same rate, is seen here because the foregoing argument applies equally in figure 12.2 to an export subsidy at an identical rate (MR/VR). Meade notes the artificiality of having to assume here that the government magically produces the required goods to pay the subsidy just as a magician pulls a rabbit out of a hat.

Revenue Redistributed as Lump-Sum Transfer to Consumers

When a tariff or a trade subsidy is imposed, the shift in the offer curve is best approached in two steps. First, as does Meade, we will observe the relationship between the trade-indifference curve of a country and the domestic price ratio. Since the free-trade offer curve (as we saw in chapter 5) is nothing but a locus of the tangencies of different terms of trade with the country's trade-indifference curves, this enables us to trace the relationship between the external and domestic price ratios on the tariff-distorted offer curve. Then we can utilize this and related insights to see how the offer curve would shift in the presence of a tariff or a subsidy.

Step 1

Let us begin with country I. Take the right quadrant in figure 12.3 which relates to country I. Pick an arbitrary point R. The trade-indifference curve U_T of country I goes through R. Draw line α tangent to U_T at R, cutting the horizontal axis in D. Join OR, and call it β. (RJC is the production-possibility block of country I and C is the consumption chosen

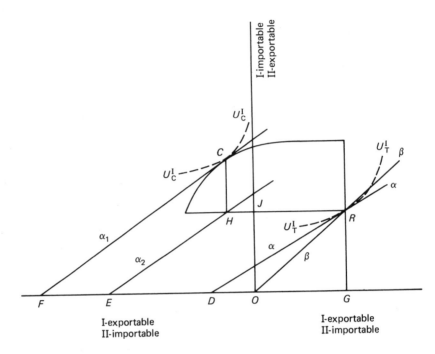

Figure 12.3

at domestic price ratio $\alpha_1 = \alpha$, as explained later.) Now the following proposition holds: *R will be a point of trade equilibrium for country I, given its production and consumption decisions if the national expenditure by the consumers equals the national income plus the amount DO.* (Figure 12.4 is identical to figure 12.3 except that D is to the right of O, so this proposition holds with the amendment that the national expenditure equals national income minus the amount DO.) In figure 12.3 the distance DO can then be shown, in the case of a trade tariff, to be the tariff revenue that must be added to national income DF to give national expenditure OF, with the duty at rate DO/OG. To see this, note that β represents the average external terms of trade, with GR importables being exchanged by country I for GO exportables, and α represents the domestic terms of trade, RG being exchanged for DG. Thus $\beta = \alpha(1 + t)$, where $\beta = GD/GR$, $\alpha = OG/GR$, and $t\ (= DO/OG)$ is the tariff rate. With the domestic goods-price ratio α, it is evident that for a given production block with R as the origin, RH and HC will be produced.

Consumption however is measured from O in the left quadrant, and the consumption-indifference curves are referenced to O as their origin. At α the consumption of the two goods will be JH and $(HC + JO)$. National income at α will then be DF, whereas national expenditure will

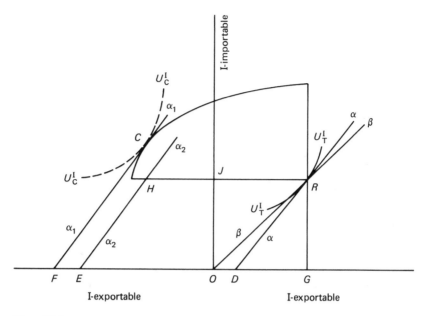

Figure 12.4

be OF (to sustain consumption at C). The difference DO is given to consumers as tariff revenue. Trade is seen as the difference between consumption and production, amounting to OG of exportables ($OG = JR = (HR - HJ)$) for RG of importables ($RG = HC + JO - HC$). With the import duty DO/OG, this trade will generate revenue DO. Therefore our illustration of trade-tariff equilibrium is consistent and complete. The argument applies equally to figure 12.4 for an import subsidy at rate DO/OG, with DO construed as the lump-sum taxation to pay the import subsidies. (See the alternative illustration of a trade tariff in figure 17.1 below.)

Step 2

We now turn to the shift of the offer curve when a tariff is levied at a given rate. In figure 12.5 we set the task of deriving the trade point R of figures 12.3 and 12.4 corresponding to a specified tariff or subsidy rate. A number of trade-indifference curves of country I are drawn in the right quadrant. We draw a straight horizontal line cutting them successively at $C_1, \ldots, C_6$. Draw tangents $\alpha_1, \ldots, \alpha_6$ to the trade-indifference curves at these points, meeting the horizontal axis at $E_1, \ldots, E_6$. Drop perpendiculars from $C_1, \ldots, C_6$ to $D_1, \ldots, D_6$. Now, following Meade, take an arbitrary point C_3. We have just shown that α_3 then represents the domestic price ratio in country I, when the tariff rate is E_3O/OD_3 and E_3O is

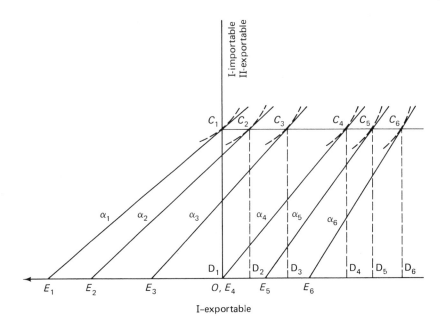

Figure 12.5

the tariff revenue. Meade next shows that $E_2O/OD_2 > E_3O/OD_3$ as $OD_2 < OD_3$ and $E_2O > E_3O$, as the slope of α_2 cannot be steeper than the slope of α_3 without the I-importable being an inferior good in country I's consumption. Therefore, we can conclude that C_2 represents a trade point with a higher tariff rate than C_3. Indeed, C_1 represents an infinite tariff rate, whereas at C_4 the tariff is zero. Therefore, successive moves from C_1 to C_4 represent reducing tariffs, but moves from C_4 toward C_6 and further, imply increasing trade subsidies, from E_5O/OD_5 to E_6O/OD_6 and beyond.

To find the tariff-shifted offer curve, we lower the $C_1 - C_6$ horizontal line and trace out a locus of points such as C_2 corresponding to the tariff rate E_2O/OD_2, and so on. Thus we can get offer curves corresponding to these tariff and subsidy rates. All the curves go through the origin O. The curve traced by C_2 will always be between the vertical axis and the free-trade offer curve. Increasing tariffs will shift the offer curve further to the left, whereas increasing subsidies will shift it to the right.

12.4   Metzler Paradox

Now that we have seen how to infer the domestic terms of trade from the trade-indifference curves, we can consider the Metzler paradox. Figure

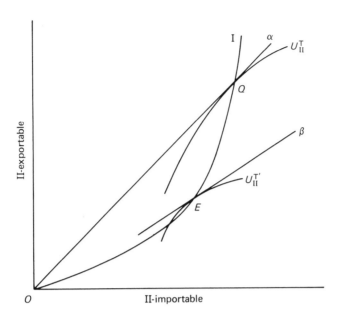

Figure 12.6

12.6 illustrates the case where the foreign offer curve OI facing the tariff-imposing country II is elastic. In this case, as will be recalled from section 12.2, the II-importable good has to be inferior in country II's consumption. Figure 12.7 illustrates the other case, where the foreign offer curve OI is inelastic.

For simplicity in figure 12.6 we draw only country I's offer curve, OI. Q is the free-trade equilibrium, and α represents the domestic and external terms of trade for country II. Country II levies a tariff that shifts its (undrawn) offer curve to cut OI at E. We can draw a line β tangent to country II's trade-indifference curve $U_{II}^{T'}$ at E in order to obtain the domestic terms of trade in country II at the tariff equilibrium. If β is flatter than α, as in figure 12.6, then we have the Metzler paradox: The tariff in country II lowers the domestic relative price of the importable good. (As Meade shows by examining the relative slopes of the trade-indifference curves U_{II}^{T} and $U_{II}^{T'}$, this implies that the importable good is inferior in country II's consumption, as was proved in section 12.2.)

Figure 12.7 illustrates the other possibility for the Metzler paradox to arise, namely when the foreign offer curve OI facing the tariff-imposing country is inelastic. Here the free-trade equilibrium at Q shifts to E with the tariff. The domestic terms of trade then shift from α to β, and β is again flatter than α (also drawn through E to show the relative slopes clearly).

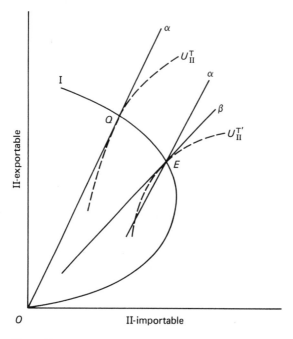

Figure 12.7

12.5   Some Extensions: Metzler Production Paradox

The conditions leading to the Metzler paradox have been analyzed in models that adapt in varying ways the analysis we presented in section 12.2. The effects of government spending its revenue in domestic and external terms of trade, of initial positive tariffs instead of free trade, of income distribution, and of variable factor supply have been worked out in the literature (see especially Bhagwati and Johnson 1961).

In chapter 34 we will also discuss the case where the tariff revenue is competed for by "revenue-seeking" lobbyists instead of being redistributed in a lump-sum fashion by the government or spent on its own consumption of goods and services. In that case the tariff has the added effect of reducing production of one or both of the produced goods in a two-good model. Therefore, even if the country imposing the tariff is small and the Metzler paradox cannot arise, the net production of the protected importable good may fall. In this way we may distinguish between the Metzler price paradox and the Metzler production paradox. In the classical model, given the concavity of the transformation function, the price paradox automatically leads to, and indeed must obtain to cause, deprotection (reduced output) of the importable good. This is not

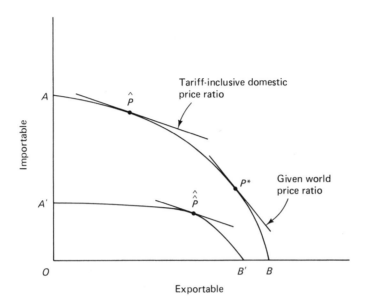

Figure 12.8

so if revenue seeking is assumed to occur. This is illustrated in figure 12.8, where the small country's tariff cannot lead to the Metzler price paradox; it will initially shift production from P^* to $\hat{P}$, which implies a primary, protective effect. However, with resources diverted to revenue seeking, the production of goods falls to $\hat{\hat{P}}$. So, even though the Metzler price paradox is absent, the final output of the importable falls, thanks to the revenue seeking that attends on the tariff. Therefore the Metzler production paradox obtains.

12.6   Lerner Symmetry Theorem

We conclude this chapter with yet another important result in trade theory, the Lerner symmetry theorem. According to this result, proved originally by Lerner (1936), an across-the-board ad valorem tariff is identical *in all respects* to an across-the-board ad valorem export tax at the same rate. From a policy perspective this is not an altogether intuitive result. For it says that the import-competing sector as a whole can be protected as easily by an export tax as by an import duty. Or that exportables as a whole can be subsidized by subsidizing imports.

The Lerner symmetry theorem is easily proved for the small-country case using the excess expenditure function introduced in chapter 9. Suppose that there are n goods of which the country imports the $1, \ldots, k$ and exports the remaining $k + 1, \ldots, n$ goods. Then, assuming that tariff proceeds are redistributed to consumers in a lump-sum fashion, under an ad valorem tariff on all importables at rate t, equilibrium is given by

$$Z((1 + t)p_1^*, (1 + t)p_2^*, \ldots, (1 + t)p_k^*, p_{k+1}^*, \ldots, p_n^*; U) = \sum_{i=1}^{k} tp_i^* Z_i(\cdot),$$

(12.17)

where the p_i^* denote the exogenously given world prices. To economize on notation, we have suppressed the factor endowments as arguments in the excess-expenditure function. Note that the assumption of lump-sum redistribution of tariff revenue is not required. What is required is that the revenue be spent in the same way under the tariff as under the export tax.

Given t, we can solve (12.17) for U and then derive the equilibrium values of quantities consumed by evaluating the derivatives of the expenditure function at that value of U. Equilibrium quantities produced require the knowledge of prices and endowments, which are already given.

Suppose now that we replace the import tariff by an export tax at rate t. Since the export tax is levied on the domestic price p_i, we have $p_i + tp_i = p_i^*$ for $i = k + 1, \ldots, n$. Thus equilibrium is given by

$$Z\left[p_1^*, \ldots, p_k^*, \frac{p_{k+1}^*}{1 + t}, \frac{p_{k+2}^*}{1 + t}, \ldots, \frac{p_n^*}{1 + t}; U\right] = - \sum_{i=k+1}^{n} \frac{tp_i^*}{1 + t} Z_i(\cdot). \qquad (12.18)$$

We need to show now that (12.18) yields an identical value of U to that yielded by (12.17). Recalling that $Z(\cdot)$ is linear homogeneous in prices, we can rewrite (12.18) as

$$Z((1 + t)p_1^*, (1 + t)p_2^*, \ldots, (1 + t)p_k^*, p_{k+1}^*, \ldots, p_n^*; U)$$

$$= -t \sum_{i=k+1}^{n} p_i^* Z_i(\cdot).$$

(12.18′)

Using the trade-balance condition, $\sum_{1}^{n} p_i^* Z_i(\cdot) = 0$, this equation reduces to (12.17). With identical values of all exogenous variables, we obtain identical solutions for U. Thus the equivalence is established. The intuitive explanation of the Lerner symmetry theorem lies in the fact that an across-the-board tariff and export tax distort the relative prices of exportables and importables identically. The tariff raises the domestic prices of importables, while the export tax lowers the prices of exportables; in either case the relative price of importables in terms of exportables rises by $1 + t$. Of course the trade-balance condition plays a crucial role. A tariff lowers imports which, through the trade-balance condition, also lowers exports. Similarly an export tax lowers exports which, through the trade-balance condition, lowers imports.

It is important to appreciate both the strengths and limitations of the Lerner symmetry theorem. As long as the trade balance is fixed at an exogenous level with balanced trade a special case, the theorem can be generalized to a multicountry world, to the case involving nontraded goods and quotas, and to a dynamic context. The generalization to a multicountry world is straightforward. From what we have just shown, it is evident that an across-the-board ad valorem tariff or export tax at the same rate leads to the same demands for exports and imports at a given set of world prices. It is then immediate that the two sets of interventions will yield identical terms of trade in a multicountry world and hence identical equilibria.

By generalization to nontraded goods and quotas (see Lopez and Panagariya 1995), if a subset of goods is subject to binding import or export quotas or is nontraded, the Lerner symmetry theorem applies to the remaining set of goods. That is to say, an across-the-board ad valorem tariff on imports not subject to binding quotas has the same effect as an across-the-board ad valorem export tax at the same rate on exports not subject to binding quotas. Once again the tariff and export tax give rise to identical relative prices of exportables and importables not subject to binding quotas and, given the trade-balance condition, the same equilibrium domestic prices.

In a multiperiod model, the symmetry holds in the sense that given that the intertemporal trade balance must be maintained at an exogenous level, an ad valorem tariff on all imports in all periods (i.e., an across-the-board *permanent* tariff) has the same effect as an export tax at the same rate on all exportables in all periods (i.e., an across-the-board permanent export tax). The symmetry does not hold, however, for an across-the-board tariff and export tax applying in a *subset* of periods only (i.e., a *temporary* tariff and export tax). For example, in a two-period model a temporary tariff that applies in the first period but not the second has very different effects from those of a temporary export tax (Lopez and Panagariya 1990; Razin and Svensson 1983).

On the face of it, the Lerner symmetry theorem looks quite robust, giving rise to temptation to use import duties and export taxes as substitutes. Or, when trade liberalization is the goal and import duties are difficult to remove, there is temptation to counter them by export subsidies. In the limit one could even consider reproducing the free trade equilibrium by neutralizing tariffs by export subsidies. But, for a variety of reasons, extreme caution is needed in going down that road.

First, in practice, trade taxes are almost never uniform across all imports. Even in rare cases where the rate of tariff is uniform, there are sectors that are not subject to the tariff or alternative instruments of protection such as when antidumping or technical barriers are present. Once we recognize that true protection is not at a uniform rate across the board, strictly speaking, the Lerner symmetry cannot be invoked. In general, a free-trade equilibrium cannot be reproduced by a combination of tariffs and export subsidies. Second, even if there is a single rate of tariff that covers all imports and no alternative instruments of protection are present, in most circumstances, agents engage in tariff evasion (smuggling). In that case the true tariff paid is likely to be nonuniform, and the symmetry between tariffs and export taxes will, once again, fail to obtain. Finally, when tariff evasion and subsidy-seeking activities are both present, countering a tariff by export subsidies can prove to be doubly damaging. Real resources can get used up in both tariff evasion and subsidy seeking. In such a situation a uniform import tariff and export subsidy at the same rate will entirely fail to reproduce the free-trade equilibrium.

Recommended Readings

Baldwin, R. E. The effects of tariffs on international and domestic prices. *Quarterly Journal of Economics* 74 (1960): 65–78.

Bhagwati, J., and H. G. Johnson. A generalised theory of the effects of tariffs on the terms of trade. *Oxford Economic Papers* N.S., 13 (1961): 225–53.

Bhagwati, J., and T. N. Srinivasan. Revenue seeking: A generalization of the theory of tariffs. *Journal of Political Economy* 88 (1980): 1069–87.

Johnson, H. G. Income distribution, the offer curve and the effects of tariffs. *Manchester School of Economic and Social Studies* 28 (1960): 215–42.

Johnson, H. G. The standard theory of tariffs. *Canadian Journal of Economics* 2 (1969): 333–52.

Jones, R. The Metzler tariff paradox. In *Trade, Stability, and Macroeconomics*, ed. by G. Horwich and P. A. Samuelson. New York: Academic, 1974.

Lerner A. P. The symmetry between import and export taxes. *Economica* N.S., 3 (1936): 306–13. Reprinted in *Readings in International Economics*, ed. by R. E. Caves and H. G. Johnson. Homewood, IL: Irwin, 1968.

Lopez, R., and A. Panagariya. Temporary trade taxes, welfare and the current account. *Economics Letters* 33 (1990): 347–51.

Lopez, R., and A. Panagariya. The Lerner symmetry and other results in the presence of quotas and nontraded goods. Working Paper 11. Center for International Economics, University of Maryland at College Park, 1995.

MacDougall, I. Tariffs, protection and the terms of trade. *Economic Record* 37 (1961): 73–81.

Meade, J. E. *A Geometry of International Trade*. London: Allen and Unwin, 1952, ch. 6.

Metzler, L. Tariffs, the terms of trade and the distribution of national income. *Journal of Political Economy* 57 (1949): 1–29. Reprinted in *Readings in International Economics*, ed. by R. E. Caves and H. G. Johnson. Homewood, IL: Irwin, 1968.

Metzler, L. Tariffs, international demand and domestic prices. *Journal of Political Economy* 57 (1949): 345–51.

Mundell, R. A. The pure theory of international trade. *American Economic Review* 50 (1960): 86–92.

Razin, A., and L. Svensson. Trade taxes and the current account. *Economics Letters* 13 (1983): 55–57.

Stolper, W., and P. A. Samuelson. Protection and real wages. *Review of Economic Studies* 9 (1941): 58–73.

13 Tariffs versus Quotas

In the preceding chapter we considered tariffs. However, many countries use quotas extensively.[1] In analyses of commercial policy, it is necessary to know whether quotas can be treated as equivalent to tariffs.

13.1 Equivalence Argument

Until recently it was customary in analytical discussion to argue that tariffs and quotas were equivalent—that if a tariff were to be replaced by a quota equal to the import level associated with the tariff, the quota would lead to a domestic price that would exceed the landed c.i.f. price of the imported good by an implicit tariff that would equal the explicit tariff that the quota replaced, so the real outcome would be identical. The only difference, it was argued, would be that in the case of the tariff the revenue would accrue to the government, whereas in the case of an equivalent quota an equal amount of windfall premia or "rents" would accrue to those receiving the import quotas.[2] This is illustrated in figure 13.1, which shows a Marshallian diagram for price and quantity of good 2 that can be interpreted as a general-equilibrium depiction of the economy. DD and $S_D S_D$ are the domestic demand and supply curves. S_F is the foreign supply curve, drawn for simplicity as a horizontal line at price p^* so that the economy is small in Samuelson's sense. With a tariff at rate t, the foreign supply curve S_F becomes S_F^t. Imports are therefore reduced from RS to VX. The domestic price p equals $p^*(1 + t)$, and the government secures tariff revenue equal to the shaded area.

Now replace the tariff by a quota at the tariff-associated import level VX. The market will evidently clear at domestic price p, whereas the CIF landed price for the imports is p^*. The difference between p and p^* then constitutes an implicit tariff at rate t, and the real equilibrium is identical to when the (explicit) tariff was instead imposed at rate t.

One implicit assumption, if we treat this as a general-equilibrium analysis, is that the government disposes of the tariff revenue in one case in the same way as the recipients of the premia on import licenses in the other case. In general equilibrium we also need to note explicitly that (as noted by Falvey 1975) both an import quota and an export quota cannot always be found that will yield the same equilibrium as a particular tariff.

---

1. See, for example, Bhagwati (1978) and Krueger (1978) on the analysis of exchange controls (quantitative restrictions or quotas) in ten semideveloped developing countries studied intensively under a National Bureau of Economic Research project.

2. It is assumed that the quotas are not auctioned.

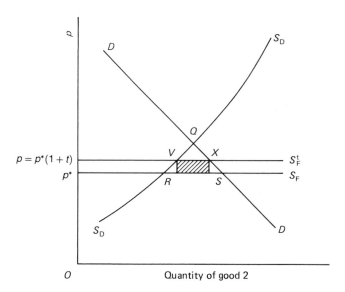

Figure 13.1

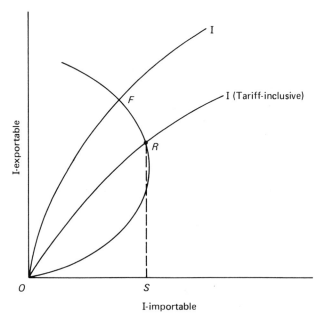

Figure 13.2

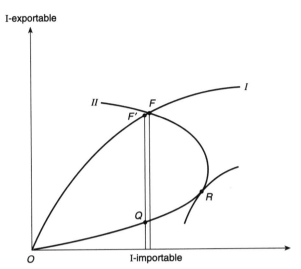

Figure 13.3

Thus, in figure 13.2, let country I be at free-trade equilibrium at *F*. If an export duty or a symmetric import duty is levied, it will shift the equilibrium to *R*. An export quota of *RS* will equally shift the equilibrium to *R*. However, since imports are greater at *R* than at *F*, an import quota cannot be used to reach *R*. Also, when the foreign offer curve is inelastic, an import quota is consistent with two points on the curve.

The latter observation can in fact be shown to offer a way out of the difficulty noted by Falvey when the foreign offer curve is inelastic. Thus, consider figure 13.2b which builds on figure 13.2a. Assume that country I wants to move to point *R* on country II's offer curve, starting under free trade at *F* but using only import restrictions rather than a tariff. The Falvey difficulty then can be surmounted, as noted by Ed Tower (1975), by first reducing imports a little by quota so that I's offer curve becomes *OF'Q*, shifting the world economy from equilibrium at *F* to a Walras-stable equilibrium at *Q*. Then, relaxing the quota little by little, one moves up from one Walras-stable equilibrium to another, crawling up along II's offer curve until *R* is reached.

13.2 Breakdown of Equivalence

Bhagwati (1965, 1969) first raised the question of the breakdown of the equivalence proposition by noting that the proposition was valid in the context of a model assuming competitive foreign supply, perfect competition in domestic production, and a quota allocated to ensure perfect competition among quota holders in the disposal of the quotas. The equivalence could break down if any of these conditions did not hold.

Take, for example, the case where the domestic producer is a monopolist in the model underlying figure 13.1. The replacement of a tariff by a quota set equal to the tariff-associated import level will lead to an implicit tariff that exceeds the explicit tariff according to the following argument: Marginal revenue at any given output is higher under the tariff than under a quota. Under the tariff the fall in domestic price due to an increase in domestic output reduces the quantity of imports supplied, so the increased domestic sales are partly at the expense of imports. However, under the quota imports are fixed, and the whole increase in domestic sales must come from an increase in quantity demanded. With this difference in marginal revenue, output will be higher and domestic price lower under a tariff than it would be under a quota for the same level of imports. (This case is illustrated, and other imperfectly competitive market structures are discussed, in Bhagwati 1969.)

An alternative, general-equilibrium analysis of the breakdown of equivalence in the sense defined above is presented in Rodriguez (1974). Rodriguez compares a tariff-retaliation process of the Cournot type (discussed in chapter 21 below) with a similar retaliation process where, instead of using optimal tariffs each time, the countries use optimal quotas. Rodriguez demonstrates that the quota-retaliation process leads to a different equilibrium outcome than the tariff-retaliation process, even though the initial conditions and the rules defined for retaliation are identical.

Finally a truism: Although a tariff can be replaced by an equivalent quota in figure 13.1, this pair of equivalent tariff and quota will not generally remain equivalent if the supply curves or the demand curves change exogenously.

What the above three examples of nonequivalence indicate is that the equivalence proposition may not hold if the supply curves or the demand curves shift exogenously and the tariff and the quota cannot be adjusted once set (as may be institutionally the case), or if the supply curves or the demand (i.e., offer) curves shift endogenously and differentially to the tariff and the quota. The Bhagwati market-structure example and the Rodriguez retaliation example belong to the latter genre. Thus, in the Rodriguez case, at each stage of the retaliatory process a country can equivalently set an optimal tariff or an optimal quota. However, depending on which policy instrument is used, the choice set open to the other country is different and therefore the retaliatory processes go different routes under the tariff and the quota regime.[3]

13.3 An Alternative Question

In view of the fact that tariffs and quotas can be nonequivalent in the Bhagwati sense as was shown above, let us ask an altogether different and equally interesting question: If one now focuses on one parameter, can one compare a tariff and a quota that both imply a target level of that parameter and then, by reference to a utility function, rank-order them in terms of welfare?[4]

In the context of uncertainty and the inflexibility of policy instruments once set in the face of resolved uncertainty, Pelcovits (1976) considered the welfare ranking of tariffs and quotas in the presence of noneconomic objectives such as constraining the expected imports to a specified level. In either case, the use of the policy instrument must be made under uncertainty regarding the demand and supply schedules. As a result of the uncertainty, the tariff and the quota at the same expected levels of imports will generally produce different welfare outcomes. Pelcovits uses a simple partial-equilibrium model such as the one underlying our figure 13.1 where the foreign supply is perfectly elastic while the import demand curve is linear. First, he shows that when the foreign supply curve is stochastic but the import demand curve is certain, the tariff is not always preferable to a quota, contrary to general intuition. In fact the tariff is preferable to a quota if the *ad valorem* rate is below 100 percent but not if it is higher. The intuitive reason for this is nicely set forth by Pelcovits: When a tariff is used to restrict imports, the country varies imports as prices change depending on how the stochastic supply curve turns out, but the actual response is to the change in the price magnified by the *ad valorem* tariff. The market therefore leads to an "overreaction" to the price change, introducing the loss element that can overturn the general presumption in favor of the price change. When the tariff exceeds 100 percent, the loss becomes sufficiently large to reverse the welfare superiority of the tariff over the quota. Second, in the case where the foreign

3. See chapter 34 on the nonequivalence between tariffs and quotas under lobbying activities generated by both. The nonequivalence arises there because the production functions in lobbying may not be identical for tariff-revenue-seeking lobbying and for quota-premium-seeking lobbying. Again, the fraction of tariff revenues lobbied for may be different from the fraction of import premia lobbied for. These differences imply that the supply curve and/or the demand curve shift differentially and endogenously to the tariff and quota instruments.

4. When equivalence obtains, such welfare ranking necessarily yields weak ordering.

supply curve is certain but the import demand curve is stochastic, the tariff always dominates the quota, since there is no price magnification or "overreaction" effect when the foreign supply price is constant.

A noneconomic objective considered by Pelcovits and also by Dasgupta and Stiglitz (1977) is the collection of revenue under uncertainty. Pelcovits is careful to note that ranking tariffs and quotas for this objective is artificial because it presupposes that the quota is auctioned off (a practice that is so rare in the real world that one of the major advantages of a tariff over a quota is simply assumed to be the revenue it generates). Nevertheless, assuming auctioned quotas, Pelcovits shows that in the stochastic foreign-supply case a tariff will yield less revenue than a quota while admitting the same expected level of imports. But a tariff in excess of 100 percent will also yield less welfare. Now, assume the parametric case where the tariff is varied to increase the revenue. This will further lower welfare where the country is small. Therefore, for an identical revenue, a tariff may well show lower welfare than a quota. This conclusion contradicts the general validity of the Dasgupta-Stiglitz proposition that a tariff is always better than a quota for a revenue target.

13.4   Applicability of Analysis to Other Forms of Tariffs and Quotas

The analysis above of *ad valorem* tariffs is applicable, with obvious modifications, to alternative ways in which tariffs are levied in practice. Tariffs come in many forms.

The most common variety is the *specific* tariff. Economists are conditioned to think of tariffs in *ad valorem* forms (i.e. percentage duties). But in the United States, for instance, until recently specific duties (i.e. a fixed duty specified in nominal value per unit) were the most frequently employed method of taxing imports. For about a century after the Civil War, as noted by Irwin (1996a), specific duties were levied on about two-thirds of dutiable imports. While the foregoing (static) theoretical analysis can be readily adapted to accommodate specific tariffs, it is important to note that the use of specific tariffs has important implications. Thus, fluctuations in import prices can lead to significant changes in the degree of protection afforded. For example, Irwin (1996b) has shown that the adverse effects of the notorious Smoot-Hawley tariff of 1930 were exacerbated by rapidly falling import prices that helped to push the average *ad valorem* U.S. tariff on dutiable imports up from about 40 percent in 1929 to nearly 60 percent in 1932. Again, import price inflation during and after the Second World War contributed to U.S. trade liberalization by eroding the protective effect of specific duties. By one calculation of Irwin, a remarkable 80 percent of the post–Smoot-Hawley decline in U.S. tariffs was driven by higher import prices and only the rest by negotiated tariff reductions.

Again *ad valorem* tariffs may be calculated on f.o.b (i.e., at origin) value instead of c.i.f. (i.e., landed) value as assumed in this chapter. This distinction involves transport costs, inclusive of insurance; Johnson (1966) and Diamond and Mitchell (1971) have analyzed this issue. Then again, there are tariff quotas where the duty is assessed until an upper bound of imports is reached, beyond which the quota restriction applies. This technique has been widely used in agricultural protection.

Also there have been "proportionally distributed" quotas under which import rights are assigned to producers or consumers in proportion to their individual production or consumption of the restricted good (as originally with U.S. oil quotas). This case has been analyzed elegantly by McCulloch and Johnson (1973), who compare and rank-order a tariff or an equivalent quota with a proportionally distributed quota as an alternative means of implementing various noneconomic objectives, such as targeted reduction of the ratio of imports to domestic production.

Equally, quotas of intermediates have usually been distributed in developing countries pro rata to installed capacity on the argument that this is "fair." On the other hand, since quotas fetch premia, this method of allocation is understood now to be one that creates economic loss because it creates an inducement to add to capacity when in fact there may even be excess capacity.[5]

Recommended Readings

Bhagwati, J. On the equivalence of tariffs and quotas. In *Trade, Growth, and the Balance of Payments*, ed. by R. Caves et al. Chicago: Rand-McNally, 1965.

Bhagwati, J. N. *Anatomy and Consequences of Exchange Control Regimes*. Cambridge, MA: Ballinger, 1978.

Dasgupta, P., and J. Stiglitz. Tariffs vs. quotas as revenue raising devices under uncertainty. *American Economic Review* 67 (1977): 975–81.

Diamond, P. A., and F. Mitchell. Customs valuation and transport choice. *Journal of International Economics* 1 (1971): 119–26.

Falvey, R. E. A note on the distinction between tariffs and quotas. *Economica* 42 (1975): 319–26.

Irwin, D. Changes in U.S. tariffs: The role of prices and policies. NBER Working paper 5665. July 1996a.

5. See Bhagwati (1978) for an extended discussion of such trade regimes, based on the findings of an NBER project, directed by Bhagwati and Krueger, on the trade and industrial policies of several developing countries.

Irwin, D. The Smoot-Hawley Tariff: A quantitative assessment. *Review of Economics and Statistics*. Mimeo. University of Chicago Business School. 1996b.

Johnson, H. G. A note on tariff valuation bases, economic efficiency and the effects of preference. *Journal of Political Economy* 74 (1966): 401–402.

Krueger, A. O. *Liberalization Attempts and Consequences*. Cambridge, MA: Ballinger, 1978.

McCulloch, R., and H. G. Johnson. A note on proportionally distributed quotas. *American Economic Review* 63 (1973): 726–32.

Pelcovits, M. D. Quotas versus tariffs. *Journal of International Economics* 6 (1976): 363–70.

Rodriguez, C. A. The non-equivalence of tariffs and quotas under retaliation. *Journal of International Economics* 4 (1974): 295–98.

Sweeney, R. J., E. Tower, and T. D. Willett. The ranking of alternative tariff and quota policies in the presence of domestic monopoly. *Journal of International Economics* 7 (1977): 349–62.

Tower, E. The optimum quota and retaliation. *Review of Economic Studies* 42 (1975): 623–30.

Young L. Ranking optimal tariffs and quotas for a large country under uncertainty. *Journal of International Economics* 9 (1979): 249–64.

Takacs, W. E. The non-equivalence of tariffs, import quotas, and voluntary export restraints. *Journal of International Economics* 8 (1978): 565–73.

This chapter extends the analysis of commercial policy to a variety of instruments that supplement the conventional trade barriers, namely trade taxes and quotas, that we have considered so far. In particular, we need to distinguish between:

1. Trade protection imposed by the import competing country and that imposed by the exporting country (at the insistence of the importing country). The exporting country then operates the so-called voluntary export restrictions (VERs) and orderly market arrangements (OMAs), among other restraints on exports.

2. Protection imposed to secure a larger share for one's firms in the *domestic* market, which is the conventional trade protection whether imposed by the importing country or the exporting country (VERs), and the protection that is imposed to secure a larger share of the *foreign* market. The latter consists of import targets, characterized initially by Bhagwati (1993) as, and now generally called, voluntary import expansions (VIEs). They have been deployed, typically by the United States in its trade with Japan.

3. Conventional protection and the new, "administered" protection in the form of antidumping (AD) actions and VERs. Under the latter, import duties are levied or export restraints are secured that reflect administrative or executive decisions, and the resulting level of trade restraint is administratively determined within the process invoked.

Modern protectionism, we might safely generalize, is characterized by greater reliance on administered protection, by a mix of importing and exporting country restraints, and by repeated attempts at imposing VIEs on Japan. The use of tariffs as trade restricting devices has generally been reduced through a progression of multilateral trade negotiations (MTN) under GATT auspices throughout the postwar period. In this chapter we therefore discuss these forms of commercial policy instruments.

14.1   Voluntary Export Restraints

Voluntary export restraints (VERs) shift the jurisdiction over trade restraint to the exporting country. There are two economic aspects of analytical consequence in regard to VERs.

VERs administered by the Exporting Country

The inherent feature is that VERs are undertaken by the exporting country, whereas import restrictions are undertaken by the importing country.

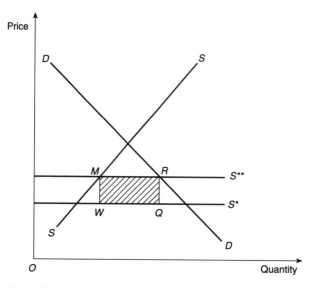

Figure 14.1

This is not to say that VERs are voluntarily imposed by the exporting country, as the nomenclature suggests. The exporting country is often left by the importing country with the choice of imposing VERs or having to suffer import restrictions.[1] The principal consequence is that the scarcity premium on restricted trade then accrues to the exporting, not the importing, country. This is shown in figure 14.1 by the conventional partial-equilibrium diagram with domestic demand curve as DD, the domestic supply curve as SS, and the foreign supply curve as S^*.

With a tariff raising the foreign supply to S^{**}, imports are restricted to MR, and the striped area $MRQW$ is the tariff revenue that accrues to the importing government. If imports are restricted instead by import quotas, then we have already seen that under perfect competition this revenue accrues instead to those who get the import licenses. Again, if the import licenses are auctioned off in a competitive marketplace, then the government earns the revenue, but in the form of the auction proceeds.

When we consider a VER, however, the striped area proceeds $MRQW$, which are rents, accrue instead to the foreign holder of the licenses. If the foreign government holds them, then it gets the proceeds. If they simply hand over the quota rights to the suppliers, then the suppliers get them. Typically foreign governments hand over the task of meeting VER re-

---

1. The origin of VERs, as also the different reasons why they may appeal to the exporting and to the importing countries, are discussed in Bhagwati (1987).

quirements, and hence exporting rights, to the industry in question, so that the rents do accrue almost always to the foreign industry.

This analysis is in partial equilibrium. Hence revenue disposal assumptions do not affect outcomes differentially among different instruments. It is easy to see, however, that relaxing this assumption can introduce nonequivalences among the different instruments despite the assumption of perfect competition. Thus the propensity to spend on different goods out of revenues or rents may be different among foreign governments, foreign producers, domestic governments, and domestic industry.

Once nonequivalence arises, recall that the analyst can ask the question: Which instrument, a VER or an import quota, will leave the importing country with higher welfare while meeting a specified target for which the restriction is being imposed? We can also ask if, compared to an import restriction, a VER will, regardless of the objective chosen, benefit the exporting country and harm the importing country, as in the partial-equilibrium analysis.

The analysis of the so-called "rent transfer" (from the importing to the exporting country under VERs) has been undertaken in the usual two-good general-equilibrium model by Bhagwati and Brecher (1987). These authors consider two alternative policies, VERs and import restrictions, and two possible policy targets: fixing the volume of imports and fixing the domestic price ratio instead. The authors show that the conventional, partial-equilibrium-analysis-based wisdom holds for the case where the target is a fixed volume of imports, requiring the added assumption of normality in importing country's consumption when the target is a fixed home price ratio.

The Bhagwati-Brecher analysis is cast in the two-country mold. This simplification however, omits an important aspect of restraints on trade that are imposed by exporting countries: VERs are typically used in multi-country contexts to "hit" specific exporting countries in a discriminatory fashion.[2] This selectivity is at the heart of the VERs and accounts partly for their popularity with importing countries. Even though import restraints will generally take the form of nondiscriminatory tariff duties that hit every exporter identically, VERs enable the importing country to restrain imports by selectively targeting some exporters at the expense of others. This then implies (Bhagwati 1987) that VERs can be confidently expected to be a more porous form of protection than import restraints (whose porosity has been discussed insightfully by Baldwin 1985): The targeted exporting countries can shift production to nontargeted coun-

---

2. See Dinopoulos and Kreinin (1990) for an extension of the Bhagwati-Brecher analysis of VERs in a three-country context.

tries, and they can also cheat by disguising origin. Thus VERs may be preferred by an importing country that seeks to convey the political message that it will restrain, owing to domestic industry pressures, but really wishes to leave the door open to imports in reality (Bhagwati 1987). Of course, to the extent that VERs become porous, they become ineffective trade restraints, so the rent transfer analysis above, where the scarcity rents ($MRQW$ in figure 14.1) go under VERs to the exporting country, is correspondingly inapplicable; the rents themselves tend to diminish as porosity gets larger.

VERs as Quantity Instruments

VERs are also typically quantity instruments in practice, though they are *not inherently* so. Thus, while the exporting country will almost always undertake to restrict exports of an item to agreed levels by imposing a *quantity* measure, there is nothing that requires the exporting country not to use a *price* measure, such as an export tax, to arrive at the same outcome (though the price policy will suffer more acutely from the problem of achieving the actual amount of desired restriction of exports).

As it happens, Canada did recently use a tax on lumber exports to achieve the restriction of exports demanded by the United States. But this is relatively rare. As we have noted, the use of quantity measures in levying VERs, and the inevitable allocation of them to exporters by foreign governments, ensures that the rents accrue to the foreign industry, whereas the use of a price measure to achieve the desired restraint by the exporting country would ensure that the foreign government would get the rents instead. Where the foreign industry is considered to be the source of market distress, clearly the quantity version of the VER is then inferior to the price version, from the viewpoint of the importing country.

Another difference of consequence between VERs designed as quantity instruments and VERs as price instruments follows again from the fact that the former are operated by industry. They can thus encourage cartelized behavior by the industry, changing the market structure of the exporting country endogenously. This outcome is avoided if the exporting government uses export tariffs to achieve the desired restraint when the exporting industry is perfectly competitive.[3]

Yet another implication of VERs used as quantity instruments, which has been observed empirically,[4] is that they will generally lead to quality

---

3. That the market structure may be endogenous to VERs is also the key insight in the important papers by Harris (1985) and Kala Krishna (1989).

4. See, for example, the classic study of the effects of VERs on U.S. autos in 1980 and 1981 by Feenstra (1984).

upgrading of imports, compared to price restraints that do not discriminate among different qualities. Falvey (1979) has argued that the quality upgrading will occur because the quantity restraint will de facto become a differentially higher tariff on lower-quality items. This is because the quota licenses carry a premium that applies like a specific tax on imports of all qualities, whereas higher quality indexes into higher landed price, so that the uniform quota premium amounts to a higher tariff on imports of lower-quality items.[5]

The quality upgrading can also be explained by the fact that many exporting countries, faced by quantity constraints on their exports, will typically encourage, even subsidize, the exporting firms to utilize the quotas in such a way as to maximize foreign exchange earned, implicitly valuing foreign exchange at a shadow value that exceeds the parity (Yoffie, 1983; Bhagwati, 1987).

As a result VERs, which have been around since the 1930s and whose analysis has been extensive as we just saw, are now outlawed at the WTO, with the transition period allowing each member country only one. Whether this will amount to anything like a substantive change in practice is debatable, for they may still work as informal constraints. Thus, when the U.S. VERs on Japanese autos formally expired in 1985, the Japanese exports did not rise for years thereafter. This could well have been because the VERs having been invoked earlier, the Japanese were aware of the threat that they might be revived if the Japanese exports rose beyond the caps that the VER had laid down earlier. A more intriguing hypothesis, which does not seem plausible given the highly competitive nature of the world auto industry, is that the earlier VER had helped cartelize the Japanese car industry in regard to exports, and they were holding back exports so as to maximize revenues, as under an optimal tariff.

14.2 Voluntary Import Expansions

But if VERs, which seek to increase the share of one's firms in domestic markets, have been around since the 1930s, this cannot be said of the new trade policy instrument which seeks to increase their share in foreign

---

5. Feenstra (1987, p. 229) has, however, argued that if quality change is modeled, not along the neoclassical lines, as in Falvey, but along hedonic lines, then the upgrading conclusion does not follow. He cites theoretical work by many others along these lines, including Carlos Rodriguez (1979) who however assumed a particular form for utility and derived the upgrading result for quotas as contrasted with ad valorem tariffs, Das and Donnenfeld (1985), and Kala Krishna (1985).

markets and which, therefore, has been christened by symmetry as voluntary import expansions (VIEs; see Bhagwati, 1987). This policy instrument came into attempted use by the United States in trading with Japan. Arguing that Japan's markets were closed in some inscrutable fashion, and asserting that the market shares of U.S. firms should be larger than observed, the U.S. government proceeded to seek the imposition of VIEs in different sectors, starting with semiconductors. Attempts at multiplying VIEs manifold, which was an integral part of the Clinton administration's trade policy in the first term, were to fail as the Japanese government refused to accept such targets.[6]

The main problem with VIEs is that while they claim virtuously to be dismantling unobserved barriers to trade by resorting to obligations to import quantities that a "truly functioning, competitive" market would yield, they amount in practice to "managed trade" (i.e., to substituting rules-determined trade by quantity-targeted trade). In imposing VIEs, the country simply assumes that the industry lobbying for them knows what the share "should" be in the foreign market. There is no good way to determine this. Even the macro-level studies of Japan's "closedness" have yielded mixed results, leave aside micro-level studies for individual industries. The politics then turns VIEs into straightforward demands to fix market shares in order to guarantee shares in the foreign market the way VERs seek to increase the domestic firms' share in the home market. VIEs then become "export protectionism," just as VERs are "import protectionism." None of this follows if, on the suspicion that our exports are being shut out, we proceed to identify how this happens and then proceed to address the removal of the practices that lead to the protectionist outcome.

As it happens, VIEs have been used in conjunction with Section 301 of the 1988 Omnibus Trade and Competitiveness Act, which authorizes the USTR to issue threats to foreign nations to fall in line with U.S. demands whether or not justified by treaty obligations and whether or not impartially determined by international procedures to be legitimate. This practice has now come to be known as aggressive unilateralism, to distinguish it from conventional unilateralism such as that embraced by Prime Minister Robert Peel when repealing the Corn Laws and unilaterally ushering in Free Trade in 1846.[7]

---

6. The history of these attempts has been traced well in Irwin (1994, ch. 2). For a detailed analysis of the failure of the Clinton-Hosokawa Summit in Washington over this issue, and of the defeat of the United States in the high-profile car dispute where VIEs were also sought and not obtained, see the various essays reprinted on the subject in Bhagwati's (1998) essays on public policy.

7. For aggressive unilateralism, see Bhagwati and Patrick (1991, ch. 1) and Bhagwati (1992).

VIEs have now been analyzed, in symmetry with VERs, in terms of how they affect the trade equilibrium: see, in particular, Irwin (1994) and Greaney (1996). But, in keeping with nonequivalence analysis of tariffs and quotas, Pravin Krishna (1996) has compared the welfare outcomes of a country when, in an imperfectly competitive setting, it chooses between a VER and a VIE as instruments with which to increase the share of its own firm in the aggregate world sales of the industry: The VER would increase world share by seeking to raise the home firm's share in the domestic market, whereas the VIE would do this by raising the home firm's share in the foreign market.

14.3   Antidumping (AD) Actions

Finally the most popular policy instrument of the protectionists today needs to be mentioned. This is the time-honored remedy against "unfair" trade: the tool of antidumping actions.

In theory, the argument against dumping is that it is predatory, eliminating an efficient (domestic) producer and replacing it with an inefficient (foreign) producer. Thus it distorts worldwide efficiency. Showing that such predatory pricing occurs would naturally be difficult, since the analyst would have to show that without governmental subsidy a firm should be able to price a more competitive firm out of the market by predatory pricing and yet earn normal profit (which in turn would require raising prices again and that would then invite the priced-out, more efficient firm back into production).

In practice, the AD actions have deteriorated into determinations of whether the price charged in the importing country is below the price charged at home (i.e., into price discrimination) or whether it is below cost. Neither of these definitions has anything to do with predatory pricing, but each opens up the possibility of zeroing in on a successful foreign supplier and slapping a protective duty on him in the guise of countervailing unfair trade.[8] The actual practice of AD actions, in the United States and even more so in the European Union, is yet more absurdly protective insofar as the price discrimination is measured deliberately in ways that exaggerate the dumping margin calculated.[9]

The use of AD actions for protectionist purposes has become such as major problem that many analysts argue that the fall of tariff barriers over successive rounds of multilateral trade negotiations under GATT

8. For important theoretical analyses of AD, see Ethier (1982) and Clarida (1993).

9. See, in particular, the writings of Hindley (1988, 1997) and Messerlin (1989) for the EU.

auspices in the postwar period has been offset by resort to AD actions and VERs, in particular. The problem with these instruments, which are now described as administered protection, is that the protection they provide is selective and elastic. Thus AD actions can be mounted not just against specific countries but against specific firms within those countries, thus enabling action against the most potent rival firms that a domestic firm must compete with. Again, the dumping margin that is calculated is subject often to "reconstructed" costs and "estimated" prices so that the room for discretion is large in practice. So the antidumping duties that follow are essentially made to order, providing elasticity in protection that a given tariff rate cannot. It is therefore not surprising that AD actions have become a favored instrument of protectionists and that attempts at reforming the AD code at the GATT, and now the WTO, encounter huge resistance from many business lobbies.[10]

Recommended Readings

Applebaum, H. The antidumping laws—Impact on the competitive process. *Antitrust Law Journal* 43 (1974): 590–600.

Areeda, P., and H. Hovenkamp. *Antitrust Law: An Analysis of Antitrust Principles and Their Application.* Boston: Little Brown, 1992.

Areeda, P., and D. Turner. Predatory pricing and related practices under Section 2 of the Sherman Act. *Harvard Law Review* 88 (1975): 697–733.

Baldwin, R., and M. Moore. Political aspects of the trade remedy laws. In *Down in the Dumps*, ed. by R. Boltuck and R. Litan. Washington: Brookings, 1991.

Baldwin, R., and J. Steagall. An analysis of factors influencing ITC decisions in antidumping, countervailing duty, and safeguard cases. NBER Working Paper, 1993.

Bhagwati, J. Quid pro quo DFI and VIEs: Political-economy-theoretic analyses. *International Economic Journal* 1 (1987): 1–14.

Bhagwati, J. *Protectionism.* Cambridge: MIT Press, 1988.

Bhagwati, J., and H. T. Patrick, eds. *Aggressive Unilateralism: America's 301 Trade Policy and the World Trading System.* Ann Arbor: University of Michigan Press, 1990.

Boltuck, R., and R. Litan. *Down in the Dumps.* Washington: Brookings, 1991.

Bovard, J. *The Fair Trade Fraud.* New York: St. Martins Press, 1991.

Brander, J., and P. Krugman. A reciprocal dumping model of international trade. *Journal of International Economics* 15 (1983):

Cass, R., and S. Narkin. Antidumping and countervailing duty law: The United States and the GATT. In *Down in the Dumps*, ed. by R. Boltuck and R. Litan. Washington: Brookings, 1991.

Clarida, R. Entry, dumping and shakeout. *American Economic Review* 83 (1993):

Clarida, R. Dumping: In theory, in policy, and in practice. In *Fair Trade and Harmonization*, vol. 1, ed. by J. Bhagwati and R. Hudec. Cambridge: MIT Press, 1996, ch. 9.

10. A brief review of administered protection, drawing on the pioneering writings of Michael Finger, is provided in Bhagwati (1988). A fine recent review is by Clarida (1996).

Das, S. P., and S. Donnenfeld. Trade policy and its impact on the quality of imports: A welfare analysis. Mimeo. University of Wisconsin-Milwaukee and New York University, December 1985.

de Melo, J., and P. Messerlin. Price, quality and welfare effects of European VERs on Japanese autos. *European Economic Review* 32 (1988): 1527–46.

Dinopoulos, E., and M. Kreinin. An analysis of import expansion policies. *Economic Inquiry* 28 (1990): 99–108.

Eichengreen, B., and H. van der Ven. US antidumping policies: The case of steel, *The Structure and Evolution of Recent US Trade Policy*, ed. by R. Baldwin and A. Kreuger. Chicago: University of Chicago Press, 1984.

Ethier, W. Dumping. *Journal of Political Economy* 90 (1982): 487–506.

Falvey, R. E. The composition of trade within import-restricted product categories. *Journal of Political Economy* 87 (1979): 1105–14.

Feenstra, R. Voluntary export restraints on US autos, 1980–81: Quality, employment and welfare effects. In *The Structure and Evolution of Recent US Trade Policies*, ed. by R. Baldwin and A. Krueger. Chicago: University of Chicago Press, 1984.

Feenstra, R. C. Automobile prices and protection: The U.S.–Japan trade restraint. *Journal of Policy Modelling* 7 (1985): 49–68.

Greaney, T. Import now! Analysis of VIEs to increase US market shares in Japan. *Journal of International Economics* 40 (1996): 149–63.

Gruenspecht, Howard. Dumping and dynamic competition. *Journal of International Economics* 25 (1988): 225–48.

Hamilton, C. European Community protection and 1992: Voluntary export restraints added to Pacific Asia. *European Economic Review* 35 (1991): 378–87.

Harris, R. Why voluntary export restraints are voluntary. *Canadian Journal of Economics* 18 (1985): 799–809.

Hartigan, J. Dumping and signaling. *Journal of Economic Behavior and Organization* 23 (1994): 69–81.

Hemmendinger, N. Comment on Murray. In *Down in the Dumps*, ed. by R. Boltuck and R. Litan. Washington: Brookings, 1991.

Hindley, B. Dumping and the Far East trade of the European Community. *World Economy* 11 (1988): 445–64.

Hindley, B. EU anti-dumping: Has the problem gone away? *Trade Policy Review 1996/97*. London: Center for Policy Studies, 1997.

Horlick, G. The United States antidumping system. In *Antidumping Law and Practice: A Comparative Study*, ed. by J. Jackson and E. Vermule Ann Arbor: University of Michigan Press, 1989.

Irwin, D. *Managed Trade: The Case against Import Targets*. Washington: American Enterprise Institute, 1994.

Joskow, P., and A. Klevorick. A framework for analyzing predatory pricing policy. *Yale Law Journal* 89 (1979): 213–70.

Kaplan, G., L. Kamarck, and M. Parker. Cost analysis under the antidumping law. *George Washington Journal of International Law and Economics* 21 (1988): 351–409.

Klevorick, A. The current state of the law and economics of predatory pricing. *AEA Papers and Proceedings* 83 (1993): 162–67.

Krishna, K. Tariffs vs. quotas with endogenous quality. NBER Working Paper 1535. January 1985a.

Krishna, K. Protection and the product line: Monopoly and product quality. NBER Working Paper 1537. January 1985b.

Krishna, K. Trade restrictions as facilitating practices. *Journal of International Economics* 26 (1989): 251–70.

Krishna, K., S. Roy, and M. Thursby. Implementing market acceso. NBER Working Paper 5593. 1996.

Krishna, P. On the Choice of instrument: Voluntary import expansions (VIEs) vs. voluntary export restraints. Mimeo. Brown University. 1996.

Liebeler, W. Wither predatory pricing? From Areeda and Turner to Matsushita. *Notre Dame Law Review* 61 (1986): 1052–76.

Lloyd, P. *Antidumping Actions and the GATT System*. Thames Essay 9. London: Trade Policy Research Center, 1977.

McGee, R. The case to repeal the antidumping laws. *Northwestern Journal of International Law and Business* 13 (1993): 991–1062.

Messerlin, P. The EU anti-dumping regulations: A first economic appraisal. *Weltwirtschaftliches Archiv* 25 (1989): 563–87.

Murray, T. The administration of the antidumping duty law by the Department of Commerce. In *Down in the Dumps*, ed. by R. Boltuck and R. Litan. Washington: Brookings, 1996.

Palmeter, N. D. The antidumping law: A legal and administrative non-tariff barriers. In *Down in the Dumps*, ed. by R. Boltuck and R. Litan. Washington: Brookings, 1991.

Rodriguez, C. A. The quality of imports and the differential welfare effects of tariffs, quotas, and quality controls as protective devices. *Canadian Journal of Economics* 12 (1979): 439–49.

Rosendorff, P. Voluntary export restraints, antidumping procedures and domestic politics. *American Economic Review* 86 (1996): 544–61.

Santoni, G. J., and T. N. Van Cott. Import quotas: The quality adjustment problem. *Southern Economic Journal* 46 (1980): 1206–11.

Staiger, R., and F. Wolak. Strategic use of antidumping law to enforce tacit international collusion. Mimeo. Stanford University, 1991.

Saxonhouse, G. What does Japanese trade structure tell us about Japanese trade policy? *Journal of Economic Perspectives* 7 (1993): 21–43.

Stewart, T. Administration of the antidumping law: A different perspective. In *Down in the Dumps*, ed. by R. Boltuck and R. Litan. Washington: Brookings, 1991.

Viner, J. *Dumping*. Chicago: University of Chicago Press, 1923.

Wares, W. *The Theory of Dumping and American Commercial Policy*. Lexington, MA: Heath, 1977.

Weinstein, D. Competition and unilateral dumping. *Journal of International Economics* 32 (1992): 379–88.

Effective Rate of Protection

Traditional trade-theoretic models are concerned with trade in final goods. However, trade in intermediate goods and raw materials forms a significant proportion of world trade. In contrast with the traditional models domestic primary factors are combined with traded intermediate goods or raw materials to produce final goods for trade or domestic use. Since tariffs and other interventions in trade can affect outputs (final goods) as well as inputs (intermediate goods and raw materials), trade theorists have recently focused on whether the entire protective structure can somehow be collapsed into meaningful indexes of protection so that we can analyze more readily the traditional matters, such as the resource-allocational implications of protection.

Toward this end, trade theorists, following Corden (1966), Johnson (1965), Balassa (1965), and others, have focused on the protection conferred by the protective structure on the domestic value added in various productive activities. The reason for this can be seen from a simple example. Suppose that the home economy is producing automobiles using steel (an intermediate good) as well as labor and capital, and both autos and steel are traded in world markets at fixed prices. A tariff on imports of automobiles can be expected to encourage domestic auto production, but a simultaneous imposition of a tariff on steel could more than offset the protective, resource-allocational effect of the tariff on automobiles.

In the absence of any imported intermediate goods such as steel, the nominal tariff on automobiles would have indicated accurately the protective effect on automobiles. Underlying the attempt to define the effective rate of protection (ERP) when intermediates are imported is the hope that it would be able to perform analytically the role that nominal tariffs play in traditional models without intermediate imports. Thus in the traditional model, with two traded goods produced with standard restrictions on the production functions by two primary factors in given endowment and with the small-country assumption, a tariff on a good would lead to a rise in the gross output of the protected good, a rise in the nominal value of the output, a rise in the use of each primary factor therein, a rise in the real value added therein (which coincides with output when real value added is defined as deflated by the price of "own output"), and a rise in the nominal value added therein (which coincides with the nominal value of output). For two traded goods and n ($n > 2$) primary factors, a tariff on one good will continue to imply increases in output and nominal value of output, though not necessarily in each of the primary factors used therein. For n ($n > 2$) traded goods and m ($m \geq n$) primary factors, a tariff on one good will still increase output and nominal value of output, but when more than one tariff is imposed (implying more than one price change), even this cannot be asserted for the good with the highest tariff.

The objective of ERP theory, then, consists in devising a concept of protection that, in the presence of tariff structures involving the imports of intermediate goods, constitutes in effect an index that will perform the same tasks nominal tariffs perform in the nominal tariff theory: predicting accurately the changes in gross output, nominal value of output, primary factor allocation, real value added, and/or nominal value added.

15.1   Two Definitions

Two basic definitions of an ERP index have been developed in the literature. In Corden (1966) and Anderson and Naya (1969) it is defined as the proportionate increment in value added per unit level of an activity brought about by the tariff structure over its free-trade value, whereas in Corden (1969) and Leith (1968) it is defined as the proportionate change (due to the tariff structure) in the "price" of value added (with the assumption that such a price can be defined meaningfully).

Corden-Anderson-Naya Definition

The first definition can be stated formally as follows: The ERP on an activity $y = (y_1, \ldots, y_n)$ involving n internationally traded goods (y_i is the net output of good i at a unit level of this activity) is defined as

$$\text{ERP} = \frac{\sum_1^n p_i y_i}{\sum_1^n p_i^* y_i} - 1, \tag{15.1}$$

where p_i is the domestic price of good i and p_i^* is its world price. If the activity produces one traded output using only primary factors, one element of y (e.g., i) will be unity and all other elements will be zero. In such a case

$$\text{ERP} = \frac{p_i}{p_i^*} - 1. \tag{15.2}$$

If tariffs were the only form of trade intervention, then p_i would equal $p_i^*(1 + t_i)$, where t_i is the *ad valorem* tariff rate on good i and ERP reduces to t_i the nominal tariff on good i.

The ERP definition embodied in equation 15.1 considers only the traded-goods components of a productive activity; it assumes that either there are no nontraded inputs and outputs or there are some and their value is treated as part of the value added. There is controversy in the literature as to whether nontraded goods should be implicitly treated as value added, as in equation (15.1), or whether they should be "decomposed" into their traded-goods and value-added contents, with the traded-goods content added to the y_i in equation (15.1) so that the modified y_i can be interpreted as total (direct and indirect) net output of traded good i for a unit level of this activity. Clearly, except in the case of a Leontief input-output technology, this attempt at decomposition can lead to difficulties.[1]

Corden-Leith Definition

An operationally meaningful "price" of value added is necessary to give content to the second definition. Production functions relating output Q to n primary factors (F) and m intermediates (M) are separable in the sense that Q can be written as $Q = G(\phi(F), M)$, where G is concave and homogeneous of degree 1 in ϕ and M while ϕ is homogeneous of degree 1 and concave in F. So one can meaningfully talk of $\phi(F)$ as the "quantity" of "value added" with a price per unit $p_v = pG_1(\phi, M)$, where p is the price per unit of output of Q in terms of some numéraire and G_1 is the partial derivative of G with respect to its first argument.

These "price" and "quantity" definitions can better understood if one views the production process as consisting of two stages. In the first stage, primary factors are combined to produce an intermediate unit called "value added" using the production function ϕ; in the second stage, this intermediate unit is combined with other intermediates M to produce Q. In a competitive equilibrium the marginal value product of the intermediate value added, pG_1, must equal its price; our definition p_v of the price of value added ensures precisely that. Given p_v of the first stage, in a competitive equilibrium the vector of marginal value products of primary factors, $p_v\phi_1$, will equal the factor price vector w. If one were to view the production process in an integrated manner by collapsing the two stages into one, the vector of marginal value products of primary factors, $pG_1\phi_1$, would equal the price vector w in a competitive equilibrium. Our definition of p_v ensures this because $pG_1\phi = w$. Thus, in defining ϕ as the quantity of value-added and p_v as the price unit of value added, we get definitions that are both meaningful and mutually consistent. (The separability of the production process is clearly crucial for this.)

The proportionate increment definition and the proportionate change definition generally yield different ERP numbers. However, in the special

---

1. For an extended treatment of the issue see Corden (1966), Balassa (1965), and Ray (1973).

case of a separable production function where the intermediates are used in a fixed proportion to output, both definitions amount to the same thing.

15.2   Predictive Power of ERP Indexes

Many theorists have shown that except in the case of separability, the predictive power of ERP indexes is severely limited in primary factor re-allocation and gross output changes. That is, if $ERP_1 > ERP_2$ in a two-activity model, one cannot necessarily infer that activity 1 will have attracted more of the primary factors (an inference that is valid in the 2×2-model nominal tariff framework, as evidenced by the Stolper-Samuelson theorem) or will have more gross output.[2]

We have suggested, however, that ERP theory cannot be seriously expected to do everything that nominal tariff theory does; for example, it is extremely improbable that an ERP index is able to predict gross output changes despite the presence of intermediates.[3] Hence we need to pause and consider whether we can ask a somewhat different question, founded on an analytically more meaningful analogy, of ERP theory so as to compare it more sensibly with nominal-tariff theory.

In the traditional analysis of nominal tariffs, the tariff leads to a change in the price of output and hence to a change in output quantity. The change in value added follows because value added coincides with gross output. In the case of two primary factors, the unidirectional change in each primary factor used also follows, by the Stolper-Samuelson theorem. The basic proposition, however, consists in relating the change in the quantity of output to the change in the price of output, thanks to the nominal tariff structure. Indeed this may be taken as the primary proposition of the traditional theory concerning the effect of a tariff structure on resource allocation.

Question 1

The task of the theory of effective protection may then be conceived essentially as one of examining, in a model allowing imported inputs, the following question: Is it possible to devise a "price" of value added that can be used as an index to rank different activities such that, in exact

---

2. See, in particular, Ramaswami and Srinivasan (1971), Jones (1971), and Bhagwati and Srinivasan (1973).

3. In Bhagwati and Srinivasan (1973), which should be read for the full analysis and to supplement the highly abbreviated review below.

analogy with the nominal-tariff theory, the change in the "quantity" of value added can be predicted correctly? If such an index can be devised, then we will be able to treat it as the exact analogue of the nominal tariff in the traditional model.

Question 2

One more dimension of the problem, which does not exist with nominal-tariff theory, is the following: Can such an index be measured from observed or observable data without the need to solve the general-equilibrium (production) system for the two situations between which the resource-allocational shift is being predicted? If it cannot be, the index will not be of practical value. Indeed, to compute it, one has to solve the full system and will thus already know the shift in value added brought about by the tariff structure.

Having clarified these two central questions, we can proceed to answer question 1.[4] In a general-equilibrium model with any number of primary factors, traded intermediates, and goods, one can express the proportionate change in nominal value added (consequent to a change in tariff structure) in an activity as the sum of two terms. The first term is a suitably weighted average of the proportionate changes in the prices of inputs and outputs involved in that activity; the second is a suitably weighted average of the proportionate changes in the quantities of primary factor inputs.

Further, under two alternative sets of sufficient conditions, the first term can indeed be treated as a workable ERP index, with the second term serving as the measure of the change in quantity of value added that the ERP index is to predict. What are these two sets of sufficient conditions? The first set of conditions restricts the class of production functions to separable production functions. In this case a physical measure of value added can be defined so that the first term (the ERP index) represents the proportionate change in the price of a physical unit of value added and the second term represents the proportionate change in the quantity (in physical units) of value added. The other set of conditions restricts the tariff changes to a range and restricts the number of final goods to two so that the first term (the ERP index)[5] helps in predicting the sign of the second term (which, again, in the absence of separable production functions, no longer represents the proportionate change in value added in physical units).

4. The formal argumentation and proofs are in Bhagwati and Srinivasan (1973).

5. In the absence of separable production functions, this index no longer represents the proportionate change in "price" of value added.

Now we can answer question 2. The answer is not helpful to the proponents of the ERP theory, for even the use of separability assumptions will not suffice, in general, to allow one to calculate the "price" of value added when noninfinitesimal tariffs are involved, without first having to solve for the resource-allocational effects of the protective tariff structure in general equilibrium.[6] (This is demonstrated at length in Bhagwati and Srinivasan 1973.)

Even though the theoretical validity of ERP as an indicator of resource pull is somewhat less than was initially asserted or hoped for, it continues to be a nice way to summarize the information on the protective structure resulting from tariffs on inputs and outputs. It is thus of descriptive value in many empirical studies of protection, especially in the developing countries. If ERPs are used with some care, and subject to the caveats noted above, even their analytical use can be somewhat suggestive.

There have been attempts to use the ERP also as a criterion for social cost-benefit analysis. If the ERP for a project is below those for other activities, it is said that the project should be accepted. This is generally an inappropriate method, however.

Recommended Readings

Anderson, J., and S. Naya. Substitution and two concepts of effective rate of protection. *American Economic Review* 59 (1969): 607–12.

Balassa, B. Tariff protection in industrial countries: An evaluation. *Journal of Political Economy* 73 (1965): 573–94. Reprinted in *Readings in International Economics*, ed. by R. E. Caves and H. G. Johnson. Homewood, Il: Irwin, 1968.

Basevi, G. The U.S. tariff structures: Estimate of effective rates of protection of U.S. industries and industrial labor. *Review of Economics and Statistics* 48 (1966): 147–60.

Bhagwati, J., and T. N. Srinivasan. The general equilibrium theory of effective protection and resource allocation. *Journal of International Economics* 3 (1973): 259–81.

Bruno, M. Protection and a tariff change under general equilibrium. *Journal of International Economics* 3 (1973): 205–25.

Corden, W. M. Effective protective rates in the general equilibrium model: A geometric note. *Oxford Economic Papers* 21 (1969): 135–41.

Corden, W. M. The structure of a tariff system and the effective protective rate. *Journal of Political Economy* 74 (1966): 221–37. Reprinted in Bhagwati, J., ed., *International Trade: Selected Readings*, 1981, Cambridge, MA: MIT Press.

Ethier, W. J. General equilibrium theory and the concept of effective protection. In *Effective Tariff Protection*, ed. by H. G. Grubel and H. G. Johnson. Geneva: General Agreement on Tariffs and Trade and Graduate Institute of International Studies, 1971.

Finger, J. M. Substitution and the effective rate of protection. *Journal of Political Economy* 77 (1969): 972–75.

---

6. Exceptions are production functions with fixed coefficients on imported inputs or of Cobb-Douglas form in all inputs.

Grubel, H. G. Effective tariff protection: A non-specialist introduction to the theory, policy implications, and controversies. In *Effecitve Tariff Protection*, ed. by H. G. Grubel and H. G. Johnson. Geneva: General Agreement on Tariffs and Trade and Graduate Institute of International Studies, 1971.

Grubel, H. G., and P. J. Lloyd. Factor substitution and effective tariff rates. *Review of Economic Studies* 38 (1971): 95–103.

Johnson, H. G. The theory of tariff structures with special reference to world trade and development. In *Trade and Development*, ed. by H. G. Johnson and P. B. Kenen. Geneva: Institut des Hautes Etudes Internationales, 1965.

Jones, R. W. Effective protection and substitution. *Journal of International Economics* 1 (1971): 59–82.

Khang, C. Factor substitution in the theory of effective protection: A general equilibrium analysis. *Journal of International Economics* 3 (1973): 227–44.

Kreinin, M. E., J. B. Ramsey, and J. Kmenta. Factor substitution and effective protection reconsidered. *American Economic Review* 61 (1971): 891–900.

Leith, J. C. Substitution and supply elasticities in calculating the effective protective rate. *Quarterly Journal of Economics* 82 (1968): 588–601.

Ramaswami, V. K., and T. N. Srinivasan. Tariff structure and resource allocation in the presence of factor substitution. In *Trade, Balance of Payments and Growth: Papers in International Economics in Honor of Charles P. Kindleberger*, ed. by J. Bhagwati et al. Amsterdam: North-Holland, 1971.

Ray, A. Non-traded inputs and effective protection: A general equilibrium analysis. *Journal of International Economics* 3 (1973): 245–58.

Sendo, Y. The theory of effective protection in general equilibrium: An extension of the Bhagwati-Srinivasan analysis. *Journal of International Economics* 4 (1974): 213–15.

Tan, A. H. H. Differential tariffs, negative value-added and the theory of effective protection. *American Economic Review* 60 (1970): 107–16.

Travis, W. P. The effective rate of protection and the question of labor protection in the United States. *Journal of Political Economy* 76 (1968): 443–61.

Uekawa, Y. The theory of effective protection, resource allocation and the Stolper-Samuelson theorem. *Journal of International Economics* 9 (1979): 151–71.

16 Transfer Problem

We can now examine the effects on international equilibrium of a transfer (e.g., a reparation payment) from one trading country to another. Dealing with this problem in the framework of two tradable goods, we find that the major difference made to the model is that Walras's law no longer holds at the country level; each country will spend differently from its income by the amount of the transfer.

The transfer problem can be analyzed simply by differentiating the classical system of chapter 12 and appendix C with respect to the transfer and solving it for the variable in which we are interested. If we solve the system for the new equilibrium terms of trade, we can solve the problem also in two stages by working out the excess demand (supply) for a good (the other good) at the pretransfer terms of trade and then inferring the direction of the price change by reference to the stability condition.

In this chapter we solve the system directly and also use the Samuelsonian two-stage derivation to get the basic criterion for the effect of the transfer on the terms of trade. Next we analyze the effect of the transfer on the welfare of the transferor country by way of the transferee country. Finally we discuss some extensions of the basic analysis.

16.1 Direct Solution

Assume that the home country I is the transferor and the foreign country II the transferee. With the transfer fixed in terms of good 1 initially at level T, we must rewrite the classical system of thirteen equations as follows: Equation (12.7) becomes

$$D_i = D_e + T, \tag{16.1}$$

equation (12.10) becomes

$$D_i^* = D_e^* - \frac{T}{p}, \tag{16.2}$$

and equation (12.13c′) becomes

$$M = \left(\frac{1}{p}\right) \cdot M^* - \frac{T}{p}. \tag{16.3}$$

It is then easy to see that the effect on international equilibrium of the transfer can be derived simply by differentiating equation (16.3) with respect to T and setting the initial T equal to zero on the assumption that the pretransfer situation was characterized by balanced trade. Thus, noting that $T = 0$ initially and $pM = M^*$, denoting the marginal propensities to import as

$$m = p \cdot \frac{\partial M}{\partial D_e}$$

and

$$m^* = \frac{1}{p} \cdot \frac{\partial M^*}{\partial D_e^*},$$

and recalling that

$$\varepsilon = -\frac{p}{M} \cdot \frac{dM}{dp}$$

and

$$\varepsilon^* = \frac{1/p}{M^*} \cdot \frac{dM^*}{d(1/p)},$$

we can derive

$$1 - m - m^* = M(\varepsilon + \varepsilon^* - 1) \cdot \frac{dp}{dT},$$

which yields the counterpart of equation (12.14):

$$\frac{dp}{dT} = \frac{1 - m - m^*}{M(\varepsilon + \varepsilon^* - 1).} \tag{16.4}$$

The transfer by country I to country II will therefore lead to an improvement in the terms of trade of country I, or leave them unchanged, or cause their deterioration according as

$$m + m^* \gtreqless 1 \tag{16.5}$$

provided that the stability condition is satisfied.

16.2 Two-Stage Derivation

The same result can be derived more readily by examining the impact of the transfer at a constant goods-price ratio and developing the excess demand function for a good. With the goods-price ratio constant, the production in both countries in our model will not change; the excess demand changes will be wholly due to demand changes. As for demand changes, if we assume the pretransfer goods-price ratio as given, the transfer T by country I will change the demand in country I for good 2, which is country I's importable good, by

$$\frac{m}{p} \cdot dD_e.$$

On the other hand, the change in the demand for good 2 in country II, which receives the transfer, is

$$q^* \cdot dD_e^*,$$

where $q^* = \partial C_2^* / \partial D_e^*$, the marginal propensity to consume the exportable good 2 in country II.

The total change in the demand for good 2 in the world as a whole therefore is

$$\frac{M}{p} \cdot dD_e + q^* \cdot dD_e^*,$$

and the transferor country, I, will have excess demand for or supply of the importable good according as $q^* \gtreqless m$. If stability is satisfied, the transferor's terms of trade will improve remain unchanged, or worsen according as

$$q^* \lesseqgtr m. \tag{16.6}$$

But $dD_e = -dT$ and $dD_e^* = dT/p$. Therefore the total change in the demand for good 2 reduces to $(q^* - m)(dT/p)$. However, $q^* + m^* = 1$ and $q + m = 1$, where $q = \partial C / \partial D_e$. Thus equation (16.6) can be rewritten as

$$(1 - m - m^*) \lesseqgtr 0, \tag{16.5'}$$

or as

$$m + m^* \gtreqless 1 \tag{16.5''}$$

(which is identical to 16.5). The full formula for the transfer-induced change in the terms of trade can be derived by noting that the excess demand for good 2, $(1 - m - m^*)(dT/p)$, has to be eliminated by an excess supply of good 2 induced by a change in the terms of trade. With (initial) $T = 0$, we can show that $(M/p)(\varepsilon + \varepsilon^* - 1)dp$ is the excess supply of good 2 resulting from the change in the terms of trade, and the transfer-induced constant-price change in the excess demand for good 2 which it must equal is $(1 - m - m^*)(dT/p)$. We can then deduce that

$$\frac{dp}{dT} = \frac{1 - m - m^*}{M(\varepsilon + \varepsilon^* - 1)}. \tag{16.7}$$

16.3   Welfare Impact

The welfare impacts of a transfer on the transferor and the transferee in the above model are readily derived. Note, however, that a decline in the terms of trade for the transferee will reduce the welfare improvement of the transfer; the "primary gain" from the transfer will be reduced by the "secondary loss" from the worsened terms of trade. Can the transferee actually be immiserized? Following Leontief (1936) and Samuelson (1954), we can show that market stability will rule out this paradox; however, it can be resurrected for modifications of the model, even if stability is assumed.

Let the social-utility function be

$$U^* = U^*(C_1^*, C_2^*),$$

with standard properties. Then we can derive

$$\frac{dU^*}{dT} = \frac{\partial U^*}{\partial C_1^*}\left(\frac{\partial Q_1^*}{\partial p} + p\frac{\partial Q_2^*}{\partial p} + \frac{M^*}{p}\frac{dp}{dT} + 1 - \frac{T}{p}\frac{dp}{dT}\right).$$

By profit maximization,

$$\frac{\partial Q_1^*}{\partial p} + p\frac{\partial Q_2^*}{\partial p} = 0.$$

Evaluating at $T = 0$, we then have

$$\frac{dU^*}{dT} = \frac{\partial U^*}{\partial C_1^*}\left(\frac{M^*}{p}\frac{dp}{dT} + 1\right). \tag{16.8}$$

Substituting for dp/dT from equation (12.7), we get

$$\frac{dU^*}{dT} = \frac{\partial U^*}{\partial C_1^*}\left(\frac{1 - m - m^*}{\varepsilon + \varepsilon^* - 1} + 1\right) \tag{16.9}$$

$$= \frac{\partial U^*}{\partial C_1^*}\left(\frac{\varepsilon' + \varepsilon'^*}{\varepsilon + \varepsilon^* - 1}\right) \tag{16.10}$$

$$> 0 \quad \text{if } \varepsilon + \varepsilon^* > 1,$$

since the compensated elasticities in the numerator are necessarily posi tive. Therefore stability rules out the paradox of an immiserizing trans feree (and equally that of a welfare-improving transferor).

16.4 Immiserizing Transfers: Other Models

Stability can be shown to be consistent with the paradox of immiserizing transfers in two classes of cases. First, as the analysis of Brecher and Bhagwati (1981a) immediately indicates, a bilateral transfer in a multi-country world could immiserize the transferee, consistent with stability. This is seen by noting that if country I is the transferor and country II is the transferee and country III is neither, equation (16.9) is no longer applicable, since the elasticity terms in the denominator will now refer to all three countries whereas the primary-impact marginal propensity terms will refer only to the countries that engage in the transfer process. Therefore equation (16.9) will no longer yield (16.10), with only compensated terms in the numerator. Immiserizing transfers will therefore arise, consistent with stability, under conditions spelled out in Brecher and Bhagwati (1981a).

Yet another instance of immiserizing transfers is provided in Brecher and Bhagwati (1982), where the transfer takes place with a (production) distortion in place, but in the two-good, two-country model analyzed above. Brecher and Bhagwati show that for the paradox to arise in the stable case, it is necessary for the importable good of the transferee country to be an inferior good for the world as a whole (in fact this inferiority must exist specifically in the transferor country). The intuitive explanation for this immiserization is that the deterioration in the transferee country's terms of trade leads (as usual) to an increased output of the transferee's importable good. This good, however, is already "overproduced" at home because of the distorting production tax *cum* subsidy. Thus the change in relative prices has the additional effect of exacerbating the existing "overproduction." The resulting extra cost may be enough to ensure a decline in welfare for the transferee country.[1]

Brecher and Bhagwati also note that in the case of aid, there may be "aid tying." This may mean that the transfer of aid itself would require the transferee to impose a distortion to satisfy the aid-tying constraint. The cost of this transfer-induced endogenous distortion may then be sufficient to enable the transfer to immiserize the transferee, consistent with stability.[2]

---

1. These results have been further analyzed and synthesized with the multicountry results by Bhagwati, Brecher, and Hatta (1983).

2. Another instance of an endogenous distortion is considered by Bhagwati, Brecher, and Hatta (1985). They allow for the transfers to be lobbied for by potential recipients in the transferee country, modeling transfer disposal therefore as a DUP activity that directly wastes real resources (a phenomenon more centrally dealt with in chapter 34).

16.5   Transfer Criterion in Other Models

Some extensions of the criterion for transfer-induced change in the terms of trade have arisen, primarily in the context of the old, classical "presumption" that the terms of trade would turn against the transferor (that $m + m^* < 1$ or, equivalently, that $q + q^* > 1$).

Johnson (1956) has argued that given only that the sum of the marginal propensities to spend on the importable and the exportable is unity, the "equal ignorance" argument suggests that there is no presumption that the average marginal propensity to spend on exportables is either greater or less than half. Therefore, for the classical presumption to be resurrected, one would have to introduce other factors such as tariffs and transport costs. Following Samuelson (1956), it is easy to see, for instance, that if the transport costs are incurred in the form of the exportable good of the importing country, the classical presumption will indeed arise. That is, the "effective" $\hat{m}$ and $\hat{m}^*$ will be reduced below the "primary" m and m^* by this leakage from propensities to spend on importables. Now, since the equal-presumption argument applies to the primary m and m^*, it follows that $\hat{m} + \hat{m}^* < 1$, so the transferor's terms of trade will deteriorate.

Another interesting variant is Samuelson's (1971) use of a model where income is substituted for leisure in a Ricardian-Marshallian framework with labor as the only factor. With all prices unchanged, and with the Marshallian assumption of a constant marginal utility of income, we find that the effect of a transfer must fall fully on the (nontraded) good—leisure—with absolutely no change in the amounts consumed of the two goods, wheat and cloth, in either country. At the same time complete specialization in production implies that the payers in the transferor country are all working more, so there should be an increment in the output of the exportable good. Similarly the recipients in the transferee country will work less, and the production of their exportable good will fall. With consumptions unchanged, an increase in the output of the transferor's exportable and a fall in the output of the transferee's exportable can only result in a deterioration in the terms of trade of the transferor country, given stability. In this model, the "propensities" to produce replace the propensities to consume as the determinants of the sign of the terms of trade change after a transfer.[3]

3. Samuelson's model was inspired by a desire to produce the "classical presumption" that the terms of trade would turn against the transferor. Johnson (1956) argued that no such presumption could be established, since only ignorance can come from ignorance. However, Jones (1970) argued that a presumption may be established in favor of a demand bias at the margin in favor of the importable good, which would produce an "anticlassical" result.

The reader should also consult the extension of the transfer-problem criterion by Jones (1970) to a model with a nontraded good and that by Johnson (1956) to the Keynesian framework with transfer-induced changing output levels rather than changing terms of trade.

Recommended Readings

Bhagwati, J. N., R. A. Brecher, and T. Hatta. The generalized theory of transfers and welfare Bilateral transfers in a multilateral world. *American Economic Review* 73 (1983): 606–18.

Bhagwati, J. N., R. A. Brecher, and T. Hatta. The generalized theory of transfers and welfare Exogenous (policy-imposed) and endogenous (transfer-induced) distortions. *Quarterly Journal of Economics* 100 (1985): 697–714.

Brecher, R., and J. Bhagwati. Foreign ownership and the theory of trade and welfare. *Journal of Political Economy* 89 (1981): 497–511.

Brecher, R., and J. Bhagwati. Immiserizing transfer from abroad. *Journal of International Economics* 13 (1982): 353–64.

Chipman, J. S. The transfer problem once again. In *Trade, Stability, and Macroeconomics: Essays in Honor of L. A. Metzler*, ed. by G. Horwich and P. A. Samuelson. New York: Academic, 1974.

Johnson, H. G. The transfer problem: A note on criteria for changes in the terms of trade. *Economica*, N. S., 22 (1955): 113–21.

Johnson, H. G. The transfer problem and exchange stability. *Journal of Political Economy* 64 (1956): 212–25. Reprinted in H. G. Johnson, *International Trade and Economic Growth*. London: Allen and Unwin, 1958.

Jones, R. W. The transfer problem revisited. *Economica*, N. S., 37 (1970): 178–84.

Jones, R. W. Presumption and the transfer problem. *Journal of International Economics* 5 (1975): 263–74.

Keynes, J. M. The German transfer problem. *Economic Journal* 39 (1929): 1–7. Reprinted in *Readings in the Theory of International Trade*, ed. by H. S. Ellis and L. A. Metzler. Philadelphia: Blakiston, 1949.

Leontief, W. Note on the pure theory of capital transfer. In *Explorations in Economics: Notes and Essays Contributed in Honor of F. W. Taussig*. New York: McGraw-Hill, 1936.

Metzler, L. A. The transfer problem reconsidered. *Journal of Political Economics* 50 (1942): 397–414. Reprinted in *Readings in the Theory of International Trade*, ed. by H. S. Ellis and L. A. Metzler. Philadelphia: Blakiston, 1949.

Metzler, L. A. A multi-country theory of income transfers. *Journal of Political Economy* 59 (1951): 14–29.

Mundell, R. A. The pure theory of international trade. *American Economic Review* 50 (1960): 75–80.

Ohlin, B. The reparation problem: A discussion. *Economic Journal* 39 (1929): 172–78. Reprinted in *Readings in the Theory of International Trade*, ed. by H. S. Ellis and L. A. Metzler. Philadelphia: Blakiston, 1949.

Samuelson, P. A. The transfer problem and transport costs: The terms of trade when impediments are absent. *Economic Journal* 62 (1952): 278–304. Reprinted in *Readings in International Economics*, ed. by R. E. Caves and H. G. Johnson. Homewood, IL: Irwin, 1968.

Samuelson, P. A. The transfer problem and transport costs: Analysis of effects of trade impediments. *Economic Journal* 64 (1954): 264–89. Reprinted in *Readings in International Economics*, ed. by R. E. Caves and H. G. Johnson. Homewood, IL: Irwin, 1968.

Samuelson, P. A. On the trail of conventional beliefs about the transfer problem. In *Trade, Balance of Payments, and Growth: Papers in International Economics in Honor of Charles P. Kindleberger*, ed. by J. Bhagwati et al. Amsterdam: North-Holland, 1971.

III TRADE AND WELFARE IN AN OPEN ECONOMY

We now turn to the oldest issues in the theory of international trade: the desirability of alternative types of policy intervention (including the limiting case of free trade) in an open economy. This area of international economic theory is best described, as by Meade, as the theory of trade and welfare.

17.1 Major Concepts and Distinctions

Before we can discuss the effect of alternative policies on welfare, we must define *welfare*. The traditional economic approach is to define welfare, or utility, as derived from the consumption of goods and services. Thus, a typical utility function would be written as $U = U(C_1, C_2, \ldots, C_n)$, where there are n goods and services and C_i stands for their consumption levels $(i = 1, \ldots, n)$. However, it is perfectly sensible to consider societies as deriving welfare also from what economists like to call "noneconomic" objectives. Thus, for example, certain types of production (e.g., for defense) may be deemed politically important and may be desired even though they involve a cost in terms of goods and services. Or, a nation's politicians and planners may like self-sufficiency and may therefore require the economist to consider the level of imports as an additional argument in their objective function. In principle, trade theorists have therefore distinguished among four major types of such "noneconomic" objectives: production, consumption, factor employment in specific sectors, and trade level (or self-sufficiency). We will address the implication of these objectives in chapter 28.

Again, even when the utility function for society is defined, we have to distinguish between static and dynamic welfare analyses. In the typical trade-theoretic analysis the effect of trade policy on current welfare is analyzed. However, as in optimal-growth theory we can optimize over more than one period and discuss intertemporal optimization, as in chapter 36.

Next, in discussing the welfare impact of different policies, we need to be clear as to the groups over which welfare is defined. Typically trade theorists distinguish between *national* and *world* welfare. However, when we consider discriminatory trade arrangements, such as customs unions or free-trade areas, we must also add the member countries as a relevant group in order to analyze the welfare impact of, say, tariff change.

The concept of *national* welfare itself is not unambiguous. The distributional impact of different policies has to be considered, and we will see in the next chapter how we can get around this thorny issue and still rank one policy as unambiguously superior to another. Specifically we will argue for such rankings by appealing to the notion that a policy change will be considered potentially desirable if, for every income distribution, it is possible to increase the welfare of one member of the group without reducing the welfare of the others.

However, we may well be interested in the specific income-distributional outcomes of two policies where such redistribution is not possible and where the market-determined outcomes must be treated as final. If so, the impact on the real incomes of specific individuals or factor classes would become important to look at in policy evaluations, and interpersonal comparisons of utility would become necessary.

Yet another complication would arise from the fact that the individuals over whom welfare is defined may become ambiguous. Aside from intergenerational issues, this problem arises typically when we consider international labor migration. Should "national" welfare then include or exclude migrants' welfare? This issue comes up in chapter 33.

17.2   Alternative Policy Instruments and Hierarchy of Policies

Our typical procedure will be to analyze different market structures characterized by alternative types of market imperfections, technological pathologies, and government-imposed distortions. For these different situations we will wish to consider the optimal (first-best) policy intervention that is called for. At the same time we will also proceed frequently to discuss whether in the absence of the first-best policy the government can use alternative second-best policies to improve welfare. A logical consequence of this analysis is to investigate whether we can rank-order these second-best policies, saying that one is generally better than the other. Where such rank ordering is possible, we will be able to define a hierarchy of alternative policies, going from the best to the second-best to the third-best, and so on. Therefore it is necessary now to define the alternative policies that we will consider in investigating the nature of optimal and next-best policy intervention for a variety of situations.

Endogenous Policy

We need to note at this stage that we have assumed so far, and will continue to do so for the bulk of the book, that policy can be chosen by the economist and sold to the government, which acts simply as a "puppet" government, implementing the economist's prescription. In reality, policy is endogenously determined. Recent political-economy-theoretic models, considered in chapter 34 and in sections of other chapters as well, assume instead that lobbies act on a "clearinghouse" government or that governments have a life of their own, being "self-willed," and that their preferences also must be taken into account in determining policy outcomes.

As we will see below, endogenizing policy raises a variety of questions, including the unhappy possibility of losing the degree of freedom to vary policy at will. Thus, if a tariff is fully determined in political-economy equilibrium, then an economist "outside" the model is unable to say how welfare will be affected if the tariff is eliminated and free trade restored. If this dilemma is not resolved, then we cannot rank-order different policies in the manner indicated above and practiced for much of the rest of the book. We merely note these problems here and will return to them later in the text.

Tariffs and Trade Subsidies

We discussed in chapter 12 the impact of a tariff or a trade subside on trade equilibrium and on the offer curve of a country adopting such a policy.

Figure 17.1 illustrates simply the equilibrium that would arise in the presence of a tariff, so as to remind the reader of the basic production,

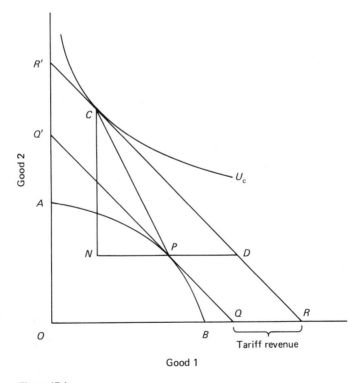

Figure 17.1

consumption, and trade aspects of such a policy equilibrium. *AB* is the production-possibility curve, and there is a tariff at an *ad valorem* rate *PD/PN*. With a world price ratio *PN/CN* (defined as the relative price of the importable good 2), *CP* is the world price line. The domestic price ratio is *DN/CN*, with *CDR* as the domestic price line. Evidently therefore

$$\frac{DN}{CN} = \frac{PN}{CN}\left(1 + \frac{PD}{PN}\right);$$

that is, the domestic relative price of the importable good equals the world price plus the tariff. National income is *OQ* in units of good 1, expenditure is *OR*, and the difference is *QR* (the tariff revenue, which is assumed to be redistributed as an income subsidy to consumers). When *OR* is spent at domestic prices, tariff revenue worth *QR* is generated by the resulting trade of *CN* imports and *PN* exports, so that our illustration is consistent.

Production Tax *cum* Subsidy

The next policy instrument we illustrate is a production tax *cum* subsidy. The "*cum*" means that since we wish to refer to a policy that affects the relative incentive to produce alternative goods, we may either tax the good(s) we wish to discourage in production or subsidize the good(s) we wish to encourage in production or use a suitable combination of the taxes and subsidies. The phrase "tax *cum* subsidy" enables us therefore to leave open the precise combination of taxes and subsidies that will be used to change the relative price ratio that we seek to change.

A production tax *cum* subsidy is evidently aimed at changing the relative goods-price ratio faced by producing agents in the economy. For a small, open economy, the resulting equilibrium is illustrated in figure 17.2. There, with the world price line at *PC*, consumption continues to occur at the world prices, since the production tax *cum* subsidy does not affect the consumers' ability to consume at world prices. (This was not true for the tariff illustration in figure 17.1, because a tariff clearly would change equally the prices faced by both producers and consumers in the domestic markets.) Production, however, now reflects the tax-*cum*-subsidy inclusive price line *PR*, which is flatter than the world price line *PC* because we are assuming that production of good 1 is being taxed and/or that production of good 2 is being subsidized.

National income at factor cost will be *OR* in units of good 1. Expenditure at market prices will be *OQ*, with *QR* representing the production subsidy payments in the case of a pure subsidy on production of good 2. If we were considering a tax on producing good 1 instead, it would be appropriate to look at the vertical axis; then, by identical argu-

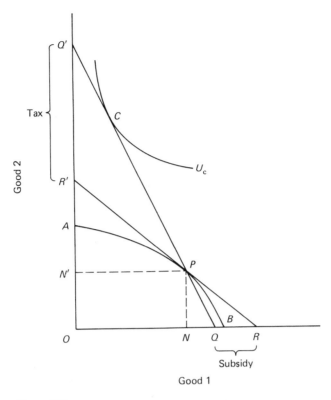

Figure 17.2

ment, we would see that national income measured in terms of good 2 is OQ', expenditure is OR', and tax payments by producers of good 1 amount to $Q'R'$. The real equilibrium is identical in these alternatives. The tax rate on production of good 1 is $Q'R'/Q'N'$, with the relationship between world and domestic relative prices of good 2 given by

$$\frac{PN'}{Q'N'(1-t)} = \frac{PN'}{R'N'}.$$

The equivalent subsidy rate on production of good 2 is QR/QN, with the relationship between world and domestic prices given by

$$\frac{QN}{PN}(1+s) = \frac{RN}{PN}.$$

Consumption Tax *cum* Subsidy

The consumption-tax-*cum*-subsidy equilibrium can be shown as in figure 17.3. Production will take place at world prices, but consumption choice

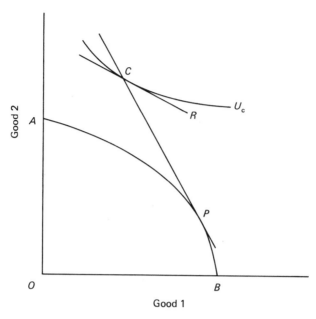

Figure 17.3

will be at the tax-*cum*-subsidy inclusive prices. Thus figure 17.3 shows production at tangency of the production-possibility curve at P with the world price line CP, whereas consumption is at nontangency with the world price line but at tangency with the domestic tax-*cum*-subsidy inclusive price line CR. It will be evident now that the consumption tax *cum* subsidy illustrated shows a net increase in the price of good 2 relative to world prices and therefore reflects a tax on consuming good 2 or a subsidy on consuming good 1, or a combination of the two policies.

Equivalences

As can be seen from a comparison of figures 17.1–17.3 and our analysis based on them, under free trade a tariff affects both consumption and production decisions equally (by changing the domestic prices faced by producers and consumers equally), whereas the production tax *cum* subsidy does not affect consumption choices and the consumption tax *cum* subsidy does not affect production choices. Thus evidently a tariff (or a trade subsidy) can be decomposed into a combination of production- and consumption-tax-*cum*-subsidy policies. A production-tax-*cum*-subsidy policy may be equivalently decomposed into uniform tax *cum* subsidy on all factors of production (including intermediates); it does not matter whether one "tax-*cum*-subsidizes" the gross value of ouput or the gross cost of factors. But we will also want to consider differential factor tax

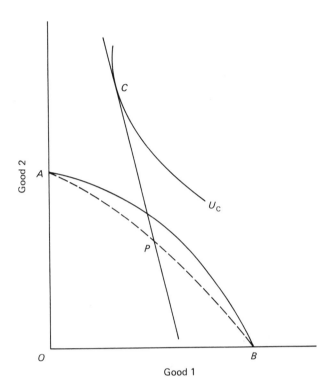

Figure 17.4

cum subsidies, where only some of the factors of production are taxed or subsidized (as in the United Kingdom's Selective Employment Tax, which taxes labor use by the service sector).

Factor Tax *cum* Subsidy

We will therefore use factor tax *cum* subsidy to denote only differential (as distinct from uniform) tax *cum* subsidies. Such a factor tax *cum* subsidy may be given everywhere in the economy or may be confined to specific sectors (like the Selective Employment Tax).

Figure 17.4 illustrates the equilibrium for the case where a tax *cum* subsidy is given selectively to the use of a factor in one sector alone. In this case it is intuitive that the economy will not be able to operate on the Edgeworth-Bowley contract curve and hence on the (best) production-possibility curve.[1] Moreover, with *APB* as the newly feasible production-possibility curve, the domestic and (equivalently) world price line *PC* will be nontangent to it at *P* because producers of good 1 (2) are having to

---

1. This is discussed formally in chapter 25.

pay more (less) for the same factor than the producers of the other good. But consumption is unaffected; consumers can consume at world prices, and therefore U_C can be tangent to the world price line at C.

We have now discussed the principal policy instruments we will be analyzing in different situations through the rest of part III. We will now proceed immediately to develop the basic propositions that underlie the classical analysis of gains from trade.

18 Gains from Trade

The bulk of this chapter deals with the basic propositions concerning the gains from trade from the viewpoint of one country; world welfare is addressed only at the end. Furthermore the analysis here does not extend to dynamic notions of efficiency and gains, nor to the implications of trade under uncertainty, nor to inclusion in the social-utility function of arguments other than the flow of goods and services. These aspects will be dealt with in later chapters.

The ideas developed here can be given very rigorous treatment. However, the treatment here will be considerably more intuitive. For pedagogic purposes, it will rely on familiar two-dimensional illustrations.

18.1 Basic Theorem without Prices

The basic proposition concerning the gains from trade is that *some trade is better than no trade*. This proposition can be discussed in technological terms or in terms of utility. In the technological version, the theorem essentially states that it is possible to exploit a trade opportunity in such a way that one can have more of one good and no less of the other for every vector of autarkic outputs. In the utility version, one can make one consumer better off and none of the others worse off.

Technological Version

Let AB be the production-possibility curve in figure 18.1. For the general case of a "large" country, we can then derive the Baldwin envelope CD,

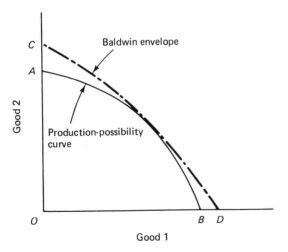

Figure 18.1

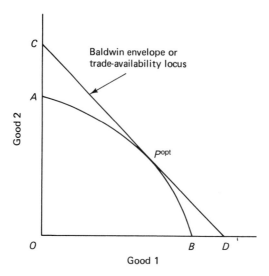

Figure 18.2

which represents the locus of points representing the maximum amount of good 2 that can be obtained (through domestic production and trade along the foreign-offer curve) for good 1. By definition, it will Pareto-dominate AB technologically. For a "small" country, CD would be a straight line, as in figure 18.2; the production point on which the line is then anchored is P^{opt}.[1] In either case it is evident that for every efficient production bundle feasible under autarky (along AB), there is a Pareto-better (strictly speaking, a not Pareto-worse) bundle under trade (along CD). This technological theorem is not really surprising. Trade is, after all, only a technology for transforming one good into another. Hence it should always be possible to use it to advantage, or at least not to disadvantage. Whether a particular set of institutions (e.g., a decentralized competitive price mechanism) will so use the trade opportunity is another matter.

Utility Version

From the Pareto-noninferiority of the technological trade situation, we can infer (without reference to prices) that since 1 and 2 are "goods" rather than "bads," it should be possible to make one consumer better off and no one else worse off. If we use Samuelson's two-person utility-

---

1. The Baldwin envelope is different from the Baldwin free-trade locus derived in section 5.4, and in fact Pareto-dominates it. The latter also Pareto-dominates AB.

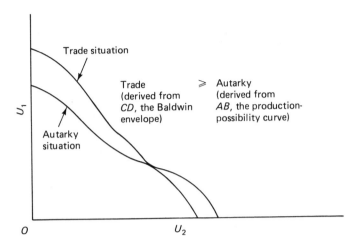

Figure 18.3

possibility curve, we see (in figure 18.3) that the utility-possibility locus in the trade situation will Pareto-dominate the utility-possibility locus in the autarkic situation.

The theorem applies only to situation ranking, not to "point" ranking. That is, a policy of trade may result in a particular vector of availabilities that cannot be redistributed to make everyone as well off as or no worse off than before (e.g., as when a trade equilibrium arises that makes a desired good unavailable at any price).

We are using the compensation principle to rank trade and autarky. However, if no redistribution is actually possible or undertaken, one may prefer the "point" outcome under autarky to that under trade. For example, if in figure 18.4 individual 1 is a pauper and individual 2 is a prince, the policymaker may well prefer autarky to trade. In fact Rawls (1971), in propounding the maximin principle, provides philosophical justification for preferring autarky to trade in "point" terms.

Instead of using the utility-possibility curve to rank-order different policies, we will generally use the Samuelson (1956) social-indifference curves,[2] which enable us to write a well-behaved social-utility function (not a social-welfare function) $U = U(C_1, C_2, \ldots, C_n)$ as if society were Robinson Crusoe. In this case we can assert that society is getting better off as we move up the social-indifference curves. Besides, all the standard properties with respect to demand obtain. Welfare-theoretic propositions

2. An individualistic social-welfare function has as its arguments the individual utilities, whereas the Samuelsonian social-utility function has the vector of aggregate consumption as its argument.

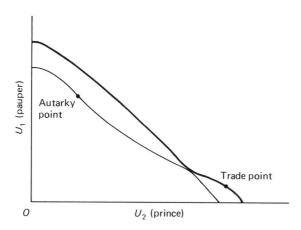

Figure 18.4

proved by use of social-indifference curves can generally also be proved by use of the utility-possibility curve, and since the former technique is simpler, we will generally use it in our analysis.

18.2 Basic Theorem with Prices

We can now introduce the price mechanism. Consider a decentralized economy where economic agents respond to market prices and profit-maximizing entrepreneurs make resource-allocational decisions by refer-ence to the prices they face. In this case we can translate the theorem that *some trade is better than no trade* into the theorem that *free trade is better than no trade*. By free trade we mean a policy such that when trade is opened up, the world prices of goods translate freely into domestic prices for the country in question and therefore no artificial impediments such as tariffs, trade subsidies, and quotas are present in the economy. This theorem can be proved either by assuming a social-utility function valid for a Robinson Crusoe or Samuelson economy or by going directly to a many-person economy. The former is the simpler method, and we present it immediately.

Social-Utility-Function Approach

Consider figure 18.5 for a large country where EF is now the Baldwin free-trade locus (as in figure 5.17). Under autarky, production and con-sumption are at Q and social utility is at U^A. With free trade, production is at P' and consumption at Q' on EF, with social utility at $U^{FT} > U^A$.

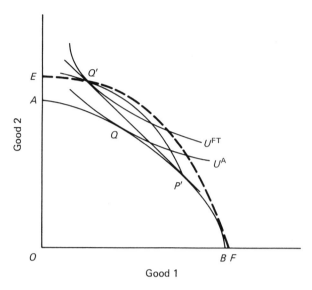

Figure 18.5

With free-trade policy foreign prices are equal to domestic prices, so $P'Q'$ is both the foreign and the domestic price line. $P'Q'$ is tangent to the production-possibility curve AB at P', since for a decentralized price economy the domestic prices are equal to the marginal domestic rate of transformation.[3]

An alternative illustration of $U^{FT} > U^A$ is obtained with the aid of the trade-indifference curves derived in chapter 2 (figure 2.10 and 2.11). Consider figure 18.6, where country I trades with country II and their offer curves are OI and OII, respectively, with trade at F. Country I's autarkic trade-indifference curve U_T^A is evidently dominated by its free-trade trade-indifference curve U_T^{FT}, which is tangent to the terms of trade OF at F.

Many-Consumer-Economy Approach

Following Grandmont and McFadden (1972), we can state the gains-from-trade theorem for free trade by decentralized multiple-consumer nations with competitive domestic markets as follows:

PROPOSITION 1   Given a world competitive trade equilibrium allocation, any alternative allocation that is feasible under autarky and makes some

3. This is derived in appendix B (proposition 4).

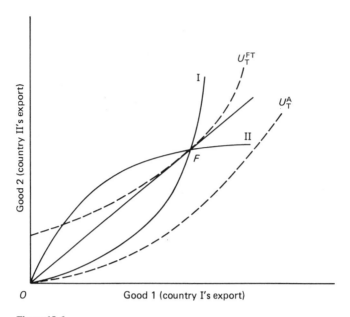

Figure 18.6

consumers in a nation better off must make some other consumers in that nation worse off.

PROPOSITION 2   Given an allocation achieved under autarky, one can find a system of world trade prices and domestic lump-sum transfers for which there will exist a competitive equilibrium allocation that will be at least as satisfactory as autarky for every consumer.

Proposition 1 follows quite generally from properties of competitive equilibria as discussed by Samuelson (1962) and Kemp (1962). It is known from the work of Debreu (1959) and Koopmans (1957) that a competitive equilibrium allocation in a world in which all consumers have locally nonsatiating preferences and no consumer is satiated while externalities are absent is in the core of an economy; that is, no feasible alternative for any coalition can be preferable in the Pareto sense for all coalition members. Applied to the coalition of consumers in each nation for a world competitive trade equilibrium, this result implies proposition 1. This conclusion requires only the mild (from a neoclassical viewpoint) conditions of local nonsatiation and no externalities. There are no explicit requirements that traders be "small," that nonincreasing returns prevail, or that factors be immobile. In particular, this argument applies independently of whether nations are infinitesimal traders in world markets.

Proposition 2, discussed by Samuelson (1956) and Kenen (1957), has been proved rigorously by Grandmont and McFadden. This proposition, being an extension of the so-called second theorem of neoclassical welfare economics of closed economies, requires a set of rather restrictive sufficient conditions, such as convexity of consumer preferences and technology of production.

18.3   Optimality of Free-Trade Policy for a Small Country

We may now go beyond the simple rank ordering of free trade and autarky and establish the central proposition relating to optimality for a competitive, small economy: that *free trade is the optimal policy for a competitive, small economy.*

This is seen by first maximizing a social-utility function subject to the domestic production-possibility curve and the foreign transformation curve (and deriving thus the first-order conditions for a maximum) and then showing that these conditions will be satisfied by the adoption of a free-trade policy in a competitive, small economy.

To begin, we will derive the first-order conditions for a maximum. These are

$$\text{DRT} = \text{FRT} = \text{DRS},$$

by which we see that for an interior maximum the (marginal) domestic rate of transformation (in production) ought to be equated to the foreign rate of transformation (in external trade), and these ought to be equated to the domestic rate of substitution in consumption. $\text{DRT} = \text{FRT}$ ensures that the economy is maximizing the availability of a good subject to a given availability of all other goods in the economy.[4] Having achieved this technological efficiency, the economy then maximizes utility by equating the resulting efficient transformation rate between goods with their rate of substitution in consumption.

The formal maximization involved here is simply as follows:

$$\max U = U(C_1, C_2)$$

subject to

$$Q_1 = \phi(Q_2),$$

$$E_1 = \psi(M_2),$$

---

4. We are assuming here that the second-order conditions for a maximum are satisfied.

$C_1 = Q_1 - E_1,$

$C_2 = Q_2 + M_2.$

Form the Lagrangian Φ, and take partial derivatives with respect to $Q_1, Q_2, E_1, M_2, C_1,$ and C_2:

$$\Phi = U - \lambda_1[Q_1 - \phi(Q_2)] - \lambda_2[E_1 - \psi(M_2)]$$
$$- \lambda_3(C_1 - Q_1 + E_1)$$
$$- \lambda_4(C_2 - Q_2 - M_2).$$

This yields

$$\frac{\partial \Phi}{\partial C_1} = \frac{\partial U}{\partial C_1} - \lambda_3 = 0, \tag{18.1}$$

$$\frac{\partial \Phi}{\partial C_2} = \frac{\partial U}{\partial C_2} - \lambda_4 = 0, \tag{18.2}$$

$$\frac{\partial \Phi}{\partial Q_1} = -\lambda_1 + \lambda_3 = 0, \tag{18.3}$$

$$\frac{\partial \Phi}{\partial Q_2} = \lambda_1 \phi' + \lambda_4 = 0, \tag{18.4}$$

$$\frac{\partial \Phi}{\partial E_1} = -\lambda_2 - \lambda_3 = 0, \tag{18.5}$$

$$\frac{\partial \Phi}{\partial M_2} = \lambda_2 \psi' + \lambda_4 = 0. \tag{18.6}$$

Now

$DRT = -\phi',$

$FRT = \psi',$

$DRS = \dfrac{\partial C_1}{\partial C_2}.$

Therefore, from equations 18.1 and 18.2 we have

$$\frac{\lambda_4}{\lambda_3} = \frac{\partial C_1}{\partial C_2} (= DRS),$$

from 18.3 and 18.4 we have

$$\frac{\lambda_4}{\lambda_3} = -\phi'(= \text{DRT}),$$

and from 18.5 and 18.6 we have

$$\frac{\lambda_4}{\lambda_3} = \psi'(= \text{FRT}).$$

This yields the first-order conditions for an interior maximum,

$$\text{DRT} = \text{FRT} = \text{DRS},$$

which we have already observed intuitively.

From here it is easy to see that a free-trade policy will satisfy these conditions for a maximum for a small competitive economy. A "small" economy (one with given external prices) will have FRT = FP (foreign prices) where the marginal and average terms of trade are identical. The free-trade policy will ensure that FP = DP (domestic prices), that DP = DRT for a competitive economy, and that DP = DRS in consumption. Therefore a small competitive economy will be characterized by DRT = FRT = DRS.

This central theorem concerning the optimality of free trade for a small, competitive economy will prove in the succeeding chapters to be the departure point for considering the theory of optimal and second-best policy interventions in the presence of distortions.

18.4   Optimality of Free Trade from World Viewpoint

It can be argued that free trade will maximize world welfare, for it will equalize DRT and DRS around the world (with appropriate modification for transport costs) and thus satisfy the first-order conditions for a world-welfare maximum. However, this merely means that free trade is Pareto-optimal from the world-welfare viewpoint. That is to say, there will generally be an infinity of such optimal solutions, with different income distributions among the member countries as illustrated in figure 18.7. Free trade at F is Pareto-optimal, but the same is true at S and R, for all these points lie on the efficiency locus SFR defined by the tangency of the trade-indifference curves of the two countries.

Although free trade is optimal from the viewpoint of world welfare, it is not so from the viewpoint of a single country unless the country is small. In figure 18.7 each country is large, so each faces an offer curve from the other that implies varying terms of trade as the volume of trade changes (see chapter 21).

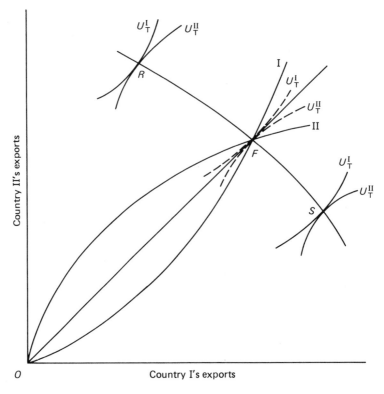

Figure 18.7

18.5   Superiority of Trade over Autarky, without Lump-Sum Transfers

Dixit and Norman (1980) argue that trade can always be exploited to produce a better outcome (in the Pareto sense) than autarky even if lump-sum taxes and transfers are unavailable.

Consider an economy in which consumers supply factors inelastically up to the limit of their availability. In the autarkic competitive equilibrium, let the aggregate production vector be x^A, which is also the consumption vector c^A. Let the goods-price vector be p^A and the factor-price vector be w^A. Then $p^A x^A = p^A c^A = w^A \bar{L}$ (where $\bar{L}$ is the aggregate factor-endowment vector) if the technology set exhibits constant returns to scale, no intermediate goods are present, and there is nonsatiation in consumption. Suppose that an opportunity arises to trade with the rest of the world at prices $p^* \neq p^A$. Let x^* denote the production vector, and let p^* and w^* be the equilibrium goods-price and factor-price vectors, respectively, that correspond to the free-trade competitive equilibrium.[5] Let the government announce taxes and subsidies such that consumers continue to pay p^A for goods they buy and receive w^A for factors they supply. From producer maximization it follows that

$$p^* x^* \geq p^* x^A = p^* \cdot c^A. \tag{18.7}$$

Because consumers face prices p^A and w^A, their aggregate demand continues to be c^A. Equation (18.7) shows that it is feasible to obtain c^A through trade, given the production vector x^*. From a budgetary viewpoint, the government "buys" goods c^A at prices p^* from domestic producers or from the world market and "sells" at price p^A to consumers, thereby earning a net revenue of $(p^A - p^*)c^A$. It "buys" factors $\bar{L}$ from consumers at prices w^A and "sells' at prices w^* to producers, thereby earning a net revenue of $(w^* - w^A)\bar{L}$. Thus total net revenue is

$$(p^A - p^*)c^A + (w^* - w^A)\bar{L} = w^* \bar{L} - p^* c^A$$

because of consumer budget constraint at autarky. Now, by definition of w^*, we have $p^* x^* = w^* \bar{L}$; that is, factor rewards completely exhaust the value of output. Hence, from equation 18.7,

$$\text{Net revenue} = w^* \bar{L} - p^* c^A = p^*(x^* - c^A) \geq 0. \tag{18.8}$$

In the above comparison each consumer is left with the same consumption and welfare in free trade as under autarky, while the needed taxes and subsidies produce nonnegative revenue to the government and therefore are feasible. If the revenue produced is strictly positive (as it would be, since in the free-trade equilibrium the value of output is greater that the autarky output valued at free-trade prices), then the government can reduce some consumer taxes or raise factor subsidies, thereby improving consumer welfare without violating its budget constraint. Thus, with trade and appropriate taxes and subsidies, a position superior in the Pareto sense to that with autarky can always be attained.

The discussion so far has treated all goods (no matter how many) as tradable, but the argument can be easily extended to allow for any number of nontraded goods as well. All one needs to do is consider a free-trade equilibrium in which the output of nontraded goods is kept at the same level as in the autarky equilibrium and show that such a constrained free-trade equilibrium is Pareto-superior to autarky. Then it

5. For the single-country analysis of this and the next section, we use a superscript asterisk to distinguish the equilibrium value of a variable under free trade rather than foreign-country variables.

would follow that the unconstrained equilibrium is, *a fortiori*, Pareto-superior to autarky.

Following Dixit and Norman and also anticipating the discussion in chapter 36 on gains from trade in an intertemporal context, we note that by distinguishing goods according to the date of their availability, one can interpret the same argument showing the Pareto-superiority of trade over autarky in a dynamic context as well. Starting from any historically given initial situation, an autarkic economy could gain a Pareto-superior path by moving to trade and using appropriate tax and subsidy policies. Conversely, an economy in such appropriate trade cannot achieve a Pareto-superior path by changing to autarky.

18.6   Illustrating the Dixit-Norman Argument

We can illustrate the Dixit-Norman argument of section 18.5 in the context of two-good model as shown in figures 18.8 and 18.9 where we successively consider the small-country and large-country cases under the simplifying assumption of fixed factor supplies.

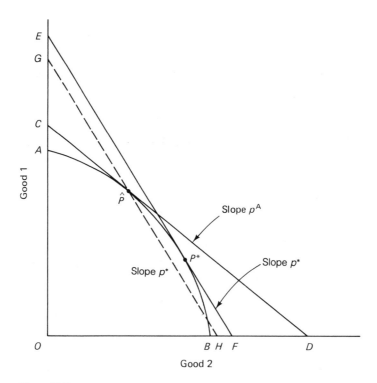

Figure 18.8

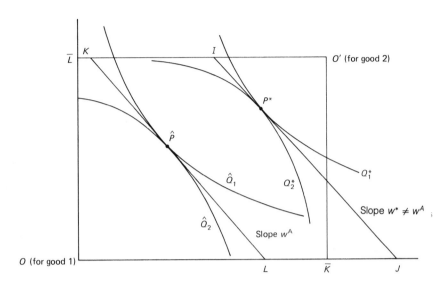

Figure 18.9

Small-Country Case

Let producers face world price p^* for commodities and an associated factor-price vector w^*; that is, they produce $Q^* = (Q_1^*, Q_2^*)$ at the point P^* in figure 18.8; the associated factor price w^* is the slope of IJ in figure 18.9. Let consumers face the autarky price ratio p^A and receive autarky factor price w^A (the slope of KL in figure 18.9). Hence they consume (supply) the same amount of each commodity (factor) as in autarky. The difference $p^A - p^*$ represents the set of commodity taxes, and $w^* - w^A$ represents the set of factor taxes. The government collects $(p^A - p^*)\hat{c}$ in commodity taxes and $(w^* - w^A)\hat{L}$ in factor taxes, where $\hat{L}$ is the autarky factor supply (the dimensions of the box in figure 18.9) and $\hat{c}$ is autarky consumption. Thus total tax revenue is

$$(p^A - p^*)\hat{c} + (w^* - w^A)\hat{L} = (p^A\hat{c} - w^A\hat{L}) + w^*\hat{L} - p^*\hat{c}.$$

However, $\hat{c} = \hat{Q} \equiv$ autarky production. Hence $p^A\hat{c} = p^A\hat{Q} = w^A\hat{L}$. Now $p^*Q^* = w^*\hat{L}$, since w^* is the factor price associated with the goods price p^*, with Q^* the output corresponding to p^* and with $\hat{L}$ the unchanged factor supply. Thus total revenue is

$$(w^*\hat{L} - p^*\hat{c}) = (p^*Q^* - p^*\hat{Q}) \geq 0,$$

since Q^* maximizes the value of output given p^* while $\hat{Q}$ is still feasible. Hence total revenue is nonnegative, and moving to free trade makes no consumer worse off compared with autarky, since with nonnegative revenue the government can subsidize consumption. This is in essence the Dixit-Norman argument, and the nonnegativity of governmental revenue can be shown in terms of figure 18.8 as follows:

$$p^A \hat{c} = OD \qquad \text{in terms of good 1}$$
$$= OC \qquad \text{in terms of good 2,}$$
$$p^* \hat{c} = OH \qquad \text{in terms of good 1}$$
$$= OG \qquad \text{in terms of good 2,}$$
$$(p^A - p^*)\hat{c} = OD - OH = HD \qquad \text{in terms of good 1}$$
$$= OC - OG = -CG \qquad \text{in terms of good 2,}$$
$$w^* \hat{L} = p^* Q^* = OF \qquad \text{in terms of good 1}$$
$$= OE \qquad \text{in terms of good 2,}$$
$$(w^* - w^A)\hat{L} = OF - OD = -FD \qquad \text{in terms of good 1}$$
$$= OE - OC = EC \qquad \text{in terms of good 2,}$$
$$(p^A - p^*)\hat{c} + (w^* - w^A)\hat{L} = HD - FD = HF \quad \text{in terms of good 1}$$
$$= EC - GC = EG \quad \text{in terms of good 2.}$$

Hence

$$\text{Revenue} = HF \qquad \text{in terms of good 1}$$
$$= EG \qquad \text{in terms of good 2}$$
$$= p^* Q^* - p^* \hat{Q} \geq 0.$$

Large-Country Case

Let consumers face autarky prices p^A and receive autarky factor rewards w^A so that they consume $\hat{c}$ and supply $\hat{L}$. As terms of trade move away from p^A, the production point moves along the PP curve AB. Since consumption is fixed at $\hat{c}$, the "offer" corresponding to each terms of trade can be derived as the difference between production and $\hat{c}$. Thus we get an "offer curve" (the quotation marks denote that this curve differs from the traditional offer curve in that consumption is not allowed to vary with changes in terms of trade). The intersection of this offer curve with the foreign offer curve generates an equilibrium-price vector p^*. With this p^*, the earlier argument establishes a weak Pareto superiority of such trade; we have found a post-trade equilibrium in which no consumer is worse off compared with autarky. (This is not the full free-trade equilibrium in the sense that consumers and producers face the same equilibrium terms of trade; it is a trade equilibrium, with commodity and factor taxes, that is not Pareto-inferior to autarky.) And this is all one needs to establish the Dixit-Norman gains-from-trade proposition.

Recommended Readings

Bhagwati, J. The theory and practice of commercial policy: Departure from unified exchange rates. (Frank Graham Lecture). *Special Papers in International Economics* 8. Princeton: Princeton University Press, 1968.

Chipman, J. S., and J. C. Moore. Social utility and the gains from trade. *Journal of International Economics* 2 (1972): 157–72.

Debreu, G. *Theory of Value*. New York: Wiley, 1959.

Dixit, A., and V. Norman. *Theory of International Trade*. Cambridge: Cambridge University Press, 1980.

Grandmont, J. M., and D. McFadden. A technical note on classical gains from trade. *Journal of International Economics* 2 (1972): 109–25.

Kemp, M. C. The gains from international trade. *Economic Journal* 72 (1972): 803–19.

Kenen, P. B. On the geometry of welfare economics. *Quarterly Journal of Economics* 71 (1957): 426–47.

Kenen, P. B. Distribution, demand and equilibrium in international trade: A diagrammatic analysis. *Kyklos* 12 (1959): 629–38.

Koopmans, T. C. *Three Essays on the State of Economic Science*. New York: McGraw-Hill, 1957.

Otani, Y. Gains from trade revisited. *Journal of International Economics* 2 2 (1972): 127–56.

Rawls, J. *A Theory of Social Justice*. Cambridge: Harvard University Press, 1971.

Samuelson, P. A. Social indifference curves. *Quarterly Journal of Economics* 70 (1956): 1–22.

Samuelson, P. A. The gains from international trade once again. *Economic Journal* 72 (1962): 820–29.

Wan, H. Y., Jr. A note on trading gains and externalities. *Journal of International Economics* 2 (1972): 173–80.

The gains from trade (and hence the cost of autarky) can be measured, and the measured gains can be decomposed into a "production" gain and a "consumption" gain, omitting terms-of-trade effects.

19.1 Gains from Free Trade

Consider figure 19.1. The economy (assumed small) produces and consumes at S under autarky, whereas it produces at P and consumes at C under free trade. U^{FT} is greater than U^A, and we now wish to measure this gain from trade despite the assumption of ordinal utility.

Consider now the Hicksian concepts of equivalent variation and compensating variation in the case of a shift from autarky to free trade. The equivalent variation may then be defined as the transfer or bribe that would have to be provided to society in autarky to improve its welfare to the level equivalent to that attainable by a shift from autarky to free trade. The compensating variation is defined as the penalty (or transfer) that would have to be extracted from society such that, while continuing in the free-trade situation, its welfare would be reduced to the same level as under autarky.

It is evident that the equivalent (compensating) variation for a move from autarky to free trade is the compensating (equivalent) variation for a move from free trade to autarky. Moreover each measure has two estimates: one each in terms of either good in the two-good economy of figure 19.1.

Thus, in figure 19.1, for a move from autarky to free trade, the equivalent-variational measure of the gains from free trade is QR in terms of good 1 and $Q'R'$ in terms of good 2, whereas the compensating variational measure is WV in terms of good 1 and $W'V'$ in terms of good 2. For a move from free trade to autarky, the cost of protection is symmetric; QR and $Q'R'$ are now the compensating-variational measures and WV and $W'V'$ the equivalent-variational measures.[1]

19.2 Decomposing Gains from Trade

Consider now the compensating-variational measure of gains from trade, WV, in figure 19.2. WV can be decomposed into WN (the consumption gain) and NV (the production gain) as follows: Suppose that the

---

1. For a recasting of these measures in terms of trade-indifference curves and an extension of the analysis to include a Marshallian surplus concept, see Bhagwati and Johnson (1960, sec. III).

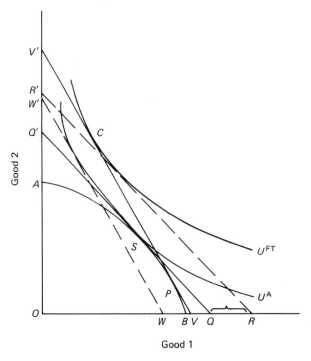

Figure 19.1

economy, in free trade, was constrained in its production such that only the autarkic production bundle was permitted, whereas consumption was allowed to be at international prices. In that event the economy would consume at C^{ps}, and welfare would be at U^{ps}. NV would then be the compensating-variational measure of the gain that would accrue from being allowed to shift production under free trade from the autarkic S to P. Similarly we can argue that WN is the compensating-variational measure of the further gain to be had from letting consumers consume at international prices rather than at the autarky-distorted prices at S.

19.3   Factor Immobility

From figures 19.1 and 19.2 it is immediately evident that factor immobility cannot be an impediment to gains from trade—free trade will still dominate autarky, for factor immobility between sectors merely eliminates the production gain but leaves open consumption gain. Thus we have figure 19.3 where the production-possibility curve is APB, with a kink at P because resources are fully immobile and sector-specific. A

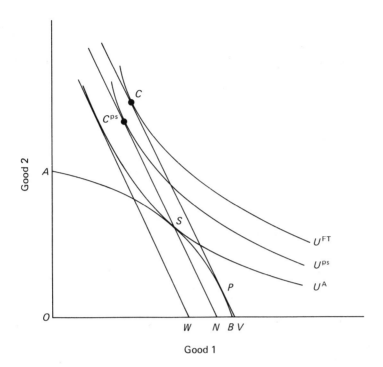

Figure 19.2

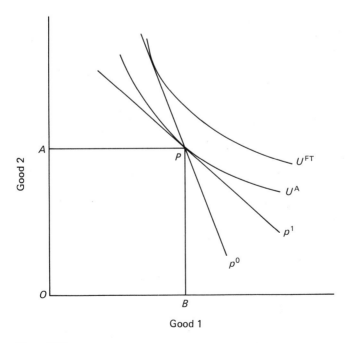

Figure 19.3

move from autarky to free trade shifts the goods-price ratio from p^0 to p^1, but production cannot move from P. However, there is still consumption gain, and $U^{FT} > U^A$.

19.4   Other Considerations

We will consider later in this book the modifications to be introduced in the measurement of the gains from trade when there is domestic monopoly in production (chapter 23) and when lobbying activities exist such that "tariff seeking" has led to the creation of the tariff or "revenue seeking" has been generated by the presence and disposal of the revenue proceeds of a protectionist tariff (chapter 34).[2]

Recommended Readings

Bhagwati, J. Lobbying and Welfare. *Journal of Public Economics* 14 (1980): 355–63.

Bhagwati, J., and H. G. Johnson. Notes on some controversies in the theory of international trade. *Economic Journal* 70 (1960): 74–93.

Bhagwati, J., and T. N. Srinivasan. Revenue-seeking: A generalisation of the theory of tariffs. *Journal of Political Economy* 88 (1980): 1069–87.

Feenstra, R. C. How costly is protectionism? *Journal of Economic Perspectives* 6 (1992): 159–78.

Haberler, G. Some problems in the pure theory of international trade. *Economic Journal* 60 (1950): 227–40. Reprinted in *Readings in International Economics*, ed. by R. E. Caves and H. G. Johnson. Homewood, IL: Irwin, 1968.

Johnson, H. G. The cost of protection and the scientific tariff. *Journal of Political Economy* 68 (1960): 327–45.

Michaely, M. *Theory of Commercial Policy, Trade and Protection*. Chicago: University of Chicago Press, 1977.

Romer, P. New goods, old theory and the welfare costs of trade restrictions. *Journal of Development Economics* 43 (1994): 5–38.

2. For more recent contributions dealing with the subject matter of this chapter, see Feenstra (1992) and Romer (1994). The lobbying issues, bearing on estimating cost of protection, are considered in Bhagwati (1980) and Bhagwati and Srinivasan (1980).

In chapter 18 we established the proposition that free trade is the optimal policy for a small, decentralized, competitive economy. This proposition followed from the fact that for an interior maximum, free trade satisfies the first-order conditions for a maximum: $DRT = FRT = DRS$. It follows immediately that in the case where the second-order conditions are not satisfied as a result of technological phenomena such as sufficiently increasing returns to scale, the proposition ceases to be valid. But beyond this complication it is easy to see that free trade will cease to be the optimal policy as soon as one or more of the following happens in free-trade equilibrium:

1. $FRT \neq DRT = DRS$.

2. $DRT \neq FRT = DRS$.

3. $DRS \neq DRT = FRT$.

4. Nonoperation of the economy on the efficient production-possibility curve.

Situations where one or more of the above outcomes prevails under free trade may be described as *distortionary*. The theory of distortions in international trade concerns itself with the effects of different policy interventions when, owing to different types of distortions such as those distinguished below, the free-trade competitive equilibrium is characterized by a suboptimal solution such as one or more of those categorized above.

Where "market failure" leads to such a distortionary situation under free trade, the distortion may be described as *market-determined*. Where the outcome is due to governmental policies, the distortion may be described as *policy-imposed*. Policy-imposed distortions may be *autonomous* or *instrumental*; in the latter case the analyst takes into account the reasons for imposing the distortion.[1]

As we will see in the next chapter, a market-determined distortion of type 1 will develop for a decentralized competitive economy that has monopoly power in trade so that it can affect its terms of trade. For such a country $FP \neq FRT$ by assumption (where FP is the foreign price ratio), and therefore free trade ceases to be optimal. This may be described as a situation where there is a *foreign* distortion in the economy. Similarly, if the economy is characterized by a simple version of production externality that implies an inequality between social and private opportunity costs, we have $DP \neq DRT$ (where DP is the domestic price ratio), and it

---

1. This set of definitions was developed by Bhagwati (1971).

follows that under free trade we will get a market-determined distortion of type 2. A consumption externality would lead to a market-determined distortion of type 3.

If at a suboptimal level a government had imposed a tariff "inadvertently", the analyst will encounter an autonomous policy-imposed distorted situation such as type 1 under a policy of free trade everywhere except for this tariff. Substituting a production tax *cum* subsidy and a consumption tax *cum* subsidy in place of the tariff in the foregoing generates autonomous policy-imposed distortion of type 2 or 3, respectively.

Where free trade would be optimal (since the decentralized competitive economy is small) but the government decides that it should add a "noneconomic" objective so that the economy is made to depart from the "economist's" maximum, the question of interest is which type of distortion (from among those distinguished above) should be chosen to be imposed on the economy so that the noneconomic objective will be satisfied at least cost. If the political leaders want the importation of importables to be reduced below the level that would emerge under free trade, should this be done through a tariff (which would impose on the economy a distortion of type 1), or through a production subsidy for the import-competing industry (bringing about distortion of type 2), or through a tax on consuming the importables (bringing about distortion of type 3)? These become choices among different "instrumental" policy-imposed distortions, since the distortions are instruments for achieving the satisfaction of the noneconomic objective.

In the bulk of what follows in part III of the text, we will consider different distortions and policy instruments for dealing with them. We will use Samuelsonian social-indifference curves, so we will not consider income-distributional questions directly. Nor will we consider questions of second-best analysis which arise from not being able to utilize lump-sum transfers (questions that arise because otherwise the collection of revenue to pay for subsidies itself can create a distortionary loss). Nor will we consider the direct costs of raising revenues and disbursing them (though the revenue-seeking analysis of chapter 34 can be utilized toward that end).

The analysis of economic policymaking throughout the rest of the book, except for chapter 34 on directly unproductive profit-seeking activities, assumes that policy can be set exogenously. That is to say, governments are, as Bhagwati (1990) has put it, "puppets" of the economist. Where the policymaking gets to be endogenously specified and determined, as in the recent models of political economy, the question does arise critically: Where and how do we then get the required degree of freedom to choose among policy alternatives as in the conventional theory of economic policy?[2]

Recommended Readings

Bhagwati, J. *The Theory and Practice of Commercial Policy: Departure from Unified Exchange Rates.* 1968, ch. 1.

Bhagwati, J. The generalized theory of distortions and welfare. In *Trade, Balance of Payments, and Growth: Papers in International Economics in Honor of Charles P. Kindleberger.* Amsterdam: North-Holland, 1971, ch. 12.

Bhagwati, J., R. Brecher, and T. N. Srinivasan. DUP activities and economic theory. In *Neoclassical Political Economy*, ed. by David Colander. Cambridge, MA: Ballinger, 1984.

Bhagwati, J. The theory of political economy, economic policy, and foreign investment. In *Public Policy and Economic Development*, ed. by M. Scott and D. Lal. Oxford: Clarendon Press, 1990.

Johnson, H. G. Optimal trade intervention in the presence of domestic distortions. In *Trade, Growth, and the Balance of Payments: Essays in Honour of G. Haberler*, ed. by R. E. Baldwin et al. Chicago: Rand McNally and Amsterdam: North-Holland, 1965, ch. 11.

O'Flaherty, B., and J. Bhagwati. Will free trade with political science put normative economists out of work? Mimeo. Economics Department, Columbia University, June 27, 1994.

Srinivasan, T. N. Distortions. In *The New Palgrave*, ed. by J. Eatwell, M. Newgate, and P. Newman. MacMillan: London. 1987.

2. This is the determinacy paradox noted in Bhagwati, Brecher, and Srinivasan (1984); it is the subject of a symposium published in *Economics and Politics*, September 1997, with contributions by Brendan O'Flaherty and Bhagwati (1994), Kaushik Basu, Avinash Dixit, and Isaac Levi.

21 Monopoly Power in Trade

When we give up the assumption of a "small," atomistic country, we postulate that a country can affect its terms of trade by altering its volume of trade. Since the offer curve facing it has less than infinite elasticity (it is not a straight line), FP ≠ FRT. In this case the free-trade situation will be characterized by suboptimality: DRT = DRS ≠ FRT. This is because DP = DRT = DRS, FP ≠ FRT, and DP = FP, (by the free-trade assumption).

In this chapter we will deal with the following questions: What is the optimal policy intervention? Since a tariff is the optimal policy, at what level should it be set? Can the optimal tariff be negative? What is the optimal tariff structure when there are several traded goods? Would the tariff policy be optimal if retaliation were possible or if extortion were feasible? How do we rank alternative policy instruments if the optimal tariff is unavailable?

21.1 Optimal Policy Intervention

Clearly the optimal policy intervention in the presence of monopoly power in trade is a tariff. A suitable tariff, by breaking the equality between domestic and foreign prices, would make possible the equation of DRT, DRS, and FRT, thus satisfying the first-order conditions for an interior maximum (because we would then have DP = DRT = DRS, FP ≠ FRT, and, by virtue of tariff policy, DP ≠ FP).

A production-tax-*cum*-subsidy policy and a consumption-tax-*cum*-subsidy policy, on the other hand, could equate DRT with FRT and DRS with FRT, respectively; however, in each case, the equality of DRT with DRS would be destroyed, so we would be left with a suboptimal situation.

An optimal tariff situation is illustrated in figure 21.1. AB is the production-possibility curve, DRT = DRS are given by the parallel domestic price lines tangent to AB at P_t and to U_C at C_t, and FRT is given by the line tangent to the foreign offer curve $P_t C_t Q$ at C_t (thus showing that DRT = DRS = FRT). The tariff rate is defined by the difference between the domestic price ratio and the foreign price ratio $P_t C_t$.

21.2 Tariff Level

The optimal tariff formula can be derived by noting that

$$(\text{DRS} = \text{DRT} =) \frac{p_2}{p_1} (= \text{DP}) = \frac{p_2^*}{p_1^*} (1 + t^{\text{opt}})$$

$$= \frac{dM^*}{dE^*} (= \text{FRT}).$$

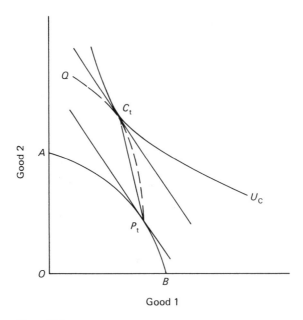

Figure 21.1

In words, the domestic relative price of the importable good 2 is higher than the foreign price thanks to a tariff at rate t^{opt}, and since t^{opt} is the optimal tariff, the domestic price ($= \text{DRT} = \text{DRS}$) must equal FRT ($= dM^*/dE^*$ along the foreign offer curve, where II denotes the foreign country). Therefore we have

$$t^{\text{opt}} = \frac{dM^*}{dE^*} \cdot \frac{p_1^*}{p_2^*} - 1$$

$$= \frac{dM^*}{dE^*} \cdot \frac{E^*}{M^*} - 1 \quad \text{(given balanced trade)}$$

$$= E_{\text{frd}}^* - 1,$$

where E_{frd}^* is the foreign country's elasticity of reciprocal demand for imports.

The same formula can be derived by reference to the offer-curve technique, as in figure 21.2. *OI* and *OII* are the free-trade offer curves of countries I and II. In free-trade equilibrium at F, the trade-indifference curves of countries I and II would be tangent to one another and to the free-trade price ratio *OF*; for country I, this trade-indifference curve is U_{T}^{f}. Optimality, however, obtains for country I, given country II's offer curve, at T, where U_{T}^{t} is tangent to *OII* and represents the highest

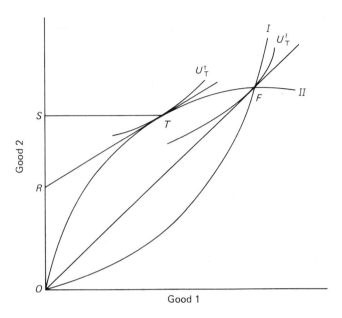

Figure 21.2

attainable welfare for country I. A suitable tariff would shift country I's offer curve to the left so as to intersect OII at T. That tariff is measured as follows:

$$\text{DP in country I} = \frac{p_2}{p_1} = \frac{ST}{RS},$$

$$\text{FP} = \frac{ST}{OS},$$

$$\text{DP} = \text{FP}(1 + t^{\text{opt}}).$$

Therefore the optimal tariff is

$$t^{\text{opt}} = \frac{\text{DP}}{\text{FP}} - 1$$

$$= \frac{ST}{RS} \cdot \frac{OS}{ST} - 1$$

$$= \frac{OS}{RS} - 1$$

$$= E^*_{\text{frd}} - 1,$$

where

$$E_{\text{frd}}^* = \frac{dM^*}{dE^*} \cdot \frac{E^*}{M^*}$$

is country II's reciprocal demand elasticity for imports. E_{frd} can be translated into other equivalent elasticity formulations, and so can the optimal tariff formula; see appendix A.

Clearly income-distributional considerations will influence the optimal tariff rate. As income distribution changes abroad, the foreign offer curve will shift, thus changing generally the optimal tariff rate. In figure 21.2 a shift in OII will generally shift T and hence the elasticity of OII at this new point. Similarly a shift in the distribution of own income must generally affect T, given OII, by shifting U_T^t and hence shifting the optimal tariff rate (unless OII is a constant-elasticity offer curve).

The case we have argued for the optimal tariff rests on the assumption that production and trade are competitive. If, however, it happens that the perception of national monopoly power leads to the private exercise of that monopoly power (as when Indian jute producers coordinated their foreign sales), then there will be no need for the government to intervene. Foreign trade will be carried on with the marginal revenue rather than the average foreign prices taken into account, so the market itself will equate the (marginal) FRT with DP = DRT = DRS. The only snag in this neat case for a return to laissez-faire is that that a private coalition to exercise external monopoly power is likely to result simultaneously in domestic monopoly, and if that happens we have replaced one welfare problem with another.

21.3   Can the Optimal Tariff Be Negative?

Can the optimal tariff be an optimal (trade) subsidy? Clearly it can. This is shown in figure 21.3 where country II's offer curve has multiple equilibria (alternative offers at the same terms of trade) and where a shift from I^f to I^s due to an export subsidy by country I yields the maximum welfare level at U_T^s. As Kemp (1967) has argued, and as we have discussed above, this phenomenon can arise in the presence of income distribution, factor-market imperfections, and externalities in country II. It can also arise when multiple equilibria obtain for similar reasons in country I, as noted by Riley (1970).

It is thus manifest that the occasional argument found in both the theoretical literature on the "new" theory of imperfect competition and in the media, that until the former arrived in the 1980s, economists could not think of arguments for subsidizing exports, is, like many such claims of the proponents of that theory, not valid.

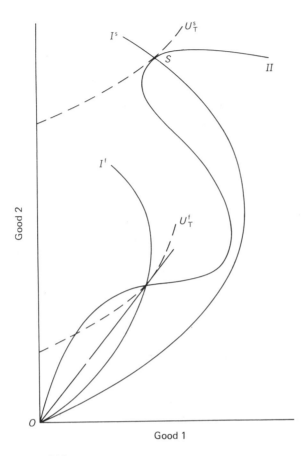

Figure 21.3

21.4   Optimal Tariff Structure with Several Traded Goods

What happens when we extend the analysis to multiple commodities? We can then show, based on Graaff's (1949–50) pioneering analysis, that there is an optimal tariff structure to be imposed. (Whether such an optimal tariff structure would show uniform or nonuniform tariffs is parts of a more general question on uniformity of policy-instrument structures in open economies, which is taken up in chapter 28.)

21.5   Retaliation or Extortion

The derivation of the optimal tariff is subject to two critical assumptions: that the foreign country does not "retaliate" in any way and that the

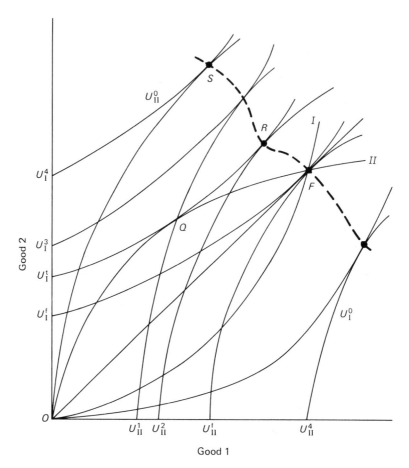

Figure 21.4

foreign country's offer curve defines the trade offers that can be "extracted" from it. These assumptions need to be relaxed, since neither is necessarily realistic; countries do retaliate, and powerful countries (e.g., Nazi Germany and the Soviet Union) have been known to impose "uneven" trade treaties on countries subject to their influence or domination.

The latter issue is easily analyzed via figure 21.4, where F represents the free-trade equilibrium and Q shows the optimum-tariff equilibrium for country I, which would take country I to U_I^t.[1]

Although the exercise of monopoly power improves the welfare of country I from U_I^f to U_I^t, this is a suboptimal policy for the world as a

1. Since the trade-indifference curves of both countries have to be shown, the subscript on U_T is changed to I and II in figure 21.4 to indicate which country's trade-indifference curve is involved.

whole. Thus it is clear that a movement from F to R via income transfer from country II to country I is preferable to a movement from F to Q via the imposition of an optimal tariff by country I. In each case country I's welfare improves to level U_I^t, but in the move to R, country II is better off ($U_{II}^2 > U_{II}^1$). Thus it would pay country II to bribe country I into not exercising its monopoly power.

The optimal tariff succeeds only partially in appropriating further gains from trade with respect to the free-trade-policy level. Since free trade has improved both countries from zero-gains-from-trade levels U_{II}^0 and U_I^0 to U_{II}^f and U_I^f, one can impose the "political" solution that the more "powerful" country, I, is able to extract as much gain from trade as possible subject to the constraint that country II does not become worse off than under self-sufficiency. In this case country I will be able to reach maximum welfare level U_I^4 subject to country II's being at U_{II}^0. This implies equilibrium at S, which requires that appropriate policies be devised to enable the two countries to transact at this point which is on neither country's free-trade offer curve.

Next consider the possibility of tariff retaliation. In a seminal paper, Johnson (1953–54) considered this question subject to the assumption that each country takes turns (as in a Cournot model) at setting optimal tariffs until equilibrium is reached when neither country changes its tariff level. Johnson showed that by these rules the two-country model we have been discussing can result in an equilibrium where a country, despite retaliation, remains better off than under free trade—contrary to what Scitovsky (1949) had asserted. Thus the case for levying an optimal tariff when there is monopoly power does not necessarily disappear if retaliation is admitted into the analysis.

The Johnson result is illustrated in figure 21.5. For each level of the foreign tariff we first determine the trade equilibrium when the home country imposes its optimal tariff, taking the foreign tariff as given. Thus Q_0 and Q_1 are the equilibria when the foreign country has a tariff of zero and some positive amount, respectively. Joining up these equilibria, which are optimal for the home country, we obtain that country's reaction curve OR_I. Repeating this procedure for each level of the home country's tariff, while the foreign country chooses its tariff optimally, we obtain OR_{II}. Then the Johnson-Cournot-Nash equilibrium, where each country sets its tariff optimally while taking the other country's tariff as given, occurs at G. By construction, the reaction curves OR_I and OR_{II} must have the same slope at the origin as OI_0 and OII_0 (the free-trade offer curves), respectively, and so G cannot occur at the origin; that is, tariff retaliation by both countries cannot eliminate trade. In general, all we can say about G is that it must lie inside the area OQ_0FSO and that it

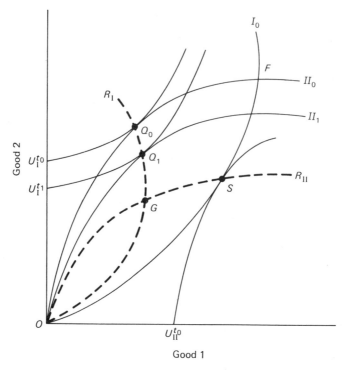

Figure 21.5

certainly may lie above the free-trade-indifference curve of one (but not both) countries, as asserted above. Finally, when countries "take turns" at setting their optimal tariffs, they may never reach G but get caught in a "tariff cycle," as Johnson notes.

Tower (1977) has analyzed tariff retaliation on the assumption that each country retaliates by imposing a tariff equal to the other country's.

21.6   Ranking Alternative Policies

We finally come to the question of how to rank alternative policies. To examine this question, we will assume again for simplicity two goods, 1 and 2, and use the following notation:[2] C_i and Q_i denote consumption and domestic output, respectively, of commodity i $(i = 1, 2)$. DRS denotes the rate of substitution in consumption, dC_1/dC_2. DRT denotes $-dQ_1/dQ_2$, and p^* denotes the ratio of the world price of good 2 to that of good 1, that is, the average terms of trade. The marginal terms of trade

2. The following analysis is based on Bhagwati, Ramaswami, and Srinivasan (1969).

FRT equal p^* only in the special case in which national monopoly power does not exist.[3]

The welfare function $U(C_1, C_2)$ and the production functions are assumed to be differentiable as required. U_i denotes the marginal utility of commodity i ($i = 1, 2$). It is assumed throughout the analysis that under laissez faire there is nonspecialization in consumption and production, and that some trade takes place.

Our procedure is as follows: We derive the expression for the change in welfare when there is a slight movement away from an initial equilibrium in which there is no intervention. If the levy of some tax (subsidy) at a low rate will secure a positive value for this expression, we can conclude that welfare can be raised above the laissez-faire level by applying this tax (subsidy). In such a case some finite (and not merely infinitesimal) tax (subsidy) rate will yield greater welfare than laissez-faire. If the derivative of welfare with respect to the rate of some tax (subsidy) is nonzero at the laissez-faire point, then by continuity it is nonzero for some finite interval of values of the tax (subsidy) rate around the laissez-faire point. If, on the other hand, the levy of some tax (subsidy) at a low rate does not change welfare, then there may not exist any rate of this tax (subsidy) that secures more welfare than under nonintervention.[4]

The change in welfare due to a small deviation from an initial laissez-faire equilibrium is

$$dU = U_1 dC_1 + U_2 dC_2 = U_1 \left(\frac{U_2}{U_1} dC_2 + dC_1 \right). \tag{21.1}$$

The marginal condition for utility maximization is that

$$\frac{U_2}{U_1} = \frac{dC_1}{dC_2} \equiv \text{DRS}.$$

Thus we get by substitution

$$
\begin{aligned}
dU &= U_1 (\text{DRS} \cdot dC_2 + dC_1) \\
&= U_1 [p^* dC_2 + dC_1 + (\text{DRS} - p^*) dC_2] \\
&= U_1 [d(p^* C_2 + C_1) - C_2 dp^* + (\text{DRS} - p^*) dC_2].
\end{aligned}
\tag{21.2}
$$

3. DRS, DRT, and FRT denote, respectively, the marginal domestic rate of substitution in consumption, the marginal domestic rate of transformation in production, and the marginal rate of transformation through trade.

4. If the function relating the level of welfare and the rate of a specified tax (subsidy) is concave and has a local maximum at the laissez-faire point, then this local maximum is a global maximum, and a finite tax (subsidy) must reduce welfare below the laissez-faire level. If this function is not concave, however, the local maximum need not be a global maximum and therefore some finite tax (subsidy) may exist that raises welfare above the laissez-faire level.

Assuming balanced trade, we have

$$p^*C_2 + C_1 = p^*Q_2 + Q_1. \tag{21.3}$$

Therefore, by substitution into (21.2), we get,

$$
\begin{aligned}
dU &= U_1[d(p^*Q_2 + Q_1) - C_2 dp^* + (\text{DRS} - p^*)dC_2] \\
&= U_1[p^*(dQ_2 + dQ_1) + (Q_2 - C_2)dp^* + (\text{DRS} - p^*)dC_2] \\
&= U_1\left[dQ_2\left(p^* + \frac{dQ_1}{dQ_2}\right) + (Q_2 - C_2)dp^* + (\text{DRS} - p^*)dC_2\right] \\
&= U_1[dQ_2(p^* - \text{DRT}) + (Q_2 - C_2)dp^* + (\text{DRS} - p^*)dC_2]. \tag{21.4}
\end{aligned}
$$

We will be using this equation to analyze other distortions in different chapters. In this chapter, however, we wish to concentrate on the problem arising from monopoly power in trade. in this case, assuming that there are no other distortions in the system, we have $\text{DRS} = \text{DRT} \neq \text{FRT}$ under laissez-faire. Then $\text{DRS} = \text{DRT} = p^*$ and $dp^* \neq 0$, so equation 21.4 reduces to

$$dU = U_1(Q_2 - C_2)dp^*. \tag{21.5}$$

Thus it is clear that production, consumption, and factor-use taxes *cum* subsidies will exist that will raise welfare above the laissez-faire level by changing the marginal rate of transformation through trade. Our analysis, however, shows that it is not possible to determine a priori what the second-best optimal policy will be. And the ranking of the three tax-*cum*-subsidy policies that are available when the first-best tariff policy is ruled out will depend on the specific situation being considered.

Recommended Readings

Baldwin, R. E. The new welfare economics and gains in international trade. *Quarterly Journal of Economics* 66 (1952): 91–101. Reprinted in *Readings in International Economics*, ed. by R. E. Caves and H. G. Johnson, Homewood. IL: Irwin, 1968.

Bhagwati, J., V. K. Ramaswami, and T. N. Srinivasan. Domestic distortions, tariffs, and the theory of optimum subsidy: Some further results. *Journal of Political Economy* 77 (1969): 1005–10.

Friedlaender, A. F., and A. L. Vandendorpe. Excise taxes and the gains from trade. *Journal of Political Economy* 76 (1968): 1058–68.

Gorman, W. M. Tariffs, retaliation and the elasticity of demand for imports. *Review of Economic Studies* 25 (1958): 133–62.

Graaff, J. On optimum tariff structures. *Review of Economic Studies* 17 (1949–50): 47–59.

Horwell, D. J., and I. F. Pearce. A look at the structure of optimal tariff rates. *International Economic Review* 11 (1970): 147–61.

Johnson, H. G. Optimum tariffs and retaliation. *Review of Economic Studies* 21 (1953–54): 142–53. Reprinted in H. G. Johnson, *International Trade and Economic Growth*, London: Allen and Unwin, 1958.

Johnson, H. G. The gain from exploiting monopoly and monopsony power in international trade. *Economica*, N. S., 35 (1968): 151–56.

Kemp, M. C. Notes on the theory of optimal tariffs. *Economic Record* 43 (1967): 395–403.

Kemp, M. C., and T. Negishi. Domestic distortions, tariffs and the theory of optimum subsidy. *Journal of Political Economy* 77 (1969): 1011–13.

Panchmukhi, V. A theory for optimum tariff policy. *Indian Economic Journal* 9 (1961): 178–98.

Riley, J. Ranking of tariffs under monopoly power in trade: An extension. *Quarterly Journal of Economics* 84 (1970): 710–12.

Scitovsky, T. A reconsideration of the theory of tariffs. *Review of Economic Studies* 9 (1942): 89–110. Reprinted in *Readings in the Theory of International Trade*, ed. by H. S. Ellis and L. A. Metzler. Philadelphia: Blakiston, 1949.

Tower, E. Ranking the optimum tariff and the maximum revenue tariff. *Journal of International Economics* 7 (1977): 73–79.

Production Externalities

We now turn to domestic distortions. Although it may appear at first that a production externality may have the simple consequence that DP $\neq$ DRT and that therefore, in a small open competitive economy, free trade would be characterized by a situation where DRT $\neq$ FRT $=$ DRS, the analytical problems arising from production externalities can be more complex. To see this, we concentrate on two major cases below: where the externality is output related and where it is factor-use related.

22.1 Output-Related Externality

The level of output in one sector (e.g., producing good 1) affects the production possibilities of the other sector, so the level of output of good 1 that can be produced with given amounts of capital and labor depends not only on these amounts but also on Q_2, the output of good 2. In other words, the two production functions are

$$Q_1 = F(K_1, L_1, Q_2) \tag{22.1}$$

and

$$Q_2 = G(K_2, L_2). \tag{22.2}$$

A special case of equation (22.1) arises when

$$Q_1 = \phi(Q_2)\bar{F}(K_1, L_1). \tag{22.1'}$$

22.2 Factor-Use-Related Externality

The level of factor (e.g., capital) use in one sector affects the output of the other sector. The two production functions in this case will be

$$Q_1 = F(K_1, L_1, K_2) \tag{22.3}$$

and

$$Q_2 = G(K_2, L_2). \tag{22.4}$$

Again, a special case arises when

$$Q_1 = \psi(K_2)\bar{F}(K_1, L_1). \tag{22.3'}$$

In each, case, one must ask the three familiar questions:

1. Given competition in the factor markets, will unit-cost minimization by producers lead the economy to operate on the production-possibility curve (PPC)?

2. If so, would competition in the goods markets ensure that the result-ing production choice[1] will be characterized by equality of the goods-price ratio with the absolute value of the slope of the PPC? That is, will the familiar tangency condition still hold in production?

3. Is the PPC concave or not?

These questions bear on the issue of whether a competitive economy with the stated production externality will be maximizing the value of output evaluated at the goods-price ratio arrived at in competitive equilibrium.

22.3   Output-Related Externality

Consider now the case of externalities of the type embodied in equations (22.1) or (22.1') and (22.2). The familiar, necessary condition for unit-cost minimization, if producers of both goods face the same factor prices be-cause of competition in factor markets, is that the marginal rate of factor substitution, as seen by the producers, equals the factor-price ratio. That is,

$$\frac{\partial F/\partial L_1}{\partial F/\partial K_1} = \frac{w}{r} = \frac{\partial G/\partial L_2}{\partial G/\partial K_2}, \tag{22.5}$$

where $w(r)$ is the wage (rental) rate in terms of the numéraire. On the other hand, for a given factor allocation to lead to a production point on the PPC (i.e., for it to be an efficient allocation from the social or the economywide view), the social marginal rates of factor substitution (with full allowance for externalities) must be the same across sectors:

$$\left(\frac{\partial F}{\partial L_1} - \frac{\partial F}{\partial Q_2} \cdot \frac{\partial G}{\partial L_2}\right) \Big/ \left(\frac{\partial F}{\partial K_1} - \frac{\partial F}{\partial Q_2} \cdot \frac{\partial G}{\partial K_2}\right) = \frac{\partial G}{\partial L_2} \Big/ \frac{\partial G}{\partial K_2}. \tag{22.6}$$

It is easily seen that any factor allocation (K_i, L_i) that satisfies equation (22.5) will satisfy (22.6) as well. Thus, the answer to the first question above is in the affirmative: The economy will indeed operate on the PPC.

Now, if there is competition in the goods markets as well, the goods-price ratio will equal the unit-cost ratio, which in turn equals the ratio of the marginal physical product of either factor in the two sectors as per-ceived by the producers.[2] Thus

---

1. One assumes that it will be an interior choice: incomplete specialization or, in other words, diversification in production.

2. Assume an interior solution in all relevant dimensions.

$$\frac{\partial F}{\partial K_1} \bigg/ \frac{\partial G}{\partial K_2} = \frac{\partial F}{\partial L_1} \bigg/ \frac{\partial G}{\partial L_2} = p_\mathrm{p}, \tag{22.7}$$

where p_p is the price of good 2 in terms of good 1 as faced by domestic producers. But the slope of the PPC at the point corresponding to the factor allocation (K_i, L_i) is given by

$$\left(\frac{\partial F}{\partial K_1} - \frac{\partial F}{\partial Q_2} \cdot \frac{\partial G}{\partial K_2}\right) \bigg/ \frac{\partial G}{\partial K_2} = \left(\frac{\partial F}{\partial L_1} - \frac{\partial F}{\partial Q_2} \cdot \frac{\partial G}{\partial L_2}\right) \bigg/ \frac{\partial G}{\partial L_2} \equiv p^\mathrm{S} \ (\equiv \mathrm{DRT}). \tag{22.8}$$

Substituting from equation (22.7), we get

$$p_\mathrm{p} - \frac{\partial F}{\partial Q_2} = p^\mathrm{S} \qquad (\equiv \mathrm{DRT}). \tag{22.9}$$

Thus the answer to the second question listed above is in the negative as long as externalities are present. That is, as long as $\partial F/\partial Q_2 \neq 0$, $p_\mathrm{p} \neq p^\mathrm{S}$, so the goods-price line will not be tangent to the PPC at the point of production.

If the PPC is concave, then we have a simple situation such as that depicted in figure 22.1 for a small, open, competitive economy. With the production externality implying overpricing of good 2 relative to its true social transformation rate (equation 22.9), free trade in this small economy will lead to nontangency in production on the PPC at P^F,

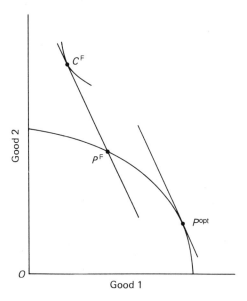

Figure 22.1

consumption at C^F, and welfare at U^F, with $P^F C^F$ the given international goods-price ratio. Thus we have DRT $\neq$ DRS $=$ FRT, since free trade equalizes the international and domestic goods-price ratios.

The optimal solution is evidently at P^{opt}, which does imply that DRT $=$ DRS $=$ FRT. This will evidently require a suitable production tax *cum* subsidy to increase the relative price facing the producers of good 2, with consumers continuing to enjoy access to international prices. A tariff would be an inferior policy to a production tax *cum* subsidy because it would, like the production tax *cum* subsidy, bring production from P^F to P^{opt}, but in so doing, it would add a gratuitous and unnecessary consumption cost. Finally, as we noted at the end of chapter 21, we can show in this case that some tariff would necessarily exist that would improve welfare over the free-trade level U^F. Therefore a tariff would be a welfare-improving policy in the case of the present production externality, but it would be inferior to the (optimal) production-tax-*cum*-subsidy policy.

Equation (22.9) yields the nature and the magnitude of the appropriate policy intervention. If private producers of good 2 are subsidized at an *ad valorem* rate of

$$\frac{\partial F / \partial Q_2}{p^{opt}}, \qquad p^{opt} \equiv \frac{p_2^{opt}}{p_1^{opt}}$$

so that the relative price of good 2 faced by private producers is

$$P_p = \frac{p_2^{opt}}{p_1^{opt}} + \frac{\partial F}{\partial Q_2} = p^s + \frac{\partial F}{\partial Q_2},$$

the social optimum will be achieved. In other words, if

$$\frac{\partial F}{\partial Q_2} > (<) \, 0,$$

so that sector 2 creates positive (negative) externalities for sector 1, either the output of good 1 is taxed (subsidized) or the output of good 2 is subsidized (taxed) relative to the prices p_1^{opt} and p_2^{opt} for achieving the social optimum.

Our analysis of policy intervention so far has been based explicitly on the assumption that the PPC is concave. However, even with output-related production externality, this may not be necessarily so. Thus it is easy to construct an example showing that $d^2 Q_1 / dQ_2^2$ could well be negative, implying that the PPC is convex. Figure 22.2 shows the kind of PPC that can result in this case; it rises up to A and then is convex between A and B. Of course the economically relevant PPC then is AB.

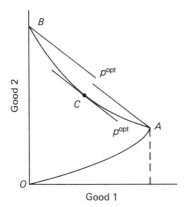

Figure 22.2

In this case it is easy to see that the economy can wind up specializing on the wrong good or being incompletely specialized and actually minimizing, rather than maximizing, welfare. Thus in figure 22.2, at given international goods-price ratio p^{opt}, specialization in producing good 1 at A is wrong in the sense that specialization in good 2 at B is superior and indeed optimal. Incomplete specialization at the tangency point at C to AB produces the least welfare;[3] the corresponding social-budget or availability line is the closest to the origin. A suitable production tax *cum* subsidy, in the event that the economy is competitively at A or C, can shift production to B and hence produce the maximal welfare.

22.4 Factor-Use-Related Externality

We will now consider briefly the factor-use-related production externality described by equations (22.3) and (22.3′), confining ourselves to the question of optimal policy intervention.

From equations (22.3) and (22.4) it is easy to see that, with competitive factor markets and no intervention, private producer behavior will lead (as before) to equation (22.5). But things change now in regard to the efficiency of factor allocation, which requires that the social marginal rates of factor substitution be the same in the two sectors, so that

$$\frac{\partial F}{\partial L_1}\bigg/\left(\frac{\partial F}{\partial K_1}-\frac{\partial F}{\partial K_2}\right)=\frac{\partial G}{\partial L_2}\bigg/\frac{\partial G}{\partial K_2}. \tag{22.10}$$

Comparison of equations (22.5) and (22.10) shows that in contrast with

3. Note that C is Marshallian-unstable.

the situation in which the externality was output-related, the equality of private marginal rates of factor substitution does not now imply equality of the corresponding social rates of factor substitution. This is not surprising, since the externality in this case manifests itself through factor use levels. It also implies that private cost minimization at given factor prices will not lead the economy to operate on the PPC. Thus further questions based on the private economy operating on the PPC become uninteresting.

Equation (22.10) also suggests the appropriate or optimal intervention to overcome this market failure. A subsidy on the private use of capital in the production of good 2 to the extent of $\partial F/\partial K_2$ (the effect of the externality created by K_2) would enable the economy to operate on the PPC. This will be sufficient to ensure optimality, with no production tax *cum* subsidy required in the goods markets.

To see that no supplementary intervention is required in the goods markets for optimality, denote the slope of the PPC at some point on it by p^s, as before. Then, at the corresponding factor allocations,

$$p^s = \frac{\partial F}{\partial L_1} \bigg/ \frac{\partial G}{\partial L_2} = \left(\frac{\partial F}{\partial K_1} - \frac{\partial F}{\partial K_2} \right) \bigg/ \frac{\partial G}{\partial K_2}. \qquad (22.11)$$

Now let $w^{\mathrm{opt}} = \partial F/\partial L_1 = p^s \partial G/\partial L_2$ be the wage rate faced by private producers of either good. Let the rental rate for producers for good 1 be $r_1^{\mathrm{opt}} = \partial F/\partial K_1$, and let that for producers of good 2 be $r_2^{\mathrm{opt}} = r_1^{\mathrm{opt}} - \partial F/\partial K_2$. From equation (22.11) it follows that

$$p^s \frac{\partial G}{\partial K_2} = \frac{\partial F}{\partial K_1} - \frac{\partial F}{\partial K_2}$$

$$= r_1^{\mathrm{opt}} - \frac{\partial F}{\partial K_2}$$

$$= r_2^{\mathrm{opt}}.$$

This implies that

$$\frac{\partial G/\partial L_2}{\partial G/\partial K_2} = \frac{w^{\mathrm{opt}}}{r_2^{\mathrm{opt}}}$$

and

$$\frac{\partial F/\partial L_1}{\partial F/\partial K_1} = \frac{w^{\mathrm{opt}}}{r_1^{\mathrm{opt}}}. \qquad (22.12)$$

From equation (22.12) it follows immediately that private producers facing factor prices $(w^{\mathrm{opt}}, r_1^{\mathrm{opt}})$ in sector 1 and $(w^{\mathrm{opt}}, r_2^{\mathrm{opt}})$ in sector 2 will reach socially optimal factor allocations and that operations on the PPC will be ensured.

Finally the private transformation ratio (the relative unit costs of production) is given by

$$\frac{\partial F / \partial L_1}{\partial G / \partial L_2} = p^s,$$

so no intervention in the commodity markets is evidently called for.

Recommended Readings

Bhagwati, J., and V. K. Ramaswami. Domestic distortions, tariffs, and the theory of optimum subsidy. *Journal of Political Economy* 71 (1963): 44–50.

Bhagwati, J., V. K. Ramaswami, and T. N. Srinivasan. Domestic distortions, tariffs, and the theory of optimum subsidy: Some further results. *Journal of Political Economy* 77 (1969): 1005–10.

Bhagwati, J. The generalized theory of distortions and welfare. In *Trade, Balance of Payments, and Growth: Papers in International Economics in Honor of Charles P. Kindleberger*, ed. by J. Bhagwati et al. Amsterdam: North-Holland, 1971.

Haberler, G. Some problems in the pure theory of international trade. *Economic Journal* 60 (1950): 223–40.

Herberg, H., and M. C. Kemp. Factor market distortions, the shape of the locus of competitive outputs, and the relation between product prices and equilibrium outputs. In *Trade, Balance of Payments, and Growth: Papers in International Economics in Honor of Charles P. Kindleberger*, ed. by J. Bhagwati et al. Amsterdam: North-Holland, 1971.

Johnson, H. G. Optimal trade intervention in the presence of domestic distortions. In *Trade, Growth, and the Balance of Payments*. ed. by R. E. Baldwin et al. Chicago: Rand McNally and Amsterdam: North-Holland, 1965.

23 Monopoly in Production

The distortionary case where there is monopoly in domestic production is relatively easy to analyze.

23.1 Nontangency

Unless there is associated monopsonistic behavior on the part of the monopolist (as discussed in chapter 24), monopoly in production will not affect the factor markets at all. Cost minimization by the monopolist in its industry, and perfect competition elsewhere, will still be compatible with operation of the economy on the efficient-possibility curve. However, monopoly in an industry will create a divergence between the domestic price ratio and the domestic, marginal rate of transformation in production. As shown in figure 23.1, for the autarkic case under monopoly in the production of good 1, autarkic equilibrium will lie at $(C_{A,M}, P_{A,M})$ and welfare at $U_{A,M}$.

23.2 Welfare Analysis

It would be tempting to conclude that—as with the identical case of production externalities (chapter 22) where the only result is nontangency—free trade ceases to be the optimal policy and a production tax *cum* subsidy is required as a first-best intervention. But this is no longer so, for here we have a case of a distortion that is not exogenous to the policy being discussed. In autarky, it is indeed true that the domestic monopoly will be protected from foreign competition. However, as soon as this small economy becomes open, the domestic monopoly itself will be destroyed. The result will be that free trade will take the economy, in figure 23.1, to P_F, consumption to C_F, and welfare to its maximum, U_F^*. Free trade thus remains the optimal policy, paradoxical as this may appear.

23.3 Gains from Trade

It follows that the gains from trade in the case of a domestic monopoly consist of two elements: the gain from the destruction of the distortionary monopoly and the standard gains from trade (analyzed in chapters 18 and 19). Thus, in figure 23.2, $C_{A,M}$ is the actual autarkic equilibrium consumption and C_A is the hypothetical autarkic equilibrium consumption on the assumption that the monopoly is destroyed. The total gains from trade (defined again as the Hicksian equivalent variation) are then QS in terms of good 1, and they can be decomposed as the sum of the

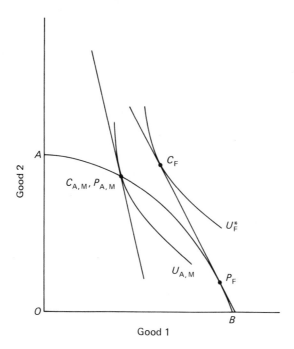

Figure 23.1

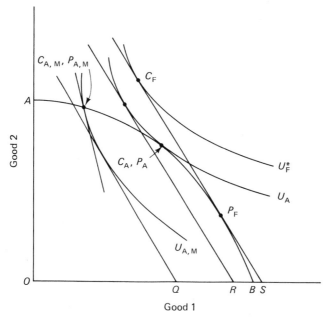

Figure 23.2

gain from destruction of monopoly (measured as QR) and the standard gain from trade (measured as RS).

For a small country, the argument that free trade will destroy domestic monopoly will also extend, generally, to nonprohibitive, *ad valorem* tariffs, but quotas will tend to shelter domestic monopoly from foreign competition.

For a large country where domestic monopolies take advantage of market power in the domestic and international markets, the above analysis of the gains from trade does not apply. In particular, Melvin and Warne (1973) have shown that with monopolies in one or both of the industries and identical market structure across the countries, a large country may be worse off in the trade-monopoly situation than in autarky. On the other hand, they show that eliminating all monopolies in both countries under trade, which certainly raises world welfare, may leave one country worse off. Thus, in general, we cannot rank a large country's welfare in the trade-monopoly situation with either autarky-monopoly or trade and perfect competition in both countries.

Recommended Readings

Caves, R. E. International cartels and monopolies in international trade. In *International Economic Policy: Theory and Evidence*, ed. by R. Dornbusch and J. A. Frenkel. Baltimore: Johns Hopkins University Press, 1979.

Fishelson, G., and A. L. Hillman. Domestic monopoly and redundant tariff protection. *Journal of International Economics* 9 (1971): 47–55.

Melvin, J. R., and R. D. Warne. Monopoly and the theory of international trade. *Journal of International Economics* 3 (1973): 117–34.

Panagariya, A. Quantitative restrictions in international trade under monopoly. *Journal of International Economics* 11 (1981): 15–31.

Panagariya, A. Tariff policy under monopoly in general equilibrium. *International Economic Review* (1982): 143–56.

Schydlowsky, D. M., and A. Siamwalla. Monopoly under general equilibrium: A geometric exercise. *Quarterly Journal of Economics* 80 (1966): 147–53.

Monopoly power in the domestic markets was analyzed in chapter 23 on the assumption that it did not simultaneously imply the exercise of monopsony power. However, as Bishop's 1966 analysis noted formally, this assumption is not necessarily realistic. Now Feenstra (1980), McCulloch and Yellen (1980), and Markusen and Robson (1980) have treated this problem in the context of an open economy.

Here we draw on the analysis of Feenstra, which uses our 2×2 analytical framework, but we amend it so that one industry is perfectly competitive in all markets while the other industry consists of a single firm with absolute control over entry. Profit maximization implies then that this firm recognizes its monopoly *and* monopsony power. To concentrate on the problem of monopsony, we will assume with Feenstra that in trade the economy is small and hence faces fixed terms of trade; therefore in free trade the firm loses its monopoly power but retains its (domestic) monopsony power. However, in autarky it will retain its monopoly power and may exercise it.

24.1 Positive Analysis of Monopsony Distortion

A number of pathologies follow from the exercise of monopsony power in this model. The major ones to note are that the economy will operate on a shrunken-in distorted, rather than on the "best," production-possibility curve (this contrasts with the case where there is exercise of domestic monopoly power alone) and that the economy will operate with non-tangency on the distorted production-possibility curve. While we establish these propositions at length, following Feenstra closely, we should note that Feenstra also shows that in contrast with the wage-differentials type of factor-market imperfection (chapter 25 below), the output responses to change in the goods-price ratio will always be "normal"—that is, the rise in the relative price of a good will always increase its output.[1]

Distorted Edgeworth Locus and PPC

Let the monopolized industry be industry 2 and the perfectly competitive industry be industry 1. The production functions are assumed to be concave and homogeneous of degree 1 in inputs, with positive marginal products, and they are given by $Q_1 = F(K_1, L_1)$ and $Q_2 = G(K_2, L_2)$,

---

1. This is because the second-order conditions of the monopsony problem imply that marginal costs are rising in equilibrium. However, Feenstra shows that the possible lack of monotonicity in marginal costs can lead to multiple equilibria and hence to discontinuous jumps in equilibrium output even when the change in the goods-price ratio is infinitesimal.

where Q_i denotes the output of industry i and $K_i(L_i)$ denotes the capital (labor) employed by industry i $(i = 1, 2)$. We choose the price of good 1 as the numéraire, so $p, r,$ and w denote the relative prices of good 2, capital, and labor, respectively. Let $\bar{K}(\bar{L})$ denote the fixed endowment of capital (labor), and define the maximum outputs $\bar{Q}_1 = F(\bar{K}, \bar{L})$ and $\bar{Q}_2 = G(\bar{K}, \bar{L})$. The monopolist's cost-minimization problem is then

$$\min_{K_2, L_2} rK_2 + wL_2 \tag{24.1}$$

subject to

$$Q_2 = G(K_2, L_2),$$

$$r = F_K,$$

$$w = F_L,$$

$$K_1 + K_2 = \bar{K},$$

$$L_1 + L_2 = \bar{L},$$

where Q_2 is given exogenously in the first constraint, $0 < Q_2 < \bar{Q}_2$. The next two constraints are the first-order conditions for profit maximization in the perfectly competitive industry, and the last two constraints are the full-employment conditions. Geometrically the monopolist's problem is to find the position on its Q_2 isoquant in the Edgeworth-Bowley box at which costs are minimized—where the factor-price ratio is determined by the slope of the competitive industry's isoquant at that point.

After some simplification the first-order conditions for cost minimization can be written as

$$\frac{G_K}{G_L} = \frac{F_K}{F_L} t(K_2), \tag{24.2}$$

where

$$t(K_2) = \frac{\sigma + \theta_L(K_2/K_1 - L_2/L_1)}{\sigma - \theta_K(K_2/K_1 - L_2/L_1)} > 0 \tag{24.3}$$

and $\sigma \equiv F_L F_K / F_{LK} F, \theta_K \equiv F_K K_1 / F, \theta_L \equiv F_L L_1 / F$ are, respectively, the elasticity of substitution and cost shares in the perfectly competitive industry. Condition (24.2) implicitly defines a cost-minimizing or distorted Edgeworth locus in the Edgeworth-Bowley box. Concerning the position of this locus, (24.2) implies that

$$\frac{G_K}{G_L} \gtreqless \frac{F_K}{F_L} \quad \text{according as} \quad \frac{K_2}{K_1} - \frac{L_2}{L_1} \gtreqless 0,$$

so the distorted Edgeworth locus must lie between the nondistorted efficiency locus (where $G_K/G_L = F_K/F_L$) and the diagonal line joining their end points. Thus the presence of a monopsony distortion will not reverse the factor intensities in the economy. Without loss of generality, we can assume henceforth that the monopolist is capital-intensive, so $K_2/K_1 - L_2/L_1 > 0$ and $t(K_2) > 1$ for $0 < K_2 < \bar{K}$.

The lower bound on $t(K_2)$ is unity, since otherwise the factor intensities are reversed. The upper bound on $t(K_2)$ is

$$z = \frac{G_K(\bar{K}, \bar{L})F_L(\bar{K}, \bar{L})}{G_L(\bar{K}, \bar{L})F_K(\bar{K}, \bar{L})},$$

since substituting $t(K_2) = z$ into the equilibrium condition (24.3) implies that $K_2/L_2 = K_1/L_1 = \bar{K}/\bar{L}$ so that the distorted Edgeworth locus is coincident with the diagonal of the Edgeworth-Bowley box, whereas $t(K_2) > z$ implies that the factor intensities are again reversed. We can show that $t(K_2)$ will equal its lower and upper bound when the economy is specialized in production of good 2 and good 1, respectively. The distorted Edgeworth locus and the nondistorted efficiency locus are illustrated in figure 24.1.

Feenstra's intuitive explanation for the shape of the distorted Edgeworth locus is as follows: For given Q_2 a movement off the distorted Edgeworth locus has two effects on the monopolist's costs: a price effect in which movements off the efficiency locus change the factor-price ratio

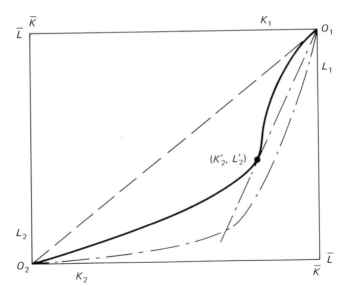

Figure 24.1

as given by the slope of the competitive industry's isoquant, and an efficiency effect in which movement off the efficiency locus leads to non-tangency of the factor-price ratio and a marginal rate of substitution in production of the monopolized industry. When the monopolized industry is very small, the competitive industry's isoquants are "flat" relative to its own, and so the efficiency effect dominates, leading to a very small divergence from the efficiency locus. When the monopolized industry is very large, its own isoquants are "flat" relative to those of the competitive industry, and so the price effect dominates; this implies strong monopsony power and a large movement off the efficiency locus.

The corresponding shrunk-in distorted production-possibility curve (PPC) must lie between the nondistorted PPC and the chord joining its end points, since the diagonal line of the Edgeworth-Bowley box corresponds to this chord. The distorted PPC has a slope equal to the slope of the nondistorted PPC when $Q_2 = 0$ and $-\bar{Q}_2/\bar{Q}_1$ when $Q_2 = \bar{Q}_2$, as illustrated in figure 24.2. Given the region within which the distorted PPC must lie, its end point slopes, and the fact that the nondistorted PPC is concave, one can see that the distorted PPC must be concave for sufficiently small values of Q_2 and convex for sufficiently large values (its shape for intermediate values of Q_2 is indeterminate and can alternate between concave and convex more than once).

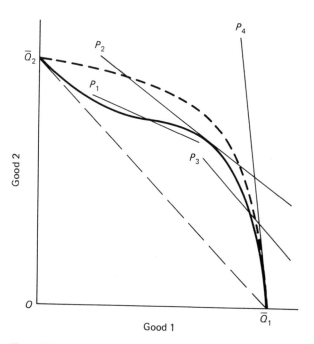

Figure 24.2

distorted and nondistorted PPCs are similar for small Q_2,
stortions are unimportant when the monopolized industry
s can also be established by varying σ in equation (24.3). A
nopolized industry can be expected to face very elastic excess-
curves for inputs, which is equivalent to saying that the elasticity
substitution in the competitive industry is large. As σ increases in
equation (24.3), t approaches unity and the distorted Edgeworth locus and
PPC shift toward the nondistorted curves; in the limit as σ approaches
infinity, the distorted and nondistorted curves coincide.

Nontangency of Goods-Price Ratio and Distorted PPC

Let p, the price of good 2 relative to good 1, be given as a parameter by
world trade. Then the monopolist's profit-maximization problem is

$$\max_{K_2, L_2} pG(K_2, L_2) - rK_2 - wL_2,$$

subject to

$$r = F_K, \quad w = F_L, \quad K_1 + K_2 = \bar{K}, \quad L_1 + L_2 = \bar{L}.$$

The first-order conditions for profit maximization can be written as

$$pG_K = r\left(\frac{1 + \theta_L(K_2/K_1 - L_2/L_1)}{\sigma}\right),$$

$$pG_L = w\left(\frac{1 - \theta_K(K_2/K_1 - L_2/L_1)}{\sigma}\right). \tag{24.4}$$

Thus the factor used intensively by the monopolist is "exploited," receiving a factor payment less than its marginal value product. The other
factor is "rewarded," receiving a payment greater than its marginal value
product in the monopolized industry.

Using conditions (24.4), it can be shown that

$$p = -\frac{dQ_1}{dQ_2}\left[1 + \left(\frac{L_1}{K_1} - \frac{dL_2}{dK_2}\right)\frac{F_{LK}K_1(K_2/K_1 - L_2/L_1)}{F_K + F_L(dL_2/dK_2)}\right], \tag{24.5}$$

where $K_2/K_1 - L_2/L_1 \geq 0$ by our assumption that the monopolist is
capital-intensive. If the economy is not specialized in the production of
the competitive industry, so that $K_2/K_1 - L_2/L_1 > 0$, the nontangency
of the goods-price ratio and the distorted PPC in equilibrium can be
expressed as

$$p \gtreqless \text{DRT} \quad \text{according as} \quad \frac{dL_2}{dK_2} \gtreqless \frac{L_1}{K_1}, \tag{24.6}$$

where the marginal rate of transformation DRT $\equiv -dQ_1/dQ_2$. Feenst[a]
shows that $p > $ DRT when the output of the monopolized industry is sufficiently small (but nonzero), and $p < $ DRT when Q_2 is sufficiently large.
These two cases are divided by a point such as (K_2', L_2') in figure 24.1, at
which $dL_2/dK_2 = L_1/K_1$ and $p = $ DRT.[2] The maximum value of p at
which the economy is specialized in the production of the competitive
industry, so that $K_2/K_1 - L_2/L_1 = 0$ in equation (24.5), is given by the
slope of the distorted or (equivalently) the nondistorted PPC at that
point. The nontangency conditions are illustrated in figure 24.2. The output responses are "normal" in the sense that $dQ_2/dp > 0$, and so the
goods-price lines in figure 24.2 are successively steeper as Q_2 falls.

Analysis of Autarkic Equilibrium

How is autarkic equilibrium to be depicted in this economy? It is clear
that we must show the economy operating on the distorted PPC plus a
nontangency with the goods-price ratio, but something more needs to be
added. Two points must be noted, in particular.

First, the monopsonist has simultaneously monopoly power. If he does
not exercise it, what happens to autarkic equilibrium in contrast to the
case where he does exercise it? This comparison is important when we
come to discuss the gains from trade (in the next section), for free trade
in a small economy will eliminate monopoly power but will leave
the monopsony power unaffected. Therefore relevant elements in the
gains from trade will be the comparison of autarky with monopoly versus
autarky without monopoly and the comparison between autarky without
monopoly and free trade. Solving for the price and quantity changes in
the first comparison is our concern here.

Second, the monopsonist, whether or not he exercises monopoly power,
can be modeled for autarkic equilibrium in two ways: Either he treats
national income as exogenous to his policies, or he takes into account
the link between output and goods demand via national income. In the
following we concentrate on the former case, where national income is
treated as exogenous by the monopsonist.[3] We then contrast the case
where the monopsonist exercises his monopoly power with the case where
he does not.

2. This point always exists but is not unique in general, so for intermediate values of Q_2 the
nontangency can alternate between $p > $ DRT and $p < $ DRT more than once. Though
(K_2', L_2') is nonunique in general, it is unique for the special case of Cobb-Douglas production functions.

3. The latter case has also been analyzed by Feenstra (1980, p. 223) and does not make any
essential difference to the analysis below.

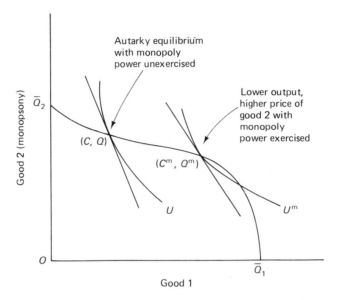

Figure 24.3

Now, if he does exercise his monopoly power, the marginal cost of the monopsonist will equal the goods-price ratio, deflated in the usual Joan Robinsonian fashion by $1 - 1/e_2$, where e_2 is the price elasticity of demand for good 2. If the monopsonist fails to exercise this monopoly power, this deflation does not apply. Utilizing this contrast, we can follow Feenstra, who further shows that the exercise of monopoly power by the monopsonist in autarky must lead (as long as neither good is inferior and marginal costs are increasing) to a lower output and a higher goods-price ratio than when the monopoly power is not exercised. That is, in figure 24.3 the autarky equilibrium (C^m, Q^m) with monopoly power exercised will imply a lower output and a higher price of the monopsonist's good 2.

24.2 Welfare Implications

Gains from Free Trade

If free trade is introduced into this economy, monopoly power is destroyed. Therefore the gains or losses from free trade for a small economy can be decomposed into two component elements: (1) the gain or loss due to moving from autarky with monopoly power exercised to autarky with monopoly power not exercised, and (2) the gain or loss due to moving from autarky with monopoly power not exercised to free trade (which

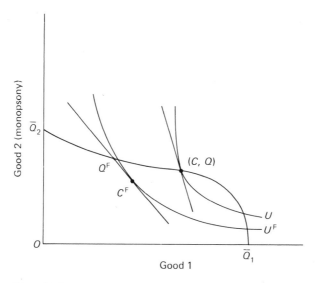

Figure 24.4

eliminates the monopoly power).[4] It turns out that neither of these two components can be signed definitively and that the overall gain from free trade therefore may be a loss instead. To see this clearly, recall from equations (24.5) and (24.6) that the economy can have $p \gtreqless$ DRT and also that the outputs in the economy will respond normally to a change in the goods price (a rise in the price of good 2 will increase its output).

It follows that component 1 may imply a loss from eliminating the exercise of monopoly power by the monopsonist, for this elimination will raise the output and lower the price of the monopsonist's good. But this may actually worsen welfare by pushing the economy toward increased production of the wrong good. This possibility is illustrated in figure 24.3, where $U < U^m$ (i.e., social utility under autarky is less when monopoly power is not exercised than when it is).

As figure 24.4 shows, component 2 may also be "perversely" signed; that is, a move from autarky without exercise of monopoly power to free trade may reduce welfare. Thus in figure 24.4 free trade increases the relative price of good 2, and its output is correspondingly higher at Q^F than at Q. The resulting welfare U^F is less than welfare U at autarky without monopoly.

Optimal Policy Intervention

Evidently, if we assume lump-sum taxation, the optimal policy intervention here must be a factor-use tax *cum* subsidy specific to the monopo-

---

4. The latter might be called the "normal" gains from trade, as in chapters 18 and 19.

lized industry 2 and favoring the use of the factor used intensively by that industry. Such a policy would take the economy back onto the undistorted PPC and equate $p = DRT = FRT = DRS$ for this small, open economy, and would thereby achieve full optimality as discussed in chapter 20.

Recommended Readings

Bishop, R. L. Monopoly under general equilibrium: Comment. *Quarterly Journal of Economics* 80, (1966): 652–59.

Feenstra, R. C. Monopsony, distortions in an open economy: A theoretical analysis. *Journal of International Economics* 10 (1980): 213–35.

Markusen, J. R., and A. J. Robson. Simple general equilibrium and trade with a monopsonized sector. *Canadian Journal of Economics* 13 (1980): 668–82.

McCulloch, R., and J. L. Yellen. Factor market monopsony and the allocation of resources. *Journal of International Economics* 10 (1980): 237–47.

25 Wage Differentials

There are many types of factor-market distortions. The three major varieties that have been analyzed in international trade theory are that where wages rates are fully flexible but unequal, for identical factors, between sectors; that where wage rates for identical factors are equal between sectors but inflexible downward; and that where the wage rate is sticky in only a subset of the sectors in the economy.

25.1 Nature of the Distortion

If the same factor of production commands differential wages between sectors, is there necessarily a distortion? Data on rural and urban wages in many underdeveloped countries show that the latter exceed the former (Hagen 1958), but this differential may not be distortionary for any of several reasons. For example, if rural labor is migrating to the cities, the capitalized value of the differential may wholly reflect the cost of the movement. On the other hand, it may reflect the fact that the urban sector is unionized and maintains a wage differential in favor of itself in comparison with the nonunionized rural sector; this amounts to a distortion. Governmental wage-regulating legislation may result in such a differential as well, since the industrial proletariat may have greater political clout than the impoverished and unorganized landless laborers.

While the issue of differential wages for identical labor, and its implication for trade policy, in particular, and for economic policy, in general, arose in the early postwar period in the context of developing countries and can be traced to the early writings of the Romanian economist Mihaïl Manoïlescu,[1] recently the argument has been revived in the context of developed countries instead by Katz and Summers (1989). Thus, referring to the United States, these authors have argued that a significant, unexplained residual remains when cross-industry remuneration of labor is analyzed, after adjustments have been made for a variety of explanatory characteristics. In their view, a distortionary wage differential exists, leading them to distinguish between "good" and "bad" jobs. The labor economist, Jacob Mincer, on the other hand, has argued that this residual, and hence implied distortion, can be significantly reduced by adding other variables. Disagreement remains therefore, on the empirical relevance of the wage differential argument of the United States.[2]

1. Douglas Irwin's (1996) classic work on the intellectual history of free trade contains an extended discussion of these early writings.

2. Katz and Summers (1989) prefer to explain the wage differential in terms of the "efficiency wage" theory. Bulow and Summers (1986) have an early examination of this theory. Brecher (1992) has explored the theory and its implications for commercial policy in general equilibrium, much like our discussion of several factor market distortions, and we urge the reader to work through this careful paper.

Assuming that there is a distortionary wage differential, we can consider two polar alternatives: where the differential is constant at a relative value [e.g., where the urban wage is $\bar{\lambda}$ (>1) times the rural wage] and where it is constant at an absolute value (e.g., when the urban wage exceeds the rural by $\bar{\lambda}$). We will concentrate on the former case, which has been analyzed in considerable detail in the literature.[3] For simplicity, and following the major contributions, the 2×2 model will be utilized.

25.2   Analysis

The Model

Now, the basic 2×2 model, using the average-product-of-labor production functions, is again

$$Q_1 = L_1 f(k_1), \tag{25.1}$$

$$Q_2 = (1 - L_1)g(k_2), \tag{25.2}$$

$$L_1 k_1 + (1 - L_1)k_2 = k, \tag{25.3}$$

$$f_K(k_1) = pg_K(k_2), \tag{25.4}$$

$$(f - k_1 f_K)\lambda = p(g - k_2 g_K), \tag{25.5}$$

where the endowment of labor is put at unity by choice of units and where f_K and g_K are the marginal physical products of factor K in the production of goods 1 and 2, respectively. This model yields the factor-price ratio as

$$\omega = \frac{f - k_1 f_K}{f_K}, \tag{25.6}$$

and

$$\lambda\omega = \frac{g - k_2 g_K}{g_K}, \tag{25.7}$$

where λ is the wage differential; that is, the relative reward of factor L in good 2 is λ times that in good 1.

Under concavity assumptions, equations (25.6) and (25.7) can be solved uniquely to yield k_1 and k_2 as functions $k_1(\omega)$ and $k_2(\omega)$. Thus,

---

3. The major contributions here, aside from Hagen (1958), are Johnson (1966), Bhagwati and Srinivasan (1971), Jones (1971), Herberg and Kemp (1971), and Magee (1973). The constant-absolute-differential case is analyzed in Schweinberger (1979).

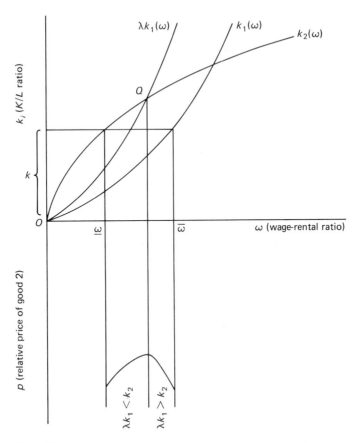

Figure 25.1

for any ω, we can solve for the corresponding k_1 and k_2, and as before, we can define the feasible range of factor-price ratios, $[\underline{\omega}, \bar{\omega}]$, given the overall factor endowment (k) as illustrated in the top half of figure 25.1. The value of L_1, and hence the allocation of factors between the two goods, corresponding to any ω, is then obtained from equation (25.3), whereas the value of ω can be obtained from (25.4) once p is specified exogenously.

Relationship between Goods-Price and Factor-Price Ratios

Now rewrite equation (25.4) as

$$p = \frac{f_K(k_1)}{g_K(k_2)}, \tag{25.8}$$

where the right-hand side is evidently a function of ω alone. Thus, writing

p as $p(\omega)$ and differentiating, we can derive[4]

$$\frac{p'(\omega)}{p(\omega)} = -\frac{f_K(k_1)}{f(k_1)} + \frac{\lambda g_K(k_2)}{g(k_2)}$$

$$= -\frac{1}{\omega + k_1} + \frac{\lambda}{\lambda\omega + k_2} \qquad \text{(using equations 25.6 and 25.7)}$$

$$= \frac{\lambda k_1 - k_2}{(\omega + k_1)(\lambda\omega + k_2)}. \qquad (25.9)$$

This basic equation shows immediately that the relationship between goods-price and factor-price ratios need no longer be unique even if the Samuelsonian factor-intensity condition is satisfied, for if the value of the numerator $\lambda k_1 - k_2$ changes sign within the interval of feasible factor-price ratios $[\underline{\omega}, \bar{\omega}]$, then $p'(\omega)$ will also change sign. This is illustrated in figure 25.1, where the sign of $\lambda k_1 - k_2$ changes from negative to positive within the interval $[\underline{\omega}, \bar{\omega}]$, and hence the lower half of the figure shows the curve relating ω to p turning up as long as $\lambda k_1 < k_2$ but coming down after $\lambda k_1 > k_2$.

Role of Differential-Weighted Factor Intensities

What becomes critical to the behavior of the system therefore is not the relationship between k_1 and k_2 (the Samuelsonian factor intensities) but the relationship between λk_1 and k_2 (the differential-weighted factor intensities). Jones (1971) describes the former as *physical* and the latter as *value* factor intensities.

An interesting implication of equation (25.4) is that even if all the usual sufficient conditions for factor-price equilization are assumed to hold in this $2 \times 2 \times 2$ model and it is also assumed that both countries have an identical wage differential (identical λ for the same factor in the same good), factor-price equalization may break down, for the two countries may have factor endowments on different sides of the crossover point of differential-weighted factor intensities (different sides of Q in figure 25.1).

Other Pathologies

One obvious implication of the wage-differential model is that the economy's feasible production-possibility set shrinks. This follows immediately from the fact that entrepreneurs face differential factor-price ratios and hence the rates of marginal substitution among factors will not be

---

4. The detailed steps of this derivation are spelled out in Bhagwati and Srinivasan (1971, pp. 22–23).

equated between them. The economy will therefore not operate on the efficient Edgeworth-Bowley contract curve in the box diagram.

It is also intuitively clear that the good that must pay more for an identical factor will be "overpriced" and that the marginal rate of transformation in domestic production (DRT) will no longer equal the goods-price ratio. Bhagwati and Srinivasan (1971, pp. 23–25) derive the relationship between DRT and the goods-price ratio as

$$\frac{dQ_1}{dQ_2} = -p\left(\frac{(\omega + k_2)(k_2 - k)\sigma_1 k_1 + (\omega + k_1)(k - k_1)\sigma_2 k_2}{(\lambda\omega + k_2)(k_2 - k)\sigma_1 k_1 + (\lambda\omega + k_1)(k - k_1)\sigma_2 k_2}\right), \qquad (25.10)$$

where σ_i is the Hicksian elasticity of substitution of the two factors in the production of the ith good. In the standard case where there is no wage differential, $\lambda = 1$, and hence equation (25.10) reduces to

$$\frac{dQ_1}{dQ_2} = -p,$$

the usual tangency condition. However, when $\lambda \neq 1$, the wage differential results in nontangency of the price line with the (feasible) production-possibility curve. Rewriting (25.10) as

$$p - \left(-\frac{dQ_1}{dQ_2}\right)$$

$$= p(\lambda - 1)\omega\left(\frac{(k_2 - k)\sigma_1 k_1 + (k - k_1)\sigma_2 k_2}{(\lambda\omega + k_2)(k_2 - k)\sigma_1 k_1 + (\lambda\omega + k_1)(k - k_1)\sigma_2 k_2}\right),$$

$$(25.10')$$

we see immediately that

$$p \gtreqless -\frac{dQ_1}{dQ_2} \quad \text{according as} \quad \lambda \gtreqless 1,$$

since the term in large parentheses on the right-hand side of (25.10') is always positive. Thus the relative price of good 2 will exceed the marginal rate of transformation (along the feasible production-possibility curve) if $\lambda > 1$—that is, if the cost of factor L is λ times higher in the production of good 2.[5]

---

5. Equation (25.10) implies that the degree of divergence between the goods-price ratio and DRT (the degree of nontangency) is not constant at all points on the feasible production-possibility curve. Even with a constant λ and CES production functions such that σ_1 and σ_2 are also constant, this nonconstancy of the degree of divergence between $-dQ_1/dQ_2$ and p will persist in general.

Yet another resulting pathology is that output response to goods-price change may no longer be normal. It can again be shown (Bhagwati and Srinivasan 1971, pp. 26–28) that the wage-differential economy will be characterized by a fall (rise) in the output of a good when its relative price rises (falls) only when the Samuelsonian and the differential-weighted factor-intensity rankings are different. That is, the perverse possibilities arise if and only if

$$k_1(\omega) > k_2(\omega) \quad \text{but} \quad \lambda k_1(\omega) < k_2(\omega)$$

or

$$k_1(\omega) < k_2(\omega) \quad \text{but} \quad \lambda k_1(\omega) > k_2(\omega).$$

Finally the feasible production-possibility set may no longer be convex when a wage differential is present. Besides, the production-possibility curve may have both convex and concave stretches. The formula for d^2Q_1/dQ_2^2, and hence its sign, is relevant to this issue; however, as shown by Bhagwati and Srinivasan (1971, pp. 29–33) and Kemp and Herberg (1971), the formula is fairly complex, and (in general, with the usual restrictions) it is not possible to determine the sign of this derivative.

Stability Conditions

The pathologies derived and described above follow from comparative-static analysis. However, Neary (1978) argues that, for a variety of plausible adjustment mechanisms, the pathology of perverse output response to a price change can be ruled out as dynamically unstable and hence unlikely to be observed.[6]

Welfare Analysis

The ranking of policy interventions in the presence of wage differentials was touched upon in chapter 20. Our analysis now shows that a distortionary wage differential will imply (under the usual assumptions of costless lump-sum taxation and transfers) that the first-best policy is to offset the differential by a wage subsidy to the sector penalized by the differential. This will restore full optimality, including operation on the efficient production-possibility curve. The second-best policy is to take the differential and hence the restricted production-possibility curve as

6. Murray Kemp has noted, however, that Neary's arguments relate to models where the goods-price ratio is given. Therefore they leave open the possibility that in more "complete" models where the goods-price ratio is endogenously determined, the perversities may resurrect themselves. In short, instability of a "partial" system does not preclude stability of the larger system. Therefore the question raised by Neary must still be considered open if this view is accepted.

given but to then offset the nontangency by a suitable production tax *cum* subsidy, thus maximizing social utility subject to the restricted production-possibility curve. A tariff will be the third-best policy, since it will unnecessarily impose a consumption cost while offsetting the production distortion along the restricted production-possibility curve. A consumption tax *cum* subsidy will evidently be irrelevant, only imposing a consumption cost (for large changes).

Recommended Readings

Batra, R. Factor market imperfections and gains from trade. *Oxford Economic Papers*, N. S., 23 (1971): 182–88.

Batra, R. Factor market imperfections, The terms of trade and welfare. *American Economic Review* 61 (1971): 946–55.

Batra, R., and P. K. Pattanaik. Domestic distortions and the gains from trade. *Economic Journal* 80 (1970): 638–49.

Bhagwati, J. The generalized theory of distortions and welfare. In *Trade, Balance of Payments, and Growth: Papers in International Economics in Honor of Charles P. Kindleberger*, ed. by J. Bhagwati. Amsterdam: North-Holland, 1971.

Bhagwati, J., and V. K. Ramaswami. Domestic distortions, tariffs and the theory of optimum subsidy. *Journal of Political Economy* 71 (1963): 44–50.

Bhagwati, J., V. K. Ramaswami, and T. N. Srinivasan. Domestic distortions, tariffs and the theory of optimum subsidy: Some further results. *Journal of Political Economy* 77 (1969): 1005–10.

Bhagwati, J., and T. N. Srinivasan. The theory of wage differentials: Production response and factor price equalisation. *Journal of International Economics* 1 (1971): 19–35.

Brecher, R. A. An efficiency-wage model with explicit monitoring: Unemployment and welfare in an open economy. *Journal of International Economics* 32 (1992): 179–91.

Bulow, J. I., and L. H. Summers. A theory of dual labor markets with applications to industrial policy, discrimination, and Keynesian unemployment. *Journal of Labor Economics* 4 (1986): 376–414.

Hagen, E. An economic justification of protectionism. *Quarterly Journal of Economics* 62 (1958): 496–514.

Herberg, H., and M. Kemp. Factor market distortions, the shape of the locus of competitive outputs, and the relation between product prices and equilibrium outputs. In *Trade, Balance of Payments and Growth: Papers in International Economics in Honor of Charles P. Kindleberger*, ed. by J. Bhagwati et al. Amsterdam: North-Holland, 1971.

Johnson, H. G. Factor market distortions and the shape of the transformation curve. *Econometrica* 34 (1966): 686–98.

Johnson, H. G. Optimal trade intervention in the presence of domestic distortions. In *Trade, Growth, and the Balance of Payments: Essays in Honour of G. Haberler*, ed. by R. E. Baldwin et al. Chicago: Rand McNally and Amsterdam: North-Holland, 1965.

Jones, R. W. Distortion in factor markets and the general equilibrium model of production. *Journal of Political Economy* 74 (1971): 437–59.

Irwin, D. *Against the Tide: An Intellectual History of Free Trade*. Princeton: Princeton University Press, 1996.

Katz, L., and L. H. Summers. Can interindustry wage differentials justify strategic trade policy? In *Trade Policies for International Competitiveness*, ed. by R. C. Feenstra. Chicago: University of Chicago Press, 1989, pp. 85–116.

Kemp, M. C., and T. Negishi. Domestic distortions, tariffs, and the theory of optimum subsidy. *Journal of Political Economy* 77 (1969): 1011–13.

Neary, J. P. Dynamic stability and the theory of factor-market distortions. *American Economic Review* 68 (1978): 671–82.

Magee, S. P. Factor market distortions, production and trade: A survey. *Oxford Economic Papers*, N. S., 25 (1973): 1–43.

Magee, S. P. *International Trade and Distortions in Factor Markets*. New York: Marcel Dekker, 1976.

Schweinberger, A. G. The theory of factor price equilisation, the case of constant absolute differentials. *Journal of International Economics* 9 (1979): 95–115.

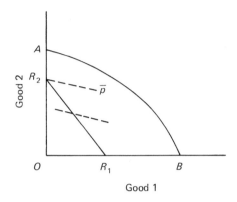

(a)

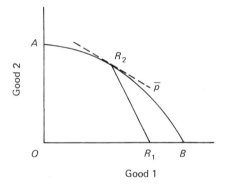

(b)

Figure 26.4

lead the economy from maximal unemployment at $\bar{k}_1$ to full employment at $\bar{K}/\bar{L}$.[2]

Figure 26.4a shows the resulting impact on the production-possibility curve. For all $p > \bar{p}$ the economy will specialize at R_2, which represents complete specialization on good 2 and corresponds to the unemployment level $\bar{k}_2$ in figure 26.3. The move from R_2 down to R_1 in figure 26.4a corresponds to the move from $\bar{k}_2$ to $\bar{k}_1$ in figure 26.3 and represents increasing unemployment at constant $\bar{p}$.[3] Finally the move from R_1 to B

2. For fuller details, especially on regions of complete specialization, see Brecher (1974b).

3. R_2R_1 is the Rybczynski line discussed in chapter 29. The equation characterizing it is derived formally in Brecher (1974a).

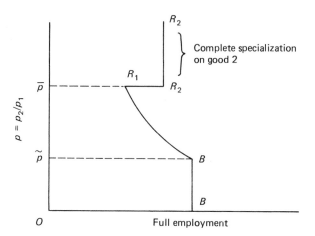

(a)

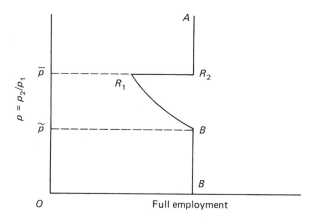

(b)

Figure 26.5

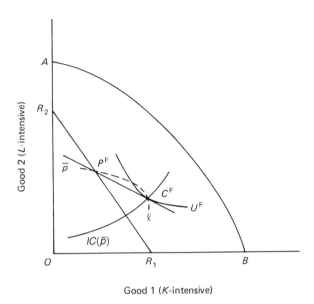

Figure 26.6

corresponds to successive reductions in p below $\bar{p}$, which take the economy in figure 26.3 from $\bar{k}_1$ to $\bar{K}/\bar{L}$ (the overall factor-employment ratio).
Figure 26.5a shows the corresponding relationship between p and the
level of employment. Thus, for all $p > \bar{p}$, there is constant but less than
full employment with complete specialization on good 2. At $\bar{p}$ the level of
unemployment can vary up from R_2 to R_1. Then, for $p < \bar{p}$, as p falls the
level of unemployment falls all the way from R_1 until full employment
is reached at B at some $\tilde{p}$. For all further p values below $\tilde{p}$ the economy
remains in place, with maximal possible employment, continued specialization in producing good 1, and increasing real wage in terms of good 2
as p declines.

Figures 26.4b and 26.5b essentially modify the above analysis for the
situation where there is a stretch AR_2 on the production-possibility
curve AB where the minimum wage would not be a binding constraint.
Then the feasible production-possibility curve changes from R_2R_1B in
figure 26.4a to AR_2R_1B in figure 26.4b, and now, for $p > \bar{p}$, as shown
in figure 26.5b, the economy will be fully employed, with all the rest as
in figure 26.5a.

Evidently, if the economy can operate on AR_2, the standard analysis
takes over, and there is no problem left. Therefore we will follow Brecher
in disregarding that possibility and concentrate on the situation depicted
in figures 26.3, 26.4a, and 26.5a.

Free-Trade Equilibrium

Free-trade equilibrium is then depicted as in figure 26.6. For simplicity it has been shown to occur at incomplete specialization in production—that is, along the line $R_2 R_1$ rather than at R_2 or along $R_1 B$.

Along $R_2 R_1$ the goods-price ratio must be $\bar{p}$ and nontangent to $R_2 R_1$ at P^F, the production point. Since free trade equalizes domestic and foreign goods-price ratios, $\bar{p}$ must also be the equilibrium foreign price ratio and the price ratio faced by consumers. Thus the consumption point C^F must lie on $\bar{p}$ through P^F and must be tangent to the social-indifference curve U^F at price ratio $\bar{p}$. C^F in fact satisfies both properties. Note that C^F would lie on an income-consumption path $IC(\bar{p})$ that is defined on the goods-price ratio $\bar{p}$ and can simply be derived as the intersection of $IC(\bar{p})$ with $\bar{p}$ through P^F. The equilibrium trade is then defined in the usual way by the triangle constituted by production at P^F and consumption at C^F, the terms of trade being $P^F C^F$.

If this is a small open economy with fixed terms of trade, $P^F C^F$ is also the foreign-offer curve superimposed on P^F in the Baldwin sense (chapter 5). However, if it is a large economy with monopoly power in trade, the foreign-offer curve is $P^F \ell$ (and FRT is not equal to the foreign price ratio at C^F).

For the small-economy case, equilibrium is not unique along $R_2 R_1$; $\bar{p}$ could be placed at any point P^F along $R_2 R_1$, and the intersection of $\bar{p}$ so shifted with the income consumption curve $IC(\bar{p})$ would define the equilibrium C^F and hence the equilibrium volume of trade. This nonuniqueness is identical to that noted for the Ricardian economy in chapters 2 and 3, and of course along $R_2 R_1$ the Brecher economy *is* Ricardian. For the large-country case, this nonuniqueness of free-trade equilibrium will generally not arise; the linear stretch in the foreign-offer curve of the Brecher economy in the $R_2 R_1$ region can still be cut uniquely by the foreign-offer curve facing the Brecher economy, yielding a unique free-trade equilibrium.[4]

Small-Country Case

Under free trade, if production is on $R_2 R_1$ at P^F in figure 26.6 DRT does not equal $\bar{p}$, since $\bar{p}$ is nontangent to $R_2 R_1$. However, $\bar{p}$ is the foreign price ratio and equals FRT for a small country under free trade. Consumption is also at $\bar{p}$, so $\bar{p}$ equals DRS. Therefore free trade leads to a situation where DRT $\neq$ FRT $=$ DRS along the restricted production-possibility curve $R_2 R_1 B$.

---

4. See Brecher (1974b) for the derivation of offer curves for a Brecher economy with $R_2 R_1 B$ as its production-possibility curve.

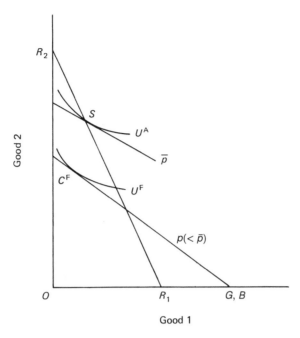

Figure 26.7

Two familiar points then can be made. First, free trade is evidently a suboptimal policy, as just noted, so it should be easy to show that free trade may immiserize an initially autarkic economy. Thus, in figure 26.7, let the autarkic equilibrium be at S on R_2R_1 at $\bar{p}$. Free trade for this small, now open economy results then in production at G with complete specialization in producing good 1. Consumption is then at C^F. Welfare is at U^F, and evidently falls below U^A at autarky. One new angle in this economy that does not arise in other cases considered so far is that autarky has unemployment and free trade has less. If we attach a negative welfare weight to unemployment, then the specific free-trade equilibrium portrayed in figure 26.7 may, despite $U^F < U^A$, be considered a "better" equilibrium. Second, the optimal, first-best policy is evidently a wage subsidy to all employment, which will eliminate at the source the wage stickiness and the consequent problems analyzed above. But if this cannot be instituted, a production tax *cum* subsidy is evidently the second-best policy in this economy. If the economy is as in figure 26.8a, the production tax *cum* subsidy that increases p above $\bar{p}$ will lead to specialization on good 2 at R_2, and the production tax *cum* subsidy that reduces p below $\bar{p}$ to an appropriate level can shift specialization onto good 1 at B. In figure 26.8a, specialization at R_2 dominates that at B, except that R_2 is also characterized by unemployment whereas B is not. Thus there may

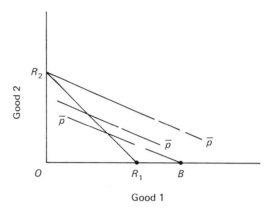

(a)

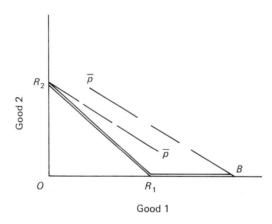

(b)

Figure 26.8

be a conflict between maximizing welfare as implied by the conventional social-utility function and maintaining full employment. This conflict disappears in the parametric case depicted in figure 26.8b, where specialization on good 1 at B maximizes welfare and ensures full employment.

Large-Country Case

For the large-country case, such as that described in figure 26.6 with the foreign offer curve as $P^F\ell$, the free-trade equilibrium is characterized by DRT $\neq$ FRT $\neq$ DRS. The domestic and foreign goods-price ratios equal $\bar{p}$, but DRT $\neq \bar{p}$ (since DRT is given by the slope of R_2R_1), FRT $\neq \bar{p}$ (since FRT equals the slope of $P^F\ell$ at C^F), and DRS $= \bar{p}$. This is a

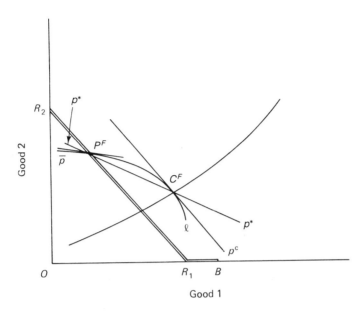

Figure 26.9

situation of suboptimality, but with two distortions occurring simultaneously. It is seen then that two policy instruments can be utilized to achieve (second-best) optimality in this situation.[5] If such an optimal solution were to occur along R_2R_1, at incomplete specialization, it would be as illustrated by figure 26.9.

Figure 26.9 portrays the following equilibrium situation, characterized by an optimal combination of a tariff and a production tax *cum* subsidy or (equivalently) a tariff and a consumption tax *cum* subsidy. In our notation,

$$\text{DRT} = \text{Slope of } R_2R_1 \neq \bar{p} \ (= p^{\text{p}}),$$

$$\text{DRS} = \text{Slope of } R_2R_1 = p^{\text{c}},$$

and

$$\text{FRT} = \text{Slope of } R_2R_1 \neq p^* \neq \bar{p}.$$

That is, the three rates of transformation are equalized, so the first-order conditions for an interior maximum are met. This solution is supported competitively by a price mechanism that shows a world or foreign goods-price ratio p^* that is not equal to $\bar{p}$. In turn $\bar{p}$ equals the domestic goods-

5. First-best optimality is achieved by a uniform wage subsidy.

price ratio faced by producers p^p but not the price ratio faced by consumers p^c (which instead equals the slope of R_2R_1). Evidently, this price configuration can be a result of either a tariff implied by the difference between p^c and p^* (with an adjusting production tax *cum* subsidy so that producers wind up facing $\bar{p}$ as the full consequence of these two policy interventions) or a tariff implied by the difference between $\bar{p}$ $(= p^p)$ and p^* (with an adjusting consumption tax *cum* subsidy which results net in consumers facing a market price ratio p^c equal to the slope of R_2R_1). Brecher (1974a) considers the latter formulation; he also considers the case where only the tariff (or trade subsidy) is employed as a policy instrument.

Recommended Readings

Brecher, R. Optimal commercial policy for a minimum-wage economy. *Journal of International Economics* 4 (1974a): 139–49.

Brecher, R. Minimum wage rates and the pure theory of international trade. *Quarterly Journal of Economics* 88 (1974b): 98–116.

Haberler, G. Some problems in the pure theory of international trade. *Economic Journal* 60 (1950): 223–40.

Johnson, H. G. Optimal trade intervention in the presence of domestic distortions. In *Trade, Growth, and the Balance of Payments: Essays in Honour of G. Haberler* ed. by K. E. Baldwin et al. Chicago: Rand McNally and Amsterdam: North-Holland, 1965.

Johnson, H. G. Minimum wage laws: A general equilibrium analysis. *Canadian Journal of Economics* 2 (1969): 599–604.

Lefeber, L. Trade and minimum wage rates. In *Trade, Balance of Payments, and Growth: Papers in International Economics in Honor of Charles P. Kindleberger*, ed. by J. Bhagwati et al. Amsterdam: North-Holland, 1971.

27 Sector-Specific Sticky Wages

Suppose now that, instead of there being a generalized sticky wage such that labor requires a minimum wage regardless of which sector it is employed in, stickiness of the wage obtains only in one of two or more sectors. This happens, for example, when a government successfully imposes a minimum wage in the urban-industrial sector but does not extend the policy to the larger rural-agricultural sector. This is the case in countries of East Africa; indeed it was in reflecting on this empirical reality that Harris and Todaro (1970) constructed their model for analyzing the implications of such a sector-specific sticky wage for optimal policy intervention. In this chapter we follow their basic model, even though it is built on the simplifying assumption of only one mobile factor between two sectors with diminishing returns to the mobile factor within each sector.

The first-best policy intervention will have to be identical to that in the Brecher-type generalized sticky-wage model discussed in the preceding chapter. That is, the grant of a uniform wage subsidy to both sectors should offset the distorting effect of the minimum wage; the grant of the subsidy to the sector with the minimum wage would have to be matched by the grant of the same subsidy to the other sector, or else the social- and private-opportunity costs of labor would be unequal. Therefore, although the first-best policy prescription is identical for the generalized sticky-wage and minimum-wage models, the analysis of second-best interventions necessarily diverges. It makes sense now to consider, as a second-best policy instrument, the use of a wage subsidy only to the minimum-wage sector.

27.1 Harris-Todaro Model

Here we will consider the basic Harris-Todaro model, stripped to its essentials (as in Bhagwati and Srinivasan 1973, 1974). First, there are two production functions,

$$Q_1 \leq f_1(L_1) \tag{27.1}$$

and

$$Q_2 \leq f_2(L_2), \tag{27.1}$$

with standard properties but diminishing returns to labor input (so that there is a "hidden" factor in the background). An explicit second factor, "capital," could be introduced,[1] with some interesting and substantive

---

1. This was done by some later authors, including Corden and Findlay (1975).

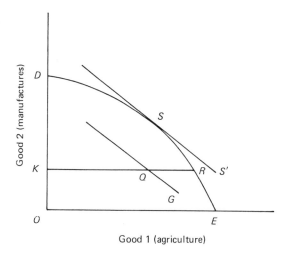

Figure 27.1

differences, but here we concentrate on the original one-factor model. Assuming labor supply to be fixed at unity by choice of units, we have

$$L_1 + L_2 \leq 1, \tag{27.3}$$

and the social utility function is

$$U = U(Q_1, Q_2), \tag{27.4}$$

defined on production of the goods so that we can apply our analysis below to either an autarkic economy or a small open economy (which can be treated as equivalent to the case of a linear utility function).

In a competitive economy the equilibrium will be at S in figure 27.1, where

$$\frac{U_1}{U_2} = \frac{f_2'}{f_1'}. \tag{27.5}$$

U_1/U_2 is the negative of the slope of SS', and U_1 and U_2 are the partial derivatives of U with respect to Q_1 and Q_2, respectively.

The sector-specific sticky-wage problem is then readily introduced under the assumption that we must have the wage in sector 2 (the manufactures sector) fixed at

$$f_2'(L_2) = \bar{w}. \tag{27.6}$$

If this constraint is binding at S, then clearly the sector-specific sticky wage matters. Harris and Todaro then have the economy adjust to this constraint by permitting the economy to have unemployment (or under-employment) in sector 2 with the sticky wage and, in effect, writing the critical equilibrium conditions in the model as

$$f_2' = \bar{w}, \tag{27.7}$$

and

$$\frac{U_1}{U_2} f_1' = \frac{\bar{w} L_2}{1 - L_1}, \tag{27.8}$$

where the consumption and production prices of good 1 are identical and equal to U_1/U_2.

With $\bar{w}$ specified, equations (27.7) and (27.8) can be solved for L_2 and L_1. The laissez-faire equilibrium, with unemployment ($L_2 < 1 - L_1$), will then lie at Q along RK; Q_2 and L_2 are fixed at values that make f_2 equal to $\bar{w}$.

Equation (27.8) implies that the actual wage in sector 1 equals the expected wage in sector 2. The latter is defined as the actual wage ($\bar{w}$) in sector 2 deflated by the average probability ($L_2/(1 - L_1)$) of finding a job at that actual wage.

27.2 Policy Implications

Optimal Policy

In this model the use of a uniform wage subsidy will help the economy get back to S, the optimal solution, in figure 27.1. Thus assume that

$$s^{\text{opt}} = \bar{w} - f_2'(L_2^{\text{opt}})$$

is the manufacturing (sector 2) wage subsidy, financed by lump-sum taxation. With this subsidy also extended to agriculture (sector 1), we have the following modified equilibrium conditions in production:

$$f_2' = \bar{w} - s^{\text{opt}} \tag{27.9}$$

and

$$\pi_{\text{c}}^{\text{opt}} f_1' = \bar{w} - s^{\text{opt}}, \tag{27.10}$$

where $\pi_{\text{c}}^{\text{opt}} = U_1(Q_1^{\text{opt}}, Q_2^{\text{opt}})/U_2(Q_1^{\text{opt}}, Q_2^{\text{opt}})$ is the consumption price (equal to the production price, f_2'/f_1') of good 1. With this uniform wage subsidy, the wage in sector 2 is at $\bar{w}$ and the wage rates are equalized at production prices in both sectors. Thus the constraints of the model are met and full-employment equilibrium is reached. S in figure 27.2 is this optimal, full-employment equilibrium, with $\pi_{\text{c}}^{\text{opt}} = \pi_{\text{p}}^{\text{opt}}$ and DRS = DRT at S.

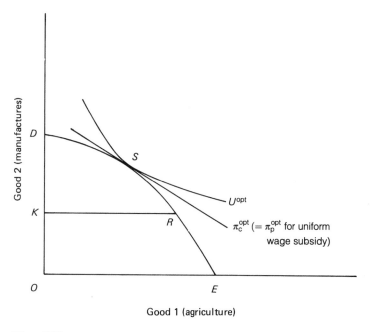

Figure 27.2

Second-Best Wage-Subsidy Intervention

Consider now a wage subsidy only to manufactures (sector 2). In this case, equation (27.7) and (27.8) become

$$f_2' = \bar{w} - \hat{s} \tag{27.11}$$

and

$$\frac{U_1}{U_2} f_1' = \bar{w} \cdot \frac{L_2}{1 - L_1}, \tag{27.12}$$

where $\hat{s}$ is the wage subsidy to the sticky-wage sector 2. Given $\bar{w}$ and $\hat{s}$, we can solve equations (27.11) and (27.12) for L_2 and L_1 and for the two outputs. It can then be shown[2] that a wage subsidy will necessarily improve welfare; $dU/d\hat{s} > 0$ at $s = 0$. Also successive wage-subsidy increases will evidently lead production steadily along QH to full employment at H in figure 27.3. However, the full-employment-achieving subsidy $\hat{s}^F$ will produce lower welfare than the (second-best) welfare-maximizing subsidy $\hat{s}^{opt}$, leading to J in figure 27.3. In this case there will be a trade-off between increased welfare and increased employment.

2. Detailed argumentation and proofs are given in Bhagwati and Srinivasan (1973).

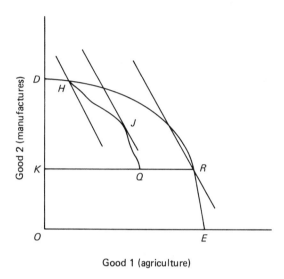

Figure 27.3

Second-Best Production Subsidy to Agriculture

Yet another second-best policy would be to subsidize agriculture (sector 1). In this case equations (27.7) and (27.8) become

$$f_2' = \bar{w}$$

and

$$\pi_p f_1' = \frac{w L_2}{1 - L_1},$$

where π_p is the producer price of good 1 and the implied production subsidy is

$$\frac{\pi_p - U_1/U_2}{U_1/U_2}.$$

It is then evident that successive production subsidies to agriculture will take the economy along QR until full employment is reached at R. Manufactures production will be frozen at OK, since $\bar{w}$ determines it. Welfare will also successively increase with the production subsidy, so the full-employment and the welfare-maximizing production subsidies are necessarily identical here (in contrast with the manufactures-wage-subsidy case). Again, the second-best wage subsidy in manufactures (welfare at J) cannot be ranked uniquely with respect to the second-best production subsidy to agriculture (welfare at R). Figure 27.3 shows the latter to be superior, but it could equally have been shown otherwise.

27.3   Other Extensions

The Harris-Todaro analysis has been developed by many writers. Of particular interest to students of international economics is the extension of the analysis by Corden and Findlay (1975) to the 2×2 model, with capital introduced and also mobile between both sectors. To see some of the differences in positive analysis that result from this extension, note that equilibrium is now determined fairly simply as follows. The fixed minimum wage in manufactures determines uniquely the capital-labor ratio as well as the rental to capital in the sector. With capital mobile, the rental on capital in agriculture must equal that in manufactures. This condition determines the capital-labor ratio, as well as the agricultural wage uniquely, if the terms of trade are unchanged. In the original Harris-Todaro model set out in this chapter, once the minimum wage in manufactures is set above its full-employment, competitive equilibrium level, it leads unambiguously to a lower level of output of manufactures in equilibrium than in the case of competitive equilibrium. With capital mobile, however, the minimum wage can paradoxically lead to a rise in manufacturing output if the elasticity of factor substitution in the two sectors is very low and manufacturing is capital-intensive. Again, in contrast with the standard Harris-Todaro model, a wage subsidy to manufacturing necessarily increases the unemployment rate in manufacturing. The effect of a wage subsidy to agriculture, on the other hand, is to leave the output of manufacturing unchanged in the standard model while lowering it in the case of capital mobility.

The work of Calvo (1978) is more significantly different in its extension of the standard model and has serious effects on the welfare implications of the sticky-wage assumption. Calvo endogenizes the determination of the manufacturing wage through the actions of an urban trade union whose objective is to maximize the difference between its members' urban income and what they would get in the rural sector at the ruling prices. Two alternative situations are examined: one where the union behaves as a monopolist in the urban labor market, with firms reacting as price-taking profit maximizers, and one where an arbitrator mediates between firms and the union by setting the urban wage and employment according to a Nash criterion. In contrast with the standard Harris-Todaro model, the urban-to-rural wage ratio tends to be harder to change in the Calvo model, so some of the traditional policies that reduce urban unemployment (such as wage subsidy) have no effect. Moreover a first-best optimum cannot be attained in the Calvo model unless the set of policy instruments includes migration barriers (e.g., a tax).

Khan (1980) generalizes the Harris-Todaro analysis in several directions. He relates urban to rural wages through a function that depends on the rural wage itself, urban unemployment, the common rental rate on capital, and a shift parameter. This particular formulation of wage determination includes as special cases the standard model, the Corden-Findlay model, the Calvo model, and various wage-differential models.

Recommended Readings

Bhagwati, J., and T. N. Srinivasan. The ranking of policy interventions under factor market imperfections: The case of sector-specific sticky wages and unemployment. *Sankhya* Ser. B., 1973.

Bhagwati, J. N., and T. N. Srinivasan. On reanalyzing the Harris-Todaro model: Policy ranking in the case of sector-specific sticky wages. *American Economic Review* 64 (1974): 502–508.

Calvo, Guillermo A. Urban unemployment and wage determination in LDCs: Trade unions in the Harris-Todaro model. *International Economic Review* 19 (1978): 65–81.

Corden, W. M., and R. Findlay. Urban unemployment, intersectoral capital mobility and development policy. *Economica* 62 (1975): 59–78.

Harris, J. R., and M. P. Todaro. Migration, unemployment and development: A two-sector analysis. *American Economic Review* 60 (1970): 126–42.

Khan, M. A. The Harris-Todaro hypothesis and the Heckscher-Ohlin-Samuelson trade model, a synthesis. *Journal of International Economics* 10 (1980): 527–47.

Stiglitz, J. E. Alternative theories of wage determination and unemployment in LDCs: The labour-turnover model. *Quarterly Journal of Economics* 88 (1974): 194–227.

Srinivasan, T. N., and J. N. Bhagwati. Alternative policy rankings in a large, open economy with sector-specific minimum wages. *Journal of Economic Theory* 11 (1975): 356–71.

Srinivasan, T. N., and J. N. Bhagwati. Shadow prices for project selection in the presence of distortion: Effective rates of protection and domestic resource costs. *Journal of Political Economy* 86 (1978): 97–116.

Wellisz, S. Dual economies, disguised unemployment and the unlimited supply of labour. *Economica*, N. S., 35 (1968): 22–51.

We turn now to the theory of policy intervention in the presence of "noneconomic" objectives. Before we turn to the analytics, a few general remarks are in order.

The distinction between noneconomic and economic is a matter of convenience. Economists have traditionally looked at social utility functions defined on the flow of final consumption of goods and services. Therefore, when we use the term "noneconomic" to describe additional arguments that we put into the utility function, it is a simple matter of drawing attention to the fact that we are departing from the conventional. It would be equally appropriate to eliminate the distinction between economic and noneconomic altogether and merely discuss the theory of policy intervention when the objective function has "successively augmented" arguments.

The noneconomic objectives themselves can often be interpreted as really economic. For instance, the objective of increasing self-sufficiency is a noneconomic one when taken by itself. However, it may be looked upon as essentially a result of economic maximization, with the objective function defined only in terms of goods and services. Thus, in a two-period analysis, self-sufficiency may be desired in the first period because it leads to a superior outcome (e.g., by preventing exploitation via trade embargos) in the second period and hence to a full two-period maximization of a utility function defined only on goods and services.[1]

Analytically we may treat the noneconomic objectives either by entering them as added arguments in the social utility function or by treating them as additional constraints. We will begin by treating them as additional constraints; in a later section we will show how formally identical qualitative results follow naturally when they are treated instead as added arguments in the utility function.

28.1   Different Objectives

Different noneconomic objectives can be considered for an open economy. In the simple trade-theoretic model where there are two primary factors producing two final traded goods, we can distinguish four classic types of noneconomic objectives:

1. Production of a good should not fall below a certain level.

2. Consumption of a good should not exceed a certain level.

3. Import (or export) of a good should not exceed a certain level.

4. Level of factor use in a good should exceed a certain level.

1. A two-period model does not necessarily turn all noneconomic objectives into economic objectives. The noneconomic objective can be applied to all periods, for example.

These are the noneconomic objectives one runs across in the policy writings. Policy-makers seem to want a production objective for ideological or related reasons. The production level in certain sectors is often regarded as strategically important on defense or related grounds, the consumption objective often arises from a desire to reduce luxury consumption in poor countries, the import objective often arises from a desire to reduce external reliance on defense and "national sovereignty" grounds, and the factor-use argument often arises in developing and developed countries that want more people in the manufacturing sector and in some other developed countries that would rather have more people in the agricultural sector.

The number of noneconomic objectives can be easily augmented. For example, staying within the 2 × 2 model, we can think of another objective affecting the ratio of imports to production. But other noneconomic objectives can follow if the model is changed suitably. If we let in international capital flows, we can think of a constraint on capital inflow arising on noneconomic grounds and forcing the policy-maker to modify the optimal capital inflow determined on economic maximization alone. If we allow for imported intermediates, we can distinguish between value added and gross value in considering a production objective. Also the analysis can be extended to optimal policy structures if we let in many traded goods; for example, we can ask whether the use of a production tax *cum* subsidy shown to be optimal in the 2 × 2 analysis for a production objective will turn out to be uniform or selective if in a many-good economy the production objective is suitably redefined so that it requires the total value of production of importables to increase by a certain value above its trade value.

In the following we discuss the noneconomic objectives within the 2 × 2 structure and then extend the analysis to several other questions outlined above. The analysis will be intuitive and geometric initially, and will assume a small country. Later various noneconomic constraints as arguments in the social utility function will be analyzed mathematically. Again extension of the argumentation to other production *cum* trade models, permitting other noneconomic objectives to be analyzed, will be undertaken. Next, we will consider how several of the noneconomic objectives can be reinterpreted in appropriate multiperiod fashion as economic objectives. Finally, applicability of the analysis to current policy problems will be shown.

Production Objective

For the small competitive economy depicted in figure 28.1, P^{opt} is the optimal production point if a traditional social-utility function is being

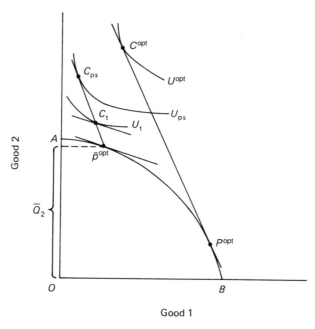

Figure 28.1

maximized. However, we now have the added constraint that the production of good 2 not fall below level $\bar{Q}_2$; that is, $Q_2 \geq \bar{Q}_2$. This constraint is clearly binding at P^{opt}. Therefore we must depart from the economist's maximum at P^{opt}. The least costly way to do this is to use a production tax *cum* subsidy to shift production to $\bar{P}^{\mathrm{opt}}$. This leaves consumption to be undertaken at the given world prices at C_{ps} with the associated utility at U_{ps}. If a tariff had been used instead to shift production to $\bar{P}^{\mathrm{opt}}$, consumption would also have had to be at the distorted prices, at C_{t}, resulting in a further loss of welfare to U_{t} because of the consumption cost.

A production tax *cum* subsidy policy is therefore evidently superior to a tariff in meeting the production constraint, for the associated production cost is unavoidable when a production constraint is binding. However, what a tariff does is add to this unavoidable cost a gratuitous consumption cost as well, since the tariff distorts prices for producers and consumers equally. By contrast, a production tax *cum* subsidy is a "clean" instrument, affecting production alone (Corden 1957).

Consumption Objective

By an analogous argument, when the noneconomic objective concerns consumption, a consumption tax *cum* subsidy is preferable to a tariff,

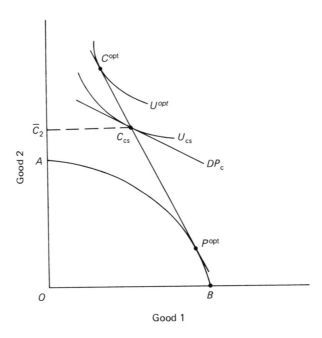

Figure 28.2

since the tariff would add to the unavoidable consumption cost a gratuitous production cost.

In figure 28.2 let the noneconomic objective take the form of a binding constraint that the consumption of good 2 cannot exceed level $\bar{C}_2$. This constraint can be met at minimum cost by consuming at C_{cs}. Any other way of doing it will imply lower welfare than at U_{cs}. The way to arrive at C_{cs} in this small competitive economy is to produce at world prices under free trade but to use a consumption tax *cum* subsidy to enable consumers to consume at a suitably "distorted" price ratio DP_C rather than at the world prices.

Self-sufficiency or Import-Export Objective

Consider now a self-sufficiency objective where the policy-maker wishes to cut down the level of imports or exports below the optimal level determined under free trade. The minimum-cost way to do this is to use an import tariff. Thus the rank-ordering of tariffs and production tax *cum* subsidy is the reverse of that which obtains under the production objective. This apparent paradox can be traced to the fact that the self-sufficiency objective can be attained by operating on both production and consumption of the importable good, since imports are the difference between consumption and production of the importable good. A tariff,

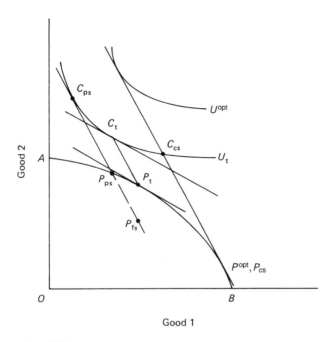

Figure 28.3

which affects both production and consumption, is now at an advantage because it exploits both ways of reducing imports, whereas a production or consumption tax *cum* subsidy would only exploit one route. The fact that a tariff enters both production and consumption markets in the model is therefore helpful now. This same property was a disadvantage when the objective of the exercise was to fix a domestic distortion in production or in consumption, for instance, since a tariff could do that only by disrupting another market simultaneously.

Johnson analyzed the self-sufficiency objective via figure 28.3 in a comparison of three policies: a tariff, a production tax *cum* subsidy, and a consumption tax *cum* subsidy. For an identical loss of welfare from U^{opt} to U_t, the comparison shows that the tariff yields the lowest level of imports (implying that the tariff costs the least in welfare loss for an identical import level). Thus, with a given U_t, the tariff leads to production at P_t and consumption at C_t, a production tax *cum* subsidy leads to production at P_{ps} and consumption at world prices at C_{ps}, and a consumption tax *cum* subsidy leads to consumption at C_{cs} and production at world prices at P^{opt}, P_{cs}. Since the trade triangles in the three cases are similar (owing to the small-country assumption), we can rank-order the import levels in the three cases by looking at the hypotenuses. It is then evident that the tariff yields the lowest import level, that is, the greatest import reduction for the same loss of welfare down to U_t.

Eliminating substitution in production will eliminate the superiority of the tariff over the consumption tax *cum* subsidy, and eliminating substitution in consumption will eliminate the superiority of the tariff over the production tax *cum* subsidy. Again the consumption tax *cum* subsidy cannot be rank-ordered relative to the production tax *cum* subsidy.

How does one bring the use of a factor tax *cum* subsidy into figure 28.3? Since this will leave consumption at world prices, consumption will be at C_{ps}, and since a factor tax *cum* subsidy must imply production off the production-possibility curve AB, the production point must lie somewhere along $C_{ps}P_{ps}$ at a point such as P_{fs}. That would imply a higher level of imports than under the production tax *cum* subsidy.

Employment Objective

Figure 28.4 illustrates a situation where labor employment in production of good 2 cannot fall below $\bar{L}_2$. The production-possibility curve AB reflects the Edgeworth-Bowley efficient locus O_1O_2 in the box diagram in figure 28.4b. As one moves down from A to Q in 28.4a, one moves up from O_1 to Q in 28.4b. At Q, however, the employment of labor in good 2 falls to the constraint level $\bar{L}_2$. Any further move from Q to B along the production-possibility curve is therefore ruled out, since it would imply that $L_2 \le \bar{L}_2$, as in the case with the free-trade solution P^{opt}. The feasible production-possibility curve, which satisfies the $\bar{L}_2$ constraint, can therefore be derived simply by moving in 28.4b along the horizontal line QB' (which implies that capital, but not labor, is being moved out of good 2 into good 1). The corresponding feasible production-possibility curve therefore is QB' in 28.4a, which is concave to the origin because only capital is being varied between sectors, with labor in each sector fixed at $\bar{L}_2$ and $\bar{L} - \bar{L}_2$.

The first-best policy can then be derived. First, note that the optimal solution now involves maximizing subject to the feasible production-possibility curve AQB'. With the world prices given, this implies production at $\bar{P}^{opt}$ and consumption taking place at world prices at $\bar{C}^{opt}$. From figure 28.4b, however, it is immediately clear that to operate at $\bar{P}^{opt}$ the economy must be characterized by differential factor-price ratios. It is also easy to see that the production of good 2 requires payment of a higher wage than the production of good 1; that is, a subsidy would have to be paid to employment of labor in production of good 2. Therefore the first-best policy for meeting an employment objective is to use a factor tax *cum* subsidy, thus conforming to the rule that the optimal

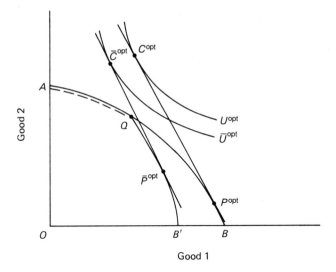

(a)

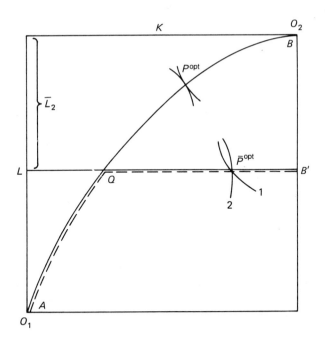

(b)

Figure 28.4

policy intervention should be addressed to the market where the non-economic objective is focused. The second-best policy would be to use a production tax *cum* subsidy that brings production to Q on the production-possibility curve AB, just satisfying the factor-employment constraint. The availability line through Q would be dominated by that through $\bar{P}^{opt}$. The third-best policy would be a tariff that would equally bring production to Q but would gratuitously impose a consumption cost on the economy.

Other Noneconomic Objectives

Within the same model as above we can distinguish another objective by reformulating the self-sufficiency objective not in terms of the level of trade but in terms of the ratio of imports to domestic production. In this case the optimal policy intervention will be to use both a tariff and a production tax *cum* subsidy, for the objective will involve both imports and production and each will require a corresponding policy intervention. The main point of the analysis above is the need to intervene directly in the particular market to which the noneconomic objective is addressed, just as the "market failure" distortions required that the policy intervention be addressed directly to the markets where the failure arose.

Yet other noneconomic objectives can be distinguished in the context of different production *cum* trade models. Tan (1971) noted that if interindustry flows are allowed, two types of production objectives can be distinguished: gross output levels and net output levels. The latter would require the (gross) production tax *cum* subsidy to be offset by a tax *cum* subsidy on interindustry usage. Again, in this augmented model, there is no reason why the optimality of the trade, factor, and consumption tax *cum* subsidies (respectively) for the trade, factor-employment, and consumption objectives should be altered. Tan also considered a model with imported intermediates,[2] and there one has to be careful to see that self-sufficiency is not identifiable with reduced import of final imports, since material imports have to be paid for as well. However, a tariff policy (which taxes imports for final consumption and for intermediate use uniformly) continues to be the correct way to minimize the cost of self-sufficiency. Again one has to distinguish between net and gross production; the latter requires a production tax *cum* subsidy, whereas the former requires a value-added tax *cum* subsidy. Tan also extends the argument, with no surprises, to a model with nontraded goods.

---

2. Specifically, he considers a 2×2 model augmented to allow for a purely imported intermediate good.

Finally, we consider the question of an optimal policy structure. Suppose that we have more than one importable. The production objective can be redefined so as to increase the aggregate valuation, at given prices, of the production of importables. Thus, a country's planner may be interested in import substitution as such, and not in the precise composition of the different industries in this total. Then the questions of importance are whether a production tax *cum* subsidy remains the optimal policy and whether the resulting tax structure can be characterized by uniformity of, say, subsidies on production to all importables. The answers to both questions are in the affirmative, though we do need the small-country assumption for the uniformity to be optimal. Vandendorpe (1974) considered this question of optimal policy structures in the presence of all noneconomic objectives using the 2×2 model above, and he extended the uniformity argument to all of them at a fairly general level. The fact that uniformity of the optimal policy structure arises (in the presence of fixed prices) on the basis of strictly economic criteria is a dividend for the policy-maker; generally, the argument for uniformity has had to be made on grounds of political economy. Thus it is argued that admitting selectivity in policy-making will lead to selectivity administered on purely self-serving, pressure-group grounds rather than on the grounds developed in the trade-and-welfare theory in the classroom, and so it is best to advise policy-makers against allowing selectivity and to opt instead for uniformity. Vandendorpe's demonstration of the optimality of uniform policy structures therefore greatly strengthens the hands of those who would recommend uniformity to governments that seek objectives such as import substitution, self-sufficiency, incremental employment of a factor in a sector, or changed levels of consumption of a class of goods.

28.2 Formal Mathematics of the Problem

The formal mathematics underlying the problem is straightforward and can be illustrated by reference to the production objective.[3] We begin with the small-country case and then extend it to monopoly power in trade. We end with an alternative approach that treats the noneconomic objective as an additional argument in the objective function rather than as an added constraint.

3. For solutions for the other noneconomic objectives, refer to Bhagwati and Srinivasan (1969). Tan (1971) and Vandendorpe (1974) can be consulted for a formal analysis of the other models discussed in the text.

Small Country with Production Objectives

The basic problem is to maximize

$$U = U(C_1, C_2) \tag{28.1}$$

subject to

$$C_1 \le F(K_1, L_1) - p^* M_2, \tag{28.2}$$

$$C_2 \le G(K_2, L_2) + M_2, \tag{28.3}$$

$$-G(K_2, L_2) \le -\bar{Q}_2, \tag{28.4}$$

$$L_1 + L_2 \le \bar{L}, \tag{28.5}$$

$$K_1 + K_2 \le \bar{K}, \tag{28.6}$$

$$C_i, K_i \ge 0, \tag{28.7}$$

where U is the social-utility function with the aggregate consumptions C_i as arguments, F and G are the two production functions, M_2 is the net imports of good 2 (with a fixed world price of p^* in terms of good 1), (K_i, L_i) is the input (capital and labor) vector in the production of good i, and $\bar{Q}_2$ is the specified minimum level of production of good 2.

The Lagrangian for this maximization problem is

$$\phi = \theta U - \lambda_1[C_1 - F(K_1, L_1) + p^* M_2] - \lambda_2[C_2 - G(K_2, L_2) - M_2]$$
$$- \lambda_3[-G(K_2, L_2) + \bar{Q}_2] - w(L_1 + L_2 - \bar{L}) - r(K_1 + K_2 - \bar{K}). \tag{28.8}$$

Maximizing the Lagrangian with respect to the choice variables C_i, K_i, L_i, and M_2 and denoting the partial derivative of a function with respect to its ith argument by the same function with the subscript i, we get the following necessary conditions:

$$\theta U_1 - \lambda_1 \le 0 \quad \text{with equality if} \quad C_1 > 0, \tag{28.9}$$

$$\theta U_2 - \lambda_2 \le 0 \quad \text{with equality if} \quad C_2 > 0, \tag{28.10}$$

$$-\lambda_1 p^* + \lambda_2 = 0, \tag{28.11}$$

$$\lambda_1 F_1 - r \le 0 \quad \text{with equality if} \quad K_1 > 0, \tag{28.12}$$

$$\lambda_1 F_2 - w \le 0 \quad \text{with equality if} \quad L_1 > 0, \tag{28.13}$$

$$(\lambda_2 + \lambda_3) G_1 - r \le 0 \quad \text{with equality if} \quad K_2 > 0, \tag{28.14}$$

$$(\lambda_2 + \lambda_3) G_2 - w \le 0 \quad \text{with equality if} \quad L_2 > 0. \tag{28.15}$$

The concavity of U, F, and G and the fact that the constraint set has a nonempty interior implies that conditions (28.9)–(28.15), with positive Lagrangian multipliers, are also sufficient for a maximum. It is to be noted that (28.11) is not an inequality, since there are no sign restrictions on M_2.[4] It is also clear from (28.11) that $\lambda_2 = \lambda_1 p^* > 0$, for the reason that $\lambda_1 = 0$ will imply that $\theta U_1 \leq 0$ (which in turn means that either $U_1 = 0$ or $\theta = 0$, since both are nonnegative). This can happen only if there is satiation in consumption overall or in the consumption of good 1. Ruling these possibilities out, we get $\theta > 0$ and $\lambda_1 > 0$. This enables us to normalize λ_1 conveniently as unity so that λ_2 becomes p^*, the world price of good 2. Assuming that both goods are consumed in positive amounts at the optimum, we get $U_2/U_1 = p^*$—that is, the marginal rate of substitution in consumption equals the world price ratio p^*. If both factors are essential in the production of each good and if both goods are produced in positive amounts[5] at the optimum, (28.12)–(28.15) become equalities implying that

$$\frac{F_1}{F_2} = \frac{G_1}{G_2} = \frac{r}{w}$$

for each good (i.e., the marginal rate of factor substitution is the same in the production of each good).

It is also clear from the foregoing that the above optimum can be described as a competitive equilibrium. With good 1 as the numéraire, the consumer price of good 2 is its world price p^*, with w as the wage rate, r as the rental rate on capital, and (as seen from 28.14 and 28.15) $p^* + \lambda_3$ as the producer price of good 2. Since the specified production level $\bar{Q}_2$ of good 2 adds the binding constraint (28.4)—otherwise, the production objective will be achieved under free trade without intervention—it follows that $\lambda_3 > 0$. Thus the producer price of good differs from its consumer price (which equals the world price p^*) by λ_3. We could therefore interpret λ_3 as the optimal production subsidy per unit of output of good 2.

Monopoly Power in Trade

If we consider the presence of monopoly power in trade, the average terms of trade p^* will no longer be fixed but will depend on the volume of trade. Let us denote by $T(M_2)$ the number of units of net exports of good 1 needed to obtain M_2 units of net imports of good 2; that is, we

---

4. There is no presumption that good 2 is imported; it could be exported ($M_2 < 0$) or imported ($M_2 > 0$) at an optimum.

5. The output of good 2 has to be positive as long as $Q_2 > 0$.

replace $p^* M_2$ in equation (28.2) by $T(M_2)$. Assume that $T_1(M_2) > 0$ and $T_{11}(M_2) < 0$ for all M_2, where T_1 and T_{11} indicate derivatives. This means that the marginal revenue derived from exports is positive but declines as the volume of exports increases.[6] With this modification in (28.1), (28.11) is modified to

$$-\lambda_1 T_1(M_2) + \lambda_2 = 0.$$

Again, for the same reasons as before, we have $\theta > 0$, $\lambda_1 > 0$, and $\lambda_2 > 0$. Therefore we can normalize λ_1 at unity, obtaining

$$\lambda_2 = T_1(M_2)$$

$$= p^*(M_2) + M_2 p_1^*(M_2).$$

Thus U_2/U_1 is equated not to the average terms of trade p^* but to the marginal terms of trade $T_1(M_2)$. For this to be achieved in a competitive equilibrium, an optimal tariff at the *ad valorem* rate of $M_2 p_1^*(M_2)/p^*(M_2)$ is required. Then, to achieve the specified level of production of good 2, we need an additional optimal subsidy of λ_3 per unit of output of good 2. This follows from (28.14) and (28.15), which are unaffected by the introduction of monopoly power in trade.

Alternative Approach

An alternative approach to the problem of noneconomic objectives is to incorporate them directly into the social-utility function, even though the distinction between economic and noneconomic objectives will thereby get blurred. We illustrate this approach again for the case of the production objective discussed above. Let us define a new concave social-utility function $W(C_1, C_2, Q_2)$ with the following properties:

$$W(C_1, C_2, Q_2) = U(C_1, C_2) \qquad \text{for all } Q_2 \geq \bar{Q}_2 \text{ and all } (C_1, C_2),$$

$$W(C_1, C_2, Q_2) < U(C_1, C_2) \qquad \text{for all } Q_2 < \bar{Q}_2 \text{ and all } (C_1, C_2),$$

$$\lim_{Q_2 \to \bar{Q}_2-} W(C_1, C_2, Q_2) = U(C_1, C_2) \qquad \text{for all } (C_1, C_2),$$

$$W_3(C_1, C_2, Q_2) > 0 \qquad \text{for all } Q_2 < \bar{Q}_2 \text{ and all } (C_1, C_2),$$

$$\lim_{Q_2 \to \bar{Q}_2-} W_3(C_1, C_2, Q_2) = 0 \qquad \text{for all } (C_1, C_2).$$

This formulation means that Q_2, the level of output of good 2, is relevant

---

6. Formula (28.2) is consistent with good 2 being an exportable good (Bhagwati and Srinivasan 1969).

for welfare only when $Q_2 < \bar{Q}_2$. The marginal social utility of the output of good 2 falls to zero as Q_2 increases to $\bar{Q}_2$ from below. Also the social utility of the consumption bundle (C_1, C_2) is less when the noneconomic objective is present than when it is absent. More important, this formulation accommodates a trade-off between economic and noneconomic objectives in the sense that an optimal solution could result in $Q_2 \geq \bar{Q}_2$, whereas in the earlier approach $Q_2 < \bar{Q}_2$ is a binding constraint and as such cannot be violated.

Now, maximizing $W(C_1, C_2, Q_2)$ subject to (28.2)–(28.7) and noting that $Q_2 \equiv G(K_2, L_2)$, we get, in part,

$$\theta W_1 - \lambda_1 \leq 0 \qquad \text{with equality if} \quad C_1 > 0, \qquad (28.9')$$

$$\theta W_2 - \lambda_2 \leq 0 \qquad \text{with equality if} \quad C_2 > 0, \qquad (28.10')$$

$$(\theta W_3 + \lambda_2)G_1 - r \leq 0 \qquad \text{with equality if} \quad K_2 > 0, \qquad (28.14')$$

$$(\theta W_3 + \lambda_2)G_2 - w \leq 0 \qquad \text{with equality if} \quad L_2 > 0. \qquad (28.15')$$

Inequalities (28.11)–(28.13) remain unchanged.

Comparison with (28.9), (28.10), (28.14), and (28.15) shows that (28.9′) and (28.10′) have the same form as (28.9) and (28.10), since W_1 and W_2 represent the same things as U_1 and U_2, respectively (i.e., the marginal social utilities of consumption of goods 1 and 2). Inequalities (28.14′) and (28.15′) differ from (28.14) and (28.15) in that θW_3 occurs in (24.14′) and (24.15′) instead of the λ_3 that occurred in (28.14) and (28.15). But a moment's reflection will suggest that θW_3 and λ_3 represent the same thing, for W_3 is the marginal social utility of Q_2 (the output of good 2) and by definition W_3 is different from zero only when $Q_2 < \bar{Q}_2$. Thus, given a sufficiently small $\varepsilon > 0$, εW_3 is nothing but the utility loss of a reduction in output by ε (i.e., the utility cost of an ε deviation away from or the utility gain in an ε deviation toward $\bar{Q}_2$). As before, θ is the shadow price of social utility in terms of good 1 if we normalize by setting $\lambda_1 = 1$. Then $\varepsilon \theta W_3$ is the shadow cost or benefit of a deviation of ε from or toward $\bar{Q}_2$. Of course $\varepsilon \lambda_3$ represents the shadow price of an ε increase or decrease in $\bar{Q}_2$ when the noneconomic objective is stated as $Q_2 \geq \bar{Q}_2$.

Thus both approaches yield estimates of the marginal cost of the noneconomic objective. However, the utility approach permits Q_2 to fall below $\bar{Q}_2$, whereas the constraint approach will not permit this. In other words, the two approaches are not equivalent unless W is such that, even though it is feasible to have Q_2 fall below $\bar{Q}_2$, it is not optimal to do so.

28.3   Turning Noneconomic Objectives into Economic Objectives

So far the new objectives considered have been treated as noneconomic in character, essentially standing in contrast to the economic objectives defined conventionally as the pursuit of happiness via goods and services. However, these noneconomic objectives may reflect, in an essential way, concern with economic objectives.

Thus it may be argued that reduction of imports below the one-period myopic level may be called for as a rational response to many-period maximization of a conventional social-utility function if the prospect of a trade embargo in future periods is a function of the first-period import level. Similarly the probability of a market-disruption-related adoption of import restrictions may be an increasing function of first-period "market penetration" in the shape of a country's exports, and hence it may be economically rational to reduce exports below the myopic first-period optimum. Similarly, if elements of a putty-clay model are assumed, the allocation of resources between sectors in the first period will constrain the reallocation that can be achieved in the next period. This again will make departure from the myopic first-period optimal pattern of production desirable on strictly economic grounds. Again, if it is argued that externalities of the Verdoorn-Kaldor type obtain in manufacturing as a function of the labor force employed therein, a many-period maximization would require that the myopic first-period optimal level of manufacturing employment be lower relative to what it should be for maximization of welfare over many periods.

All this can be seen more clearly in a formal analysis of the market-disruption problem. As we show in considerable detail in chapter 39 (where we draw on Bhagwati and Srinivasan 1976, among other models with uncertainty), it is possible to construct a theoretical model with a two-period time horizon such that the level of exports E in the first period affects the probability $P(E)$ of a quota $\bar{E}$ being imposed at the beginning of the next period. The market-disruption-induced quota-imposition possibility requires the imposition of an optimal tariff in period 1. This means that there is now an economic reason for restraining first-period trade, and this in turn requires tariff-policy intervention. The noneconomic objective has therefore been turned theoretically into an economic policy intervention.[7]

___

7. For the production noneconomic objective turning into an economic objective, also see Bhagwati and Srinivasan (1976, sec. 4 and 5) and Findlay (1973, ch. 8).

"Voluntary" export restraints, when truly voluntary, represent a real-world example of such policy-imposed restraint on trade so as to reduce the threat of protection. Another excellent example of a noneconomic objective turned into an economic one is provided by the Selective Employment Tax enacted in the United Kingdom in 1966 under Nicholas Kaldor's auspices. Kaldor believed that labor should be taxed out of retailing and other services and into the manufacturing sector, since the latter sector is characterized by greater technical change.[8] Apparently therefore myopic maximization should be departed from, since it would produce an inadequately small manufacturing sector from the viewpoint of many-period maximization or (in simplistic terms) of "growth." The analysis of this chapter shows clearly that, in order for this argument to imply as a first-best measure a Selective Employment Tax rather than a production subsidy to manufacturing (or a tax on nonmanufacturing output), it would have to be fairly explicit that the alleged externalities are related to labor employment rather than to production in the manufacturing sector. This important lesson of the theory of policy intervention in the presence of noneconomic objectives does not appear to have been understood by the proponents of the now-defunct Selective Employment Tax.

28.4 Environment and Labor Standards

The theory of noneconomic objectives has immediate bearing on the question of achieving certain environment and labor standards in open economies. Clearly the optimal way to do this is to seek these objectives directly with policies addressed to them, while retaining free trade to maximize the gains from trade.

Thus, if there are domestic pollution externalities, for instance, the optimal way to address them is not by introducing tariffs but by using the "polluter pay" principle of taxing the producer of pollution and then maintaining free trade (for a small, open economy).[9] Many environmental groups fail to understand this principle of economic policy intervention and wind up wrongly seeking to depart from free trade instead. This and other aspects of the current debates over the freeing of trade

8. For a controversial argument on the "facts," see Kaldor (1975) and Rowthorn (1979).

9. The use of trade policy as a "second-best" intervention tool has been discussed in the context of international externalities, such as in the case of global warming and ozone layer depletion, by Markusen (1975) and more fully in the appendix authored by T. N. Srinivasan in Bhagwati and Srinivasan (1996, ch. 4). Also see the various contributions in Anderson and Blackhurst (1992).

and the protection of the environment and safeguarding of workers' rights and standards are discussed extensively in Bhagwati (1993), Bhagwati and Srinivasan (1996), Brown, Deardorff, and Stern (1996), GATT (1992), and Srinivasan (1996).[10]

Recommended Readings

Anderson, K., and R. Blackhurst, eds. *The Greening of World Trade Issues.* New York: Harvester Wheatsheaf, 1992.

Bhagwati, J. The case for free trade. *Scientific American* 269 (1993): 17–23.

Bhagwati, J. Non-economic objectives and the efficiency properties of trade. *Journal of Political Economy* 75 (1967): 738–42. Reprinted in J. Bhagwati, *Trade, Tariffs, and Growth.* Cambridge: MIT Press, 1969.

Bhagwati, J. The generalised theory of distortions and welfare. In *Trade, Balance of Payments, and Growth: Papers in International Economics in Honor of Charles P. Kindleberger* ed. by J. Bhagwati et al. Amsterdam: North-Holland, 1971.

Bhagwati, J., and T. N. Srinivasan. Optimal intervention to achieve non-economic objectives. *Review of Economic Studies.* 36 (1969): 27–38.

Bhagwati, J., and T. N. Srinivasan. Optimal trade policy and compensation under endogenous uncertainty: The phenomenon of market disruption. *Journal of International Economics.* 6 (1976): 317–36.

Bhagwati, J., and T. N. Srinivasan. Trade and the environment: Does environmental diversity detract from the case for free trade? In *Fair Trade and Harmonization: Prerequisites for Free Trade?* vol. 1, ed. by J. Bhagwati and R. Hudec. Cambridge: MIT Press, 1996, ch. 4.

Brown, D., A. Deardorff, and R. Stern. International labor standards and trade: A theoretical analysis. In *Fair Trade and Harmonization: Prerequisites for Free Trade?* vol. 1, ed. by J. Bhagwati and R. Hudec. Cambridge: MIT Press, 1996, ch. 5.

Corden, W. M. Tariffs, subsidies and the terms of trade. *Economica,* N. S., 24 (1957): 235–42.

Findlay, R. *International Trade and Development Theory.* New York: Columbia University Press, 1973, ch. 8.

GATT. *Trade and the Environment.* Annual Report. Geneva. 1992.

Grossman, G., and A. Krueger. Environmental impacts of a North American Free Trade Agreement. In *The Mexico–U.S. Free Trade Agreement,* ed. by P. Garber. Cambridge: MIT Press, 1993.

Johnson, H. G. The cost of protection and the scientific tariff. *Journal of Political Economy* 68 (1960): 327–45.

Johnson, H. G. Optimal trade intervention in the presence of domestic distortions. In *Trade, Growth, and the Balance of Payments: Essays in Honour of G. Haberler,* ed. by R. E. Baldwin et al. Chicago: Rand McNally and Amsterdam: North Holland. 1965, ch. 11.

Kaldor, N. *Causes of the Slow Economic Growth of the United Kingdom.* Cambridge: Cambridge University Press, 1966.

Kaldor, N. Economic growth and the Verdoorn law—A comment on Mr. Rowthorn's article. *Economic Journal* 85 (1975): 891–96.

Markusen, J. International externalities and optimal tax structures. *Journal of International Economics* 5 (1975): 15–29.

10. The "positive" question whether growth leads to more environmental pollution was discussed in a much-cited paper by Grossman and Krueger (1993) and in GATT's (1992) annual report on trade and the environment. It is now a subject of much research interest.

Rowthorn, R. What remains of Kaldor's law? *Economic Journal* 85 (1975): 10–19.

Rowthorn, R. A reply to Lord Kaldor's comment. *Economic Journal* 85 (1975): 879–901.

Rowthorn, R. A note on Verdoorn's law. *Economic Journal* 89 (1979): 131–33.

Srinivasan, T. N. International trade and labor standards. In P. van Dijck and G. Faber, eds., *Challenges to the New World Trade Organization*. The Netherlands: Klewer Law International, 1996, pp. 219–43.

Tan, A. Optimal trade policies and non-economic objectives in models involving imported materials, inter-industry flows, and non-traded goods. *Review of Economic Studies* 38 (1971): 105–12.

Vandendorpe, A. L. On the theory of non-economic objectives in open economies. *Journal of International Economics* 4 (1974): 15–24.

We now turn to the concept and theory of immiserizing growth. This has proved to be a remarkably important development in the theory of trade and welfare, with a bearing on several significant aspects of the subject. We begin with a historical account of the evolution of the concept, and then develop the essential insight underlying the phenomenon. Finally we relate the concept to several problem areas in the theory of trade and welfare.

29.1 Original Case

That growth can immiserize an economy is a paradox first noted in the context of the postwar discussion of the dollar shortage. Following Hicks's (1953) initiation of the theoretical analysis of the dollar shortage in terms of differential productivity change between the United States and the rest of the world, a number of trade theorists (among them Johnson 1954, 1955) developed a "real" analysis of the effects of growth on the terms of trade of the growing country.[1] It was then but a short step to argue that the welfare impact of growth in an open economy could be reduced because the primary gain from growth might be offset by the secondary loss from a possible deterioration in the terms of trade. This argument could be extended to assert that the secondary loss may even outweigh the primary gain, resulting in immiserizing growth.

The conditions for such immiserizing growth were established by Bhagwati (1958) in the context of the 2×2 model of trade theory. Bhagwati showed that such immiserizing growth can occur even in the presence of market stability, in contrast with the Leontief case of a transfer-induced immiserization, which had been shown by Samuelson to require market instability. Bhagwati (1958) also showed that the immiserization can occur even if the foreign-offer curve facing the growing country is elastic; this paradox flew in the face of intuition and constituted a paradox within a paradox.

Here we content ourselves with illustrating the immiserizing-growth outcome in figure 29.1, where AB and $A'B'$ are the pregrowth and postgrowth production-possibility curves. Production, consumption, and welfare before growth are at P, C, and U, respectively. After growth they are

---

1. Hicks was essentially trying to build on ideas developed earlier by John Williams and Thomas Balogh. Johnson's two classic papers were the first successful theoretical analyses of the problem ventilated by Balogh and Williams.

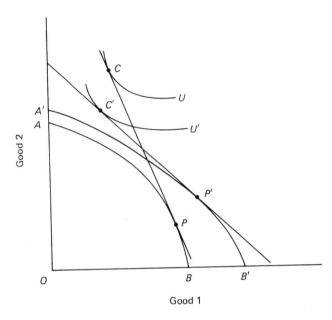

Figure 29.1

at P', C', and U'. The terms of trade have deteriorated from PC to $P'C'$, and the result is a decline in welfare from U to U' (or immiserizing growth).

29.2   Immiserizing Growth for a Small Country with a Tariff

Johnson (1967) considered the case of a small, competitive economy with a distortionary tariff in place. This country experiences growth and is immiserized as shown in figure 29.2, where the tariff moves production from P^{opt} to $\hat{P}$ before growth takes place. As growth occurs, and with the tariff and hence the domestic price ratio unchanged, production shifts to $\hat{\hat{P}}$ (which is given by the tangency of the fixed domestic price ratio and the undrawn, new production-possibility curve). Because this is a small country, the availability line at given world price ratio moves back, with the shift from $\hat{P}$ to $\hat{\hat{P}}$. Hence, with unchanging consumption distortion, we can conclude that the economy is immiserized. ($\hat{P}$ and $\hat{\hat{P}}$ will lie on a Rybczynski line $\hat{P}R$, which is the locus of tangencies of the fixed domestic price ratio with the production-possibility curves resulting from successive augmentation of capital if the source of the growth is capital accumulation and good 2 is capital-intensive.)

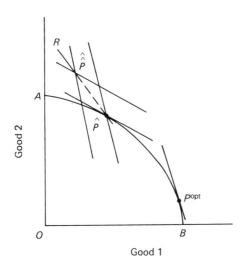

Figure 29.2

29.3 Generalized Theory

What is in common between these two paradoxes of immiserizing growth? Immiserizing growth must involve some form of suboptimality: Growth merely enlarges a country's opportunity set, and if the country follows optimal policies, it should be impossible for it to be immiserized. By this line of thought, it becomes obvious that what underlies the phenomena of immiserizing growth is the fact that the country experiences growth subject to some distortion. The distortion (in the Johnson case the presence of a tariff, which is necessarily distortionary since the country is assumed to be small) imposes a loss in comparison with the situation where an optimal policy is being followed (free trade, in the Johnson case). When growth takes place, this same distortion may impose an accentuated loss in comparison with the optimal postgrowth situation. If this incremental loss from the distortion outweighs the primary gain from growth (this gain is measured as the difference between pregrowth and postgrowth situations at optimal policies—free-trade policies in the Johnson case), then immiserizing growth will follow (Bhagwati 1968).

Thus let U_1^{opt} and U_2^{opt} be the before-growth and after-growth welfare levels if the economy follows optimal policies in each situation. Let $\hat{U}_1$ and $\hat{U}_2$ be the corresponding actual welfare levels with the distortion in place. Then, using (say) the Hicksian equivalent-variational measures, we can decompose the net change in welfare of the growth in this distorted economy as follows:

$$\{\hat{U}_2 - \hat{U}_1\} \quad \equiv \{U_2^{\text{opt}} - U_1^{\text{opt}}\}$$

Net change   Primary gain from
in welfare   growth at optimal
from growth   policies (positive)

$$+ \begin{bmatrix} \{\hat{U}_2 - U_2^{\text{opt}}\} - & \{\hat{U}_1 - U_1^{\text{opt}}\} \\ \text{Loss from} & \text{Loss from} \\ \text{distortion in} & \text{distortion in} \\ \text{after-growth} & \text{before-growth} \\ \text{situation} & \text{situation} \\ \text{(negative)} & \text{(negative)} \end{bmatrix} .$$

Change in loss
from distortion
due to growth

Evidently, when immiserizing growth obtains, the second bracketed term on the right-hand side in this decomposition is sufficiently negative to outweigh the primary gain from growth (the first bracketed term on the right-hand side).

Thus immiserizing growth can arise whenever growth occurs subject to distortions. In the original Bhagwati case where the terms of trade deteriorate sufficiently to immiserize the growing economy, the distortion comes from the fact that the economy evidently has monopoly power in trade and ought to have an optimal tariff but instead has a (distorting) free-trade policy. In the later Johnson case, the distortion is the tariff when the smallness of the country implies that free trade is the optimal policy. Indeed the cases of immiserizing growth can be multiplied; they can be constructed around any distortion.[2]

Once this underlying essence of immiserizing growth is understood, it is also easy to resolve another paradox that characterizes the Johnson case. Johnson noted that the probability of immiserizing growth occurring in his small, tariff-distorted economy was increased if growth occurred through technical change in the protected, importable industry. This implies that if an "infant industry" is protected and becomes technically progressive in consequence, technical progress is harmful rather than helpful.[3] But this paradox is now seen to be only apparent: The technical progress in the protected importable industry implies that the tariff in question now leads to a substantially accentuated loss; the pull power of the tariff is augmented now, and it draws a disproportionately greater

2. See Bhagwati (1968) for more such cases.

3. Here one has to assume that the tariff continues to be in place even after the infant industry has experienced technical progress.

amount of resources away from the optimal allocation to the protected industry.

29.4 Two Caveats

The preceding analysis does not apply without modification to cases where the source of the growth is population expansion, for in that case the economy can be construed as being immiserized under less stringent conditions. Even when GNP increases, per-capita GNP can fall when population has grown.

Our argument that the optimal pursuit of policies excludes immiserizing growth is also subject to the caveat that the opportunity set does expand with growth, but it may not if the foreign transformation curve facing the growing country changes with growth. This may be trivially the case when the foreign country experiences its own growth or a parametric shift in its demand simultaneously (Melvin 1969; Bhagwati 1969), but it can also happen nontrivially as follows: Consider a tariff-retaliation model of the Cournot-Johnson variety (discussed in chapter 31). In this case the growing country will achieve an optimal tariff-retaliation-process equilibrium welfare level, which may dominate its free-trade welfare level. After growth, there will be another such optimal tariff-retaliation-process level. The latter (after-growth) level may well be below the former (before-growth) level despite the optimality of each, for the reason that the external offer curve is no longer given as exogenous to the country's optimal policy.

29.5 Diverse Applications of Immiserizing-Growth Theory

The theory of immiserizing growth illuminates a number of significant theorems in the theory of trade and welfare whenever distortions figure in an essential manner. We indicate some of these applications here.

Ranking Free Trade and Autarky

We know from chapter 20 that free trade and autarky cannot be rank-ordered uniquely when distortions are present.[4] It is easy to see why: Consider the Baldwin free-trade locus. It dominates the production-possibility curve for the autarky situation. Therefore the free-trade situation might be viewed as an after-growth situation and the autarky situation as the

4. Haberler (1950) is probably the seminal paper on the subject.

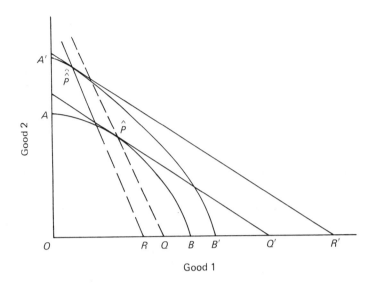

Figure 29.3

before-growth situation. It should be immediately obvious then that the proposition that a shift to free trade from autarky causes a welfare loss in the presence of distortions is nothing more than an application of the theory of immiserizing growth.

Measuring Growth Rates

Should growth rates be measured at world prices or at domestic prices when trade distortions are present? The issue is clearly seen in figure 29.3, which centers on the Johnson case of figure 29.2. Growth pushes out the production-possibility curve from AB to $A'B'$. If the growth rate were measured at domestic prices, it could be shown as $Q'R'/OQ' > 0$ when in fact the economy has been immiserized and its "true" growth rate (at world prices) is $QR/OQ < 0$. This is an important, policy-relevant implication of the theory of immiserizing growth, and also a major contribution to the theory of national income measurement.[5]

Immiserizing Foreign Investment

Another insight from immiserizing-growth theory is that inducing the inflow of foreign capital by erecting a tariff, as is often done, can immiserize the economy. In fact, if some foreign capital flows in when the tariff-ridden economy's importable good is capital-intensive in the stan-

5. The issues raised by this problem are dealt with in depth in Bhagwati and Hansen (1973).

dard 2×2 model, immiserization is inevitable (chapter 32).[6] This application of immiserizing growth is also of considerable policy relevance because it implies that one of the major sources of the inferiority of the import-substituting strategy of development relative to the export-promoting strategy may well be that the former is characterized by foreign investments coming into capital-intensive industries protected by tariffs and quantitative restrictions (Bhagwati 1978, ch. 8).

Lobbying and Welfare

An equally significant application of immiserizing-growth theory has been to the question of whether lobbying activities addressed to imposing a distortion (for example, lobbying for a distortionary tariff) add to the cost imposed by that distortion.[7] In other words, is the welfare cost of an exogenously specified distortion necessarily less than that of the same distortion arrived at by expenditure of real resources in lobbying to get that distortion implemented by the government? Since the comparison is being made subject to a given distortion (e.g., a tariff in a small economy as in the Johnson case above), and since the resource-using lobby situation and the nonlobbying situation are equivalent to before growth and after growth situations, respectively (because lobbying itself is a directly unproductive activity), it follows from the theory of immiserizing growth that the lobbying-inclusive distortionary situation can be characterized—paradoxically—by higher welfare.

29.6   Algebra of the Bhagwati and the Johnson Cases

We finally turn to the formal analysis of the two celebrated cases of immiserizing growth in the literature: the Bhagwati and the Johnson cases.

Bhagwati Case

Consider the 2×2 model discussed in part I and formally developed in chapters 9 and 12 and appendix C. This model was used also in our analyses of tariffs (chapter 12) and of the transfer problem (chapter 16), and we utilize here the same notation.

First, consider the effect of growth in country I on its terms of trade, which are assumed to adjust so as to accommodate the effects of growth. At constant terms of trade, the effect of growth on country I's excess

---

6. This result was established by Uzawa (1969), Hamada (1974), and Brecher and Díaz-Alejandro (1977).

7. This is explored in chapter 34.

demand for the importable is

$$m \cdot dD_e = (c - \gamma)dD_e, \tag{29.1}$$

where (as will be recalled) c is the marginal propensity to consume the importable and γ is the marginal propensity to produce the importable, both with respect to the change in domestic expenditure (D_e) and income ($D_i = D_e$) resulting at constant goods-price ratio as a result of the growth.

The excess demand for the importable good must be cleared by change in the terms of trade, p, so we get, as in the analysis of the impact of tariffs and transfers,

$$\frac{dp}{dD_e} = \frac{c - \gamma}{M(\varepsilon + \varepsilon^* - 1)}. \tag{29.2}$$

We can now derive the effect of growth on country I's welfare:

$$\frac{dU}{dD_e} = \frac{\partial U}{\partial C_1} \left(\frac{dC_1}{dD_e} + p \cdot \frac{dC_2}{dD_e} \right)$$

$$= \frac{\partial U}{\partial C_1} \left(\frac{d(Q_1 - M^*)}{dD_e} + p \cdot \frac{d(Q_2 + M)}{dD_e} \right)$$

$$= \frac{\partial U}{\partial C_1} \left(\frac{\partial Q_1}{\partial D_e} + \frac{\partial Q_1}{\partial p} \cdot \frac{dp}{dD_e} - \frac{dM^*}{dD_e} \right.$$

$$\left. + p \cdot \frac{\partial Q_2}{\partial D_e} + p \cdot \frac{\partial Q_2}{\partial p} \frac{dp}{dD_e} + p \cdot \frac{dM}{dD_e} \right)$$

$$= \frac{\partial U}{\partial C_1} \left[\left(\frac{\partial Q_1}{\partial D_e} + p \cdot \frac{\partial Q_2}{\partial D_e} \right) + \left(\frac{\partial Q_1}{\partial p} + p \cdot \frac{\partial Q_1}{\partial p} \right) \frac{dp}{dD_e} \right.$$

$$\left. + p \cdot \frac{dM}{dD_e} - \frac{dM^*}{dD_e} \right].$$

But

$$\left(\frac{\partial Q_1}{\partial p} + p \cdot \frac{\partial Q_2}{\partial p} \right) = 0$$

by profit maximization, and

$$\left(\frac{\partial Q_1}{\partial D_e} + p \cdot \frac{\partial Q_2}{\partial D_e} \right) = 1,$$

since these two production effects add up to the change in domestic income and therefore expenditure. Therefore

$$\frac{dU}{dD_e} = \frac{\partial U}{\partial C_1}\left(1 + \frac{pdM}{dD_e} - \frac{dM^*}{dD_e}\right).$$

However, $pM = M^*$. Differentiating and substituting, we get

$$\frac{dU}{dD_e} = \frac{\partial U}{\partial C_1}\left(1 - M \cdot \frac{dp}{dD_e}\right). \tag{29.3}$$

Substituting (29.2) into (29.3), we then get

$$\frac{dU}{dD_e} = \frac{\partial U}{\partial C_1}\left(1 - \frac{c - \gamma}{\varepsilon + \varepsilon^* - 1}\right)$$

$$= \frac{\partial U}{\partial C_1}\left(\frac{\varepsilon' + (\varepsilon^* - 1) + \gamma}{\varepsilon + \varepsilon^* - 1}\right). \tag{29.4}$$

Now immiserizing growth implies that $dU/dD_e < 0$. With market stability ($\varepsilon + \varepsilon^* > 1$), and with $\varepsilon' > 0$ because it is the compensated elasticity, immiserizing growth requires that either

$$\varepsilon^* - 1 = \eta^* < 0$$

or

$$\gamma < 0.$$

In the expression above $\eta^* < 0$ means that the foreign country's elasticity of supply of exports with respect to the change in the terms of trade must be negative; that is, geometrically the growing country I operates on country II's offer curve in the inelastic range QR in figure 29.4. On the

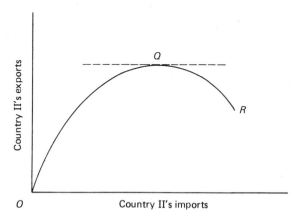

Figure 29.4

other hand, $\gamma < 0$ means that the "output effect" on supply of the importable good, at constant goods-price ratio, is negative. That is, production of the importable good falls off absolutely with the productivity change or factor-supply augmentation that constitutes growth. Recall from chapter 5 that $\gamma < 0$ will arise if capital accumulates with the exportable good capital-intensive or if Hicks-neutral technical progress occurs in the exportable activity. Evidently it is therefore incorrect to assert that inelasticity of the foreign offer curve ($\eta^* < 0$) is a necessary condition for immiserizing growth. However, if we were to assume complete specialization on the exportable good, we would have $\gamma = 0$; hence $\eta^* < 0$ would become a necessary condition for immiserizing growth. (For further discussion, see Bhagwati 1958.)

Johnson Case

The formal condition for the Johnson case of immiserizing growth to arise can now be established, as was done for the case of factor accumulation by Bertrand and Flatters (1971) and by Martin (1977).

As figure 29.2 showed, immiserizing growth will arise if and only if the Rybczynski line $\hat{P}R$ is flatter than the international price line $\hat{P}Q$. By deriving the equations for the slopes of these two lines, we can get the necessary and sufficient condition for the Johnson case of immiserizing growth.

Now it can be readily shown that the slope of the Rybczynski line for augmentation of factor K is

$$-\frac{dQ_1}{dQ_2}\bigg|_{dL=0} = \frac{Q_1/L_1}{Q_2/L_2}$$

(the ratio of average products of the nonaugmenting factor). On the other hand, the goods-price ratio equals the ratio of marginal products thereof. Since the condition for immiserizing growth is that the slope of the Rybczynski line be less than that of the international price line, this condition translates into

$$\frac{Q_1/L_1}{Q_2/L_2} < \frac{p_2^*}{p_1^*}. \tag{29.5}$$

That is, output per factor L employed, evaluated at world prices, must be greater in the L-intensive good 1 than in the K-intensive good 2 (Bertrand and Flatters 1971, eq. 4). However, under competition in factor markets, the wage rate w is equal in both activities. Thus, dividing both sides of equation (29.5) by w and noting that the domestic and foreign goods-price ratios stand in the relation

$$\frac{p_1}{p_2} = \frac{(1+t)p_1^*}{p_2^*}$$

(since good 1 is the importable), we get the following equivalent condition for immiserization:

$$1 + t > \frac{wL_2}{p_2Q_2} \frac{p_1Q_1}{wL_1} \equiv \frac{\alpha_2}{\alpha_1}, \qquad (29.6)$$

where α_1 and α_2 are the labor shares in the two activities (Martin 1977, eq. 7). That is, an increase in the stock of capital will reduce welfare if and only if the ratio of domestic to foreign price of the imported good, $1 + t$, exceeds the ratio of the labor share in the imported good to the labor share in the exported good. With the usual restrictions on production functions, this means that immiserization in the Johnson case cannot arise with capital accumulation if the imported good is labor-intensive.

Recommended Readings

Bhagwati, J. Immiserizing growth: A geometric note. *Review of Economic Studies* 25 (1958): 201–205.

Bhagwati, J. Distortions and immiserizing growth: A generalization. *Review of Economic Studies* 35 (1968): 481–85.

Bhagwati, J. Optimal policies and immiserizing growth. *American Economic Review* 59 (1969): 967–70.

Bhagwati, J. The generalised theory of distortions and welfare. In *Trade, Balance of Payments, and Growth: Papers in International Economics in Honor of Charles P. Kindleberger*, ed. by J. Bhagwati et al. Amsterdam: North-Holland, 1971.

Bhagwati, J., and B. Hansen. Should growth rates be evaluated at international prices? In *Development and Planning: Essays in Honour of Paul Rosenstein-Rodan*, ed. by J. Bhagwati and R. Eckaus. Cambridge: MIT Press, 1973.

Bhagwati, J. *Foreign Trade Regimes and Economic Development: The Anatomy and Consequences of Exchange Control*. Cambridge: NBER/Ballinger, 1978.

Batra, R., and P. K. Pattanaik. Domestic distortions and the gains from trade. *Economic Journal* 80 (1970): 638–49.

Bertrand, T. and F. Flatters. Tariffs, capital accumulation and immiserizing growth. *Journal of International Economics* 1 (1971): 453–60.

Brecher, R., and C. Diaz-Alejandro. Tariffs, foreign capital and immiserizing growth. *Journal of International Economics* 7 (1977): 317–22.

Haberler, G. Some problems in the pure theory of international trade. *Economics Journal* 9 (1950): 223–40. Reprinted in *Readings in International Economics*, ed. by R. E. Caves and H. G. Johnson. Homewood, IL: Irwin, 1968.

Hamada, K. An economic analysis of the duty-free zone. *Journal of International Economics* 4 (1974): 225–43.

Hicks, J. R. An inaugural lecture. *Oxford Economic Papers*, N. S., 2 (1953): 117–35.

Johnson, H. G. Increasing productivity, income-price trends and the trade balance. *Economic Journal* 64 (1954): 462–85.

Johnson, H. G. Economic expansion and international trade. *Manchester School of Economic and Social Studies* 23 (1955): 95–112.

Johnson, H. G. The possibility of income losses from increased efficiency or factor accumulation in the presence of tariffs. *Economic Journal* 77 (1967): 151–54.

Martin, R. Immiserizing growth for a tariff-distorted, small economy. *Journal of International Economics* 3 (1977): 323–26.

Melvin, J. Demand conditions and immiserizing growth. *American Economic Review* 59 (1969): 604–606.

Tan, A. H. Immiserizing tariff-induced capital accumulation and technical change. *Malayan Economic Review* 13 (1968): 1–7.

Uzawa, H. Shihon Jivuka to Kokumin Keizai (Liberalization of Foreign Investments and the National Economy). *Ekonomisuto* (December 23, 1969): 106–22.

We consider two categories of imperfect competition: oligopoly and monopolistic competition. The literature on oligopoly and trade policy has grown rapidly since its inception in early 1980s. However, broadly speaking, there are two types of models. In the first model type, firms located in two different countries compete in the third market. These models are designed to focus on export policy. In the second type, firms located in the two countries compete against each other in each other's market.[1] In these models the menu of policies is wide and includes tariffs, export subsidies, and subsidies on home sales.

Competition in each category of models may take the Cournot or Bertrand form; the marginal cost may be increasing, constant, or decreasing; the product may be homogeneous or differentiated; demands may be concave, linear, or convex; the number of firms may be small or large in one or both countries; entry may be free or restricted; any markets may be integrated or separated. Because of the interdependence in the firms' decisions, results depend crucially on which combination of assumptions is chosen along these dimensions. The literature, though interesting in its own right, does not yield any robust results.

For this reason our approach in this chapter is illustrative rather than general. Where the sensitivity of results to specific assumptions can be illustrated with specific demand or cost functions, we have done so. We also do not attempt to cover all possible cases. A more comprehensive treatment of the subject is available in Helpman and Krugman (1989). In addition many of the important original articles on the subject have been brought together in a recent volume edited by Grossman (1992).

30.1 Competition in the Third-Country Market

Perhaps the most influential contribution to the literature on oligopoly and trade policy is Brander and Spencer (1985). These authors demonstrate that when a home firm and a foreign firm engage in Cournot competition in a third-country market, the optimal trade policy is likely to be an export subsidy. We begin by establishing this result and the conditions under which it arises. We then proceed to discuss several qualifications to

---

1. Within the two-country context, we can also consider optimal policy for a country facing a domestic oligopoly with or without competitive foreign suppliers. Conversely, there can be a foreign oligopoly with or without domestic competitive suppliers. These cases are analyzed in Helpman and Krugman (1989).

the result. Following the general practice in the literature, we present the analysis in a partial equilibrium setting.[2]

Basic Brander-Spencer Analysis

Let there be three countries, a home country, a foreign country, and a third country. There is a single homogeneous product produced in home and foreign countries only and consumed in the third country only. There is one firm each in the home and foreign countries. The two firms compete against each other in the third country. The welfare in home and foreign countries is determined by profits earned by their respective firms, exclusive of any government subsidy. The welfare in the third country depends on the consumers' surplus, but it will not concern us in our analysis.

To minimize notation, we refer to the firm in the home country as home firm and that in the foreign country as foreign firm. Variables associated with the foreign firm are distinguished from those of the home firm by an asterisk. Variables associated with the third country are without an asterisk. Throughout the chapter, Q stands for market demand and supply. Lowercase q and q^* are used to represent supplies of individual firms. The inverse demand function is denoted $P \equiv P(Q)$ where, in the present duopoly case, $Q = q + q^*$. Total cost functions facing the home and foreign firms are $C(q)$ and $C^*(q^*)$.

We solve the problem facing the home firm in detail. The foreign firm's problem can be solved by analogy. Assuming no policy intervention for the moment, the home firm's problem is

$$\max_{q} \pi(q, q^*) \equiv P(q + q^*)q - C(q). \tag{30.1}$$

As a Cournot player, the firm takes q^* as given. The first- and second-order conditions are given by

$$\pi_q \equiv P(q + q^*) + P'(q + q^*)q - C'(q) = 0, \tag{30.2a}$$

$$2P' + qP'' - C'' < 0, \tag{30.2b}$$

respectively. Equation (30.2a) defines home firm's reaction function: for each exogenous q^*, it gives the optimal value of q.

---

2. A general-equilibrium setting introduces complexities that are not central to the issues of concern in the presence of oligopoly. Two problems stand out in a general-equilibrium context. First, market power in the goods market necessarily implies market power in factor markets (Feenstra 1980). Second, in a multiple-goods, general-equilibrium context, the equilibrium is sensitive to the choice of the numéraire. Authors who embed their oligopoly models in general equilibrium (e.g., Brander and Spencer 1985) usually ignore the first problem and allow for only one other good which serves as the natural numéraire.

Before we discuss the reaction function in detail, it is useful to relate (30.2a) to the conventional profit maximization condition of a monopolist. We can rewrite (30.2a) as

$$C'(q) = P\left[1 + \frac{P'(q + q^*)}{P} q\right]$$

$$\equiv P\left(1 - \frac{1}{\eta/\alpha}\right),$$

(30.2a')

where η is the "total" elasticity of demand in the third country and α is the share of the home firm in total sales. Formally

$$\eta \equiv \frac{-1}{P'(\cdot)} \frac{P}{q + q^*}, \quad \alpha \equiv \frac{q}{q + q^*}.$$

We will treat η/α as the home firm's "perceived" elasticity of demand and hence the right-hand side of (30.2a') as the firm's perceived marginal revenue. Then (30.2a') says that the firm equates the marginal cost of production to its perceived marginal revenue. Because α is smaller than unity, the perceived elasticity is higher than the total elasticity of demand.

Differentiating (30.2a), we can obtain the slope of the reaction function in (q, q^*)-space. We have

$$\frac{dq^*}{dq}\bigg|_{HC} = -\frac{\pi_{qq}}{\pi_{qq^*}} \equiv -\frac{2P' + P''q - C''}{P''q + P'},$$

(30.3)

where HC is used to indicate that the slope relates to home country's reaction curve. The numerator of (30.3) is negative by the second-order condition, but the denominator may be positive or negative. Sufficient conditions for the denominator to be negative are that P'' be negative, zero, or positive but not too large. These imply, respectively, that the demand curve be strictly concave to the origin, linear or not "too convex" to the origin. For now we will assume that one of these conditions is satisfied so that

$$\pi_{qq^*} \equiv P''q + P' < 0.$$

(30.4)

We will later see that even within the framework of Cournot duopoly, this assumption limits considerably the validity of the subsidy argument.

Given (30.4), the home firm's reaction function is negatively sloped as shown by RR in figure 30.1. For each q^* the reaction function shows the optimal value of q. The optimal q is smaller the larger is q^*, and vice versa. Intuitively, as the foreign firm increases q^*, the demand curve

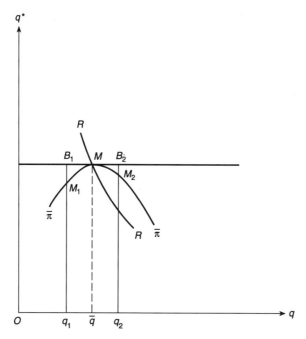

Figure 30.1

facing the home firm shifts to the left, and given (30.4), the marginal revenue curve facing it shifts down (see the discussion below for more details).

The next step in the analysis is to introduce iso-profit curves. Take an exogenous value of q^*, say $\bar{q}^*$. The optimal response of the home firm is shown by point M in figure 30.1. The associated output and profits are $\bar{q}$ and $\bar{\pi}$, respectively. Holding q^* at $\bar{q}^*$, if the firm deviates from $\bar{q}$, the profit will be lower than $\bar{\pi}$. Two such points are shown by B_1 and B_2 with the firm's outputs q_1 and q_2, respectively. Holding now the output at q_1 or q_2, if we want to restore profits back to $\bar{\pi}$, we must lower the value of q^* as shown by points M_1 and M_2. Joining all points such as M_1 and M_2 with M, we obtain the iso-profit curve $\bar{\pi}\bar{\pi}$. The curve is positively sloped to the left of M and negatively sloped to the right of it. At M the iso-profit curve is horizontal. These properties of the iso-profit curve can be verified by differentiating π in (30.1) with respect to q and q^*, setting $d\pi = 0$, and calculating dq^*/dq.

We can draw a family of iso-profit curves with their slopes equal to 0 at the reaction curve. Profits rise as we move down the reaction curve. This is because the firm's maket share rises as we move down the reaction curve.

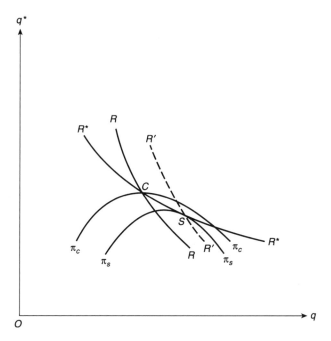

Figure 30.2

The reaction curve and iso-profit curves of the foreign firm can be drawn in analogous fashion. Assuming a condition equivalent to (30.4), the reaction curve slopes down. The iso-profit curves take an inverted-U shape relative to the q^*-axis with a slope equal to infinity relative to the q-axis.

In figure 30.2 we represent the reaction curves of home and foreign firms by RR and R^*R^*, respectively. The intersection of these curves, C, gives the Cournot equilibrium. Note that as drawn R^*R^* is flatter than RR at C. This requires the additional condition that the right-hand side of (30.3) be larger in absolute value than the analogous expression for the foreign firm. The condition is satisfied if and only if equilibrium C is Cournot stable.[3] Though the concept of stability in static games is tenuous, we will assume that the condition is satisfied.[4]

In figure 30.2 we show two iso-profit curves for the home firm: $\pi_C\pi_C$ and $\pi_S\pi_S$. The former is associated with the Cournot equilibrium and

---

3. See Dixit (1986) for more on stability conditions under oligopoly.

4. The stability analysis proceeds as follows. For a given Q^* in the neighborhood of C, firm A chooses Q on RR. Taking, this output of firm A as given, firm B chooses the output along R^*R^*. This process keeps repeating until we reach C. The problem with this analysis is that at each step of the way, each firm sees its rival reacting; yet, in making its optimal choice, it

the latter with Stackelberg equilibrium. The Stackelberg equilibrium is obtained by maximizing the home firm's profits along the foreign firm's reaction function and is represented by point S. By definition, a firm earns a higher profit at its Stackelberg equilibrium than at the Cournot equilibrium.

Suppose that the firms are Cournot players. In the absence of intervention, the equilibrium must be C. Now allow the home-country government to precommit itself to an export subsidy to the home firm at rate s per unit. Given that all output is sold abroad, the export subsidy is equivalent to an output subsidy. Adding the term $s \cdot q$ to the right-hand side of (30.1) and rederiving (30.2), it is easy to verify that, with subsidy, the home firm's reaction curve lies to the right of its original position. If the subsidy is given at just the right rate, the reaction curve is $R'R'$ and passes through point S in figure 30.2. Under this "optimal" subsidy, Cournot behavior leads to the Stackelberg outcome for the home country. Profits for the firm, exclusive of the subsidy, rise to π_S. Subsidy-inclusive profits are given by a new iso-profit curve (not shown) passing through point S along $R'R'$.

What is the intuition behind this result? At the Cournot equilibrium, the firm equates its marginal cost to its "perceived" marginal revenue which assumes that the rival will maintain its current level of output. Given the equivalent of condition (30.4), the foreign firm reduces its output in response to output expansion by the home firm. By assuming that the foreign firm is passive, the home firm underestimates the size of its market and produces below its true optimum.

It may be asked why the subsidy is necessary. Why can the home firm not become a Stackelberg leader on its own? The reason is that the foreign firm comes to the market assuming that the home firm is playing the Cournot game and produces the output associated with point C. If the home firm now chooses the output associated with point S, its profit will be below π_C. The home firm, acting on its own, cannot establish the equilibrium at S if the foreign firm believes firmly that it (home firm) is a Cournot player.

---

disregards the reaction and assumes that the latter's output is fixed at its current level. This story is internally inconsistent and has led to a reinterpretation of the model as a one-shot game. Accordingly, firms are viewed to play a simultaneous-move, one-shot game. Knowing the optimal output of the rival, each firm enters the market with its Cournot output. Though this interpretation is internally consistent, it robs the reaction curves and the traditional stability analysis of their meaning. More important, the condition that RR be steeper than R^*R^* in figure 30.2 can no longer be justified on the basis of stability.

How does a precommitment to subsidy change this situation? If the government is credible to the foreign firm, the latter will be forced to recognize that Cournot equilibrium in the presence of the optimal subsidy is S, not C. Credibility is at the heart of this conclusion. If the foreign firm believes that the subsidy is a gimmick and that it will be recovered later by the government through a tax, it will continue to stick to point C as the optimal solution.

It may be noted that the home country benefits from the subsidy by shifting profits away from the foreign firm. Thus the foreign firm is worse off at S than at C in figure 30.2. It can be verified that the subsidy expands the home firm's supply more than it reduces the foreign firm's supply. Therefore the importing country—the third country—experiences an improvement in its terms of trade and benefits unambiguously.

Within the framework of the present model, the export subsidy result is able to withstand at least two modifications: the introduction of domestic consumption and the possibility of intervention by the government in the foreign country. If domestic consumption is introduced, we must take into account the distortion in the home market given by the difference between the price and the marginal cost of production. A consumption subsidy will typically improve welfare in this situation. Assuming that the home firm has monopoly over the domestic market in each country and can price discriminate vis-à-vis the third country, it remains true that an export subsidy, regardless of the consumption subsidy at home, is welfare improving. If the marginal cost is constant, the previous analysis remains virtually unchanged. The export subsidy has no effect on profit-maximizing sales in the domestic market, and the optimal level of export subsidy is the same in the presence of domestic consumption as in its absence. If the marginal cost is decreasing, an export subsidy reduces the marginal cost for domestic as well as foreign market so that the optimal subsidy is higher in the presence of domestic consumption than in its absence. If the marginal cost is increasing, the optimal subsidy is lower in the presence of domestic consumption than in its absence.

The subsidy also remains desirable when the foreign-country government also intervenes. Assuming Nash behavior on the part of both governments, the optimal policy for them remains export subsidy if there is no domestic consumption. An important qualification to this result, however, is that at the Nash subsidy equilibrium joint welfare of the exporting nations rises if subsidy levels are reduced. Indeed it can be shown that if there is no domestic consumption of the product as assumed in the original story, joint welfare of the two nations is maximized by an export tax rather than export subsidy (proposition 5, Brander and Spencer 1985).

Thus, in the Nash policy equilibrium, export subsidies harm rather than benefit the two countries.

Convexity-of-Demand Assumption

The key feature of the Brander-Spencer model which drives the export-subsidy argument is that the reaction functions are negatively sloped. The optimal response of a firm to an increase in the rival's output is to lower its own output, and vice versa. In game theorists' jargon, the game is characterized by "strategic substitutability."

The strategic-substitutability property of the reaction curves depends critically on condition (30.4). If the condition is violated for the foreign firm, the latter's reaction curve is positively sloped, and the optimal policy for the home country becomes an export tax. The crucial question then is how likely is condition (30.4) to be violated.

Before addressing this question, let us explain the role of condition (30.4) in determining the slope of the reaction curve. In figure 30.3 DD shows the net demand facing the firm, given a specific level of q^*, say q_1^*. The marginal revenue curve associated with DD is represented by MR. Given the marginal cost curve MC, the firm's optimal q is q_1.

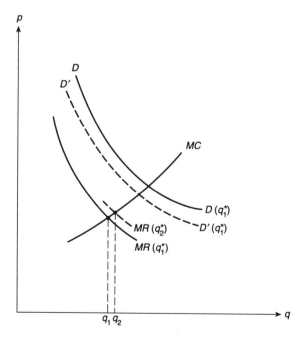

Figure 30.3

Consider now a higher value of q^*, say q_2^*. The net demand curve facing the home firm shifts horizontally to the left by $q_2^* - q_1^*$ and is represented by curve $D'D'$. This shift increases or reduces the optimal value of q as the marginal revenue curve shifts up or down.

Given that the total revenue is $P(q + q^*)q$, the marginal revenue facing the home firm (for a given q^*) is $P'(q + q^*)q + P(q + q^*)$. The vertical shift in the marginal revenue due to a rise in q^* is then given by $P''(\cdot)q + P'(\cdot)$. But this is exactly the expression appearing in (30.4). If this expression is negative as required by (30.4), the MR curve shifts down and q falls, and if it is positive, q rises. The reaction curve slope down or up as (30.4) is satisfied or violated. In figure 30.3 condition (30.4) is assumed to be violated.

Bandyopadhyay (1997) addresses the issue of the convexity of the demand function using a constant-elasticity-of-demand model. He shows that if the two firms face identical, constant unit costs of production and one government does not intervene, the optimal policy for the other government is an export subsidy, free trade, or tax, according as the demand is elastic, unit elastic, or inelastic. The results alter under asymmetric cost conditions. Thus under unit-elastic demand the optimal policy is a tax or subsidy, according as the firm on whose behalf intervention takes place has a higher or lower unit cost of production.

To see how this works, consider the case of unit-elastic demand and constant average and marginal costs. Let the inverse-demand function be written

$$P(q + q^*) \equiv (q + q^*)^{-1}. \tag{30.5}$$

We have

$$P' = -(q + q^*)^{-2}, \tag{30.6a}$$

$$P'' = 2(q + q^*)^{-3}. \tag{30.6b}$$

Substituting these into (30.4), we obtain

$$P''q + P' = (q + q^*)^{-3}(q - q^*) \tag{30.7}$$

which is positive, zero, or negative as q is larger than, equal to, or smaller than q^*. That is, whenever q along the reaction curve exceeds or equals q^*, condition (30.4) is violated. The relevant question then is whether there are portions of the reaction curve such that q is larger than or equal to q^*.

Substituting from (30.5) and (30.6a) into (30.2a), the reaction function can be written

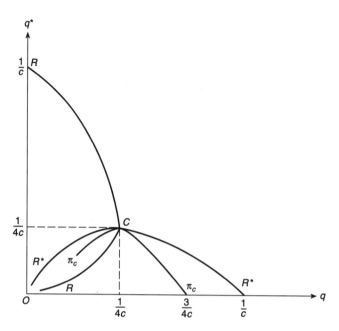

Figure 30.4

$$q = \sqrt{\frac{q^*}{c}} - q^*, \tag{30.8}$$

where c is the constant marginal and average cost of production. The shape of this reaction function is shown by RR in figure 30.4. The reaction curve slopes positively up to $q^* = 1/(4c)$ and negatively thereafter. At $q^* = 1/(4c)$ the reaction curve is vertical. As q^* approaches zero, q also approaches zero. Because P approaches infinity as q and q^* approach zero (see the demand function 30.5), the reaction function is not defined at the origin.

Take first the symmetric case such that the foreign firm's unit cost of production, c^*, equals c. The firm's reaction curve can be represented by R^*R^* which is symmetric to RR. Cournot equilibrium obtains at point C where each reaction curve is vertical relative to the own-output axis. Furthermore each firm's iso-profit curve at Cournot equilibrium lies inside the rival's reaction curve as shown by $\pi_C\pi_C$. It is then immediate that if one government chooses not to intervene, the other government will find it optimal not to intervene as well.[5]

---

5. Locally it can be verified by that the change in home firm's profit at Cournot equilibrium as we move along foreign firm's reaction curve is zero. A similar statement applies to foreign firm's profits as we move along home firm's profits.

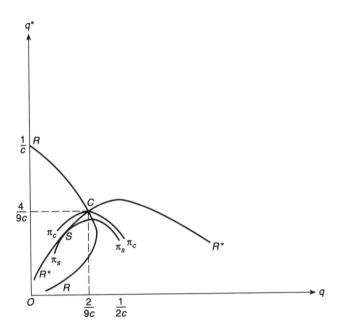

Figure 30.5

Next, suppose that foreign firm's unit cost is lower than that of the home firm, $c^* < c$. For concreteness, assume that $c^* = (1/2)c$. Then the foreign firm's reaction curve is positively sloped up to $q = 1/(2c)$ and meets q-axis at $q = 2/c$. As shown in figure 30.5, Cournot equilibrium now obtains at $q = 2/(9c)$ and $q^* = 4/(9c)$. At the equilibrium the re-action curve of the home firm is negatively sloped and that of the foreign firm is positively sloped. As shown, assuming no intervention by the for-eign government, the home government now has an incentive to pre-commit to an export tax. Drawing appropriate iso-profit curves of the foreign firm, it can also be shown that if the home government does not intervene, the foreign government has an incentive to precommit to an export subsidy.

The story gets more complicated when both governments intervene in a simultaneous-move Nash game. For example, assuming unit-elastic demand and symmetric, constant unit costs, there is a continuum of equi-libria characterized by a subsidy by one country and a tax at the identical rate by the other country. Thus free trade involving a subsidy at rate 0 by one country and tax at rate 0 by the other country is a possible outcome. If costs are asymmetric, a Nash policy equilibrium does not exist at all under a unit-elastic demand. In the elastic case the country whose firm has a higher cost subsidizes its firm at a lower rate than the other country (de Meza 1986; Neary 1994) and may even tax it (Bandhyopadhyay 1997).

Bertrand Competition

Next let us turn to Bertrand price competition. Eaton and Grossman (1986) have made the important point that under Bertrand duopoly the optimal policy for governments is an export tax. To show this, we employ a differentiated products model.[6] We denote by P and P^* the prices of products sold by the home and foreign firms, respectively. $D(P, P^*)$ and $D^*(P, P^*)$ are the demand functions in the third country for products of the home and foreign firms. $D_P(\cdot)$ and $D_{p^*}(\cdot)$ denote the first partials of $D(\cdot)$ with respect to P and P^*, respectively. The cost function may be writtent $C(D(P, P^*))$ with $C'(\cdot)$ and $C''(\cdot)$ positive. The home firm's problem is

$$\max_P \pi(P, P^*) = PD(P, P^*) - C(D(P, P^*)). \tag{30.9}$$

Taking P^* as given, the first-order condition is

$$\pi_P(\cdot) \equiv [P - C'(\cdot)]D_P(\cdot) + D(\cdot) = 0. \tag{30.10}$$

This is the home firm's reaction function. Differentiating (30.10) totally, we have

$$\left.\frac{dP^*}{dP}\right|_{HC} = -\frac{\pi_{PP}}{\pi_{PP^*}}. \tag{30.11}$$

From the second-order condition, $\pi_{PP} < 0$. In addition a sufficient condition for $\pi_{PP^*} > 0$ is $D_{PP^*} > 0$. Assuming this to be true, the reaction function is positively sloped.

In figure 30.6 RR shows the home firm's reaction function. Price increases by the foreign firm induce the home firm to increase its own price. Intuitively a price increase by the foreign firm shifts the demand curve facing the home firm to the right. The likely result is an increase in the output as well as price. (The condition $D_{PP^*} > 0$ ensures that the equilibrium output does not rise so much as to actually lower or leave P unchanged.)

The iso-profit curves are now U-shaped relative to the own-price axis. To see this, consider an arbitrary price of the foreign firm, say $\bar{P}^*$. The home firm's optimal response, given by point M on RR, is $\bar{P}$. The asso-

---

6. If the product is assumed to be homogeneous, the Bertrand equilibrium cannot be defined in a straightforward manner. The demand shifts entirely in favor of the firm offering to sell the product at an infinitesimally smaller price.

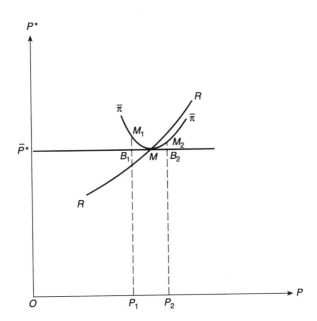

Figure 30.6

ciated profit is $\bar{\pi}$. If the home firm deviates from this value of P to, say, P_1 or P_2 indicated by points B_1 and B_2, respectively, profits decline. Holding the price now at P_1 or P_2, if we want to restore profits back to $\bar{\pi}$, we must raise P^* as shown by points M_1 and M_2. Joining points such as M_1 and M_2 with M, we obtain the iso-profit curve $\bar{\pi}\bar{\pi}$. Other iso-profit curves can be derived similarly. Because both price and market share rise with a rise in P^*, profits rise as we move up the reaction curve.

Figure 30.7 introduces the reaction curve of the foreign firm along with that of the home firm. This curve is also upward sloped. As in the Cournot case we impose the stability condition, which requires that the home firm's reaction curve be steeper than that of the foreign firm. The Bertrand equilibrium is represented by B. The home firm's iso-profit curve through this point is denoted $\pi_b\pi_b$. We also show the home firm's iso-profit curve which is tangent to the foreign firm's reaction curve at point S. If the home firm was a Stackelberg leader, it would choose the price associated with point S.

Suppose that the behavior is characterized by Bertrand competition on the part of both firms. As just noted, in the absence of intervention, the equilibrium will be B. But if the home government precommits itself to an export tax, it can increase the home firm's net profits by shifting the latter's reaction curve to the right. The optimal export tax shifts the reaction curve to $R'R'$ and pushes the Bertrand equilibrium to S. An

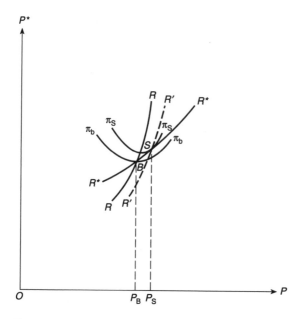

Figure 30.7

analogous point can be made for the foreign country by introducing the foreign firm's iso-profit curves which are U-shaped relative to the P^*-axis.

The intuitive reason behind why the Stackelberg equilibrium is associated with a higher price than the Bertrand equilibrium is as follows: When a firm raises its price, the rival also raises the price and confers a positive externality on the former. But under Bertrand behavior the rival's reaction is ignored and the externality is not internalized. Under Stackelberg behavior the leader internalizes this externality.

An important point to note is that unlike the Brander-Spencer case depicted in figure 30.2, both the leader and follower are better off at the Stackelberg equilibrium than at the Bertrand equilibrium in figure 30.7. Thus, while the Brander-Spencer case exhibits strategic substitutability, the Eaton-Grossman case exhibits strategic complementarity. The higher price at S charged by the home firm benefits the foreign firm directly by giving the latter a larger market. The latter also benefits by raising its own price. The cost of increased benefits to both firms is borne by the importing country.

A final interesting point, not recognized by Eaton and Grossman, is that if the home and foreign firms are identical in the sense that their reaction curves are symmetric, at S, the follower's profits are higher than those of the leader. To see this, suppose that the reaction curves in figure 30.7 are symmetric. It is then immediate that the follower—the foreign firm—can earn as much profits as the leader if it sets P^* at P_S. But the foreign firm actually charges a lower price than P_S and takes a bigger free ride on the home firm than it gives the latter.[7] Graphically at $P^* = P_S$ the foreign firm's profits are shown by its iso-profit curve (not shown) intersecting the 45-degree line through the origin at $P^* = P_S$. This iso-profit curve shows lower profits than that passing through S.

Beyond Duopoly: The Case of Many Firms

In the international context we are likely to encounter more than two firms producing a given product. Therefore we now turn back to the Cournot case but allow for n firms in the home country and n^* in the foreign country. We assume that the product in question is homogeneous and that the demand curve is linear. The latter assumption implies that condition (30.4) is automatically satisfied. Unit costs of production are constant at c for home firms and c^* for foreign firms. As in the basic Brander-Spencer case, the product is produced in the home and foreign countries only and consumed in the third country only.

The inverse demand function is written

$$P = \alpha - \beta Q$$
$$= \alpha - \beta(\textstyle\sum_i q_i + \sum_j q_j^*), \qquad i = 1, \ldots, n, j = 1, \ldots, n^*, \qquad (30.12)$$

where q_i is the output produced by firm i in the home country and q_j^* that produced by firm j in the foreign country. Parameters α and β are positive. Letting s and s^* be the export subsidies, $\alpha > c - s, c^* - s^*$ to ensure that equilibrium output is positive.

Let us consider firm k's problem in the home country. The firm solves the problem

$$\max_{q_k} \pi^k \equiv (P + s - c)q_k. \qquad (30.13)$$

The first-order condition associated with (30.13) is

$$P + q_k \frac{dP}{dq_k} = c - s, \qquad (30.14)$$

where the left-hand side represents the firm's perceived marginal revenue and the right-hand side its private marginal cost. The derivative dP/dq_k is calculated by differentiating (30.12), holding outputs of all firms other than k constant. This leads to $dP/dq_k = -\beta$, allowing us to rewrite

---

7. In a symmetric equilibrium, the Stackelberg equilibrium lies below the 45-degree line through the origin.

Though the nature of intervention (i.e., subsidy or tax) depends only on the relative number of firms, the magnitude of intervention depends on the initial level of output. From (30.20) we see that ceteris paribus, the larger the home output, the larger the optimum subsidy or tax. The magnitude of the home output in turn varies positively with home firms' cost advantage $(c - (c^* - s^*))$. Thus, ceteris paribus, the greater the cost advantage, the larger the optimum subsidy or tax.

A final point worthy of note can be made with the help of the case when $c = c^*$ and $s = s^* = 0$ initially. In this case the country with smaller market share has smaller number of firms and has an incentive to subsidize exports while the larger one has the incentive to tax exports (or do nothing).[10] This result contrasts with the one obtained in the duopoly case based on unit-elastic demand. In that case the country with smaller market share had the incentive to tax and that with larger market share to subsidize exports.

Entry and Increasing Returns

So far we have assumed that entry into the industry is not permitted. In practice, pure economic profits attract entry. More important, even when profits are absent, the presence of subsidies is likely to induce entry. This is the issue we turn to next.

It is clear that as long as unit costs are nondecreasing, free entry will lead to the competitive outcome. With constant unit costs, the price will be equated to the marginal cost with the number of firms and size indeterminate. With rising marginal costs, each firm will be forced to operate at the infinitesimally small level of output and price equated to the marginal and average cost at that level of output. Clearly, if entry is to lead to a nonstandard outcome, we must interact it with decreasing costs.

The first point to note is that the results of the basic duopoly case considered by Brander and Spencer remain valid under decreasing costs. Recall that in deriving the optimal subsidy earlier in this section, we never imposed the assumption $C''(\cdot) > 0$. The results of the multi-firm oligopoly case also extend to the case of decreasing costs provided that we retain the assumption of constant marginal costs. This can be seen by noting that if fixed costs are present, all we need to do is subtract them from the firm's profit function in (30.13). The remainder of the analysis is entirely unaffected.

The more interesting case is the one where decreasing costs and free entry are simultaneously present. To illustrate, we take the simple case

10. Under the assumed conditions, $q = q^*$, and the country with less firms has the smaller market share.

where production requires a fixed cost f and a constant marginal cost c. The other assumptions of the previous section are retained with the modification that n and n^* are now endogenous. As just noted, we can formulate the problem of a representative firm by subtracting the fixed cost from profits. The first-order condition associated with this problem remains the same as (30.15). In addition free entry implies zero profits. This condition yields

$$P + s = \sqrt{\beta f} + c. \tag{30.21a}$$

Remarkably, according to (30.21a), the price received by producers is independent of the subsidy. Putting (30.21a) into (30.15), we get the output of the represetative firm

$$q = \left(\frac{f}{\beta}\right)^{1/2}. \tag{30.21b}$$

The firm's output is independent of the subsidy. Any expansion or contraction of the total output takes place through entry or exit.

An immediate consequence of these results is that given identical cost functions across countries, the country subsidizing exports at the higher rate will drive the other country entirely out of the market. More generally, by (30.21a) home firms offer the product for sale at $(\beta f)^{1/2} + c - s$ and will outcompete foreign firms if this expression is smaller than $(\beta f)^{1/2} + c^* - s^*$.

Remembering that welfare depends on profits exclusive of the export subsidy in the present context, it is not surprising that it will never pay the country to subsidize. Each dollar's worth of subsidy results in an equivalent reduction in the consumer price so that all benefits from the subsidy accrue to the importing country. Put differently, profits are zero in the initial equilibrium. With a subsidy, entry drives subsidy-inclusive profits to zero and, hence, negative subsidy-exclusive profits.

Specific versus *Ad valorem* Subsidies

It is useful at this point to clarify an important difference between the operation of a per-unit or specific subsidy and an *ad valorem* one. In models of perfect competition these instruments are equivalent in the sense that there is for each specific tax or subsidy *an advalorem* tax or subsidy that yields the same outcome. This is not true in models of imperfect competition. A specific tax or subsidy does not change the slope of the demand curve, but an *ad valorem* one does. This differnece implies that for the same prices a specific tax or subsidy leads to a different output than an *ad valorem* tax or subsidy.

This distinction is brought out most clearly with the help of the model of increasing returns and free-entry model introduced above. We know that given zero profits, the firm's equilibrium is characterized by a tangency between the demand curve and the average-cost curve.[11] The specific subsidy has no effect on the slope of the demand curve and hence the output and the supply price. The *ad valorem* subsidy makes the average revenue curve steeper and hence raises the supply price and lowers the output.

To see this formally, suppose for a moment that the home country has a cost advantage over the foreign country and that it is the sole supplier of the product. Consider now the effect of an *ad valorem* subsidy. Letting $\tilde{s}$ be the *ad valorem* subsidy rate, the profit function in (30.13) is rewritten by replacing $P + s$ by $P/(1 - \tilde{s})$ and subtracting f from the right-hand side. Maximization with respect to q_k yields

$$P - \beta q = c(1 - \tilde{s}),$$

where we have dropped subscript k. The zero-profit condition is given by

$$\{P - (1 - \tilde{s})c\}q = f(1 - \tilde{s}).$$

Solving the first of these equations for q and substituting in the second one, we can obtain the supply price of the firm,

$$\frac{P}{1 - \tilde{s}} = \left(\frac{f\beta}{1 - \tilde{s}}\right)^{1/2} + c.$$

Comparing with (30.21a), for a given P the supply price is higher under an *ad valorem* subsidy than under a specific subsidy. Whereas the specific subsidy is passed on entirely to consumers, an *ad valorem* subsidy goes to partially raise the producer price and hence increased average cost. The equilibrium output in the latter case is obtained by substituting the value of P into the profit-maximization or zero-profit condition. We have

$$q = \left[(1 - \tilde{s})\frac{f}{\beta}\right]^{1/2}.$$

Comparing with (30.21b), the firm-level output under an *ad valorem* subsidy is below that under a specific subsidy. This means that for s and $\tilde{s}$ which yield the same P, there is more entry under the latter.

---

11. Letting AR stand for average revenue ($= P + s$ under a specific subsidy and $P/(1 - \tilde{s})$ under an *ad valorem* subsidy) and AC for the average cost, the total revenue and costs are $AR \cdot q$ and $AC \cdot q$, respectively. Then the marginal revenue and cost are given by $AR + q \cdot AR_q$ and $AC + q \cdot AC_q$, respectively. The firm's profit miximixzation condition requires that these be equal. Moreover the zero-profit condition says that $AR = AC$. Together the two conditions imply that $AR_q = AC_q$.

30.2 Oligopoly in Two-Country Models

Let us now turn to models with increasing returns and oligopoly within the more conventional two-country models. In these models, firms belonging to the two countries compete in each other's markets. This naturally gives rise to consumption effects that must be included in our welfare calculations. The set of possible interventions is also enlarged with the subsidy on home sales, export subsidy, and tariff playing separate roles.

Based on whether markets are segmented or integrated and whether entry is free or restricted, four cases can be distinguished. The case of segmented markets without entry is analyzed by Dixit (1984). Venables (1985) extends Dixit's model to allow for free entry. Horstmann and Markusen (1986) consider the case of integrated markets with free entry. Finally Markusen and Venables (1986) unify the literature within a single framework.

We will focus primarily on the segmented markets model and deal with the integrated markets model only briefly. If entry is assumed to be restricted, the segmented markets model is able to capture the basic features of the multi-firm model discussed in the preceding section. In addition, due to the distortion in consumption, the model allows for a richer interaction of domestic and foreign-trade policies. In the following we rely on the linear version of Dixit's (1984) model. Though Dixit (1984) considers the case of restricted entry only, drawing upon Venables (1985), we also consider the case of free entry.

Segmented Markets with No Entry

There are n identical home firms and n^* identical foreign firms. Firms in each country sell in the home as well as foreign market. We let Q denote the demand in the home market and R^* that in the foreign market. Throughout this section it may be convenient to think of the home market as the Q-market and the foreign market as the R^*-market. Sales by representative home and foreign firms in the home (or Q) market are denoted q and q^*, respectively. Sales in the foreign (R^*) market are denoted r and r^*. The total sales in the home country are $Q \equiv nq + n^*q^*$, and in the foreign country $R^* \equiv nr + n^*r^*$.

The inverse demand functions in the two countries are

$$P = \alpha - \beta Q, \quad Q \equiv nq + n^*q^*, \tag{30.22a}$$

$$P^* = \alpha^* - \beta^* R^*, \quad R^* \equiv nr + n^*r^*. \tag{30.22b}$$

As before, fixed costs are denoted f and f^* and marginal costs c and c^*. We consider policies applicable to the home market only; policies applicable to the foreign market can be understood by analogy. There are three possible instruments that can influence sales in the home market: a tariff t imposed by the home country on sales by foreign firms, an export subsidy s_q^* given by the foreign country to its firms, and a subsidy s_q given to home firms on home sales by the home government. All policy parameters are defined on a per unit rather than *ad valorem* basis.

Remembering that each firm operates in both markets, the representative home and foreign firms' profits, respectively, may be written

$$\pi = (P - c + s_q) \cdot q + (P^* - c) \cdot r - f, \tag{30.23a}$$

$$\pi^* = (P - c^* + s_q^* - t) \cdot q^* + (P^* - c^*) \cdot r^* - f^*. \tag{30.23b}$$

In the home market, under Cournot behavior, profit maximization by the representative home and foreign firm, respectively, yields

$$P - \beta \cdot q = c - s_q, \tag{30.24a}$$

$$P - \beta \cdot q^* = c^* - s_q^* + t. \tag{30.24b}$$

Note the resemblance between these equations and equation (30.15). A home firm's share in the market will be larger than, equal to, or smaller than that of a foreign firm according as $c - s_q$ is smaller than, equal to, or larger than $c^* - s_q^* + t$.

In the foreign market there are no policy interventions by assumption. Therefore profit-maximizing conditions for home and foreign firms are

$$P^* - \beta^* \cdot r = c, \tag{30.25a}$$

$$P^* - \beta^* \cdot r^* = c^*. \tag{30.25b}$$

Substituting for P from (30.22a), equations (30.24a) and (30.24b) can be solved for q and q^* independently of (30.25a) and (30.25b). Similarly, substituting for P^* from (30.22b), we can solve (30.25a) and (30.25b) for r and r^* independently of (30.24a) and (30.24b). Markets are not only segmented in the sense that P and P^* are different, but they are entirely independent of each other. Two key assumptions leading to the independence are a lack of entry or exit and constant marginal costs. If there is free entry and exit, changes in one market change the number of firms that has feedback effects in the other market. Similarly, if c depends on the firm's total output, changes in sales in one market change the marginal cost and hence affect sales in the other market. Formally we can no longer solve for q independently of r.

As noted earlier, we will focus exclusively on policies directed at the home market and, till the introduction of free entry, work exclusively with (30.22a), (30.23a), (30.24a), and (30.24b). Observe that these equations do not look particularly different from the corresponding equations in section 30.1. The only difference is the presence of additional policy instruments. Equations (30.22a), (30.24a), and (30.24b) can be solved explicitly for P, q, and q^*. For future reference we note here the equilibrium price and the comparative static effects of policy changes on q, q^*, and Q.

$$P = \frac{1}{n + n^* + 1}[\alpha + n(c - s_q) + n^*(c^* + t - s_q^*)], \tag{30.26}$$

$$dq = \frac{1}{\beta}\frac{1}{n + n^* + 1}[(n^* + 1)\,ds_q + n^*(dt - ds_q^*)], \tag{30.27a}$$

$$dq^* = -\frac{1}{\beta}\frac{1}{n + n^* + 1}[(n\,ds_q + (n + 1)(dt - ds_q^*)], \tag{30.27b}$$

$$dQ \equiv n \cdot dq + n^* \cdot dq^* = \frac{1}{\beta}\frac{1}{n + n^* + 1}[n\,ds_q - n^*(dt - ds_q^*)]. \tag{30.27c}$$

From (30.26) we see that P varies directly with α, implying that $P - c$ rises with α. According to (30.27a)–(30.27c) the subsidy on home sales by the home government raises the domestic and total output and lowers the foreign output. The expressions for comparative static effects of the subsidy in these equations are identical to those obtained for the export subsidy, s, in section 30.1 (see equation 30.17). A tariff raises home output and lowers the foreign and total output. An export subsidy by the foreign government has the opposite effects of the tariff.

We are now ready to discuss the effects of the policy changes on welfare. In the present setting welfare is measured by the sum of consumers' surplus, profits, and net government revenue. Denoting by $g(Q)$ the gross benefit of home consumers (i.e., the area under the inverse demand curve), the consumers' surplus is $g(Q) - PQ$. Since the marginal benefit function represents the inverse demand function, we have $g'(Q) = P$. Welfare is now written

$$U \equiv [g(Q) - PQ] + n\pi + [tn^*q^* - s_q nq], \tag{30.28}$$

where the first term stands for the consumers' surplus, the second for total profits, and the last one for the net government revenue. Substituting for π from (30.23a), the expression for welfare becomes

$$U \equiv [g(Q) - PQ] + n[(P - c)q + (P^* - c)r - f] + tn^*q^*$$

$$\equiv CS + n\tilde{\pi} + R. \tag{30.28'}$$

The subsidy on home sales, being a pure transfer from home government to home firm, drops out of U. The subsidy does have an effect on welfare through an effect on output choices, however. We denote the first term by CS (consumers' surplus), the second term by $n\tilde{\pi}$ (total profits exclusive of the subsidy on home sales), and the third one by R (tariff revenue).

Due to market segmentation, policies directed at the home market have no effect on foreign-market variables. Because we change only the policies aimed at home market, variables related to the foreign market do not change. Then, differentiating the CS, $n\tilde{\pi}$, and R, we have

$$d(CS) = -Q\,dP = \beta Q\,dQ, \tag{30.29a}$$

$$n\,d\tilde{\pi} = n[(P-c)\,dq + q\,dP] = n[(\beta q - s_q)\,dq - \beta q\,dQ], \tag{30.29b}$$

$$dR = n^*[t\,dq^* + q^*\,dt]. \tag{30.29c}$$

In deriving (30.29a), we use $g'(Q) = P$. The second equality in (30.29b) follows from (30.24a).

From (30.27a)–(30.27c) the subsidy on home sales raises Q and q and lowers q^*. The rise in Q lowers P and raises the CS. Given a rise in q but fall in P, the effect on $n\tilde{\pi}$ is ambiguous. Because the fall in P increases the consumers' surplus more than it reduces home profits, the effect of the subsidy on $CS + n\tilde{\pi}$ is positive.[12] R does not change if $t = 0$ initially but falls otherwise. These results are summarized in the first row of table 30.1.

Figure 30.8 illustrates the effects of the subsidy to home firms on homes sales at $t = 0$. The introduction of a subsidy lowers the price from P^0 to P' and raises home sales from $(nq)^0$ to $(nq)'$. The CS rises by areas 1 and 2. Profits, exclusive of the subsidy, fall by area 1 and rise by area 4 with net effect on them being ambiguous. Because the lost area 1 is picked up by consumers, the net effect on $CS + n\tilde{\pi}$, and hence welfare is positive. The net gain equals the sum of areas 2 and 4.

An increase in the tariff lowers Q and q^* and raises q. Therefore the CS falls and $n\tilde{\pi}$ rises. The effect on the CS and $n\tilde{\pi}$ combined is ambiguous, however. R rises for low initial values of t but falls otherwise. The second row of table 30.1 shows these results.

Finally the export subsidy by the foreign country raises Q and q^* and lowers q. The CS rises and $n\tilde{\pi}$ falls, and the joint effect is ambiguous. R is

12. The increase in Q reduces P, which increases the CS by $Q \cdot dP$ and reduces $n\tilde{\pi}$ by $nq \cdot dp$. Given $Q = nq + n^*q^*$, the former change is larger.

Table 30.1
Effects of policy changes on home welfare

	CS	$\tilde{\pi}$	TR	$CS + n\tilde{\pi}$	U
s_x	+	+/− as $n^* + 1 - n$ is +/− at $s_x = 0$	− (0 at $t = 0$)	+	+ (at $t = 0$)
t	−	+	? (+ at $t = 0$)	?	+ (at $t = 0$)
s_x^*	+	−	+ (0 at $t = 0$)	?	?

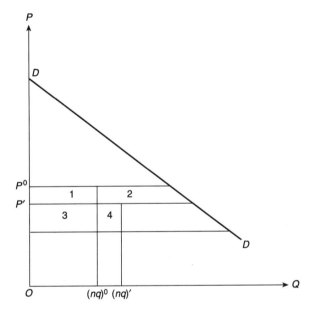

Figure 30.8

unaffected if $t = 0$ initially but rises otherwise. These results are shown in the last row of table 30.1.

Before turning to the discussion of the first- and second-best policies to maximize U, note the equivalence between (30.29b) above and (30.19). Remembering that the output effects of s_q in the present model are identical to those of s in the model discussed in section 30.1, from the viewpoint of home firms' profits, the two instruments work identically. Indeed, substituting for dq/ds_q and dQ/ds_q from (30.27a) and (30.27c), we can shown that the s_q which maximizes $n\tilde{\pi}$ is positive zero or negative according as n is smaller than, equal to, or larger than $n^* + 1$. A similar result holds for the foreign country with respect to its export subsidy, s_q^*.

First-Best Home Policies

By (30.24b) we have $t = P - (c^* - s_q^*) - \beta q^*$. Differentiating this totally, we obtain $dt = (dP + ds_q^* - \beta \, dq^*) = -(\beta \, dQ - ds_q^* + \beta \, dq^*)$. Substituting these values of t and dt into (30.29c) and adding the resulting expression to (30.29a) and (30.29b), we obtain

$$dU = n(P - c) \, dq + \{(P - c) + [c - (c^* - s_q^*) - 2\beta q^*]\} n^* \, dq^*$$

$$+ \, n^* q^* \, ds_q^*. \tag{30.30}$$

Keeping the foreign export subsidy fixed ($ds_q^* = 0$), equation (30.30) can directly serve as the basis of the discussion of optimal choices of s_q and t. There are only two endogenous variables that must be chosen optimally: q and q^*. Once these are determined, Q and P are automatically determined. Therefore the home government can manipulate the two policies to control q and q^* optimally; namely we can think of q and q^* as exogenous variables and choose them to maximize U.

Assuming that q is positive, the first condition for optimality is that the coefficient of dq be set equal to zero:

$$P - c = 0. \tag{30.31}$$

By (30.24a) this condition can be satisfied by setting $s_q = \beta q$.

To understand the second condition, derived from the coefficient of dq^*, we must consider two cases: c is smaller than $c^* - s_q^*$, and the opposite. Taking the case where $c < c^* - s_q^*$ first, we see that, given $P - c = 0$, the coefficient of dq^* in (30.30) is unambiguously negative. The optimal policy is not to import the good at all. Interestingly it turns out that this outcome is ensured by the optimum subsidy on home sales alone, and no trade-policy intervention is required. With domestic subsidy set to yield $P = c$, the assumption $c < c^* - s_q^*$ implies that $P < c^* - s_q^*$. Foreign firms fail to cover their marginal costs even if $t = 0$.

To explain why this policy is Pareto optimum, note that in the absence of intervention, the market equilibrium is characterized by two distortions: The price exceeds the social marginal cost of the product, and trade is nonoptimal. The optimal subsidy on home sales corrects both of these distortions by equating P to c and ousting entirely imports that cost more than c.

Next take the case where $c > c^* - s_q^*$. As long as q is positive, (30.31) remains a valid optimality condition. But P is now larger than $c^* - s_q^*$, and the subsidy on home sales does not oust imports entirely. Indeed, by inspection of (30.30), it appears that for small values of q^*, the coefficient of dq^* can be positive, and it may be optimal to subsidize imports in this case. This conjecture is false, however. By (30.24b) and (30.31) the co-efficient can be shown to equal $t - \beta q^*$ which, at $t = 0$, is necessarily negative. Therefore the optimal trade policy still is to restrict imports.[13] The optimum tariff can be obtained by setting the term in square brackets equal to zero and substituting it into (30.24b) to solve for t. We have

$$t_{\text{opt}} = \frac{c - (c^* - s_q^*)}{2}. \tag{30.32}$$

On the one hand, the tariff contributes to home country's welfare by generating revenue and shifting profits in favor of home firms, but on the other, it reduces the consumers' surplus. The optimum tariff strikes a balance between these two effects.[14]

Second-Best Policies for the Home Country

We now consider each of s_q, t, and s_q^* in isloation assuming that other two policies are unchanged. It is now convenient to bring the policies explicitly into our algebraic expressions. Adding (30.29a)–(30.29c) and substituting for dq, dq^*, and dQ from (30.27a)–(30.27c), the change in welfare can be determined by evaluating

$$\beta(n + n^* + 1)\, dU = n[(P - c)(n^* + 1) + n^*(\beta q^* - t)]\, ds_q$$
$$+ n^*[(P - c)n + (n + 1)(\beta q^* - t)]\, dt$$
$$+ n^*[-(P - c)n + n^*\beta q^* + t(n + 1)]\, ds_q^*. \tag{30.33}$$

This equation is equivalent to (30.30).

Consider first the subsidy on home sales by setting $t = dt = ds_q^* = 0$. We already know that if $c < c^* - s_q^*$, the subsidy on home sales can achieve the Pareto efficient outcome. This conclusion also follows from (30.33). The more interesting case is the one where $c > c^* - s_q^*$. The co-efficient of ds_q is unambiguously positive at least so long as $P - c$ is non-negative. Given $c > c^* - s_q^*$, q^*, and hence the coefficient of ds_q, remains positive even after the subsidy on home sales is chosen to yield $P - c = 0$. This means that the optimum subsidy must be so large that P is below c. From our discussion of the Pareto-efficient outcome, we know that if the tariff was available, we would restrict imports beyond the level achieved

---

13. If c is very large in relation to $c^* - s_q^*$, it may be optimal to let the entire home market be supplied by imports. Because $q = 0$ and $P = c$ is not a valid optimality condition in this case, an import subsidy can be optimum. This case is ruled out by assumption in the text.

14. Given $P - c = 0$, the net contribution of the tariff to welfare is less than the revenue. Therefore the optimum tariff in (30.32) falls short of the revenue-maximizing tariff.

at $P - c = 0$ and $t = 0$. This still remains true except that we must rely on the second-best instrument—subsidy on home sales—to achieve further reductions in imports. Setting the coeffficient of ds_q in (30.33) equal to 0, substituting $\beta q^* = P - (c^* - s_q^*) - t$ from (30.24b), and recalling that $t = 0$ by asumption, we obtain the optimum-subsidy rule

$$P = \frac{n^* + 1}{2n^* + 1} c + \frac{n^*}{2n^* + 1} (c^* - s_q^*). \tag{30.34}$$

Thus the price is set between the home and foreign net marginal cost.

Next consider the tariff when the subsidy on home sales is not available. By (30.33), starting at $t = 0$, the coefficient of dt is positive as long as at least one of $P - c$ and βq^* is positive. Setting the coefficient of dt in (30.33) equal to 0, the second-best optimum tariff is

$$t = \frac{n}{n + 1} (P - c) + \beta q^*$$

$$= \frac{2n + 1}{n + 1} (P - c) + \frac{1}{2} [c - (c^* - s_q^*)]. \tag{30.35}$$

We use (30.24b) to obtain the second equality. P, an endogenous variable, is given by (30.26). The first equality shows that if q^* is positive, the optimum tariff is necessarily positive. Recall that when $c < c^* - s_q^*$ and the ouput subsidy is available, the Pareto optimum is characterized by $P - c = 0$ and $q^* = 0$. Then (30.35) also reduces to 0 as expected. If the subsidy on home sales is not available, at the second-best optimum, imports are positive but restricted. On the one hand, the tariff raises revenue and transfers profits to home firms, while on the other, it reduces the consumers' surplus. Formula (30.35) ensures that at the margin the extra gain equals the extra cost. It does not pay to impose a prohibitive tariff because the lost revenue and reduced consumers' surplus more than outweigh the increased profits to home firms.

Given $c > c^* - s_q^*$, if the subsidy on home sales is set optimally ($P - c = 0$), the above formula reduces to (30.31). If the subsidy on home sales is not available, the optimum tariff is higher than that in (30.31). The subsidy on home· sales acts partially like a tariff by discouraging imports. When the subsidy is not available, the higher tariff must compensate for it.

Foreign Export Subsidy and Home Welfare

Let us now turn to the foreign export subsidy. In a conventional model with perfect competition, a foreign subsidy is always beneficial to the home country. From (30.33) we see that the effect of such a subsidy in the present model is ambiguous. A rise in the foreign subsidy lowers P and q, which in turn increase the consumers' surplus but reduces home profits. The net result is also ambiguous.

To understand the implications of the foreign subsidy fully, it is helpful to focus on the case when $t = s_q = 0$. Substituting $P - c = \beta q$ from (30.24a) and setting $dt = ds_q = 0$, (30.33) yields

$$\beta(n + n^* + 1)\, dU = -n^*\beta[nq - n^*q^*]\, ds_q^*. \tag{30.36}$$

Given $t = 0$, the change in welfare equals the change in the consumers' surplus plus profits. Foreign subsidy lowers P and raises q. The impact of the change in P on the consumers' surplus and profits is $Q\, dP - nq\, dP = \beta n^*q^*\, dQ$ and that of the change in q on profits is $n(P - c)\, dq = n\beta q\, dq$ (using 30.24a). Since $dQ/ds_q^* = -dq/ds_q^* > 0$ by (30.27c), welfare rises or falls as n^*q^* is larger or smaller than nq. This makes intuitive sense in that the larger the foreign firms' share in the market, the smaller the loss in home profits due to increased foreign competition.

An interesting nonmonotonicity property of the effect of the change in s_q^* on U may be noted. Suppose that $n = n^*$ and $c < c^*$. Then $nq > n^*q^*$ in the absence of any interventions. Let the foreign country introduce a small export subsidy. According to (30.36) this lowers U. The subsidy also increases n^*q^* and lowers nq, however. Therefore, if we keep increasing the export subsidy, eventually, n^*q^* becomes larger than nq, and further increases in the subsidy raise home welfare.

Impact on the Foreign Country

Change in policies aimed at home market affect foreign country's welfare through profits only. Foreign country's consumers' surplus and government revenue are independent of those policies. Formally we can write

$$dU^* = (P - c^*)\, dq^* + q^*\, dP = (\beta q^* - s_q^* + t)\, dq^* - \beta q^*\, dQ. \tag{30.37}$$

Consider first the export subsidy s_q^*. It has already been stated that the this policy variable works in the same way as in section 30.1. Therefore the optimal trade policy for the foreign country is an export subsidy, no intervention or export tax as n^* is smaller than equal to or larger than $n + 1$.

The effect of a subsidy on home sales by home country on U^* is negative. This is because the subsidy lowers q^* and expands Q thereby lowering P. Both changes are harmful for the foreign country. Finally the effect of a tariff on U^* is ambiguous. From (30.27b) and (30.27c) we note that $dQ/dt = \{n^*/(n + 1)\}\, dq^*/dt$. Substituting this into (30.37) and evaluating at $t = s_q^* = 0$, we see that the introduction of a tariff has a positive, zero, or negative effect on welfare according as $n + 1$ is larger than, equal to, or smaller than n^*. Recalling that the introduction of a small tariff always benefits the home country, we find that in the case $n^* > n + 1$, both countries are better off with a tariff. This is, of course, due to the fact that the initial equilibrium is globally suboptimal.

Segmented Markets with Free Entry

Let us now assume that entry is free. We must now determine n and n^* endogenously. The zero-profit conditions provide two additional equations for this purpose.

For reasons that will become clear shortly, we also introduce transport costs now. In particular, we assume that the cost of shipping goods from one country to the other is g per unit. Profit functions are now modified as follows:

$$\pi = (P - c + s_q)q + (P^* - c - g)r - f, \tag{30.23a$'$}$$

$$\pi^* = (P - c^* + s_q^* - t - g)q^* + (P^* - c^*)r^* - f^*. \tag{30.23b$'$}$$

Equation (30.24a) remains unchanged, but (30.24b) is modified so that we have

$$P - \beta q = c - s_q, \tag{30.24a}$$

$$P - \beta q^* = c^* - s_q^* + t + g. \tag{30.24b$'$}$$

Since our purpose is merely to illustrate how the model works, we assume that preferences are identical in the two countries. This assumption, along with the presence of transport costs, allows us to modify (30.25a) and (30.25b) as follows:

$$P^* - \beta r = c + g, \tag{30.25a$'$}$$

$$P^* - \beta r^* = c^*. \tag{30.25b}$$

Substituting for q from (30.24a) and for r from (30.24b$'$), the zero-profit condition $\pi = 0$, we write

$$(P - c + s_q)^2 + (P^* - c - g)^2 = \beta f. \tag{30.38a}$$

This zero profit condition now links P and P^*. Though markets are still segmented in the sense that P and P^* remain different, there is interaction among them. The link comes from the number of firms, which is now endogenous. A change in one market induces entry or exit which feeds into the other market.

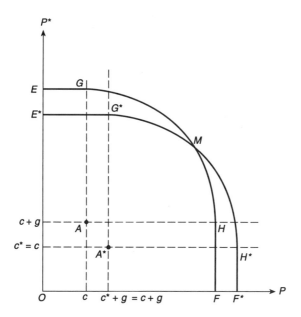

Figure 30.9

By analogy with (30.38a), the zero-profit condition for the foreign country may be written

$$(P - c^* + s_q^* - g - t)^2 + (P^* - c^*)^2 = \beta f^*. \tag{30.38b}$$

Equations (30.38a) and (30.38b) can be solved for P and P^*. Given P and P^*, the four first-order conditions (30.24a)–(30.25b) determine the firms' outputs q, q^*, r, and r^*, and the demand functions yield total quantities Q and Q^*. The number of firms in each country is then obtained by solving $Q = nq + n^*q^*$ and $R^* = nr + n^*r^*$. The model is fully determined.

The zero-profit conditions are circles and can be graphed precisely. Setting all policy variables equal to zero initially, (30.38a) is a circle with center at $(c, c + g)$ and radius $(\beta f)^{1/2}$ in (P, P^*) space. In figure 30.9, EF shows this zero-profit condition.

Along EF, P and P^* are related inversely over the range GH. Starting at a point on the stretch GH, suppose that we raise P but hold P^* constant. Pure economic profits emerge and new firms enter. Since new firms sell also in the foreign market, P^* falls. To maintain zero profits, a rise in one price must be compensated by a fall in the other price. The absolute value of the slope of GH equals q/r. This can be verified by differentiating (30.38a) and using (30.24a) and (30.25a'). A rise in P/P^* is associated with a rise in q/r.

Below point H on EF, P^* is less than $c + g$, and foreign sales cease entirely. Once sales are limited to one market, the trade-off between P and P^* vanishes, and as in section 30.1 the supply price, which is also the autarky price, becomes constant at $OF = c + (\beta f)^{1/2}$. Given zero profits, constancy of the supply price also implies constancy of the firm's output. Over the range HF, changes in the total output come entirely from entry and exit of firms. To the left of G, P is less than c, and home sales cease. Once again the supply price becomes constant at OE ($= OF + g$).

To determine equilibrium P and P^*, we must draw (30.38b) in figure 30.9. Assuming that $c = c^*$ and $f = f^*$, we draw (30.38b) as a circle with its center at $(c + g, c)$ and radius $(\beta f)^{1/2}$. In figure 30.9 this is shown by E^*F^*. Because of the assumed symmetry, the home and foreign circles intersect at $P = P^*$.

Before turning to the discussion of policy, note that if transport costs are zero $(g = 0)$, EF and E^*F^* will completely overlap each other. The two zero-profit conditions degenerate to one, and the solution becomes $P = P^*$. Though we can determine the total number of firms, $n + n^*$, the number of firms in individual countries is indeterminate in this case.

Holding g still equal to 0, assume that the marginal or fixed cost is higher in the foreign country. Then the foreign country's zero profit condition will lie entirely outside that of the home country. In this case, as in section 30.1, firms of the lower-cost country, the home country, will become the sole suppliers of product in both markets.[15] This case illustrates the importance of transport costs in the present model. Unlike the case of no entry, the absolute advantage of one country in supplying the product to both markets rules out reciprocal dumping. Each country must have a cost advantage in its own market over the rival.

Assume, however, that the conditions necessary to obtain a recipocal-dumping equilibrium are satisfied. Consider the effects of small policy changes. In figure 30.9 the introduction of a dollar's worth of subsidy on home sales by the home country shifts the origin of the home-country circle horizontally to the left by a dollar. This raises equilibrium P^* and, interestingly, lowers P by more than a dollar. The expansion of home firms that enjoy a cost advantage in "own" market and entry of new firms allows price to fall by more than the subsidy. The foreign price rises because the decline in P must be compensated by a rise in P^* to maintain the zero-profit condition. The subsidy raises the slope of the zero-profit condition of the home country lowers that of the foreign country. Therefore q/r rises and q^*/r^* falls as a result of the subsidy.

---

15. Given that endowment differences of countries are likely to give rise to systematic cost advantages for one country, this possibility is quite real.

The present model generates tariff effects that are rather perverse. The introduction of the tariff by the home country moves the origin of the foreign firm's zero-profit condition horizontally to the right and leads to a *fall* in P and rise in P^*. The outcome is necessarily what is referred to as the Metzler paradox. Within the context of the model, the tariff reduces profits of foreign firms and leads to exit of firms there. P^* rises and, by the zero-profit condition, P falls. Looked at from the home market's viewpoint, by restricting foreign sales, the tariff induces entry of new firms and also allows expansion of the existing firms. Because home firms enjoy a cost advantage in their own market, these changes allow a reduction in the price.[16]

Turning to the welfare effects, we must now modify the welfare function. The consumers' surplus (CS) and tariff revenue (R) enter the welfare function as before, but profits exclusive of subsidy are replaced by $-s^q nq$. Given $\pi = 0$, we have $n\tilde{\pi} = n(\pi - s^q q) = -s^q nq$. Starting at $t = s^q = 0$, the change in home welfare can be written

$$dU = -Q\,dP - nq\,ds^q + n^*q^*\,dt. \tag{30.39a}$$

Consider first the home subsidy. The subsidy generates leads to entry, which adds to fixed costs, but lowers P, which raises the consumers' surplus. These effects are, respectively, captured by the second and first terms in (30.39a). We saw above that a subsidy on home sales lowers P by more than the subsidy, $-dP/ds^q > 1$. Then, since $Q > nq$, the favorable effect necessarily dominates, and the subsidy is welfare-improving.

Next let us take the tariff. The introduction of a small tariff lowers P and generates revenue. Both effects are favorable, and welfare improves. Because tariff lowers the domestic price, it improves welfare even if the social value of tariff revenue is zero. An immediate implication of this observation is that if tariff revenue had zero social value, the optimal tariff in this model is the one that ousts all imports. If tariff revenue has social value, the optimal tariff will still be high: higher than the revenue-maximizing tariff. Intuitively, after the tariff has reached the revenue-maximizing level, there are still gains from tariff increases in the form of reduced domestic price. At the margin we still want to trade the price reduction for a small loss in revenues.

A foreign export subsidy affects welfare through P. The introduction of such a subsidy lowers P and raises U. Recall that in the absence of entry, this effect is ambiguous (see table 30.1).

---

16. The effects of export subsidy are opposite to those of the tariff and left for the reader to analyze.

Finally the change in foreign country's welfare at $s_q^* = 0$ can be written

$$dU^* = -R^* dP^* - n^* q^* ds_q^*. \tag{30.39b}$$

The subsidy on home sales and the tariff by home country raise P^*. Therefore the effect of those policies on the foreign country is negative. The export subsidy by the foreign country has a positive and a negative effect. But because $-dP^*/ds_q^* > 1$ and $R^* > n^* q^*$, the positive effect dominates and welfare improves.

Declining Marginal Costs: Protection as Export Promotion

In the previous section the home and foreign markets were linked by free entry. An alternative way to link the two markets is to assume that the marginal cost declines with output. This is the approach taken by Krugman (1994). Without presenting this model in detail, we state the central result emerging out of it. Suppose that the home and foreign countries have one firm each and that the condition for the existence and stability of a segmented markets equilibrium with reciprocal dumping are satisfied. Then a tariff by home country leads to an expansion of the home firm and contraction of the foreign firm. This in turn lowers the marginal cost of the former and raises that of the latter. The result is an expansion of sales by the home firm not only in the home market but also in the foreign market. Protection leads to export expansion.

Integrated Markets and Product Differentiation

Last we come to the case of integrated markets. We now assume that if the product is homogeneous, prices in the home and foreign markets can differ by no more than the per-unit transport cost. An immediate implication of this assumption is that if there is even an infinitesimally small transport cost, reciprocal dumping cannot occur. Trade is one way. Moreover, under free entry and exit and linear cost and demand functions, the supply price of firms becomes constant as in section 30.1. In the absence of intervention, production gets concentrated in the country with lower supply price.

Even within this simple framework, one important result can be readily seen. Suppose that there is no market intervention, and the supply price is lower in the foreign country. Production gets concentrated in that country. Suppose now that the home country introduces a tariff that is large enough to make the foreign country's supply price plus tariff larger than the home country's potential supply price. All foreign firms are now forced to exit, and production gets concentrated in the home country. In the new equilibrium the price is higher than before. Moreover, because home firms supply both markets, no tariff revenues is collected. Welfare necessarily declines. This is in stark contrast to the results obtained in the segmented markets model with free entry. In that model the tariff raises welfare even if tariff revenue has no social value.

Horstmann and Markusen (1986) offer a richer analysis of the integrated markets case than in the above example. To resurrect the basic setting of the reciprocal-dumping model within the integrated markets framework, they switch to a model with product-differentiation. Introducing two varieties of the product, they assume that each variety is produced in exactly one country. Given positive demand for both varieties in both countries, there is necessarily two-way trade.

Assuming linear demand and total-cost functions, the Horstmann-Markusen model works very much along the lines of the model with free entry discussed in section 30.1. Denoting by X the home variety and by Y the foreign variety, a per-unit tariff on Y in the home country has no effect on the slope of the firms' perceived average revenue curves in either industry. The supply price and the firm-level output in both industries remain unchanged. The natural outcome is a rise in the home country's domestic price of Y by the full amount of the tariff. The entire burden of the tariff falls on home consumers who must pay a higher price for Y. Substitution in demand toward X leads to entry of new firms with the price of X and per-firm output unchanged. The response is similar to that obtained in the small-country model under perfect competition. For an infinitesimally small tariff, welfare in the home country is unaffected, but for a finite tariff, it declines. Welfare in the foreign country is unchanged.

An export subsidy worsens welfare. A per-unit export subsidy has no effect on supply prices so that the terms of trade of the country deteriorate by the full amount of the subsidy, and internal home prices are unchanged. The home country is worse off and foreign country better off.

A per-unit subsidy on home sales improves the home country's welfare. Such a subsidy lowers the consumer price of X at home but does not affect its terms of trade. The reduction in the home price reduces the marginal-cost-price differential in X and generates a welfare gain.

If we replace per-unit taxes and subsidies by ad valorem taxes or subsidies, as explained at the end of section 30.1, the output per firm becomes responsive to policy changes. This alters our results. For example, an ad valorem tariff by the home country makes the demand curve for Y facing foreign firms flatter. Per-firm output expands, lowering the supply price. The home country's terms of trade improve, and the home price rises by less than the tariff. For small values of the tariff, the terms of trade effect dominates and welfare improves. The result is once again reminiscent of the competitive model, albeit the large-country one.

30.3   Monopolistic Competition

Let us now turn to optimal trade policy in a world of monopolistic competition. This problem is analyzed by Gros (1987) and also considered by Helpman and Krugman (1989). Following these authors, we rely on the model in Krugman (1980) to address the issue. Denoting the consumption of variety i by c_i, recall that the utility function in this model is assumed to take the form $\sum_i c_i^\theta$ where $0 < \theta < 1$.

We saw in chapter 11 that the solution to the closed-economy version of this model is quite simple. To recapitulate, denoting by c and x the consumption and output of a representative variety and by n the number of varieties produced, full-employment and market-clearing conditions yield

$$n(\alpha + \beta x) = L, \tag{30.40}$$

$$x = cL, \tag{30.41}$$

respectively. In addition the representative firm's profit-maximization condition and free entry together lead to

$$x = \alpha(\sigma - 1)/\beta. \tag{30.42}$$

Given this value of x, (30.40) and (30.41) determine c and n.

The first question we may ask is whether the closed-economy equilibrium is Pareto-efficient, or whether it offers any opportunities to increase welfare via intervention. Symmetry ensures that despite price-cost margin, the marginal rate of transformation between any two varieties and marginal substitution between them are equalized. This suggests that the equilibrium is distortion-free. There is, however, the issue of the number of varieties. Given economies of scale, monopolistic competition is traditionally thought to lead to excessive variety and, hence, suboptimal output of each variety.

It turns out, however, that even the number of varieties is at its optimal level in the closed-economy version of this model. The conclusion is verified easily by solving the following problem:

$$\max_{x,c,n,\lambda,\mu} \Omega = nc^\theta L + \lambda(x - cL) + \mu[L - n(\alpha + \beta x)]. \tag{30.43}$$

The first-order conditions with respect to x, c, and n can be combined to yield

$$\theta(\alpha + \beta x) = \beta cL, \tag{30.44}$$

which, together with the constraints, yields the same solution as (30.40)–

(30.42). Thus in the closed-economy context there is no room for welfare-improving intervention. Due to free entry the market-power aspect of imperfect competition is entirely absent in this model. The only potential distortion, as in external economies models, arises due to average-cost pricing of each product variety. However, since this distortion is uniform across varieties, there is no net economywide distortion. Such distortion would arise if we were to introduce, for example, a sector producing a homogeneous good subject to marginal-cost pricing. As in externalities models, we would then have a distortion between the differentiated goods sector taken as a whole and the homogeneous good such that the former would operate below the socially optimum level. A production subsidy to the differentiated good or tax on the homogeneous good would then be optimal.

The conclusion that there is no distortion when the only sector in the economy is that producing symmetric varieties of a differentiated good changes when we move to the open-economy context. Because each country, no matter how small, is the sole producer of its varieties, it necessarily has market power abroad. Because firms fail to exercise this market power due to free entry, there is room for the government to step in. Not surprisingly the optimum tariff is necessarily positive.

To proceed with the analysis, let us now introduce two countries: home and foreign. By assumption, the home-country government chooses its tariff optimally while the foreign-country government is passive. Because we must distinguish between the consumption of home variety in the home and foreign country and likewise for the foreign variety, we will use subscripts H and F when referring to consumption and price variables. For other variables, the notation is the same as in chapter 11.

Given that the number of varieties is *ex post* fixed in the model and marginal rates of transformation and substitution between each pair of varieties are equalized, the optimum tariff will have the conventional form, $1/(\eta^* - 1)$, where η^* is the foreign elasticity of demand for the representative variety of home country. The key task therefore is to derive this elasticity. Foreign country's budget constraint is given by

$$np_{\mathrm{H}}^* c_{\mathrm{H}}^* + n^* p_{\mathrm{F}}^* c_{\mathrm{F}}^* = n^* p_{\mathrm{F}}^* x^*, \tag{30.45}$$

where p_{H}^* and c_{H}^* denote the price and quantity demanded of home variety in foreign country and similarly for p_{F}^* and c_{F}^*. Denoting by $p^* \equiv p_{\mathrm{H}}^*/p_{\mathrm{F}}^*$ the price of home variety in terms of foreign variety in the foreign country, we can rewrite (30.45) as

$$np^* c_{\mathrm{H}}^* + n^* c_{\mathrm{F}}^* = n^* x^*. \tag{30.45'}$$

In addition, given the assumed preference structure, the equality of the marginal rate of substitution between home and foreign varieties to their relative prices yields

$$\left(\frac{c_F^*}{c_H^*}\right)^{1-\theta^*} = \frac{p_H^*}{p_F^*} \equiv p^*, \tag{30.46}$$

where we allow for the possibility that foreign preferences may differ from domestic preferences (i.e., θ^* may be different from θ). Remembering that n, n^*, and x^* are fixed in this model, equations (30.45') and (30.46) together allow us to determine the foreign elasticity of demand for home country's goods. Differentiating the two equations totally and using a caret ($\hat{}$) to denote a proportionate change in a variable, we have, respectively,

$$np^* c_H^*(\hat{p}^* + \hat{c}_H^*) + n^* c_F^* \hat{c}_F^* = 0, \tag{30.47}$$

$$\hat{c}_H^* - \hat{c}_F^* = -\sigma^* \hat{p}^*, \tag{30.48}$$

where $\sigma \equiv 1/(1 - \theta)$. Substituting for the proportionate change in c_F^* from (30.48) into (30.47), we can obtain the elasticity of demand for the home variety with respect to its relative price in the foreign country. We have

$$\eta^* \equiv -\frac{\hat{c}_H^*}{\hat{p}^*} = (1 - s^*)(1 - \sigma^*) + \sigma^*, \tag{30.49}$$

where $s^* \equiv n^* c_F^*/(nC_H^* + n^* c_F^*)$ is foreign country's share in national income measured at that country's prices. The optimum tariff can now be written as

$$t^{opt} = \frac{1}{\eta^* - 1} = \frac{1}{s^*(\sigma^* - 1)}. \tag{30.50}$$

The optimum tariff varies inversely with foreign country's share in the world income and its elasticity of substitution between home and foreign varieties. As was noted earlier, even if we make foreign country's share in income close to 1, thus making home country very tiny, the optimum tariff remains positive.

This basic analysis can be and has been extended in a variety of directions. The most obvious extension is to introduce a homogeneous goods sector into the model just discussed. But, as discussed in chapter 11, this modification gives rise to indeterminacy in the structure of trade and production. Though this indeterminacy can be resolved by introducing transport costs, such a recourse makes the model complicated.

An alternative, pursued by Francois (1992, 1994), is to work with Ethier's (1982) two-sector, two-factor model. As we saw in chapter 11, this model has a constant-returns good, and an increasing-returns good that uses differentiated intermediate inputs. The latter good is subject to external economies that depend on the number of inputs available, while inputs themselves are subject to internal scale economies. In this setting, if we assume that only final goods are traded, the model behaves similarly to models with external scale economies at the sectoral level (Markusen 1990). However, once we introduce trade in intermediate inputs, national externalities are supplemented by cross-border spillovers (international externalities) with policy in one country directly (i.e., independently of the terms-of-trade effects) affecting sectoral efficiency in other countries. Francois (1992, 1994) shows that as in the national scale-economy case, average cost pricing implies potential gains from subsidy schemes that favor the increasing-returns sector. There are potential benefits from a cooperative subsidy scheme, for the group can then internalize some of the cross-border spillovers of externalities. Since this model has four traded goods—two final goods, home intermediate inputs, and foreign intermediate inputs—there are up to three trade-tax instruments available. This fact turns the derivation of optimal trade tax structure into a complicated exercise.

Recommended Readings

Bandyopadhyay, S. Demand elasticities, asymmetry and strategic trade policy. *Journal of International Economics*, 42 (1997): 167–77.

Brander, J. A., and B. J. Spencer. Export subsidies and market share rivalry. *Journal of International Economics* 18 (1985): 83–100.

de Meza, D., Export subsidies and high productivity: Cause or effect? *Canadian Journal of Economics* 19 (1986): 347–50.

Dixit, A. International trade policy for oligopolistic industries. *Economic Journal* 94, suppl. (1984): 1–16.

Dixit, A. Comparative statics for oligopoly. *International Economic Review* 27 (1986): 107–22.

Eaton, J., and G. M. Grossman. Optimal trade and industrial policy under oligopoly. *Quarterly Journal of Economics* 101 (1986): 383–406.

Ethier, W. J. National and international returns to scale in the modern theory of international trade. *American Economic Review* 72 (1982): 389–405.

Feenstra, R. C. Monopsony distortion in an open economy: A theoretical analysis. *Journal of International Economics* 10 (1980): 213–35.

Francois, J. F. Optimal commercial policy with international returns to scale *Canadian Journal of Economics* 23 (1992): 109–24.

Francois, J. F. Global production and trade: Factor migration and commercial policy with international scale economies. International *Economic Review* 35 (1994): 565–81.

Gros, D. A note on the optimal tariff, retaliation and the welfare loss from tariff wars in a framework with intra-industry trade. *Journal of International Economics* 23 (1987): 357–67.

Grossman, G. M., ed. *Imperfect Competition and International Trade*. Cambridge: MIT Press, 1992.

Helpman, E., and P. Krugman. *Trade Policy and Market Structure*. Cambridge: MIT Press, 1989.

Horstmann, I., and J. R. Markusen. Up the average cost curve: Inefficient entry and the new protectionism. *Journal of International Economics* 20 (1986): 225–47.

Krugman, P. Scale economies, product differentiation, and the pattern of trade. *American Economic Review* 70 (1980): 950–59.

Krugman, P. R. Import protection as export promotion: International competition in the presence of oligopoly and economies of scale. In *Monopolistic Competition and International Trade*, ed. by H. Kierzkowski. Oxford: Oxford University Press, Oxford, 1994.

Markusen, J. R. Microfoundations of external scale economies. *Canadian Journal of Economics* 23 (1990): 495–508.

Markusen, J. R., and A. J. Venables. Trade policy with increasing returns and imperfect competition: Contradictory results from competing assumptions. *Journal of International Economics* 24 (1988): 299–316.

Neary, J. P. Cost asymmetries in international subsidy games: Should government help winners or losers? *Journal of International Economics* 37 (1994): 197–218.

Venables, A. J. Trade and trade policy with imperfect competition: The case of identical products and free entry. *Journal of International Economics* 19 (1985): 1–20.

31 Uniform versus Preferential Tariff Reduction

This chapter is addressed to the welfare issues raised by customs unions, free-trade areas, and related preferential tariff reductions. We begin by discussing the economics of uniform tariff reductions by a country in order to make the special and contrasting features of preferential tariff reductions more manifest.

31.1 Unitorm Reduction

For uniform tariff reduction, applied to all other countries equally, it is easy to demonstrate the following propositions.[1]

PROPOSITION 1   For a small country, a higher tariff is inferior to a lower tariff.

This proposition is valid in the sense that it is always possible to find a welfare-improving equilibrium under a lower tariff. However, in the case of inferior goods, multiple equilibria can arise, and it is possible for some competitive equilibrium under a higher tariff to be better than under a lower tariff. Therefore we can rank two suboptimal policies, while free trade is the optimal policy for a small country. From a practical policy viewpoint, proposition 1 tells us as well that a move toward free trade—as distinct from fully free trade—is desirable. This insight is not applicable to the case of preferential tariff reduction where a move toward free trade by a small country may be welfare-worsening.

Proposition 1 should be evident from the mathematical formulation in chapters 12 and 21. Using equation (21.2) for our present purposes and noting that the small-country assumption means that $dp^* = 0$, we see that the expression for the change in welfare as a tariff is lowered reduces to

$$dU = U_1[d(Q_1 + p^*Q_2) + (p - p^*)\, dC_2]. \tag{31.1}$$

Note that a tariff reduction improves the social-budget line reflecting world prices $[d(Q_1 + p^*Q_2) > 0]$, and this in turn means $dC_2 > 0$ (if inferior goods are ruled out). It then follows that $dU > 0$, since $p > p^*$ because of the tariff.

Figure 31.1 illustrates the case of a small country I facing the offer curve OII. With normality of the goods in consumption, a tariff will shift the offer curve OI to OI' and trade equilibrium to F'. A further tariff will shift the offer curve to OII'' and trade equilibrium to F''. Successive tariff increases will mean closer moves toward autarky at O. Evidently the

1. This section is based on Bhagwati (1968), Bhagwati and Kemp (1969), and Riley (1970).

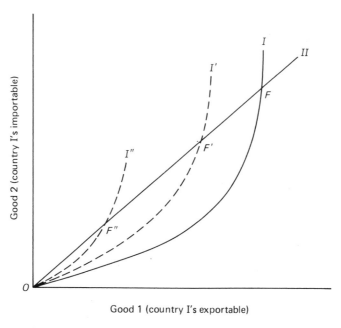

Figure 31.1

successive tariff increases yield lower welfare as the trade-indifference curves (not drawn in) through F, F', and F'' show.

Now let us introduce inferiority of country I's exportable good 1 in figure 31.2. With the higher tariff this small economy produces and consumes at P_H and C_H, respectively, with welfare at U_H. With the lower tariff, the equilibrium shifts to P_L and C_L, and welfare to U_L. Now $U_H > U_L$, but this perverse outcome depends critically on, and can arise only if, the exportable is inferior in social consumption.

But this qualification to the proposition concerning the superiority of a lower tariff must be qualified. Even though the presence of an inferior good can create a paradoxical loss from lowering a tariff, inferiority in consumption then leads to multiple equilibria. Some lower-tariff equilibrium that dominates the higher-tariff equilibrium can always be found. Thus consider figure 31.3, which reproduces C_L and C_H from figure 31.2. To the left of C_H, on U_H, we can find C'_L, where the low-tariff-inclusive price ratio is tangent to U_H. C_L and C'_L therefore lie on the income-consumption (dashed) curve for this price ratio. But now extend this income-consumption line beyond C'_L. If inferiority of good 1 continues, the curve will continue to bend back until it meets and goes up the vertical axis. If inferiority disappears, the curve will move northeast instead. In the latter case the social-budget line in the low-tariff situation will cut

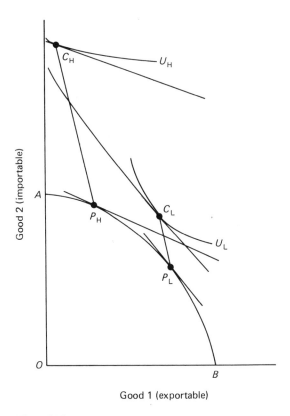

Good 2 (importable)

Good 1 (exportable)

Figure 31.2

the income-consumption curve at a point such as C_L'', and this low-tariff equilibrium will clearly yield a higher welfare level than U_H. Alternatively, in the former case, such an intersection yielding higher welfare will occur at C_L''' on the vertical axis, at complete specialization in consumption on good 2. In either polar case we see that in addition to the perverse lower-welfare equilibrium at C_L, there will be at least one more higher-welfare equilibrium in the low-tariff case.

All this can be seen also in terms of the offer-curve diagram in figure 31.4. There OI and OI' are the low-tariff and high-tariff offer curves, respectively. As chapter 12 showed, the offer curve with a higher tariff must always lie inside the offer curve with a lower tariff. Thus, while the low-tariff equilibrium at W shows greater welfare than the high-tariff equilibrium at W', it shows lower welfare than the high-tariff equilibrium at W'''; the "best" low-tariff equilibrium at W'' dominates all high-tariff equilibria. That the best low-tariff equilibrium will have a higher trade volume associated with it than the best high-tariff equilibrium should be

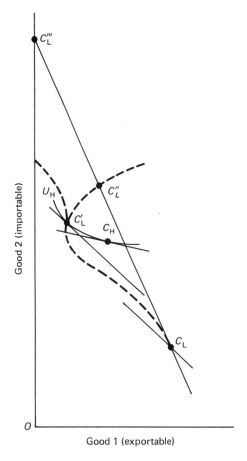

Figure 31.3

evident from figure 31.3; with either of the two income-consumption paths there, and taking the world-price-determined budget lines through P_H, C_H and P_L, C_L for the high-tariff and low-tariff cases, it is plain that the maximal trade volume for the high-tariff case must be less than that for the low-tariff case.

We now complete our analysis by examining how tariffs may be ranked for a large country with monopoly power in trade. Again, excluding inferior goods and now imposing certain "reasonable" conditions on the foreign offer curve facing the country, we can argue the following: Let the optimum tariff be t^{opt}, the zero tariff t_0, and the (just) prohibitive tariff t_p. Then two propositions follow:

PROPOSITION 2   Successive increases in the tariff from the level t_0 will raise welfare until the level t_w is reached; successive increases in the tariff

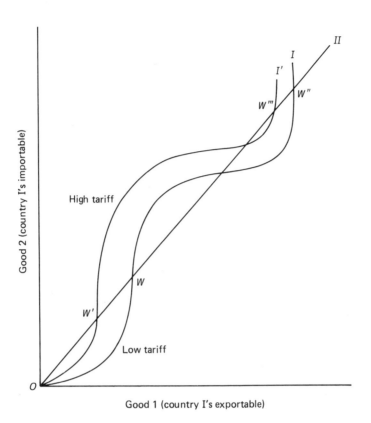

Figure 31.4

thereafter will reduce welfare until the level t_p is reached; higher tariffs merely involve continuing autarky and hence are weakly ordered.

PROPOSITION 3 For a country with monopoly power in trade, the choice of a social-utility function will merely determine the magnitudes of t^{opt} and t_p; hence tariffs may be seen as continually laid in a chain from zero to infinity, with the social-utility function for a specific country serving as a "spike" that lifts this chain up to the level of the optimal tariff and drops it to the floor at the level of the appropriate prohibitive tariff.

Figure 31.5 shows how these propositions depend on the volume of imports falling with tariff increases. The fact that country I is large is reflected in the bowed-out offer curve of country II. Illustrated are the trade-indifference curves U_T^{opt}, U_T^0, and U_T^p reached by country I successively under an optimum tariff, a zero tariff, and a prohibitive tariff. It is clear that proposition 2, and hence proposition 3, will hold if and only if an increase in country I's tariff will necessarily reduce the demand for imports; in such a case an increase in the tariff, starting from zero

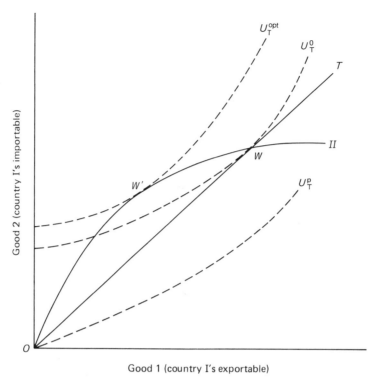

Good 1 (country I's exportable)

Figure 31.5

tariff at W, will take the economy through successively higher trade-indifference curves until it reaches W' and then through successively lower trade-indifference curves to O and U_T^p.

Therefore exceptions to proposition 2 (and hence to proposition 3) must constitute exceptions to the rule that an increase in the tariff will reduce the demand for imports. We know that this rule admits of exceptions when the exportable commodity is inferior.

To see how "irregularities" in the foreign offer curve (resulting from phenomena such as inferiority of a good in foreign consumption) can also invalidate propositions 2 and 3, consider figure 31.6. With multiple equilibria built into OII (the foreign offer curve), let the free-trade offer curve of country I be OI, with two possible equilibria at W at W''. Propositions 2 and 3 will hold relative to W but evidently not with respect to W'', since the welfare level at W'' exceeds even that at W' (the optimal tariff, locally), and the *optimum optimorum* policy is in fact a trade subsidy that takes the economy to W''' and hence to U_T^{OPT} (thus the situation requires a negative optimal tariff as noted in chapter 21).

Multiple equilibria in the foreign offer curve resulting in multiple trade equilibria, as in figure 31.7, are not necessary for invalidating proposi-

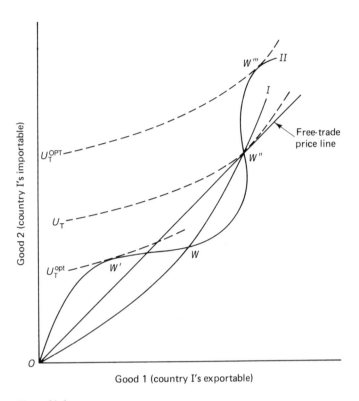

Figure 31.6

tions 2 and 3. As Tower (1975) shows, inflection points in it are sufficient to give rise to counterexamples to propositions 2 and 3. This is shown in figure 31.7. Starting from the unique free-trade (zero-tariff) equilibrium at W with welfare level U_T, imposition of a positive tariff reduces welfare until a local minimum is reached at W' where country II's offer curve touches the trade-indifference curve U_T^{opt} of country I from below. Further increases in tariff raise welfare until optimal tariff and welfare U_T^{OPT} are reached at W''. Any further increases in tariff will reduce welfare until the prohibitive tariff is reached.

Finally in the small-country case the assumption of fixed terms of trade for an atomistic country automatically rules out such perversities from afflicting the foreign offer curve facing the country.

31.2   Preferential Reduction

The theory of uniform tariff cuts is basically in accord with the intuition that a tariff reduction ought to be welfare-improving (except below the

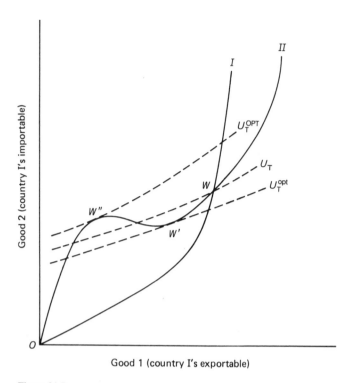

Figure 31.7

optimal tariff level for the large-country case), and the complexities noted in the foregoing section were at a somewhat deeper analytical, and perhaps empirically not important, level. This is, however, not true of preferential tariff reductions.

The theory of preferential tariff cuts has developed mainly as a result of the post–World War II moves toward customs unions and free-trade areas.[2] These represented partial moves toward free trade and posed a problem for the GATT (General Agreement on Trade and Tariffs), which had been constituted in order to regulate trade in the postwar world. Under GATT each member country is required to extend most-favored-nation (MFN) treatment to other GATT members: The lowest tariff applicable on an item imported into a member country must be extended by that country to all GATT members. A customs union or a free-trade area, with zero tariff on members of the union or area but positive tariffs on outside countries, would conflict with GATT, since some of the out-

2. The discussion in this section is mainly based on Viner (1950), Lipsey (1957, 1960), Bhagwati (1971, 1973), Kirman (1973), Johnson (1974), and Kemp and Wan (1976). Viner's analysis predates the Treaty of Rome that set up the European Common Market leading to the current European Union.

side countries are GATT members and hence entitled under GATT's MFN rule to zero tariff. To resolve this conflict, GATT was drafted so as to accommodate customs unions and free-trade areas. Thus Article 24 makes any preferentially tariff-reducing arrangements involving any but not all GATT members admissible provided that the tariff reductions are not partial but go all the way to free trade among the members, either immediately or in a phased program. Since free-trade areas and customs unions do precisely that, with the major trading difference being that the former do not require a common external tariff while the latter do, they are both accommodated by this Article.

From an economic viewpoint the interesting question that arose at the time was whether such a preferential reduction of tariffs in favor of a subset of countries in the world economy would be welfare-improving or whether it could worsen member countries and/or world welfare conventionally defined. This "static" question is considered here and again in section 31.3 and distinguished from the recent, "dynamic" time-path question, posed and analyzed in section 31.4.

Trade-Diverting and Trade-Creating Unions

Viner (1950) distinguished between trade-diverting and trade-creating customs unions. He argued that the case for customs unions was a mixed bag, since trade-diverting customs unions would worsen, and only trade-creating unions would improve, world efficiency (welfare). Viner defined a trade-diverting union as one that would shift production from a lower-cost nonmember country to a higher-cost member country, and a trade-creating union as one that would do the opposite. The simplest model of this, and one that corresponds to Viner's notions and helps illustrate his insightful distinction to advantage, is a three-country, two-good model.

Let the three countries be home (H), partner (P), and outside (O) countries. Country H has a uniform tariff on import of good 1 from both P and O before the union. Assume constant costs so that the production-possibility curve for H is Ricardian and the external offer curves from countries P and O are linear. If then the preunion tariff of country H is prohibitive, and the elimination of it with country P on forming the union with it leads to imports from P at the expense of domestic production of the importable, this is clearly a Vinerian trade-creating union, for the lower-cost P production of the importable replaces the higher-cost H production.

Must a Trade-Diverting Union Worsen Welfare?

However, consider the case where the preunion tariff was not prohibitive and the member country P is higher-cost relative to the outside country, so that preunion imports were from the outside country. The union now eliminates the tariff on imports from P alone. Let this make the price to consumers of imports from P less than that for imports from O, since the latter still carry the tariff. This switches trade from the cheaper source O to the higher-cost source P. The result, in Vinerian language, is a trade-diverting customs union.

Now, focusing on the welfare of the home country H, let us ask a question that was widely discussed in the later 1950s: Would such a trade-diverting union *necessarily* harm the home country? And, if we assume that the impact on the rest of the world is negligible, since it is "large," would it correspondingly amount to deterioration of world welfare?

The answer to this question is best developed formally in an explicit general-equilibrium model reflecting the assumptions detailed above. In figure 31.8 assume that at all equilibrium goods-price ratios, the home country's Ricardian production-possibility curve (not drawn) will lead to specialization on good 2 at A. Production will therefore not vary from A. Let the fixed terms of trade with the outside country be given by the

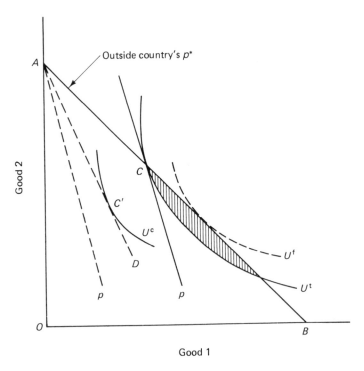

Figure 31.8

line ACB, and let the inferior terms of trade with the partner country be indicated by the broken line AD.

With a common tariff, imports of good 1 from both sources will be taxed equally, and hence the cheaper supplier, the outside country, will be the source of imports. Therefore the preunion equilibrium consumption will be at C, tangent to the tariff-inclusive domestic price ratio p, as determined by the external terms of trade with the partner country and the tariff. Evidently the corresponding welfare level U^t is dominated by the free-trade welfare level U^f.

Suppose that we eliminate the tariff only on imports from country P because of a union between the home and partner countries. Then, as the relative steepness of Ap (the tariff-inclusive domestic price line for imports from the partner country) and AD (the tariff-free domestic price line for imports from the partner country) demonstrates, imports from the partner country will become cheaper to consumers in the home country. Trade will shift to the partner country; consumption will be at C' and welfare at U^c.[3] Now $U^c < U^t$, so this trade-diverting union has lowered welfare for the home country. A little reflection will show that if the partner country's price line, while steeper than AB, had gone through the striped area, then $U^c > U^t$ would have been the outcome.

The dividing line between the welfare-improving and welfare-worsening trade-diversion zones in figure 31.8 is then provided by the partner-country terms-of-trade line that is tangent to U^t and would equate the union and preunion welfare levels at U^t. This is shown in figure 31.9. The cone pAC defines the range of possible partner-country price ratios. If it is less steep than AC, the partner country will be cheaper than the outside country, contradicting the assumption underlying our analysis; if it is steeper than Ap, trade diversion to the partner country will not take place with the formation of the union. The possible price ratio $A\bar{P}$ then clearly divides this cone into the welfare-improving zone $CA\bar{P}$ and the welfare-worsening zone $\bar{P}Ap$.

It will be evident that the home country can improve welfare even though the union diverts trade. Why? The reason is what we earlier called, in chapter 19, the consumption gain. The union implies that although there is a loss from the terms-of-trade deterioration implied by shifting imports of good 1 to the higher-cost partner country, the consumers wind up consuming at a lower relative price of the importable, which is closer to its "true" world price as defined by the least-cost outside country.

---

3. The social-indifference curve is tangent to AD at C', whereas it was not tangent to AB at C. This is because the union, with zero tariff on partner-country imports, means that consumers consume at world prices set by the partner country.

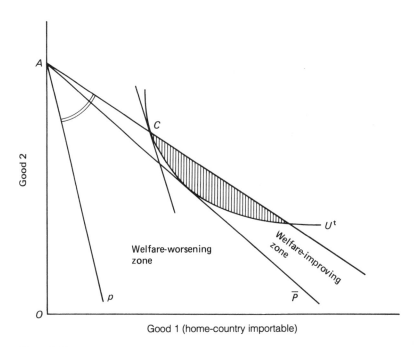

Good 2

Good 1 (home-country importable)

Welfare-worsening zone

Welfare-improving zone

Figure 31.9

Hence the (secondary) consumption gain may more than offset the (primary) terms-of-trade loss from the trade diversion.

Why did Viner miss this argument and imply that trade diversion was necessarily harmful? There has been much ink spilled over this issue, with Lipsey (1957, 1960) claiming that Viner had in mind fixed consumption coefficients, Bhagwati (1971) claiming that Viner assumed a constant volume of imports shifting from the outside country to the partner country,[4] and Michaely (1976) arguing that Viner's writings generally show insufficient attention to consumption effects anyway (and that probably, as Bhagwati argued, he had not thought through the consumption-change-related implications systematically). What is clear is that unless one rules out consumption gain in one way or another, a trade-diverting union can be welfare-improving. Furthermore the model can be extended to include production gain as well if domestic production of the importable good, if any, is allowed to shrink in response to its reduced relative price after the union. This more general case, which permits the (primary) terms-of-trade loss from a shift in import source to a higher-cost partner country to be offset by the (secondary) consumption and production re-

4. Each of these assumptions is sufficient to take the economy into the welfare-worsening zone in figure 31.9.

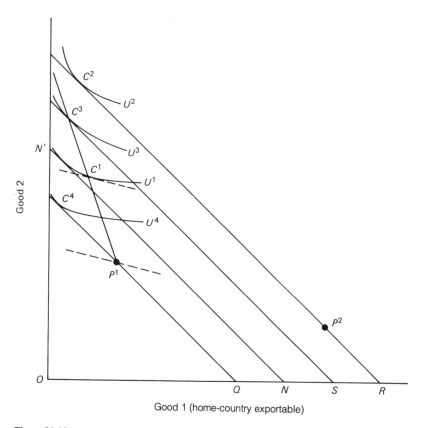

Figure 31.10

allocational gains, is illustrated in figure 31.10. The production-possibility curve has been omitted to avoid cluttering up the diagram. The union shifts production from P^1 to P^2 and consumption from C^1 to C^2, and winds up improving welfare. The broken lines are the preunion tariff-inclusive domestic price, with P^1C^1 the terms of trade with the outside country. With the union, the domestic price line becomes identical with the terms of trade P^2C^2 from the partner country. Welfare is at U^2 with the union and at U^1 before the union.

We can then decompose the welfare change from U^2 to U^1 by using the Hicksian compensating variation, starting from the union equilibrium. Evidently the measure of this welfare change, in terms of good 1, is RN. Indeed withdrawal of RN units of good 1, starting from the union equilibrium, would shift the budget line from P^2C^2 to NN', thus eliminating fully the gain from the union. This measure of the gain from the union, or the loss from giving up the union, can be decomposed into production gain, terms-of-trade loss, and consumption gain by decomposing the shift from U^2 to U^1 into moves from U^2 to U^4, from U^4 to U^3, and from U^3 and U^1, respectively. Thus QR is the production gain from the union,[5] QS is the terms-of-trade loss from the initial trade diversion,[6] and SN is the consumption gain from the union.[7]

Evidently, then, the gain from the union is

$$
\begin{array}{ccccc}
RN = & QR & - & QS & + & SN \\
\text{(Net} & \text{Production} & \text{(Terms-of-trade} & \text{(Consumption} \\
\text{gain)} & \text{gain)} & \text{loss)} & \text{gain)}
\end{array}
$$

$$= RS + SN.$$

In the present model, the production and consumption effects improve welfare whereas the terms-of-trade effect worsens it. If we interpret Viner to mean that the production effect is trade creation (since domestic higher-cost production yields to lower-cost imports from the partner country), we have to conclude with the possibility that an initially trade-diverting union eventually leads to trade creation (production gain) and to consumption gain. Johnson suggests that it would be best to group the consumption and production effects together and call them the "trade creation" effect, as each component would be welfare-improving here. This seems sensible; however, when Johnson suggests that Viner himself must have thought so, others disagree.

Ambiguity of Consumption Effect with More than Two Goods

The qualifications to Viner's original analysis in the two-good model imply that the consumption effect of a trade-diverting customs union is welfare-improving—an invalid inference when more than two goods are introduced into the analysis. The simplest way to see this is to take a model with complete specialization where good 1 is imported from the partner country and good 3 from the outside country, in exchange for good 2 by the home country. An identical tariff rate applies to all imports. Before the union, the pairwise price ratios faced by consumers imply that

5. A withdrawal of QR units of good 1 from the economy in the union equilibrium would lead to the budget line through P^1, equilibrium consumption at C^4, and welfare at U^4 (down from U^2) and therefore measures the gain that follows from being able to reallocate production from P^1 to P^2 after the union.

6. With production at P^1 and consumption at union prices, the preunion terms of trade P^1C^1 will mean an improved welfare from U^4 to U^3; therefore, at union prices, the measure of the loss from the worsened terms of trade is QS.

7. The move from U^3 down to U^1 reflects the fact that the consumption before the union is at the distorted (broken) price line, whose the measure is SN at union prices.

$$\frac{p_3}{p_2} \neq \frac{p_3^*}{p_2^*},$$

$$\frac{p_1}{p_2} \neq \frac{p_1^*}{p_2^*},$$

$$\frac{p_1}{p_3} = \frac{p_1^*}{p_3^*}. \text{[8]}$$

The union then replaces this situation with another suboptimal situation where free trade with the partner country turns the second inequality into an equality, $p_1/p_2 = p_1^*/p_2^*$, but turns the last equality into an inequality, since good 1 now carries no tariff while good 3 still does: $p_1/p_3 \neq p_1^*/p_3^*$. In this case no rank-ordering of the two situations in terms of their implied consumption gain is possible, in general. The scope of Samuelsonian "qualitative economics" is then circumscribed, and one must estimate with specific utility functions to get answers for particular parametric cases.

As a consequence of the argument just presented, it would be wrong to infer that a trade-diverting customs union, characterized by an unchanged total value of imports, must necessarily have worsened its welfare. An unchanged aggregate can permit, if there is more than one importable, a reallocation among different imports that can yield a consumption gain that, even with no production gain, may still outweigh the postulated terms-of-trade loss. This apparent paradox can be made even more striking: Even a reduced value of aggregate imports, in a trade-diverting union, could be shown to result in increased welfare through the consumption gain (if sufficiently great) from reallocation of consumption and hence imports.

Possible Qualifications and Extensions

The above analysis abstracts from a number of aspects of real-life customs unions. The following, in particular, may be noted:

First, we assumed that the partner country's offer curve to the home country remained unchanged before and after the union. This is nearly always not true, for the partner country's own tariffs must be eliminated by the union. This implies, for instance, that the possible terms-of-trade loss to the home country from a trade-diverting union is likely to be less than otherwise. In figure 31.9 the improved offer curve of the partner

8. The last equality holds because imports of goods 1 and 3, from partner and outside countries, respectively, carry a uniform tariff rate.

country clearly makes it flatter and more likely to enter the welfare-improving zone.

Second, many empirical analysts have claimed that the principal advantages of free trade and moves to free trade may consist in elimination of domestic monopoly, exploitation of economies of scale, and the like. One can incorporate these effects into the simple Vinerian general-equilibrium analysis presented above, using the tools developed in chapters 23 and 30 above for domestic monopoly and increasing returns, respectively.

Third, we have taken an arbitrary external tariff, after the union is formed. Essentially we took the initial home-country tariffs on the nonmember countries as continuing unchanged after the union and examined the consequences of reducing the tariffs to zero on the member countries. But we could approach the analysis of customs unions from a very different angle and consider the following question: Given a set of nonpreferential tariffs by a subset of countries of the world economy, can they eliminate these tariffs preferentially on one another to their advantage while devising a suitable common tariff on nonmember countries? This question, subject to the important proviso that nonmember countries are not hurt, has been posed by Kemp and formally resolved by Kemp and Wan. They show the following:

PROPOSITION 4   Consider any competitive world trading equilibrium, with any number of countries and commodities and with no restrictions whatever on the tariffs and with costs of transport fully recognized. Now let any subset of the countries form a customs union. Then there exists a common tariff vector and a system of lump-sum compensatory payments, involving only members of the union, such that each individual, whether a member of the union or not, is not worse off than before the formation of the union.

The intuitive argument underlying this proposition is clear enough. If the actual, preunion trade is frozen, the nonmember countries cannot be hurt. Then, treating this trade vector as an endowment, one can imagine that the union members can dismantle their tariffs with respect to one another to reach an optimal equilibrium with an associated domestic price vector. The assumption of lump-sum transfers ensures that no member country gets hurt. The difference between the domestic price vector associated with this equilibrium and the foreign price vector yields the common, external tariff structure for the union. Therefore this tariff structure plus the lump-sum transfers within the union ensure that the outside countries are not hurt and that some member countries are better off while others are not worse off.

The formal proof of this proposition is as follows: Assume that the consumption set of each individual is closed, convex, and bounded below; that the preferences of each individual are convex and representable by a continuous ordinal utility function; that each individual can survive with a consumption bundle each component of which is somewhat less than his preunion consumption bundle; and that the production set of each economy is closed, is convex, contains the origin, and is such that positive output requires at least one positive input (impossibility of free production). Consider a fictitious economy composed of the member economies but with a net endowment equal to the sum of the member endowments plus the equilibrium preunion net excess supply of the rest of the world. In view of these assumptions, the economy possesses an optimum, and any optimum can be supported by at least one internal price vector. Either the preunion equilibrium of the member countries is a Pareto-optimal equilibrium of the fictitious economy (that is, corresponds to a maximal point of the utility possibility set), or it is not; in the latter case, a preferred Pareto-optimal equilibrium can be attained by means of lump-sum transfers among individuals in the fictitious economy. Proposition 4 then follows immediately.

Proposition 4 is of great interest because it does provide analytical support to the general view that customs unions are a welfare-improving device, for member countries and for world welfare, even though they fall short of free trade. What the proposition shows is that, if one does not eliminate by assumption the choice of a suitable external tariff, reasonable restrictions suffice to make a customs union among any subset of economies in the world a welfare-improving device for the member countries without affecting the terms and volume of trade (and hence affecting the welfare) of the nonmember countries. (Unfortunately, beyond proving the "existence" of such unions, we do not know anything about the analytical properties of such unions, such as whether the average tariff rate would rise or fall with such a union.)

Fourth, in addition to the Kemp-Wan approach, there is yet another important development which offers an analytical handle on customs-union analysis. Bhagwati and Tironi (1980), Bhagwati and Brecher (1979), and Brecher and Bhagwati (1981) have examined the question as to how, in the presence of "foreign-owned" factors of production, the usual analysis of policy and parametric shifts needs to be modified to reach the correct welfare conclusions. For instance, trade liberalization for a small country may be immiserizing, rather than welfare-improving as suggested by section 31.1 here, if the effect of the lower tariff is to divert income disproportionately to foreign-owned factors of production via, say, a Stolper-Samuelson effect. This Bhagwati-Brecher type of analysis is immediately applicable to a customs union with full factor mobility and a common external tariff. Thus, the Bhagwati-Brecher analytical approach can answer questions such as these: Within the European Economic Community, if the common external tariff is changed, how does Britain's welfare change? If Germany experiences technical change, how does that affect Italy's welfare? If France receives a transfer payment, does that help or harm the Netherlands? The traditional approaches of the Viner-Lipsey-Meade or the Kemp-Wan type cannot handle these questions, as they do not allow for intermember factor mobility in their formal structure. Thus this Bhagwati-Brecher approach must be considered an effective way to investigate customs unions in their natural format with full factor mobility, and it certainly opens up an approach to the analysis of questions that are important to the members of such unions (as when the contribution of a member to the community has to be decided in light of the decision to change agricultural support prices).

We conclude this section with another approach to customs-union theorizing, which has now been formalized by Krishna and Bhagwati (1996). In the context of import-substituting industrialization by less developed countries, it has been argued that if a subset of LDCs were to form a union, they could maintain their desired size of the industrial sector *in toto* but could specialize with respect to one another to advantage. In such a union, Tanzania could produce $120 million worth of shoes and trade shoes for cloth from Kenya, which would produce $80 million worth of cloth, with both countries exploiting economies of scale, special skills, and natural resources to advantage. By contrast, in the absence of a union, Tanzania would have to produce $80 million worth of shoes and $40 million worth of cloth to satisfy the domestic target of import substitution, and Kenya would have to produce $40 million each of shoes and cloth. It has been argued that any objective such as an aggregate target of import substitution could be satisfied at lower cost by any member of a subset of LDCs by entering into union than by not doing so.[9] This argument can be formalized, without invoking scale economies (as the early writings did), by simply combining the insights of the Kemp-Wan theorem and of the theory of noneconomic objectives. Thus Krishna and Bhagwati (1996) have shown that any subset of countries forming a customs union can improve their welfare and achieve a given domestic-industrialization (production) target, without hurting the outside world,

9. This approach was developed by Cooper and Massell (1965). It was explored in the context of tariff bargaining by Johnson (1965) and in the context to GATT rules on preferential tariff reductions by Bhagwati (1968).

by combining a production tax-*cum*-subsidy with an external tariff chosen endogenously à la Kemp and Wan.

31.3   Recent "Static" Analyses

Among the recent extensions of the "static," Vinerian analysis, which have come about as a result of the revival of interest in forming more preferential trade agreements (PTAs), especially FTAs, under GATT Article 24, the most important ones have related to the examination of the assertions that trade diversion is unimportant and that this is particularly so if the member countries are so-called natural trading partners.

The natural trading partners phrasing and hypothesis about its benign character originated in Wonnacott and Lutz (1989). Based on the work of Viner (1950), Lipsey (1960), and Johnson (1962), these authors provided detailed criteria for determining whether or not a given set of countries constituted natural trading partners. In their view, trade creation is likely to be great, and trade diversion small, if the prospective members of an FTA are natural trading partners. There are two points that are relevant to their defining criteria:

1. Are the prospective members already major trading partners? If so, the FTA will be reinforcing natural trading partners, not artificially diverting trade to them.

2. Are the prospective members close geographically? Groupings of distant nations may be economically inefficient because of the high transportation costs (Wonnacott and Lutz 1989, p. 69).

These two criteria—one, a higher initial volume of trade, and the other, a closer geographic proximity or lower transport cost—as guides to forming benign PTAs were embraced by leading economists such as Krugman (1991) and Summers (1991) and can be found as influential arguments in the public domain. But they are wrong, as Bhagwati and Panagariya (1996) have demonstrated. Some of the key criticisms are discussed in what follows.[10]

Volume-of-Trade Criterion

The volume-of-trade criterion for choosing natural trading partners and treating them as likely to be welfare-enhancing to their members seems plausible at first glance but is in fact treacherous.

---

10. For a full theoretical analysis, see Bhagwati and Panagariya (1996, ch. 1).

First, the criterion is neither symmetric nor transitive. A lack of symmetry implies that country A may be a natural trading partner of country B, but the reverse may not hold true. A lack of transitivity implies that even if A is a natural trading partner of B, and B is a natural trading partner of C, A may not be a natural trading partner of C. Lest this be viewed as a purely academic point, we note that the United States is Mexico's largest trading partner, but the reverse is not true. Similarly the United States is the largest trading partner of both Canada and Mexico, but Canada and Mexico have little trade with each other.

Second, the volume-of-trade criterion is premised on the view that a larger initial volume of trade between potential partners implies a lower likelihood of loss because of trade diversion. This is, however, an unsupported inference from the fact that for any given volume of initial imports, the higher is the partner country's initial share, the lower is the outside country's share and hence the smaller is the *scope* for diverting trade. Instead, what one needs to determine is how likely is the *actual* trade diversion. The underlying model that defines the trade volumes in different equilibriums may well imply then that the relationship between the initial volume of imports from the partner country and the trade to be diverted to it may be altogether tenuous.[11]

Third, while the volume-of-trade criterion for judging FTAs to be benign is clearly to be rejected, linking it to *regionalism* and thus declaring regional FTAs to be more benign than nonregional FTAs is also wrong. There is no evidence that pairs of contiguous countries, or countries with common borders, have larger volumes of trade with each other than do pairs that are not so situated or that trade volumes of pairs of countries, arranged by distance between the countries in the pair, will show distance to be inversely related to trade volumes.[12]

---

11. As shown originally in Panagariya (1995, 1996) and developed fully in Bhagwati and Panagariya (1996), if we look at the welfare effect of preferential liberalization from an *individual* country's viewpoint, the outcome is exactly the opposite of what the natural trading partners hypothesis asserts: The larger the imports from the partner, the greater is the loss or the smaller is the gain to a country from its own preferential liberalization. Under the small union assumption, as long as imports from the rest of the world are not eliminated entirely, the tariff revenue collected on imports from the partner in the original equilibrium is transferred in its entirety to partner-country exporters. And the larger the imports from the partner, the greater is the transfer. The country can, of course, recover this loss through a reverse transfer resulting from preferential liberalization by the partner, but if the latter's tariffs are low to begin with, on net, it will lose from the arrangement. For this reason Panagariya (1996) argues that static welfare effects of NAFTA went against Mexico which has much higher external tariffs than the United States.

12. This would not be generally true even if we were to take the measure for just one particular country with every other country instead of pooling all possible pairs together.

This is evident from just one telling example. Chile shares a common border with Argentina, but in 1993 it shipped only 6.2 percent of exports to Argentina and in turn received only 5 percent of its imports (Panagariya 1996, tables 3 and 4). By contrast, the United States does not have a common border with Chile but in 1993 accounted for 16.2 percent of its exports and 24.9 percent of its imports. The volume-of-trade criterion then would make the United States, *not* Argentina, the natural trading partner of Chile, clearly controverting the claim that the volume-of-trade criterion translates into a regional criterion.

As contended by Bhagwati (1993a), the equation by Krugman (1991) and Summers (1991a) of the two concepts of volume of trade and regionalism (whether of the distance or the common border or contiguity variety) is therefore simply wrong. Nonetheless, Frankel and Wei (1995) have recently argued otherwise, claiming that their empirical work favors the Krugman-Summers assertion. They use the gravity model as their basic tool to conclude that "proximity is in general an important determinant of bilateral trade around the world, notwithstanding exceptions like India-Pakistan and other cases."

But this misses the point at issue. What is at stake is not whether distance, interpreted through the gravity model and/or common border modeled through a dummy, matters. There does seem to be a *partial* correlation between distance, proximity, common border, and so on, on the one hand, and trade volumes on the other. But what we have to look at is the *total* initial volume of trade, and this does not correlate simply with distance as the right-hand side variable, as required by the "natural trading partners" assertion of the volume-of-trade criterion for forming PTAs.

Next we have the difficult problem of endogeneity of initial trade volumes with respect to preferences. If the large volumes are themselves attributable, in significant degree, to preferences granted earlier, then they are not "natural," nor is it proper to think that additional preferences are therefore harmless. The point is best understood by thinking of high trade barriers by a country leading to a larger within-country relative to external trade. To deduce that added barriers are harmless is to compound the harm done by existing barriers that are, of course, preferences in favor of trade within the country.

This is not an idle question. Offshore assembly provisions between the United States and Mexico and the longstanding GATT-sanctioned free trade regime in autos between Canada and the United States are certainly not negligible factors in pre-NAFTA U.S. trade with these NAFTA members. In granting preferences under the Generalized System of Preferences, the United States, EC, and Japan have all concentrated on their regions. Thus the partial correlation between distance and trade volumes (in gravity models) may be a result of preferences granted to proximate neighbors, rather than a "natural" phenomenon justifying (new) preferences.[13]

Finally we need to raise a different objection to the argument that a high initial volume of imports from a partner country will work to protect a country against trade diversion. Quite aside from the fact that aggregate volumes shift significantly in practice over time, the comparative advantage in specific goods and services often changes in different locations.[14] Consistent with a given aggregate trade volume, its composition may shift so as to yield greater trade diversion when a PTA is present.

Consider a case, based on constant costs for simplicity, in which the United States imports a product from Canada under a nondiscriminatory tariff. If a PTA is formed between the two countries, the product will continue to be imported from Canada. But suppose that on a future date Canada loses its comparative advantage to Taiwan ever so slightly so that the preferential advantage enjoyed by her outweighs this loss. There will be trade diversion, and imports into the United States will continue to come from Canada with the volume of trade remaining unchanged.[15] Observe that there is an asymmetry here between a shift in comparative advantage away from the partner and that toward it. If Canada experiences a reduction in the cost of production of a product imported by the United States from Taiwan under a PTA, there can still be trade diversion. Because of the preference Canada will replace Taiwan as the supplier of this product even before Canada's costs fall below those of Taiwan. The volume of trade will rise, and at the same time there will be trade diversion.[16] The proponents of the "high initial import volume" thesis are thus trapped in a static view of comparative advantage that is particularly at odds with today's volatile, kaleidoscopic comparative advantage in the global economy.

---

13. Of course, even if the relationship were "natural," it would not justify preferences.

14. Bhagwati, in several writings, for example, Bhagwati and Dehejia (1994) and Bhagwati (1996a), has argued that comparative advantage has become "kaleidoscopic;" it has become thin and volatile as technical know-how has converged, multinationals have become global, interest rates have become closer across nations, and access to different capital markets has become more open. More and more industries are thus footloose.

15. In this paragraph we abstract from the demand effects. The inclusion of demand effects will modify the discussion but not the fundamental point.

16. If costs were to fall below those of Taiwan, there would be no extra gain from the PTA because Canada would replace Taiwan as the supplier even under a nondiscriminatory tariff.

Transport-Cost Criterion

But if the volume-of-trade criterion is conceptually inappropriate and must be summarily rejected, what about the transport-cost criterion? This criterion maps directly into distance and hence into regionalism. However, the question to be analyzed is: Should PTA partners be chosen on the basis of lower transport costs, and hence greater proximity, to maximize gains to members or to minimize losses to them?

The earliest reference we could find to transport costs in the context of trade liberalization is from Johnson (1962, p. 61): "If the separate markets of various members are divided by serious geographical barriers which require high transport costs to overcome them, the enlargement of the market may be more apparent than real." All he seems to be arguing is the truism that trade liberalization may be meaningless if high transport costs prevent trade from breaking out.

But the natural trading partners hypothesis is altogether different and incorrect. There is in fact no reason to think that greater distance increases the likelihood of gain for members in a PTA. This can be seen simply by constructing a counterexample where a union with a country (C) that is more distant produces more gain (for A) than a union with the country (B) that is less distant but otherwise identical (to C).

To construct the counterexample noted above, consider a world consisting of three countries: A, B, and C. Country A has the option to form an FTA with either B or C. Countries B and C are identical in all respects except that the latter is located farther away. We assume that supply curves of B and C are upward sloped.[17] In figure 31.11 we draw three panels. In the first two panels, we show the export supply curves of C and B as $E_C E_C$ and $E_B E_B$, respectively. In the third panel, we have their combined supply obtained by summing horizontally the individual supplies from the first two panels. The supply curves of C and B are identical in all respects except that C's supply price includes a constant per-unit transportation cost. Thus, for each quantity, C's supply price exceeds that of B by the per-unit transportation cost.

To avoid clutter, we do not draw A's demand curve. Instead, imagine that there is an arbitrary nondiscriminatory tariff initially that yields the total demand for imports as represented by point Q_{B+C}. The price paid for this quantity to B and C is P^*. Individual supplies of B and C can be obtained by intersecting their supply curves with P^* and are shown by Q_B and Q_C. Not surprisingly, imports are larger from the geographically proximate country B than from C.

---

17. This complicates the analysis because the countries now wield market power, and unilateral free trade is no longer optimal.

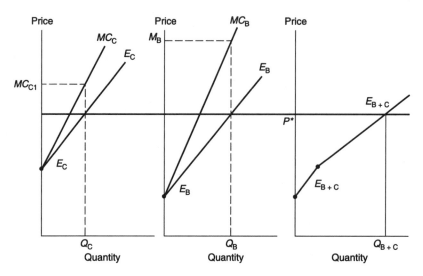

Figure 31.11

Now consider the introduction of preferential trading. To see which way preferences should be given, draw the *marginal* cost curve associated with each supply curve. These are shown by MC_B and MC_C. It is then immediate that, at the initial nondiscriminatory tariff, the marginal cost of imports is higher on imports from B than from C. We then obtain the dramatic conclusion that if A wants to give a tariff preference, it should opt for the distant partner C rather than the proximate B. The transport-cost criterion for choosing partners in a PTA is exactly wrong in this instance.

The explanation of this result is straightforward. The discriminating monopsonist model says that for any quantity of total purchases, the supplier with higher elasticity should be paid a higher price. In the present problem, this prescription translates into a lower tax on the supplier with higher elasticity. And transportation costs make C's supply curve more elastic than that of B.

31.4   Recent "Dynamic" Time-Path Analyses

Much of the recent ferment in the theory of PTAs has derived, however, from the fact that the United States decided in 1982, after the refusal of Europe and developing countries to launch a new multilateral trade-negotiating (MTN) round at the November 1981 GATT Ministerial. Not able to get MTN going, which would mean that trade barriers would be reduced on an MFN basis, the United States turned to Article 24 as the only available, alternative route to worldwide reductions of trade barriers. This meant that in place of the "static" question as to whether a PTA was beneficial in itself, the analytical question now was what Bhagwati (1993) has called a "dynamic" time-path question relating to the continued reductions of trade barriers.

The question thus relates not to whether the immediate (static) effect of a PTA is good or bad, but whether the (dynamic) effect of the PTA is to accelerate or decelerate the continued reduction of trade barriers toward the goal of reducing them worldwide. This question as to whether, in Bhagwatti's (1991) conceptualization and terminology, PTAs are "building blocks" or "stumbling blocks" to worldwide freeing of trade, may be formulated analytically in two separate ways.

Question 1

Assume that the time-path of MTN (multilateral trade negotiations) and the time-path of PTAs are separable and do not influence each other. The two policies are "strangers" to (independent of) one another: Neither hurts nor helps the other. Will then the PTA time-path be characterized by stagnant or negligible expansion of membership? Or will we have expanding membership, with this turning eventually into worldwide membership as in the WTO and thus arriving at nondiscriminatory free trade for all? A similar question can be raised for the MTN time-path. And the analysis can be extended to a comparison of the two time-paths, ranking the efficacy of the two methods of reducing trade barriers to achieve the goal of worldwide free trade for all.

Question 2

Assume instead, as is more sensible, that if both the MTN and the PTA time-paths are embraced simultaneously, they will interact. In particular, the policy of undertaking PTAs will have a malign impact on (be a "foe" of) the progress along the MTN time-path, or it will have a benign effect on (be a "friend" of) the MTN time-path.[18]

Question 1 can be illustrated with the aid of figure 31.12, which portrays a sample of possibilities for the time-paths in question. World (rather than individual member) welfare is put on the vertical axis and time along the horizontal axis. For the PTA time-paths drawn, an upward movement along the path implies growing membership; for the MTN (or what are described as "process-multilateralism") time-paths, it implies nondiscriminatory lowering of trade barriers among the nearly worldwide

---

18. Similarly the MTN path may facilitate or obstruct the expansion of PTA membership, so the interaction between the two paths may be mutual.

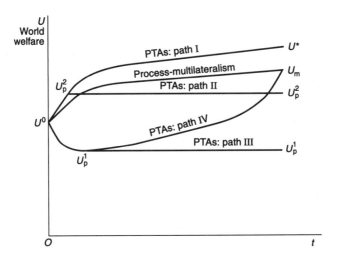

Figure 31.12

WTO membership instead. The PTA and MTN time-paths are assumed to be independent of each other; the PTA time-path neither accelerates nor decelerates the course of MTN (thus ruling out question 2-type issues). The goal can be treated as reaching U^{opt}, the worldwide freeing of trade barriers on a nondiscriminatory basis at a specified time. As figure 31.12 illustrates, PTAs may improve welfare immediately from U^0 to U_p^2 or, because of net trade diversion, reduce it to U_p^1. The time-path with PTAs, in either case, could be stagnant (paths II and III), implying a fragmentation of the world economy through no further expansion of the initial trade bloc. Or it could lead (paths I and IV) to multilateral free trade for all at U^{opt} through continued expansion and coagulation of PTAs. Under process-multilateralism, the time-path may fail to reach U^{opt} and instead fall short at U_m because of free-rider problems. Or it may overcome both and reach U^{opt}. Assumed in the diagram is that the time-paths are independent: Embarking on the PTAs path does not affect the process-multilateralism path.

Question 1 can be illustrated by reference to the PTA paths I–IV. Thus PTAs may improve welfare immediately, in the static sense, from U^0 to U_p^2 or reduce it to U_p^1. In either case the time-path will become stagnant (as with time-paths II and III), implying a fragmentation of the world economy through no further expansion of the initial PTA. Else, it will lead (as in time-paths I and IV) to multilateral free trade for all at U^{opt} through continued expansion and coagulation of the PTAs. Under "process multilateralism," that is, in treating the negotiating to reduce trade barriers as a multilateral process distinct from multilateralism as the desired goal, the time-path may fail to reach U^{opt} and instead fall short at U_m because of free-rider problems.

As indicated, if the PTA and MTN time-paths are interdependent, we can address question 2. In that case the MTN time-path becomes a function of whether the PTA time-path is traveled simultaneously. These questions, identified and discussed in Bhagwati (1991, 1993), have been extensively explored recently in a burgeoning theoretical literature which is briefly reviewed now.

"Exogenously Determined" Time-Paths: A Diversion

Let us first consider and turn aside certain theoretical approaches that are not particularly suited to thinking about the dynamic time-path questions at hand, even though they have often been mistaken to be so.

Kemp-Wan

The seminal approach of Kemp and Wan (1976) to Customs Union theory seems to be pertinent to our two questions but in fact is not. Recall that unlike the Vinerian approach, Kemp and Wan made the external tariff structure (of the Customs Union) endogenously chosen so that each member country's welfare would be improved, while that of the non-members was left unchanged. The beauty of this approach was that it restored the commonsense intuition prior to Viner that a CU should be welfare-improving for members and for the world. This is, of course, a "possibility" theorem, no more and no less.[19]

It is then immediately apparent that the PTA time-path to U^* in figure 31.12 can be made monotonic provided that expanding membership of a PTA always satisfies the Kemp-Wan rule for forming a Customs Union. But what this argument does not say, and indeed cannot say, is that the CU will necessarily expand and, if so, in this Kemp-Wan fashion.

For that answer, to what is obviously question 1, we must turn to the *incentive structure* that any CU/PTA provides, through interests, ideology, and institutions, for expansion or stagnation of its membership.

Krugman

The same argument applies to the theoretical approach to the question of PTAs recently used by Krugman (1991a, 1991b, 1993). Again the expansion of membership is treated as exogenously specified, as in Viner, and the welfare consequences of the world mechanically dividing into a

---

19. Bliss (1994) has tried to give the argument some structure. More recently, Srinivasan (1995) has done so in the context of examining the question of the impact of PTAs on nonmember welfare.

steadily increasing number of symmetric blocs—clearly demarcated countries are then not even the natural constituents of these "blobs"-*cum*-blocs—are considered and, for particular specifications, the monotonicity of world welfare examined, including even calculations concerning the "optimal" number of such symmetric PTAs/blocs. This symmetry assumption has led to critiques, as by Srinivasan (1993) who essentially shows that the specific Krugman conclusions are easily reversed by abandoning symmetery, and to further variations by a few others.[20] Yet it is hard to see the analytical relevance of this approach to the compelling (incentive-structure) questions today concerning the membership expansion of PTAs. For the analysis of the dynamic time-path questions of the type introduced above, we must turn elsewhere.

Incentive Structure Arguments

Bhagwati (1993a), advanced several arguments concerning the incentive structure within specific PTAs, once formed, to expand or to stagnate. Before we discuss the theoretical modeling of such ideas by Baldwin (1995), Krishna (1998), and Levy (1997), among others, it is worth recapitulating the principal arguments distinguished by Bhagwati.[21]

We need to recognize, of course, that the incentives may be political rather than (narrowly) economic. A PTA may be formed, and even expanded, to seek political allies by using trade as foreign policy and to target the benefits of trade to politically favored nations. Politics is not a negligible factor in the discriminatory trade arrangements implemented by the EU via association agreements with the smaller countries on its periphery and beyond, and it certainly cannot be ignored in the transformation of the original Canada–U.S. Free Trade Agreement into NAFTA with Mexico and then into the proposed Free Trade Area of the Americas.

Clearly that is not the whole story. We can learn much by thinking carefully about the incentive structure for membership expansion in political-economy-theoretic terms. To do this, Bhagwati (1993a) distinguishes among three different types of "agents" and offered the following analysis:

1. *Governments of member countries.* PTAs may not have an incentive to expand where governments feel that they already have a large market ... and therefore do not stand to gain by going through the hassle of adding more members. This is the "our market is large enough" syndrome, emphasized by Martin Wolf, who has often noted that large

---

20. See Deardorff and Stern (1994).

21. Bhagwati (1993a, pp. 40–44) also discussed skeptically the claims that PTA formation is quicker, more efficient, and more certain than MTN.

countries tend to opt for inward-looking trade and investment strategies, while the small ones go the outward-looking route.

2. *Interest groups in member countries.* The interest groups in member countries may be for or against new members. Whereas the internationally oriented exporting firms may be expected to endorse new members, whose markets then become preferentially available to them vis-à-vis nonmember exporters to these new members,[22] the firms that are profiting from access to preferential markets in the member (partner) countries will not want new members whose firms are exporters of the same or similar products in the member markets. Both incentives reflect the preferential nature of the PTAs.

The former incentive was clear in the NAFTA debate in the United States and reflected in many pronouncements, including that of pro-NAFTA economists (and even President Clinton, who played the Japanophobic card that the United States would have preferential access to Mexico vis-à-vis Japan). It is also evident in the statement of Signor Agnelli of Fiat: "The single market must first offer an advantage to European companies. This is a message we must insist on without hesitation."

3. *Interest groups in nonmember countries.* The third set of agents is in the nonmember countries. Here the example of a PTA may lead others to emulate, even to seek, entry. Then again, the fear of trade diversion may also induce outsiders to seek entry.

Recent Theoretical Analyses

Subsequently the analysis of the dynamic time-path question has moved into formal political economy-theoretic modeling.

The single contribution that focuses on question 1 (the incentive to add members to a PTA) that was posed earlier is by Richard Baldwin (1995), who concentrates on the incentive of nonmembers to join the PTA. He constructs a model to demonstrate that this incentive will be positive: The PTA will create a domino effect, with outsiders wanting to become insiders on an escalator. The argument is basically driven by the fact that the PTA implies a loss of cost competitiveness by imperfectly competitive nonmember firms whose profits in the PTA markets decline because they must face the barriers that member countries' firms do not have to face.

---

22. In comparing incentives for export-oriented firms, for lobbying for a PTA (for example, NAFTA) as against MTN (for example, the Uruguay Round), a dollar's worth of lobbying would go a longer way in the former case because any preferential opening of the Mexican market would be better for the U.S. exporter than such an opening on an MFN basis that yields the benefits equally to U.S. rivals in Japan, the EU, and elsewhere. This argument applies only to the extent that the MTN process simultaneously does not open other markets to the U.S. exporter on a reciprocal basis.

These firms then lobby for entry, tilting the political equilibrium at the margin toward entry demands in their countries. The countries closest to the margin will enter the bloc, assuming that the members have open entry. This enlarges the market and thereby increases the cost of non-membership and pulls in countries at the next margin. Given the assumptions, including continuity, this domino model can take the PTA time-path to U^{opt} in figure 31.12.

While Baldwin formalizes the incentive of nonmembers to get inside the PTA, interestingly there is no formalization of the incentives of members to add or reject new members that have been discussed in the literature, as by Bhagwati (1993a). Indeed the Baldwin model itself shows, on the flip side, that member firms will gain from the cost advantage that they enjoy vis-à-vis the nonmember firms and hence will have an opposed interest in not admitting the nonmembers to the PTA. A full analysis of the political economy of both members and nonmembers in the Baldwin model could then lead to specific equilibrium outcomes that leave the PTA expansion imperiled.

The rest of the theoretical contributions address question 2, that is, whether the PTA possibility and/or time-path helps or harms the MTN time-path. Krishna (1998) and Levy (1997) address directly and quite aptly this question and reach the "malign-impact" conclusion, unfavorable to the exhortation to "walk on both legs."

Krishna models the political process in the fashion of the government acting in response to implicit lobbying by firms, what Bhagwati (1990) has called a "clearinghouse"—government assumption where the government is passive, as in Findlay and Wellisz (1982). Krishna shows in his oligopolistic-competition model that the bilateral PTA between two member countries reduces the incentive of the member countries to liberalize tariffs reciprocally with the nonmember world and that with sufficient trade diversion this incentive could be so reduced as to make impossible an initially feasible multilateral trade liberalization.

Levy models the political process instead in a median-voter model à la Mayer (1984); the government is not what Bhagwati (1990) has called "self-willed" with its own objectives but acts again as a clearinghouse. Using a richer model with scale economies and product variety, Levy demonstrates that bilateral FTAs can undermine political support for multilateral free trade.[23]

---

23. For a synthesis of several analytical contributions to the PTA literature beginning with Viner (1950), including the recent work of Grossman and Helpman (1995), Bagwell and Staiger (1998), and others, see the Introduction and reprinted essays in Bhagwati, Krishna, and Panagariya (1998). Additional key contributions to the literature include Bond and Syropoulos (1996), Ethier (1996), and Deardorff and Stern (1994).

Recommended Readings

Arndt, S. W. Customs unions and the theory of tariffs. *American Economic Review* 59 (1969): 108–18.

Arndt, S. W. On discriminatory vs. non-preferential tariff policies. *Economic Journal* 78 (1968): 971–78.

Bagwell, K., and R. Staiger. Will preferential agreements undermine the multilateral trading system? *Economic Journal* 1998, forthcoming.

Baldwin, R. E. Customs unions, preferential systems and world welfare. In *International Trade and Money*, ed. by M. B. Connolly and A. K. Swoboda. Toronto: University of Toronto Press, 1973.

Baldwin, R. A domino theory of regionalism. In Baldwin, R. A., P. Haaparnata, and J. Kiander, eds., *Expanding Membership of the European Union*. Cambridge: Cambridge University Press, 1995.

Berglas, E. Preferential trading: The *n* commodity case. *Journal of Political Economy* 87 (1979): 315–31.

Bhagwati, J. Trade liberalization among LDCs, Trade Theory and GATT Rules. In *Value, Capital, and Growth: Papers in Honour of J. R. Hicks*, ed. by J. N. Wolf. Oxford: Oxford University Press, 1968.

Bhagwati, J. Trade-diverting customs unions and welfare improvement: A clarification. *Economic Journal* (1971): ch. 63.

Bhagwati, J. A reply to Professor Kirman. *Economic Journal* (1973): ch. 64.

Bhagwati, J., and R. Brecher. National welfare in an open economy in the presence of foreign-owned factors of production. *Journal of International Economics* (1979): ch. 53.

Bhagwati, J. *The World Trading System at Risk*. Princeton: Princeton University and Harvester Wheatsheaf, 1991.

Bhagwati, J. Regionalism and Multilateralism: An Overview. In *New Dimensions in Regional Integration*, ed. by J. de Melo and A. Panagariya. Cambridge: Cambridge University Press, 1993. (1993a)

Bhagwati, J. Beyond NAFTA: Clinton's trading choices. *Foreign Policy* (Summer 1993): 155–62. (1993b)

Bhagwati, J., and M. C. Kemp. Ranking of tariffs under monopoly power in trade. *Quarterly Journal of Economics* (1969): ch. 16.

Bhagwati, J., P. Krishna, and A. Panagariya, eds. *Trading blocs: alternative approaches to analyzing preferential trade agreements*, Cambridge: MIT Press, 1998.

Bhagwati, J., and E. Tironi. Tariff change, foreign capital and immiserization. *Journal of Development Economics* (1980): ch. 52.

Bhagwati, J. and A. O. Krueger. *The Dangerous Drift to Preferential Trade Agreements*. Washington: American Enterprise Institute for Public Policy Research, 1995.

Bhagwati, J. and A. Panagariya. The theory of preferential trade agreements: Historical evolution and current trends. *American Economic Review* 86 (1995): 82–87.

Bliss, C. *Economic Theory and Policy for Trading Blocs*. Manchester: Manchester University Press, 1994.

Bond, E., and C. Syropoulos. Trading blocs and the sustainability of inter-regional cooperation. In M. Canzoneri, W. J. Ethier and V. Grilli, eds., *The New Transatlantic Economy*, Cambridge: Cambridge University Press, 1996, 118–41.

Brecher, R., and J. Bhagwati. Foreign ownership and the theory of trade and welfare. *Journal of Political Economy* (1981): ch. 54.

Cooper, C. A., and B. F. Massell. A new look at customs union theory. *Economic Journal* 75 (1965): 742–47. (1965a)

Cooper, C. A., and B. F. Massell. "Toward a General Theory of Customs Unions for Developing Countries." *Journal of Political Economy* 73, no. 5 (1965): 461–76. (1965b)

Deardorff, A., and R. Stern. Multilateral trade negotiations and preferential trading arrangements. In A. Deardorff and R. Stern, eds., *Analytical and Negotiating Issues in the Global Trading System*. Ann Arbor: University of Michigan Press, 1994.

de Melo, J., and A. Panagariya, ed. *New Dimensions in Regional Integration*. Cambridge: Cambridge University Press, 1993.

de Melo, J., A. Panagariya, and D. Rodrik. The new regionalism: A country perspective. In *New Dimensions in Regional Integration*, ed. by J. de Melo and A. Panagariya. Cambridge: Cambridge University Press, 1993, ch. 6.

Ethier, W. Regionalism in a multilateral world. Working paper, Department of Economics, University of Pennsylvania, 1996, forthcoming in *Journal of Political Economy*.

Frankel, J., and S.-J. Wei. The new regionalism and Asia: Impact and options. In Panagariya, A., M. Quibria, and N. Rao. eds., *The Global Trading System and Developing Asia*. Oxford: Oxford University Press, 1997.

Frankel, J., E. Stein, and S.-J. Wei. Trading blocs and the Americas: The natural, the unnatural and the supernatural. *Journal of Development Economics* 47 (1995): 61–96. (1995b)

Grossman, G., and E. Helpman. The politics of free trade agreements. *American Economic Review* (September 1995): 667–90.

Haberler, G. The political economy of regional or continental blocs. In *Postwar Economic Problems*, ed. by S. E. Haris. New York, 1943.

Johnson, H. G. An economic theory of protectionism, tariff bargaining, and the formation of customs unions. *Journal of Political Economy* 73 (1965): 256–83.

Johnson, H. G. Trade-diverting customs unions: A comment. *Economic Journal* 84 (1974): 618–21.

Johnson, H. G. A note on welfare-increasing trade diversion. *Canadian Journal of Economics and Political Science* 8 (1975): 117–23.

Kemp, M. C., and H. Wan, Jr. An elementary proposition concerning the formation of customs unions. *Journal of International Economics* (1976): ch. 19.

Kirman, A. P. Trade diverting customs unions and welfare improvement: A comment. *Economic Journal* 83 (1973): 890–93.

Krauss, M. B. Recent developments in customs union theory: An interpretive survey. *Journal of Economic Literature* 10 (1972): 413–36.

Kreinin, M. E. On the dynamic effects of a customs union. *Journal of Political Economy* 72 (1964): 193–95.

Krishna, P. Regionalism and multilateralism: a political economy approach. *Quarterly Journal of Economics* 113 (1998).

Krueger, A. O. Rules of origin as protectionist devices. In *International Trade Theory: Essays in Honour of John Chipman*, ed. by J. Melvin, J. Moore, and R. Riezman. London: Routledge, 1996.

Krugman, P. The move to free trade zones. In *Symp. on Policy Implications of Trade and Currency Zones*. Federal Reserve Bank of Kansas City, 1991.

Krugman, P. Is bilateralism bad? In E. Helpman and A. Razin, eds., *International Trade and Trade Policy*. Cambridge: MIT Press, 1991.

Levy, P. A political economic analysis of free trade agreements. *American Economic Review* 87 (1997).

Lipsey, R. G. The theory of gustoms unions: Trade diversion and welfare. *Economica*, N. S., 24 (1957): 40–46.

Lipsey, R. G. The theory of customs unions: A general survey. *Economic Journal* (1960): ch. 18.

Lloyd, P. J. 3 × 3 theory of customs unions. *Journal of International Economics* 12 (1982): 41–63.

Meade, J. E. *The Theory of Customs Unions*. Amsterdam: North-Holland, 1955.

Michaely, M. On customs unions and the gains from trade. *Economic Journal* 75 (1965): 577–83.

Michaely, M. The assumptions of Jacob Viner's theory of customs unions. *Journal of International Economics* 6 (1976): 75–93.

Mundell, R. A. Tariff preferences and the terms of trade. *Manchester School of Economic and Social Studies* 32 (1964): 1–13.

Panagariya, A. Should East Asia go regional? No, no and maybe. WPS 1209. Washington: World Bank, 1993.

Panagariya, A. East Asia and the new regionalism. *World Economy* 17 (1994): 817–39.

Panagariya, A. Rethinking the new regionalism. Paper presented at the Trade Expansion Program Conference of the United Nations Development Programme and World Bank, January 1995.

Panagariya, A. The free trade area of the Americas: Good for Latin America? *World Economy* (1996): 485–515.

Panagariya, A. Preferential trading and the myth of natural trading partners. *Japan and the World Economy* 9 (1997): 471–89.

Panagariya, A., and R. Findlay. A political economy analysis of free trade areas and customs unions. In *The Political Economy of Trade Reform, Essays in Honor of Jagdish Bhagwati*, ed. by R. Feenstra, G. Grossman, and D. Irwin. Cambridge: MIT Press, 1996.

Polak, Jacques J. Is APEC a natural regional trading bloc? A critique of the "gravity model" of international trade. *World Economy* 19 (1996): 533–43.

Richardson, M. Why a free trade area? The tariff also rises. *Economics and Politics* 6 (1994): 79–95.

Riezman, R. A 3×3 model of customs unions. *Journal of International Economics* 9 (1979): 341–54.

Riley, J. Ranking of tariffs under monopoly power in trade: An extension. *Quarterly Journal of Economics* 84 (1970): 710–12.

Srinivasan, T. N. Discussion. In *New Dimensions in Regional Integration*, ed. by J. de Melo and A. Panagariya. Cambridge: Cambridge University Press, 1993.

Srinivasan, T. N. Common external tariffs of a customs union: Alternative approaches. *Japan and the World Economy* 9 (1997): 447–70.

Summers, L. Regionalism and the world trading system. *Symposium on Policy Implications of Trade and Currency Zones*. Federal Reserve Bank of Kansas City, 1991.

Vanek, J. *General Equilibrium of International Discrimination: The Case of Customs Unions*. Cambridge: Harvard University Press, 1965.

Viner, J. *The Customs Union Issue*. New York: Carnegie Endowment for International Peace, 1950.

Wonnacott, P., and M. Lutz. Is there a case for free trade areas? In *Free Trade Areas and U.S. Trade Policy*, ed. by J. J. Schott. Washington: Institute for International Economics, 1989, pp. 59–84.

We turn now to the analysis of international factor mobility. This chapter will focus on capital flows, and in chapter 33 we will turn to international labor migration. (Labor mobility, though it is often modeled in the same way as capital flows, has important differences and raises additional questions of interest; hence it merits separate treatment.) We first discuss the two questions that have attracted the most attention on the positive side: whether factor mobility can substitute for trade in goods and whether international capital mobility can permit two countries to be incompletely specialized in production. We then turn to the welfare impact of international capital flows.

32.1 Goods-Price Equalization: Turning Factor-Price Equalization on Its Head

Mundell (1957) showed that Samuelson's factor-price-equalization (FPE) theorem implied equally that if goods trade were prohibited and one of the factors were fully mobile internationally instead, the resulting FPE would imply goods-price equalization (GPE). Both theorems would follow, of course, once the Samuelson assumptions for FPE were made.

It is evident that if (in the Samuelson case) GPE $\Rightarrow$ FPE, the arrow can be equally reversed so that (in the Mundell case) FPE $\Rightarrow$ GPE. Mundell presented his argument by assuming a small country I in free trade, with FPE in place, and imposing a tariff on its import of capital-intensive good 2. He then argued that this would raise the rental on capital in country I and induce capital inflow from country II, as the Stolper-Samuelson theory suggests. As long as there is import of good 2 into country I, however, the incentive for capital to flow into country I will be present. Equilibrium can be reached only if trade is eliminated by the capital inflow. But it is possible to show that this elimination of trade can occur at the pretariff, pre–resulting-capital-movement world goods-price ratio, for at this price ratio, with identical and homothetic production functions, world production is unchanged as long as both economies remain diversified (as indeed the FPE theorem requires). The transfer of $\bar{K}$ units from country II to country I in the new equilibrium then merely transfers an appropriate amount of the resulting production from II to I, the changes in II and I being fully offsetting. National welfare too remains unchanged at the pretariff, free-trade level, in view of the assumption that each factor earns the value of its marginal product. (The one snag to this neat argument is that the transmission of interest payments is required, since the owners of the capital that flowed from country II to country I are resident in country II where their consumption would presumably take place. This poses no problem if the tariff is imposed in country I alone, but Mundell rightly points out that if the tariff were in both countries, the factor and goods prices could not be equalized completely. This implies a possible asymmetry between international labor and capital mobility, for it seems likely that labor, once it has moved from country II to country I, will consume in country I. However, it may again be necessary to consider associated international transfers due to remittances.)

Mundell's argument generalizes to the case where both countries are large as long as the assumptions necessary for FPE are made, including the assumption that both countries remain diversified in production.

32.2   Diversification with Different Technologies

A related but distinct question is whether, in the presence of international capital mobility, two countries in a 2×2 model would both exhibit diversification (instead of at least one being forced to complete specialization). This question has been raised by trade theorists since Jones (1967) asserted that this was unlikely in the presence of international differences in technology. Chipman (1971), Inada and Kemp (1970), and Uekawa (1972) analyzed this question at length, permitting technology to differ across countries, and concluded that diversification in production by both countries is by no means unlikely.

Brecher and Feenstra (1982) greatly simplified the analysis of this question, showing clearly why diversification in both trading countries is not unlikely. Essentially they show that even if one assumes a unique capital rental at which goods-price ratios are identical across the two countries with diversification in each country, the world production-possibility curve corresponding to this unique (capital rental and) goods-price ratio will be characterized by a flat segment (or a "Chipman flat") such as $R_2 R_1$ in figure 32.1. This segment is linear because multiple values of world production of good 1 and good 2 are possible at the same relative goods-price ratio when each economy produces both goods using a different technology. This multiplicity arises quite simply from the facts that the equalization of capital rentals (through capital mobility) and of the goods-price ratio (through free trade) in the two countries is consistent with any international capital-stock allocation that leaves each country within its cone of diversification and that different allocations give rise to different world-output combinations when Rybczynski effects differ between countries.

The flat segment immediately establishes the proposition that dual diversification is not a *curiosum* in the presence of international technological differences. Brecher and Feenstra (1982) also examine conditions

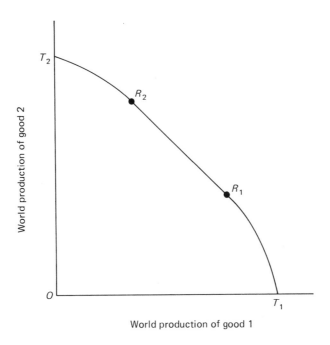

Figure 32.1

under which a goods-price ratio will exist consistent with a stable free-trade equilibrium under dual (global) diversification. Their conditions concern international technological differences of the Hicks-neutral type, whereas Uekawa (1972) considered a different set of technological differences.

32.3   Welfare Analysis: Inflows without Optimal Policy Intervention

Two fundamental types of questions concerning the welfare impact of international capital flows have been analyzed: How do they affect welfare under laissez-faire or free trade? What are the optimal and the second-best interventions in the presence of such capital mobility? After addressing these questions, we will turn to some novel welfare-theoretic questions that have been raised recently. Since the effects of an inflow and an outflow can be analyzed symmetrically, we will focus only on the former.

Capital Inflow under Laissez-Faire

How would capital inflow, left to itself without policy intervention designed to exploit it to the host country's advantage, affect the welfare of the host country?

Nondistortionary Case

The simplest way to address this question is to build the analysis around the central proposition that in the absence of distortions, a "small" inflow of foreign capital will neither harm nor benefit the recipient nation, for the rental on such capital (r) will then equal the value of its private marginal product (PMP), which in turn will equal the social marginal product (SMP):

$$r = \text{PMP} = \text{SMP}.$$

The rental represents the cost, and the social marginal product the gross gain, to the recipient country; their equality ensures the absence of gain or loss.

This paradoxical outcome, that the inflow of capital or its absence is a matter of indifference to the recipient country, reflects the assumption that the influx is infinitesimally small. When it is "large" (finite), the presence of diminishing returns and the ensuing decline in the rental on foreign capital leaves the economy with a surplus: The rental equals the private marginal product for the marginal inflow, but the total return to all capital is less than its contribution to national product; the difference accrues to the economy as a gain in income and hence in welfare. This is seen readily for a one-sector economy, where the standard measure of the gain to the economy from a large inflow of foreign capital is the area under the marginal-product-curve net of the return to the capital. This is the shaded area in figure 32.2, where $\bar{K}_f$ is the magnitude of the inflow, r is its competitive rental, $OSRT$ is the total increase in product from the capital inflow, and $OQRT$ is the total return to foreign capital, with SR the marginal-product curve as foreign capital inflow is varied.

The role of diminishing returns in this welfare-improving outcome is critical. If the capital inflow can be absorbed without diminishing returns, the no-impact proposition will resurrect itself even though the inflow is not small. Consider a typical 2×2 model. With a given goods-price ratio, factor prices and therefore factor proportions in the two activities will remain unchanged if complete specialization or factor-intensity reversal does not occur. The inflow and the resulting change in the factor-endowment ratio will then produce a change only in relative outputs of the two goods, with the relative and the absolute output of the labor-intensive good falling and those of the capital-intensive good rising (in the Rybczynski manner). The capital inflow therefore will not cause a decline in the reward to capital; diminishing returns will have been frustrated. More generally, as long as the economy remains within the

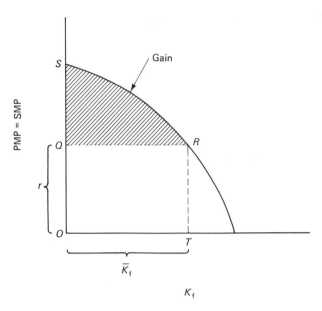

Figure 32.2

McKenzie-Chipman diversification cone (defined on the pre-inflow factor prices), rewards to factors will not change no matter how large is the capital inflow, and correspondingly the no-impact proposition will hold. This is illustrated in figure 32.3. At the pre-inflow factor-price ratio AB, the factor proportions in production of goods 1 and 2 are given by OQ and OR, respectively. The overall factor-endowment ratio $\bar{K}/\bar{L}$ is only a weighted sum of the factor proportions in X and Y, given full employment. Any increase in the total endowment ratio via a capital inflow that leaves the economy still in the diversification cone QOR, as does the inflow raising the endowment ratio to $\bar{K}'/\bar{L}$, will permit the economy to remain at factor-price ratio AB, with factor proportions in goods 1 and 2 unchanged.

Distortionary Cases

When there is a distortion in the host country, the equality between PMP and SMP may break down, resulting in a possible loss from the influx of capital into the economy. We discuss here two interesting cases of this phenomenon.

As noted in chapter 29, a small inflow of capital into a small country with a distortionary tariff in place will necessarily immiserize the country if its importable is capital-intensive. This result, implying that the distortion leads to PMP > SMP, has been established independently by Uzawa

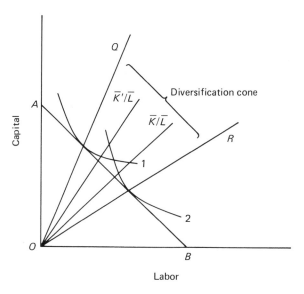

Figure 32.3

(1969) and by Brecher and Díaz Alejandro (1977). It can be demonstrated as follows. In figure 32.4, let the given foreign goods-price ratio be FP. Production at the tariff-inclusive domestic goods-price ratio DP is at $\hat{P}$. When foreign capital comes in, the production of good 2 (assumed to be capital-intensive) rises and that of good 1 falls along the capital Rybczynski line $\hat{P}R$ at constant DP. Let $\hat{P}$ be the new production point. (The tangency of the tariff-inclusive DP with the augmented production-possibility curve is not shown to avoid cluttering the diagram.) With foreign capital being paid the value of its domestic marginal product, it is clear that the national net-production point shifts from $\hat{P}$ to G if foreign capital consumes only good 1, to H if it consumes only good 2, and along GH if it consumes some of each good. It is then clear that national consumption, and hence welfare, must lie along the social-budget FP line through some point on GH. In all cases it is to the left of the pre–influx-of-capital social-budget FP line through $\hat{P}$, so immiserization of the host country is inevitable. The preceding argument is developed in the context of the $2 \times 2 \times 2$ HOS model, but Brecher and Findlay (1983) extended it to an examination of the welfare impact of an endogenously determined inflow of foreign capital in the context of the sector-specific factor model. They showed that the original Brecher–Díaz Alejandro results are robust and that foreign-investment inflow will be injurious to a small, tariff-distorted economy when the inflow augments the specific factor used only in the importable good.

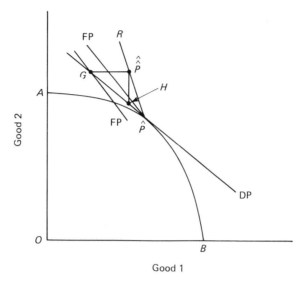

Figure 32.4

Consider next the case where an exogenously specified amount of foreign investment flows into a large country with variable terms of trade. Brecher and Choudhri (1982) show that in this case the host country can get immiserized, depending entirely on the effect on the terms of trade. Intuitively it is easy to see why. Foreign capital earns the value of its domestic marginal product, thus leaving the host country no better or worse off if terms of trade do not change. Any deterioration in the terms of trade is then a net loss. For instance, in figure 32.5 let AB be the pre-inflow production-possibility curve, with production, consumption, and welfare at P^0, C^0, and U^0 respectively. At detrimental terms of trade, foreign capital inflow shifts the production point to P^2. The national income of the host country remains along $P^1 C^1$, net of the increment in production that must fully accrue to foreign capital (Bhagwati and Brecher 1980).[1] Thus the post-inflow equilibrium production, consumption, and national welfare are at P^1, C^1, and U^1, respectively, and the deterioration in the inflow-induced terms of trade has harmed the host country: $U^1 < U^0$. An interesting implication of this argument is that whereas free trade is mutually beneficial to all freely participating economic agents, this cannot be asserted for free international mobility of capital when free trade obtains initially. In popular discussions and in scholarly discourse

---

1. They show this to be the case where equilibrium occurs throughout at the non-end points of AB and $A'B'$, though they also extend the analysis to cases of complete specialization.

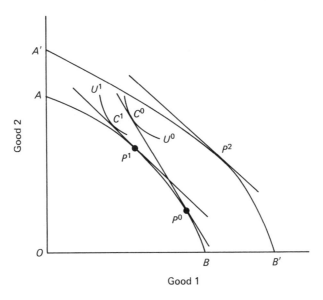

Figure 32.5

the two propositions are put on the same level of acceptability, but that is simply an error.

32.4 Welfare Analysis: Optimal and Second-Best Interventions

Consider now a different question: What is the optimal policy intervention when capital flows in? We will address this question with increasing complexity.

For a one-product economy, assume that capital flows in at a fixed rental. For example, QR in figure 32.2 is the supply curve of foreign capital. It is also then the marginal-cost curve for foreign capital and the free-trade inflow OT is clearly optimal. No intervention is necessary.

However, where the foreign supply of capital is subject to a rising cost, it is plain that the host country will profit from restricting the inflow. In figure 32.6, with a rising supply price of foreign capital, unrestricted inflow will overshoot to OT, while the optimal level of inflow is OS (given by the intersection of the marginal-product and the marginal-cost curves at Q). Optimal restriction then requires that the inflow be reduced by amount ST by a tax that takes the tax-inclusive average curve through Q.

Kemp (1966) and Jones (1967) generalized this analysis to the 2×2 model where capital mobility cannot be interfered with without influencing the goods market. Their analysis thus integrates two diametrically opposed problems: the levy of an optimal goods tariff when factors do

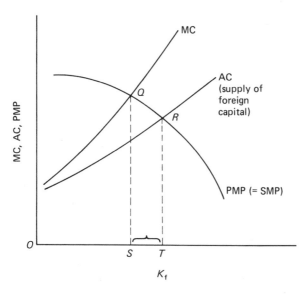

Figure 32.6

not move and the levy of an optimal factor tax *cum* subsidy when the traded-goods aspect does not obtain (as in a one-product model). As one would expect from Tinbergen (1952) and Meade (1951) or from the theory of distortions and commercial policy (Bhagwati and Ramaswami 1963; Johnson 1965), Kemp's analysis shows that two policy instruments —capital and trade taxes and subsidies—generally will be necessary to handle the impact in two markets (the factor market and the goods market). Jones essentially extends Kemp's argument to the second-best context by examining the optimal level of one of these instruments when the other one is arbitrarily set at zero. Brecher (1982) has shown that the Jones policy problem is in fact a third-best rather than a second-best problem as is generally believed. If only one of the tariff and capital-mobility taxes (*cum* subsidies) can be used, it is generally possible to improve welfare further by admitting an altogether different domestic policy instrument: a production or consumption tax *cum* subsidy, which-ever the case may be. This result is consonant with the results of Bhagwati, Ramaswami, and Srinivasan (1968) for the case without international capital mobility, which was analyzed in chapter 21 above.

32.5 Other Welfare-Theoretic Questions

Recently other novel questions have been raised in regard to the implica-tions of international factor mobility. The more important of these are discussed briefly here.

Foreign Ownership and the Theory of Trade and Welfare

If part of the factor endowment is foreign-owned, analysis of the effect of policy changes on national welfare must take into account the redistribution of income that can occur away from or toward the foreign-owned factors of production. Standard theorems such as that free trade is superior to autarky are no longer valid. As Bhagwati and Tironi (1980) noted, this is easily demonstrated by taking an extreme example where free trade immiserizes a country relative to autarky if it raises (in the Stolper-Samuelson manner) the real wage of the foreign-owned factor and reduces the real rental of the domestic factor in a 2×2 model where one factor is wholly foreign-owned and the other is wholly national. Bhagwati and Brecher (1980) and Brecher and Bhagwati (1981) analyzed this problem more fully and considered questions such as the impact of foreign transfers, production growth, and tariff change on national welfare when some of the factor endowment is foreign-owned. Since international labor and capital flows imply that foreign-owned factors must always be reckoned with, this analysis represents an important extension and qualification of the conventional trade-and-welfare insights based on the assumption that all domestically resident factors are national in ownership.

Licensing Technology from Abroad

Related to the theory of international capital flows is the question of analyzing optimal policy when there is licensing of technical know-how from abroad. A pioneering analysis of this kind of question was that of Rodriguez (1975), who adopted the perspective of the technology-exporting country and assumed that it was the sole owner of the technology for one of the two goods in the model. Brecher (1982) examined the question from the viewpoint of the technology-importing country, with the less restrictive assumption that technology in one of the goods is Hicks-neutrally inferior in one country. The handicapped country can then import the superior technology by paying royalties, and these are assumed to equal the amount of extra output made possible by using foreign rather than domestic technology. Brecher shows that the maximization of national income by the technology-importing country requires the joint use of a trade tariff and a domestic production or consumption tax *cum* subsidy. Brecher's analysis also demonstrates that the technology-inferior country may reach a lower welfare level while importing technology than when not importing it at all—that is, that the optimal use of imported technology may simply be at zero level. This happens, not implausibly, when the technology is imported in the activity that produces the exportable good.

Recommended Readings

Bhagwati, J. N., and R. A. Brecher. National welfare in an open economy in the presence of foreign-owned factors of production. *Journal of International Economics* 10 (1980): 103–15.

Bhagwati, J. N., and V. K. Ramaswami. Domestic distortions, tariffs and the theory of optimum subsidy. *Journal of Political Economy* 71 (1963): 44–50.

Bhagwati, J. N., and E. Tironi. Tariff change, foreign capital and immiserization. *Journal of Development Economics* 7 (1980): 71–83.

Bhagwati, J. N., V. K. Ramaswami, and T. N. Srinivasan. Domestic distortions, tariffs and the theory of optimum subsidy: Some further results. *Journal of Political Economy* 77 (1969): 1005–10.

Brecher, R. A. Optimal policy in the presence of licensed technology from abroad. *Journal of Political Economy* 90 (1982): 1070–78.

Brecher, R. A. Second-best policy for international trade and investment. *Journal of International Economics* 14 (1983).

Brecher, R. A., and J. N. Bhagwati. Foreign ownership and the theory of trade and welfare. *Journal of Political Economy* 89 (1981): 497–511.

Brecher, R. A., and E. U. Choudhri. Immiserizing investment from abroad: The Singer-Prebisch thesis reconsidered. *Quarterly Journal of Economics* 97 (1982): 181–90.

Brecher, R. A., and C. F. Díaz Alejandro. Tariffs, foreign capital and immeriserizing growth. *Journal of International Economics* 7 (1977): 317–22.

Brecher, R. A., and R. C. Feenstra. International trade and capital mobility between diversified economies. *Journal of International Economics* 14 (1983): 321–39.

Brecher, R. A., and R. Findlay. Tariffs, foreign capital and national welfare. *Journal of International Economics* 14 (1983): 277–88.

Chipman, J. S. International trade with capital mobility: A substitution theorem. In *Trade, Balance of Payments and Growth, Papers in International Economics in Honor of Charles P. Kindleberger*, ed. by J. N. Bhagwati et al. Amsterdam: North-Holland, 1971.

Hamada, K. Strategic aspects of taxation of foreign investment income. *Quarterly Journal of Economics* 80 (1966): 361–75.

Hamada, K. An Economic analysis of the duty-free zone. *Journal of International Economics* 4 (1974): 225–41.

Inada, K., and M. C. Kemp. International capital movements and the theory of international trade. *Quarterly Journal of Economics* 83 (1970): 524–28.

Jasay, A. E. The choice between home and foreign investment. *Economic Journal* 70 (1960): 105–13.

Johnson, H. G. Optimal trade intervention in the presence of domestic distortion. In *Trade, Growth and the Balance of Payment*, ed. by R. Caves et al. ed. by R. F. Baldwin et al. Chicago: Rand McNally and Amsterdam: North-Holland, 1965.

Jones, R. W. International capital movements and the theory of tariffs and trade. *Quarterly Journal of Economics* 81 (1967): 1–38.

Kemp, M. C. Foreign investment and the national advantage. *Economic Record* 38 (1962): 56–62.

Kemp, M. C. The gain from international trade and investment: A neo-Heckscher-Ohlin approach. *American Economic Review* 56 (1966): 788–809.

MacDougall, G. D. A. The benefits and costs of private investment from abroad: A theoretical approach. *Bulletin of the Oxford University Institute of Statistics* 22 (1960): 189–211. Reprinted in *International Trade*, ed. by J. Bhagwati. Baltimore: Penguin, 1969.

Meade, J. *The Balance of Payments*. Oxford: Oxford University Press, 1951.

Minabe, N. Capital and technology movements and economic welfare. *American Economic Review* 64 (1974): 1088–1100.

Mundell, R. A. International trade and factor mobility. *American Economic Review* 47 (1957): 321–35.

Mundell, R. A. International trade and factor mobility. *American Economic Review* 47 (1967): 321–25. Reprinted in *Readings in International Economics*, ed. by R. E. Caves and H. G. Johnson. Homewood, IL: Irwin, 1968.

Negishi, T. Foreign investment and the long-run national advantage. *Economic Record* 41 (1965): 628–32.

Rodriguez, C. A. Trade in technological knowledge and the national advantage. *Journal of Political Economy* 83 (1975): 121–35.

Singer, H. W. The distribution of gains between investing and borrowing countries. *American Economic Review* 40 (1950): 473–85. Reprinted in *Readings in International Economics*, ed. by R. E. Caves and H. G. Johnson. Homewood, IL: Irwin, 1968.

Srinivasan, T. N. International factor movements, commodity trade and commercial policy. *Journal of International Economics* 14 (1983): 289–312.

Tinbergen, J. *On the Theory of Economic Policy.* Amsterdam: North-Holland, 1952.

Uekawa, Y. On the existence of incomplete specialization in international trade with capital mobility. *Journal of International Economics* 2 (1972): 1–23.

Uzawa, H. Shihon jiyuka to kokumin keizai (Liberalization of foreign investments and the national economy). *Economisuto* 23 (1969): 105–22.

Wong, K. Y. On choosing among trade in goods and international capital and labor mobility: A theoretical analysis. *Journal of International Economics* 14 (1983): 223–50.

In many ways, while international labor mobility poses many significant asymmetries, it can be analyzed in the same way as international capital mobility. A key similarity is that the fundamental proposition that a small capital inflow in an economy without distortions will neither harm nor help the host country resurrect itself in the well-known argument that a small emigration will not harm nor help those left behind. The emigrant will have been earning his social marginal product, and therefore his departure will reduce his contribution to national product and his own earned share in it by identical amounts.

33.1 Asymmetries

Minor asymmetries arise from the fact that in the analysis of international labor mobility some of the distortions are likely to be different from those relevant to questions of international capital mobility. For instance, Bhagwati and Hamada (1974) model the effects of the "brain drain" in a model where private mortgage product (PMP) $\neq$ social mortgage product (SMP) because emigration leads to integration of the domestic market for professional labor into the higher-paid world market for it and hence to an escalation of the fixed wage in a Harris-Todaro-type model. Such a distortionary problem, embodying what they call the "keeping-up-with-the-Joneses effect," is evidently not appropriate in the capital-mobility context.

More fundamental asymmetries arise from the fact that migration raises the question of the appropriate manner in which to define national welfare. Should the migrant or mobile population be counted as part of the population set of the country of "origin" or of the country of "destination," or neither, or both? We can see the differences between international mobility of capital and labor that can arise from this fundamental question by borrowing from Hamada (1977) an argument based on the analysis of factor flows in a single-product model. Take figure 33.1, which portrays a factor flow occurring from an LDC (less developed country) to a DC, the world endowment of the factor being $O_1 O_2$ and the marginal-product schedule of the factor for the DC being measured from O_1 and that for the LDC from O_2. Assume away all distortions so that one can legitimately concentrate on gains and losses within the framework of the figure.

Let $O_1 A$ and $A O_2$ then be the national endowments of the factor in the DC and in the LDC before migration, respectively. Assume now that the factor in question is labor. When migration is allowed, an amount AB of labor will migrate from the LDC to the DC. Therefore the domestic

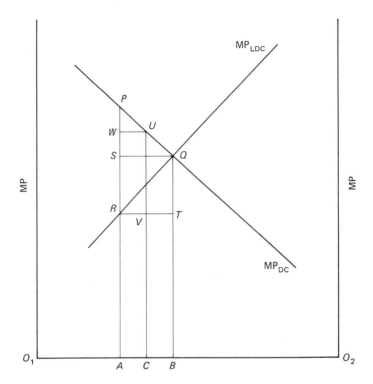

Figure 33.1

product of the LDC will reduce by the area $QRAB$, and the income received by those left behind will diminish by the area of the triangle QRT, reflecting the "large"-flow effect that has been discussed in relation to capital mobility. The domestic product of the DC will increase by $PABQ$, and the income received by those originally living in the DC will increase by PSQ. The gain obtained by the emigrants themselves is equal to $SRTQ$.

If we were considering capital on the horizontal axis, the welfare gain due to the movement of capital, amounting to the triangle PQR, would be distributed to the two countries in amounts PSQ and SRQ. Thus both countries gain from the free movement of capital. On the other hand, in the case of labor migration, not only is this total gain PQR (plus QRT) distributed to the premigration population of the DC and the migrants who constitute the new residents there, but there is actually a loss of an amount equal to the area QRT suffered by the nonmigrants in the LDC.

Thus we have an asymmetry between foreign capital outflow and labor emigration arising from the fact that the income earned on capital invested abroad is part of the national income, whereas we are assuming here that the migrant labor and its income are falling outside of the definition of LDC income. In brief, the total world gain PRQ decomposes into an LDC gain of SRQ and a DC gain of PSQ in the case of capital outflow, and into an emigrants' gain of $SRTQ$, an LDC (net of emigrants) loss of QRT, and a DC (net of immigrants) gain of PSQ for the case of labor outflow.

This asymmetry would disappear if the migrants were to be treated as part of the population over which national welfare is defined, despite the unavoidable income-distributional issues as migrants benefit and non-migrants lose. The income-distributional implication of outmigration of labor, when present, provides a rationale for proposals to extend the domestic tax jurisdiction to incomes earned abroad by nationals. On the ground of the familiar compensation principle alone, a policy of free out-migration of labor would need in these circumstances to be accompanied by a policy that taxes the welfare-improving migrants to compensate those left behind. This argument for taxing the migrants presupposes that the nonmigrants in the country of emigration suffer a loss, as built into the model of figure 33.1. However, a number of alternative rationales[1] have been provided for such taxation—for example, that the migrants (especially the highly skilled) enjoy windfall gains, due to severe immigration restrictions, that should be taxed for spending on socially agreeable purposes and that equity demands that nationals who work abroad should not altogether escape the domestic tax net.[2]

33.2   Choice between International Labor and Capital Mobility

The consideration of labor mobility introduces a further problem: While the Kemp-Jones-Brecher-type analysis discussed in chapter 32 focuses on optimal policies in the presence of one factor's (capital's) international mobility, there is now the interesting choice-theoretic question of which factor's mobility would yield the greater national advantage.[3]

Suppose that we have a capital-rich country, the United States, and a capital-poor country, Mexico. Assume that the United States must uni-

---

1. For a comprehensive statement of these rationales, and the economic and ethical arguments involved, see Bhagwati (1979) and Bhagwati and Partington (1976). The theoretical issues raised by the presence of international labor mobility for the modern theory of optimal income taxation have been discussed in a symposium issue of the *Journal of Public Economics* 18, no. 3 (1982).

2. This equity notion underlies the American practice of taxing citizens no matter where they reside, under Internal Revenue Code Section 911, ensuring that there is "no representation without taxation."

3. This theoretical problem has been posed, in the context of policy issues, by Bhagwati and Srinivasan (1983).

laterally decide between two alternative feasible courses of action: It can allow its capital to migrate to Mexico while effectively closing the border to immigration, or it can prohibit capital outflow but permit immigration of Mexican labor. If the United States must also choose optimal taxes and subsidies on such factor flows, so that we would wind up comparing optimal ways of choosing between the two forms of mobility, which would be to its greater national advantage? This is a complex problem, which could be considered in a model that permits both goods and factor movements. However, in an early analysis, Ramaswami (1968) considered this very issue in a one-sector model with no goods trade. He showed that optimal restriction of immigration of Mexican labor by the capital-rich United States was preferable for U.S. welfare to optimal restriction of capital outflow to Mexico. As has become evident from the later analyses of Calvo and Wellisz (1983) and Bhagwati and Srinivasan (1983), this rank ordering is attributable to the fact that the optimal restriction of immigration permits the United States to impose a tax policy on immigrants that discriminates between them and American citizens.[4] It therefore raises, from a policy standpoint, legal, political, and ethical questions similar to those discussed in Bhagwati and Partington (1976) concerning the possibility of developed countries taxing skilled immigrants from the developing countries in order to raise resources for developmental spending in the developing countries of their origin.[5]

33.3   Response to Import Competition

Yet another analytical and policy-relevant question that has been recently posed relates to variations in immigration quotas as they reflect the response by economic agents in the import-competing industries to the phenomenon of import competition. Bhagwati (1982b) and Sapir (1983) consider how in technologically stagnant traditional industries, import competition can result from newly industrializing countries gaining comparative advantage due to lower wages (in the manner of the HOS theory). In this case a possible response may well be to import more

---

4. It also presupposes that Mexican labor in the United States is not part of U.S. welfare. For a full treatment of the Ramaswami model, including the complications introduced by differences in assumptions about how migrant labor is viewed, see Bhagwati and Srinivasan (1983).

5. See Wong 1983 for an analysis, in the $2 \times 2 \times 2$ framework and using appropriate new techniques, of the relative merits of alternative policies such as free trade without international factor mobility, free labor mobility without goods trade, free capital mobility without goods trade, and free trade plus labor or capital mobility.

labor by relaxing immigration barriers. Bhagwati (1982b), using the HOS model, the sector-specific-factors model, and the fixed-wage Haberler-Brecher model successively, analyzes the differential advantage that capitalists, wage-earners, and the government could gain by responding to such import competition by tariff protection and instead by labor importation.

Recommended Readings

Berry, R. A., and R. Soligo. Some welfare aspects of international migration. *Journal of Political Economy* 77 (1969): 778–94.

Bhagwati, J. N., ed. *The Brain Drain and Taxation: Theory and Empirical Analysis.* Amsterdam: North-Holland, 1976.

Bhagwati, J. N. International factor movements and national advantage. *Indian Economic Review* N. S., 14 (1979): 73–100.

Bhagwati, J. N. International migration of the highly skilled: Economics, ethics and taxes. *Third World Quarterly* 1, (1979): 17–30.

Bhagwati, J. N. Introduction. (Symposium on the Exercise of Income Tax Jurisdiction over Citizens Abroad) *Journal of Public Economics* 18 (1982): 285–89.

Bhagwati, J. N. Shifting comparative advantage, protectionist demands, and policy response. In *Import Competition and Response*, ed. by J. Bhagwati, 1982b. Chicago: University of Chicago Press, 153–84.

Bhagwati, J. N., and K. Hamada. The brain drain, international integration of markets for professionals and unemployment: A theoretical analysis. *Journal of Development Economics* 1 (1974): 19–24.

Bhagwati, J. N., and K. Hamada. Tax policy in the presence of emigration. *Journal of Public Economics* 18 (1982): 291–317.

Bhagwati, J. N., and M. Partington, ed. *Taxing the Brain Drain: A Proposal.* Amsterdam: North-Holland, 1976.

Bhagwati, J. N., and C. Rodriguez. Welfare-theoretical analyses of the brain drain. *Journal of Development Economics* 2 (1975): 195–221.

Bhagwati, J. N., and T. N. Srinivasan. On the choice between capital and labour mobility. *Journal of International Economics* 14 (1983): 209–21.

Calvo G., and S. Wellisz. International factor mobility and national advantage. *Journal of International Economics* 14 (1983): 65–81.

Grubel, H. B., and A. D. Scott. The international flow of human capital. *American Economic Review* 56 (1966): 268–74.

Hamada, K. Taxing the brain drain: A global point of view. In *The New International Economic Order*, ed. by J. N. Bhagwati. Cambridge, MIT Press, 1977.

Hamada, K., and J. N. Bhagwati. Domestic distortions, imperfect information and the brain drain. In *The Brain Drain and Taxation*, ed. by J. N. Bhagwati. Amsterdam: North-Holland, 1976.

Kenen, P. B. Migration, the terms of trade, and economic welfare in the source country. In *Trade, Balance of Payments, and Growth, Papers in International Economics in Honor of Charles P. Kindleberger*, ed. by J. Bhagwati et al. Amsterdam: North-Holland, 1971.

Ramaswami, V. K. International factor movement and the national advantage. *Economica*, N. S., 35 (1968): 309–10.

Ramaswami, V. K. International factor movement and the national advantage: Reply. *Economica*, N. S., 37 (1970): 85.

Rodriguez, Carlos A. On the welfare aspects of international migration. *Journal of Political Economy* 83 (1975): 1065–72.

Sapir, A. Foreign competition, immigration and structural adjustment. *Journal of International Economics* 14 (1983).

Webb, L. R. International factor movement and the national advantage: A comment. *Economica*, N. S., 37 (1970): 81–84.

Wong, K. Y. On choosing among trade in goods and international capital and labor mobility: A theoretical analysis. *Journal of International Economics* 14 (1983): 223–50.

IV RECENT THEORETICAL DEVELOPMENTS

In reality tariffs are accompanied by three phenomena that have recently received analytical attention:

1. *Tariff evasion* (smuggling) in which profit is made by getting around the tariffs.

2. *Tariff-seeking lobbying* by pressure groups that expect to profit from protection.

3. *Revenue-seeking lobbying* to get a share of the revenue disbursement expected to follow the receipt of the tariff revenue. Tariffs imposed for protectionist reasons as a result of tariff-seeking lobbying almost always generate revenue.

When quantitative restrictions (QRs) are used in lieu of tariffs, the above three phenomena arise as QR evasion, QR seeking, and premium seeking, respectively.

All these activities are profitable without being directly productive. Economic agents earn incomes, using real resources, but without contributing directly or indirectly to output that enters the utility function. In short, these activities are tantamount to a contraction of the availability set of the economy, defined on goods and services entering the utility function. In thinking of such activities, we therefore resurrect the physiocratic distinction between productive and unproductive activities—but on a sound basis.

Many of these activities are attempts to make profit by either getting around governmental policies (e.g., by tariff evasion) or getting governmental policies modified (e.g., by replacing free trade with a protective tariff). But one can equally think of nongovernmental activities such as theft or seeking a share of private altruistic grants. We have deliberately inserted the qualification that the activities we are discussing are "directly unproductive" (not *directly* productive). As this chapter will show, they can be indirectly and ultimately welfare-improving. Following Bhagwati (1982a), we describe these activities as directly unproductive profit-seeking (DUP, pronounced "dupe") activities—an appropriate acronym for resource-using activities that, directly, yield zero output.

The generic class of what Krueger (1974) calls "rent-seeking" activities is easily seen to be a subset of such DUP activities. She defines the rent-seeking activities as lobbying activities generated by the existence of policy interventions such as QRs or licenses and restrictions, which carry premia or windfall profits (in the nature of Marshallian rents) that accrue to the successful lobbyist. Hence follows the rent-seeking activity, much as a missile seeks heat. These rent-seeking activities, however, are not the only category of DUP activities. In addition there are DUP activities that reflect lobbying triggered by price instruments (e.g., tariffs lead to revenues that generate revenue seeking). Rent-seeking also presupposes rents on existing interventions, but there are also DUP activities that seek to impose or influence the policy intervention itself, as when tariff seeking is considered. Again DUP activities can involve evading a policy instrument. A functional classification of DUP activities, with a proper delineation of where Krueger's rent seeking belongs, is presented in figure 34.1.[1]

The DUP activities can be further divided into those that are legal and those that are illegal. Tariff evasion or smuggling is illegal, but tariff seeking and revenue seeking in pluralistic democracies are usually legal. This distinction is important, since illegal activities carry risk of detection and punishment, whereas legal ones do not; thus the former open up for analysis further questions about the optimal levels of enforcement expenditures by the government, whereas the latter do not.

In the analyses below we consider the positive and welfare implications of DUP activities in a fashion now already familiar to the reader. Having dealt with three major types of DUP activities—tariff evasion, revenue seeking, and tariff seeking—we will then present a general welfare-theoretic analysis of DUP activities.

34.1   Tariff Evasion

Bhagwati-Hansen Model

The analysis of tariff evasion was initiated by Bhagwati and Hansen (1973). The distinctive feature of their analysis was that they made Samuelson's "melting ice" assumption on the cost of illegal trade confining themselves to the 2×2 model. They assumed that illegal trade is characterized by a lower rate of transformation between exports and imports than that associated with legal trade. This model makes sense when the illegal trade implies some "attrition"—such as when goods perish in transit or are thrown overboard when detection is feared. If it is assumed additionally that the market prices of legally and illegally traded goods are identical, the model reduces to that in figure 34.2.

In figure 34.2 the tariff shifts production from P^* to P_t, and consumption and welfare are at C_t and U_t, respectively. With a small country

---

1. Krueger appears to have assumed that the policy interventions she studied were distortionary in nature, but they need not be so. Thus figure 34.1 holds even if the interventions are optimal. For example, the Krueger-type premium seeking may involve QRs, which are the quantity equivalent of the optimal tariff under monopoly power, or smuggling, representing a policy-intervention-evading DUP activity, may be around an optimal tariff.

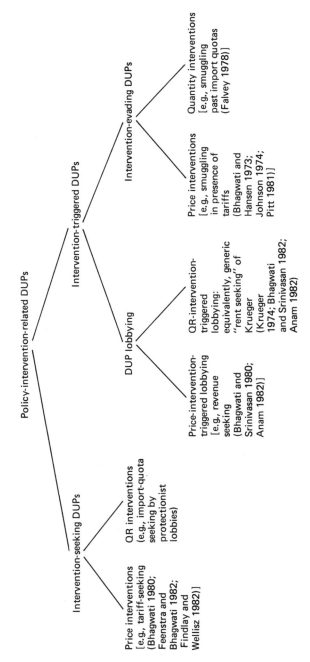

Figure 34.1

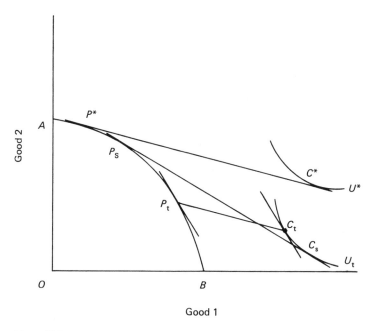

Figure 34.2

assumed and with constant costs in smuggling, the inferior transformation rate is supposed to be $P_S C_S$ in tariff-evading illegal trade, which is steeper than the $P^* C^*$ for legal trade. Trade is fully diverted to illegal trade because the illegal-trade price ratio $P_S C_S$, which avoids the tariff, dominates the tariff-inclusive legal-trade price ratio $P_t C_t$. The situation is therefore fully equivalent to that of a trade-diverting customs union (chapter 31) if we substitute "illegal trade" for "partner country" in the union and "legal trade" for the "outside country" that is subject to the external tariff of the union. Figure 34.2 shows the break-even case where the shift to illegal trade leaves the country as well off as under legal trade. Better terms of illegal trade will be then welfare-improving; worse terms will be welfare-worsening.

Figure 34.3 illustrates the case where illegal and legal trade coexist, and the same assumptions as in figure 34.2 continue to apply. Now the illegal terms of trade are just equal to the tariff-inclusive legal-trade price ratio, which implies that illegal and legal trade can coexist, since neither dominates the other in this model with constant rate of transformation illegal and legal foreign offer curves. In this case the respective levels of illegal and legal trade are clearly indeterminate, but it is clear that a positive level of illegal trade will lower welfare below the legal-trade level and that the larger the illegal trade, at the inferior terms of trade, the

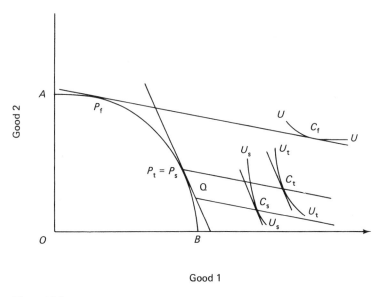

Figure 34.3

lower is the welfare level. In figure 34.3, with both trades coexisting, illegal trade takes place up to Q from P_t, P_S and legal trade from Q to C_S, leaving the economy ultimately at U_S (which is evidently less than U_t). The reason is that illegal trade is conducted at inferior terms of trade, which imposes the standard terms-of-trade loss on the economy. At the same time, since internal prices faced by consumers and producers do not change at all from their legal-trade level, there is no offsetting production or consumption gain. Thus illegal trade merely causes loss in this coexistence situation.

Sheikh Model

In an alternative model, Sheikh (1974) basically retains the Bhagwati-Hansen approach, but instead of using the "melting ice" assumption to model the direct real costs of smuggling, he assumes that illegal trade uses the primary resources directly (though he uses the device of embodying them in a third good that is "used up" *pro rata* to the level of illegal trade). Furthermore Sheikh introduces risk in illegal trade, using a rising cost of smuggling owing to risk in order to arrive at a determinate level of illegal trade, as when Bhagwati and Hansen introduce increasing costs (in contrast with the brief analysis of constant-rate-of-transformation illegal-trade offer curve presented in the preceding subsection). The central difference between the Bhagwati-Hansen model and the Sheikh model emerges from the fact that the "melting-ice" assumption in the

Bhagwati-Hansen model implies that the production-possibility curve for producing the tradable goods is invariant to smuggling, whereas the Sheikh model implies that it will change with smuggling. The former implies, as we have just seen, that if illegal and legal trade coexist, the country must necessarily be immiserized. This follows from the fact that the illegal trade will impose a terms-of-trade loss, whereas no production or consumption gain will follow (because the coexistence of legal and illegal trade implies that in this small country the tariff-inclusive legal-trade price remains unchanged despite illegal trade). In the Sheikh model, however, the presence of illegal trade does utilize primary factors and therefore affects the tradable outputs that are produced. This means that one has to contend with the possibility of immiserizing growth. The withdrawal of resources into the illegal trade means that fewer resources are available for producing the tradables that enter the utility function. However, since the situation is distortionary in view of the tariff, this reduction in available primary factors means that there may be an improvement, rather than a deterioration, in welfare. Thus, when illegal and legal trade coexist, a situation in which gain is possible remains in the Sheikh model, whereas it does not in the Bhagwati-Hansen model. This illustrates well the differences in outcomes that can result from differences in the structure of production and trade that are modeled.

Pitt Model

Yet another model of smuggling has been developed by Pitt (1981). He notes that in some classes of smuggling, such as the Indonesian export trade which has been studies fairly intensively, the Bhagwati-Hansen and Sheikh models are inapplicable. They assume that the domestic price of tradables will always reflect the tariff-inclusive price for importables and the net-of-duty price of exportables with respect to their foreign prices.[2] In the Indonesian case, however, the domestic prices of the export-smuggled items (evading the export duties) are generally higher than what profitable legal trade would imply. Thus, if the export duty for an exportable is at an *ad valorem* rate t_x and the foreign FOB price is p_i^x, the domestic price in the case of legal trade should be $p_i^x(1 - t_x)$, whereas in Indonesian markets it is usually above that, implying that legal trade is carried on at a loss.

Reflecting on this, Pitt argues that legal trade may be necessary for illegal trade to be carried out without excessive fear of detection, and that

2. They also assume that goods, whether illegally traded or legally traded internationally, fetch an identical price in the market. This is not always the case, for illegally traded goods are sometimes cleared at a lower price because of the risk.

therefore illegal trade and legal trade coexist and the losses on legal trade, as observed in Indonesia, are really generating more-than-offsetting profits on the illegal trade that this legal trade helps to camouflage and therefore make feasible. For instance, as long as any illegal import trade exists in a small economy, the domestic price ratio that results must lie between the zero-tariff and tariff with no illegal import domestic price ratios. Therefore the illegal-trade situation must be characterized by production and consumption gains over the situation without illegal trade. Now, if the Bhagwati-Hansen "melting ice" assumption is made such that the illegal trade is characterized by an inferior transformation rate, any positive level of illegal trade imposes a corresponding terms-of-trade loss. Therefore (in view of the production and consumption gains) the Pitt model also leads to the conclusion, in common with Sheikh but contrary to that of Bhagwati and Hansen, that the coexistence of legal and illegal trade can improve welfare over the situation where only legal trade obtains. At the same time the Pitt model leads to a "price disparity" between the legal-trade tariff-inclusive domestic price ratio and the actual domestic price ratio, as observed for Indonesian trade. This is contrary to both the Sheikh model and the Bhagwati-Hansen model.

The above analysis of the three models focuses on their contrasting features and their implications for welfare impact when legal and illegal trade coexist. However, the literature on the subject has extended the analysis to related issues, such as the effect of illegal trade on the rank ordering of optimal and maximum-revenue tariffs, the effect on maximum-revenue levels (Johnson 1974; Bhagwati and Srinivasan 1973), and the rank ordering of legal-trade and illegal-trade situations where the society has noneconomic objectives such as target protection of the importable activity (Ray 1978). The implications of alternative types of illegal trade for their economic consequences and statistical detection have also been explored by Bhagwati (1981), and Anam (1982) has an interesting analysis of smuggling in the presence of revenue seeking.

34.2   Revenue Seeking

The theory of revenue seeking has been developed by Bhagwati and Srinivasan (1980) under the assumptions of the 2×2 model for productive activities and a "nontraded" sector representing lobbying for the revenue generated by the tariff (which is assumed to be exogenously specified, so that any "tariff seeking" has been already solved for).

For a small open economy, using the simplifying assumptions of the 2×2 model, consider then figure 34.4. The standard representation of a

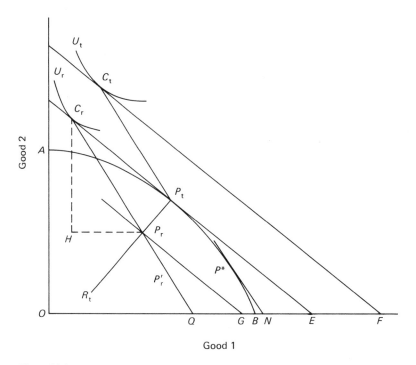

Figure 34.4

tariff equilibrium in this case is with world price ratio (equal to minus the slope of the line) $P_t C_t$, free-trade production at P^*, tariff-policy production and consumption at P_t and C_t, and the associated tariff revenue EF in terms of good 1. Lump-sum transfer of revenues to consumers is assumed.

Now introduce revenue seeking into this model. Envisage a production function in revenue seeking that uses factors K_r and L_r. It is evident that with competition in this activity, the K_r/L_r ratio will be chosen to minimize costs, given the market values of the rental (r) and the wage (w).

In the 2×2 model, as long as we confine ourselves to incomplete specialization in production, the tariff-inclusive domestic goods-price ratio $(C_t F = P_t E$ in figure 34.4) will determine the factor-price ratio (i.e., the w and r faced by the revenue seekers) and the K_r/L_r ratio.

With this choice of K_r/L_r ratio, the total factors withdrawn from use in goods production at P_t will equal the amount of tariff revenue that we assume to be subject to seeking. This follows from our assumption of competitive revenue seeking. Our analysis will divide the total tariff revenue into the revenue sought and the Meade-type lump-sum transfer that escapes the seeking. However, we first consider the case of full revenue seeking.

The withdrawal of K_r and L_r for revenue seeking will reduce the total amount of factors available for production of goods 1 and 2. On the other hand, it is equally evident from the fixity of goods and factor prices that the domestic consumption of goods will lie on the domestic-expenditure line, which is identical to the national-income-at-factor-cost line $P_t E$ in figure 34.4. Domestic expenditure must equal domestic income in the revenue-seeking equilibrium, and the latter is nothing but the value of factors used in goods production plus the value of factors diverted to revenue-seeking, which adds up to the value of all factors at w and r associated with P_t and hence to national income at factor cost at P_t.

The resulting revenue-seeking equilibrium is illustrated in figure 34.4. The domestic-expenditure (or national-income-at-factor-cost) line is $P_t E$. Consumption must therefore occur at C_r. Moreover the world price line must pass through C_r, so $C_r Q$ is the world price line through C_r. At the same time the new production point must lie on $C_r Q$; it also lies on the generalized Rybczynski line $P_t R_t$ (which is the locus of successive production points, at constant domestic goods-price ratio $P_t E$, since factors are successively withdrawn for revenue seeking in the proportion K_r/L_r). The production point that satisfies both the requirements is therefore P_r. The difference between C_r and P_r defines $C_r H$ as the import level, with tariff revenue now at GE; the value of factor income in goods production is OG, that in revenue seeking is GE, and that in aggregate is OE.

Welfare falls, with the introduction of competitive revenue seeking, from U_t to U_r. This appears to be a thoroughly intuitive conclusion in that resources are being diverted by revenue seeking to a "wasteful" activity with zero output (in terms of social valuation). However, this intuition needs correction: The welfare-worsening outcome is not the only possibility, since the withdrawal of resources to revenue seeking is from a distorted situation.

To see this, consider the possibility that part of the revenue is handled as a Meade-type lump-sum transfer, and only the remainder is competitively sought, so that the value of factors diverted to revenue seeking is less than the total revenue. Consider figure 34.5, which uses much the same lettering as figure 34.4, and the income-consumption line at the tariff-inclusive domestic price ratio. The difference is that the Rybczynski line $P_t R_t$ is now flatter than the international price line $P_t N$. A possible revenue-seeking equilibrium is shown at P_r, C'_r, with total revenue collected at GE, revenue offered and sought at GJ, and the lump-sum Meade-type transfer at JE. Thus welfare improves with revenue seeking to $U'_r (> U_t)$ and the proportion of tariff revenue disbursed to revenue seekers is less than unity (the proportion is GJ/GE).

The necessary condition for the paradoxical welfare-improving revenue seeking to arise is that the output of the "underproduced" good should

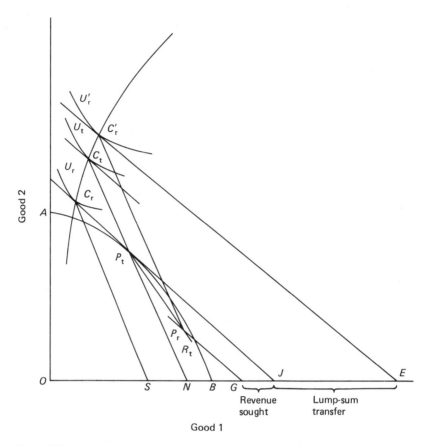

Figure 34.5

increase because of the revenue seeking. Thus in figure 34.6, if the revenue-seeking production point P_r shifts to within the shaded zone I, that will suffice to improve welfare over P_t (the tariff equilibrium without revenue seeking) for this small open economy with world price line P_tQ, for under free trade production will be at P^* whereas the tariff leads to reduction of good-2 output at P_t. If revenue seeking takes production into zone I, the output of good 2 gets back closer to its optimal level at P^*, the source of the welfare-improving paradox. However, increase in the output of good 1 is only a necessary condition, not a sufficient one, for the paradox. Thus P_r could move into zone II. In light of the world price ratio, this is not sufficient to improve welfare over the level at P_t.[3]

3. A more detailed analysis of these conditions governing the paradox will be found in Bhagwati and Srinivasan (1980, sec. IV). Also, recall the discussion of immiserizing growth and negative shadow factor prices in chapter 29. These are precisely the phenomena involved in the paradox of welfare-improving revenue seeking.

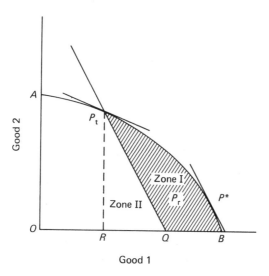

Figure 34.6

34.3   Tariff Seeking

The Bhagwati-Srinivasan analysis of revenue seeking, which takes the tariff as exogenously given, is conceptually distinct from the analysis of tariff seeking, which aims at endogenizing the imposition of the tariff. Formal analysis of tariff seeking began with Brock and Magee (1978) and has led to recent work by Findlay and Wellisz (1982), Feenstra and Bhagwati (1982), and Bhagwati (1982b).

The Findlay-Wellisz model takes one factor as mobile between two sectors, each of which also has a sector-specific factor in addition (in the manner of Jones 1971). They then model lobbying for and against a tariff by the sector-specific factors, since in the simple model structure the tariff will raise the real wage of one such factor and reduce that of the other. Lobbying itself uses up the mobile factor. The model is solved for the endogenous tariff that results from this set of assumptions.

Feenstra and Bhagwati, on the other hand, work with a 2 × 2 model and permit tariff seeking on the part of the factor that loses from a shift in the terms of trade. Then, given a cost function for tariff seeking, they solve for the tariff that will yield to this lobby maximum income. They introduce a novel twist by assuming that the government will intervene as an actor seeking national interest. To pursue this interest, the government is assumed to utilize the tariff revenues in this equilibrium to bribe the lobby into accepting a socially less expensive tariff such that at this tariff the lobby is still earning an income (wage-plus-tariff revenue) identical to that before the tariff-revenue distribution. This tariff, which yields higher social welfare in the presence of tariff-seeking lobbying by utilizing tariff revenues as a bribing policy instrument, is called by these authors the *efficient tariff.*

Bhagwati (1982b) considers tariff-seeking lobbying in the context of international factor mobility by modeling tariffs, importation of more foreign labor, and exportation of capital (direct investment abroad) as three possible lobbying responses to the fact of import competition. He distinguishes between two classes of industries facing import competition: the "senile" labor-intensive industries and the Schumpeterian technically innovative industries. He notes that in the labor-intensive industries the entrepreneurs and labor in the import-competing industry are likely to be divided in their responses, since the entrepreneurs will be happy to consider not just tariffs but also asking the government to import more cheap foreign labor by relaxing immigration restrictions, whereas labor would clearly be interested only in tariff protection. On the other hand, in the Schumpeterian industries it is likely that (as in the U.S. auto industry) the entrepreneurs who are losing out to technologically smarter competitors abroad would prefer tariff protection, whereas labor would equally consider forcing (via protectionist threats) the foreign entrepreneurs to shift their production via foreign investment to where the labor is.[4] Bhagwati utilizes the 2×2 model to analyze the former choice between labor importation via relaxed immigration quota and tariff protection as objects of lobbying activities by entrepreneurs and labor in response to import competition. Sapir (1983) considers similar problem in the context of the specific-factors Jones-type model discussed in chapter 7.

34.4 General Theory of DUP Activities

In regard to welfare consequences the DUP activities examined above sometimes create paradoxes such that while being directly unproductive, they sometimes indirectly are "productive" (welfare-improving). Evidently a general theoretical framework is required to embrace these divergent outcomes. Bhagwati (1982a) has provided this, arguing that the most fruitful taxonomy must build on the distinction between distorted (or suboptimal) and nondistorted (or optimal) situations. Thus a DUP activity that uses up resources in the context of a distortion may be paradoxically

4. For example, the United Auto Workers union does not care whether its members are employed by Nissan or Ford, but Ford does care.

welfare-improving, whereas a similar DUP activity that destroys a distortion and achieves a first-best, optimal outcome may be paradoxically welfare-worsening. But when a DUP activity arises and uses up real resources in the context of a nondistorted situation, it must always cause a loss.[5]

Let us then turn to the following taxonomy which, with an eye on welfare analysis, is built on the fact that all such DUP activities will involve either a distorted or a distortion-free situation before and after the undertaking of the activity. Four critical classes of DUP activities are distinguished:[6]

Category I: The initial and final situations are both distorted.

Category II: The initial situation is distorted, but the final situation (thanks to the DUP activity) is distortion-free.

Category III: The initial situation is distortion-free, but the final situation is distorted.

Category IV: The initial situation is distortion-free, and so is the final situation (despite the DUP activity).

The fundamental distinction remains that between categories I and II (which relate to initially distorted situations) and categories III and IV (which relate to initially distortion-free situations).

For DUP activities falling into categories I and II, a beneficial rather than immiserizing outcome is (paradoxically) feasible, whereas for those falling into categories III and IV, it is not. The critical difference is that the former set have initial situations that are distorted, whereas the latter set start with distortion-free initial situations. The existing analyses of DUP activities, many of which were detailed above, are then assigned to these four categories.

The critical analytical point at issue is simply that the diversion of resources from directly productive to directly unproductive activities, when undertaken in the context of initially distorted situations, is fundamentally different from such diversion occurring in the context of initially distortion-free situations. In the latter case, the loss of resources is occurring from a first-best situation and hence must represent a social loss,

---

5. Noting that when distortions exist almost anything can happen, we emphasize that the theory and the resulting taxonomy presuppose that the world is indeed distortion-free except for the distortions with which the directly unproductive profit-seeking activity in question is related in an essential way. Thus, if one considers revenue seeking as analyzed above, the revenue sought by the lobbyists is on a distortionary tariff already in place in the model. In that model therefore there is an unchanging distortion in place when the directly unproductive premium seeking is introduced, but there are no other distortions.

6. In each category, activities can be legal or illegal.

whereas in the former case, it is occurring in a second-best situation and hence need not represent a social loss but may well be beneficial.

Category I

In this class of cases, the DUP activities are triggered by initially distortion-ridden situations. Two legal activities so discussed in the literature are the Krueger (1974) phenomenon of premium seeking and the Bhagwati-Srinivasan (1980) phenomenon of revenue seeking. Krueger's premium-seeking analysis postulates that presumably as a result of protectionist demands, import quotas have materialized and characterize the initial situation. The premium-fetching import licenses then generate resource-using competition among potential beneficiaries of the license allocation, and the analysis presupposes that the initial quota level remains unchanged. Therefore the Krueger analysis of premium seeking is essentially of a legal process of DUP activity undertaken in the context of a distorted situation where the distortion triggering off the DUP activity remains unchanged through the analysis. The same features characterize the Bhagwati-Srinivasan (1980) analysis of revenue-seeking: Legal directly unproductive competition for a share in the disbursement or transfer of tariff revenue results incidentally from the imposition of a tariff, thanks to protectionist lobbying, the tariff thus being an exogenously specified, unchanging distortion that triggers off the revenue seeking being analyzed.

We have already noted, in the context of revenue seeking, that the lobbying activity being modeled can be paradoxically beneficial despite being directly unproductive. This possibility can also arise in the premium-seeking case unless the quota is defined purely in quantitative terms (in which case the second-best possibility of welfare improvement through DUP-activity-induced changes in outputs will be prevented by the pure trade constraint from spilling over into the paradoxical outcome). General propositions concerning the contrast between DUP activities triggered by price and quantitative distortions have been developed by Anam (1982) and Bhagwati and Srinivasan (1982) and will be discussed below.

The analyses of illegal trade above also fit immediately into category I of DUP activities, for they assume that there is an initially distorting tariff and that the tariff-evading activity is undertaken with this tariff remaining in place through the analysis. In view of the theoretical analysis developed above, it follows immediately that these analyses ought to yield the conclusion that such tariff evasion may be welfare-improving (even allowing for the fact that the illegality carries an extra, negative dimension), as they in fact do. Recall that smuggling can be beneficial rather than immiserizing in the Bhagwati-Hansen model, for instance, even though it uses up real resources, since it confers production and consumption gains when the effective tariff is cut by the smuggling. The negative weight attached to the illegality may be considered to be out-weighted by the gain noted above, leaving the net evaluation beneficial. The paradox thus exists also in the context of illegal trade.

The foregoing examples of category I DUP activities—premium-seeking, revenue seeking, and tariff or QR evasion—assume that the specified distortion that triggers off such activity remains exogenous to the activity. However, it is easy to imagine phenomena where the distortion may be endogenous to such activity. Thus revenue seeking may affect adversely the protection implied by the tariff that triggered off the revenue seeking. Bhagwati and Srinivasan (1980) demonstrate in the context of their general-equilibrium analysis of revenue seeking that the revenue seeking may lead to a Metzler production paradox: The protectionist tariff plus revenue seeking may lead to a lower output of the importable than under free trade. If so, the protectionist lobby may well seek greater protection, thus influencing in principle the original tariff distortion and making the eventual tariff level endogenous to revenue seeking. Even this complexity would leave the phenomenon of revenue seeking squarely within category I of DUP activities, with its attendant paradox of possible welfare improvement from such activities.

Category II

In this class of DUP activities, the initial situation that triggers such activities is still distorted but the outcome turns out to be distortion-free. This category is easily analyzed in light of the foregoing analysis of category I. The overall welfare impact of a DUP activity starting from a distorted situation but ending in a distortion-free situation is the sum of two effects: the welfare impact of a withdrawal of resources into the directly unproductive activity, with the distortion held unchanged (category I type analysis), and the welfare impact of the elimination of the distortion in the final situation. The former effect is either positive or negative; the latter is necessarily positive. The net outcome may therefore be positive or negative. The welfare-improving paradox obtains again, and so does the opposite quasi-paradox that a distortion-destroying lobbying activity may lead to immiserization and hence be only a Pyrrhic victory.[7]

---

7. Remember the caveat concerning pure quantity distortions, discussed in Bhagwati and Srinivasan (1982) and Anam (1982).

Category III

The paradox of beneficial DUP activities disappears as soon as these activities are undertaken in the context of initially distortion-free situations. Category III relates to these when the final situation is the successful creation of a distorted situation. Two classic examples of such legal DUP activities are successful lobbying for the creation of a government-sanctioned monopoly and lobbying to get tariff protection. In each such case, the total social loss imposed by the DUP activity in question can be decomposed into the sum of two effects: the negative welfare effect of the withdrawal of resources into the directly unproductive activity if no distortion has resulted, and the negative welfare effect of the imposition of the distortion if the resources have already been diverted to the directly unproductive activity. Evidently there is no source of gain here and hence no room for the paradox of welfare improvement as with categories I and II.

Figure 34.7 illustrates the tariff-seeking case. The protectionist lobby, starting from free trade at P^*, manages in this small economy to spend resources to get a tariff enacted. With only the diversion of resources to lobbying taken into account, at free-trade prices production would shift from P^* to $\hat{P}_l^*$ on the shrunk-in production-possibility curve $A'B'$, representing a loss of RS measured in terms of good 1. The tariff resulting

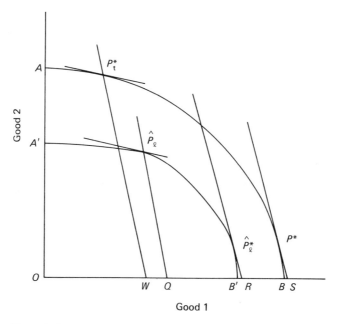

Figure 34.7

from the successful lobbying shifts the production point further to $\hat{P}_l$, which is the final, observed equilibrium under tariff seeking; this is tantamount to a further loss of QR in terms of good 1. These measures are conventional Hicksian equivalent-variational measures, as before, at world prices. Thus the overall loss QS, as explained, is decomposed into two constituent elements, each of which is unambiguously negative.

A minor paradox lurks here. In figure 34.7 suppose that the total social cost of tariff seeking, QS, were to be decomposed along an alternative route: the shift from P^* to P_t^* along AB, representing the social cost of the tariff but with the hypothetical assumption that the lobbying resources are not yet expended so that it is as if the tariff has come about exogenously, and then the shift from P_t^* to $\hat{P}_l$, from AB to $A'B'$, representing the further shift as a result of the diversion of resources to lobbying assuming the tariff distortion to be in place. In this case the first element of the decomposition will always yield a social loss (WS); however, as illustrated in figure 34.7 and reflecting the second-best considerations outlined in the analysis of categories I and II above, the second element may well yield a gain (WQ). Thus, although the overall impact of category III activities must be negative (QS), it would be incorrect to assert or imply that the social cost of a distortion imposed without the aid of directly unproductive activity must be less than that of the same distortion imposed because of such activity. For example, in figure 34.7 the shift from P_t^* to $\hat{P}_l$ need not always be a social cost, and in fact it is shown to be a social gain worth WQ.

These conclusions can be readily extended to examples of illegal activities in category III. An instance of this kind would be provided by tariff evasion or smuggling from an optimal, rather than a distortionary, tariff.

Category IV

The final category of DUP activities is provided by those activities that start with a distortion-free situation and wind up also with a distortion-free situation despite the resources expended. A simple, effective example of such an activity, provided by Findlay and Wellisz (1982) and suggested by Tullock (1967), is where tariff seeking by one lobby is offset by anti-tariff lobbying by another group, with the result that resources are used up in mutually deterring lobbying that does not affect free-trade policy for the small country in the end. Figure 34.7 would illustrate this case with a slight reinterpretation. There is evidently a shrinking in of the production-possibility set for goods 1 and 2 from AB to $A'B'$ as resources are diverted to the lobbying activities, and therewith a social loss of RS in terms of good 1 since $\hat{P}_l^*$ is now the actual, postlobbying equilibrium, characterized by continuing free trade. The diversion of resources from productive use when the first-best policy (of free trade in this small competitive economy) is in place throughout must obviously be immiserizing.[8] There is no room for paradoxes of any kind here.

Category IV then is the clearest case of DUP activities where the simple claims of the early analysts of such activities as to their negative impact can be sustained without the slightest qualification. But this is also clearly a very narrow subset of the entire range of activities that we must consider.

34.5   Price versus Quantity Distortions

We noted above that for DUP activities triggered by existing distortions (categories I and II) it was necessary to distinguish between price and quantity distortions. Bhagwati-Srinivasan-type revenue seeking is an instance of the former, and Krueger-type premium seeking is an example of the latter. The reason for this distinction is that the welfare-improving paradox will not arise if a (pure) quantity distortion is the only distortion in place. Hence, the scope of the paradox is reduced, though not eliminated.

Consider the revenue-seeking case in figure 34.8, which is similar to figure 34.3. Imagine that a tariff-seeking lobby has succeeded and a protective tariff has been put in place. Imagine next that the revenue that results from this (nonprohibitive) tariff attracts a revenue-seeking lobby. This revenue-seeking lobby therefore operates from an initially distorted, tariff-ridden equilibrium. A small country with given terms of trade $P_t C_t$ and a production-possibility curve AB is depicted. A tariff is imposed, making the importable good 2 more expensive domestically and leading to production at P_t at the point of tangency of the tariff-inclusive price ratio $P_t S$ with AB and to consumption at C_t. A DUP revenue-seeking activity generated by this tariff would lead to a shift in the production of goods from P_t to somewhere inside AB, and if this shift occurred to a point such as P_r in the shaded zone the revenue-seeking activity would paradoxically improve welfare, as at C_r^t.[9]

Now, does this paradoxical possibility, inherent in the second-best nature of the problem at hand, not arise equally if the tariff at P_t is replaced instead by an import quota? It would seem at first glance that it would, but this is not so: When a quantitative restriction on exports

8. An inference of illegal profit-seeking DUP activity in category IV would be that of theft, which utilizes real resources in attempts at both undertaking and evading it but without creating any distortion (Tullock 1967).

9. The shadow price of a factor at a tariff-distorted equilibrium such as P_t could be sufficiently negative to generate this outcome, as explained in chapter 37.

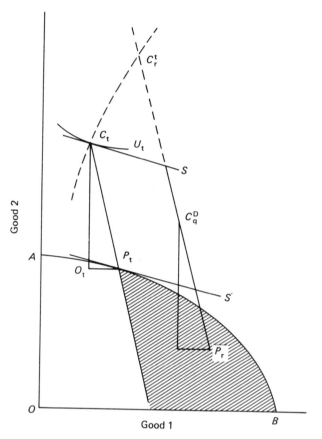

Figure 34.8

or imports is defined purely in quantity (rather than value) terms, the trade triangle is fixed for the binding quota as $C_t O_t P_t$, and no matter where P_t shifts within AB as a result of premium seeking, the attendant constrained-trade equilibrium must imply that the resulting consumption point cannot rise above $C_t S$ and hence cannot rise above U_t.

As long as imports are fixed quantitatively, premium-seeking has therefore to be immiserizing. The result holds equally for export and import quotas when the country is small. For a small country the result will hold if the quotas are defined in foreign values rather than in pure quantity. However, even for a small country, the critical constraint on import quantity may be relaxed (opening up the possibility of beneficial premium seeking) if an import quota is defined in domestic values. Indeed, as the implicit tariff falls, the same domestic-value constraint can accommodate an increasing quantity of imports. For a large country, however, the possibility of admitting the paradox of beneficial premium-seeking is enhanced. Although an import quota will close off this possibility, an export quota will not (unless one imposes the restriction that the foreign offer curve be elastic). Thus the same export level may be compatible with more than one import quantities, and the critical import-quantity constraint may not exclude the paradox of beneficial premium-seeking. Even if the import quota is fixed in foreign values, the variable terms of trade implied by the large-country assumption can relax the import constraint and open up the paradoxical possibility.

The above analysis of tariffs and trade quotas indicates that the presence of quotas, rather than *ad valorem* price distortions, may quite generally restrict the scope of paradoxical welfare improvement from premium-seeking. This is indeed a general result on price versus quantity distortions.

The critical question about the paradoxical possibility of welfare-improving DUP activity (which has zero output) is whether at least one shadow factor price (as defined in chapter 37) is negative, for that is a necessary condition for the net welfare impact of such activity to be positive. It can then be shown, as has been done by Anam (1982) and Bhagwati and Srinivasan (1982), that the following propositions hold:

PROPOSITION 1   Whenever the distortion that triggers seeking activity is the only distortion in the economy, and is a (pure) quantity constraint and remains a binding constraint in the presence of the seeking activity, the shadow price of a primary factor cannot be negative.

PROPOSITION 2   When the only distortion is instead an ad valorem price distortion, the shadow price of a primary factor may be negative (except when the distortion does not affect productive efficiency).

The essential argument underlying proposition 1 is that while the DUP activity takes place in a second-best distortionary situation, it fails to improve welfare because the quantity constraint "bottles up" the source of positive gain that might outweigh the loss implied by diversion of real resources to the DUP activity. This, on the other hand, does not happen when the distortion is instead of a price variety, proposition 2.

Recommended Readings

Anam, M. Distortion-triggered lobbying and welfare: A contribution to the theory of directly-unproductive profit-seeking activities. *Journal of International Economics* 13 (1982): 15–32.

Bhagwati, J. Distortions and immiserizing growth: A generalization. *Review of Economic Studies.* 1968, ch. 5.

Bhagwati, J., ed. *Illegal Transactions in International Trade: Theory and Policy*. Amsterdam: North-Holland, 1974.

Bhagwati, J. Lobbying and welfare. *Journal of Public Economics*. 1980, ch. 25. 14 (3), Dec. 1980: 355–63.

Bhagwati, J. Alternative theories of illegal trade: Economic consequences and statistical detection. *Weltwirtschaftliches Archiv* 117 (1981): 409–26.

Bhagwati, J. "Directly-unproductive profit-seeking (DUP) activities. *Journal of Political Economy* 90 (1982a): 988–1002.

Bhagwati, J. Shifting comparative advantage, Protectionist demands, and policy response. In *Import Competition and Response*, ed. by J. Bhagwati. Chicago: University of Chicago Press, 1982b.

Bhagwati, J., and B. Hansen. A theoretical analysis of smuggling. *Quarterly Journal of Economics* 87 (1973): 172–87.

Bhagwati, J., and T. N. Srinivasan. Smuggling and trade policy. *Journal of Public Economics* 2 (1973): 377–89.

Bhagwati, J., and T. N. Srinivasan. Revenue seeking: A generalization of the theory of tariffs. *Journal of Political Economy* 88 (1980): 1069–87.

Bhagwati, J. N., and T. N. Srinivasan. The welfare consequences of directly unproductive profit-seeking (DUP) lobbying activities: Price *versus* quantity distortions. *Journal of International Economics* 13 (1982): 33–44.

Brock, W. M., and S. Magee. The economics of special interest politics: The case of the tariff. *American Economic Review* 68 (1978): 246–50.

Falvey, R. A note on preferential and illegal trade under quantitative restrictions. *Quarterly Journal of Economics* 92 (1978): 175–78.

Feenstra, R., and J. Bhagwati. Tariff-seeking and the efficient tariff. In *Import Competition and Response*, ed. by J. Bhagwati, Chicago: University of Chicago Press, 1982.

Findlay, R., and S. Wellisz. Endogenous tariffs, the political economy of trade restrictions and welfare. In *Import Competition and Response*, ed. by J. Bhagwati. Chicago: University of Chicago Press, 1982.

Johnson, H. G. The possibility of income losses from increased efficiency or factor accumulation in the presence of tariffs. *Economic Journal* 77 (1967): 151–54.

Johnson, H. G. Notes on the economic theory of smuggling. *Malayan Economic Review* (1972). Reprinted in *Illegal Transactions in International Trade*, ed. by J. Bhagwati. Amsterdam: North-Holland, 1974.

Jones, R. W. A three-factor model in theory, trade and history. In *Trade, Balance of Payments, and Growth: Papers in International Economics in Honor of Charles P. Kindleberger*, ed. by J. N. Bhagwati et al. Amsterdam: North-Holland, 1971.

Krueger, A. O. The political economy of the rent-seeking society. *American Economics Review* 69 (1974): 291–303.

Pitt. M. Smuggling and price disparity. *Journal of International Economics* 11 (1981): 447–58.

Martin, L., and A. Panagariya. Smuggling, trade and price disparity: A crime theoretic approach. *Journal of International Economics* (1984): 201–17.

Ray, A. Smuggling, import objectives, and optimum tax structure. *Quarterly Journal of Economics* 92 (1978): 509–14.

Sapir, A. Foreign competition, immigration and structural adjustment. *Journal of International Economics* 14 (1983): 381–94.

Sheikh, M. Smuggling, production and welfare. *Journal of International Economics* 4 (1974): 355–64.

Tullock, G. The welfare cost of tariffs, monopolies, and theft. *Western Economic Journal* 5 (1967): 224–32.

In recent years the failure of import-substitution policies has led many developing countries to introduce trade reforms aimed at creating an outward oriented policy regime. Trade reforms raise interesting analytic questions in normative as well as positive economics. Below we consider each type of question in turn.

35.1 Normative Analysis

There are two broad questions addressed in the literature: Assuming that policy changes can be made only in a "piecemeal" fashion, how can we sequence them such that welfare improves every step of the way? And what is the final structure of trade policy at which the reform should aim? The theory of second best can be brought to bear on both questions.

Piecemeal Trade Reform

The major task of trade reform is to liberalize tariffs and quotas. We first deal with these instruments separately and then jointly. The analysis of piecemeal tariff reform, involving only partial liberalization of tariffs, goes back to Meade (1955).[1] Subsequent contributions to this literature include Lipsey and Lancaster (1956), Bertrand and Vanek (1971), Hatta (1977), Fukushima (1979), Lopez and Panagariya (1992), and Panagariya (1992). The problem of piecemeal quota reform, involving a product-by-product liberalization of quotas, has been considered by Corden and Falvey (1985). Finally piecemeal trade reform in the simultaneous presence of tariffs and quotas has been addressed by Falvey (1988) and extended by Anderson and Neary (1992).

Before we proceed, it is useful to spell out a general result, due to Krishna and Panagariya (1997), that distinguishes the problems involving tariff distortions from quota distortions in the present case. According to this result, if we take an optimization problem and restrict the level of a subset of choice variables directly (e.g., import quotas) or through a set of convex constraint sets (e.g., noneconomic objectives) not exceeding the number of restricted variables and reoptimize, the first-order conditions with respect to the remaining choice variables will be identical to those obtained in the initial problem. What this result says is that if a subset of variables is restricted directly, there is no need to create distortions with

---

1. An important fact that has been neglected by much of the subsequent literature is that Meade almost always analyzed the welfare effects of changes in trade policies from a global perspective. By contrast, the subsequent literature looks at the issue from a national welfare perspective. One contribution that looks at the problem precisely in the way Meade did is Hatta and Fukushima (1979).

respect to other variables. Since in most optimization problems in economics choice variables are quantities, if certain sectors are subject to production, consumption, or trade quotas, optimality requires that no distortions be introduced elsewhere. This is in sharp contrast to price distortions that typically violate the first-order conditions of the original optimization problem and open the door to intervention in other sectors as well.

A closely related result, also due to Krishna and Panagariya (1997), is that comparative statics results that are valid in the absence of direct restrictions on a subset of choice variables (e.g., import quotas) will generally be valid in the presence of such restrictions. Thus, as we will see below, theorems of tariff reform derived when tariffs are the only distortion in the system remain valid if the imports of one or more of the other goods are subject to binding quotas.

Tariff Reform

Following the general practice in the literature, we assume a small-country context. For many developing countries, this is not an unreasonable assumption. We further assume that the country in question has already removed all quotas and the only distortion is a set of tariffs. At this stage we do not take into account the reason for the existence of tariffs. We begin by demonstrating the following two results which have been most influential in recent trade reforms in many developing countries:

PROPOSITION 1   Assuming that tariffs constitute the only distortion in the economy and that the excess demand for the good with the highest tariff exhibits net substitutability with excess demands for all other goods, a lowering of the highest tariff to the next highest one is welfare-improving.

PROPOSITION 2   Under the same assumptions, suppose that the existing tariffs cannot be changed and that a subset of goods is freely traded. Then the introduction of and an increase in the tariff on an initially unrestricted good improves welfare up to a point. This point is reached before the new tariff rate reaches the highest preexisting tariff rate.

Proposition 1 appears in different forms in Meade (1955), Bertrand and Vanek (1971), and Hatta (1977) and proposition 2 in Lipsey and Lancaster (1956). Fukushima (1979) generalizes proposition 1 in the presence of non-traded goods, while Lopez and Panagariya (1992) and Panagariya (1992) discuss limitations imposed on these results by the presence of imported inputs not produced at home.

Although propositions 1 and 2 are valid in a n-good model, they can be analyzed conveniently in a model with two importables and one exportable. Denoting the goods by 1, 2, and 3, let 1 and 2 be importables and 3 exportable. Choose the units of each good such that its world price equals unity. Denoting by t_i the ad valorem tariff on good i $(i = 1, 2)$, the economy's budget constraint can be written

$$Z(1 + t_1, 1 + t_2, 1; U) = t_1 Z_1(\cdot) + t_2 Z_2(\cdot). \tag{35.1}$$

Recall that $Z(\cdot)$ is the excess expenditure function and represents the difference between the expenditure and revenue functions (see chapter 9). The $Z_i(\cdot)$ are compensated import-demand functions. Since tariff rates are exogenous, equation (35.1) can be solved for U. Differentiating (35.1) totally, we obtain

$$Z_U \, dU = t_1 \, dZ_1 + t_2 \, dZ_2. \tag{35.2}$$

From this equation we can deduce that a tariff reform that increases tariff revenue in terms of the world prices at the intial tariff rates is welfare-improving. The challenge is to come up with a simple rule that satisfies this condition. For this let us change t_1, holding t_2 constant. We can now rewrite (35.2) as

$$(Z_U - t_1 Z_{1U} - t_2 Z_{2U}) \, dU = (t_1 Z_{11} + t_2 Z_{21}) \, dt_1. \tag{35.3}$$

Assuming that all goods are normal, linear homogeneity of Z_U in all prices implies that the term in parentheses on the left side is positive.[2] Therefore the effect of the change in t_1 on welfare is determined by the term in parentheses on the right side. Due to concavity of $Z(\cdot)$, Z_{11} is negative. Z_{21} is negative or positive as import (or excess) demands for 1 and 2 exhibit net complementarity or substitutability. It follows that if import demands exhibit net complementarity, a reduction in t_1 is necessarily welfare-improving. Intuitively, given complementarity, a reduction in t_1 expands the imports of good 1 as well as good 2.[3] We reduce the impact of distortion in both sectors. This result generalizes to many imports in the sense that if the sector that is liberalized exhibits complementarity with all other imports, welfare necessarily rises.

The more interesting and realistic is the case when import demands exhibit substitutability. In this case imports of good 2 decline with a reduction in t_1, making the impact of distortion in sector 2 worse. To determine the effect on welfare, we must manipulate (35.3) further. Remembering that Z_1 is homogeneous of degree 0 in all prices, we have

2. We can also establish the positive sign of this term by recourse to stability. See Hatta (1977).

3. Strictly speaking, under net complementarity, this statement applies at a constant utility. But given stability, it also holds true in equilibrium, *ex post*.

$$(1 + t_1)Z_{11} + (1 + t_2)Z_{12} + Z_{13} = 0. \tag{35.4}$$

Solving this equation for Z_{11} and substituting into (35.3), we can obtain

$$(Z_U - t_1 Z_{1U} - t_2 Z_{2U}) \, dU = -\frac{1}{1 + t_1} [Z_{12}(t_1 - t_2) + t_1 Z_{13}] \, dt_1. \tag{35.5}$$

Given net substitutability, Z_{12} and Z_{13} are both positive. Therefore a sufficient condition for a reduction in t_1 to raise welfare is $t_1 \geq t_2$. This establishes proposition 1 above. Intuitively net substitutability between excess demands for 1 and 3 ensures that at constant utility the reduction in t_1 increases exports. Given the trade-balance condition, this means that the reduction in imports of good 2 is less than the expansion of imports of good 1. Because sector 1 is also the more distorted sector ($t_1 > t_2$), there is a net gain in efficiency.

This result, though derived in a model with two imports, generalizes to many imports in the following sense: Suppose that the net substitutability condition is satisfied. Then a reduction in the highest tariff rate to the next highest one is welfare-improving. Once this is achieved, a reduction in these two tariff rates to the next highest one is welfare-improving, and so on. This approach to tariff reform is sometimes referred to as the *concertina* approach.

On the face of it, the substitutability condition seems a relatively weak restriction. It turns out, however, that in the presence of imported inputs not produced at home, the condition necessarily breaks down. This point, made by Lopez and Panagariya (1992), can be demonstrated conveniently for the case where the imported input is used in a fixed proportion to the output.[4]

Let us choose the units of the input such that its world price equals unity. Denote by a_i the imported input-output coefficient in sector i and by τ the tariff rate on the input. Then, letting $v_i \equiv (1 + t_i) - a_i(1 + \tau)$, the revenue function can be written $R(v_1, v_2, v_3)$ where $R(\cdot)$ has all the standard properties.[5] $R_i(\cdot) \equiv \partial R / \partial v_i$ gives the output of good i and $-R_\tau(\cdot) \equiv -\partial R / \partial \tau = \Sigma_i a_i R_i$ ($i = 1, 2, 3$) gives the demand for the imported input. Since the R_i are all homogeneous of degree 0 in the v_i, $R_\tau(\cdot)$ is also homogeneous of degree 0 in the latter. We immediately have

---

4. The point remains valid, however, for a variable coefficients technology.

5. The revenue function is derived by maximizing $\Sigma_i[(1 + t_i)F_i(K_i, L_i) - (1 + \tau)a_i F_i(K_i, L_i)]$ subject to factor endowments constraint. Here the $F_i(\cdot)$ represent the value added in sector i which is combined in fixed proportions with the imported input to produce the final product. To ensure that the revenue function is strictly convex, we must assume at least as many primary factors of production as goods.

$$v_1 R_{\tau 1} + v_2 R_{\tau 2} + v_3 R_{\tau 3} = 0. \tag{35.6}$$

From (35.6) it follows that at least one $R_{\tau i}$ must be positive. Since τ does not enter the expenditure function, $Z_{\tau i} = -R_{\tau i}$; net complementarity between the imported input and at least one i necessarily obtains.

The significance of this complementarity can be explained intuitively with the help of two simple examples. First, suppose that $t_1 > t_2$ and that the imported input is used sufficiently intensively in good 1 relative to good 2 that the effective rate of protection to the former is lower than to the latter.[6] A reduction in t_1 allocates resources away from sector 1 and into sector 2 (and 3). Thus the most protected sector expands, and efficiency in production declines. Unless this loss is more than offset by the gain from increased efficiency in consumption, welfare declines.

Second, suppose that the highest tariff applies to the imported input, the effective rates protection in sectors 1 and 2 are positive, and the input is not used in the exportable. In this case a reduction in the highest tariff rate, τ, increases the effective protection to sectors 1 and 2. Moreover, since the imported input does not enter consumption, the reduction in τ confers no gains in consumption. Welfare declines unambiguously.

Two important points may be noted. First, it is not the presence of complementarity per se which makes a tariff reduction less likely to be gainful. Look back at equation (35.3) which was derived for a model without imported inputs. There we saw that if the liberalized good exhibits complementarity with all other imports, the tariff reduction improves welfare independently of whether or not this tariff is the highest. This result can be shown to be valid in the presence of imported inputs as well. It is only when complementarity between some products arises in the presence of substitutability between other products that our welfare conclusions run into a difficulty. Second, the substitutability condition in proposition 1 is only a sufficiency condition. It is quite easy to construct examples where a reduction in the highest tariff improves welfare despite the presence of complementarity between two or more importables. Unfortunately, what we cannot do is to state a set of simple sufficiency conditions that can be readily checked in a given situation to ensure that the *concertina* approach will yield an improvement in welfare every step of the way.

Next let us consider proposition 2. Suppose now that $t_1 = 0 < t_2$ initially. If net substitutability holds, according to equation (35.5), the introduction of a small tariff on good 1 is necessarily welfare-improving.

---

6. The effective rate of protection to sector i is $[v_i - (1 - a_i)]/(1 - a_i) = (t_i - \tau a_i)/(1 - a_i)$. See chapter 15.

Intuitively the infinitesimally small tariff does not cause an efficiency loss in sector 1. But increasing the imports of good 2, which is subject to a positive and finite tariff, increases efficiency in that sector.

Holding t_2 fixed, the optimum tariff on good 1 is obtained by setting $dU = 0$ in (35.5). We have

$$t_1^* = \frac{Z_{12}}{Z_{12} + Z_{13}} t_2. \tag{35.7}$$

Given substitutability, Z_{12} and Z_{13} are both positive. Therefore the optimum value of t_1 is less than the given value of t_2. By considering a model with three or more importables, it can be shown that given net substitutability and holding other tariffs constant, the optimum tariff on a good is below the highest tariff rate in the economy. This establishes the second part of proposition 2.

Because proposition 2 also relies on substitutability, the presence of imported inputs can lead to its breakdown. The simplest example arises when the freely traded good in the initial equilibrium is an input used in the exportable. The introduction of a tariff on this input is likely to lower welfare by reallocating resources further away from the exportable and into already protected import-competing goods. This type of problem is common enough that frequently inputs used in exportables are given special treatment through a duty exemption or duty drawback. As Panagariya (1992) shows, when an imported input is used in importables as well as exportables and the tariff on it is initially low or zero, there is a strong presumption that an increase in the tariff complemented by a duty drawback improves welfare.

When valid, propositions 1 and 2 together can serve as useful practical tools of reform in the presence of a revenue constraint. Proposition 1 says that a reduction in the highest tariff(s) is welfare-improving, while proposition 2 (implicitly) says that the revenue lost from such tariff reduction can be recovered by introducing tariffs on initially freely traded or low-tariff goods. Panagariya's (1992) analysis shows that if initially freely traded or low-tariff goods are inputs, increased tariffs on them must be complemented by a duty drawback or duty exemption.

For completeness, we note the following additional result on piecemeal reform due to Bruno (1972):

PROPOSITION 3   Regardless of whether import demands exhibit substitutability or complementarity, a proportionate reduction in all existing *ad valorem* tariff rates is welfare-improving.

Since, in practice, governments find it difficult to change all tariff rates at once, this result has not played a significant role in actual trade reforms.

To prove the result within our three-good model, differentiate (35.1) totally.

$$(Z_U - t_1 Z_{1U} - t_2 Z_{2U}) \, dU$$

$$= (t_1 Z_{11} + t_2 Z_{21}) \, dt_1 + (t_1 Z_{21} + t_2 Z_{22}) \, dt_2. \tag{35.8}$$

Remembering that both tariff rates change by a constant proportion, we set $dt_i = t_i \, d\lambda$. Equation (35.8) is transformed into

$$(Z_U - t_1 Z_{1U} - t_2 Z_{2U}) \frac{dU}{d\lambda} = (t_1^2 Z_{11} + 2 t_1 t_2 Z_{21} + t_2^2 Z_{22})$$

$$= [t_1 \ \ t_2] \begin{bmatrix} Z_{11} & Z_{12} \\ Z_{21} & Z_{22} \end{bmatrix} \begin{bmatrix} t_1 \\ t_2 \end{bmatrix} < 0. \tag{35.8'}$$

The sign of the right-hand side follows from the fact that the 2×2 matrix containing Z_{ij}'s $(i, j = 1, 2)$ is negative definite.[7] Thus a proportionate *reduction* in all tariff rates is shown to be welfare-improving.

Quota Reform

Let us now turn to quota reform. We begin by assuming that the only restriction in place is a set of import quotas. The following result, due to Corden and Falvey, is of interest:

PROPOSITION 4   Under the standard assumptions including constant returns and perfect competition, if import quotas are the only distortion in a small open economy, liberalization or removal of a quota is welfare-improving.

Once again, though the result is valid in an n-good model, we restrict ourselves to the three-good model. Assume now that goods 1 and 2 are subject to import quotas. Quota licenses are auctioned competitively and quota rents redistributed to consumers in a lump-sum fashion. The economy's budget constraint can be written

$$Z(1 + \varepsilon_1, 1 + \varepsilon_2, 1; U) = \varepsilon_1 Z_1(\cdot) + \varepsilon_2 Z_2(\cdot), \tag{35.9}$$

where ε_i is the *ad valorem* quota rent on good i. Because goods 1 and 2 are subject to import quotas, we also have

$$Z_i(\cdot) = \bar{Z}_i, \qquad i = 1, 2, \tag{35.10}$$

---

7. The complete substitution matrix associated with $Z(\cdot)$, $A \equiv \{Z_{ij}\}$ $(i, j = 1, 2, 3)$, is negative semidefinite. Matrices obtained by deleting the rows and cloumnns associated with elements along the diagonal of A are also negative semidefinite. Because the 2×2 matrix in (35.8') is such a matrix with full rank, it is negative definite.

where $\bar{Z}_i$ is the import quota on good i. We now have three equations in three variables, U, ε_1, and ε_2. We can use this system to analyze the welfare effect of an expansion of the quota on good 1, holding the quota on good 2 unchanged. Substituting from (35.10) into (35.9) and differentiating the resulting equation with respect to $\bar{Z}_i$, we have

$$Z_U \, dU = \varepsilon_1 \, d\bar{Z}_1. \tag{35.11}$$

That is, as long as the quota rent is positive in the initial equilibrium, welfare improves with the relaxation of the quota on one good even if the quotas on other goods are left intact. Because it is reasonable to assume that the quota rent will be positive as long as the quota is binding, we can conclude that a complete removal of quota on one good, holding other quotas fixed, will also be welfare-improving. This result remains valid in the presence of other imports not subject to distortions. The intuitive reason is that the liberalization of quota in one sector leaves the quantities imported in other quota-distorted sectors unchanged. Therefore the economy moves unambiguously closer to the free-trade equilibrium.

For policy reform this result is potentially very useful in that it says that regardless of sequencing, a removal of quotas is welfare-enhancing. Unfortunately however, the result is not robust. Shortly we will see that if some goods are subject to tariffs, the result breaks down. Presently we consider the possibility that a constant proportion of the quota rent is used up in rent-seeking activities.

Denote by α_i $(1 > \alpha_i > 0)$ the proportion of the quota rent lost in DUP activities. The right-hand side of (35.9) is now modified such that ε_i is replaced by $(1 - \alpha_i)\varepsilon_i$. Making this change and differentiating with respect to the quota in sector 1, we obtain

$$Z_U \, dU = (1 - \alpha_1)\varepsilon_1 \, d\bar{Z}_1 - \alpha_1 \, d\varepsilon_1 - \alpha_2 \bar{Z}_2 \, d\varepsilon_2. \tag{35.12}$$

An unambiguous improvement in welfare can now obtain if the liberalization of quota lowers the quota rent on all goods subject to import quotas. Without providing a proof, we note that this condition is not automatically fulfilled. In equation (35.12) sufficient but not necessary conditions for ε_2 to rise are that the excess demands for goods 1 and 2 be normal and that they exhibit net complementarity with each other.[8] Intuitively complementarity implies that liberalization of the quota on good 1 increases the demand for imports of good 2. Given no change in the quota for good 2, this raises the rent on the latter.

8. In this chapter, the excess demand for good i is defined as normal if $Z_{iU}(\cdot)$ is positive. Excess demands for goods i and j are defined to exhibit net substitutability or complementarity as $Z_{ij}(\cdot)$ is positive or negative. If the excess demands are independent, $Z_{ij}(\cdot) = 0$.

A Simultaneous Existence of Tariffs and Quotas

When tariffs and quotas exist simultaneously, the results on tariff reform survive provided that we assume quota-restricted goods to be net substitutes for all other goods. (Here nontraded goods can be included as goods subject to a prohibitive quota.) Thus, assuming that quota-ridden goods and the good with the highest tariff are net substitutes with respect to all other goods, as in proposition 1, a reduction in the highest tariff to the next highest one is welfare-improving. Proposition 2 generalizes analogously.

The results on quota reform fail to generalize when some goods are subject to tariffs. A sector-by-sector removal of quotas, regardless of sequencing, is no longer necessarily welfare-improving. Indeed, in the spirit of proposition 2, if some goods are traded freely in the initial equilibrium and are net substitutes with respect to all other goods, a small tightening of their imports through the introduction of quotas is welfare-improving. Starting with an initial quota-ridden equilibrium, the most we can show is that assuming all commodities to be net substitutes, a loosening of a quota with implict tariff higher than the highest explicit tariff is welfare-improving (Falvey 1988).

Optimal Tariff Structure and the Uniform Tariff Issue

In dealing with the optimal structure of trade policy, we will focus exclusively on tariffs. This is in the spirit of actual reforms that have generally involved a replacement of existing trade policies including quantitative restrictions by an appropriate set of tariffs.

Assuming net substitutability, proposition 1 says that a reduction in the top tariffs is welfare-improving, while proposition 2 says that the introduction of and an increase in the lowest tariffs on freely traded goods is also welfare-improving. These results together have led some policy economists to conclude that the optimal structure of tariffs is uniform. This is surely one way to explain why international institutions such as the World Bank and the IMF have frequently recommended to developing countries that they make their tariffs uniform across commodities.[9]

That a uniform positive tariff cannot be optimal under the assumed setting should be obvious. Given no distortions, the optimal trade policy for a small open economy is free trade. If tariffs are to be positive, there must be an exogenous reason for them. There are at least three possibilities. First, there may be preexisting distortions in the economy that cannot be removed. Positive tariffs may serve to soften the effects of

9. See Thomas, Nash, and Associates (1991).

those distortions. Second, in the spirit of Bhagwati and Srinivasan (1969), governments may have exogenous or noneconomic objectives such as self-sufficiency, protection, or revenue. Finally, political factors such as lobbying by firms may give rise to positive tariffs. In the following, we successively discuss the optimum tariff structure when each of these factor necessitates recourse to tariffs. Because tariff uniformity has played an important role in the trade reform during recent years, our discussion is organized around this policy.

The optimal structure in the presence of distortions depends on the nature of such distortions. Without presenting a full taxonomy, we offer a simple example in which the structure of optimal tariffs is nonuniform. Thus assume that there are two importables and one exportable. Let one good be subject to a tariff that cannot be changed. Then, as stated in proposition 1, under net substitutability the optimum tariff on the second importable is lower than the preexisting tariff. The tariff structure is nonuniform.

Noneconomic Objectives and the Optimum Tariff Structure

Johnson (1964) was perhaps the first to consider systematically the problem of optimum tariff structure in the presence of self-sufficiency and protection objectives. Ramaswami and Srinivasan (1968) analyzed the problem under a revenue constraint, paying special attention to imported inputs. A full-blown analysis of revenue-constrained optimum tariffs was presented by Dasgupta and Stiglitz (1974).[10] We begin with a discussion of the self-sufficiency constraint.

Consider a small open economy interested in holding the value of imports, measured at world prices, at a level below the free-trade level. Continuing with the two-import, one-export case for simplicity, we can formulate the problem formally as follows:

$$\max_{t_1, t_2} \psi = U + \lambda[t_1 Z_1(\cdot) + t_2 Z_2(\cdot) - Z(1 + t_1, 1 + t_2, 1; U)]$$
$$+ \mu[Z_1(\cdot) + Z_2(\cdot) - \overline{M}].$$

The first constraint in this problem is the economy's budget constraint, and the second one is the self-sufficiency objective. $\overline{M}$ denotes the desired value of imports. As before, the world prices are set equal to 1, which implies that the value of imports at world prices is the same as the quantity. Maximizing with respect to t_1 and t_2, respectively, and dividing the resulting conditions, we obtain

10. For further references and a survey of the literature, see Panagariya (1994).

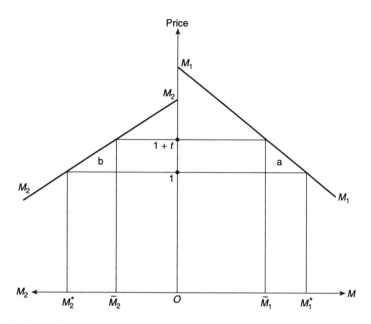

Figure 35.1

$$\frac{t_1 Z_{11} + t_2 Z_{21}}{t_1 Z_{12} + t_2 Z_{22}} = \frac{Z_{11} + Z_{21}}{Z_{12} + Z_{22}}. \tag{35.13}$$

Equation (35.13) is necessarily satisfied if $t_1 = t_2$. Optimality implies a uniform tariff across commodities. The intuition behind this result can be explained with the help of a simple partial equilibrium graph shown in figure 35.1. In the right-side panel we draw the demand for imports of good 1, and in the left-side panel the demand for imports of good 2. Imports of good 2 are measured to the left from the origin. Because the world prices are set equal to 1, the horizontal axis measures the quantity as well as the value of imports at world prices. Under free trade the value of imports equals $M_2^* M_1^*$.

Suppose now that the country wishes to restrict the value of imports at $\bar{M}_2 \bar{M}_1$. This can be accomplished with the help of a uniform tariff at rate t. The accompanying welfare cost of this restriction is area $a + b$. It is easy to verify that an alternative tariff structure which preserves the value of imports at $\bar{M}_2 \bar{M}_1$ leads to a higher welfare cost. Intuitively the uniform tariff equalizes the marginal cost of restricting imports across commodities, and any deviation from it must raise the excess burden of meeting the objective.

Next suppose that the country wishes to raise the value of output of import-competing industries, at world prices, beyond its free-trade level.

In the spirit of Bhagwati (1971), the best instrument to achieve this
objective is an output subsidy. It can be shown that if the subsidy can be
financed costlessly, its optimal structure is uniform across sectors. The
proof is similar to that in the previous case, and intuition follows closely
figure 35.1 with supply curves replacing the import-demand curves.

However, if tariffs are used to achieve the protection objective, their
optimal structure is nonuniform. To show this, take once again the case
of two importables. To introduce the protection objective, we must work
explicitly with the revenue function. The problem we solve is as follows:

$$\max_{t_1, t_2} \psi = U + \lambda[t_1 Z_1(\cdot) + t_2 Z_2(\cdot) - Z(1 + t_1, 1 + t_2, 1; U)]$$
$$+ \mu[R_1(1 + t_1, 1 + t_2, 1) + R_2(\cdot) - \bar{Q}],$$

where $\bar{Q}$ is the desired value of output at world prices. The condition
obtained by solving this problem is similar to (35.13) except that on the
right-hand side, derivatives of Z are replaced by derivatives of R:

$$\frac{t_1 Z_{11} + t_2 Z_{21}}{t_1 Z_{12} + t_2 Z_{22}} = \frac{R_{11} + R_{21}}{R_{12} + R_{22}}. \tag{35.14}$$

From (35.14) we can no longer obtain $t_1 = t_2$ as the solution to our
problem except when goods 1 and 2 are not consumed domestically. In
the latter case the tariff coincides with an output subsidy so that a uniform tariff works like a uniform output subsidy.

To gain more insight into (35.14), consider further the special case
when goods 1 and 2 are independent, $E_{12} = R_{12} = Z_{12} = 0$. Equation
(35.14) yields

$$\frac{t_1}{t_2} = \frac{Z_{22}}{Z_{11}} \frac{R_{11}}{R_{22}}. \tag{35.14'}$$

Ceteris paribus, the higher the output response (not elasticity), the larger
is the tariff, and the higher the import response, the lower is the tariff.
This is intuitively plausible since the high output response implies that a
small increase in tariff yields a large gain on the protection objective.
Similarly, holding the output response constant, a large import response
means that the harmful consumption effect of an increase in the tariff is
large.

Finally consider the revenue objective. Because many developing countries rely heavily on trade taxes for tax revenues, this objective is of
immense practical importance. The maximization problem is written

$$\max_{t_1, t_2} \psi = U + \lambda[t_1 Z_1(\cdot) + t_2 Z_2(\cdot) - Z(1 + t_1, 1 + t_2, 1; U)]$$
$$+ \mu[t_1 Z_1(\cdot) + t_2 Z_2(\cdot) - \bar{T}],$$

where $\bar{T}$ is the desired tariff revenue. As before, maximizing with respect to the two tariff rates and dividing, we obtain

$$\frac{t_1 Z_{11} + t_2 Z_{21}}{t_1 Z_{12} + t_2 Z_{22}} = \frac{Z_1 + t_1 Z_{11} + t_2 Z_{21}}{Z_2 + t_1 Z_{12} + t_2 Z_{22}}. \tag{35.15}$$

Once again, the relationship between t_1 and t_2 is complex. More insight into (35.15) can be obtained by considering the special case where the two imports demands are independent, $Z_{12} = 0$. Letting $\tau_i \equiv t_i/(1 + t_i)$ $(i = 1, 2)$, we can show that

$$\frac{\tau_1}{\tau_2} = \frac{(1 + t_2) Z_{22}/Z_2}{(1 + t_1) Z_{11}/Z_1} \equiv \frac{\tilde{\eta}_{22}}{\tilde{\eta}_{11}}. \tag{35.15'}$$

That is, optimum tariff rates are inversely proportional to their compensated import demand elasticities. This is equivalent to the usual inverse elasticity, or Ramsey rule, encountered frequently in the public economics literature. To maximize revenue, we must tax goods with low compensated import demand elasticities at a high rate, and vice versa. The reason is that when import demand is inelastic, a tariff on it leads to a relatively small movement from its free trade level. By contrast, when the elasticity is large, the deviation from the free-trade value of imports is large. This can be shown using a construction similar to that in figure 35.1.

In the general case where import demands are not independent, it can be shown that imports that exhibit complementarity with exports should be taxed more heavily. Ideally we minimize distortion by taxing all imports, including the exportable at a uniform rate. But, since imports of the exportable are negative, under balanced trade such a uniform tariff yields no revenue. We must leave the exportable out of the tax base. An indirect way to tax the exportable, however, is to tax more heavily imports that exhibit complementarity with it. This is akin to the standard tax problem in the labor-leisure model with the exportable replacing leisure. Recall that in the tax problem we are unable to tax leisure directly, and optimality requires that we tax more heavily the consumption of goods that exhibit complementarity with leisure.

The analysis up to this point does not support the case for uniform tariffs. The only objective for which uniform tariffs are optimal is self-sufficiency. For countries reforming their trade regimes, this is rarely an important objective. This means that the case for tariff uniformity must be made on *ad hoc* criteria. For instance, one could argue that it is desirable to have transparency in the tariff structure and that transparency requires a single tariff rate. Alternatively, it could be argued that various elasticities required to calculate optimum tariffs may simply not be available and the deviations from the optimum due to bad information may be worse than those resulting from a uniform tariff. Finally, one could argue that uniform tariffs help deter smuggling.

Each of these reasons can justify at most a limited number of tariff rates but not complete uniformity. Thus transparency can be achieved as long as the number of tariff rates is small though not necessarily one. As for the information on elasticities, even if it is limited, it can be better exploited with a few tariff rates than just one. Finally, there is no evidence that the volume of smuggling is less with one tariff rate than a larger but small number of tariff rates. Nor is less smuggling necessarily welfare-superior to more smuggling.

Politics of Tariffs and the Uniform Tariff Rule

Tariffs may also exist because of lobbying pressures. Taking this to be the case, we can once again ask whether the adoption of a uniform tariff rule can lead to a superior outcome than obtained in its absence. Panagariya and Rodrik (1993) analyze this problem systematically and consider three arguments that can make uniform tariffs potentially superior to a variegated tariff structure. First, a precommitment to a uniform tariff rule (UTR) means that the tariff granted to one sector becomes available to all other sectors. This introduces a free-rider problem for those choosing to lobby and restricts the level of lobbying. Second, if there are imported inputs used in final importables, a tariff granted on the latter becomes automatically applicable to the former under the UTR. This, once again, reduces the incentive for lobbying. Finally, if a future government is expected to protect certain import-competing sectors, a UTR may restrain it by requiring that all import-competing sectors be protected equally. In the following, we look at the first of these models in detail.

Suppose that there are $n + 1$ sectors with the first n being importables and the last one exportable. All import-competing sectors use a sector-specific factor denoted K_i and labor. The exportable uses only labor. By appropriate choice of units, all world prices are set equal to 1. Domestic prices of import competing goods are denoted $1 + t_i$, where t_i is determined endogenously through lobbying. We represent the restricted profit function in ith import-competing sector by[11]

$$\pi^i = \pi^i(1 + t_i, w), \tag{35.16}$$

11. The profit function is obtained by maximizing $(1 + t_i)F_i(K_i, L_i) - wL_i$ with respect to L_i. Here $F_i(\cdot)$ is the production function with usual properties, w the wage rate, and K_i and L_i, respectively, sector-specific capital and labor in sector i.

where, by the envelope theorem, the partial derivatives of π^i with respect to the two arguments, respectively, have the following properties:

$$\pi_1^i(1 + t_i, w) = Q_i, \tag{35.17a}$$

$$\pi_w^i(1 + t_i, w) = -L_i. \tag{35.17b}$$

Because the exportable uses only labor, by choosing the units of labor appropriately, we can set $w = 1$. This feature simplifies the model considerably. Under a nonuniform tariff regime (NTR), the tariff is determined by the lobbying function

$$\text{NTR:} \quad t_i = g(l_i), \quad g(0) = 0, \quad g'(\cdot) > 0, \quad g''(\cdot) < 0, \quad i = 1, \dots, n, \tag{35.18}$$

where l_i is the labor used in lobbying by sector i. There are diminishing returns to lobbying. Function $g(\cdot)$ is the same across sectors, implying that all sectors have "equal access" to protection. This assumption neutralizes the differences in tariff rates that may arise solely because of different lobbying functions.

The level of lobbying is chosen to maximize the return on capital net of lobbying costs, $\pi^i(1 + g(l_i), w) - wl_i$. The relevant first-order condition is

$$g'(l_i)\pi_1^i(\cdot) = w. \tag{35.19}$$

The system (35.17)–(35.19) represents $4n$ equations in $4n$ variables: Q_i, L_i, l_i, and t_i. Solving and substituting the equilibrium values of L_i and l_i into the full-employment condition (not shown), we obtain the quantity of labor employed in the exportable as a residual. Putting the latter into the production function, we can determine the output of the exportable. Thus all variables are determined.

Now suppose that the government adopts a uniform tariff rule such that the level of the tariff is endogenous but whatever tariff is granted to one sector is also granted to all sectors. The lobbying function is now written

$$\text{UTR:} \quad t = h(\Sigma_i l_i) = h(l), \quad h(0) = 0, \quad h'(\cdot) > 0, \quad h''(\cdot) < 0, \tag{35.20}$$

where l is the total quantity of labor employed in lobbying by all sectors. To preserve neutrality in lobbying technology, $g(\cdot)$ and $h(\cdot)$ are assumed to be related as follows:

$$h(l) = g\left(\frac{l}{n}\right), \quad h'(l) < g'(l). \tag{35.21}$$

The first restriction says that l/n workers employed in sector i generate the same level of protection under NTR as l workers employed economy-wide under UTR. Put differently, if every sector employes m workers in lobbying, the level of protection is the same under NTR and UTR. The second restriction in (35.21) says that for equal quantity of labor, the marginal product of lobbying is higher under NTR. This restriction is needed to sign some of the comparative statics.

Once again each sector chooses the level of lobbying to maximize the return to capital net of lobbying cost, given the lobbying function in (35.20). For reasons that will become clear shortly, we must now allow for $l_i = 0$ as a possible solution and write the first-order conditions as

$$h'(l)\pi_1^i(1 + h(l^U), w) - w \leq 0,$$
$$l_i[h'(l^U)\pi_1^i(1 + h(l^U), w)) - w] = 0,$$

(35.22)

where recall that l^U is the economywide level of lobbying. The first term in the inequality in (35.22) is the marginal benefit from lobbying and second term, w, the marginal cost. Given the UTR, the marginal benefit depends not on the level of lobbying *within* the sector but on *economy-wide* lobbying. Consequently the only factor distinguishing marginal benefits across sectors is the level of output, $\pi_1^i(\cdot)$. Indexing goods such that $\pi_1^1(1 + g(l^U), w) > \pi_1^2(1 + g(l^U), w) > \cdots > \pi_1^n(1 + g(l^U), w)$, marginal benefit curves can be stacked as in figure 35.2.[12]

Because the marginal benefit from lobbying is the highest in sector 1, that sector will necessarily lobby. Setting (35.22) as an equality for $i = 1$, we can solve it for l^U. Let the solution be $\bar{l}^U$. It is then clear that the marginal benefit from lobbying for sectors $2, \ldots, n$ is below the wage rate, and assuming Nash behavior, these sectors will choose $l_i = 0$. In equilibrium, only sector 1, the sector with the largest value of output at world prices, chooses to lobby.

With equilibria under NTR and UTR thus defined, Panagariya and Rodrik (1993) show that the level of lobbying by sector 1 under the latter regime is lower. This means that the total resources employed in lobbying under UTR are necessarily less than under NTR. Also the level of tariff under UTR is lower than the tariff in sector 1 under NTR.

These results point in the direction of superiority of the UTR. But the conclusion is not clear-cut. Though the highest tariff (in sector 1) under NTR is higher than the uniform tariff under UTR, tariffs in other sectors can well be lower under the former regime. For example, if sector 1 ac-

12. Recall that since all world prices are equal to 1, this ranking is by the value of output at world prices.

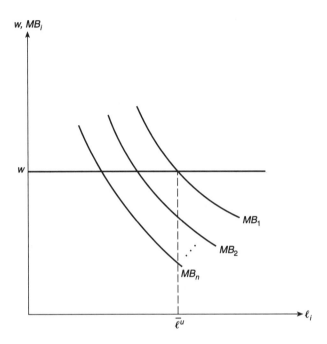

Figure 35.2

counts for a large proportion of the GDP valued at world prices while the other sectors are small, the uniform tariff under UTR will be higher than the tariff rates sought by sectors $2, \ldots, n$ under NTR. Thus it is entirely possible for the UTR to yield an inferior outcome than NTR. Only when no single industry is dominant in the economy, the UTR yields a superior outcome.

Positive Analysis

The positive economics of policy reform focuses on issues such as why reforms that increase the national income and/or benefit the majority segments are resisted and why some reforms are subsequently reversed. The subject goes well beyond trade policy and includes, among other topics, stabilization and privatization policies. Our treatment below is restricted to trade reform.

The simple answer to why a trade reform that increases the country's aggregate real income is resisted relies on nonneutrality of the distribution of gains and losses. A reform benefits some and hurts others. If losers are politically more powerful than gainers and nondistorting transfers are not feasible, the former will block the reform. Take, for example, a median voter model where the gains from a reform are limited to, say, capitalists who are a few and losses are suffered by workers who are numerous.

Then, even if there is a net gain in income, the median voter will turn down the reform. Observe that this argument is symmetric in the sense that if losses are concentrated and benefits are diffused, the reform can be accepted even if the net gain in income is negative.

Fernandez and Rodrik (1991) address the more difficult question: Why are reforms that affect favorably large and/or politically powerful segments of the society resisted? Trade reforms in Taiwan and South Korea in early 1960s, in Chile in 1970s, and in Turkey in 1980s were initially resisted by business groups. Surprisingly, once the authoritarian regimes of these countries had introduced the reform, business groups became its staunchest supporters.

To answer the puzzle, Fernandez and Rodrik offer the following argument: Suppose that the country under consideration is a democracy based on a majority vote.[13] There are 100 voters. A given trade reform is known to increase the income of 51 voters by $5 and lower that of 49 by $1. In the absence of uncertainty, the reform will be voted in.

Suppose now that 49 voters know for sure that they will gain but the remaining 51 are in the dark. The latter know that two of them will gain $5 each and 49 will lose $1 each but do not know the identities of the gainers and losers. This makes them identical *ex ante* with an expected benefit per person equaling $[(5 \times 2) - 49 \times 1]/51 = -39/51$ dollars. Assuming risk neutrality, all of these 51 voters will vote against the reform!

This argument can also explain why some reforms are eventually reversed. Suppose now that 51 voters stand to lose $5 each from the reform while 49 stand to gain $1 each. This reform not only hurts the majority but also lowers the national income overall. Assume this time that 49 voters know that they will lose but the other 51 are in the dark. *Ex ante*, the latter's expected benefit per person is $[49 \times 5 - 2 \times 1]/51 = 243/51$. All of these 51 voters will vote in favor of the reform. After the reform is in place and the identity of the remaining two losers is revealed, they (along with other 49 losers) will vote to reverse the reform when such an opportunity arises.

Note that there is nothing in the Fernandez-Rodrik argument to prevent a reform that reduces the national income from being voted in and sustained. Thus, if 51 voters gain $1 each and know it while 49 voters lose $2 each and know it, the reform will be voted in and sustained. The national income is of course reduced in this case by $(49 \times 2 - 51 \times 1) = $47. Symmetrically a reform that increases national income may never take place even if all voters know their gains and losses with certainty.

---

13. The argument is applicable in other political settings as well.

Recommended Readings

Anderson, J. E., and J. P. Neary. Trade reforms with quotas: Partial rent retention and tariffs. *Econometrica* 60 (1992): 57–76.

Bertrand, T. J., and J. Vanek. The theory of tariffs, taxes and subsidies: Some aspect of the second best. *American Economic Review* 61 (1971): 925–31.

Bhagwati, J. The generalized theory of distortions and welfare. In *Trade, Balance of Payments and Growth: Papers in International Economics in Honor of Charles P. Kindleberger*, ed. by J. Bhagwati et al. Amsterdam: North-Holland, 1971.

Bhagwati, J., and T. N. Srinivasan. Optimal interventions to achieve non-economic objectives. *Review of Economic Studies* 36 (1969): 27–38.

Bruno, M. Market distortions and reform. *Review of Economic Studies* 39 (1972): 373–83.

Corden, W. M., and R. E. Falvey. Quotas and the second best. *Economics Letters* 18 (1985): 67–70.

Dasgupta, P. S., and J. E. Stiglitz. Benefit-cost analysis and trade policies. *Journal of Political Economy* 82 (1974): 1–33.

Falvey, R. E. Tariffs, quotas and piecemeal policy reform. *Journal of International Economics* 25 (1988): 177–83.

Fernandez, R., and D. Rodrik. Resistance to reform: Status quo bias in the presence of individual-specific uncertainty. *American Economic Review* 81 (1991): 1146–55.

Fukushima, T. Tariff structure, non-traded goods and theory of piecemeal policy recommendations. *International Economic Reviews* 20 (1979): 427–35.

Hatta, T. A recommendation for a better tariff structure. *Econometrica* 45 (1977): 1859–69.

Hatta, T., and T. Fukushima. The welfare effects of tariff rate reductions in a many country world. *Journal of International Economics* 9 (1979): 503–11.

Johnson, H. G. Tariffs and economic development: Some theoretical issues. *Journal of Development Studies* 1 (1964): 3–30.

Krishna, P., and A. Panagariya. A unification of the theory of second best. Mimeo. University of Maryland, College Park.

Lipsey, R., and K. Lancaster. The general theory of second best. *Review of Economic Studies* 24 (1956): 11–32.

Lopez, R., and A. Panagariya. On the theory of piecemeal reform: The case of pure imported intermediate inputs. *American Economic Review* 82 (1992): 615–25.

Meade, J. *Trade and Welfare.* Oxford: Oxford University Press, 1955, ch. 13.

Panagariya, A. Input tariffs, duty drawbacks and tariff reform. *Journal of International Economics* 32 (1992): 131–47.

Panagariya, A., and D. Rodrik. Political-economy arguments for a uniform tariff. *International Economic Review* 34 (1993): 685–703.

Panagariya, A. Why and why not of uniform tariffs. *Economic Studies Quarterly* (September 1994): 303–21.

Ramaswami, V. K., and T. N. Srinivasan. Optimal subsidies and taxes when some factors are traded. *Journal of Political Economy* 76 (1968): 569–82.

Thomas, V., J. Nash, and Associates, *Best Practices in Trade Policy Reform.* New York: Oxford University Press, 1991.

Does growth affect the welfare conclusions derived in part III, and especially in chapter 18? It is important to distinguish between two different types of questions:

• If an economy transits from autarky to free trade, we may ask how this will affect the economy's growth path given the technology and institutions in that economy (which may well be distortionary in the sense defined in part III) and whether free trade can still be considered welfare-superior to autarky for an open economy.

• If the economy can follow everywhere-optimal policies, can free trade remain a superior policy for an open economy (as in the static discussion of chapter 18), or can there be a deadweight loss in the free-trade situation in the context of a growing economy?

36.1 Distortionary Situations

The first question is readily answered. When a country's other policies are not fully optimal, the welfare superiority of free trade over autarky for an open growing economy cannot be asserted—exactly as in the static analysis of part III. For a large economy free trade is superior to autarky, but it is not optimal (chapter 21).

These points are familiar to economists from the literature on choice of techniques in development theory, in which it is now agreed that if the savings rate cannot be chosen independently of the choice of technique (e.g., by resorting to a nondistortionary fiscal policy), maximization of the value of current output will not necessarily result in an optimal-growth solution for the economy. The reason is that the lack of separability of the savings and choice-of-technique decisions implies the presence of a distortion so that present-output-maximizing techniques or associated resource allocations are not necessarily optimal. This is best seen in the context of the Harrod-Domar model, in which the rate of growth of income is

$$\frac{\dot{Y}}{Y} = \frac{s}{\alpha},$$

(36.1)

where Y is income, s is the average savings ratio, and α is the marginal capital-output ratio. In this essentially one-good model of a closed economy, combining the productive factors so as to minimize the capital-output ratio (by maximizing current output) should yield the highest rate of growth of output for any chosen savings ratio. Thus current or myopic or static efficiency can be combined with—indeed, is a prerequisite to—

intertemporal or farsighted or dynamic efficiency, since there is no trade-off between current and future output. Now trade is also, as we have noted, a policy that essentially chooses a technique. It follows then for a small open economy that free trade, in maximizing current efficiency, is also maximizing dynamic efficiency when lump-sum fiscal policy is available. Free trade therefore Pareto-dominates autarky (and other forms of protection) for a small open economy.

On the other hand, owing to a lack of lump-sum fiscal policy or other suitable policies, achievable savings ratios may be dependent on the techniques chosen. Then, as equation (36.1) implies, it may pay an economy maximizing welfare intertemporally to incur current inefficiency by choosing a resource-allocation mix or a set of techniques that offset the resulting increase in the capital-output ratio by increasing the savings ratio. Thus, in an open economy, autarky would involve a lower current income relative to free trade ($OA < OB$ in figure 36.1), but if s/α is increased, it would imply more rapid growth of income so that autarky

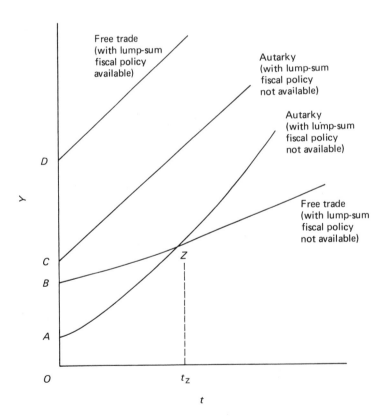

Figure 36.1

might well dominate free trade in welfare terms, given an intertemporal social-welfare function. Thus in figure 36.1 the autarkic and free-trade growth paths, in the distortionary situation of a lump-sum fiscal policy being unavailable, cross over at Z on the assumption that autarky increases s/α relative to free trade. An intertemporal social-welfare function that attaches negligible weight to income beyond time t_Z will lead the planner to choose free trade, but shifting the weights in favor of the future could lead to the choice of autarky. Free trade no longer dominates autarky, given the distortion in the shape of an unavailable lump-sum fiscal policy.[1]

A formal analysis of how autarky changes the savings ratio in a 2×2 framework is provided by Pattanaik (1974), who establishes necessary and sufficient conditions for a switch from autarky to free trade to reduce total savings in terms of both goods, irrespective of the pattern of trade. Pattanaik uses the 2×2 model with the added assumption that there are constant average propensities to save from wages (S_w) and profits (S_γ). He assumes further that the country is exporting the labor-intensive good 1, and denotes by Z_i^A the capital-labor ratios in $i = 1, 2$ in autarky and by Z_i^F those in free trade. He proves that a change from autarky to free trade will reduce savings in terms of the importable good 2 if Z/Z_2^F is greater than S_w/S_γ and only if Z/Z_2^A is greater than S_w/S_γ, whereas it will always reduce saving in terms of exportables.

36.2   Optimal Policies Everywhere: Absence of Deadweight Loss under Free Trade

The basic argument that in the absence of other distortions in the economy free trade will be superior to autarky in an open economy should evidently apply as much to intertemporal as to static gains-from-trade analysis; that is, there should be no deadweight loss under free trade in a growing, open economy. This argument was developed more formally by Smith (1979) and Dixit and Norman (1980), and needs to be borne in mind because the writings of Emmanuel (1972), Metcalf and Steedman (1974), Mainwaring (1974), and Steedman (1979) have been construed, not entirely without plausibility, as suggesting or asserting otherwise.[2]

In particular, it needs to be understood that free trade is superior to autarky in a dynamic context. From any historically given initial situation, an autarkic economy can always gain a Pareto-superior path by

---

1. Note that $OC < OD$ for a small country (because free trade is the optimal policy) and for a large country (because free trade is suboptimal but superior to autarky).

2. The Dixit-Norman argument was developed in chapter 18 in its static form, and as we noted, it applies equally to intertemporal gains from trade.

moving to free trade and using otherwise-optimal policies; conversely, an economy in free trade cannot achieve a Pareto-superior path by changing to autarky. However, this does not necessarily mean that if an autarkic economy converges to some steady state in the long run and the same economy under free trade converges to a different steady state, the latter steady-state path is Pareto-superior to the former. Indeed it can be Pareto-inferior.

As is well understood from the writings of Smith (1979) and others, and sharply noted by Stiglitz (1970), Samuelson (1978), and Srinivasan and Bhagwati (1980), this inability to rank-dominate the free-trade over the autarkic steady-state path does not imply that there is a dynamic deadweight loss under free trade. To assert otherwise, as seems to have happened, is to make the error of ignoring the fact that, with the levels and compositions of capital stock of different steady states being different, movement from one steady state to another involves traversing a non-stead-state path. The relevant welfare comparison therefore is not between the ultimate steady states to which actual paths of the economy (under free trade and autarky) starting from given conditions converge, but rather between these paths themselves. And the latter comparison must show that free trade does dominate autarky even in a growing economy.

36.3   Steady States, Trade, and Welfare

To see (in the 2×2 model) that the source of error in asserting a deadweight loss under free trade relative to autarky appears to be the fact that the steady-state per-capita consumption under free trade can be lower than under autarkic steady-state conditions, we turn now to the analysis of Srinivasan and Bhagwati (1980), which was stimulated by Samuelson's (1978) far more complex treatment of this issue in a time-phased capital-theoretic model. We will adopt only that form of the Srinivasan-Bhagwati analysis that demonstrates free trade being dominated by autarky in terms of its associated steady-state per-capita consumption.

For simplicity, we assume that there is just one consumer in this economy who has inherited a capital stock of k_0 units. He lives forever and supplies e^{nt} units of labor at instant t of time. He is interested in maximizing the sum of the discounted stream of instantaneous utilities (per unit of labor provided),

$$\int_0^\infty e^{-\rho t} u(c_t) \, dt,$$

where ρ (> 0) is the discount rate and c_t is his consumption at time t. Let good 2 be the consumer good and good 1 be the capital good. In autarky this single-consumer economy is assumed to maximize

$$\int_0^\infty e^{-\rho t} u(c_t)\, dt \tag{36.2}$$

subject to

$$c_t = l_2(t) g(k_2(t)), \tag{36.3}$$

$$l_2(t) k_2(t) + [1 - l_2(t)] k_1(t) = k(t), \tag{36.4}$$

$$\dot{k}(t) = [1 - l_2(t)] f(k_1(t)) - nk(t), \tag{36.5}$$

where $k_i(t)$ is the capital-labor ratio, $l_i(t)$ is the fraction of labor employed in the production of good i $(i = 1, 2)$, and $k(t)$ is the aggregate capital-labor ratio. The relevant nonnegativity conditions are assumed.

Equation (36.3) states that consumption per unit of labor equals output of consumer goods per unit of labor. Equation (36.4) states that the aggregate capital-labor ratio is a weighted average of the sectoral capital-labor ratios, the weights being the sectoral labor-use proportions. This ensures that total capital in use equals total capital available. Equation (36.5) is the investment equation, which shows that the rate of change of the aggregate capital-labor ratio is the output of capital goods per unit of labor net of the amount needed to maintain the capital-labor ratio, given that labor grows at the proportionate rate n.

It is well known that the optimal time path from given initial stock k_0 satisfies (with subscripts of functions u, f, and g denoting their first derivatives)

$$\frac{d}{dt} u_1(c_t) = n + \rho - f_1(k_1(t)), \tag{36.6}$$

$$\frac{f - k_1 f_1}{f_1} = \frac{g - k_2 g_1}{f_2}. \tag{36.7}$$

This optimal path converges to a steady state given by

$$f_1[k_1^{*A}] = n + \rho \tag{36.8}$$

$$\frac{f(k_1^{*A}) - k_1^{*A} f_1(k_1^{*A})}{f_1(k_1^{*A})} = \frac{g(k_2^{*A}) - k_2^{*A} g_1(k_2^{*A})}{g_1(k_2^{*A})}, \tag{36.9}$$

where the superscript A denotes autarky and, in the present single-country context, superscript * denotes steady state rather than foreign-country variables. With n and ρ given, (36.8) uniquely determines k_1^{*A} and

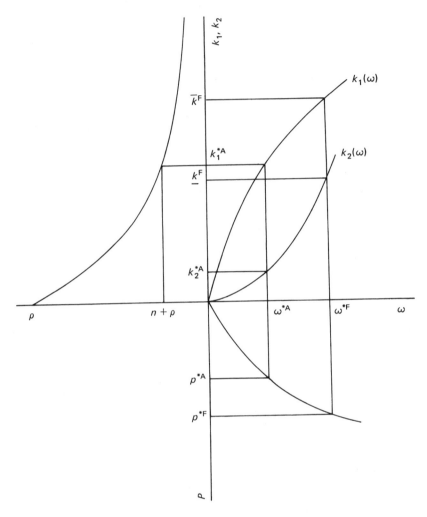

Figure 36.2

(36.9) determines k_2^{*A}. With k_1^{*A} and k_2^{*A} given, (36.4) and (36.5) with $\dot{k} = 0$ determine k^{*A} and l_2^{*A}. Substitution in (36.3) yields the steady-state consumption c^{*A}.

This solution could be interpreted as a competitive equilibrium with the common value of the marginal rate of substitution in the two sectors as the wage/rental ratio ω^* and with the ratio $f_1[k_1^{*A}]/g_1[k_2^{*A}]$ as the price p^{*A} of the consumer good in terms of the capital good. This is illustrated in figure 36.2, where the first quadrant depicts the optimal capital intensities corresponding to alternative capital-labor ratios. With good 1 always capital-intensive, the second quadrant depicts the marginal product of capital in the production of capital goods (or, equivalently, the own rate of interest on capital good), and the fourth quadrant depicts the relative cost of production of the consumer good in terms of the capital good.

Let us now introduce trade. The free-trade optimal path and the steady state it converges to can then be determined as follows: The opportunities available to the economy can be viewed as enabling it to use foreign trade to separate production and consumption decisions, in the sense of choosing a production pattern that will maximize income at world prices and a consumption pattern that is consistent with intertemporal welfare maximization. Thus, instead of a two-sector economy, we consider a one-sector economy that produces "income," consumes part of it, and saves the rest to accumulate capital. With the world price p^{*F} of the consumer good in terms of the capital good, the production function $Y(k)$ for "income" is obtained by

$$Y(k) = \max p^{*F} l_2 g(k_2) + (1 - l_2) f(k_1) \tag{36.10}$$

subject to

$$l_2 k_2 + (1 - l_2) k_1 = k. \tag{36.11}$$

With $Y(k)$ thus determined, the optimal growth problem is to maximize

$$\int_0^\infty e^{-\rho t} u(c_t) \, dt \tag{36.12}$$

subject to

$$\dot{k}_t = Y(k_t) - p^{*F} c_t - n k_t \qquad (k_0 \text{ given}). \tag{36.13}$$

The steady-state aggregate capital-labor ratio under free trade is $Y_1(k^{*F}) = n + \rho$, and the steady-state consumption is $c^{*F} = Y(k^{*F})/p^{*F}$. It is straightforward to sketch the argument that yields $Y(k)$ by using figure 36.2. Equating the relative domestic cost of production of good 2 to its world price p^{*F}, we first determine the associated equilibrium wage-rental ratio ω^{*F}, which in turn determines two limiting capital-labor ratios, $\underline{k}^F$ and $\bar{k}^F$, through $\underline{k}^F = k_2(\omega^{*F})$ and $\bar{k}^F = k_1(\omega^{*F})$. It is obvious from figure 36.2 that the maximized income $Y(k)$ at world prices p^{*F} is achieved by specializing in the production of good 2 (good 1) if $k < \underline{k}^F (> \bar{k}^F)$. For values of k in the interval $[\underline{k}^F, \bar{k}^F]$, the economy is incompletely specialized.[3] Hence

3. This analysis is based on figure 36.2, in which $k_1(\omega) > k_2(\omega)$ for all ω. It should be appropriately changed if $k_2(\omega) > k_1(\omega)$ for all ω. The steady-state analysis can be carried out even if factor-intensity reversals occur.

$$Y(k) = p^{*\mathrm{F}} g(k) \qquad \text{for } 0 \le k < \underline{k}^{\mathrm{F}}$$

$$= p^{*\mathrm{F}} \left(\frac{\bar{k}^{\mathrm{F}} - k}{\bar{k}^{\mathrm{F}} - \underline{k}^{\mathrm{F}}} \right) g(\underline{k}^{\mathrm{F}}) + \frac{k - \underline{k}^{\mathrm{F}}}{\bar{k}^{\mathrm{F}} - \underline{k}^{\mathrm{F}}} f(\bar{k}^{\mathrm{F}}) \qquad \text{for } \underline{k}^{\mathrm{F}} \le k \le \bar{k}^{\mathrm{F}}$$

$$= f(k) \qquad \text{for } k > \bar{k}^{\mathrm{F}}. \tag{36.14}$$

Since in a steady state $Y_1(k)$ equals $n + \rho$, by (36.14) we see that incomplete specialization is consistent with the steady state only if $f_1(\bar{k}^{\mathrm{F}})$ [which equals $Y_1(k)$ in such a case] equals $n + \rho$. This in turn means that since in the autarky steady state $f_1(k^{*\mathrm{A}})$ equals $n + \rho$, we must have $\bar{k}^{\mathrm{F}} = k^{*\mathrm{A}}$. However, $\bar{k}^{\mathrm{F}} = k^{*\mathrm{A}}$ implies $p^{*\mathrm{F}} = p^{*\mathrm{A}}$. Thus only in the uninteresting case of the autarkic steady-state domestic price ratio equaling the world price ratio will the economy be incompletely specialized in the free-trade steady state. Otherwise, the economy will be specialized in the production of good 2 (the consumer good) if $f_1(\bar{k}^{\mathrm{F}})$ is less than $n + \rho$ and in the production of good 1 (the capital good) if $f_1(\bar{k}^{\mathrm{F}})$ is greater than $n + \rho$.

Now that our model is solved for the steady-state solutions under autarky and under free trade, we can proceed to construct parametric cases such that the free-trade steady-state per-capita consumption is "paradoxically" below that for autarky. For example, if we assume that the production function in each sector is of the Cobb-Douglas type, we can choose a combination of values of the parameters including the world price of the consumer good such that our economy is specialized in producing the capital good in the free-trade steady state and exhibits the required, superficially paradoxical result of autarkic per-capita consumption being greater.

In the derivation of the steady states, the economy's planners are presumed to optimize accumulation or saving policies all along the path that converges to the steady state. These planners, in a decentralized fashion, ensure optimality of savings within each situation during the approach to the steady state (within the free-trade and autarky situations). Trade is optimally exploited by free trade since the country is assumed to face a constant world price ratio. Hence the "paradox" of autarkic steady-state per-capita consumption being greater than free-trade steady-state per-capita consumption is more interesting than, for instance, the Bertrand (1975) demonstration that, for an arbitrarily fixed savings ratio, such a paradoxical steady-state rank ordering of per-capita consumption could result.

The intuitive explanation of our, and Samuelson's, result is that the welfare loss in moving from a free-trade steady state to the autarky steady state through a non-steady-state path outweighs the gain in welfare due to higher per-capita consumption once the autarky steady state is attained. Conversely, starting from an autarky steady state and moving to a free-trade steady state will result in sufficient gain in welfare in the non-steady-state transitory stage to outweigh the loss once a steady state is reached under free trade.

Recommended Readings

Bardhan, P. K. Optimum accumulation and international trade. *Review of Economic Studies* 32 (1965): 241–44.

Bertrand, T. The gains from trade: Steady-state solutions in an open economy. *Quarterly Journal of Economics* 89 (1975): 556–68.

Black, J. Trade and the natural growth rate. *Oxford Economic Papers* 22 (1970): 13–23.

Corden, W. M. The effects of trade on the rate of growth. In *Trade, Balance of Payments, and Growth: Papers in International Economics in Honor of Charles P. Kindleberger*, ed. by J. N. Bhagwati et al. Amsterdam: North-Holland, 1971.

Deardorff, A. V. Trade reversals and growth stability. *Journal of International Economics* 4 (1974): 83–90.

Dixit, A., and V. Norman, *Theory of International Trade*. Cambridge: Cambridge University Press, 1980.

Emmanuel, A. *Unequal Exchange: A Study of the Imperialism of Trade*. New York: Monthly Review Press, 1972.

Findlay, R. Efficient accumulation, international trade, and the optimum tariff. *Oxford Economic Papers* 20 (1968): 208–17.

Findlay, R. Implications of growth theory for trade and development. *American Economic Review* 65 (1975): 323–28.

Johnson, H. G. Trade and growth: A geometrical exposition. *Journal of International Economics* 19 (1971): 83–102.

Johnson, H. G. The theory of trade and growth: A diagrammatic analysis. In *Trade, Balance of Payments, and Growth: Papers in International Economics in Honor of Charles P. Kindleberger*, ed. by J. N. Bhagwati et al. Amsterdam: North-Holland, 1971.

Mainwaring, L. A neo-Ricardian analysis of international trade. *Kyklos* 27 (1974): 537–53.

Metcalf, J. S., and I. Steedman. A note on the gain from trade. *Economic Record* 50 (1974): 581–95.

Pattanaik, P. K. Trade, distribution and saving, *Journal of International Economics* 4 (1974): 77–82.

Samuelson, P. A. Trade pattern reversals in time-phased Ricardian systems and intertemporal efficiency. *Journal of International Economics* 5 (1975): 309–64.

Samuelson, P. A. Free trade's intertemporal Pareto optimality. *Journal of International Economics* 8 (1978): 147–49.

Smith, M. A. M. Trade, growth, and consumption in alternative models of capital accumulation. *Journal of International Economics* 6 (1976): 371–84.

Smith, M. A. M. Capital accumulation in the open two-sector economy. *Economic Journal* 87 (1977): 273–82.

Smith, M. A. M. Intertemporal gains from trade. *Journal of International Economics* 9 (1979): 239–48.

Srinivasan, T. N., and J. Bhagwati. Trade and welfare in a steady state. In *Flexible Exchange Rates and the Balance of Payments: Essays in Memory of Egon Sohmen*, ed. by J. Chipman and C. Kindleberger. Amsterdam: North-Holland, 1980, ch. 9.

Steedman, I. *Trade among Growing Economics*. Cambridge: Cambridge University Press, 1979.

Stiglitz, J. Factor price equalization in a dynamic economy. *Journal of Political Economy* 78 (1970): 456–88.

Togan, S. The gains from international trade in the context of a growing economy. *Journal of International Economics* 5 (1975): 229–38.

Vanek, J. Economic growth and international trade in pure theory. *Quarterly Journal of Economics* 85 (1971): 377–90.

37

The model of the preceding chapter is an open-economy version of the conventional neoclassical growth models of Solow (1956), Cass (1965), and Koopmans (1965). Also in an open economy along the steady path, whether under autarky or under free trade, output, consumption, and capital stock grow at the same rate as the exogenous growth rate of the labor force. A once-and-for-all change in trade policy, for example, opening the economy to free trade from a position on its autarky steady-state path, has only *transitional* effect on the growth rate of output, consumption, and capital stock. As the economy converges to its free-trade steady state, the growth rates of all three converge to their autarky steady-state values, namely in the rate of growth of the economy's labor force. However, such a policy change has a *level effect* on the steady-state growth path, as was shown in chapter 38 in the differences in consumption per capita in autarky and free-state steady states.

It is well known in the literature on closed-economy neoclassical growth models that if labor-augmenting technical progress at an *exogenous* constant proportional rate per unit time is used to characterize the technology of production, steady-state paths exist (as long as the utility discount rates are sufficiently high). Along these paths output, consumption, and capital stock grow at the same exogenous rate, and the common growth rate is the sum of the rates of growth of labor force and technical progress. In contrast to the steady states in the absence of technical progress, output, capital stock, and consumption per worker grow at the same rate as that of technical progress. The initial level of capital stock has no influence on the steady state: Economies that start from different levels of capital stock converge to the same steady state as long as their technologies (i.e., production functions and tastes, instantaneous utility function, and the utility discount rate) are the same.

The desire to escape from some of these implications of the neoclassical model motivated the recent revival of growth theory initiated by the influential papers of Lucas (1988) and Romer (1986).[1] Romer looked for alternatives to the neoclassical model in order to escape from its implications:

initial conditions or current disturbances have no long-run effect on the level of output and consumption ... In the absence of technical change, per capita output should converge to a steady state value with no per capita growth. (Romer 1986, pp. 1002–1003)

---

1. A good summary of the evolution of the new growth theory and its antecedents in (as well as contrasts with) conventional growth theory, is provided in the Symposium on New Growth Theory in *Journal of Economic Perspectives* 8 (winter 1994).

Lucas wished to escape also from the implications of the neoclassical model of an open economy, arguing that

> In the absence of differences in pure technology then, and under the assumption of no factor mobility the neoclassical model predicts a strong tendency to income equality and equality in growth rates, tendencies we can observe within countries, but which simply cannot be seen in world at large. When factor mobility is permitted, this prediction is reinforced. (Lucas 1988, pp. 15–16)

37.1 Endogenous Growth and Trade

Apart from the primary goal of escaping the long-run growth implications of the conventional neoclassical model, recent research is also aimed at endogenizing the long-run rate of growth. Endogenization means that long-run growth rate depends not only on the exogenous parameters of technology and taste as in the conventional model but also on the endogenous choice of fiscal policies, foreign trade policies, research and development policies, population policies, and so on. In particular, the rate of technical progress itself is an outcome of *endogenous* decisions of entrepreneurs with respect to investment in research and development and also of government policy interventions in influencing that investment. For these reasons the recent growth theories are almost universally called endogenous growth theories or models. A simple model of such endogenous technical progress follows in the next section.

In many endogenous growth models the primary goal is accomplished through increasing scale economies in aggregate production. The resulting nonconvexities lead to multiple equilibria and hysteresis in some models so that history (i.e., initial conditions as well as any past shocks experienced by the economy) and policies have long-term effects. The scale economies arise in some models in the production functions of individual firms, and in others, only in the aggregate production function from externalities (e.g., learning by doing), spillover effects of innovation, or possible nonrivalrous nonexcludable public-goods features of knowledge accumulation, and the like. Naturally, in so far as perfect competition is incompatible with the presence of scale economies, imperfectly competitive market structure is postulated in these models.

The models of innovation that generate sustained growth in the long run in per-capita income are of interest in themselves. Before describing one of them in section 37.2, it is worth showing that policy changes, such as liberalization of trade, can have *level as well as growth effects* in the long run even in conventional growth models. It is also the case that scale economies are neither necessary to generate sustained growth in the long run nor sufficient to make it endogenous.

Consider the standard Solow (1956) model:

Output: $Y(t) \equiv K(t)^a L(t)^b + cK(t),$ (37.1)

$0 < a < 1, 0 < b < 1, a + b \geq 1, c \geq 0,$

Net investment: $\dot{K}(t) = sY(t) - \delta K(t),$ (37.2)

Labor force: $L(t) = e^{nt},$ (37.3)

where n is the geometric rate of growth at each instant t of time.

Now as long as $nb \neq (sc - \delta)(1 - a)$, there exists a unique steady-state solution for $K(t)$ with its rate of growth being $(sc - \delta)$ if $(sc - \delta)(1 - a) > nb$ and $(nb)/(1 - a)$ if $(sc - \delta)(1 - a) < nb$. Three special cases are of interest.

The first case is one where $a + b = 1$ and $c = 0$, the production function exhibits constant returns to scale, and the marginal product of capital diminishes to zero as the capital-labor ratio increases indefinitely. Along the unique steady state, capital stock, consumption, and output grow at the same exogenous rate, with n being the rate of growth of the labor force.

The second is one where $c = 0$ and $a + b > 1$. The production function exhibits increasing scale economies, and the property that the marginal product of capital diminishes to zero (since $0 < a < 1$) as the capital-labor ratio increases indefinitely. Along the unique steady state, capital stock grows at the rate $(nb)/(1 - a) > n$, and output per worker grows at the rate $n(a + b - 1)/(1 - a) > 0$. Thus, with increasing scale economies, there is positive but exogenous growth in per worker output in the long-run steady state.

The third is the case where $a + b = 1$ and $c > 0$. The production function now exhibits constant returns to scale, but the marginal product of capital is bounded below by $c > 0$. If c is sufficiently large so that $(sc - \delta)(1 - a) > nb = n(1 - a)$ or $sc > (n + \delta)$, then in the steady state capital stock grows at the rate $(sc - \delta) > n$ and output per worker grows at the rate $(sc - \delta - n)a > 0$.

Almost all contributors to traditional neoclassical growth theory worked with production functions, such as in the first case of constant returns to scale and absence of a positive floor to the marginal product of capital. Indeed it is this combination that is responsible for the steady-state implications of neoclassical growth models from which modern growth theorists had wished to escape.

It is clear from the second case that although increasing scale economies yield a positive rate of growth in per worker output in the steady state, this rate is exogenous. As such, increasing scale economies alone are not sufficient to generate endogenous growth.

In the third case, since the savings rate s can be endogenous, one obtains positive, endogenously determined growth in per worker output in the long run. This case demonstrates that increasing scale economies are not necessary to generate endogenous and positive growth of output per worker in the long run. It is enough if a high positive growth lower than the marginal product exists, although there are no scale economies.

It should now be evident from the third case that one can generate long-run growth effects of trade liberalization if the production function is such that there is a sufficiently high floor for the marginal product of capital. This can be demonstrated with two well-known models, the one-sector Harrod-Domar model and the two-sector Feldman-Mahalanobis model.

Consider the simplest version of the workhorse of early development planning, namely the Harrod-Domar (Domar 1957) model in which capital is the sole factor of production.[2] Output Y at any time t is the product of capital stock K in existence at that time and a constant output-capital ratio β. The economy is assumed to be closed to foreign trade. A constant proportion s of output is assumed to be saved and invested so that, given a constant proportional rate of depreciation at the rate δ per unit of time of capital stock, the growth rate g of the economy is $s\beta - \delta$. As long as s is exogenous, so is the growth rate g.

Let us introduce foreign trade into the model in a very simple way. Suppose that the economy can trade with the rest of the world at a constant terms of trade of π ($\pi > 1$) units of investment per unit of output in contrast with domestic terms of trade of unity under autarky. In other words, under autarky, the economy can transform each unit of output into one unit of consumption or one unit of investment; with trade, it gets the same consumption but more (i.e., $\pi > 1$) investment per unit of output. Implicit in this way of introducing trade is that the economy is too small to influence the world relative price (in terms of home output) of the investment good and that it has a comparative advantage in its home output or, equivalently, the consumption good. Thus with capital as its sole factor of production, this Ricardian economy specializes in producing the consumption good under free trade.

2. Strictly speaking, corresponding to this model is only Harrod's "warranted equilibrium path," along which available savings are continually absorbed into investment without changing the capital-output ratio.

Let us also make savings (equivalently consumption c_t) endogenous (and thus growth endogenous) through the maximization of intertemporal welfare

$$W \equiv \int_0^\infty e^{-\rho t} u(c_t)\, dt, \tag{37.4}$$

where, for simplicity of analysis, we can assume that the instantaneous felicity function $u(c_t)$ is $(c^{1-\sigma} - 1)/(1 - \sigma)$ (with $\sigma > 0$). Let us assume, again for simplicity, that international lending or borrowing is infeasible, so trade has to be balanced at each t. Thus W is to be maximized subject to the constraint investment goods imports equals the value of exports or

$$\dot{K}_t + \delta K_t = \pi[\beta K_t - c_t], \tag{37.5}$$

and the nonnegativity constraints $c_t \geq 0$, $\dot{K}_t + \delta K_t \geq 0$.

An optimal solution to this problem exists, and is unique, as long as $\rho + (\sigma - 1)(\pi\beta - \delta) > 0$. It is given by

$$K_t = K_0 e^{gt} \quad \text{and} \quad c_t = \left[\frac{\rho + (\sigma - 1)(\pi\beta - \delta)}{\pi\sigma}\right] K_0 e^{gt}, \tag{37.6}$$

where

$$g = \left(\frac{\pi\beta - \delta - \rho}{\sigma}\right). \tag{37.7}$$

The short- and long-run growth rate g of consumption and capital stock will be positive as long as $\pi\beta - \delta - \rho > 0$. Now $\partial g/\partial \pi = \beta/\sigma > 0$. Since opening the economy to trade involves an increase in the relative price of the consumption good in which the economy has comparative advantage from its value of 1 under autarky to $\pi > 1$ under free trade, it follows from $\partial g/\partial \pi > 0$ that the short- and long-run growth rate of the economy, g, is increased by such opening. Thus trade liberalization (which in this case means moving to free trade from autarky) has positive growth effects.

Now the gross domestic product (GDP) valued in units of investment goods is

$$(\dot{K}_t + \delta K_t) + \pi c_t = \beta\pi K_0 e^{gt} \tag{37.8}$$

Clearly, as π under free trade is raised above its autarky value of unity, there is a *positive level effect* (through $\beta\pi$), and a *positive growth effect* (through g) from the move to free trade on the value of GDP in units of investment goods. The value of GDP in units of consumption goods (or equivalently output) is $\beta K_0 e^{gt}$. Therefore moving to free trade has only a growth effect and no level effect on the value of GDP in units of consumption goods.

It is seen from (39.6) that moving to free trade has a positive growth effect—but an ambiguous level effect (it is positive, zero, or negative according as $(\sigma - 1)\delta - \rho$ is positive, zero, or negative)—on consumption in physical units. This reflects the conflict between a positive income effect and a negative substitution effect as the economy moves to freer trade, arising from the rise in relative price of consumption good in which the economy has comparative advantage. The value of consumption, in terms of investment goods, is

$$\pi c_t = \left[\frac{\rho + (\sigma - 1)(\pi\beta - \delta)}{\sigma} \right] K_0 e^{gt}.$$

Hence, moving to free trade has a positive growth effect on it as well. The level effect is positive if and only if the intertemporal elasticity of substitution $1/\sigma < 1$. However, whether or not the level effect on consumption is positive (in value or in physical units), it can be shown that intertemporal welfare W increases under free trade relative to autarky, the reason being that even if the *level effect* on consumption of a move to free trade is negative, the positive growth effect is more than enough to raise W under free trade above its autarky level.

One of the influential development models was formulated independently by Fel'dman (1928) for the Soviet Union and the physicist-statistician Mahalanobis (1955). It is a model of a closed economy in which there are two sectors, one of which produces a consumption good, and the other, a capital good. Capital is the only factor of production, and the output of each sector is the product of the stock of capital in existence in that sector and its output-capital ratio. While the flow of output of the investment goods sector can be allocated in any fashion to augment the stock of capital in either sector, capital, once installed in that sector, cannot be shifted to the other sector.

Consider an expanded open economy version of this model (section 37.3). Let there be two consumer goods as well as two investment goods (instead of one each) with the marginal product of capital being constant in the production of each good. Let the utility function, and the aggregation function that transforms the output of the two investment goods into aggregate investment, be Cobb-Douglas. Let capital stock be freely shiftable within each sector but with no intersectoral shiftability. Assume, for simplicity only, that the share of investment devoted to the accumulation of capital stock in the capital goods sector is exogenously fixed rather than endogenously determined through intertemporal welfare maximization.

It is easily seen that under autarky all four goods will be produced in positive amounts. Suppose now that this economy is opened to free trade in consumer goods, with the relative price of the two consumer goods being fixed in world markets. Then the economy will specialize in producing one of the two consumer goods in which it has a comparative advantage and trade some of it for the other. However, as long as the share of investment devoted to the capital goods sector is unchanged and that sector is closed to foreign trade, even though the welfare of the economy will rise relative to autarky, the long-run growth rate of the economy will be unchanged. In contrast, if the capital goods sector is opened to free trade (again at fixed world relative prices) while the consumer goods sector is kept closed, there will be a positive long-run growth effect and a welfare effect relative to autarky. The implication is that from a growth perspective, keeping the growth-inducing sector (which is the capital goods sector in this model) closed to international competition is costlier than closing the consumer goods sector. Of course, keeping neither closed would be even better, since for this small economy there is no market power to be exploited through a tariff policy nor any dynamic externalities due to learning effects to be internalized in the model.

37.2   Innovation-Based Growth and Technology Diffusion among Countries

One of the simplest models of innovation based growth is well-exposited by Helpman (1990).[3] He first considers a closed economy with labor as the only factor of production. Labor can be used as an input into research and development, or it can be used to manufacture differentiated products. Consumers have a constant elasticity substitution (CES) among these products which enter symmetrically in their utility function, implying a constant price elasticity, $1/(1 - \alpha)$, for demand for each of the products. Manufacturing requires a_{LX} units of labor per unit of output, while product development requires a_{Ln}/K units of labor per product, where K is an index of the stock of knowledge capital in product development. This stock reflects learning by doing in that the higher the stock K, the lower is the cost (in terms of labor) of development per product. Thus its rate of change, $\dot{K}$, is the same as the rate of change in the number of products in existence, namely n. By proper choice of units, Helpman sets $K = n$.

---

3. Grossman and Helpman (1991) is a comprehensive treatise on models of innovation, growth, and trade. It includes the exposition of the so-called quality-ladders model developed by the two authors in which each variety of a differentiated product is also distinguished by its quality. Improvements in quality, which come in discrete steps, involve investment in research.

With competition in product development and choosing the cost of development per product as the numéraire, it is seen that

$$1 = \frac{w(t)a_{Ln}}{K},\tag{37.9}$$

where $w(t)$ is the wage rate in numéraire units at time t.[4] With Chamberlinian monopolistic competition ruling in the market for differentiated products, markup pricing prevails so that

$$p = \frac{wa_{LX}}{\alpha},\tag{37.10}$$

where p is the price of each differentiated product in numéraire units and $1/\alpha$ is the markup over marginal cost. As noted, the price elasticity of demand is $1/(1-\alpha)$.

With L units of labor available, factor market clearance implies that

$$\frac{a_{Ln}}{n}\dot{n} + a_{LX}X = L,\tag{37.11}$$

where $\dot{n}$ is the rate of development of new products and X is the total output of differentiated products. Total expenditure pX on differentiated products equals consumer spending E on such products. Denoting by η the expenditure per product, E/n, and using (37.10), the factor market clearance condition yields

$$\frac{\dot{n}}{n} = \frac{L}{a_{LN}} - \alpha\eta.\tag{37.12}$$

Recall that the utility U of the consumer from consuming X_i units of product i $(i = 1, \ldots, n)$ is

$$U(t) = \log \sum_{i}^{n} \{X_i\}.\tag{37.13}$$

So, noting that the same amount will be consumed of each variety, we set $X_i = X/n$ and get

$$U(t) = (1 - \alpha)\log n + \alpha \log X.\tag{37.14}$$

Maximizing intertemporal welfare $\int_0^\infty e^{-\rho\tau} U(\tau)\, d\tau$ with respect to $X(t) = E/p$ subject to the budget constraint $\int_0^\infty e^{-r\tau} E(\tau)\, d\tau = Z$, where Z is consumer wealth (i.e., discounted present value of wage income), we get[5]

---

4. For ease of notation in what follows the time argument of variables are omitted except where it is needed for clarity.

5. For simplicity the interest rate r is assumed to be constant.

$$\frac{\dot{E}}{E} = (r - \rho).\tag{37.15}$$

Now, by (37.10) and the definition of E and η, the profits per product π equaling the difference between revenue pX/n and costs $wa_{LX}X/n$, can be written

$$\pi = (p - wa_{LX})\frac{X}{n} = (1 - \alpha)\frac{pX}{n} = (1 - \alpha)\frac{E}{n}$$

$$= (1 - \alpha)\eta.\tag{37.16}$$

Since the cost of a product developed at any time t is unity, which under free entry into that industry equals the discounted present value of the profit streams, we get

$$1 = \int_t^\infty e^{-r(\tau - t)} \pi(\tau) \, d\tau\tag{37.17}$$

This implies that

$$\pi(t) = r.\tag{37.18}$$

From $\eta = E/n$, it follows that $\dot{\eta}/\eta = \dot{E}/E - \dot{n}/n$, or

$$\frac{\dot{\eta}}{\eta} = r - \rho - \frac{\dot{n}}{n} = (1 - \alpha)\eta - \rho - \frac{\dot{n}}{n}.\tag{37.19}$$

Substituting for $\dot{n}/n$ from the labor market clearance obtains

$$\frac{\dot{n}}{n} = \eta - \rho - \frac{L}{a_{Ln}}.\tag{37.20}$$

The only solution to (37.20) that satisfies the transversality condition of the consumer welfare maximization is the stationary solution $\eta = $ constant. This means that $\dot{\eta} = 0$, and hence the growth rate products $g \equiv \dot{n}/n$ is given by

$$g = (1 - \alpha)\frac{L}{a_{Ln}} - \alpha\rho\tag{37.21}$$

Thus the larger the labor employed in R&D (L/a_{Ln}), the lower the discount rate ρ, and higher the market power (as represented by higher markup factor $1/\alpha$), the higher is the growth rate g of the economy.

Treating the economy described above as the innovating North, Helpman introduces an imitating economy, called the South. At any time t of the n products in existence, n_S denotes the number that have been imitated by the South. Thus $n_N = n - n_S$ the number of products in which the North still has monopoly. The instantaneous rate of imitation is $\mu \equiv \dot{n}_S/n_N$, so every Northern brand has the same chance by being imitated. Once a product is imitated, the Northern entrepreneur loses his monopoly on that product. Therefore he has to take into account the risk that his product will be imitated. His product development cost equals the expected value of the discounted stream of profits until it is imitated, the expectation being taken over the uncertain time of future imitation. Thus, with development cost as the numéraire, the profit rate has to include a risk premium as well. This turns out to imply that

$$\pi = r + \mu, \tag{37.22}$$

where r is the interest rate.

South needs $a_{LI/ns}$ units of labor per variety imitated. Having imitated a variety, South needs a_{LX} units (same as in the North) of labor to produce a unit of the product. Assuming that the Southern wage (and hence Southern cost of production) is sufficiently below that of the North in order for the South to be able to charge a monopoly price and still shut-out the Northern suppliers from the market for an imitated product, Helpman derives the market-clearing conditions for Southern labor as

$$a_{LI}\frac{\dot{n}_S}{n_S} + a_{LX}X_S = L_S$$

where X_S is the output of imitated products in the South leading to the steady-state growth equation

$$g = (1 - \alpha)\frac{L_S}{a_{LI}} - \alpha\rho. \tag{37.23}$$

Now taking into account the risk premium, the corresponding equation for the North turns out to be

$$g + \mu + \rho = (1 - \alpha)\frac{(L_N/a_{LN} - g)(g + \mu)}{\alpha g} \tag{37.24}$$

The two equations together determine g as in figure 37.1.

Helpman draws several implications from figure 37.1. First, if innovation in the South requires more resources than imitation, as seems reasonable, trade with the North speeds up long-run growth in the South. This can be seen by replacing a_{LI} by a larger coefficient representing the cost of innovation in equation (37.21). Second, trade with the South speeds up long-run growth in the North. Third, while a larger South raises both the rate of innovation and the rate of imitation, a larger North does not affect the rate of innovation but reduces the rate of imitation.

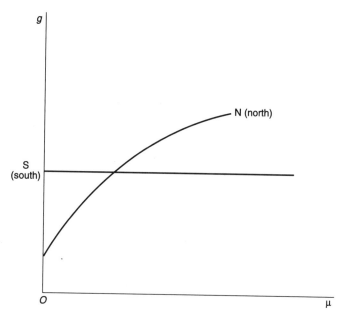

Figure 37.1

In addition to analyzing the interaction between innovating North and an imitating South, Helpman also considers the interaction between two identical countries. In the case where the R&D experience of one country contributes the same amount of knowledge capital to both countries, the two economies can be aggregated into one double-sized economy and proceed as if it is the only country in the world. The common long-run growth rate will depend on *aggregate* world employment in innovation. With nonidentical countries the situation becomes complicated. Long-run growth will be influenced by asymmetries in size, comparative costs, and differential dissemination of rates of knowledge at home and abroad.

Helpman points out that every policy that induces a long-run resource allocation affecting employment in R&D also changes long-run growth rates. In a one-country world given the uninternalized learning-by-doing externality, some degree of growth promotion through R&D subsidies is desirable. However, it turns out that in a multicountry world, one country's policies can affect R&D levels at home and abroad in opposite directions so that the net effect on growth can be positive or negative.

In addition to policies toward R&D, commercial policy can accelerate long-run growth rate if it succeeds in diverting resources toward innovation. But given monopolistic competition, which is a distortion by the well-known general theory of distortions, a growth-enhancing trade policy could turn out to be welfare-reducing if it aggravates the distortion.

37.3   Appendix: Expanded Open-Economy Model

Consumption-Goods Sector

Output of good $i = Q_i^c$, $i = 1, 2$.

Domestic use of good $i = C_i^c$, $i = 1, 2$.

Stock of capital $= K^c$.

Production frontier, $\beta_1 Q_1^c + \beta_2 Q_2^c = K^c$. $\hspace{3cm}$ (37.25)

Utility function, $U = (C_1^c)^\alpha (C_2^c)^{1-\alpha}$. $\hspace{3cm}$ (37.26)

Investment-Goods Sector

Output of good $i = Q_i^I$.

Domestic use of good $i = A_i^I$.

Stock of capital $= K^I$.

Production frontier, $\gamma_1 Q_1^I + \gamma_2 Q_2^I = K^I$. $\hspace{3cm}$ (37.27)

Aggregate investment, $I = (A_1^I)^\delta (A_2^I)^{1-\delta}$. $\hspace{3cm}$ (37.28)

Capital Accumulation

Let λ be the share of investment devoted to accumulation of K^I. Then

$$\dot{K}^I \equiv \frac{dK^I}{dt} = \lambda I, \hspace{3cm} (37.29)$$

$$\dot{K}^c \equiv \frac{dK^c}{dt} = (1 - \lambda) I. \hspace{3cm} (37.30)$$

Autarky

$C_i^c = Q_i^c$ and $A_i^I = Q_i^I$, $i = 1, 2$.

Maximization of (37.26) subject to (37.25) leads to

$$C_1^c = \frac{\alpha K^c}{\beta_1}, C_2^c = \frac{(1 - \alpha) K^c}{\beta_2} \quad \text{and} \quad U = \left(\frac{\alpha}{\beta_1} \right)^\alpha \left(\frac{1 - \alpha}{\beta_2} \right)^{1-\alpha} K^c. \hspace{1cm} (37.31)$$

Maximization of (37.28) subject to (37.27) leads to

$$A_1^I = \frac{\delta K^I}{\gamma_1}, \quad A_2^I = \frac{(1 - \delta) K^I}{\gamma_2} \hspace{3cm} (37.32)$$

Substituting (37.32) in (37.33), we get

$$I = \left(\frac{\delta}{\gamma_1} \right)^\delta \left(\frac{1 - \delta}{\gamma_2} \right)^{1-\delta} K^I \hspace{3cm} (37.33)$$

$$\equiv \eta K^I$$

where

$$\eta = \left(\frac{\delta}{\gamma_1} \right)^\delta \left(\frac{1 - \delta}{\gamma_2} \right)^{1-\delta} \hspace{3cm} (37.33')$$

Using (37.33)' in (37.29) and (37.30) and solving

$$K^I = K_0^I e^{\lambda \eta t} \tag{37.34}$$

yields

$$K^c = K_0^c + \left(\frac{1-\lambda}{\lambda}\right) K_0^I (e^{\lambda \eta t} - 1) \tag{37.35}$$

Thus the long-run growth rates of K^I, K^c, I, and U are the same and equal $\lambda \eta$

Free trade in Consumer Goods at a Relative Price π^C of Good 2 in Terms of Good 1 and Autarky in Investment Goods

Without loss of generality assume $\pi^c > \beta_2/\beta_1$. Then it is optimal to produce only good 2, export part of the output, and import good 1. It is easy to show that

$$Q_1^c = 0,$$

$$Q_2^c = \frac{K^c}{\beta_2},$$

$$C_1^c = \frac{\alpha \pi^c K^c}{\beta_2},$$

$$C_2^c = \frac{(1-\alpha)K^c}{\beta_2},$$

$$U = \alpha^\alpha (1-\alpha)^{1-\alpha} (\pi^c)^\alpha \frac{K^c}{\beta_2}.$$

It is easy to verify that given $\pi^c > \beta_2/\beta_1$ welfare U under free trade is higher than under autarky for any K^C. Since the investment goods sector is closed to trade, the dynamics of the system are unaffected, so the paths of K^C and K^I continue to be given by (37.34) and (37.35). Hence the long-run growth rates of K^C, K^I, I, and U are still $\lambda \eta$ though the level of U at each t is higher than under autarky.

Free Trade in Investment Goods at a Relative Price of π^I of Good 2 in Terms of Good 1 and Autarky in Consumption Goods

Without loss of generality assume that $\pi^I > \gamma_2/\gamma_1$. Then it is optimal to produce only good 2, export part of the output, and import good 1. It is easy to show that

$$Q_1^I = 0,$$

$$Q_2^I = \frac{K^I}{\gamma_2},$$

$$A_1^I = \frac{\delta \pi^I K^I}{\gamma_2},$$

$$A_2^I = \frac{(1-\delta)K^I}{\gamma_2},$$

$$I = \delta^\delta (1-\delta)^{1-\delta} (\pi^I)^\delta \frac{K^I}{\gamma^2}.$$

It is easy to verify that given $\pi^I > \gamma_2/\gamma_1$, investment I under free trade is higher than under autarky for any K^I. Now using (37.29) and (37.30) and solving,

$$K^I = K_0^I e^{\lambda \mu t}, \qquad \mu = \frac{\{\delta^\delta (1-\delta)^{1-\delta}(\pi^I)^\delta\}}{\gamma_2}$$

$$K^C = K_0^C + \left(\frac{1-\lambda}{\lambda}\right) K_0^I (e^{\lambda \mu t} - 1)$$

Given $\pi^I > \gamma_2/\gamma_1$ it follows that $\mu > \eta$. Hence the values of K^I and K^C at each time t under free trade in investment goods are higher than their corresponding values under autarky, and the long-run growth rate of K^C, K^I and I are the same at $\lambda \mu$, which is also higher than its value $\lambda \eta$ under autarky.

The consumption goods sector under autarky by given by

$$K^c, Q_1^c = C_1^c = \frac{\alpha K^c}{\beta^1},$$

$$Q_2^c = C_2^c = \frac{(1-\alpha)K^c}{\beta^2},$$

$$U = \left(\frac{\alpha}{\beta_1}\right)^\alpha \left(\frac{1-\alpha}{\beta_2}\right)^{1-\alpha} K^c.$$

Since K^C is higher at each t under free trade in investment goods than under autarky, U is higher as well. Since K^C grows faster, U grows faster as well.

Recommended Readings

Cass, D. T. Optimum growth in an aggregative model of capital accumulations. *Review of Economic Studies* 32 (1965): 233–40.

Domar, E. *Essays in the Theory of Economic Growth*. London: Oxford University Press, 1957.

Fel'dman, G. A. *K teorii tempov narodnogo dokhoda. Planovoe Khoziaistvo* 11 (1928): 146–70 and 12 (1929): 152–78. (This is discussed in Domar 1957, ch. 9.)

Grossman, G., and E. Helpman. *Innovation and Growth in the Global Economy*. Cambridge: MIT Press, 1991.

Helpman, E. Monopolistic competition in trade theory. Special Papers in International Finance, 16. Department of Economics, Princeton University, 1990.

Koopmans, T. C. On the concept of optimal growth. In *The Econometric Approach to Development Planning*. Amsterdam: North-Holland, 1965.

Lucas, R. E. On the mechanics of economic development. *Journal of Monetary Economics* 22 (1988): 3–42.

Mahalanobis, P. C. The approach of operational research to planning in India. *Sankhya: The Indian Journal of Statistics* 16 (1955): 3–62.

Romer, P. M. Increasing returns and long-run growth. *Journal of Political Economy* 94 (1986): 1002–37.

Solow, R. M. A contribution to the theory of economic growth. *Quarterly Journal of Economics* 70 (1956): 65–94.

Trade theory has recently been extended to the questions raised by cost-benefit analysis. As is evident from our analysis in part III, trade theorists have generally considered second-best problems in characterizing the nature of optimal policy intervention when the given distortions cannot be directly removed. Project analysis poses a related but different question: If the given distortions defining current resource allocations cannot be removed, will the introduction of a project that withdraws resources from this existing allocation for project use improve welfare? In short, we need a social-valuation criterion utilizing "true" or shadow prices of inputs and outputs to determine whether the project should be implemented or rejected. The market prices are distorted and are, in principle, not useful.[1]

38.1 "World-Price"–Valuation Rule

Little and Mirrlees (1974) proposed that the shadow prices of traded goods (whether inputs or outputs) should be treated as their world prices and that the shadow prices of nontraded factors be derived by evaluating their marginal product at world prices.[2] This prescription reflects their basic criterion for project acceptance by a small country in a world of traded goods and nontraded factors: The project is accepted if it adds to national income valued at world prices.

In the 2×2 model, the intuition and logic behind this are clear: If the project, withdrawing factors to itself from existing allocation, results in an outward shift of society's budget line (which is evidently defined at world prices for a small country), welfare is improved, given a well-behaved social-utility function and constant consumer prices. If there is no distortion—that is, if the economy is producing optimally in free trade at P^* in figure 38.1 (with world price ratio WP^*)—there is no way that a project producing either good 1 or good 2 can improve welfare. Only in a distorted economy, with production distorted to $\hat{P}$, withdrawal of resources from $\hat{P}$ toward use in a project producing good 1 or good 2 will the postproject social-budget line shift from WP_1 to WP_2. The Little-Mirrlees (LM) criterion for project acceptance simply formalizes this

1. However, an interesting question posed by Bhagwati and Srinivasan (1980) and considered further by Smith (1982) is: Are there conditions when the use of market prices for factors would nonetheless yield the correct answer that the use of shadow prices for factors always would?

2. What we call the Little-Mirrlees rule is qualified by these authors when factor-market and intertemporal distortions are involved. The LM rule is therefore, strictly, only a component of their full analysis. For extension to nontraded goods and monopoly power in trade, see Little and Mirrlees (1974) and Bhagwati and Srinivasan (1981).

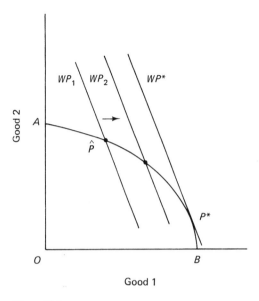

Figure 38.1

notion and states that a project is socially advantageous if it results in the social-budget line (which is defined at world prices) moving outward. An acceptable project should add to national income valued at world prices.

The LM shadow prices of goods and factors reflect this criterion. If a project uses factors and goods and produces goods, the social benefit of the project is the goods produced (valued at world prices), whereas its social cost is the goods used in production (valued at world prices) plus the shadow price of the factors (which must be derived as their marginal product or the production forgone when these factors are withdrawn from existing use toward project use) valued at world prices.

The LM shadow prices for factors are therefore based on their opportunity cost in terms of production forgone, valued at world prices. They are different from the shadow prices of factors based on the utility impact of factors withdrawn for project use.[3] We will concentrate on the LM shadow factor prices because the LM procedure for cost-benefit analysis has been widely practiced and because it reflects trade-theoretic principles beautifully. Also this procedure's use of limited, objective data (world prices) for project appraisal—whereas going to utility impact requires explicit specification of utility information—raises the question whether cost-benefit analysis should not be replaced, once all information is available, by overall general-equilibrium computation of the nth-best solution

---

3. The relationship between these is considered at length in Bhagwati and Srinivasan (1981).

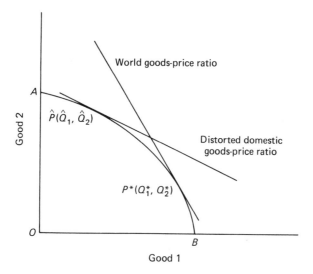

Figure 38.2

that would automatically yield the project choice as part of the total activity-allocational choice.[4]

38.2   Derivation of World-Price–Valuation Shadow Prices with Given Distortion

To see how the world-price–valuation shadow prices are to be derived, consider a simple model with three traded goods (1, 2, and 3) and two nontraded factors (K and L). Let the project produce good 3, and let the existing equilibrium production of goods 1 and 2 be at $\hat{P}$ in figure 38.2, the cause being a production-distorting tax that shifts production from optimal P^*. For simplicity we ignore intermediate use of goods.

Starting from $\hat{P}$, some factors are withdrawn for use in good-3 production. Under the project being evaluated, the problem at hand assumes that the distortion is in place and cannot be removed; if it could be removed, one would go straight to P^* and social cost-benefit analysis would not be required. Therefore we must proceed in two steps: First, we have to evaluate the change in outputs of goods 1 and 2, starting from $\hat{P}$, as factors K_3 and L_3 are withdrawn to produce one unit of good 3. We have to do this in general equilibrium and assume that the goods-price ratio facing producers is the distorted one. Next, we have to value these changes in outputs of goods 1 and 2, from $\hat{P}$, at the world price ratio.

---

4. This point was sharply raised by Rudra (1972) and discussed by Bhagwati and Wan (1979).

If the changes in outputs at $\hat{P}$ are ΔQ_1, ΔQ_2, the social cost of the project is evidently $\Delta Q_1 + \Delta Q_2 p^*$. The social gain is $Q_3 \cdot p_3^*/p_1^*$. Therefore the project-acceptance criterion is that

$$\Delta Q_1 + \Delta Q_2 p^* \leq \frac{Q_3 p_3^*}{p_1^*}. \tag{38.1}$$

The shadow prices of factors can be defined, for marginal withdrawal of factors for project use from $\hat{P}$, as

$$\hat{w}^* = \frac{\partial Q_1}{\partial L} + \frac{\partial Q_2}{\partial L} p^* \tag{38.2}$$

and

$$\hat{\gamma}^* = \frac{\partial Q_1}{\partial K} + \frac{\partial Q_2}{\partial K} p^*, \tag{38.3}$$

where the caret on the wage and the rental indicates that they refer to the distorted situation at $\hat{P}$ and the asterisk indicates that they are shadow prices.[5] Alternatively, they can be derived as solutions to the equations

$$1 = \hat{w}^* \left(\widehat{\frac{L_1}{Q_1}}\right) + \hat{\gamma}^* \left(\widehat{\frac{K_1}{Q_1}}\right) \tag{38.4}$$

and

$$\frac{P_2^*}{P_1^*} = \hat{w}^* \left(\widehat{\frac{L_2}{Q_2}}\right) + \hat{\gamma}^* \left(\widehat{\frac{K_2}{Q_2}}\right), \tag{38.5}$$

where the unit-output factor requirements (in parentheses) are fixed at $\hat{P}$, since with the distortion in place the distorted goods-price ratio is fixed and so therefore are the factor coefficients. These equations clearly equate the social valuation of factors to the valuation of their marginal output (at the distorted prices and factor coefficients) at world prices. Therefore, the project-acceptance criterion (38.1), for small changes, can be written also as

$$\hat{w}^* L_3 + \hat{\gamma}^* K_3 \leq \frac{P_3^*}{P_1^*}, \tag{38.6}$$

where the left-hand side is the social cost of the factors L and K withdrawn to produce unit output of good 3 in the project and the right-hand side is the project output valued at its world price.

---

5. The partial derivatives have to be calculated at the distorted situation namely by holding the distorted goods-price ratio and therefore the factor coefficients unchanged at $\hat{P}$.

38.3   Negative Shadow Prices

An examination of equations (38.4) and (38.5) shows that one of the shadow prices can be negative. This implies, as we have already noted in chapters 29 and 34, that the economy is so badly distorted, with such serious misallocation of resources resulting therefrom, that the withdrawal of a factor from existing use for project use actually produces a net gain, which should be added to the gain implied by the output of the project.

Brecher has adapted the Lerner-Findlay-Grubert-Wellisz technique to illustrate this possibility beautifully. In figure 38.3 assume (as in figures 38.1 and 38.2) that producers of good 2 receive a domestic price higher than the world price, whereas for producers of good 1 the domestic and world prices are identical. The actual market wage-rental ratio $\hat{w}/\hat{\gamma}$ then is given by the line RS, which is tangent to the unit-value-at-domestic-prices isoquants Q_1 and Q_2 at factor ratios $\hat{K}_1/\hat{L}_1$ and $\hat{K}_2/\hat{L}_2$, respec-

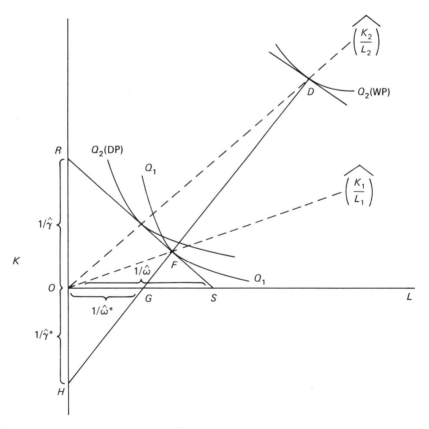

Figure 38.3

tively. Then OS and OR are evidently $1/\hat{w}$ and $1/\hat{\gamma}$, respectively, since they represent the unit-value amounts of each factor that can be hired if none of the other factor's services is purchased. The unit-value-at-world-prices isoquants, however, are $Q_1(\text{WP})$ and Q_2. It follows that by connecting D and F and projecting the line down to cut the L axis at G and meet the K axis at H, we get a positively sloped factor-price line DH, which corresponds to world goods prices (but factor proportions chosen at domestic prices), and thus reflects the shadow factor prices, $\hat{w}^*$ and $\hat{\gamma}^*$. More precisely, OH is $1/\hat{\gamma}^*$ and OG is $1/\hat{w}^*$, and evidently $\hat{\gamma}^*$ is negative.

How are negative shadow prices related to the phenomenon of "value subtraction" at world prices in certain activities, noted by empirical analysts for many trade-distorted economies? The two phenomena are related in an essential way, since they both reflect world-price valuation. Value subtraction at world price must imply that total factor valuation must be negative; hence value subtraction requires some negative shadow factor price. However, as is evident from equations (38.4) and (38.5), a negative shadow factor price does not necessarily result in value subtraction.[6]

38.4   Other Issues and Extensions

The shadow prices of factors have been derived so far for a model with all traded goods and for a country with no monopoly power in trade. The method, however, must be amended to accommodate nontraded goods and monopoly power in trade. Since nontraded goods have no world prices, they must be decomposed into equivalent traded goods in equilibrium and then evaluated at the latter's world prices. This can be appropriately done if we have nontraded goods produced at constant costs, as in the Komiya (1967) model. In the Komiya model, the $n \times n$ structure of tradables and nontraded factors determines the domestic factor prices reflecting the domestic prices of the tradable goods. The factor prices in turn determine the unit cost of each nontraded good. Hence, as long as the withdrawal of factors into project use leaves the economy at unchanged factor prices (i.e., as long as the economy remains in the McKenzie-Chipman diversification cone), the unit cost of each nontraded good will remain constant as factors are withdrawn for project use.[7]

---

6. Further analysis of the relationship between these two concepts is to be found in Bhagwati, Srinivasan, and Wan (1978).

7. This and related questions on how monopoly power in trade affects the LM shadow factor prices are treated informally in Little and Mirrlees (1974) and examined further in Bhagwati and Srinivasan (1981).

The LM approach can break down when quantitative restrictions affect the prices faced by consumers. The LM procedure assumes that we can go on from a shift in the social-budget constraint at world prices to infer a change in social utility, but this cannot necessarily be done if the prices faced in consumption change. Thus, with quantitative restrictions in trade, the domestic prices faced by consumers may be distorted further from world prices when the project is introduced, and the loss from this added consumption distortion may well outweigh the gain implied by the shift in national income at world prices.[8]

Finally the project-acceptance criterion (38.6) can be written

$$\text{DRC}_3 = \frac{\hat{w}^* L_3 + \hat{\gamma}^* K_3}{P_3^*} \leq 1, \tag{38.7}$$

where DRC_3 is the domestic resource cost (at the appropriate shadow prices, $\hat{w}^*$ and $\hat{\gamma}^*$) of producing a unit of foreign exchange via good 3 in the project. If we rewrite equations (38.4) and (38.5) in the DRC form, we can see immediately that for goods 1 and 2 at the preproject equilibrium $\hat{P}$,

$$\text{DRC}_1 = \text{DRC}_2 = 1.$$

Therefore the project-acceptance criterion (38.7) implies that

$$\text{DRC}_3 \leq \text{DRC}_1 = \text{DRC}_2;$$

that is, the DRC in the project should not be greater than in the existing factor allocation.[9]

Recommended Readings

Bacha, E., and L. Taylor. Foreign exchange shadow prices: A critical review of current theories. *Quarterly Journal of Economics* 85 (1971): 197–224.

Bhagwati, J., and T. N. Srinivasan. On inferring resource-allocational implications from DRC calculations in trade-distorted small open economies. *Indian Economic Review* 14 (1979): 1–16.

Bhagwati, J., and T. N. Srinivasan. Domestic resource costs, effective rates of protection, and project analysis in tariff-distorted economies. *Quarterly Journal of Economics* 96 (1980): 205–209.

Bhagwati, J., and T. N. Srinivasan. The evaluation of projects at world prices under trade distortions: Quantitative restrictions, monopoly power in trade and nontraded goods. *International Economic Review* 22 (1981): 385–99.

8. See Bhagwati and Srinivasan (1981) for further analysis of quantitative restrictions.

9. More on this, and on the inappropriateness of using effective rate of protection as a project-evaluation criterion, is to be found is Srinivasan and Bhagwati (1978).

Bhagwati, J., and H. Wan, Jr. Shadow prices in project evaluation, with and without distortions, and with many goods and factors. *American Economic Review* 69 (1979): 261–73.

Bhagwati, J., T. N. Srinivasan, and H. Wan, Jr. Value subtracted, negative shadow prices of factors in project evaluations, and immiserizing growth: Three paradoxes in the presence of trade distortions. *Economic Journal* 88 (1978): 121–25.

Bruno, M. The optimal selection of import-substituting and export-promoting projects. In *Planning the External Sector: Techniques, Problems and Politics.* New York: United Nations, 1967.

Diamond, P. A., and J. A. Mirrlees. Private constant returns and public shadow prices. *Review of Economic Studies* 43 (1976): 41–48.

Findlay, R., and S. Wellisz. Protect evaluation, shadow prices, and trade policy. *Journal of Political Economy* 84 (1976): 543–52.

Joshi, V. The rationale and relevance of the Little-Mirrlees criterion. *Bulletin of Oxford Institute of Economics and Statistics* 34 (1972): 3–33.

Komiya, R. Non-traded goods and the pure theory of international trade. *International Economic Review* 8 (1967): 132–52.

Little, I. M. D., and J. A. Mirrlees. *Project Appraisal and Planning for Developing Countries.* New York: Basic Books, 1974.

Rudra, A. Use of shadow prices in project evaluation. *Indian Economic Review* 7 (1972): 1–15.

Smith, M. A. M. Some simple results on the gains from trade, from growth, and from public investment. *Journal of International Economics* 13 (1983): 163–67.

Srinivasan, T. N., and J. Bhagwati. Shadow prices for project selection in the presence of distortions: Effective rates of protection and domestic resource costs. *Journal of Political Economy* 86 (1978): 97–116.

In the preceding chapters we discussed the positive and normative aspects of international trade in a world of complete certainty. Agents (producers, consumers, and factor owners) decided on their actions (inputs into production, allocations for consumption, and factor offers) with certain knowledge of outcomes (outputs, welfare, and factor employment) of each action and of the signals (prices, taxes, and transfers) to which their actions responded. In this chapter we explore the consequences of introducing uncertainty into this system.

The propositions that were derived from the characterization of equilibrium with international trade as a competitive equilibrium continue to hold, even if we introduce uncertainty, as long as there is a complete set of contingent commodity markets. Existence of a complete set of markets means that agents can contract to buy or sell goods or factor services contingent on a specific date and any (and every) specified realization of the event or events they are uncertain about. Thus perfect insurance is feasible. Each agent enters into contingent contracts prior to the resolution of uncertainty. Once the realized state of nature becomes known to every agent, each agent carries out the contracts he had made contingent on that state of nature being realized; contracts contingent on other unrealized states of nature then become irrelevant. Thus markets open and contracts are made prior to the resolution of uncertainty. Once uncertainty is resolved, contracts are carried out (production takes place, contracted deliveries and purchases are made), but no further market transactions need to take place and none will take place even if markets reopen. To reinterpret in this fashion the theory of competitive equilibrium in a static world without uncertainty in the context of uncertainty, one has to assume a finite number of alternative states of nature, a finite time horizon, and a finite number of commodities involved in each possible combination of time period and state of nature. Even then, the number of possible contingent commodities could be very large, so a complete set of markets is unlikely to exist. An alternative to the existence of a complete set of contingent commodity markets is the existence of a sequence of spot markets—one for each date and state of nature at that date—and a set of markets for securities that enable agents to transfer wealth across states of nature and over time. Helpman and Razin (1980) work with a framework in which securities as well as commodities are traded internationally.

It is easy to see that familiar theorems continue to hold in such a world. For instance, if a country is "small" in the wider sense that it is a price taker in each market in the complete set of contingent markets (or in the market for securities, as well as in spot commodity markets), free trade in contingent commodities (in securities and commodities) is the optimal policy. Versions of the Stolper-Samuelson, Rybczynski, and factor-price-equalization theorems hold. Thus, if trade in contingent commodities equalizes their prices across countries, contingent factor prices also will be equalized under the same set of assumptions as in the traditional model. As Anderson (1981) showed, even the Heckscher-Ohlin theorem can be shown to be valid in the Helpman-Razin model if consumers are identical, are rational in their expectations, and have utility functions that exhibit a constant Arrow-Pratt (Arrow 1971; Pratt 1964) measure of relative risk aversion.

Since the framework discussed above is very special and unlikely to be a convincing enough abstraction of the real world, it is fruitful to assume that only a small subset of the complete set of markets exist, even though this avoids the deeper issue of why only the observed set of markets are active and others are not. Since a model with an incomplete set of markets involves (loosely speaking) a departure from "first best," it is to be expected that some of the first-best results do not obtain and that paradoxes emerge. Among these paradoxes are that tariffs do not protect and that the Heckscher-Ohlin or the Stolper-Samuelson theorem does not hold. Moreover Hart (1975) has shown that in such a context a competitive equilibrium (given the active markets) might be Pareto-dominated by some other feasible competitive equilibrium. Further a competitive equilibrium with a given set of markets may be Pareto-dominated by another with an additional market opened up.

Any discussion of models with an incomplete set of markets must involve a taxonomic approach. First, one has to specify the markets that are active, the actions that have to be taken prior to the resolution of uncertainty, and the markets and actions that are relevant only after the resolution. For instance, factor markets may be active and production decisions made prior to the realization of the state of nature, whereas consumption and trading decisions may be taken after. Second, one has to specify the information available to an agent at the time he makes a decision and the way he uses that information. In particular, a clear distinction has to be made between information that is available only to an agent or a group of agents and the information that is available to all agents and known to be available to all agents. In the previous example a producer's information may include the common knowledge on prices that cleared the markets in previous periods as well as private information about his own production possibilities. His use of this information in forming his expectations about future prices may be static, adaptive, or rational. Third, in the specification of feasible actions prior to the resolution of uncertainty, the alternative market and nonmarket ways of sharing or pooling risks have to be specified. Fourth, it must be specified whether uncertainty is exogenous (e.g., due to weather or other natural phenomena) or endogenous to the system.

39.1   Ricardian Model for Complete Set of Markets

In that follows we present a few models to illustrate the issues involved without being comprehensive. (See Pomery 1979 for a more detailed discussion.) Consider a Ricardian model in which the technology permits the production of two goods using a single factor: labor. Introduce uncertainty into the system by postulating that the productivity of labor (e.g., in the production of one of the goods) depends on the weather. There are only two possible states of weather: good and bad. In bad weather productivity is half as much as in good weather. Thus the technology in labor input per unit of output is as follows:

	Good weather	Bad weather
Good 1	l_1	l_1
Good 2	l_2	$2l_2$

Let the total labor endowment of the economy be one unit in both types of weather. Let there be a single consumer who owns the labor endowment. To begin with, assume that a complete set of markets exists. Clearly, for the set of markets to be complete, we must have six markets, one for each state of weather for each good and labor. Thus, if prices p_1^j, p_2^j, and w^j (for good 1, good 2, and labor, respectively) were quoted contingent on weather being $j = ((\text{G})\text{ood}, (\text{B})\text{ad})$, producers would decide their production and employment plan for each j so as to maximize profits and the consumer would choose his consumption plan (c_1^j, c_2^j) so as to maximize his welfare subject to a budget constraint $\sum_j (p_1^j c_1^j + p_2^j c_2^j) \leq \sum_j w^j$. It is easily seen that the production problem reduces to analyzing a standard Ricardian model for each j. Thus, except when p_2^j / p_1^j equals the factor-input ratio corresponding to j, there will be complete specialization in production in each state of the weather, though the economy could specialize in different goods in good and in bad weather. Hence standard theorems that relate to the supply side of the Ricardian economy continue to hold.

More specifically, since labor is not mobile across countries, labor markets have to clear within each country. This implies that the output vector (Q_1^j, Q_2^j) has to satisfy

$$Q_1^j = \frac{1}{l_1}, \quad Q_2^j = 0 \qquad \text{if } \frac{p_1^j}{p_2^j} > \frac{l_1}{\theta^j l_2}, \tag{39.1}$$

or

$$Q_1^j = z, \quad Q_2^j = \frac{1 - l_1 z}{\theta^j l_2}, \qquad 0 \le z \le \frac{1}{l_1} \qquad \text{if } \frac{p_1^j}{p_2^j} = \frac{l_1}{\theta^j l_2}, \tag{39.2}$$

or

$$Q_1^j = 0, \quad Q_2^j = \frac{1}{\theta^j l_2} \qquad \text{if } \frac{p_1^j}{p_2^j} < \frac{l_1}{\theta^j l_2}, \tag{39.3}$$

where $\theta^j = 1$ if $j = G$ and $\theta^j = 2$ if $j = B$. Labor-market clearance implies that $w^j = p_1^j / l_1$ in case (39.1), $w^j = p_1^j / l_1 = p_2^j / \theta^j l_2$ in case (39.2), and $w^j = p_2^j / \theta^j l_2$ in case (39.3).

The consumer's welfare is represented by his expected utility

$$\sum_j \pi^j u(c_1^j, c_2^j),$$

where π^j is the probability of state j occurring. It is more convenient to write the actual welfare achieved in state j by the indirect utility function

$$v^j = v(p_1^j, p_2^j, e^j),$$

where e^j is the consumer's expenditure in state j. The consumer's problem then is to maximize $\sum \pi^j v^j$ subject to the budget constraint $\sum e^j = \sum w^j$. If he spends a positive sum in each state, it is necessary for an optimum that $\pi^j v_3^j = \lambda$, where λ is the Lagrangian multiplier associated with the budget constraint and v_3^j is the marginal utility of income in state j. Using the budget constraint, we see that $\lambda \sum w^j = \sum \pi^j v_3^j e^j$. The difference between (Q_1^j, Q_2^j) and (c_1^j, c_2^j) represents net trade, which is balanced when both states are taken together.

39.2   Ricardian Model for Securities and Spot Markets

Now modify the model so that producers make their employment and production decisions prior to the resolution of uncertainty, whereas the consumption and trading decisions take place after the resolution. One could then view the producer's employment-production decision in respect of good 1 as if he "produces" a real security, using one unit of labor per unit of security. A unit of type 1 security yields a return of $1/l_1$ units of good 1 in all states of nature and nothing of good 2. Similarly security type 2 yields $1/l_2$ units of good 2 in good weather, $1/2l_2$ units in bad, and nothing of good 1 in either state. Clearly, if the production of securities is competitive and if their prices are $\tilde{q}_1$ and $\tilde{q}_2$, then

$$\tilde{q}_j \le \tilde{w}, \qquad j = 1, 2,$$

where $\tilde{w}$ is the wage rate. A consumer who holds x_j units of security type j will have an endowment of $(x_1/l_1, x_2/l_2)$ of the two goods in good weather and $(x_1/l_1, x_2/2l_2)$ in bad. Because consumption and trade take place after the resolution of uncertainty, the consumer maximizes his utility, given the price vector (p_1^j, p_2^j) in the spot markets and income y^j, which equals the value of his endowment in state j at prices $(\tilde{p}_1^j, \tilde{p}_2^j)$. Thus

$$\tilde{y}^j = \frac{\tilde{p}_1^j x_1}{l_1} + \frac{\tilde{p}_2^j x_2}{\theta^j l_2}.$$

Denote the consumer's indirect utility in the two states of nature as

$$\tilde{v}^j = v(\tilde{p}_1, \tilde{p}_2, \tilde{y}^j).$$

The portfolio-choice problem of the consumer is to choose (x_1, x_2) so as to maximize his expected utility $\sum \pi^j \tilde{v}^j$ subject to his budget constraint that he spends no more than his wage income w on the securities; that is,

$$\tilde{q}_1 x_1 + \tilde{q}_2 x_2 \le \tilde{w}.$$

An interior solution to this problem leads to

$$\sum \pi^j \tilde{v}_3^j \left(\frac{\tilde{p}_j^1}{l_1} \right) = \mu \tilde{q}_1 \tag{39.4}$$

and

$$\sum \pi^j \tilde{v}_3^j \left(\frac{\tilde{p}_j^2}{\theta^j l_2} \right) = \mu \tilde{q}_2. \tag{39.5}$$

If securities are traded internationally, $\tilde{q}_1$ and $\tilde{q}_2$ are the world-market prices of the two securities. If they are not traded, the market for securities has to clear within the country. Consider the latter case. If it takes one unit of labor to "produce" each security, and if positive amounts of each are demanded and supplied in an interior equilibrium, we have

$$\tilde{q}_1 = \tilde{q}_2 = \tilde{w}. \tag{39.6}$$

The equilibrium of this economy when there is no international trade in securities is depicted in figure 39.1. Any portfolio (x_1, x_2) of the consumer determines an expected utility $\sum \pi^j v^j(\tilde{p}_1^j, \tilde{p}_2^j, \tilde{y}^j)$ for him. This determines a set of asset-indifference curves in (x_1, x_2) space. The marginal rate of substitution along an indifference curve is

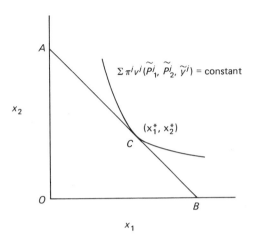

Figure 39.1

$$-\frac{\partial \Sigma \pi^j \tilde{v}^j / \partial x_1}{\partial \Sigma \pi^j \tilde{v}^j / \partial x_2} = \frac{\pi^G \tilde{v}_3^G \tilde{p}_1^G / l_1 + \pi^B \tilde{v}_3^B \tilde{p}_1^B / l_1}{\pi^G \tilde{v}_3^G \tilde{p}_2^G / l_2 + \pi^B \tilde{v}_3^B \tilde{p}_2^B / 2l_2},$$

where $\tilde{v}_3^G$ is the marginal utility of income in good weather, and so on. If the consumer exhibits strict aversion to risk in income, the indifference curves will have the usual strict convexity toward the origin. In an interior equilibrium, the marginal rate of substitution will equal the marginal rate of transformation (unity, since by assumption each security is "produced" by one unit of labor). With an aggregate endowment of labor of 1, the transformation curve is AB (with a slope of 1) in figure 39.1. An equilibrium portfolio (x_1^*, x_2^*) is represented by point C. Thus, in equilibrium,[1]

$$\tilde{y}^{j*} = \frac{\tilde{p}_1}{l_1} x_1^* + \frac{\tilde{p}_2}{\theta^j l_2} x_2^* \quad \text{and} \quad \frac{\sum \pi^j \tilde{v}_3^{j*} \tilde{p}_1^j / l_1}{\sum \pi^j \tilde{v}_3^{j*} \tilde{p}_2^j / \theta^j l_2} = 1.$$

The latter equation can be derived from equations (39.4)–(39.6).

39.3   Ricardian Model: Equivalence of Equilibria in Spot and Securities Markets and in a Complete Set of Contingent Commodity Markets

To relate the securities model with the contingent commodity model, let us first construct Arrow-Debreu type securities (i.e., a portfolio that has a unit payoff in one state of nature and none in the other). Now, without

---

1. In the single-country analysis of this chapter, we use superscript * to denote equilibrium values of variables rather than foreign-country variables.

loss of generality, let

$$\frac{\tilde{p}_1^{\mathrm{G}}}{\tilde{p}_2^{\mathrm{G}}} \neq \frac{\tilde{p}_1^{\mathrm{G}}}{\tilde{p}_2^{\mathrm{B}}}$$

so that the relative price of good 1 in terms of good 2 is different when the weather is good than when it is bad. Then the portfolio $(x_1^{\mathrm{B}}, x_2^{\mathrm{B}})$ yields a unit payoff when the weather is bad and none when it is good, where

$$x_1^{\mathrm{B}} = \frac{-2l_1\tilde{p}_2^{\mathrm{G}}}{\tilde{p}_1^{\mathrm{B}}\tilde{p}_2^{\mathrm{B}} - 2\tilde{p}_1^{\mathrm{B}}\tilde{p}_2^{\mathrm{G}}}, \qquad x_2^{\mathrm{B}} = \frac{2l_2\tilde{p}_1^{\mathrm{G}}}{\tilde{p}_1^{\mathrm{G}}\tilde{p}_2^{\mathrm{B}} - 2\tilde{p}_1^{\mathrm{B}}\tilde{p}_2^{\mathrm{G}}}. \tag{39.7}$$

Implicitly we are permitting short sales in forming these portfolios. Now the cost q^{B} of the portfolio $(x_1^{\mathrm{B}}, x_2^{\mathrm{B}})$ is

$$\tilde{q}_1 x_1^{\mathrm{B}} + \tilde{q}_2 x_2^{\mathrm{B}} = \frac{1}{\mu}\left[x_1^{\mathrm{B}}\left(\sum \pi^j \tilde{v}_3^j \frac{\tilde{p}_1^j}{l_1}\right) + x_2^{\mathrm{B}}\left(\sum \pi^j \tilde{v}_3^j \frac{\tilde{p}_2^j}{\theta^j l_2}\right) \right]$$

$$= \frac{\pi^{\mathrm{B}} \tilde{v}_3^{\mathrm{B}}}{\mu}. \tag{39.8}$$

Similarly the cost $\tilde{q}^{\mathrm{G}}$ of the portfolio $(x_1^{\mathrm{G}}, x_2^{\mathrm{G}})$ is $\pi^{\mathrm{G}} \tilde{v}_3^{\mathrm{G}}/\mu$.

If we set the contingent commodity price

$$p_k^j = q^j \tilde{p}_k^j, \qquad j = \mathrm{G}, \mathrm{B}, \; k = 1, 2, \tag{39.9}$$

and also set

$$e^j = w^j = \tilde{q}^j \tilde{y}^{j*}, \qquad \mu = \lambda, \tag{39.10}$$

then

$$v_3(p_1^j, p_2^j, e^j) = v_3(\tilde{q}^j \tilde{p}_1^j, \tilde{q}^j \tilde{p}^j, \tilde{q}^j \tilde{y}^{j*})$$

$$= \frac{1}{\tilde{q}^j} v_3(\tilde{p}_1^j, \tilde{p}_2^j, \tilde{y}^{j*}) \tag{39.11}$$

because the indirect utility function is homogeneous of degree 0 in prices and income, and so its partial derivative are homogeneous of degree -1. Hence

$$v_3(p_1^j, p_2^j, c^j) = \frac{1}{\tilde{q}^j}\tilde{v}_3^j = \frac{\mu}{\pi^j} \quad \text{or} \quad \pi^j v_3 = \mu = \lambda. \tag{39.12}$$

It follows from equations (39.10) and (39.12) that the equilibrium with markets for securities and spot markets for commodities is identical to the equilibrium in contingent commodity markets. It is important that this equivalence of the equilibrium with a complete set of contingent commodity markets and that with spot markets for commodities and securities markets holds when the underlying source of uncertainty is multiplicative. Our Ricardian model satisfies this requirement, since uncertainty manifests itself in multiplying the productivity of labor in one sector by a random factor. (This feature is used at several points in the proof of equivalence.)

39.4   Models with an Incomplete Set of Markets

Commitment Model

We now turn to four models with an incomplete set of markets in order to illustrate the implications of uncertainty in realistic situations. Consider the following model due to Ruffin (1974): For simplicity assume that there is no production but only exchange from a given endowment of two commodities. Terms of trade are uncertain, but trading decisions have to be made prior to the resolution of uncertainty. Thus opportunities for covering risk through a stock market or contingent markets are absent. This model is not as unrealistic as it may seem, since many commodities are often shipped on consignment to export markets where they are auctioned off. Thus the size of the consignment has to be decided before the auction that determines prices. Similarly contracts for import of a given quantity *ex ante* may be made with prices being determined *ex post*. Autarky is still inferior to trading in such an environment, and trades may involve simultaneous commitments to export both commodities.

Assume that the social-utility function $U(c_1, c_2)$ is concave. Committing to export e_1 (e_2) units of commodity 1 (2) before terms of trade p is known, with an initial endowment (x_1, x_2), leads to a random consumption of the first commodity of $c_1 - x_1 - e_1 + e_2/p$ and a consumption of the second commodity of $c_2 = \{x_2 + pe_1 - e_2\}$. The expected welfare is $EU(c_1, c_2)$. Taking the derivative EU with respect to e_1 (e_2) and evaluating it at $e_1 = e_2 = 0$, we get

$$\left.\frac{\partial EU}{\partial e_e}\right|_{e_1=e_2=0} = U_2(x_1, x_2)(Ep - p^A)$$

and

$$\left.\frac{\partial EU}{\partial e_2}\right|_{e_1=e_2=0} = U_2(x_1, x_2)\left[p^A E\left(\frac{1}{p}\right) - 1\right],$$

where p^A denotes the autarky price ratio $U_1(x_1, x_2)/U_2(x_1, x_2)$. If $Ep >$

p^A and $E(1/p) > 1/p^A$, then positive commitment to export small amounts of both commodities is welfare-improving compared with autarky.

These results are also intuitively obvious. Committing to export a specific commodity prior to the knowledge of p can result in exporting it when it would have been optimal to import it had the trade decision been taken after p was known. In the above example, if p were less than p^A and trade took place after p was known, commodity 1 would have been imported rather than exported. Thus, even though p could take values greater than p^A and make exporting commodity 1 optimal, concavity ensures that there is still a loss in expected welfare as long as the average price Ep is less than p^A. It is also clear why a simultaneous commitment to export both commodities may improve welfare: This way one bets and hedges at the same time.

Market-Disruption Model

Next we discuss the market-disruption model of Bhagwati and Srinivasan (1976) in which the level of a country's exports in one period determines the probability that its trading partner will impose a quota of known size in the next period.[2] Consider a two-commodity model of international trade, and assume a two-period time horizon such that the level of exports E in the first period affects the probability $P(E)$ of a quota $\bar{E}$ being imposed at the beginning of the next period. Let $U[C_1, C_2]$ be the standard social-utility function defined in terms of the consumption C_i of commodity i $(i = 1, 2)$. By assumption, $U[C_1, C_2]$ is known at the beginning of the next period whether the quota $\bar{E}$ has been imposed or not. Thus the policy in the next period will be to maximize U subject to the transformation function $F[X_1, X_2] = 0$ and the terms-of-trade function π if no quota is imposed, with an additional constraint $E \leq \bar{E}$ if the quota is imposed.

Let the maximal welfare with and without the quota be $\underline{U}$ and $\bar{U}$, respectively. Clearly then $\bar{U} > \underline{U}$ when the quota is binding. The expected welfare in the second period is then

$$\underline{U}P(E) + \underline{U}[1 - P(E)].$$

The objective function for the first period therefore is

$$\phi = U[X_1 - E, X_2 + \pi E] + \rho[\underline{U}P(E) + \bar{U}[1 - P(E)]],$$

2. This method of introducing market disruption presupposes that the QR level is pre-specified but that the probability of its being imposed will be a function of how deeply the market is penetrated in the importing country and therefore how effective the import-competing industry's pressure for protection will be with respect to the importing country's government.

where ρ is the discount factor. This is to be maximized subject to the domestic transformation constraint, $F[X_1, X_2] = 0$. In doing this, one assumes that $P(E)$ is a convex function of E (i.e., the probability of a quota being imposed increases at an increasing rate as E is increased) and that, in the case where π depends on E, πE is concave in E. Then the first-order conditions for an interior maximum are

$$\frac{\partial \phi}{\partial X_1} = U_1 - \lambda F_1 = 0, \tag{39.13}$$

$$\frac{\partial \phi}{\partial X_2} = U_2 - \lambda F_2 = 0, \tag{39.14}$$

$$\frac{\partial \phi}{\partial E} = -U_1 + U_2(\pi + E\pi') - \rho(\overline{U} - \underline{U})P'(E) = 0. \tag{39.15}$$

Equations (39.13) and (39.14) yield the familiar result that the marginal rate of substitution in consumption equals the marginal rate of transformation, and equation (39.15) can be written as

$$\frac{U_1}{U_2} = (\pi + \pi'E) - \frac{\rho\{\overline{U} - \underline{U}\}}{U_2} P'(E). \tag{39.15'}$$

If monopoly power is absent ($\pi' = 0$) and if the first period's exports do not affect the probability of a quota being imposed in the second period, then (39.15') reduces to the standard condition that the marginal rate of substitution in consumption equals the (average = marginal) terms of trade. If only the second of these conditions holds, then U_1/U_2 equals the marginal terms of trade ($\pi + \pi'E$), leading to the familiar optimal tariff. If both conditions hold, there is an additional tariff element:

$$\frac{\rho[\overline{U} - \underline{U}]}{U_2} P'(E).$$

This term can be explained as follows: If an additional unit of exports takes place in period 1, the probability of a quota being imposed, and hence a discounted loss in welfare of $\rho(\overline{U} - \underline{U})$ occurring, increases by $P'(E)$. Thus at the margin the expected loss in welfare is $\rho(\overline{U} - \underline{U})P'(E)$, since there is no loss in welfare if the quota is not imposed. Converted to numéraire terms, this equals

$$\frac{\rho(\overline{U} - \underline{U})P'(E)}{U_2}$$

and must be subtracted from the marginal terms of trade $(\pi + \pi'E)$, the effect of an additional unit of exports on the quantum of imports.[3]

It is then clear that the market-disruption-induced QR possibility requires optimal intervention in the form of a tariff (in period 1). It is also clear that compared with the optimal situation without such a QR possibility, the resource allocation in the QR-possibility case will shift against exportable production. That is, comparative advantage, in the welfare sense, shifts away at the margin from exportable production. Moreover, if we denote the utility level under the optimal policy intervention with quota possibility as ϕ_Q^{Opt} and that under laissez-faire with the quota possibility as ϕ_{NQ}^L, we can argue that

$$\phi_Q^{Opt} > \phi_Q^L \quad \text{and} \quad \phi_{NQ}^L > \phi_Q^L.$$

This result is set out, with the attendant periodwise utility levels achieved under each option, in table 39.1, which is self-explanatory.[4]

For a small country with no monopoly power in trade (except for the quota possibility), the equilibria under alternative policies are illustrated in figure 39.2.[5] Here $\bar{U}$ represents the utility level in the absence of a

---

3. Instead of assuming that the fixed quota of $\bar{E}$ will be imposed with probability $P(E)$, one could assume that a quota of $\bar{E}$ will be imposed with probability density $P(\bar{E}, E)$. In other words, the quota level $\bar{E}$ is variable and the probability of imposition depends both on the level $\bar{E}$ and on the quantum of exports E in the first period. Let $f(\bar{E})$ denote the maximum of $U(C_1, C_2)$ subject to $F(X_1, X_2) = 0$ and $E \leq \bar{E}$, where $C_1 = X_1 - E_1$ and $C_2 = X_2 + \pi E_1$. Then the expected welfare in period 2, given the export level E in the first period, is

$$\int f(\bar{E}) P(\bar{E}, E) \, dE.$$

Denote this by $h(E)$. Thus the maximand ϕ now becomes

$$U[X_1 - E, X_2 + \pi E] + \rho h(E),$$

and condition (38.15') becomes

$$\frac{U_1}{U_2} = \pi + \pi'E + \frac{\rho h'(E)}{U_2}.$$

Now $h'(E)$ is the change in expected welfare in period 2 due to an additional unit of export in period 1, and this has to be added to the marginal terms of trade $\pi + \pi'E$. Nothing substantive changes therefore. However, if we allow for many exporting countries and if the share in the overall quota level granted in period 2 to one exporting country will increases with the export level achieved by the country in period 1, this would produce an incentive to increase rather than decrease the export level in period 1, *ceteris paribus*. Hence our analysis based on one exporting country must be modified correspondingly.

4. However, we cannot assert that $\phi_{NQ}^L > \phi_Q^{Opt}$ except in the case of a small country with no influence on the terms of trade. This follows from the fact that ϕ_{NQ}^L is no longer the first-best policy in the presence of monopoly power in trade, so U^* may well exceed $\bar{U}$ in table 38.1.

5. For a country with no monopoly power, it is not meaningful to think of market disruption leading to QRs. If the country is indeed atomistic in foreign markets, its exports surely will not cause market disruption. Our analysis allows for monopoly power.

Table 39.1
Alternative outcomes under different policies

| | Outcome | | |
	Optimal policy intervention with possible quota	Laissez-faire with possible quota	Laissez-faire with no quota possibility
Period 1	U^*	$\bar{U}$	$\bar{U}$
Period 2	$\rho[\underline{U}P^* + \bar{U}(1 - P^*)]$	$\rho[\underline{U}\bar{P} + \bar{U}(1 - \bar{P})]$	$\rho\bar{U}$
ϕ: Social utility level	$\phi_Q^{\text{Opt}}(> \phi_Q^L)$	ϕ_Q^L	$\phi_{NQ}^L(> \phi_Q^L)$

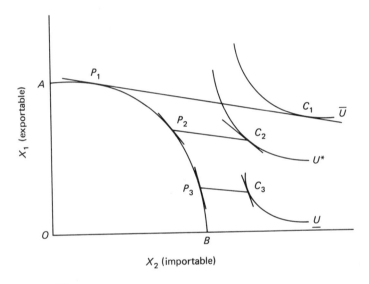

Figure 39.2

quota, $\underline{U}$ the utility level when the quota is imposed, and U^* the first-period utility level reached under the optimal-policy-intervention option. Equilibrium with U^* naturally requires that the export level be restricted below the level that would be reached (at $\bar{U}$) with nonintervention and above the level reached (at $\underline{U}$) in equilibrium when the quota is invoked. Also the optimal policy for restricting the first-period level of exports is a tariff (a conclusion that should now be familiar from the theory of optimal intervention under noneconomic objectives as set out in chapter 28).

Two Price-Stabilization Models

Newberry and Stiglitz (1981) draw on the analysis of Hart (1975) to show that in the context of a simple two-country model, free trade need not be optimal in a world with an incomplete set of markets. Suppose that two countries have negatively correlated weather in that good weather in one is always associated with bad weather in the other. For any given weather condition (good or bad) the output of either country is the same, so world output is the same in good and bad weather. Free trade between the countries will stabilize prices while destabilizing incomes, whereas autarky will stabilize income in each country while destabilizing prices, if we assume unitary price elasticity of demand. Thus under autarky producers have implicit income insurance, which is eliminated under free trade, and if in free trade producers respond to income risk by reducing supplies, consumers can be made worse off.

The literature on price stabilization is vast. A survey of welfare aspects of such schemes can be found in Turnovsky (1978). We conclude our discussion of uncertainty with one such analysis to illustrate the impact of alternative sources of uncertainty on welfare.[6] Consider two countries, with country i $(i = 1, 2)$ having the following demand (d_{it}) and supply (s_{it}) curves in period t:

$$d_{it} = \alpha_i - \beta_i p_t + u_{it},$$

$$s_{it} = \gamma_i + \delta_i p_t + v_{it},$$

where u_{iy} and v_{it} are the demand and supply disturbances. In the absence of a price-stabilization scheme, the world market will be cleared at the equilibrium price p_t given by

$$p_t = \frac{(\sum \alpha_i - \sum \gamma_i) + \sum u_{it} - \sum v_{it}}{\sum \beta_i + \sum \delta_i}.$$

In this linear model a self-liquidating buffer stock scheme will stabilize prices at $\bar{p}$ given by

$$\bar{p} = \frac{\sum \alpha_i - \sum \gamma_i}{\sum \beta_i + \sum \delta_i}.$$

On the basis of standard consumer and producer surplus measures, Hueth and Schmitz then show (assuming that the country is the net exporter) the following:

• Domestic producers gain (lose) from the stabilization of domestic supply (demand) disturbances. They lose from the stabilization of foreign demand and supply disturbances.

• Domestic consumers gain (lose) from the stabilization of domestic demand (supply) fluctuations. They lose from the stabilization of foreign demand and supply disturbances.

---

6. This is based on a model by Hueth and Schmitz (1972).

• The domestic economy (producers and suppliers together) gains (loses) from the stabilization of domestic (foreign) disturbances.

• The world as a whole (producers and consumers of the two countries together) gains from price stabilization.

Recommended Readings

Anderson, J. E. The Heckscher-Ohlin and Travis-Vanek theorems under uncertainty. *Journal of International Economics* 11 (1981): 239–48.

Arrow, K. J. *Essays in the Theory of Risk Bearing.* Chicago: Markham, 1971.

Bhagwati, J., and T. N. Srinivasan. Optimal intervention to achieve non-economic objectives. *Review of Economic Studies* 36 (1969): 27–38.

Bhagwati, J., and T. N. Srinivasan. Optimal trade policy and compensation under endogenous uncertainty: The phenomenon of market disruption. *Journal of International Economics* 6 (1976): 317–36.

Hart, O. G. On the optimality of equilibrium when the market structure is incomplete. *Journal of Economic Theory* 11 (1975): 418–43.

Helpman, E., and A. Razin. *A Theory of International Trade Under Uncertainty.* New York: Academic Press, 1980.

Hueth, D., and A. Schmitz. International trade in intermediate and final goods: Some welfare implications of destablized prices. *Quarterly Journal of Economics* 86 (1972): 351–65.

Johnson, H. G. Optimal trade intervention in the presence of domestic distortions. In *Trade, Growth, and the Balance of Payments: Essays in Honour of G. Haberler*, ed. by R. E. Baldwin et al. Chicago: Rand McNally, 1965.

Newbery, D., and J. Stiglitz. *The Theory of Commodity Price Stabilization.* Oxford: Oxford University Press, 1981.

Pomery, J. Uncertainty and international trade. In *International Economic Policy; Theory and Evidence*, ed. by R. Dornhursch and J. Frenkel. Baltimore: Johns Hopkins University Press, 1979.

Pratt, J. W. Risk aversion in the small and in the large. *Econometrica* 32 (1964): 122–36.

Ruffin, R. J. International trade under uncertainty. *Journal of International Economics* 4 (1974): 243–59.

Turnovsky, S. The distribution of welfare gains from price stabilization: A survey of theoretical issues. In *Stabilizing World Commodity Market*, ed. by F. Adams and S. Klein. Lexington, MA.: Lexington Books, 1978.

APPENDIXES

Given that the offer curve, at any point, conveys information about the terms of trade and the quantities offered, we can in principle distinguish among four different elasticities:

- Elasticities relating to change in exports supplied as terms of trade change (ε_s).

- Elasticities relating to change in imports demanded as terms of trade change (ε).

- Elasticities relating to change in exports supplied as imports demanded change (E_{frs}, described generally as the elasticity of foreign reciprocal supply, after John Stuart Mill's description of the offer curves as foreign reciprocal demand curves).

- Elasticities relating to change in imports demanded as exports supplied change (E_{frd}, described as the elasticity of foreign reciprocal demand and being the reciprocal of E_{frs}).

Since all these definitions relate to the same information, it is inevitable that they are related to one another. The precise nature of these relationships can be worked out readily. Assume that a country exports good 1 and imports good 2. Let the price ratio or the terms of trade be defined as $p_2/p_1 = p$ Then, the four elasticities can be defined as follows:

$$\varepsilon_s = \frac{1/p}{E}\frac{dE}{d(1/p)},$$

$$E_{frs} = \frac{M}{E}\frac{dE}{dM},$$

$$\varepsilon = -\frac{p}{M}\frac{dM}{dp},$$

$$E_{frd} = \frac{E}{M}\frac{dM}{dE}.$$

Because of balanced trade, pM is equal to E. Therefore

$$p\frac{dM}{dp} + M = \frac{dE}{dp} = -\frac{dE}{d(1/p)}\frac{1}{p^2},$$

$$\frac{p}{M}\cdot\frac{dM}{dp} + 1 = -\frac{1}{Mp^2}\frac{dE}{d(1/p)},$$

$$1 - \varepsilon = -\varepsilon_s,$$

$$\varepsilon - \varepsilon_s = 1.$$

Next note that

$$\varepsilon_s = \frac{1/p}{E} \frac{dE}{d(1/p)}$$

$$= \frac{M}{E^2} \cdot \frac{dE}{d(M/E)}$$

$$= \frac{M/E^2}{d(M/E)/dE}$$

$$= \frac{M/E^2}{(E(dM/dE) - M)/E^2},$$

and therefore

$$\varepsilon_s = \frac{1}{(E/M)(dM/dE) - 1}$$

$$= \frac{1}{E_{frd} - 1}.$$

Hence

$$\varepsilon_s = \frac{E_{frs}}{1 - E_{frs}}.$$

Furthermore, since $\varepsilon - \varepsilon_s = 1$,

$$\varepsilon = \frac{E_{frd}}{E_{frd} - 1}.$$

and

$$\varepsilon = \frac{1}{1 - E_{frs}}.$$

We illustrate E_{frd} and E_{frs} in figure A.1. There, at point A on the offer curve,

$$\frac{dE}{dM} = \frac{BQ}{AB} \quad \text{and} \quad \frac{E}{M} = \frac{OB}{AB}.$$

Therefore

$$E_{frs} = \frac{BQ}{OB} \quad \text{and} \quad E_{frd} = \frac{OB}{BQ}.$$

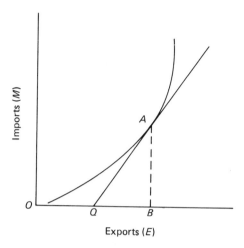

Figure A.1

For most of the analysis in this volume we use the import demand elasticity ε. We use its decomposition in several different ways, as derived in appendix C.

Basic Results of the 2 × 2 Neoclassical Model of Trade Theory

This appendix deals formally with the basic results of the 2×2 model of trade theory, which were set out more intuitively (though with sufficient rigor for most classroom discussion) in chapter 5.

ASSUMPTION 1   Two goods, 1 and 2; outputs denoted by Q_1 and Q_2.

ASSUMPTION 2   Two factors, capital and labor; aggregate endowments denoted by K and L.

ASSUMPTION 3   The production function for good 1 is $F(K_1, L_1)$ and that for commodity 2 is $G(K_2, L_2)$, where K_i and L_i denote amounts of capital and labor devoted to production of commodity i $(i = 1, 2)$.

DEFINITION 1   The production-possibility set Z of this economy is the set of commodity outputs $Q \equiv (Q_1, Q_2)$, where $Q_1 \leq F(K_1, L_1)$, $Q_2 \leq G(K_2, L_2)$, $K_1 + K_2 \leq K$, $L_1 + L_2 \leq L$, and $Q_i, K_i, L_i \geq 0$ $(i = 1, 2)$.

DEFINITION 2   A set X is said to be convex if $x^1 \in X$, $x^2 \in X$, and $0 < \lambda < 1$ imply that $\lambda x^1 + (1 - \lambda)x^2 \in X$.

DEFINITION 3   A function $f(x)$, where $x = (x_1, \ldots, x_n)$ $(n \geq 1)$ defined over a convex set X, is said to be concave (convex) if, with $x^1 \in X$, $x^2 \in X$, and $0 < \lambda < 1$, $f(\lambda x^1 + (1 - \lambda)x^2) \geq (\leq) \lambda f(x^1) + (1 - \lambda)f(x^2)$.

PROPOSITION 1   The production-possibility set Z is convex if the production functions F and G are concave.

Proof   We need to show that with concave F and G, $Q^1 \in Z$, $Q^2 \in Z$, and $0 < \lambda < 1$ imply that $Q \equiv \lambda Q^1 + (1 - \lambda)Q^2 \in Z$. Now $Q^i \in Z$ $(i = 1, 2)$ implies that there exist (K_j^i, L_j^i) $(i = 1, 2, j = 1, 2)$ such that $Q_1^i \leq F(K_1^i, L_1^i)$, $Q_2^i \leq G(K_2^i, L_2^i)$ $(i = 1, 2)$, and $K_1^i + K_2^i \leq K$, $L_1^i + L_2^i \leq L$. Consider $K_j(\lambda) = \lambda K_j^1 + (1 - \lambda)K_j^2$ and $L_j(\lambda) = \lambda L_j^1 + (1 - \lambda)L_j^2$ $(j = 1, 2)$. Clearly $K_1(\lambda) + K_2(\lambda) \leq K$ and $L_1(\lambda) + L_2(\lambda) \leq L$. By concavity of F, we have

$$F(K_1(\lambda), L_1(\lambda)) \geq \lambda F(K_1^1, L_1^1) + (1 - \lambda)F(K_1^2, L_1^2) = Q_1,$$

and by concavity of G, we have

$$G(K_2(\lambda), L_2(\lambda)) \geq \lambda G(K_2^1, L_2^1) + (1 - \lambda)G(K_2^2, L_2^2) = Q_2.$$

Hence $Q \equiv (Q_1, Q_2) \in Z$.   ∎

DEFINITION 4   A combination of feasible commodity outputs $Q \equiv (Q_1, Q_2)$ (i.e., $Q \in Z$) is said to be efficient if there exists no other feasible Q' such that $Q_1' \geq Q_1$ and $Q_2' \geq Q_2$ with at least one inequality strict.

DEFINITION 5   The curve $Q_2 = H(Q_1)$ such that (Q_1, Q_2) is efficient is called the *production-possibility* (or *transformation*) *curve*, and $H(Q_1)$ is called the *transformation function*.

PROPOSITION 2   If Z is convex, then the transformation function $G(Q_1)$ is concave.

Proof   We have to show that

$$H(\lambda Q_1^1 + (1 - \lambda)Q_1^2) \geq \lambda H(Q_1^1) + (1 - \lambda)H(Q_1^2)$$

for $0 < \lambda < 1$, given that $(Q_1^1, H(Q_1^1))$ and $(Q_1^2, H(Q_1^2))$ are both efficient points of Z. Since Z is convex, we know that

$$[\lambda Q_1^1 + (1 - \lambda)Q_1^2, \lambda H(Q_1^1) + (1 - \lambda)H(Q_1^2)] \in Z.$$

By definition,

$$[\lambda Q_1^1 + (1 - \lambda)Q_1^2, H(\lambda Q_1^1 + (1 - \lambda)Q_1^2)]$$

is an efficient point of Z. Hence

$$H(\lambda Q_1^1 + (1 - \lambda)Q_2^2) \geq \lambda H(Q_1^1) + (1 - \lambda)H(Q_1^2).$$ ∎

DEFINITION 6   A production function $f(x)$ relating the output of a good to the input vector $x = (x_1, \ldots, x_n)$ is said to exhibit constant returns to scale if $f(\lambda x) = \lambda f(x)$ for all $\lambda \geq 0$—that is, if $f(x)$ is homogeneous of degree 1 in x.

Properties of Functions Homogeneous of Degree 1

Let f_i denote the partial derivative of f with respect to x_i. Then $\sum_{i=1}^{n} f_i x_i \equiv f(x_1, \ldots, x_n)$ and f_i is homogeneous of degree 0 in x.

Proof   By definition, $f(\lambda x) = \lambda f(x)$. Differentiating both sides with respect to λ, we get $\sum f_i(\lambda x)x_i = f(x)$. Setting $\lambda = 1$, we get $\sum f_i(x)x_i = f(x)$. Differentiating partially with respect to x_i, we have $\lambda f_i(\lambda x) = \lambda f_i(x)$. Canceling $\lambda \neq 0$, we get $f_i(\lambda x) = f_i(x)$ for all $\lambda > 0$. That is, f_i is homogeneous of degree 0 in x.   ∎

In the two-good model, assume that both F and G are homogeneous of degree 1 (constant-returns-to-scale production function). Then, for instance,

$$F(K_1, L_1) \equiv F\left[L_1 \cdot \frac{K_1}{L_1}, L_1 \cdot 1\right] \equiv L_1 F\left[\frac{K_1}{L_1}, 1\right] \equiv L_1 f(k_1),$$

where $k_1 = K_1/L_1$ and $f(k_1) \equiv F(k_1, 1)$. Clearly $f(k_1)$ represents the *average* product of labor at the capital-labor ratio k_1. The marginal product of capital is, by definition, $\partial F / \partial K_1$, and from the above relationship it follows that

$$\frac{\partial F}{\partial K_1} = L_1 \cdot f_1(k_1) \cdot \frac{1}{L_1} = f_1(k_1),$$

where $f_1(k_1)$ is the derivative of $f(k_1)$ with respect to k_1. Similarly it can be shown that the marginal product of labor, $\partial F / \partial L_1$, equals $f(k_1) - k_1 f_1(k_1)$. The marginal products of capital and labor are $g_1(k_2)$ and $g(k_2) - k_2 g_1(k_2)$, respectively, in the production of good 2.

Now introduce the assumption that producers face competitive markets for factors (i.e., they behave as price takers). With w the price per unit of labor service per unit of time and r the rental per unit of capital per unit of time (both prices being defined in terms of the numéraire good 1), and with constant returns to scale, each producer minimizes his unit cost of production. That is, he chooses capital-labor ratios k_1 and k_2 such that $(w + k_1 r) / f(k_1)$ and $(w + k_2 r) / g(k_2)$ are minimized (the numerator of each of these ratios is the cost per unit of labor employed and the denominator is the output per unit of labor, so the ratio represents the unit cost of production). The optimal (unit-cost-minimizing) capital-labor ratios depend only on the factor-price ratio $w/r \equiv \omega$. If for convenience we assume the so-called Inada conditions—that the marginal rates of substitution $(f - k_1 f_1) / k_1$ and $(g - k_2 g_1) / k_2$ go to 0 (∞) as the capital-labor ratios $\{k_1, k_2\}$ tend to 0 (∞)—then the optimal capital-labor ratios k_1 and k_2 are unique functions of ω given by

$$\frac{f - k_1 f_1}{f_1} = \omega = \frac{g - k_2 g_1}{g_1}. \tag{B.1}$$

From this definition it can be easily derived that

$$k_1'(\omega) = -\frac{f_1^2}{f f_{11}} \geq 0$$

and

$$k_2'(\omega) = -\frac{g_1^2}{g g_{11}} \geq 0, \tag{B.2}$$

where $k_i'(\omega)$ is the derivative of $k_i(\omega)$ with respect to ω and where f_{11} and g_{11} represent the derivatives of f_1 and g_1, respectively, with respect to k_1 and k_2. By the concavity assumption on F and G, we have $f_{11} \leq 0$ and $g_{11} \leq 0$.

DEFINITION 7   The elasticity of substitution between capital and labor in producing commodity i is

$$\frac{d \log k_i}{d \log \omega} = \frac{\omega}{k_i} k_i'(\omega), \qquad i = 1, 2.$$

The ratio of minimal unit cost of production of good 2 in terms of good 1, denoted by $c(\omega)$, depends only on ω and is given by

$$c(\omega) = \frac{(\omega + k_2(\omega))/g(k_2(\omega))}{(\omega + k_1(\omega))/f(k_1(\omega))},$$

which, if we use equation (B.1), yields

$$c(\omega) = \frac{f_1(k_1(\omega))}{g_1(k_2(\omega))} = \frac{f - k_1 f_1}{g - k_2 g_1}. \tag{B.3}$$

It can also be shown from equations (B.1)–(B.3) that

$$\frac{c'(\omega)}{c(\omega)} = \frac{f_{11} k_1'(\omega)}{f_1} - \frac{g_{11} k_2'(\omega)}{g_1}$$

$$= -\frac{f_1}{f} + \frac{g_1}{g}$$

$$= -\frac{1}{\omega + k_1} + \frac{1}{w + k_2}$$

$$= \frac{k_1(\omega) - k_2(\omega)}{(\omega + k_1)(\omega + k_2)}. \tag{B.4}$$

Clearly $c(\omega)$ increases (decreases) as ω increases according as $k_1(\omega) > (<) k_2(\omega)$.

PROPOSITION 3   The competitive profit-maximizing decisions, with a relative price p for good 2 and a wage w and rental r (all in terms of good 1), are as follow: If (1) $[rk_1(\omega) + w]/f(k_1(\omega)) > 1$, it is unprofitable to produce any amount of good 1; if (2) $[rk_1(\omega) + w]/f(k_1(\omega)) = 1$, any amount of good 1 is equally profitable to produce; and if (3) $[rk_1(\omega) + w]/f(k_1(\omega)) < 1$, producers would like to produce as large an output of good 1 as possible. Similarly, if (4) $[rk_2(\omega) + w]/g(k_2(\omega)) > p$, no amount of good 2 is profitable to produce; if (5) $[rk_2(\omega) + w]/g(k_2(\omega)) = p$, any amount of good 2 is equally profitable to produce; and if (6) $[rk_2(\omega) + w]/g(k_2(\omega)) < p$, producers would like to produce as large an output of good 2 as possible.

Proof   With constant returns to scale and a comparison of minimal unit cost with price per unit, the results follow.   ∎

COROLLARY   From the above, it is clear that an economy will specialize in the production of good 1 (i.e., it will produce positive and finite amounts of good 1 and none of good 2) if conditions 2 and 4 hold simultaneously. With the definition of ω $(= w/r)$, $k_1(\omega)$, $k_2(\omega)$, and $c(\omega)$, conditions 2 and 4 together imply that $c(\omega) > p$. Similarly the economy will be specialized in the production of good 2 if conditions 1 and 5 hold simultaneously, that is, if $c(\omega) < p$. Positive and finite amounts of both commodities will be produced if conditions 4 and 5 hold, that is, if $c(\omega) = p$. Thus, with the constant-returns technology, the relative factor price ω and the relative commodity price p determine which commodity or commodities will be produced under competition.

Returning to the two-good model of definition 1 and utilizing the assumption of constant returns to scale in the production of the two goods, we can describe the production-possibility set Z (under full employment of labor and capital and with the aggregate endowment of labor L set at unity by choice of units of measurement of labor) by

$$Q_1 \leq l_1 f(k_1), \quad Q_2 \leq (1 - l_1)g(k_2), \quad l_1 k_1 + (1 - l_1)k_1 = k, \qquad (\text{B.5})$$

where $0 \leq l_1 \leq 1$, k is the aggregate endowment ratio of capital to labor, and l_1 is the proportion of labor force employed in the production of good 1.

Production-Possibility Curve

The production-possibility curve of this economy is derived by maximizing Q_2 subject to

$$Q_1 = \text{Specified value } \bar{Q}_1,$$

where

$$\bar{Q}_1 \leq f(k) = \text{Maximal output of } Q_1$$

when the economy is specialized in the production of good 1. Assume now that an interior maximum obtains. Sufficient conditions for this would be to assume that both factors are essential for the production of each good (in the sense that if either factor is reduced to zero, output falls to zero regardless of the amount used of the other factor) and that the marginal product of either factor is always positive in the production of each good at all finite levels of factor use. Then the first-order conditions for a maximum imply that

$$\frac{f - k_1 f_1}{f_1} = \frac{g - k_2 g_2}{g_1}. \tag{B.6}$$

These, with $\bar{Q}_1 = l_1 f(k_1)$, and

$$l_1 k_1 + (1 - l_1)k_2 = k, \tag{B.7}$$

completely determine the soultion.

Parametrization of Production-Possibility Curve

Comparison with equation (B.1) suggests that the production-possibility curve can be parametrized through ω, as follows: Assume without loss of generality that $k_1(\omega) > k_2(\omega)$ for ω in the relevant range as determined below. Start from $\omega = \underline{\omega}$ where $(f - kf_1)/f_1 = \underline{\omega}$; that is, $\underline{\omega}$ is the marginal rate of substitution in the production of good 1 when the economy is specialized in the production of it. If ω is increased from $\underline{\omega}$, both $k_1(\omega)$ and $k_2(\omega)$ increase, as already shown in equation (B.2). Solve for $l_1(\omega)$ from equation (B.7). As long as $k_1(\omega) > k_2(\omega)$, $l_1(\omega)$ will decrease from unity as ω incereases and will reach zero when ω equals $\bar{\omega}$ [given by $\bar{\omega} = (g - kg_2)/g_2$; i.e., $\bar{\omega}$ equals the marginal rate of factor substitution in the production of good 2 when the economy specializes in the production of it]. This parametrization is illustrated in figure B.1, and the production-possibility curve is shown in figure B.2.

PROPOSITION 4   The slope of the production-possibility curve is $c(\omega)$.

Proof   The slope, by definition, is

$$-\frac{dQ_1}{dQ_2} = -\frac{\dfrac{dQ_1}{d\omega}}{\dfrac{dQ_2}{d\omega}} = -\left(\frac{l_1 f_1 \dfrac{dk_1}{d\omega} + f \dfrac{dl_1}{d\omega}}{(1 - l_1)g_1 \dfrac{dk_2}{d\omega} - \dfrac{dl_1}{d\omega}} \right). \tag{B.8}$$

The right-hand side can be shown to equal $c(\omega) = f_1/g_1$ by substitution for $dk_i/d\omega$ and $dl_1/d\omega$.   ∎

PROPOSITION 5   With $c(\underline{\omega})$ denoted by $\underline{p}$ and with $c(\bar{\omega}) = \bar{p}$, the competitive production equilibrium of this economy, with an exogenous relative price p^*, will be as follows [the assumption that $k_1(\omega) > k_2(\omega)$ for ω in $(\underline{\omega}, \bar{\omega})$ ensures $\underline{p} < \bar{p}$]:

If $p^* \leq \underline{p}$, $k_1 = k$, and $l_1 = 1$, the economy specializes in producing good 1.

If $\underline{p} < p^* < \bar{p}$, $k_1 = k_1(\omega)$, $k_2 = k_2(\omega)$, $l_1 = [k - k_2(\omega)]/[k_1(\omega) - k_2(\omega)]$, and ω is determined from $p^* = c(\omega)$, the economy is incompletely specialized.

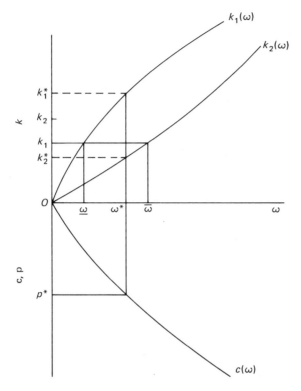

Figure B.1

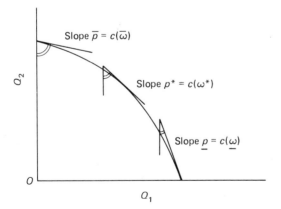

Figure B.2

If $p^* > \bar{p}$, $k_2 = k$, and $l_1 = 0$, the economy specializes in the production of good 2.

Proof Apply proposition 3, and use the resource constraint (B.7). ∎

DEFINITION 8   The technology of the two-good economy is said to be characterized by factor-intensity nonreversals if either

$$k_1(\omega) > k_2(\omega) \qquad \text{for all } \omega > 0$$

or

$$k_1(\omega) < k_2(\omega) \qquad \text{for all } \omega > 0.$$

Though a slightly more general definition could have been used, it has been avoided to simplify the following analysis.

PROPOSITION 6 (Samuelson)   If trade between two two-good economies with identical technology that does not permit factor-intensity reversals equalizes goods prices between them, and if in the post-trade competitive equilibrium both economies are incompletely specialized, then their factor prices are also equalized.

Proof Goods-price equalization means that both economies face an identical relative price p^* after trade. Incomplete specialization implies that $p^* = c(\omega)$ in each economy. Under the assumption of no factor-intensity reversal, $c(\omega)$ is either a strictly increasing or a strictly decreasing function of ω for all ω. Hence the solution to $p^* = c(\omega)$ is unique; that is, factor-price equalization obtains. In the following analysis we will assume that the technology of production does not permit factor-intensity reversals so that, with p^* given, the equilibrium ω^* is uniquely determined. ∎

Consider an economy that continues to be incompletely specialized as p^* is varied. Then, from the fact that the equilibrium wage/rental ratio ω^* corresponding to p^* is determined from $p^* = c(\omega^*)$, it follows from equation (B.4) that

$$\frac{d\omega^*}{dp^*} = \frac{1}{c'(\omega^*)} = \frac{1}{p^*}\left(\frac{k_1(\omega^*) - k_2(\omega^*)}{[\omega^* + k_1(\omega^*)][\omega^* + k_2(\omega^*)]}\right)^{-1}. \tag{B.9}$$

This leads to the next proposition.

PROPOSITION 7   The equilibrium wage/rental ratio increases (decreases), as the relative price of good 2 in terms of good 1 is increased, according as good 1 is capital-(labor-) intensive relative to good 2.[1]

1. Modify this proposition appropriately if the economy moves into or out of complete specialization as p^* is changed.

Now the equilibrium wage (rental) in terms of good i, denoted by w_i^* (r_i^*), is by definition the marginal product of labor (capital) in the production of good i. Hence

$$w_1^* = f(k_1(\omega^*)) - k_1(\omega^*)f_1[k_1(\omega^*)], \tag{B.10}$$

$$r_1^* = f_1(k_1(\omega^*)), \tag{B.11}$$

$$w_2^* = g(k_2(\omega^*)) - k_2(\omega^*)g_1[k_2(\omega^*)], \tag{B.12}$$

$$r_2^* = g_1(k_2(\omega^*)). \tag{B.13}$$

Using equations (B.2) and (B.4), we get

$$\frac{dw_1^*}{dp^*} \gtreqless 0, \quad \frac{dr_1^*}{dp^*} \lesseqgtr 0,$$

$$\frac{dw_2^*}{dp^*} \gtreqless 0, \quad \frac{dr_2^*}{dp^*} \lesseqgtr 0,$$

according as $k_1(\omega^*) \gtreqless k_2(\omega^*)$. This leads to the next proposition.

PROPOSITION 8 (Stolper and Samuelson)   The competitive reward to the factor used intensively in the production of the good whose relative price rises also increases in terms of either good.[2]

Consider next changes in the aggregate factor endowments $\bar{K}$ and $\bar{L}$ while keeping p^* constant. Assume that the economy remains incompletely specialized as $\bar{K}$ or $\bar{L}$ is varied. Since p^* remains unchanged, so do the equilibrium wage-rental ratio ω^* and the two capital intensities $k_1(\omega^*)$ and $k_2(\omega^*)$. Let $L_1(\bar{K}, \bar{L})$ denote the level of employment in the production of goods. Then, by definition,

$$k_1(\omega^*)L_1(\bar{K}, \bar{L}) + k_2(\omega^*)[\bar{L} - L_1(\bar{K}, \bar{L})] = \bar{K}. \tag{B.14}$$

Hence

$$\frac{\partial L_1}{\partial \bar{L}} = \frac{k_2(\omega^*)}{k_2(\omega^*) - k_1(\omega^*)} \tag{B.15}$$

and

$$\frac{\partial L_1}{\partial \bar{K}} = \frac{-1}{k_2(\omega^*) - k_1(\omega^*)}. \tag{B.16}$$

Since the equilibrium output levels Q_1 and Q_2 are given by

---

2. This proposition too is easily modified to account for changes in the equilibrium pattern of specialization as p^* is varied.

$$Q_1 = L_1(\bar{K}, \bar{L})f(k_1(\omega^*))$$

and

$$Q_2 = [\bar{L} - L_1(\bar{K}, \bar{L})g(k_2(\omega^*)),$$

it follows that

$$\frac{\partial Q_1}{\partial \bar{L}} = \frac{k_2(\omega^*)f(k_1(\omega^*))}{k_2(\omega^*) - k_1(\omega^*)}, \quad \frac{\partial Q_1}{\partial \bar{K}} = \frac{-f(k_1(\omega^*))}{k_2(\omega^*) - k_1(\omega^*)}, \tag{B.17}$$

$$\frac{\partial Q_2}{\partial \bar{L}} = \frac{-k_1(\omega^*)g(k_2(\omega^*))}{k_2(\omega^*) - k_1(\omega^*)}, \quad \frac{\partial Q_2}{\partial \bar{K}} = \frac{g(k_2(\omega^*))}{k_2(\omega^*) - k_1(\omega^*)}. \tag{B.18}$$

Alternatively,

$$\frac{\partial Q_2}{\partial \bar{L}} = \frac{-k_1(\omega^*)}{k_2(\omega^*)} \cdot \frac{f(K_2(\omega^*))}{f(k_1(\omega^*))} \cdot \frac{\partial Q_1}{\partial \bar{L}}, \tag{B.19}$$

$$\frac{\partial Q_2}{\partial \bar{K}} = -\frac{g(k_2(\omega^*))}{f(k_1(\omega^*))} \cdot \frac{\partial Q_1}{\partial \bar{K}}. \tag{B.20}$$

∎

Using equations (B.17) and (B.18), we can state the following:

PROPOSITION 9 (Rybczynski)   At a constant relative price of good 2 in terms of good 1, an increase in the aggregate endowment of capital (labor) will result in an increase in the equilibrium output of the capital-(labor-) intensive good and a decrease in that of the labor- (capital-) intensive good, if the economy continues to be incompletely specialized as its factor endowment changes.

This proposition is illustrated in figure B.3. Point X is the initial equilibrium on the initial production-possibility curve PP'. The slope of PP' at X equals the goods-price ratio. As the capital endowment is increased (decreased) with the labor endowment kept constant, the equilibrium output vector moves from X toward A (A') if good 1 is the capital-intensive good. At A (A') the economy specializes in good 1 (good 2). The straight line AA' can be called the *capital Rybczynski line*. Similarly, as the labor endowment is increased (decreased), the equilibrium output vector moves from X toward B' (B). At B (B') the economy specializes in good 1 (good 2). The straight line BB' is the labor Rybczynski line.

Equations (B.19) and (B.20) endable us to write down the equations of AA' and BB' in the (Q_1, Q_2) space. Since the economy is specialized in good 2 at A' while still using capital intensity $k_2(\omega^*)$ in its production, the

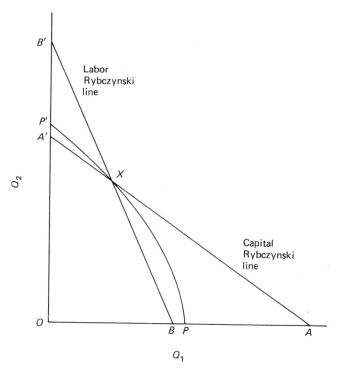

Figure B.3

coordinates of A' are $(0, \bar{L}g(k_2(\omega^*)))$. The slope of $A'A$, using (B.20), is $-g(k_2(\omega^*))/f(k_1(\omega^*))$. Hence the equation of $A'A$ is

$$Q_2 = g(k_2(\omega^*)) \left(\bar{L} - \frac{Q_1}{f(k_1(\omega^*))} \right). \tag{B.21}$$

At A the economy specializes in good 1 using capital intensity $k_1(\omega^*)$ in its production. Hence the coordinates of A are $(\bar{L}f(k_1(\omega^*)), 0)$. It is verified that A lies on the line determined by equation (B.21). Similarly the equation of the labor Rybczynski line can be shown to be

$$Q_2 = \frac{g(k_2(\omega^*))}{k_2(\omega^*)} \left(\bar{K} - \frac{Q_1 k_1(\omega^*)}{f(k_1(\omega^*))} \right). \tag{B.22}$$

DEFINITION 9 (Hicks) If a shift in the production function of a constant-returns-to-scale industry changes the marginal product of labor and capital in the same proportion at all capital-labor ratios, then such a technical change is said to be *neutral*. The production function of such an industry is of the form $\lambda F(K, L)$, where λ is the technical-change parameter.

PROPOSITION 10 (Johnson)   If Hicks-neutral technical change takes place in the two-sector neoclassical economy, the relative output at a constant relative price of the industry experiencing greater technical change (i.e., having a larger technical-change parameter) will be greater after technical change, if there is incomplete specialization before and after technical change.

Since neutral technical change does not affect the ratio of marginal product of labor to that of capital in either industry at any capital-labor ratio, the $k_i(\omega)$ $(i = 1, 2)$ curves remain unchanged. However, because $c(\omega)$ is the ratio of marginal product of capital (labor) in industry 2 to that in industry 1, the $c(\omega)$ curve is shifted up (down) as the second industry experiences greater (less) neutral technical change. Assuming, without loss of generality, that industry 1 is more capital-intensive and experiences greater technical change, we see that the wage/rental ratio corresponding to a fixed relative price of good 2 must be lower after technical change. This means that the proportion of labor employed in good 2 has to go down to maintain full employment of labor and capital. With lower capital intensity, a lower proportion of labor force employed, and less technical change, the output of industry 2 must go down relative to that of industry 1. This can be shown algebraically as follows: Let λ_1 and λ_2 be the technical-change parameters in industries 1 and 2. Then the equilibrium wage/rental ratio ω^* is determined from

$$p^* = \frac{\lambda_1 f_1(k_1(\omega))}{\lambda_2 g_1(k_2(\omega))}. \tag{B.23}$$

It is clear that ω^* depends on the ratio $\lambda \equiv \lambda_2/\lambda_1$ and that any combination of λ_1 and λ_2 that keeps λ unchanged leaves ω^* unchanged as long as p^* is constant. Hence, using (B.4), we have

$$\frac{\partial \omega^*}{\partial \lambda} = \frac{1}{\lambda} \left(\frac{k_1(\omega^*) - k_2(\omega^*)}{[\omega^* + k_1(\omega^*)][\omega^* + k_2(\omega^*)]} \right)^{-1}. \tag{B.24}$$

Now the relative output of good 2, Q_2/Q_1, is given by

$$\frac{Q_2}{Q_1} = \frac{[\bar{L}k_1(\omega^*) - \bar{K}]g(k_2(\omega^*))}{[\bar{K} - \bar{L}k_2(\omega^*)]f(k_1(\omega^*))}. \tag{B.25}$$

From (B.25) it can be shown that if good 1 is capital- (labor-) intensive, an increase in ω^* lowers (raises) Q_2/Q_1. From (B.24) it follows that if good 1 is capital- (labor-) intensive, an increase in λ raises (lowers) ω^*. Putting the two results together, we obtain proposition 10.

Assuming, without loss of generality, that good 1 is capital-intensive, and noting that $\partial\lambda/\partial\lambda_1 < 0$ and $\partial\lambda/\partial\lambda_2 > 0$, we get $\partial\omega^*/\partial\lambda_1 < 0$ and $\partial\omega^*/\partial\lambda_2 > 0$. That is, the wage/rental ratio falls (rises) according as the capital (labor-) intensive industry experiences technical change. Using equations (B.10)–(B.13), we can derive the implications of technical change in one or both of the industries for the equilibrium wages and rentals defined in terms of either good.

C   Classical Comparative-Statics Model and Analytical Relationships

In the chapters on comparative statics (especially 12, 16, and 29), we use primarily the classical model with two primary factors producing two goods traded between two countries. We have explored this model in appendix B from other viewpoints. We now examine it from the viewpoint of facilitating comparative static analysis.

This classical model can be stated in a number of ways, with varying complexity. For example, the supply side may be summarized in an implicit transformation function between the two commodities (a procedure that is quite adequate for certain purposes, such as analysis of the transfer problem). On the other hand, it may be spelled out at greater length in terms of the production functions of each commodity and the factor-endowment equations (a procedure that is necessary for detailed analysis of other problems, such as the effects of growth). We state the classical model in its simplest form here.

Classical Model

Using the notation of chapter 1, assume two countries I and II and two goods 1 and 2. Let the terms of trade be denoted by $p = p_2/p_1$. In the absence of a tariff, this price ratio represents both the external and internal terms of trade, and we need not distinguish between p^* and p.

We can then put the entire model together by reference to figure C.1, which is the familiar representation for one country's free-trade economic equilibrium. If we assume given terms of trade, then production of goods 1 and 2 is determined. OZ will be the quantity of 2, and OK the quantity of 1, produced when the terms of trade are given as GSH. Thus, using the notation and numbering of chapter 12, we can write the production functions for the two countries as

$$Q_1 = Q_1\left(\frac{1}{p}\right), \tag{12.1}$$

$$Q_2 = Q_2\left(Q_1\left(\frac{1}{p}\right)\right), \tag{12.2}$$

$$Q_1^* = Q_1^*\left(\frac{1}{p}\right), \tag{12.3}$$

$$Q_2^* = Q_2^*\left(Q_1^*\left(\frac{1}{p}\right)\right), \tag{12.4}$$

where the Qs refer to production levels and the asterisk distinguishes country II's variables.

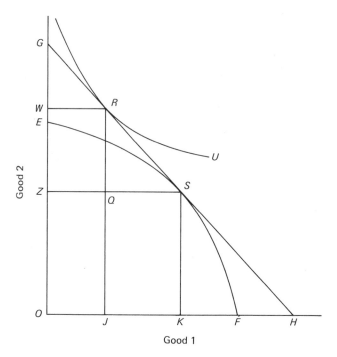

Figure C.1

Once production levels are determined, the given terms of trade will define the national income at factor cost in each country: It is equal to OH in units of good 1 and OG in units of good 2 in figure C.1. In figure C.1 we further depict national expenditure as equal to national income. This is Walras's law. Thus for the two countries we can write

$$D_i = Q_1 + pQ_2, \tag{12.5}$$

$$D_e = C_1 + pC_2, \tag{12.6}$$

$$D_i = D_e, \tag{12.7}$$

$$D_i^* = \frac{Q_1^*}{p} + Q_2^*, \tag{12.8}$$

$$D_e^* = \frac{C_1^*}{p} + C_2^*, \tag{12.9}$$

$$D_i^* = D_e^*, \tag{12.10}$$

where D_i is the national income measured at factor cost, equal in turn to D_e which is national expenditure at market prices of country I measured in units of 1, and D_i^* is identically the national income and D_e^* is the expenditure of country II measured in units of 2.[1] The consumption of each commodity is denoted by C with appropriate subscripts and superscripts.

Next we can write the demand equations for each country. In figure C.1, for example, once national expenditure is determined at OH and the budget line is GSH, consumption is determinate at R. It is also clear that given the expenditure equation and the price ratio, it is enough to specify the demand equation for one commodity; the demand equation for the other commodity is not independent. Thus we have the following two demand equations for the two countries:

$$C_2 = C_2(D_e, p), \tag{12.11}$$

$$C_1^* = C_1^*\left(D_e^*, \frac{1}{p}\right). \tag{12.12}$$

Altogether we have 12 independent equations and 12 unknowns (Q_1, $Q_2, Q_1^*, Q_2^*, C_1, C_2, C_1^*, C_2^*, D_i, D_e, D_i^*, D_e^*$) if we specify p exogenously. But we can add one more equation to determine p itself, and this completes the classical model.

We can do this, however, in one of two equivalent ways. Because the consumption and the production of both goods are determined once p is specified, we can impose the equilibrium requirement that p must be such as to clear the market for each good. We thus write the last equation to show that world production and consumption must be equal, or that the import of a good by one country equals its export by the other, or that the value of exports of a country equals the value of its imports. Since the clearance of the market for one good will necessarily imply clearance of the other, we have to write only one independent equation:

$$(C_2 + C_2^*) - (Q_2 + Q_2^*) = 0, \tag{12.13a}$$

or

$$(C_2 - Q_2) = (Q_2^* - C_2^*), \tag{12.13b}$$

or

$$(C_2 - Q_2) = \frac{1}{p}(C_1^* - Q_1^*) \qquad \text{by Walras's law.} \tag{12.13c}$$

Introducing $M = C_2 - Q_2$ as the symbol for imports of good 2 by country I and $M^* = C_1^* - Q_1^*$ as the symbol for imports of good 1 by country

---

1. If we allow each country to spend differently from its income, as when a transfer payment is involved, then $D_i \neq D_e$ and $D_i^* \neq D_e^*$.

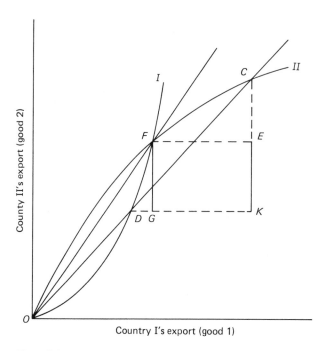

Figure C.2

II, we can then rewrite the last equation as

$$M = \left(\frac{1}{p}\right)M^*.$$ (12.13c′)

Either way, the system is complete and we have 13 equations that determine the 13 unknowns, including the terms of trade p.[2] The resulting free-trade equilibrium is depicted in the standard Marshallian offer-curve diagram, shows in figure C.2 at F.

Stability Conditions

The classical model can be used for analyzing the effects of a number of parametric shifts: shifts in demand, changes in commercial policy, shifts in production due to technological change, and so on. Essentially the procedure involved in analyzing the shift to a new trade equilibrium consists in differentiating the system with respect to the specified change and solving it for the variable in whose change we are interested.

2. If we were to count $M = C_2 - Q_2$ and $M^* = C_1^* - Q_1^*$ as two additional equations, then we would have two additional unknowns: M and M^*. Equation (12.13b) is discussed in the text with the assumption that country I imports good 2, but it clearly holds regardless of which pattern of trade holds in equilibrium, as does the alternative equation (12.13a).

However, the standard question as to whether the system will in fact converge to the new equilibrium requires the usual specification of a dynamic adjustment mechanism. In the analysis that follows, we assume that there is a Walrasian auctioneer, that no transactions take place at disequilibrium prices, and that the auctioneer's rules entail lowering the (relative) price of the commodity with positive world excess demand at the quoted price.[3]

Let us then take the classical model and derive the stability conditions subject to the rules just stated. Assume now that country I exports good 1 and imports good 2.

We assume that the equilibrium price ratio for this two-country economy (in figure C.2) is OF, where the two offer curves intersect. We then quote a different price ratio, OC, at which the relative price of good 2 is higher. If then the result is a negative excess demand for good 2, the auctioneer will call a lower price of good 2 and the system will work back to the equilibrium price ratio OF.

Hence the local-stability condition in our model is

$$\frac{d(M)}{dp} - \frac{d(E^*)}{dp} < 0, \tag{C.1}$$

where M are the home country's imports and E^* the foreign exports. Figure C.3 illustrates a stable equilibrium where raising the relative price of good 2 to OC leads to an excess supply of good 2 equal to $FG + CE = CK$ units.

The basic stability condition can now be rewritten as

$$\varepsilon + \varepsilon^* > 1, \tag{C.2}$$

where

$$\varepsilon = -\frac{p}{M} \cdot \frac{dM}{dp}$$

and

$$\varepsilon^* = -\frac{1/p}{M^*} \cdot \frac{dM^*}{d(1/p)}.$$

3. Stability conditions can be derived under alternative assumptions, including those that permit transactions at disequilibrium prices. We must also note that we are investigating *local stability* (in the sense of whether or not, given a sufficiently small disturbance from an initial equilibrium, the postulated dynamic adjustment process leads the system to converge to the original equilibrium). This also means that when applied to comparative static changes, the analysis assumes that the set of static equilibria lie within the region of local stability appropriately defined.

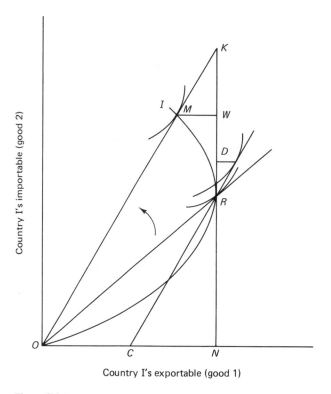

Figure C.3

These expressions are in fact the import-demand (offer-curve) elasticities of countries I and II.

To derive the inequality C.2, first multiply C.1 by $-p/M$. Since $M = E^*$ at the equilibrium point F of figure C.2, we have

$$-\frac{p}{M}\frac{dM}{dp} + \frac{p}{E^*}\frac{dE^*}{dp} > 0. \tag{C.1$'$}$$

The first term in C.1$'$ is ε. From appendix A the second term in C.1$'$ is ε_s^* (the elasticity of export supply for country II which exports good 2). In appendix A we showed that $\varepsilon_s^* = \varepsilon^* - 1$. Substituting this relationship into C.1$'$, we obtain C.2.

We can rewrite the same stability conditions in yet another way. We can bypass the offer curves and go directly to world production and world consumption as in equation (9.13a). Then C.1 becomes

$$\frac{d(C_2 - Q_2)}{dp} - \frac{d(Q_2^* - C_2^*)}{dp} < 0,$$

$$\frac{d(C_2 + C_2^*)}{dp} - \frac{d(Q_2 + Q_2^*)}{dp} < 0;$$

that is,

$$\frac{p}{C_2^{\mathrm{W}}} \cdot \frac{d(Q_2 + Q_2^*)}{dp} - \frac{p}{Q_2^{\mathrm{W}}} \cdot \frac{d(Q_2 + Q_2^*)}{dp} < 0,$$

where $C_2^{\mathrm{W}} = Q_2^{\mathrm{W}} = C_2 + C_2^* = Q_2 + Q_2^*$, since at F the world consumption and production of good 2 (and of 1, for that matter) are equal.[4] Thus we can rewrite the stability condition as

$$E_2^{\mathrm{C}} + E_2^{\mathrm{P}} > 0, \tag{C.3}$$

where

$$E_2^{\mathrm{C}} = -\frac{p}{C_2^{\mathrm{W}}} \cdot \frac{dC_2^{\mathrm{W}}}{dp}$$

and

$$E_2^{\mathrm{P}} = \frac{p}{Q_2^{\mathrm{W}}} \cdot \frac{dQ_2^{\mathrm{W}}}{dp}$$

are the price elasticity of world consumption of good 2 and the world production of good 2, respectively.

If production is well behaved in the sense that the transformation curve is concave, E_2^{P} will always be nonnegative. For instability to occur would require $E_2^{\mathrm{C}} < 0$. Thus good 2 must be a Giffen good in world consumption, this being a necessary but not a sufficient condition for instability.

We revert now to the offer-curve-elasticity criterion: $\varepsilon + \varepsilon^* > 1$. This can be reduced to a number of equivalent criteria, essentially by decomposing the import-demand elasticities into component effects or elasticities. (In what follows we have suppressed the country superscripts, which are not relevant for the decomposition of each country's import-demand elasticity.)

DECOMPOSITION 1   A simple decomposition of the offer-curve import-demand price elasticity is a weighted sum of the production and consumption price elasticities. Consider the import of good 2, for which

$$M \equiv C_2 - Q_2.$$

Therefore

$$-\frac{p}{M} \cdot \frac{dM}{dp} = -\frac{p}{M} \cdot \frac{dC_2}{dp} + \frac{p}{M} \cdot \frac{dQ_2}{dp}$$

---

4. Walras's law holds at the world level, so transfers between countries are again admissible.

and

$$\varepsilon = \frac{C_2}{M}\left(-\frac{p}{C_2}\cdot\frac{dC_2}{dp}\right) + \frac{Q_2}{M}\left(\frac{p}{Q_2}\cdot\frac{dQ_2}{dp}\right)$$

$$= \frac{C_2}{M}\cdot\varepsilon^{C} + \frac{Q_2}{M}\cdot\varepsilon^{P}, \tag{C.4}$$

where ε^{C} and ε^{P} are the total price elasticities of consumption and production of the importable good 2.

DECOMPOSITION 2   A more complete, value-theoretic decomposition is along the following lines:

$$\varepsilon = \eta + e, \tag{C.5}$$

where

$$\eta = -\frac{p}{M}\cdot\frac{\partial M}{\partial P}\bigg|_{\bar{Q}_1,\bar{Q}_2}$$

is the price elasticity of import demand, reflecting pure demand change, if production is constant $(\bar{Q}_1,\bar{Q}_2)$, and where

$$e = \frac{1/p}{E}\cdot\frac{\partial E}{\partial(1/p)}\bigg|_{\bar{C}_1,\bar{C}_2}$$

is the price elasticity of export of export supply with consumption constant $(\bar{C}_1,\bar{C}_2)$. To derive this result, take the import equation

$$M \equiv C_2(p, D_e) - Q_2\left(Q_1\left(\frac{1}{p}\right)\right),$$

where M refers to quantity of imports of good 2, $C_2 = C_2(p, D_e)$ is the consumption equation for good 2, and $Q_2 = Q_2(Q_1(1/p))$ is the production equation, as already stated in the classical model. Differentiate this equation totally with respect to p to get

$$\frac{dM}{dp} = \frac{\partial C_2}{\partial p}\bigg|_{\bar{D}_e} + \frac{\partial C_2}{\partial D_e}\cdot\frac{dD_e}{dp} - \frac{dQ_2}{dQ_1}\cdot\frac{dQ_1}{dp}. \tag{C.6}$$

Now the first term on the right-hand side of this equation can be decomposed into the Slutsky-Hicks substitution and income terms:

$$\frac{\partial C_2}{\partial p}\bigg|_{\bar{D}_e} = \frac{\partial C_2}{\partial p}\bigg|_{\overline{RI}} - C_2\frac{\partial C_2}{\partial D_e},$$

where the first term on the right-hand side is the pure substitution term with real income (RI) held constant. The second term on the right of C.6 reduces to

$$Q_2 \cdot \frac{\partial C_2}{\partial D_e}$$

because $dQ_2/dQ_1 = -1/p$ (in equilibrium, at incomplete specialization), and therefore

$$\frac{dD_e}{dp} = \frac{d(Q_1 + pQ_2)}{dp} = Q_2.$$

The third term on the right of C.6 reduces to

$$-\frac{1}{p}\frac{dQ_1}{dp} = \frac{-M}{p}\left(\frac{1}{M}\frac{dQ_1}{dp}\right) = \frac{-M}{p}\left(\frac{p}{E}\frac{dQ_1}{dp}\right),$$

since $M = (1/p) \cdot E$ in initial equilibrium. Therefore, multiplying C.6 by $-p/M$ on both sides, we get

$$\varepsilon = -\frac{p}{M}\left(\frac{\partial C_2}{\partial p}\bigg|_{\overline{\mathrm{RI}}} - M\frac{\partial C_2}{\partial D_e}\right) + \frac{1/p}{E}\cdot\frac{dQ_1}{d(1/p)}. \tag{C.7}$$

Since the change in M holding production constant equals the change in C_2, while the change in E holding consumption constant equals the change in Q_1, C.7 can be written as C.5.

Thus the offer-curve elasticity, defined as the price elasticity of import demand, is the sum of the country's elasticity of demand for imports (ignoring production changes) and its elasticity of supply of exports (ignoring consumption changes).

DECOMPOSITION 3   A more common decomposition of ε is

$$\varepsilon = \varepsilon' + m,$$

where

$$\varepsilon' = -\frac{p}{M}\cdot\frac{\partial M}{\partial p}\bigg|_{\overline{\mathrm{RI}}}$$

is the compensated price elasticity of import demand and where

$$m = p\frac{\partial C_2}{\partial D_e}$$

is the marginal propensity to spend on imports. This decomposition is readily derived by recalling from the preceding section that

$$\varepsilon = \frac{p}{M} \cdot \frac{dM}{dp}$$

$$= -\frac{p}{M} \left(\frac{\partial C_2}{\partial p} \bigg|_{\overline{\text{RI}}} - M \frac{\partial C_2}{\partial D_e} \right) - \frac{p}{M} \cdot \frac{dQ_2}{dp}$$

$$= -\frac{p}{M} \cdot \frac{\partial(C_2 - Q_2)}{\partial p} \bigg|_{\overline{\text{RI}}} + p \frac{\partial C_2}{\partial D}$$

$$= \varepsilon' + m.$$

Diagrammatic Illustrations

We now illustrate the major decompositions of the offer-curve import-demand elasticity (ε) derived so far.

Figure C.3 shows the offer curve of country I: *ORMI*. For a shift in the terms of trade from *OR* to *OM*, the import demand increases by *WR* units of good 2. The proportionate change in the terms of trade is *KR/RN*, and the proportionate change in imports is *WR/RN*. The change in income brought about by the improvement in the terms of trade is approximately *OC* units of good 1 (or *KR* units of good 2). Therefore

$$\varepsilon = \frac{WR/RN}{KR/RN},$$

$$m = \frac{WD}{KR},$$

and

$$\varepsilon - m = \frac{DR \, (= WR - WD)}{KR} = \frac{DR/RN}{KR/RN} = \varepsilon',$$

since *D* represents the point of tangency of the "compensated" budget line *CD* with a trade-indifference curve. Therefore

$$\varepsilon = \varepsilon' + m.$$

The same decomposition may be illustrated in terms of consumption and production equilibria, as in figure C.4. We can do this in two stages. First, assume that production is fixed at *Q* no matter what terms of trade are quoted. Let the terms of trade, p_2/p_1, then improve from *CQ* to *CK*. The equilibrium consumption level then shifts from *C* to *E*. The net change in imports is then *CG*. The price elasticity of import demand (ε) is therefore

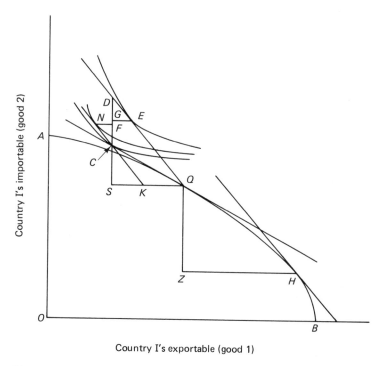

Country I's exportable (good 1)

Figure C.4

$$\frac{SQ}{CS} \cdot \frac{CG}{QK}.$$

This in turn is

$$\frac{SQ}{CS} \cdot \frac{CF}{QK} + \frac{SQ}{CS} \cdot \frac{FG}{QK} = \varepsilon' + P \cdot \frac{FG}{QK}$$

$$= \varepsilon' + m \qquad \left(\text{as } m = \frac{FG}{CD} \right).$$

Now assume that Q is variable along a production-possibility curve AB. The shift in the terms of trade from CQ to CK will then shift production from Q to H. Imports will increase still further by QZ on this account. However, the effect of this production shift on national income is of the second order of smalls, and it will not affect consumption.[5] Therefore the only change in our analysis (once production is allowed to vary) entails taking the production change QZ into account. Now we have

5. Recall that $dD_e/dp = Q_2$, the production of the importable good.

$$\varepsilon = \frac{SQ}{CS} \cdot \frac{CG + QZ}{QK}$$

$$= \frac{SQ}{CS} \cdot \frac{CF + QZ}{QK} + \frac{SQ}{CS} \cdot \frac{FG}{QK}$$

$$= \varepsilon' + m,$$

where ε' now includes the import-demand change resulting from the production change as well. Alternatively, we can rewrite ε as

$$\varepsilon = \left(\frac{SQ}{CS} \cdot \frac{CF}{QK} + \frac{SQ}{CS} \cdot \frac{FG}{QK} \right) + \frac{SQ}{CS} \cdot \frac{QZ}{QK}$$

$$= \eta + e.$$

Important Elasticities

$\varepsilon = -\dfrac{p}{M} \dfrac{dM}{dp}$ is the total, offer-curve price elasticity of demand for imports.

$\eta = -\dfrac{p}{M} \dfrac{M}{p} \bigg|_{\bar{Q}_1, \bar{Q}_2}$ is the price elasticity of demand for imports with production held constant, and hence reflects only consumption change.

$\varepsilon' = -\dfrac{p}{M} \dfrac{M}{p} \bigg|_{\overline{RI}}$ is the *compensated* price elasticity of demand for imports with real income held constant, and hence reflects only the substitution and production effects.

$e = \dfrac{1/p}{E} \dfrac{\partial E}{\partial(1/p)} \bigg|_{\bar{C}_1, \bar{C}_2}$ is the price elasticity of supply of exports with consumption held constant, and thus reflects only production change.

Recommended Readings (Appendix C)

Amano, A. Stability conditions in the pure theory of international trade: A rehabilitation of the Marshallian approach. *Quarterly Journal of Economics* 82 (1968): 326–39.

Jones, R. W. Stability conditions in international trade: A general equilibrium analysis. *International Economic Review* 2 (1961): 199–209.

Mundell, R. A. The pure theory of international trade. *American Economic Review* 50 (1960): 67–110.

Index